THE NEW COMPETITOR INTELLIGENCE

NEW DIRECTIONS IN BUSINESS

New Directions in Business books provide managers and business professionals with authoritative sources of ideas and information. They're designed to provide convenient and effective ways to upgrade your skills in today's fast-changing world of business.

New Directions books cover current topics that leaders in every business need to know about. They focus on applied techniques that can be used today and are written by authors with academic and professional experience.

New Directions in Business titles

Hands-On Strategy: The Guide to Crafting Your Company's Future by William C. Finnie

The New Competitor Intelligence: The Complete Resource for Finding, Analyzing, and Using Information about Your Competitors by Leonard M. Fuld

New Product Success Stories: Lessons from the Leading Innovators by Robert J. Thomas

The Smarter Organization: How to Build a Business That Learns and Adapts to Marketplace Needs by Michael E. McGill and John W. Slocum

Touchstones: Ten New Ideas Revolutionizing Business by William A. Band

THE NEW COMPETITOR INTELLIGENCE

The Complete Resource for Finding, Analyzing, and Using Information about Your Competitors

Leonard M. Fuld

John Wiley & Sons, Inc.

New York · Chichester · Brisbane · Toronto · Singapore

A WORD OF CAUTION

This book describes and encourages honest, ethical means of gathering competitor information. Should any of the techniques or sources in this book be used illegally, the author and publisher do not claim responsibility for such misuse. The author and publisher recommend that any reader in doubt about the use of a source or technique in a particular industry consult with an attorney before beginning research.

This text is printed on acid-free paper.

Copyright © 1995 by Leonard M. Fuld
Published by John Wiley & Sons, Inc.

Library of Congress Cataloging-in-Publication Data:

Fuld, Leonard M.
   The new competitor intelligence : the complete resource for
 finding, analyzing, and using information about your competitors /
 Leonard M. Fuld.
     p.   cm.
  Includes index.
   ISBN 0-471-58508-4. — ISBN 0-471-58509-2 (pbk.)
   1. Business intelligence. 2. Competition. I. Title.
HD38.7.F863   1994
658.4'7—dc20   94-18292

Printed in the United States of America

10 9 8 7 6 5 4 3 2

Michal and Avi, it's your turn

ACKNOWLEDGMENTS

Acknowledgments are always the most difficult part of the book for me. Since founding my firm over 15 years ago, I have learned lessons from so many individuals that at times the names and incidents become a blur. There are the seminars, the lectures, the airplane flights, the phone conversations and discussions with the various members of my family. All these conversations and meetings truly feed into this author's imagination and thinking about the intelligence concept. Nevertheless, certain individuals have helped me a great deal and spent considerable time "talking me" through this latest undertaking.

My partner, Mike Sandman, has brought a great deal of manufacturing and real-world business experience to my firm. His innovative approaches to analysis are found in cases throughout this book. Finally, Mike's steady hand in business management has given me the time and freedom to think through this manuscript. Mike, "Thank you."

Mary Morrison has dug up her English teacher's grammar rules and overlayed these with common sense to help me craft a text that is both readable and informative. Thank you, Mary, for wielding the red ink firmly but gently.

Then, there are the other professionals and support staff in my firm without whom I could not have survived this undertaking. To Jennifer Walch, Paula Privatera, and Lynn Smith, who kept me organized, generated the graphics, and told me the best way to do things. To Michelle LeMonde-McIntyre who meticulously checked each and every source and reference, I alliteratively appreciate your patience, persistence, and professionalism. To Lenore Scanlon and Paula Sullivan, considerable thanks for watching my editorial compass, making sure that I accurately portrayed a story and clearly conveyed the lessons taught. To Ginny O'Brien and June LaPointe who so thoroughly researched the international sources. This was a tough task that tried their patience—in many languages and time zones.

I especially would like to acknowledge the contributions of the experts whose advice is peppered throughout this book. Their insights make it clear that intelligence is a real-world topic, one that touches nearly every facet of business life. Thank you, one and all, for lending me some of your wisdom. In particular, I would like to thank José Salibi Neto, who used his global network to put me in touch with additional experts from around the world.

I also feel grateful to have worked closely with my editor, John Mahaney, whose sense and sensitivity helped steer this book in the right direction. Thank you, John, for your good humor and your advice.

Last, I want to thank my wife, Suzi, for having the patience to let me write and the impatience to ensure I attended to family matters. With all my love and respect, I thank you.

L.M.F.

CONTENTS

PART TWO   FIND THE BASIC AND CREATIVE SOURCES

The Intelligence Pyramid

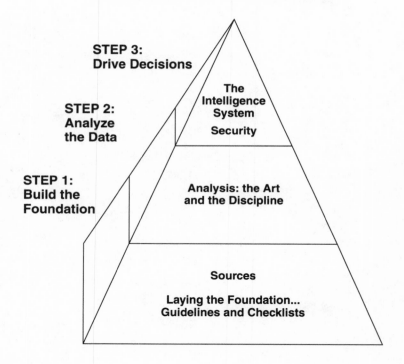

INTRODUCTION
How This Book Will Help
You Make Decisions

If you are in business, you need competitor intelligence. Whether you are a sales manager, insurance broker, manufacturer's rep, market analyst, or company president, you need business and competitor intelligence to make decisions. You need to analyze your competitors' pricing strategy, production processes, and overall strategies. This book gives you the information sources and analytical techniques to develop the intelligence you need for today's marketplace and tomorrow's competitive environment.

This book also addresses the many types of intelligence needs that exist: strategic and tactical; manufacturing and service; domestic and international. Among the questions this book will help you to answer are:

"How can I . . .

   . . . analyze privately held companies and subsidiaries?"

   . . . determine a competitor's, a supplier's, or a customer's operating costs, pricing strategies, and financials?"

   . . . build a cost-effective intelligence system using existing resources?"

   . . . corroborate rumors and improve management decision making?"

   . . . improve benchmarking success?"

   . . . anticipate competitors' R&D strategies?"

   . . . profile a competitor's management to understand how they will likely make decisions?"

   . . . identify key elements in a company's future strategy?"

A STEP-BY-STEP GUIDE: THE MEANS, NOT JUST THE SOURCES

There is no such thing as an "intelligence cookbook," but there are right ways and wrong ways, efficient means and inefficient means, to begin a competitive assessment. I have written this book to help you understand intelligence as a process of discovery, not as a formula. Sometimes, a discovery may be as small as finding a new way to sort data in some unusual but informative way, or as revealing as a regulatory filing that contains operational details on a plant or facility, or as significant as a new and better way to analyze competitor's costs or predict a new product roll-out.

To help you "discover" all these new sources and ideas, I have included dozens of War Stories that describe how to develop and apply intelligence. These stories range from the unusual, such as the Rust on Rails anecdote, to the provocative, such as the Know Thy Brothel story. The War Stories are meant to arrest your attention and help you think intelligence, not simply memorize sources.

Part One of this book opens up your intelligence tool kit by first defining the role of and the boundaries of competitor or business intelligence. It also presents the fundamental techniques that will get you started in this process.

Part Two describes the thousands of basic and creative sources available to you around the globe. Because information flows differently in different industries and in different cultures, I have given you both the sources themselves and the means for you to locate other sources and techniques. This group of chapters brings together the experience of researchers in many industries and shows how corrugated boxes, box cars, technical manuals, help-wanted ads and even the Yellow Pages can reveal a great deal about your competitor. In Chapter 7, "International Intelligence," you will learn how to create intelligence maps, an approach to conducting intelligence projects outside your home-office country.

Part Three describes both the art and the discipline of analysis through narrations of actual (but disguised) cases. By reviewing the cases, you will learn how to address questions on a competitor's cost structure, future strategies, and new product or service plans. Each case allows you to effectively look over the project manager's shoulder to see how the competitive issue was addressed, the analytical framework used, and the recommendations the client received.

Part Four discusses a critical—but an often overlooked—piece of the intelligence process: accepting and taking action on the intelligence. In this Part, you will learn how to establish an ongoing intelligence system using an approach that has worked for companies around the world. Once again, you will see many illustrations of real-world systems—not a lot of theory. The final chapter covers intelligence security. It turns to the flip side of the intelligence coin and outlines ways for you to avoid losing the vital information your business needs to survive and prosper.

THE KEY: THE STRATEGIC INTELLIGENCE INDEX

I expect that readers will use this book in different ways. For that reason, I have designed the Strategic Intelligence Index (SI Index), a unique index that immediately follows this Introduction. I have found, over the years, that clients from the United States, Japan, Germany, and other countries, whether in manufacturing or service industries, often look for markedly different and divergent types of information. The

SI Index reflects these many needs. If you are looking for ways to assess a service company, to determine a cost of operations, or to examine a company's R&D activities, the SI Index pulls together all the discussions, published sources, and available resources that touch on or explore your questions. I cannot hope to anticipate *everyone's* needs, but I believe you will find the SI Index versatile enough to help you locate at least a lead to your ultimate solution, if not the solution itself.

ADVICE FROM THE EXPERTS

I have recruited a group of internationally known experts to comment on the far-reaching applications and benefits of competitor and business intelligence. Virtually all aspects of business operations have embraced the need for intelligence in recent years—from total quality management (TQM) to benchmarking, from the purchasing function to a company's international marketing efforts. I believe you will enjoy the opinions (often iconoclastic) expressed by these business gurus. Their comments will help you to evaluate the new and very practical ways in which you might apply the intelligence process to your business and your job.

A NOTE ABOUT THE SOURCES

This book has thousands of sources, which I and my staff have spent countless hours verifying. Inevitably, over time, many of these addresses will change and some publishers will merge or go out of business. My intent is to show you where a unique source exists and where you can find others. If a particular source no longer exists or a company has gone out of business, you will have the tools and techniques available to find others.

Except for a few instances, I have placed the address and telephone number for each source in Part Five, which is an alphabetical listing by publisher or producer. Where I felt that a text section described a particular source in depth or where that source had multiple relevant addresses—such as the various filing offices for each U.S. state—I made an exception and listed these addresses in the chapter that contains the material.

Whatever your job or business, make the intelligence process a part of your daily agenda. Because each workday presents competitive opportunities—opportunities that you need to understand—fold intelligence into every task, every trade show visit, every sales meeting and scientific conference. Competitor intelligence is not just for market analysis; it is for every decision maker and everyone whose goal is business success.

STRATEGIC INTELLIGENCE INDEX

Consider this book a printed on-line database, and consider this Strategic Intelligence Index (SI Index) your tool for applying the book's thousands of sources and analytical techniques to your particular problem or question. Do you need to analyze costs or understand a competitor's R&D plans? Are you planning to begin a search for an acquisition? When you find viable candidates, how can you determine their management style and profile their financials?

The SI Index is divided into five major categories:

1. Cost/Financials
2. Management
3. Process
4. Strategy/Marketing
5. Technology/R&D.

No single listing can anticipate all the possible concepts and ancillary topics that are significant for all readers. These are the most often requested types of intelligence, based on discussions with thousands of participants who have attended my firm's seminars over the years.

1. COST/FINANCIALS   Page

1. COST/FINANCIALS   **Page**

1. COST/FINANCIALS　　　　　　　　　　　　　　　**Page**

3. PROCESS Page

4. STRATEGY/MARKETING Page

4. STRATEGY/MARKETING   Page

4. STRATEGY/MARKETING   Page

4. STRATEGY/MARKETING   **Page**

4. STRATEGY/MARKETING Page

4. STRATEGY/MARKETING   **Page**

5. TECHNOLOGY/R&D   **Page**

5. TECHNOLOGY/R&D   **Page**

5. TECHNOLOGY/R&D Page

PART ONE

LAYING THE FOUNDATION

The Intelligence Pyramid

STEP 3:
Drive Decisions

The
Intelligence
System

Security

STEP 2:
Analyze
the Data

STEP 1:
Build the
Foundation

Analysis: the Art
and the Discipline

Sources

Laying the Foundation...
Guidelines and Checklists

Whether you are a company president, a salesperson, or an intelligence analyst, you want speedy answers to your critical competitive questions. Yet, by simply charging ahead into the research thicket, without much forethought or planning, you may fail to answer even your most basic questions. "Light-Brigade" intelligence-seekers—those who rush into the process with little knowledge of how it works—encounter a lot of frustration and little intelligence.

Part One is designed to alert you to special uses of business information and how best to develop the precious commodity known as intelligence. Insights are offered and tips are given on how to approach the experts in an industry, how to enhance your intelligence library, how to conduct interviews, and how to manage an intelligence project. Above all, these chapters begin to illustrate how to use intelligence for competitive advantage.

1 UNDERSTANDING INTELLIGENCE

Are there corporate spies? Sure. Do corporate spies account for most corporate success stories—or corporate failures? No. Most corporate victories result from well-designed products or services, hard-won marketing campaigns, and the strategic use of intelligence. Most failures come from a combination of bad timing, poor judgment, and misuse or underuse of business intelligence. Protect your corporate secrets, but don't equate a competitor's market savvy with illegal activity. A competitor that knows its market, its competition, and how to leverage what it has learned is one that will continue to win legitimately in the marketplace.

To learn about the spy business, do what I do: pick up a Le Carré, Forsyth, or Ludlum novel. There is fact behind the fiction. Just don't apply too much fiction to the facts of your business.

WHAT IS COMPETITOR INTELLIGENCE?

Sometimes, it's almost easier to describe what intelligence is *not* rather than what it *is*. It is not reams of database printouts. It is not necessarily thick, densely written reports. It is most certainly not spying, stealing, or bugging. In its most basic description, intelligence is "analyzed information."

Intelligence—not information—helps a manager to respond with the right market tactic or long-term decision. For example, to say, "The competitor's plant is up to 90 percent of capacity," or "The bank is launching a new product promotion," is merely stating information. It becomes decision-producing intelligence when the statement has implications: "The manufacturer has reached a cost position that will knock us out of the market, unless we can reduce our overheads," or "The bank's new product presents no immediate threat and is only a me-too introduction. We can wait and watch for six months . . ."

Your analysis may end up being a 30-page report or just a two-sentence statement. (Don't confuse volume with value!) Whatever its length, if the resulting intelligence helps you succeed or overcome a market barrier, then it has done its job.

If you think competitor intelligence is "business babble" for the 1990s, consider the business success stories of the past—J. P. Morgan, Nathan Rothschild, John D. Rockefeller—and the present—Bill Gates, Akio Morita. They all have used intelligence; they just never gave it that name. By actively seeking intelligence and learning how to use it, you can turn information into a powerful weapon that will give you a competitive advantage.

Unfortunately, the power of the intelligence concept is often diluted because the term itself is ill-defined or misunderstood. Popular business magazines frequently use the labels "data," "information," and "intelligence" interchangeably. You will more readily recognize, and thus effectively use, intelligence if you understand how very different these terms are. As you will see, companies often have a great deal of data, but do not develop it into intelligence. The example below shows how data and intelligence can lead you to two very different conclusions about a company.

Definition	Example
Data. Scattered bits and pieces of knowledge	1990: "The Dun & Bradstreet report told us that the competitor's plant had 100 employees."
	1993: "One of our salespeople just passed by the competitor's plant and spotted only 30 cars in the lot."
Information. A pooling of these bits of knowledge	"Based on the D&B and the sales report, it appears the competitor has lost business."
Analysis. Distilled information	"After gathering more operational information and running it through a side-by-side profit and loss analysis [see Chapter 12], it appears the competitor has become highly efficient. It exceeds industry standards and has become a best-in-class facility."
Intelligence. The implication that will allow you to make a decision	"The competitor would make a good acquisition candidate. Its lean-and-mean structure would fit well with our current operations."

If you had stopped the process just short of analysis, acting only on the collected information, you likely would have drawn the wrong conclusion: "Drop in employment equals poor financial condition." Instead of considering the competitor's operation for a possible acquisition, you would have dismissed it as unprofitable. One of your other competitors might then have analyzed the very same information, recognized a profitable operation, and promptly snatched it from under you, thereby gaining a potential competitive advantage that you just missed.

The real lesson in all this is that all companies, large and small, in today's world have virtually the same access to information. The companies that convert available information into actionable intelligence will end up winning the game. Intelligence will make the difference between two competitors that sell similar products and have similar access to markets. Intelligence has helped companies, such as Compaq Computer, rise to the top. Sound business decisions are based on a combination of experience, gumption, and intelligence. Without the last item, you may succeed in winning a battle or two, but you can't expect to win the war.

As you will see from the sources and analytical techniques presented in this book, whether you are a small grocery store or a large conglomerate, information is a relatively inexpensive and easily obtainable commodity. Electronic databases, CD-ROMs, and other information vehicles allow anyone the freedom to ask almost any question imaginable about the competition. Keep asking the right questions, and remember to analyze the resulting answers.

A final point here: Much like a container of fresh cream, intelligence has a short shelf life. Use it and apply it, but don't ignore it. Once intelligence is allowed to sit around and not be used, its value declines rapidly.

On the Defensive? Don't Ignore the Intelligence!

LEONARD FULD: How are successful or unsuccessful marketing warfare campaigns influenced by intelligence—or the lack of it?

AL RIES: There is a strong relationship between marketing and warfare in the sense that the larger the scope of the enemy's planned offensive, the more important the role of intelligence becomes to the defender and, paradoxically, the easier that intelligence is to gather.

When the Allies invaded Normandy in June 1944, the Germans had a wealth of advance information on the date, scope, and general target of that invasion. You can't assemble that many men, tanks, ships, guns, without alerting enemy intelligence. The fact that the Germans failed to act on that intelligence is a management failure, not an intelligence failure.

When IBM launched the personal computer in August 1981, we were working for Digital Equipment Corporation. Yet we had picked up intelligence on the IBM move months in advance. Partly as a result of "informal" intelligence, we recommended to Digital Equipment that they launch a personal computer *before* IBM did.

Digital Equipment refused to do so. I can only speculate on their reasons, but I believe that Digital management could not deal with the "uncertainty" of the intelligence function. These are engineers who were used to dealing with facts.

Yet, if Digital had analyzed the situation, they would have realized that the odds were very high that the IBM rumors were true. You cannot "hide" a big operation like the launch of a totally new category of computer.

Al Ries is considered a leading marketing strategist. He is coauthor of the best-selling book, *Marketing Warfare,* and a partner in the firm of Trout & Ries, Inc.

CORPORATE INTELLIGENCE GATHERING: A BRIEF OVERVIEW

The word "intelligence" conjures up images of sleuths with magnifying glasses in hand, or a furtive meeting of two individuals in the back corner of a bar to exchange thousands of dollars for some valuable inside information.

Information on your competitors can be collected efficiently and accurately through totally honest and ethical methods. Admiral Ellis Zacharias, Deputy Chief of Naval Intelligence during World War II, agreed. In his book, *Secret Missions: The Story of an Intelligence Officer* (Putnam, 1946, pp. 117–18), he said that 95 percent of all necessary intelligence, corporate or military, can be found in the public arena.

In the world of commerce, this intelligence gathering goes on every day, without necessarily being called by its rightful name. An article that appeared in *Barron's* (March 19, 1979, p. 4) pointed out that gathering corporate intelligence is everyone's job and that virtually everyone collects it—knowingly and unknowingly:

Agents for Hire

Directly or indirectly, corporations deploy hundreds (thousands, by some estimates) of agents with widely divergent backgrounds and contrasting methods of operation. Here will be a Ph.D. preparing a scholarly analysis of long-range policy trends, based on private talks with government specialists. There will be a young free-lance lawyer with a phone-answering machine for an office, hustling to make it, not so much as a lawyer but as a Washington operator. Here a former newspaper reporter worming advance information or an unreleased document out of a carefully cultivated source—but for a private client now, not the reading public. And, of course, the high-prestige types—large law firms, well-established information-gathering companies and the official Washington representatives (often bearing a vice president's title) of the nation's major corporations.

In effect, the sources you need to uncover competitor information may already be there, ready for the picking, if you know where to look. Your understanding of the intelligence jigsaw puzzle will make a big difference.

THE JIGSAW PUZZLE

Corporate intelligence gathering has its roots in a number of very different, yet complementary disciplines: sales prospecting, library science, statistics, accounting, detective sleuthing, military intelligence, and jigsaw puzzles. The application of many of these disciplines to corporate intelligence gathering is easily understood. But a few may seem out of place.

Sales prospecting includes tracking down your competitor's customers. Detective sleuthing describes the common sense approach to gathering company information. Never overlook the obvious; by counting the parking spaces or spotting a building's structure, you can learn a great deal about your competitor's size and operations.

Military intelligence implies a down-to-earth, dogged pursuit of your competitor's activities. It does not imply any illegal or covert activities on your part.

The strangest of the disciplines mentioned, jigsaw puzzles, simply implies an ability to take what on the surface appear to be unrelated pieces of information and fit them together to form a complete picture. For instance, the discipline of the jigsaw puzzle might enable you to fit together the following:

1. You may come across a competitor's help-wanted ad, seeking a host of programmers to produce a new software product.
2. You discover through your sales force that this same competitor is opening a sales office in a different region.
3. You have heard rumors that certain prospective clients whom you've been wooing for months have suddenly been approached by this competitor for possible test marketing of a new product.
4. A credit report states that this same competitor has just completed four new UCC filings for major pieces of equipment.

These information items might be just a few random pieces of a jigsaw puzzle that you have come across in your daily business routine. This book suggests you take these seemingly random pieces of information and assemble a corporate intelligence picture of the competing firm. What does the information in the example suggest?

1. The competitor is planning to hire or has already hired a considerable number of new programmers for a soon-to-be-released product.
2. The product may be further along than the help-wanted ad suggests, because the company is already opening new sales offices. You should track where these new offices are located; they may form a pattern that will tell you the states or regions in which the competitor is concentrating sales.
3. The clients the competitor approached may become valuable sources of information on the new product.
4. Any UCC filings usually make clear what equipment was purchased. You should find out what the equipment is being used for; it very likely could be for the marketing or production of the new product.

This is the jigsaw puzzle discipline. If you can master the knack for spotting bits and pieces of the puzzle, then you are well on your way to assembling a much more complete picture of your competitors and their activities.

THE CARDINAL RULE OF INTELLIGENCE

Wherever money is exchanged, so is information.

We all imagine our competitors entrenched in medieval castles with 30-foot-thick walls. Surrounding those castles are deep moats infested with crocodiles and piranha. On top of the castle's parapets are the competitors' managers, wearing armor and helmets and holding steaming vats of oil, ready to pour the hot liquid down on any approaching competition. You may feel the competitor is virtually impenetrable, at least from an information standpoint.

In reality, quite the opposite is true. Each day, every competitor inadvertently throws down informational bridges over the moat, allowing outsiders to peek into its operations. These bridges are the result of the many business transactions companies conduct.

The world's mightiest multinationals hire and fire, open facilities, deal with suppliers, negotiate with national, state, and local governments, attend scientific conferences, and present papers. Each of these activities generates information about the companies involved.

The cardinal rule—wherever money is exchanged, so is information—explains a great deal about how much information is truly available in the marketplace. This rule applies to finding information on customers, suppliers, and distributors, not just competitors.

With a myriad of transactions, how can you identify the important ones? As a start, look at your own operations and see how *you* do business. For example, if your question involves your competitor's information systems, speak to your director of information systems and find out what hardware and software suppliers the systems group uses and whom they talk to in the industry. Most likely, the competitor does business with the same or similar groups of suppliers. Start your research with this thought in mind: No matter how big and powerful (or small and supposedly secretive) the company, it must deal with the outside world. The minute it does, it has to pass along information. Use this immutable intelligence law as your guide, and you will likely find the information you need. Later chapters will discuss specific interviewing, research, and analysis techniques.

HOW INTELLIGENCE TRAVELS IN THE REAL WORLD

Once you accept the fact that business information is transmitted whenever a buyer and a seller come together for a transaction, you begin to see how easily even the most guarded information becomes public. Here is an example:

Action	Actors	Public Sources	Intelligence Revealed
Purchase of property for building a new plant	Company management; seller; lawyers; industrial realtors; notary public	Filing with town assessor; bank filing (UCC)	Details on capacity; expansion plans

This company is buying a piece of property for a new plant. Look at how the intelligence flows. Beyond a seller and a buyer (company management), there are lawyers, realtors, and a notary public involved in the sale. The information they generate does not remain bottled up; it moves on. Aside from all the parties involved in talking about it, there are public filings that announce the sale—the assessor's filing and the UCC documents.

Even the casual observer will be quick to spot all kinds of information that has leaked out about the purchase. Such information may concern the company's capacity or its overall expansion plans.

Let's examine another business event. In this case, a government agency was poised to step in and regulate the chemical processes taking place in a manufacturing plant.

Action	Actors	Public Sources	Intelligence Revealed
Environmental regulation	Company; community action groups; local newspaper; state and federal EPA; realtors; neighboring plants	State notification; federal environmental impact statement; news reports; community gossip; reporters	Plant process; plant operations; capacity; product type

This example demonstrates that even one event causes a wave of information to cascade down to the surrounding community and into the public domain.

The preceding examples were in the manufacturing or production area. Now let's explore the banking industry to see whether company intelligence leaks out in the same manner. The next example traces a bank's newly announced cash-management service:

Action	Actors	Public Sources	Intelligence Revealed
Announcement of new cash-management product	Bank; corporate end-users; financial reporters	Trade news; conferences; written proposals	Features; pricing

The world of banking is actually a very small one. The announcement of a new financial product is watched closely by the competitors, and the activity is reported in the trade press. Competitors send out proposals, which in turn reveal much about the bank's marketing strategy and target market. Because many of these proposals are custom-designed, a competitor with a keen sense of organization can learn a good deal about that bank's strategy.

The idea that information leaks out is not new. Sometimes, though, it is a difficult one for the beginning researcher to grasp, especially when the closer that researcher gets to the work, the more difficult it is to see alternate sources—or any sources at all.

The lesson to learn from the examples above—and to keep in mind throughout the book—is:

> Each business transaction reveals data. By understanding the transaction, you can locate the intelligence source.

ARE THERE TRULY ANY BUSINESS SECRETS?

The answer is yes. Within the bounds of ethical and legal research techniques, there are definite secrets. The Coca-Cola formula or the source codes for a computer program are trade secrets, and the only way to obtain them is through theft or subterfuge.

According to James Pooley, in his 1982 book, *Trade Secrets* (McGraw-Hill), a trade secret is ". . . any formula, pattern, device or compilation of information used in a business that gives the owner an advantage over competitors who neither know of nor use it."

Practically speaking, a trade secret may represent only 5 percent of all the information you may need on a competitor. In many respects, it is the least important piece of that competitor's makeup.

Unearthing trade secrets is not what companies need in order to compete. They need tactical and strategic intelligence, which they can develop from the information sources all around them. For instance, does Pepsi truly need to know Coke's secret formula? What it actually needs to know is the style of its rival's vending machines, its new pricing and advertising strategy, or its distribution plans. These are not trade secrets; they are examples of intelligence that Pepsi can develop as it strives toward long-term success.

Your needs are very much like those of Pepsi. You too can determine your competitor's, customer's, or distributor's tactics and strategy. The information is out there, if you know where to look.

All this discussion of trade secrets reminds us of the other side of the intelligence coin: how to safeguard your own secrets. I will cover a number of security do's and don'ts in Chapter 14, "Security: The Flip Side."

THE POINTILLIST PAINTING—AN INTELLIGENCE METAPHOR

If you understand how impressionist paintings are created, you have a model for the fundamentals of intelligence.

Stand six inches from a Seurat or Monet pointillist painting, or look closely at a newspaper photograph. Up close, all you will see is an assembly of dots in various shades. There is no pattern, no sense of the complete image at this close range. Take a few steps back and you see an entire picture—forms, images, shadow, and light.

The same process can be applied to the development of intelligence. As you are collecting the bits and pieces of data, you often do not know how they will all fit into the larger picture. Only when you see all the "data dots" lined up next to one another will you see the entire image. Intelligence is exactly this: a combination of dots made whole by comparison.

This artistic metaphor teaches the intelligence gatherer many lessons:

1. *You must find information; it does not find you.* Eleventh-hour research assignments are almost sure to miss critical points because the information you seek is not there when you want it.

2. *Intelligence is constant.* You must track your competition (or your customers, distributors, and suppliers) constantly, otherwise you may misinterpret what you find. You need the entire picture, or at least the most complete picture you can assemble in a given time period.

3. *Competitive assessment is a 3-D picture.* Information floats in time. Just as competitors change, so does their competitive environment. You must find a way to capture competitive snapshots continuously and historically—not just during strategic planning time.

HOW DOES INTELLIGENCE FLOW?

Once the information about a particular company is released, it takes an erratic path until it reaches the public forum—if it ever reaches the public at all. Here is the usual sequence of events:

1. Rumors of an impending announcement stir within the company.
2. The event becomes known, somewhat before-the-fact, to knowledgeable sources—for example, to brokers, suppliers, and dealers.
3. The event occurs.
4. The event reaches the industry through trade shows, the trade press, and salespeople.
5. The general press picks up the news.
6. Information may be entered into a data bank.
7. Articles are printed on microfilm and cataloged in indexes to be filed away on a library shelf.

FIVE KEY INTELLIGENCE FACTORS

Often, the ease or difficulty one has in locating information on a competitor will depend on environmental factors or on the way the industry operates. Five key factors—almost barometers—can tell you your ability to gain "intelligence access" to a company. As strange as it may sound, the way an industry works very much determines how accessible company information is to the researcher. The five key factors are:

1. *Regionality.* The more local or regional a company's sales and operating territory, the easier one can find data about that company. What does this imply?

In industries where companies sell and operate nationally, where sources of supply, distribution, and sales are countrywide, one will find it extremely difficult to locate sources that are knowledgeable about one particular plant.

On the other hand, where a company or plant operates almost totally on a local level, one can expect to find out a good deal about that plant or service division. For example, one can go to the town newspaper, the county employment office, or a local trucking or shipping company for intelligence. The general rule that the regionality factor teaches is: the more local you go, the more likely you are to tap into knowledgeable sources of valuable intelligence.

2. *Dynamism.* This informative but somewhat perplexing factor states that the more dynamic and actively growing the industry, the easier it is to get the intelligence you are looking for. Yet, you will also find that, along with the information you receive, you will encounter accuracy problems.

Take the personal computer industry as an example. A lot of gossip and news circulates about all the latest personal computers. The question, though, is whether the information being received is accurate. Often, in such a dynamic industry, it is not. One may get five estimates of market share for a personal computer company, and all five may be dramatically different.

3. *Regulation.* The more regulated the industry, the higher the intelligence access for any one company. Translated into more basic terms, the more companies have

to account for their actions to a governmental authority, the more information they will disclose about their activities. Banks and airlines are examples of regulated industries.

4. *Concentration.* In industries where a few companies control a large market share, these companies will also know a lot about competitors, and vice versa. The more concentrated the industry, the greater the intelligence access to an individual corporation.

5. *Integration.* In industries where the companies operating within them control all their sources of supply and distribution—in other words, where the companies are highly integrated—one has a poor chance of finding much out about a competitor. Why? Because the competitor controls all the possible contacts and sources of information.

In reality, few companies are totally integrated. Most firms have to go outside for some supplies, or may have to contract for independent representatives to sell their wares. But in general, high integration means low access.

ETHICS AND LEGALITIES

Most of the information you will need is in the public domain and will not infringe on any laws or personal ethics. But, as most lawyers will tell you, what is legal is not necessarily ethical. Laws may vary from state to state and from country to country, but they exist and legal boundaries are clear.

Ethical boundaries, however, can become dangerously fuzzy. It is often easier to discuss and set *legal* limits on what kind of information can be gathered and how to collect that information. Personal ethics vary widely and often involve individual rather than group decisions.

For a more complete discussion on the subject of intelligence and ethics, I refer you to "Ethical and Legal Guidelines," Chapter 9 of *Monitoring the Competition* (Fuld, John Wiley & Sons, 1988).

The Legal Issues

News articles worldwide frequently describe patent infringements, outright thefts, and similar illegal acts. Some of these illegalities are easy to understand and require little discussion. Other information-related legislation, especially regarding antitrust practices and the sharing of information, enters the realm of the arcane and is little understood by the average businessperson. Every intelligence analyst needs to realize what the legal limits are and how to comply with them.

The key rule is: Contact your company's legal department or outside legal practitioner for details on laws affecting your industry or business activity. You may be surprised at how few instances involve legal restrictions. In any case, remember that ignorance is no excuse in the eyes of the law.

Antitrust laws in the United States explicitly prohibit companies from fixing prices among themselves or exchanging price information. The legislation's primary goal is to stop companies from conspiring to monopolize markets. An analyst could contribute (at least on the surface) to monopolizing these markets by swapping prices with an employee at a competing company. The U.S. Department of Justice might see this act as an attempt to control a market.

For more information on antitrust laws and their impact on overall business activities, I recommend the *Antitrust Compliance Manual: A Guide for Counsel, Management and Public Relations,* by Walker B. Comegys (Practicing Law Institute, NY, 1986).

Ethical Considerations:
What Are Your Personal Limits?

Make no mistake: A person collecting information can be as aggressive as any salesperson trying to win an account or any purchasing manager who tries to win the best deal with a supplier. Your goal is legitimate and necessary: to gather and use information properly in order to help your company. But just as a salesperson or a purchasing manager can step over the ethical line, so can an intelligence analyst. Because this dilemma potentially must be addressed on a daily basis, it's important that you consider the following questions early in the process:

- How should I represent myself?
- Do I identify my sources in a report?
- Did I "trick" the individual into giving me the information?

There are no simple answers to these questions. Often, the answer lies within particular circumstances, and to establish general rules could be dangerous. Yet, nearly everyone feels that at some moment, the questioning may be stepping over some unseen line. The quickest way to find that line is through the Harm Rule. When Michael Sandman, presently Senior Vice President at Fuld & Company, held his former position as Chief Operating Officer for a division of Dexter Corporation, he was asked to sign an agreement that included the Harm Rule:

> *I will not do anything that may now or in the future*
> *harm or embarrass the corporation.*

The rule drives home the point that unethical behavior can quickly translate into lost dollars. Most information gatherers who keep the Harm Rule in mind will find themselves stopping where this translation would occur, or at a conservative distance ahead of it. They will ask themselves whether they are possibly causing financial harm to their company by going one step or one word further. If the answer is yes, they will stop.

Do's and Don'ts for Your Company

Formal codes of ethics are only useful if they are read. If a code is vague, or difficult to memorize, it becomes an unread plaque on the wall. Organizations need to establish a candid, easily understood code, if for no other reason than to declare a position.

The Society of Competitive Intelligence Professionals, based in Alexandria, Virginia, has published the following ethical guidelines for a member's conduct:

To continually strive to increase respect and recognition for the profession at local, state, national, and international levels.

To pursue his or her duties with zeal and diligence while maintaining the highest degree of professionalism and avoiding all unethical practices.

To faithfully adhere to and abide by his or her own company's practices, objectives, and guidelines.

To comply with all applicable laws.

To accurately disclose all relevant information, including the identity of the professional and his or her organization, prior to all interviews.

To fully respect all requests for confidentiality of information.

To promote and encourage full compliance with these ethical standards within his or her company, with third-party contractors, and within the entire profession.

Some Simple Precautions

All the rules and guidelines in the world may not prevent careless—and potentially expensive—mistakes. From my clients' experiences, I offer the following precautions.

Report the facts with few adjectives. Do not editorialize, and avoid hyperbole altogether. One analyst for a large manufacturing company, perhaps a fan of Ian Fleming, punctuated his text with words such as "surreptitious," "surveillance," and "dominate." The first two imply illegal activities. In truth, the report backed up all the findings and the intelligence was developed in the open and above board. Unfortunately, the phrasing told another story. The word "dominate" can set off all kinds of antitrust alarm bells—and did.

As usually happens in such cases, the report found its way to the competitor who was the subject of the study. The competitor chose to sue. The lawsuit was costly

---

The Ten Commandments
of Legal and Ethical Intelligence Gathering

Fuld & Company has published its own guidelines, as follows:

1. Thou shalt not lie when representing thyself.
2. Thou shalt observe thy company's legal guidelines as set forth by the Legal Department.
3. Thou shalt not tape-record a conversation.
4. Thou shalt not bribe.
5. Thou shalt not plant eavesdropping devices.
6. Thou shalt not deliberately mislead anyone in an interview.
7. Thou shalt neither obtain from nor give to thy competitor any price information.
8. Thou shalt not swap misinformation.
9. Thou shalt not steal a trade secret (or steal employees away in hopes of learning a trade secret).
10. Thou shalt not knowingly press someone for information if it may jeopardize that person's job or reputation.

in two respects: (1) the client spent almost three years in court and accumulated huge legal fees; (2) the client had to disclose some trade-secret information in order to defend its case. In the end, the client successfully defended its case, but gave away a great deal of information in the process. (Remember the axiom: Wherever money is exchanged, so is information!)

These are the lessons to be learned here:

- State the facts with little or no dramatization and no "purple prose."
- Support all statements with sources (either printed documents or interview transcripts).
- Avoid flashpoint words, such as *dominate*, that could set off an antitrust lawsuit.

CREATIVE VERSUS BASIC INTELLIGENCE SOURCES

An intelligence source is really any timely, accurate source of information that can eventually be analyzed; often, it is highly specific. This definition may seem quite general, sort of a corporate cop-out, but it defines a wide variety of traditional (basic) and creative sources. Both types are very often needed to locate the necessary intelligence on a target company.

If you were to examine all the possible sources you might need to find the data on a corporation, you would look at a universe split equally between basic and creative sources. Each half of that universe would contain both primary and secondary sources.

Before I go any further, let me explain what I mean by a basic source and a creative source. As the name implies, a basic source is a source you would ordinarily think of when looking for information on a corporation. When hunting for a financial statement, you may search for an annual report or a state filing. If you want background on a company's management, you can look for relevant articles in a library index, and then actually copy the articles from microfilm.

Now, what if the search were not that simple? Let's say that no annual report or state filing is available. To compound the problem, the company was just started two years ago and very little has been printed about it. Going to a library index, in this case, will not work. What do you do? You turn to a creative source.

You may not have an entire income statement, but you can locate enough elements to create an estimated income statement. Town records or a quick count of the number of parking spaces outside the plant can give you an estimate of the number of employees. Local interviewing with state and town experts will yield labor rates. A commercial realtor in the area may tell you the value of the property and whether the company is leasing or is the owner. An inquiry at a local box supplier might tell you the plant's production or sales output. The city Chamber of Commerce or a university's alumni records may have details on some of the company's managers.

Using these creative or unusual sources, you will see an income statement taking shape.

A primary source is an original source of information. A secondary source is a source that has recorded or interpreted the information found in the primary source. An annual report or a news article is a secondary source. An interview with an expert, or an aerial photograph, is a primary source of intelligence. Yes, as I mentioned earlier, both basic and creative sources come in primary and secondary forms.

You will need both basic and creative sources to solve most difficult intelligence cases (see Chapter 2 for further details). The following example illustrates the distinction between creative and basic intelligence sources.

The intelligence question is:

I need to locate financial statements and marketing strategies on my competitor. The company is privately held and maintains a low profile. I believe, though, that I have seen some articles about it. Where do I look for details?

The answer could come from these basic and creative sources:

Basic Primary. Retrieve a state filing.

Basic Secondary. Search for articles in a library magazine index.

Creative Primary. Check the Yellow Pages for marketing information available in the display ads.

Creative Secondary. Call the local newspaper for unindexed articles about the company.

Why Basic Sources Don't Always Work

Usually, any question you may have about a competitor has two overriding requirements:

1. *Currency.* The information you collect must be up-to-date; otherwise, it is useless to you.
2. *Narrow focus.* Your questions are specific. You are looking for a highly detailed answer to a single part of a competitor's activities (for example, you need to know how one out of a competitor's 20 warehouses operates).

These two requirements will often disqualify any basic source. Why? State filings, for instance, are at least six months to one year behind their publication date. Information in magazine articles may be three to six months old before the issues hit the newsstands.

Also, publishers have to meet the needs of their readership. They cannot afford to concentrate on articles of limited interest. You, for example, may be the only reader who would be interested in a story on your competitor's warehousing operation. Keep this time frame in mind next time you are using a basic source to solve your intelligence problem. Remember, such sources can be useful, but they have well-defined limits.

What Is a Creative Source?

The word "creativity" immediately conjures up an image of an artist's canvas or a composer's scoresheet—a blank surface on which a creative person brings out a new image or theme. This same kind of creativity allows the corporate researcher to locate a piece of information that at first glance did not seem to be there.

True, most of the time you will use the same sources—directories, articles, credit reports. For most projects, all of these more basic, common sources will suffice.

But what happens when you enter a new industry or encounter a company whose inner workings you cannot even begin to imagine?

For instance, what do you do when someone asks you to find the original manufacturer of a mouthwash that has not been sold for ten years? What do you do when your supervisor asks you to find the number of retail outlets for a small regional chain, and you discover that none of the standard directories contains a listing? How do you find the number of employees in a particular plant, when the Standard & Poor's directory lists only the parent company's figures? Where do you go to look for plant-by-plant hiring patterns? How do you go about locating details on a competitor's pension trust management program, or its fee structure and services?

All of the above research problems could be relatively easy to solve, provided you take off your research blinders and try alternate sources.

For example, a simple call to a merchandising manager of a large supermarket chain could answer the mouthwash question. Finding a knowledgeable and helpful manager might take as little as 15 minutes.

Finding the number of retail outlets could lead to a stroll through the local Yellow Pages, where all the stores are listed for the metropolitan area in question.

When you need to know the number of employees in a plant, why not go to a state filing or an aerial photograph from the U.S. Geological Survey or a town assessor's office?

Plant-by-plant hiring patterns may appear in help-wanted display ads in the local newspaper. Track those ads and you can discover much more than just hiring patterns.

Should you need to understand a competitor's pension fund program, take the back-door approach. Locate the clients and interview them. Client lists in the pension fund industry happen to be readily available, and those interviewed will likely be more than willing to talk.

These are a few of the creative sources and methods that a researcher must employ to tackle difficult projects. You will find that each assignment, no matter how simple or familiar, will have some new twist or esoteric question.

The key to creativity is persistence. Don't give up when an obstacle appears. Take a step back and examine it. Ask yourself:

- Where might the information be recorded?
- Who ordinarily tracks such information (the government, an association, a newsletter publisher)?
- What are alternate indicators and where can you find them?

Remember, take those blinders off! (For more information see Part Two of this book.)

PUBLIC DOES NOT ALWAYS MEAN PUBLISHED

We all seem to learn, from elementary school on through our university training, that whatever is in print is true and whatever is not in print does not exist. This sounds absurd, but notice how people react. If a news item is in *The Wall Street Journal,* it's credible. If the same piece of news is heard in conversation, it's deemed a rumor.

In stark contrast to this notion, you will find that most competitor and market information is out there and available, but not in printed form. Based on the thousands of research projects my firm has completed, I would argue that less than 1 percent of all business information will ever find its way to print.

This brings to mind another perplexing question: If so small an amount of information is in print, why use published sources at all? The answer is that published sources (databases, government filings, news articles, and so on) can lead you to the people who know the answers or have the information you need. That is why it is so critical to know where and how to find the vital published information. Without it, you will have a hard time finding experts or other primary sources.

The next section discusses how to use published sources to develop your primary intelligence.

War Story: Rust, Chicks, and Jade: The Tale of Intelligence

A. A Case of Rust. A group of Japanese engineers pulled over to a railroad siding near a competing American manufacturing plant and measured the density of the rust that had accumulated on a piece of rail leading up to the competitor's loading dock. They did not trespass. By entering this rust density measurement into a mathematical formula they had developed, they were able to determine the number of times box cars had slid up to the loading dock over a period of time. Using that indicator, they were able to estimate the volume of shipments.

B. Hatching a New Idea. How did the Chicago Museum of Science and Industry discover that its hatching chick exhibit was the most popular exhibit in the museum? There were no turnstiles, and no counting mechanism was available. The answer lay with the floor tile. The Museum's janitors kept coming to the curators, complaining that the tile wore out far quicker around the chick exhibit than anywhere else. Eureka!

C. It's All in the Eyes. Sellers of jade in ancient China were able to tell—without words or hand motions of any sort—when a customer was interested in one piece of jade more than in another. They simply looked into their customer's eyes. When the customers' pupils dilated more for one piece of jade than for another, they had their answer.

All these stories demonstrate that human behavior, not machines, databases, or high technology, can reveal a company's behavior or strategy. In story A, for example, rust is a chemical by-product, but that by-product also reflects the number of cars someone ordered to the loading docks. The chick and jade stories follow similar lines.

All corporations—whether manufacturing or service—are the result of human beings and their transactions. Keep these stories in mind and you will be able to surmount your competitors' seemingly impenetrable castles.

THE BUSINESS LIBRARY:
YOUR FIRST INTELLIGENCE SOURCE

Know your library. Remember, never overlook the straightforward solutions to an intelligence problem. Your library is one of those solutions. It may serve to answer only 10 percent or less of your truly difficult intelligence problems, but it is also your insurance against missing a simple article or directory listing that will get you off to a fast start in your research. When doing your homework for an intelligence-gathering assignment, the library should be your first stop.

When competitor intelligence, by definition, must be current, how can a library help? What are its resources?

Most libraries offer a collection of specialty trade directories that cannot be found anywhere else. These names are leads—entries into an industry. Some of the types of directories and other sources of information you will find in a business library are:

Industry dictionaries. These will quickly bring you up to speed on insiders' lingo and terminology.

Trade magazines. Obscure periodicals that no one else may stock can often be found in a specialty business library.

Case studies and theses. Business schools generate reams of these industry cases and student theses each year. They contain a wealth of information—and perhaps some insight into your target company.

Statistical collections. A good business library will house a combination of governmental statistical publications, such as those of the U.S. Department of Labor and Department of Commerce. Almost every sizable trade association produces an annual industry statistics volume. You will find many of these at your local business library.

Literature indexes. For almost every body of industry literature there is a corresponding index that some enterprising publisher has seen fit to print. Examples include Funk & Scott (F&S), Public Affairs Information Service (PAIS), Business Periodicals Index, and Engineering Index.

Computer search service. There is hardly a business library today that does not have a computer search service available to its patrons. Although we will discuss databases in another chapter, know now that a database search—with all its problems—is still the quickest and most effective way to scan the literature.

Union catalog. Each library has a union catalog listing the library holdings by subject, title, and author. The more progressive libraries have their catalogs on microforms or online.

Special bibliographies. Librarians have compiled special bibliographies as a beginning researcher's shopping list to the best sources to look for in a particular industry.

The reference librarian. Never forget the best resource any business library has. The reference librarian works with the library's collection every day and

becomes familiar with materials you have no idea even exist. If you are
stumped, or need to bounce some of your research thoughts off someone, try
the reference desk librarian.

Corporate report collections. Some libraries may stock only the Fortune 500 annual reports; others may offer SEC filings for all publicly traded companies going back 20 years. In addition, a number of the better-endowed libraries
subscribe to the often expensive Wall Street Investment Services, which issue
reports on publicly held companies.

Tips to Finding a Business Library

There are general business libraries and specialty business libraries. Some libraries
serve a broad community; others operate within the confines of a corporation.
    There are literally thousands of these business libraries throughout the coun-
try. Most of them are small, and many are dedicated to a special industry segment.
Finding these libraries is relatively easy, provided you know where to look. Here
are some tips:

Business schools. Almost every business school will have some sort of library or
literature collection. Locate the major business schools in your area and find out
what the admissions policy is. A number of university business libraries have
begun to restrict outside public use of their collections. You may need a special
pass or may have to pay a fee (sometimes steep) to use the library.

Corporate libraries. Companies large and small have established literature collections. They can be found in all stages of organization, from those containing
a card catalog system to those that operate haphazardly out of someone's back
office. Some corporate libraries, like GTE's, may have satellite libraries at various locations linked through a computerized index network.

You can find the library you are looking for by just calling a company whose
industry you are examining, or by contacting your local chapter of the Special Libraries Association.

Special Libraries Association (SLA). This is networking at its very best. Most
SLA chapters have published their own directories, with indexed listings of
member libraries (many of them corporate and university). The New York chapter reflects the largest assembly of business libraries in the United States. The
national headquarters of SLA is in Washington, DC. There are local SLA chapters throughout the country. To locate an SLA chapter, contact your local library (corporate or public), and the reference librarian there should be able to
answer your questions.

Directories of business libraries. There are a number of these. One of the more
popular is *Subject Collections* (R. R. Bowker).

Public business libraries. Fear not. Your local public library has not deserted
you. In fact, a number of municipal libraries have excellent business collections.
In Boston, there is the Boston Public Library's Kirstein Business Branch. In
Brooklyn, there is the downtown branch of the Brooklyn Public Library, which
is considered one of the best business libraries in the country.

Major Business Libraries: Use Them!

By definition, universities with prestigious business schools will also have excellent business libraries. These repositories contain unusual magazines and trade news that you would be hard pressed to find elsewhere.

In addition to the magazine collections, business libraries are likely to house an extensive file of annual reports. Because many of these libraries were originally funded by wealthy families with interests in particular industries, certain libraries will specialize in collecting business information from industries represented by these families.

These libraries should be the starting point for any corporate research you may begin. If you are not located near one of the libraries, try a telephoned or written request for information. In many instances, they will respond, often charging only for photocopying and postage.

THE RIGHT RESEARCH STUFF: TRAITS TO WATCH FOR

Expert corporate intelligence analysts are often hard-nosed perfectionists, at least when it comes to finding and analyzing information. They can smell out a source, and they doggedly pursue answers to particularly tough questions. Good researchers are not born, they are molded and shaped. (See Chapter 14, "How To Build Your Own Intelligence System," for more details on staffing.)

Something else to note: educational degrees can be almost meaningless when it comes to succeeding as an interviewer or analyst. Education certainly can help here, but experience and talent are far more important. A business or engineering degree, for example, teaches a general body of knowledge; it does not teach how to pursue a line of questioning, or how to read the rust on competitors' rails. I have found talented intelligence analysts packing a raftload of diplomas and others with little more than a high school education. Do not ignore a prospective analyst's education, but concentrate on the following specific traits:

1. *A good listener.* I have formally interviewed scores of intelligence managers and asked them what trait they considered most important. Almost universally, they cited "listening." Your best listeners may fall far outside your own market research or intelligence group. The best salespeople are terrific listeners. Your listener may come from R&D, Customer Service, Field Engineering, or any number of groups within the corporation.

2. *Creativity.* The successful analyst spots things like rust on rails and other odd-ball or quirky information that may indeed be the smoke trail left behind by a competitor.

3. *Persistence.* Rock climbing is the image that comes to mind when I think of the high-performance analyst. He or she doesn't let go before latching on to some sort of an answer or onto another solid lead. The persistent analyst will not give up just because a contact firmly states: "If I don't know it, it just doesn't exist." Nine times of ten, I have managed to prove such a source wrong. If I couldn't find the exact answer I wanted, I found a proxy. You can, too.

4. *Strategy.* To save precious time—especially with an eleventh-hour deadline— the astute researcher will devise a plan of attack, an efficient means to find the

vital intelligence. Random research means wasted time, lost dollars, and failure to meet the deadline.

5. *Experience.* Think *fat Rolodexes.* Companies need to identify or hire analysts with 5, 10, or 20 years of industry experience. These are individuals with long lists of contacts and industry experience. They can quickly qualify an answer, add value to the information, and find someone who can confirm or disprove a rumor. A young MBA, fresh out of school, generally cannot accomplish the same feat. So take heart, if you are an engineer, salesperson, or other manager with years of industry experience; you may be a far better analyst than you ever thought you were. Knowing whom to contact and what questions to ask is critical, and that takes experience.

In all this discussion of traits and experience, be aware that to be successful as an analyst you will need some basic information-related skills. (See Chapter 13 in this book, as well as my other text, *Monitoring the Competition,* Wiley, 1988, pp. 137–146.) These skills include:

1. *Understanding databases.* Become a good consumer of intelligence, but not necessarily an information technician. Have your librarians, or a company such as Dialog, train you in the structure and use of online databases. By knowing what they are and what they can do for you, you'll ask better questions on your next literature search.

2. *Knowing your library.* Too many executives know where their library is but not what it contains. Take a detailed tour of its collection, particularly of the files and unique internal databases its staff has built.

3. *Training on software packages.* A spreadsheet package or a statistical analysis package may save you a great deal of analytical time in the long run.

4. *Writing and Interviewing.* Find ways to improve your communications skills—writing and interviewing in particular. Good analysts know how to state a fact convincingly and quickly. They also know how to make people listen and respond to their questions.

ASSEMBLING YOUR RESEARCH TEAM OR CLUSTER

We have noted that certain characteristics make a good researcher or intelligence analyst. Taking that thought a step further, ask yourself: "What individuals and roles are needed to form a well-oiled intelligence team?"

The ideal team consists of an analyst, a project manager, and a librarian. For purposes of this discussion, each position is defined as follows:

Librarian/Database searcher. This person will gather and organize all published data.

Analyst. The individual who conducts the interviews, gathers other unpublished data, and then adds value to the resulting information by analyzing it.

Manager. A manager will coordinate the research team and possibly settle any political issue with clients.

A Management Imperative:
Turning Data into Intelligence

LEONARD FULD: Why, in many large organizations, doesn't critical intelligence reach corporate management soon enough, while in other organizations intelligence seems to move up the corporate ladder very quickly? Can you identify the two or three major obstacles to successful use of competitor or business intelligence? Which corporations stand out as models of business intelligence usage?

ROBERT WATERMAN: The main opportunity in the arena of competitor intelligence is to move from masses of data to true information. That idea sounds obvious, but seems always to be missed. The problem is twofold: first, gathering too much information without focusing and, second, using the wrong lens to focus.

Take the first problem. A typical scenario is this. A newly energized manager, or hotshot planner, has heard about the value of analyzing competition. A mountain of data is gathered and presented on every facet of the competitive world out there. People are overwhelmed by the completeness of the work, but also overwhelmed because they simply cannot digest all that data. Their very effort to solve a problem has defeated their own ability to do so. Analysis paralysis.

People defeat their own effort in another way, and that has to do with the second problem: using the wrong lens to focus the data. What happens here is that people terrify themselves with the information they gather. The lens they use is an economic model that assumes the fundamentals we all learned from economics: rational competitors and customers, movement toward perfect competition, and competitors out to beat up on one another. Viewed through this sort of lens, the world out there looks very frightening. It's easy to conclude that everything will degenerate to straight commodity competition, that no profit margin will be left, and that someone else will do better—a different kind of analysis paralysis.

The most helpful lens is shaped by these assumptions: (1) The main use of competitor intelligence is to learn best practices from the outside; (2) there is no such thing as a commodity; and (3) even where commodity conditions seem to reign, the best companies can still make money.

Assumption 1: Learn Best Practices from Outside

The reason the first assumption is so important is that it leads to action. Study of best practice from the outside—that is, benchmarking—leads naturally to asking what your company has to do to be better. It's a far more upbeat and energizing approach than the usual, which is to look only at competitive threat and how to defend against it. As they say, a good offense is the best defense.

Assumption 2: There Is No Such Thing as a Commodity

The reason for the second assumption is to get people focused on the real economic transaction, and that happens when company meets customer. (In
(Continued)

(Continued)

business, organizations battle one another through fighting for common customers; they do not battle one another directly as teams would in sports or armies would in war.) Most managements fail most conspicuously in understanding their customers. Who are they—present and potential? What are they really buying? These questions seem simple. They're not. The reason is that everything a customer buys is a package of goods and services, not a commodity. Wrapped in that package are multiple appeals. Price is the obvious one. But there are a host of others: quality, features, service, delivery, and so on. With a little brainstorming, one might list as many as 30 to 40 different appeals that accompany one product offering. The crucial question, then: Which appeals are most important and for which market segments?

Innovation

My own look at some of America's best organizations and their practices suggests they distinguish themselves, from the customer's point of view, in two main ways. One is that they simply out-innovate their competitors. The second is that they are simply more reliable than the rest in delivering what their customers think they were promised. Companies from relatively low-tech Rubbermaid to very high-tech Merck are great examples of competing through raw innovation. In 1993, Rubbermaid introduced 365 new products, one for each day of the year, a statistic the people there love to talk about.

The intelligent question is: How do they do it? On close study, several themes emerge. One is extraordinary focus on market niches that leads in turn to extraordinary ability to anticipate customer needs. Another is skill in managing cross-functional teams. A third is in involving customers in not only product idea generation but also product development. There are more.

Merck, the world's largest drug company, is also the most constantly innovative. How do *these* guys do it? Big companies are supposed to kill the innovative spirit. They make it their business to stay right at the cutting edge of technology; most Merck researchers have taught or could teach in the nation's leading medical and science universities. But in dramatic contrast to university practice (and frequent industry practice), Merck links its scientists and others in uniquely interdisciplinary teams. There are more attributes of innovation at both Merck and Rubbermaid. The point is that you learn a lot by looking at the best.

Genuine Customer Satisfaction

Looking at the best also leads to the second major dimension of competitive advantage: genuine customer satisfaction. A cursory look at Motorola would suggest that their competitive advantage is their relentless pursuit of total quality. In an effort that started in 1979, this company strives to drive the defects in any process to a near-perfect three mistakes per million items handled. The cursory look would be partly right. But a deeper look would reveal that their definition of "mistake" means blunder as seen by customer, not fault as defined by engineers. A major part of their strategic edge, therefore, turns out to be what

(Continued)

they call "total customer satisfaction." The same is true for other successful total quality and total service programs: what they really are about is satisfying customers better than competition.

Assumption 3: Success Even Where Commodity Conditions Reign

While the second assumption (no such thing as commodity) yields major opportunity for those who make it, some industries (for example, natural resources, industries in over capacity) force price competition. You can still make a buck. Again, the trick is to look with the right lens. For a company in such an industry, the absolutely prime piece of competitive information is your cost compared to competition; in these industries, as the economists would predict, it's the struggling high-cost competitor who sets the price. As long as your costs are lower, you make money (total market demand keeps the high-cost competitor barely in business to meet total market needs). While competitors can't directly exchange cost data, the good companies do a remarkably good job of estimating their cost position relative to competitors. Phelps Dodge, the copper giant, almost went out of business when copper prices plunged to around 60 cents a pound, way below this company's costs. These days, aided by technology and wrenching cost cutting, the company operates well below the industry cost structure, even in bad times. Phelps Dodge makes money in a commodity business, even in bad times.

The general rule then is to pick the right lens to turn strategic data to information, and to use that lens to look at best practices. The most useful lenses help you look at your capabilities at innovation, your ability to anticipate what customers want, and your cost structure versus that of competitors.

Robert H. Waterman, Jr. is coauthor of *In Search of Excellence* and author of *The Renewal Factor*, and other books. He founded the Waterman Group, Inc., a California-based research and consulting firm, after having spent 21 years at McKinsey & Company.

What if you cannot afford the ideal three-person team? If one person has to wear all three of the above hats, which job is most critical? Which job adds the most value to the intelligence, which is the ultimate product?

The librarian serves in a critical role, as does the manager. But analysis is the watchword here. Without it, you do not develop an accurate picture of the competition. Next time you need intelligence and must hire someone to meet that need, think first of analysis and analyst. The analyst is your cornerstone for building any intelligence effort.

HOW TO STOCK YOUR OWN INTELLIGENCE LIBRARY

An intelligence library is a *directory,* not a *repository.* There is a great difference between a traditional library and an intelligence library. An intelligence library is a directory to information; traditional libraries are repositories for collections of information. A traditional reference library represents a very different philosophy and serves a different purpose.

Many corporations have built formidable libraries to serve R&D, marketing, and other functions. These become huge repositories of important industry and competitor data. I have visited a number of companies that have 20 or more libraries in different locations. They provide data in the form of reference books, magazines, and databases. Companies need repository libraries, but these libraries often fail to take the analyst into the primary arena of experts.

In contrast, intelligence libraries are lean and mean. Their major goal is to direct the analyst to outside sources of information: experts, other analysts, and unpublished resources.

Applying the principle of an intelligence library as a "directory of resources" rather than as a repository, I recommend you enhance your existing library with some of the following categories of source materials (for specific titles, database names, and other information, see the chapter noted for each category or group of categories):

General. Standard & Poor's (Chapter 4); Thomas Registers (Chapter 11); Yellow Pages (Chapter 10).

Specific. Association membership directories, buyers' guides, industry and trade show directories (Chapter 11); file of conference papers and list of internal experts (Chapter 13); international resources (Chapter 6); magazines (Chapter 4).

The list can go on and on. Most of these sources are relatively inexpensive and will serve to lead analysts to the people who have the needed information—both inside and outside your organization.

2 GETTING STARTED

The Basic Approaches and Techniques

There is something to be said for just jumping into the pool and getting wet. All well and good for a swimming lesson, but not for competitor intelligence. You need to prepare the foundation, the research strategy. Without a plan, you will waste time, resources, and—what is worse—inadvertently close many doors by asking the wrong questions in the wrong way. Believe me, I am speaking from experience! Should you choose to charge ahead without a research plan, you will likely waste potentially valuable interviews for which you won't get a second chance. Consider each tidbit of information as priceless, and each interview opportunity as a once-in-a-lifetime event. Collect each one in earnest, but follow a plan. You may go on many detours in your analysis, but as long as you start out with a reasoned approach, you will decrease missteps and increase your prospects for success.

"Never overlook the obvious."

DOING YOUR HOMEWORK

This book advocates the use of creative activities, such as examining aerial photos and corrugated boxes, and of analytical techniques, such as benchmarking or time-lining. But do not mistake the underlying rule: Always do your homework first. For instance, never overlook a simple article or an entry in a trade directory. Sometimes the most basic source will answer your questions. You may use the corrugated-box approach in one out of ten cases; you should search the literature in *every* instance, not just one out of ten. Due diligence is the name of the game in intelligence and competitive analysis.

Remember Murphy's law of intelligence gathering: "The corporate information you have been seeking is probably located in the very sources you decided to overlook because those sources were too obvious."

In reality, most news articles and trade directories only serve as leads to guide you to your answer. They usually do not provide you with the actual answer.

One way to make sure you have done your homework is to use Table 2.1's checklist of the intelligence sources you should use in any project. These are the basic research tools you should have available or at least have access to. Details on each of the sources will be discussed in upcoming pages.

The First Steps

Preparation is everything. In order to develop an accurate analysis, you need to prepare your questions, creating a research road map with which to guide yourself over the course of the assignment.

Parts Three and Four of this book describe ways to analyze the data and ultimately turn the data into intelligence. At this initial stage, you need to find the data. Here are the first steps you must take:

1. *Define the question.* Make sure you know what you and—more important— your client hope to learn.
2. *Learn the industry structure.* Assuming you know nothing or very little of the target company's industry, learn the industry's structure before you plunge into your company-specific research.
3. *Know your sources (basic and creative).* Before grabbing at the sources you always use (library indexes, Thomas Register), stop. Ask yourself what other sources might be more efficient to use and possibly more productive.
4. *Conduct a literature search.* No literature search today would be complete without using a database index. When used correctly, a database sweep can search the literature at lightning speed, much faster than one could pore manually over the *Readers' Guide to Periodical Literature* or the Funk & Scott Index.
5. *Retrieve the articles/Explore the library.* Your library can get you off to a running start with names of experts to call and references to your target company.
6. *Milk those articles.* In the articles you retrieved in your search, look for names of individuals who may know far more about your target company than was revealed in the article in which they were mentioned.
7. *Prepare a strategy.* Once you have located the potential sources and have developed a tentative experts list, begin to pair off the sources. Discriminate between the better and the best sources available, to identify the most accurate intelligence in the most efficient fashion.
8. *Begin the interview process.* Don't wait for all your library research to be completed. Begin the interviewing as soon as you can. Through the interview process, you will begin to refine your intelligence-gathering strategy, a process that continues for the duration of the project.
9. *Conduct a debriefing and record the results.* When the project is over, it's not officially over. To learn from past experience, you should debrief each other on

TABLE 2.1 Research Checklist

1. Company Financials
   - ____ Annual report
   - ____ Credit reports
   - ____ Government filings
   - ____ Moody's
   - ____ Published articles
   - ____ State filings
   - ____ *Wall Street Transcript*

2. Market Share
   - ____ Funk & Scott (F&S) Predicasts
   - ____ Literature search
   - ____ Market studies
   - ____ Nielsen/IRI reports

3. Company Background
   - ____ Annual reports/Government filings
   - ____ Credit report
   - ____ F&S indexes
   - ____ Investment reports
   - ____ Kompass directories
   - ____ Newspaper index
   - ____ Published articles
   - ____ Standard & Poor's
   - ____ *Wall Street Transcript*

4. Industry Background
   - ____ Association reports and studies
   - ____ Industry handbooks
   - ____ Investment reports
   - ____ Published articles and reports
   - ____ Special trade magazine issues
   - ____ Trade magazines
   - ____ *Industrial Outlook Handbook*
   - ____ Value Line

5. Competitors
   - ____ Standard & Poor's
   - ____ Thomas Registers
   - ____ Special trade magazine issues
   - ____ Industry buyers' guides
   - ____ Yellow Pages
   - ____ Associations
   - ____ Leading National Advertisers (LNA)

6. Industry Experts
   - ____ Articles
   - ____ Key magazines
   - ____ Biographies
   - ____ Conference listings of speakers
   - ____ Authors of technical articles
   - ____ Patent holders
   - ____ Consultants
   - ____ University professors
   - ____ Speakers' bureaus

7. Management Personnel
   - ____ Association membership directories
   - ____ Local newspapers
   - ____ PR departments
   - ____ College alumni associations
   - ____ *Wall Street Journal/Financial Times*

8. International Information
   - ____ Chambers of Commerce
   - ____ Consulates
   - ____ Embassies
   - ____ International credit reports
   - ____ International Trade Administration (ITA)
   - ____ Country-by-country data (see Chapter 6)

9. Advertising
   - ____ *Advertising Age*
   - ____ Leading National Advertisers (LNA)
   - ____ Local newspapers
   - ____ Advertising associations
   - ____ News clipping services

10. Government Experts
   - ____ Department of Commerce
   - ____ Chapters 3 and 7 of this book
   - ____ Washington researchers' guides

lessons you have learned and new creative sources you may have stumbled on. Record your new expert names in an index for future reference.

"WHO ELSE NEEDS THIS?": A BIG QUESTION

Do not imagine that you are the only person who has ever asked the vexing question, "What is the competitor's capacity—cost, exports, technology, R&D?" If your company has competition, you can bet that a host of other people are interested in your market, your competition, and your customers. They have had the same questions, and in many instances have found answers.

Here's an example. You are looking for information on a competitor's R&D plans and have run up against a wall. The trade magazines and journals contain little. Where they do have information, it is either dated or too general. You must break out of this mental box and consider who else needs to know this company's R&D activities.

Assume various roles and say to yourself:

- If I were an *equipment supplier,* I would need to know this company's R&D expenditures and direction, in order to know what equipment to sell and customize for this client. Therefore, I will send in my salespeople to ask questions. (Here is one information bridge over the moat we imagined in Chapter 1.)

- If I were a *sponsor of a scientific conference,* I would expect that the competitor's scientists will attend the major conferences and exchange information on new developments; they may even present papers. The industry or professional association probably catalogs these speeches for future reference by its members.

- If I were a *recruiter or head hunter,* I would comb client companies for new hire requests and would begin to send their inquiries throughout the scientific market in search of an appropriate applicant. These activities will, in turn, spawn help-wanted advertisements, spark conversations among professionals at conferences, and have other similar effects.

The list of information seekers goes on and on. If you are in a competitive market, many companies and individuals have reason to seek the same answers to virtually the same questions. Never think you are alone. In fact, imagine you have an invisible committee you need to convene and with whom you wish to exchange ideas and information. You may find these other information seekers within your own company; they almost certainly are within your own industry.

RESEARCH CHECKLISTS FOR THE BEGINNER

Intelligence gathering can be frustrating, especially if you are a beginner who does not know enough to distinguish among the many types of sources.

The following sets of lists should help you select the people to call and the reference books to pull off the shelf. These lists are a purely subjective ranking of the secondary and primary sources I have found most useful when conducting a search. The category labeled "first choice" does not necessarily mean the best choice. It implies only that this list is more likely to point toward the answers than are the second and third choices.

These lists will suggest both specific sources to use (e.g., Nielsen, Moody's Investors Manuals) and general categories, as found in trade magazines and the U.S. Department of Commerce publications. Both basic and creative sources are mentioned.

Each of the lists is arranged by objective. One list offers general market data on an industry, another is a list for a researcher trying to assemble an income statement on a corporation. In addition, there are lists for those who need to gather background information on a company and its management.

Not all sources will apply in every circumstance. Other sources that you may use often may not even be hinted at in these pages because it is virtually impossible to account for every intelligence-gathering situation or case.

Use these sources simply as a guide. They may save you a great deal of work and wasted time, and they may lead you to other sources that will deal directly with your specific need.

Research Priority List 1: Market Overviews

List Objective

To enable the researcher to locate general market data on the industry and the companies he or she is researching. These sources will yield information on market shares, industry size, and trends.

First Choice

Trade magazine annual issues. Almost every trade magazine published has at least one annual issue in which it reviews its industry. This issue often discusses the major players in the industry and offers statistics on sales volume and market data contained nowhere else. Examples of these magazines are *Iron Age, American Metal Market,* and *Advertising Age.*

U.S. Department of Commerce. This Cabinet department tracks industry shipments and trends. Its two major works, published annually, are *U.S. Industrial Outlook Handbook* and *Current Industrial Reports.*

Market studies. This category applies to the thousands of privately published reports produced by stock analysts, publishing houses, and market research firms. These reports may be available for the asking, or can cost thousands of dollars. The data in these reports may not contain much detail on the competition, but may prove valuable for overall market analysis.

Wall Street Transcript. This is a useful source for both specific company information and reviews of an entire industry. This newspaper's Roundtable discussions offer excellent reviews of an industry's key issues and trends.

Commercial databases. Databases, such as Predicasts' Promt file, collect market information from a wide variety of sources and display the information in either statistical or textual form.

Competitors, suppliers. If you can catch people who have been in the business for a number of years and are willing to talk about their experiences, you can learn about some of the subtler aspects of the market. In addition, these participants will be able to give you a regional feel for the market.

Second Choice

Purchasing agents. These agents know what is selling and are up-to-the-minute on the pricing of products. They are also hard to catch for an interview. Whatever your questions are, be specific and to the point. These folks have little time for chitchat and don't care much about the weather, unless it affects their product line's price.

Retailers. Although retailers don't know much about the supply and manufacturing side of the business, they can tell you what sells and what doesn't, and what product lines they are phasing out.

Nielsen/IRI (Dun & Bradstreet). Nielsen, widely known for its television rating system, also tracks retail purchases. Included in the surveys it conducts is one for *Food and Health and Beauty Aids.* Each monthly update contains the most recent data, as well as ten years' historical data. The entire subscription is pricey. If you cannot find room in your budget, you may be able to locate less expensive industry indexes. Or, you can contact your company's advertising agency, which probably subscribes to Nielsen, and ask them to let you review the data.

Stock analysts. Like purchasing agents, stock analysts are not open to much idle conversation. It is their job to watch a market and the companies within that market. Analysts publish reports on their industries. Brokers and analysts have begun cutting back on free distribution of their reports, but you can request a copy through your broker.

Office of Technology Assessment. This government group tracks the latest technology to come out of American industry. It issues reports and data that you may find helpful.

Labor unions. Although they offer information from a narrow perspective, labor unions monitor the employment climate for an industry. A union information office may give you an idea of market performance in light of industry hirings and layoffs.

Third Choice

Local newspapers. Especially in a highly regionalized industry, town newspapers will report on major corporations within an area.

Annual reports. A company's annual report will frequently compare its performance to that of its industry. In the course of making this comparison, it will describe the industry in some detail.

Research Priority List 2: Company Financials

List Objective

To help the researcher assemble a financial statement. This list includes both those sources that directly contain company financials and those that can supply a portion of a financial statement (e.g., labor costs, plant assets) where no complete statement exists in the public domain.

First Choice

SEC documents. In Chapter 3, I will discuss the array of SEC documents that publicly traded companies need to file and which filings meet your needs. At this point, realize that you no longer have to talk directly to the SEC for the appropriate filings. If you have a CD-ROM, you can subscribe to SilverPlatter Information's *SEC Online* (Newton Lower Falls, MA). Disclosure of Bethesda, MD, offers direct document retrieval and CD-ROM access, as well as fax or online databases of all SEC filings.

Annual report. Most public and some private corporations will publish their own version of the SEC's required 10-K annual report. This is usually a slick condensation of the 10-K, designed to impress current and prospective stockholders. Yet, these annuals frequently contain the same income statement and balance sheet information as one would find in the 10-K. Write to the company you are studying and ask to be placed on the mailing list for an annual.

Credit report. This source will be discussed in Chapter 9. Keep in mind that credit reports, while short on financials, can sometimes pull together all the publicly filed financial information. Occasionally, a credit report will also reveal an income statement for a privately held corporation. Beware: these sales figures are, many times, estimates or unverified information given by the company itself. When you begin a major company analysis where financials are a crucial part of the study, always order a credit report on the company.

Trade news articles. A lengthy feature piece in a trade magazine will likely disclose some financial information about a company. It may discuss plant size, number of employees, or sales. Take these reports with a grain of salt. These articles look authoritative, but they are occasionally written by the company's public relations agency with only minor editing on the part of the magazine.

Wall Street Transcript. This source is cited often in this book. It regularly publishes quarterly and annual statements released by publicly held companies. These statements are reduced to bare bones, with little text accompanying them. See "What Did the CEO Say? Ask the *Transcript*," at the start of Chapter 8, for more information on the *Transcript*.

Moody's Investors Manuals. Although rather expensive to subscribe to, this source indexes news summaries and financials for most publicly held companies, public utilities, municipalities, banks, and insurance companies.

Standard & Poor's Daily News Database. This database essentially contains the same information as the Moody's manuals, except that the information here is available online.

Second Choice

Competitors. You will find that competitors are not only knowledgeable about their competition, but may also give you a good deal of information as part of an information swap.

UCC filings. Most researchers find this source more of a tease than a helpful piece of intelligence, but UCCs can be useful in disclosing a new plant asset on which your target may have taken out a loan. See Chapter 11 for further details.

General Corporate Databases. Aside from Disclosure and the SilverPlatter products, there are other databases that cover both large and small companies in different ways. The *Dun's Market Identifiers* (Dun's Marketing Services), a Dun & Bradstreet service, offers addresses and some financial data on millions of companies—privately held and publicly traded. The InvesText database (Thomson Financial Services, Boston, MA), presents online access to scores of recent stock analyst reports.

American Business Directory Databases (American Business Information, Inc.). These two database products, based on telephone directory listings, allow for a speedy, first-cut review of a large number of businesses throughout the United States. Both the *American Business 20 Plus Directory* (containing names of businesses with 20 or more employees) and the larger American Business Directory (containing over 10 million businesses), give the searcher the power to review and sort businesses by industrial classifications, as well as by zip code and size of yellow pages advertisement.

State Filings. State governments require less information from privately held corporations located in their states than they did previously. In many states, companies do not have to do more than give their name, address, and stockholders or owners. Nevertheless, the same rule applies: where you have no other source, it is worth asking for a filing. (See Chapter 3 for more information.)

General Press. Where a company has received a lot of press, you are bound to find some financial details mentioned. A business reporter would be derelict if he or she neglected to get at least a sales or growth rate figure for an article. You will probably have more luck with newspapers located near the plant or company you are studying than you would with a major regional paper.

Town Assessor's Office. The town assessor's office can supply you with tax, ownership, and zoning information that the company may have filed. Or, the assessor can put you in touch with a local town realtor who may know more. These filings are often skimpy, but may still contain more data than are found in a state filing.

Real Estate Agents. Look for a commercial real estate agent who can give you square footage costs of a company's plant and, perhaps, specifications on the plant and equipment.

Courts. Court filings may reveal details on a company's indebtedness or problems involving trademark infringement. Bankruptcy or Chapter 11 filings contain a good amount of detail on the filing companies.

Third Choice

Industry financial ratios. If all you have are a few data items, such as sales and current assets, you can construct a more complex income statement or balance sheet using industry financial ratios. A tricky tool, they can nevertheless give you a good sense of a company's proportions if you are careful in their use. (See the "Financial Ratios" section in Chapter 9 for further discussion.)

Interviews. Although not a scientific approach, interviews can occasionally reveal good guesstimates of a company's sales and assets. Sometimes, this may be the only way you will get a set of financials on a small, privately held company.

Visual sightings. Counting the number of parking spaces and applying a rough formula for number of riders per car will give you an approximate employment figure for a plant or office. Eyeballing a plant can tell you something about its operating machinery and, perhaps, asset value. This is a highly creative, and not always accurate, tool for gauging competitor assets and employment information.

Research Priority List 3: Management Profiles

List Objective

To supply the sources most used for assembling management profiles.

First Choice

Local newspapers. Very often, a national press release on an executive's promotion will only be carried in his or her hometown newspaper or in the newspaper where the plant or office is located. Local newspapers may have also done a feature story on the executive, especially if the executive or the company he or she works for contributes to the economic health of the community.

Who's Who directories. There are many varieties of biographical directories. Some, like Marquis' *Who's Who in Finance and Industry,* cover all industries and the major executives in each. Other directories are geared toward one industry, such as *Who's Who in Electronics.* Overall, a Who's Who will list only 5 percent or fewer of those you might consider important executives, so don't be surprised if you don't find your candidate.

Dun & Bradstreet Credit Reports. D&B reports, and others like them, are designed to analyze a company, not its officers, although frequently the reports include some form of biographical sketch. It is a good place to start when assembling a biography. For example, it may tell you where an executive attended school and where he or she lives. These are both leads to follow through on: contact the alma mater and the local newspaper or Rotary Club.

Annual report and proxy. Annual reports will sometimes contain brief rundowns on the senior executives. Proxies, on the other hand, list the company's officers in some detail. These sources apply only to publicly held companies.

Second Choice

Voter registry and assessor's offices. A local town hall will record the number of occupants in a house and who owns the house, as well as the home owner's age and the number of members in his or her family. Usually, clerks in these offices are very helpful.

Colleague interviews. A touch-and-go source. Sometimes a colleague may be very helpful, especially where he or she has only good things to say about the individual.

Third Choice

Trade journals. Trade magazines will often cover many of the industry's key promotions. Occasionally, they will write up a complete profile on one of its professionals who achieved industry greatness. Instead of focusing on family life and hobbies, these articles reveal much about an executive's management style and financial wizardry.

Trade associations. Associations are very protective of their membership—and rightfully so. But when they have nothing but good things to say about one of their members, they will be happy to talk. When a trade association is unusually reticent, don't worry. They just may not know anything about an executive. One tip: smaller associations are far more helpful and knowledgeable than are larger ones in this regard. They know their members, who may number only in the hundreds, whereas an association with thousands of members is not likely to recall a particular name or face.

Research Priority List 4: Company History

List Objective

To be able to piece together company activities (e.g., acquisitions, name changes, major changes in management).

First Choice

SEC filings. The Securities and Exchange Commission's 10-Ks offer company history and management analysis sections, but only for publicly traded companies. Another filing, the initial prospectus, discusses a new corporation and its brief history.

Annual reports. Many private as well as public companies publish a fairly complete company history in their annual reports.

Corporate directories. Standard & Poor's, ValueLine, and Dun & Bradstreet each publish directories that offer company history. The companies in these listings include both publicly traded and privately held corporations.

Trade news/Special reports. Trade magazines will feature at least one company per issue, profiling the company. These articles are rich with company stories and activities. If there is no library index that covers the trade press in your industry, then select the most likely magazines and call up their editors or library. They will know whether they have recently published an article on your target company. If they have not, the editor can steer you to a competing publication that probably has. (In most industries, one trade magazine will follow its competing magazines very closely. The competing editors may even know each other socially.)

Case studies. These are summaries of a company's operations, written and compiled by various university business schools throughout the country. Case studies can very in length, some amounting to as many as 30 or 40 pages, single-spaced. They will study a particular company's operations, financials, marketing strategy, or organizational structure. Much of the information contained in a case study will come from the subject company itself. Case studies may prove a valuable way to understand an industry and its structure, as well as a single company's operations. Note, however, that the data are often dummied up—for reasons of confidentiality, financials may have been altered.

The Case Clearing House at Harvard Business School is the best known source for case studies. Stanford University also supplies case studies.

Local reporters. Regional and town newspapers will frequently cover a new company from its inception. Even if the newspapers have not written full stories about the firm, they know a great deal of hearsay about it.

Second Choice

Industry interviews. Competitors, suppliers, and those who come into contact with a company on a daily basis will have a fairly good idea of the company's background.

Stock trading statistics. Standard & Poor's daily stock reports, for instance, will allow the researcher to track the progress of a company's stock, how it was traded, and whether there were any splits.

Market studies. Capsule reports describing a company may be contained within a larger market research report. These company summaries are usually very general. The information is considerably dated. It is usually not worth your while to purchase an entire research study to obtain a one- or two-paragraph write-up of the company.

State corporate filings. Most states require a company to file initial articles of incorporation and amendments to describe the nature of the business and how it was capitalized.

Commercial databases. You can find publicly traded companies described in Disclosure's database, available on the Dialog system. These databases, discussed at length in Chapter 5, can also lead you to articles on the target company.

Third Choice

Textbooks. Occasionally, a textbook will cover the history of a company. The chance of finding the right book, with a proper index, is slim.

Local business schools. University business schools conduct their own reviews of various companies. Most likely, a professor will select a company that is close to the school so that he or she can conduct interviews and on-site visits. Therefore, you can locate a study on a local company by looking for the nearby business school.

KNOW THY INDUSTRY BEFORE THY TARGET COMPANY

You have to know something about your target company's industry before you can begin to research the target. Otherwise, you may waste a lot of time and energy speaking to the wrong contacts and asking the wrong questions. Understanding your target's industry is the first step in creating a strategy for researching a company.

When I talk about an "industry," I mean any industry, including service, health care, banking, insurance, as well as manufacturing. The same rules and concepts apply. Different industries call the same positions by different names, but their functions may be identical. In banking, for instance, substitute "licensee bank" for "distributor."

By just leafing through the scores of intelligence sources in this book, even the beginning researcher will soon realize the plethora of sources available on any one company. You can use general checklists and educated guesses as to the best person to speak to, but the question remains: Who are the best contacts and who knows the most about an industry and about a target company in particular?

The answer is simple: The best sources of information are those already involved in the industry—on almost any level. They can be manufacturers, suppliers, distributors, trade magazines, or consumer groups.

Using this concept as a premise, this section has a twofold purpose: (1) to show you the books and directories that list these industry mavens, and (2) to explain what kinds of expertise each industry group has and how each can help you in tracking down details on the target company.

Questions these mavens must answer before you can begin locating data on a particular corporation are:

1. How many importers, suppliers, manufacturers, distributors, consumer groups, trade organizations, and news media are there in the industry?
2. Of these groups, which ones control the largest share of the market?

This second question is crucial. If you can answer it, you are almost certain to locate the intelligence on your target. (See "Five Key Intelligence Factors," in Chapter 1.)

Why is this second question so crucial? Because if you can determine that, let's say, there are hundreds of manufacturers in an industry, but that this same industry has only two trade magazines, which control 80 percent of the readership for that industry, you now have some key information in your hands.

The chances that one of these hundreds of manufacturers knows anything about your target company are small. But the chances that an editor of a trade magazine knows about a company in this industry are far greater; he or she has probably spoken to the company president at some time in the past.

In other words, the group with the largest market share also knows a lot about that market.

Caveat—Do Your Homework First!

Don't forget to do your homework. Search the business literature. You may still be able to answer your intelligence questions from a straightforward press announcement or news article.

Although it provides you with alternate sources to interview, this section assumes you have done your homework and the articles you researched yielded zero or poor intelligence.

HOW TO USE INDUSTRY GROUPS TO YOUR BEST ADVANTAGE

Just knowing that an industry group exists does not mean that you can successfully get the information you need from it. This section, therefore, has two aims:

1. To show you how to speak to each of these groups, helping you to understand how their organizations work, and who or what within each organization may have the answer for you.

War Story: Soap Suds and Confusion

When it comes to understanding an industry, begin at the beginning. Bounding out of the analytical starting gate unprepared can land you in a great deal of trouble and confusion.

A number of years ago, I had to present an intelligence seminar at a detergent company before a team of managers who had an average of 20 years of industry experience. I had to learn very quickly about all the nuances of this industry.

Part of my preparation included asking our librarian to conduct a literature search on the manufacture and marketing of detergents, including the new superconcentrated detergents. What she handed me was a special issue of *Chemical Week* magazine, labeled "Soaps and Detergents." I couldn't have asked for a more wonderful start. It was as if *Chemical Week's* publisher was saying, "Here is an issue we wrote just for you." Unfortunately, the issue was filled with arcane jargon, and laced with terms such as surfactants, sulfonation, saponification. I quickly became confused and frustrated. There must be a better way, and there was.

I turned to the Encyclopedia Britannica and found a detailed description of the detergent process. The critical terms, saponification, sulfonation and the like, were all explained in great detail, in context, and in clear language.

After I had read the encyclopedia's version, I returned to *Chemical Week* armed with the right background information and quickly absorbed my newfound knowledge. If your "basic" backgrounding source is anything but basic, look for an even more basic source that will take your hand and walk you through the complex industrial maze. Often, that source is the encyclopedia.

---

2. To show you how to find the companies and organizations within each group—especially, how to find the companies that are in your target industry.

Seven industry groups are discussed in this section: (1) the media, (2) trade organizations, (3) consumer groups, (4) consultants and analysts, (5) retailers, (6) distributors, and (7) manufacturers and suppliers.

The Media

Some industries have hundreds of publications, so any one magazine or newspaper is a poor source of specific company data. On the other hand, many industries have only a handful of trade magazines representing them. Editors of these trade magazines become excellent company intelligence sources.

Tips for Using the Media

1. *Ask for the editor by topic.* If you don't have the editor's name, ask for an editor by the topic or industry segment your target company represents.

War Story: A Hot Dog Producer's Financials, or How to Avoid Coming to a Grinding Halt
(A benchmark study)

Background. The client, a leading producer of meat products, could not understand how the competitor was constantly beating it on price while apparently expanding its operations. How was this possible? Perhaps the competitor, a small, privately held corporation, was low-balling on price and absorbing a tremendous loss just to gain market share. The alternate answer was not as pleasant: perhaps the competitor is truly a low-cost producer. If so, how did it manage to produce these products and maintain quality at the same time? My firm had to determine where the gaps existed and how the competitor's operations were different.

Findings. We determined that indeed the competitor had a different and more efficient method of producing the meat product. We constructed a pro forma profit and loss statement and drafted a production flow chart for the plant, showing where and how the competitor experienced considerable savings.

The Secret—Knowing the Keystone. There were a number of "secrets," but one stood out: a critical grinding machine. Most manufacturing processes rely on one or two pieces of machinery. Without them, the process would become impossible. Finding this piece of machinery helped answer many questions about the type of process, the efficiency, and the capacity of the facility.

The project team leader was an expert on manufacturing processes and could reconstruct much of the plant's operations from the information embedded in the dozens of town filings. A combination of government documents and interviews with equipment and raw materials suppliers gave us the critical pieces of information needed to build the benchmark cost puzzle on this company.

But the key that unlocked this puzzle for our team was the discovery of a particular food processing machine. Only a half-dozen companies produced such a machine. The team leader interviewed a supplier of this machine. The answers he received brought into focus all the other information he had collected—capacity, processing speed, and efficiencies.

---

2. *Ask for the publisher's library.* If the editor cannot give you a satisfactory answer, ask to speak to the magazine's librarian. Often, trade magazines—especially from publishers that produce more than one magazine—will catalog all their articles. No one editor or writer can hope to remember every article that ever appeared in his or her magazine.

3. *Is there a special issue?* Find out whether the magazine has published a yearly special issue that may have covered the company you are interested in ("The 100 Largest . . ." or "The 50 Industry Leaders").

4. *Use an old article as a reference.* An article you dug up in your search may not answer your questions, but it can provide you with a conversation opener when

interviewing a trade editor. (See "Milking an Article for All It's Worth," later in this chapter.)

5. *Go for the magazine with the largest circulation.* The directories listed below will tell you which magazines or newspapers have the largest circulation. These magazines will have the largest staff and, in turn, the largest information base. This means they probably have the best chance of knowing something about your target company. The one exception is the local town newspaper, which can often glean a good deal of information on a regional company.

Key Media Sources

LNA Multi-Media Report Service (Leading National Advertisers, Inc., New York). This service reports the specific printed and broadcast vehicles in which companies advertise. With this information in hand, you can narrow down your research strategy and examine just those publications or radio or television stations used by particular competitors, suppliers, or others.

Gale Directory of Publications and Broadcast Media (Gale Research, Inc.). This directory organizes most North American publications by publisher, title, and city. A terrific resource if you are trying to identify newspapers that may have published local news stories on a company.

Standard Periodical Directory (Oxbridge Communications). This book offers a brief description and the circulation size for tens of thousands of magazines. As with most Gale reference sources, it is a well-indexed text.

Ulrich's International Periodicals Directory (R. R. Bowker). The master reference guide used by most librarians to locate a magazine worldwide. This three-volume work contains over 120,000 listings.

Working Press of the Nation (Reed Reference Publishing). This reference work adds yet another resource, the names of the key editors of each magazine cited. As you will see in the section on interviewing techniques, it always helps to have a name to open a door. Specifically, with busy weekly magazines, the closer you can get to the right editor, the more time you will save and the more accurate your answer will be.

Trade Organizations

A trade organization may not want to give you very much data about its members, but it is usually happy to discuss its industry. Very often, it has assembled information packets, or an officer is available to answer your probings about its market.

Most trade organizations are nothing more than lobbying groups. Most of them have their headquarters in Washington, DC. Their chief concern is to represent their members in halls of government. Many are also their industry's public and consumer relations voice. Because of their positions, trade associations must marshal the facts about their industries (but not necessarily about their member companies).

If you can find a trade association that represents a large portion of an industry's manufacturers, suppliers, or another industry segment, you have a valuable information source. Where a small number of manufacturers or trade associations hold a large share of the market, they become excellent intelligence sources.

The directories mentioned below are designed to point out which trade associations are dominant in their respective industries. By locating the largest and most powerful associations, you will have also located a likely intelligence source.

Tips for Using Trade Organizations

1. *Do not expect trade associations to give you company-specific information.* They represent their members, not you—a probing researcher. They will be happy to supply you with general industry information, but may be less than cooperative when asked for company-specific data. By giving you "insider" information, they could be compromising their membership.

2. *Ask for the information officer.* In associations where the staff numbers more than five, you will probably find an information officer. Otherwise, the association's president often doubles as the public affairs or information officer.

3. *Ask for their annual study or report.* Most associations have published some form of annual review of their industry. This study is usually available for free or for a nominal charge. Here you will find industry statistics and market share analyses.

4. *Check the data they supply you.* Many trade associations cannot afford to hire market research firms; instead, they use government data. You may have to look very carefully to find the footnotes that state that the information is from a government source. Also, make sure that the industry breakdown they are offering is the one you are looking for. For example, do you want the number of plastics manufacturers, or only those who produce polyurethane?

5. *Be prepared for smug or ignorant answers.* Although most trade associations are extremely helpful, some will discourage your research efforts. In our research, we have discovered that when one trade association claimed that no one had the information, another association was able to give us the answer. If you feel you are not being given the information you expect, then maybe you are speaking to the wrong person in the organization. You could also be speaking to the wrong association. If this is the case, return to one of the directories listed below and try again.

6. *Look for the organization with the largest membership and the largest staff.* Trade groups with the largest staff usually support a library and maintain statistics for the industry. Large size also indicates that the organization is likely to be one of the older, more established trade groups—and may have the greatest number of contacts in the industry.

Key Trade Organization Sources

Directory of Associations in Canada (Micromedia Ltd.). As the name implies, this listing contains the names of the leading Canadian industrial associations, including the names of each organization's chief executive.

Directory of European Industrial and Trade Associations (Gale Research, Inc.). This is a list of thousands of national and regional groups, including technical societies.

Encyclopedia of Associations (Gale Research, Inc.). This multivolume set cross-indexes the thousands of associations, by industry, market served, and name. The descriptions offer membership size (a wonderful tip-off to the researcher who needs to understand the popularity of the association in its own industry).

They also list active committees, key publications produced by the organizations, and names of the chief executives. This wonderful work can be found on almost every library reference shelf.

National Trade and Professional Associations of the United States and Canada and Labor Unions (Columbia Books, Inc.). This directory lists information on 6,300 national organizations.

World Guide to Trade Associations (K. G. Saur). As the name implies, this listing focuses on an international assortment of trade associations. You may want to use this as a supplement to the Gale *Encyclopedia of Associations*.

Consumer Groups

As a timely example of consumer groups, computer clubs are springing up everywhere. The Boston Computer Society, for instance, is one of the largest of its kind in the United States, with thousands of members. Here, a researcher can find out how many new models are on the market and where the users are buying their machines. The Boston Computer Society is, in effect, a giant network of computer users who can supply researchers with valuable insights into the market.

Tips for Using Consumer Groups

1. *Shop around for information.* Consumer groups and market research companies offer a wide variety of reports and findings. To the researcher in search of market data, finding the right group with the best information can be frustrating— and expensive. You may find that the data you need are free for the asking.

2. *Join consumer groups and professional societies.* Membership fees are often nominal, especially for nonprofit groups. Join the club or the society, assuming you qualify. These groups need more than just goodwill to survive. You will be amazed at the number of doors that will suddenly open when you become a member.

3. *Ask for the library or resource center.* The larger clubs and societies have been established for many years and will likely have information centers and files. The industry data you need will be found here.

Key Consumer Group Sources

Cumulative List of Organizations Described in Section 170(c) of the IRS Code (U.S. Government Printing Office). This work lists 300,000 nonprofit organizations eligible for tax-deductible contributions. Listings are alphabetically organized; there is no cross-index.

National Directory of Non-Profit Organizations (Gale Research, Inc.). This directory lists over 140,000 organizations and includes names and addresses. Unlike the above GPO publication, this version is well-indexed.

FINDEX (Cambridge Information Group). Sometimes, the best way to gauge the pulse of society is to see what the trendwatchers are watching. *FINDEX*, considered the best maintained and broadest reference listing of the latest market research studies, offers you that gauge. *FINDEX* is available as both a printed and an online reference work. The database version contains studies starting in 1985.

Yellow Pages (available through your regional Bell System operating group, or independent publishers). If the organization or club you seek has a telephone number, it will probably be listed in the local Yellow Pages. Often, speaking to local association chapters, rather than to the national headquarters, can give you more insight on societal or industrial trends.

Consultants and Analysts

Consultants abound in the business world. When a problem arises, you don't have to look far to find a consultant to solve it.

Consultants are entrepreneurial by nature and have marshaled a wealth of experience and contacts that makes them extremely valuable for company research. Any consultant who has been in business for many years has accumulated hundreds, if not thousands, of contacts. Why not use this expertise to your advantage?

Tips for Using Consultants and Analysts

1. *As a company, a consultant sees you as a prospective client.* Use this position to your advantage. Market research firms have a hard time getting data from other research firms because they are the competition. But as a company, you become a prospective client. You do not have to mislead the consultant; like anyone else, a consultant will soon see through a ruse. But by just being straightforward and explaining your position—that you are doing research on a company—you will find many a consultant offering you free information. After all, the consultant feels that this small favor will make you think of him or her in the future when you may want to hire an outside expert.

2. *Consultants appreciate receiving as well as giving information.* Swap what you've got before you ask for too much. Information is a consultant's bread and butter, a commodity to buy and sell. Add to the consultant's storehouse and he or she will be happy to give you some information you may not already have.

3. *Narrow down your field as much as possible.* Particularly in the technical fields, consultants find their own niches. Frequently, these fields are so specialized that other consultants, even in a related area, may not have heard of these specialities. Directories like the ones listed below will help you locate the consultant of your choice.

4. *Articles will help you find consultants.* A consultant's best advertising vehicle is plain old publicity in the relevant field's trade magazine or newspaper. If you are having a hard time finding a consultant in your field of interest, search for an article in that field and watch the consultants pop out—as articles' authors or subjects.

5. *Consultants are great sources of management background.* They are privy to insider information about a company; they also hear almost every rumor to come down the industrial pike. When you are looking for nonfinancial information about a company, turn to a consultant.

Key Consulting Sources

Bradford's Directory of Marketing Research Agencies and Management Consultants in the United States and the World (Denlinger's Publishers Ltd.). This text is revised every two years and contains over 2,400 listings.

Consultants and Consulting Organizations Directory (Gale Research, Inc.). This book indexes consultants in over 135 categories, as well as by location. Categories range from Sales Forecasting and Religion to Materials Science and Interior Design.

Directory of Management Consultants (Kennedy Publications). This text concentrates only on management consultants and lists them by specialty.

Dun's Consultants Directory (Dun's Marketing Services). One of the largest and most general directories of its kind, it contains approximately 25,000 listings of consultants.

European Consultants Directory (Gale Research, Inc.). You have to understand the widely varying European market to realize that this directory, even with its listing of over 5,000 businesses, is just a beginning—but a good one. As with all of the above directories, you must qualify your contacts and make sure they meet your needs—something that is more difficult when you are dealing with other cultures and languages.

Retailers

Department stores, discount houses, and mom-and-pop retail stores will offer you some extremely valuable information on your competition. Although your competitor may have already made certain moves that you might have caught earlier in the business cycle, you can still learn many details by interviewing the retailers who carry your competitor's products.

Here is some of the competitive information you can learn from a retailer.

1. Where is a product positioned in the store?
2. Has your competitor designed a special display for the product?
3. What are its price points? Do discount stores price the product differently?
4. Has your competitor tailored the product to fit different markets? Is it sold in two types of packages, one to appeal to the mom-and-pop shop and another for the mass merchandiser?
5. What is the product's retail market share?
6. Is your competitor shipping the product on time, or are there delays? Do these delays differ between small stores and large discount chains, for example?
7. Is the retailer being supported with manufacturer's co-op advertising?

Tips for Using Retailers

1. *Speak to the department manager.* The manager is likely to know such items as a product's market share in his or her department (in other words, how that product is selling in that area), product price points, and packaging and display information. The manager will also be able to tell you service and warranty conditions and where the nearest service dealership is located.
2. *Buyers are everything to a retailer.* These are backshop executives who make all the buying decisions for either a store or an entire chain. They see the factory salespeople, independent representatives, and distributors. Aside from pricing, they may also have inside knowledge of a company, its management, and how it

operates. Because they price shop, they know, probably better than anyone else, who the industry leaders are and where the market is concentrated.

Unfortunately, they are also busy people and most, when you speak with them, sound as if they are in a rush. Tell the buyer that the questions you have to ask will take no more than a minute (and stick to your promise), and that you will swap information on the company. Usually, this will open some more doors for you.

3. *Walk through the store.* There is no better way to understand how a store positions and displays a product.

4. *Speak to more than one chain store.* Although the competitor's product is being sold in an entire chain of stores, how it is displayed and marketed can differ widely from store to store.

5. *Contact the store's receiving room.* Those stocking the shelves can tell you whether they have received the product for a new promotion, and how often they restock the product.

Key Retail Trade Sources

Directory of Discount Stores/Catalog Showrooms (Lebhar-Friedman). This directory contains names of the key executives for each chain, as well as the chain's sales volume and product lines.

Directory of General Merchandise, Variety & Specialty Stores (Chain Store Age). This source lists the senior executives of each chain, as well as some information on the sales and the product lines carried.

Fairchild's Retail Stores Financial Directory (Fairchild Publications). A detailed profile and financial description for each of over 250 chains.

National Association of Chain Drug Stores (National Association of Chain Drug Stores). An unusual directory that lists both the stores themselves and the key suppliers. Each listing identifies the mix of company-owned and leased stores.

Sheldon's Major Stores & Chains (Phelon, Sheldon and Marsar, Inc.). A detailed directory that contains information on discounters, clubs, catalog showrooms, jobbers, and rack jobbers.

Distributors

How a product is distributed can tell you a good deal about the manufacturer and its marketing plans. Some companies will distribute their own products (for example, Radio Shack). Other companies may use outside, independent distributors or trucking fleets.

By tapping into these lines of distribution you, as a researcher, can learn how much a company is shipping and how it is promoting one product, for example.

When I talk about distributors, I mean railroads, trucking firms, and warehouses. In a less strict sense, these distributors can include the nonmanufacturing industries such as insurance brokers, licensee banks, and health care delivery services. These are all elements in the distribution network.

Let's say, in one research case, you are able to find out that the industry you are studying has only three distributors covering 90 percent of the industry. This should tell you that speaking to a distributor can tell you a good deal about any of the manufacturers in that industry.

Tips for Using Distributors

1. *Check to see whether your target company uses an independent trucking fleet.* Because many smaller manufacturers cannot afford to maintain an entire fleet of trucks, truck leasing can play an important role in your search. Like corrugated boxes, rented trucks are another incidental intelligence source. Find the leasing company and you may have found a source of production and shipping information on your target company.

2. *Speak to a retailer to find out how the company ships its products.* Retailers can tell you how long it takes a company to deliver an order and whether the company is back-ordered. Because retailers are sensitive to customer needs, they are inclined to keep on top of their supplier's delivery and service.

3. *Distributors can tell you which products move best.* If a distributor feels a product is not moving, it will drop that particular item quickly. Conversely, should a distributor detect that an item 'is turning over fast, the distributor will be sure to hop onto the bandwagon before demand overtakes the manufacturer's ability to supply the product and the distributor gets caught short.

4. *Ask for a distributor's line card.* Independent market representatives and distributors issue what are known in the trade as line cards. These cards indicate what product lines each distributor carries and describe the products in some detail. Line cards vary in size and detail. For example, some distributors will print their line card on the back of their business card. Others may design their card as a file folder, with the products and marketing information written on both the inside and outside of the folder. Line cards allow the researcher to quickly gauge the size of a manufacturer's product line, as well as to discern which products move the best. By ordering a number of line cards from competing distributors, you can determine which types of products are the most popular.

Key Distribution Sources

Air Freight Directory (Air Cargo, Inc.). This directory lists trucking and shipping companies that will deliver freight to and from the air carriers.

American Warehousemen's Association Membership Directory (American Warehousemen's Associations). A listing of 550 public warehousing companies throughout the United States.

American Wholesalers and Distributors Directory (Gale Research, Inc.). This directory contains a monumental list of over 20,000 wholesalers throughout the United States.

International Directory of Public Refrigerated Warehouses (International Association of Refrigerated Warehouses). A detailed listing of approximately 1,000 public refrigerated warehouses worldwide.

Thomas Food Industry Register (Thomas Publishing Company). An invaluable directory if you are doing any competitive analysis of the food industry. It lists over 45,000 companies and organizes them both by the function they serve (brokers, distributors, manufacturers) and by location.

Warehousing/Distribution Directory (K-III Information Company, Inc.). This takes the *American Wholesalers* . . . directory (listed above) a step further in one specific area: it lists approximately 800 warehousing and consolidation companies that offer truck, trailer, or other carrier services.

Manufacturers and Suppliers

Throughout this text, I discuss sources of manufacturing and manufacturer information—the Thomas Register, the Dun & Bradstreet Million Dollar Directory, and the Standard & Poor's corporate directory, among others. We will not go into depth here about the pros and cons of each source. These sources will be covered in Chapter 4.

Because manufacturers are in the center of the product cycle, they can tell a researcher about an industry's suppliers, distributors, consultants, governmental offices, trade press, and, of course, the competitors.

Aside from gleaning names from such sources as the Thomas Register, there is one book that is indispensable for determining the size and makeup of your target industry: the *U.S. Industrial Outlook Handbook*. For a list of specific industry sources, see Chapter 4.)

The *U.S. Industrial Outlook Handbook* explores and reports on hundreds of U.S. industries, giving the reader the number of companies, their concentration, and their geographical distribution. It will describe the industry's growth rate and product trends. At the end of each section, it offers a brief bibliography of other sources you may want to refer to. In addition, it states the name and phone number of the Department of Commerce analyst who compiled the report. The *Handbook* is published by the Government Printing Office and appears annually.

MILKING AN ARTICLE FOR ALL IT'S WORTH

Searching through business literature can be a frustrating experience for people who desperately want to locate details on a company. Why? Because most people have unrealistic expectations of what the literature can offer, and they generally do not understand an article's true potential.

There are two major problems with searching for corporate information in an article:

1. Your question may be too narrowly focused. No publisher in its right mind would publish an article on a very narrow subject that might interest only two or three readers. You don't sell papers or subscriptions that way. An article can *hint* at your subject, but that is all.

2. Likely as not, you need timely information about your competition. That often means that the event may have occurred literally yesterday or last week. Apart from daily publications, this kind of deadline is difficult for trade magazines to meet.

Monthly and weekly magazines may have a six-month waiting list for certain articles. Although an article appears on a particular date, it may have been written six months earlier, and researched months before that. Timeliness is not usually a trade magazine's highest virtue.

What *can* you use an article for? You can turn it upside down and inside out for valuable leads. Leads come in the form of names of experts, companies, suppliers, and so on. These are live experts, not names that have been lying in some directory or randomly assembled. These names have a direct link to your target company. Use them. Some typical types of sources you will find in a business article are: authors, competitors, suppliers, distributors, end-users, similar products, and industry experts.

Articles are especially useful when dredging up information on a company in a new and little-known industry.

INTERVIEW TECHNIQUES

The telephone is your most valuable research tool. It allows you to go outside the narrow confines of a particular city or company. In just a few brief minutes a caller can solicit answers to questions from a wide variety of sources—that is, if he or she is skilled in getting the answers.

Knowing when and how to ask the right questions takes a combination of instinct and experience. The do's and don'ts that follow are culled from Fuld & Company's experience in the field. They are not completely foolproof. Sometimes, you may hit a string of successful calls; other times, you may strike out.

My apologies for making some of the suggestions sound almost too simple, but sometimes it may pay to belabor the obvious. After all, one person's forest is another person's trees. By employing these suggestions, you will be well on your way toward using the telephone as a powerful information-gathering tool.

- ☑ *Explain who you are and why you are calling.* Play it straight. Tell who you are and why you are calling. By doing so, you become more than just a disembodied voice on the other end of the line. You become a person, accountable to some corporation or organization. You establish credibility and put the contact at ease.

- ☑ *Have a name at hand.* Ask for a specific person. By knowing the names and titles of knowledgeable sources, you eliminate fishing for experts and avoid runarounds.

- ☑ *When in doubt, ask for public relations or personnel.* If you don't know whom to talk to, ask for public relations. PR people generally know who's who and what's what in a company. They can either put you in touch with the experts in their firm or direct you to outside sources. They can also dig up organizational data or industry statistics in a hurry.

  If public relations is of no help, ask for personnel. This area's strength is in locating the right department. It has organization charts handy, as well as divisional or group locations.

- ☑ *Don't be a know-it-all; don't act tough.* Most people love to talk about their areas of expertise and will respond nicely to a disarming interviewer. Come on too strong, however, and the contact will go on the defensive and clam up. No one who feels threatened is going to offer information. Likewise, no one will talk freely if you appear to already have all the information you need, or can easily get it elsewhere.

- ☑ *Smile when you dial.* This is an old sales trick that applies to any research setting. If you have a smile on your face when you talk on the phone, your voice carries that message to the person on the other end. Human nature being what it is, people are always more receptive to exuberance than they are to ennui.

☑ *Be humble, be naive.* Play it smart by acting dumb. By claiming to know little or nothing about the subject—but desperately wanting to learn—you will probably get a respondent to offer more information. Or, the person may feel sorry for you and refer you to another source.

    This technique also allows the researcher to ask questions until the information is clearly understood. In research, the only dumb question is the one that isn't asked.

☑ *To get a response, feed information.* Remember, you are calling people out of the blue. To help orient their thought and adjust them to your thinking, tell them some of what you have found out to date and what you still need. Tell them about some of the industry gossip you have heard. Also, mention the gaps that your research still has.

☑ *Bracket data.* Many professionals refuse to give or feel hesitant in offering numbers or statistics off the top of their heads. They would rather refer to a textbook—which, of course, is never handy when you are calling.

    Help them along by giving them a range of numbers to work with. For example: "Do you think sales are between $10 million and $15 million, or are we talking more in the range of $50 million to $75 million?" Another example might be: "Are we talking about five types of wiring or 50 types?"

☑ *Say you were referred.* Referrals are door openers. Whenever you call someone based on a referral, make sure that your first sentence includes the name of the person who referred you.

☑ *Exchange information.* The maxim "You get nothing for nothing" holds very true when it comes to research.

You will encounter a lot of resistance if you are pestering someone who will gain nothing from your questions. No one likes to feel milked. U.S. government analysts may be the only exception; they are specifically hired to answer a taxpayer's questions.

    For everyone else, however, swap information or offer to send them a small portion or summary of your results (without sacrificing confidentiality or disclosing too much of the report). This is an especially effective technique when soliciting information from service professionals (marketing consultants, management consultants) who make their living dispensing advice. They are not likely to give you any information unless you can offer something in return.

Your Sense of Timing or How to Make Sure You Reach Your Expert

Bracketing your data and swapping information are excellent ways of making your interview successful. This assumes you are able to reach the interviewee in the first place. In order to better ensure your getting through, I recommend the following tactics:

☑ *Don't call on Mondays.* Mondays are the best time to reach experts and the worst time for getting them to talk to you. Imagine your own situation. You probably have left a number of pressing needs hanging from your Friday departure. In addition, you are not yet in the frame of mind to be interviewed by anyone. The expert feels the same way.

☑ *Mornings are better than afternoons.* By Tuesday, a person is in the work-week frame of mind. So, aside from Monday mornings, the early part of the workday is often the best time to reach executives. They have the fewest intrusions early in the day.

☑ *Try the contact twice, then call back once more.* Three times should be enough. Your time is precious, too. If you do not find a potential respondent cooperative, then move on to the next one. Remember, there is always more than one expert.

☑ *Don't overkill.* Although many people admire persistence, few welcome pests. Do not make yourself a nuisance. People may refuse you because they just do not have the time to give that week. Should you create ill will at this first encounter, you may be closing doors to any future contact or additional surveys you will have to conduct.

☑ *Set up a call-back time.* If you set up a time to call back, the respondent will expect to hear from you and at least has to have some kind of answer to your questions. Generally, a respondent appreciates that you respect his or her time enough to schedule the interview.

☑ *Tell the respondent how long the interview will be.* Never say the interview "will take a few minutes." Anyone who has ever received a consumer telephone survey call realizes that the "few minutes" stated by the interviewer can often run into a half hour or more. Meanwhile, your supper has gone cold and your anger has heated up.

Keep your surveys relatively short, but always state an accurate time. It is always better to give an exact time or one that sounds fairly precise. For

---

War Story: "Hello, Mr. Chairman"

A client had asked us to conduct a specialized series of interviews with a select group of CEOs, some of whom were heads of Fortune 500 corporations.

Now, when you think of the Fortune 500, you may imagine a monolithic skyscraper, on top of which is the executive suite. In that executive suite, you have visions of a mammoth office interior with a phalanx of secretaries guarding the CEO's sanctum sanctorum.

That all may have been true when we undertook the survey. Yet we still achieved a relatively high success rate. The reason was our timing.

Instead of calling during normal business hours (9 A.M. to 5 P.M.), we chose to call the CEOs at 7 or 7:30 A.M. Even the most devoted secretary had not yet appeared to screen the call. Security had answered the switchboard phone and just passed us through to the head of the company.

example, state: "This survey will take approximately two minutes and thirty seconds."

The Mason-Dixon Factor

The Mason-Dixon factor is one of those unspoken phenomena in corporate intelligence that is worth noting here. I usually find Southern contacts far more friendly and approachable than those from the North. This may sound like a gross generalization that will offend those from the North and will appear condescending to Southerners, but I find it a hard point to deny.

It becomes an especially difficult factor to ignore when you have gotten 10 turndowns from Northern contacts and then pick up the telephone again to call a Georgian or a Texan. All of a sudden, you discover, people start talking. You're asking the same questions in the same tone of voice. This time, the only difference is that people are talking to you—and they're generally polite, even when they do turn you down.

This cultural difference extends into the international arena, as well. Experienced analysts will tell you that it is much easier to interview someone from the United States than it is to interview a European. The United States is reputed to have an open, trusting culture, one that encourages people to talk to strangers on the telephone. Europeans, by varying degrees, are more closed-mouth and discrete.

I will be the first to admit that there are exceptions and shades of gray to every rule, including the Mason-Dixon factor. For example, I have found that potential contacts located in larger Southern cities may be just as unfriendly as their counterparts from the North.

Yet, in general, those experts south of the Mason-Dixon line (or those in the United States versus Europe) seem to have more time to spend, or at least give the researcher the courtesy of a thoughtful answer.

Reasonable Expectations

The following disguised interview teaches a number of very important lessons, lessons even the most seasoned analyst must review.

1. *Lesson 1, Orient Your Listener:* You need to orient the person you interview. After all, most of the time, your hoped-for expert did not expect you to call and is not necessarily clear why you are calling—even if he or she is happy to contribute information to you.
2. *Lesson 2, Limit the Scope of Your Questions:* Most experts will know only a few bits and pieces of information and not the entire answer. Do not keep pummeling the expert with questions in hopes of learning the entire answer. By doing so, you will only frustrate a possibly valuable contact. Instead, ask questions that are limited in scope and you will likely be rewarded with better-than-expected results.

In this project, the analyst must identify and assess potential generic pharmaceutical competitors who are poised to launch a new class of drugs—anti-migraine medicines, in this fictionalized case. This is the big picture the analyst

(Continued)

needs to understand. However, in the interview, the analyst lays out a far narrower set of objectives for himself. At this point, the analyst simply needs to locate potential suppliers of a bulk chemical used in the manufacture of the generic pharmaceutical product. If he can identify the bulk chemical supplier, he has a good chance of discovering who the U.S. and European generic marketers will be. The entire interview was conducted over the telephone. The expert is a regional marketing and sales manager for one of the bulk chemical supply houses:

Interviewer: Hello, my name is Tom Moore and I am trying to understand the general direction the anti-migraine market is heading. Can you help me?

[Author's comment: General opening. Asking for help, rather than sounding pompous and all-knowing is what you need to start.]

Expert: No, I'm no pharmaceutical guru. My job is just to sell the bulk chemicals to the Mercks of the world.

[Author's comment: The expert is not who the analyst thought he might be. These surprises will often startle a neophyte, and will end an interview prematurely. Don't let it. Persist and see if there is another opportunity to explore. After all, the expert did not say "no," he only said he did not feel confident enough to answer this question.]

Interviewer: I see, Let me reword my question, if I can. If I can better understand the movement of the raw chemical used in this type of medication, then I can better assess the market's growth and players in this relatively new market. Does this help?

[Author's comment: Note the analyst's response. He calmly restated his request, adjusting it to fit the knowledge base of the person he has in front of him.]

Expert: Not really. You want me to divulge my clients' marketing strategies. I'm sorry but even if I knew, I couldn't tell you. Sorry, but . . .

[Author's comment: Another potential barrier, perhaps the most difficult to overcome—confidentiality. What would you do here?]

Interviewer: No. I don't want you to reveal a confidence. Rather, if you could just tell me the general movement in this market, that would be helpful. You don't have to name names. Okay?

[Author's comment: This is the most straightforward response the analyst could offer. The "Okay" at the end definitely gives the expert the option to stop the interview right here. It is a risk worth taking. Your goal is to get the bits and pieces of information you need, but not at all costs. Think of the practical side. You may have to speak to this person again near the end of the study. You want someone who will trust you, not someone who will hang up the phone.

(Continued)

(Continued)

Expert: Okay. What I can tell you is public knowledge and was widely spoken about at the last conference, held in Paris.

Interviewer: I'd appreciate hearing more about this conference, or whatever you feel comfortable discussing.

[Author's comment: Once again, the interviewer has chosen to emphasize the unthreatening aspect of the interview.]

Expert: Poinsyntex, in San Celoni, Spain, is going back into the bulk oxyrib business. Poinsyntex had told Drugco AG in Germany that it plans to have product available by fourth quarter this year. One of Poinsyntex's big markets will be the U.S., although it's not clear to whom it will sell the oxyrib.

[Author's comment: Much of this conversation may not contain a great deal of new or valuable information. Yet it can lead the interviewer to other potentially valuable opportunities.]

Interviewer: Can you guess who the international buyers for oxyrib might be?

[Author's comment: Notice that the interviewer asked the expert to guess who the buyers are, a piece of information the expert knows well since he deals in this market every day. At the same time, the expert is giving away little information that would in any way compromise a client.]

Expert: My guess is Nippon Pharma of Japan, TJK also of Japan, Markkum in the U.S. and Rikard Veber in the Netherlands.

That's all I know. Sorry if my information is limited.

Interviewer: No problem. You gave me some insight. By the way do you have names of people I can speak to at Markkum and Veber?

[Author's comment: Why stop here? If the expert knows the companies in question, he also must know people in those companies. So . . .]

Expert: In fact, yes. At Markkum, you want to call Peter Sten and at Veber, Johan Maas.

Interviewer: Thank you, once again. By the way, I came across a great investor's report on this market. Would you like a copy for your files?

[Author's comment: In the process of conducting the research, the interviewer surely came across information he could give away without exposing his client or his client's purpose. This investment report might be in public domain, but could be considered extremely valuable to the expert who did not know it existed. Now, the information swap that took place in this interview is more even-handed. Both parties—the expert and the interviewer— have benefited.]

Expert: Sure. That would be great.

Interviewer: I'll be happy to send it to you. Thanks, again.

THE VALUE OF QUESTIONNAIRES

Questionnaires should be used as a matter of course when organizing even the simplest of projects. usually associated with political pollsters, the questionnaire is one of the most effective tools for collecting competitor information.

One of the first steps you should take when beginning a project is to design a survey form to use on the telephone. A survey form gives the interviewee a point of reference and a place from which you, the interviewer, can branch out and ask other questions.

Because the intelligence-gathering process is such a precarious one, and you can never be certain where the answer will actually come from, a written questionnaire will help guide you to the most likely places. It will take the interview step by step, hopefully leading to the answer you are seeking. In short, a well-written survey will ensure that:

Everyone involved in the project is speaking the same language and asking the same questions.

The person being interviewed is being led logically through the area of interest.

At the project's end, the answers collected can be easily organized and sorted.

This section discusses two fundamental questionnaire formats: linear and grid. Each serves a different purpose and can be designed in open- or closed-ended style. Table 2.2 describes each style. Samples of linear closed-ended and open-ended questionnaires appear as Figures 2.1 and 2.2.

A Grid Survey

Let's say you are handed an assignment to collect data on six competitors in the same industry. You realize that calling the same contacts back six times for each of the target companies would be ridiculous, not to mention a waste of your contacts' time. By the third call, you can be sure your contacts will hang up on you. Not only would

TABLE 2.2   Types of Questionnaires and Their Uses

Type of Questionnaire	Advantages for Intelligence Gathering
Linear, open-ended (Figure 2.1)	Flexible A conversation opener Allows for the unknown Doesn't box the interviewer in
Linear, closed-ended (Figure 2.2)	Easy—doesn't require industry knowledge Contains listings of products Useful for quantitative data Allows for quick response time
Grid (Figure 2.3)	Covers many companies in one interview Permits shorter answers (yet not as controlled as a linear questionnaire)

Hello, my name is _____ and I am calling from Fuld & Co. We are an independent research firm based in Cambridge, Massachusetts.

Could you give me a few minutes of your time to answer questions on the oil valve industry and a few companies that are in it?

[If YES, continue.] Thank you.

[If NO, thank the person for his or her time.]

1. Have you ever purchased products from Marko-Valves, Lead Valves, or Excel-Valve?
   _____ YES _____ NO

2. In the past year, did you buy:
   _____ 1–5 valves
   _____ 6–10 valves
   _____ 10–20 valves
   _____ 20–50 valves
   _____ 50 or more (if so, how many? _____)

3. If you could estimate Marko's regional sales (in your region), would they be:
   _____ between 50 and 100 million
   _____ between 100 and 125 million
   _____ between 125 and 150 million

4. Do you feel that the last recession:
   _____ caused Marko to lay off workers
   _____ caused Marko to shut down its plant on occasion
   _____ had no effect on Marko's operations
   _____ caused its sales to climb

5. Do you think _____'s [mention one of the above companies] market share was:
   _____ 10% or less
   _____ between 10 and 15%
   _____ greater than 25%

Thank you for your time. Should I have any other questions, may I call you back? _____ Also, whom can you refer me to who might have dealt with Marko or any of the other companies in the past? Is there another company that may have purchased a large number of their valves in this area? Whom in Excel's sales department can you recommend I speak to?

Figure 2.1 Linear, closed-ended questionnaire—The Data Gatherer.

you lose a present contact, but you would close the door to any future inquiries with this contact.

A partial solution to this dilemma is the grid survey. The grid allows a researcher to pigeonhole data into the right slots. It permits quick coverage of all the target companies and categories.

Drafting the grid is simple. In the leftmost column, you list the companies you are studying. On the top row across you label each of the categories or topics you are covering (e.g., product pricing, size of sales force, plant expansion, and so on). Figure 2.3 gives a sample.

The grid survey is a quick-and-dirty method for collecting preliminary data. It is not a good tool for in-depth inquiry, because of the limited space allotted for information on the grid itself. Compared to the straightforward, linear questionnaires

Hello, my name is _____ and I am calling from Fuld & Co. We are an independent research company based in Cambridge, Massachusetts.

Could you give me a few minutes to answer a half-dozen questions on the oil valve industry and some companies in it?

[If YES, continue.] Thank you.

[If NO, thank the respondent for his or her time.]

1. Have you ever used Marko-Valves, Lead Valves, or Excel-Valve products?
2. What do you think of their service?
3. Does this company send its salespeople out to you more than once a year? _____ If so, exactly how often? What do you think of its sales force?
4. Do you know how many salespeople operate out of this office?
5. Tell me, do you know the sales force size for _____ and _____ [the other two not discussed above]?
6. How many Marko-Valves have you bought in the past year?
7. Do you feel that Marko's market share in this line is greater than 50% or less than 50%? _____ How much less or more?
8. How do you think _____ [mention one of the above companies] weathered the recession? Were there layoffs, plant shutdowns?

Thank you for your time. Should I have any more questions, may I call you back? _____ Also, whom can you refer me to who might have dealt with Marko in the past? Is there another company that may have purchased a large number of their valves in this area? Whom in Excel's sales department can you recommend I speak to?

Figure 2.2   Linear, open-ended questionnaire—The Opinion Gatherer.

shown in Figures 2.1 and 2.2, it requires a researcher who is more attuned to the assignment.

The grid questionnaire in Figure 2.3 helped the interviewer investigate over six competitors and dozens of product lines—all on one page. Although the information entered in each box was limited, it did provide a quick means of comparison. Also, because one competitor's data fell right next to another's, the researcher could catch nuances in the data and return rapidly with further questions for the expert being interviewed.

Some Tips for Drafting an Intelligence Questionnaire

1. Always provide an introduction, where the researcher gives his or her name and affiliation, along with the project description.
2. Limit the questionnaire to five to ten questions, no more. After all, if the person on the other end of the phone wants to talk, the questionnaire will act as a springboard to further questions. (Don't limit yourself to the questions on the sheet. Don't feel tied down by the survey's structure. Use it as a starting point. You may want to have a list of additional questions on the side, in case you find an extremely valuable and talkative source.)
3. Always get the respondent's name and title or position.
4. Incorporate familiar industry terminology into the questionnaire. Make the survey as conversational as possible.

Hello, my name is _____ and I am calling from Fuld & Co. We are an independent research firm based in Cambridge, Massachusetts.

Could you give me a few minutes of your time to answer one or two questions on the oil valve industry and its product lines?

[If YES, continue.] Thank you.

[If NO, thank the person for his or her time.]

1. Have you bought any Marko, Excel, or Lead Valves in the past year?

[If YES, continue.]

2. I would like to go down a brief list of companies and their product lines. Can you tell me, to the best of your recollection, exactly how many valves you may have bought?

Company	2" Valve	5" Automatic Control Valve	2" Valve with Filter
Marko			
Excel			
Lead			
U.S. Valve			
Lockwood			
Tennessee			
Treasure			

Thank you for your time. Should I have other questions, may I call you back? _____ Also, whom can you refer me to who might have dealt with Marko or any of the other companies in the past? Is there another company that may have purchased a large number of their valves in this area? Whom in Excel's sales department can you recommend I speak to?

Figure 2.3   Grid questionnaire—The Data Gatherer for More Than One Company.

A basic questionnaire should be used when you are targeting one or two companies. When you must analyze a host of competitors using the same interview sources, use a grid survey rather than a linear or simple questionnaire.

LEARN THE LINGO: KNOW THE INDUSTRY JARGON

Learning an industry's catchall phrases and jargon can be one of the most difficult aspects of researching a company whose industry you know very little about. Have the fundamental terms at your fingertips. The experts you interview may have little patience for someone they perceive as coming to them unprepared.

These are the best three ways to quickly "get up to speed" on a new industry:

1. *Speak to an industry analyst.* This doesn't mean stockbrokers; they will not have the time to explain the intricacies of an industry. Their job is to sell stock, not lecture to a new student. Better yet, find a government analyst. The U.S. Department of Commerce has scores of them in Washington. To find the one who specializes in your category, look in the *U.S. Industrial Outlook Handbook* (available from the Government Printing Office).

2. *Locate a few key trade magazines and speak to their editors.* As long as you don't bend their ears too much, these editors will be happy to explain certain basics about their industry and its leaders. Also, it would help if, before calling them, you could read a handful of general articles on the subject and company you are investigating.

3. *Use an industry dictionary.* Almost every industry has a dictionary that contains the special production and technical terminology you will need when asking questions or writing your final report. Trade associations can steer you to the better reference sources. In addition, a well-equipped university library may have a collection of these special dictionaries. Many of the major dictionaries are mentioned in various industry sections throughout this book.

BEWARE OF TECHNOBABBLE

You need to speak and write in ways that others understand. You will miss vital pockets of information if you do not speak the right language—the language in which the sources were coded, written, or recorded. It makes no difference whether you are dealing with an electronic database or conducting a face-to-face interview; if you ask the question the wrong way, you will receive an inadequate answer, at best.

"Computer people speak a language all their own. So do plumbers, librarians and accountants, but somehow the jargon of their trades doesn't irritate the rest of us, or infiltrate our own speech, as much as technobabble does. After all, no one but a police officer calls a criminal a perpetrator," wrote L. R. Shannon in *The New York Times* (October 8, 1991, p. C5).

As part of "learning the lingo," I recommend that you consider placing on your bookshelf one or both of the books referred to in Shannon's article: *Technobabble,* John A. Barry (M.I.T. Press); and *The New Hacker's Dictionary,* Eric Raymond (M.I.T. Press).

WHO IS AN EXPERT AND WHERE TO FIND ONE—START INSIDE

An expert is anyone who lives at least 100 miles from our company.

This is one client's cynical but realistic view of human nature. The truth is, no one knows your industry and your competition as well as your company's employees; their concentration is squarely on your particular market. Unfortunately, *The Wall Street Journal, BusinessWeek,* and *The Economist* hold greater sway over most managers than does the information from within their own organizations. These publications have to appeal to millions of readers and can only touch on your market periodically—and then in a mostly superficial way. Their job is to inform readerships, not to bore them with a myriad of competitive details. Yet, these very details are the ones you need to analyze each day. Besides, the information you read in a major trade or business publication may be dated.

The lesson in all this is: Use your own organization for current, specific intelligence. Regarding your customers, your suppliers, or your competitors, you spend

---

War Story: Purchasing Insider Intelligence

A high-technology company, and a leader in its various markets, had worked for many years with a number of sole-source suppliers to ensure that its suppliers produced the highest quality product possible. One day, the company's senior management read in *The Wall Street Journal* that a supplier was about to be sold off in part or whole to an investment group. The managers who read this notice were concerned that the supplier's operations would be cannibalized or sold off in parts, and that they would lose their sole-source supplier.

After some investigation by the customer, it was discovered that its own purchasing managers had been concerned, for over the past 18 months, about the supplier's solvency and had alerted management, over one year before, of the potential loss of this key supplier. Management chose to ignore its own internal purchasing people—to its detriment.

In the end, the supplier remained intact and continued to supply this high-tech customer, but this outcome was pure luck. The sad fact remained: the information had been available but was overlooked or ignored.

---

more time and have far more experience than any other "credible" external news source. Realize this fact and take advantage of it.

Chapter 12 offers ideas and suggestions for increasing the internal information flow and credibility of your own corporate information.

The Insiders: How to Find Them

Assuming you accept the fact that your company contains hidden experts, the way to unearth and organize their expertise for easy retrieval is to conduct an Intelligence Audit. (See my earlier book, *Monitoring the Competition* (Wiley, 1988).) Fuld & Company conducted just such an audit for a pharmaceutical company, where we unearthed hundreds of experts. We tagged and indexed their expertise and placed it on a simply constructed PC-based database. For example, we noted names of former employers, scientific knowledge, regional market expertise, and so on. (See Chapter 13 for more details.)

The Outside Experts: How to Find Them

In general, outside experts are not the journalists who write the articles, but the people they write about. With that in mind, here are some ideas for identifying outside experts:

Authors. Authors of technical articles are the experts themselves, not someone ghost writing or representing the true expert.

Conference literature. Speakers are cited in conference literature. Many associations keep on hand lists of their favorite speakers on various subjects.

Speakers' bureaus. Indexing and presenting their talent is the core of their business.

Technological matchmakers. A number of companies, such as TelTech (Minneapolis, MN), have sprung up over the past ten years. Their job is to amass a large list of scientists and engineers in highly specialized fields. They may make these experts available on a per-call basis or for longer engagements.

Off-handed citations. Articles in the general press will cite experts to bolster stories and support evidence.

House committee hearings. Industry experts often testify before Congressional hearings and their names are entered into the Congressional Record. Databases, such as the Congressional Record Abstracts, will cite their names.

FRIENDLY VERSUS UNFRIENDLY SOURCES

A researcher gathering intelligence must realize that just as there are sources who will not talk, there are probably an equal number of sources who will supply answers. This is what usually occurs as the research begins:

1. A researcher lines up contacts and starts making telephone calls.
2. By midday, the researcher has not learned anything new; most contacts have turned him or her down flat.
3. By the day's end, the researcher concludes that it is impossible to get the information.

No company is an island unto itself. Chances are there are many more contacts this researcher has not yet reached who would be perfectly happy to answer questions. All the researcher has to realize is that, for every unfriendly source, there is probably a friendly one. It's only a matter of *finding* that friendly source.

What Makes a Source Friendly?

A source that is friendly to a manufacturer may be totally unfriendly to a market research firm. As an example, a market researcher for a manufacturing firm needed to collect data on her competitors. She decided to call everyone in the industry for information. Here is a list of her contacts and their reactions:

Contact	Reaction to Inquiry
Competing company	Unfriendly
Distributor	Friendly
Market research firm	Friendly
A competitor's sole-source supplier	Unfriendly
Government agency	Friendly

The distributor, market research firm, and government agency were friendly because they were: an impartial observer (the government agency), aware of a potential business relationship (the market research firm or distributor), or free of any feeling of being threatened (the distributor).

The competitor and the competitor's sole-source supplier were unfriendly because the source saw a direct threat (to the competitor), and the competitor would not compromise an existing, competing relationship (with the sole-source supplier).

By taking a step back from your research and examining which contacts you used, you will quickly distinguish between the friendly and unfriendly sources. To give yourself a better perspective and a realistic sense of who will speak to you when you make contact, draft a list of all potential sources and tag them "friendly" or "unfriendly." This little exercise will save you time, frustration, and a lot of wasted energy.

STEPS IN SETTING UP A RESEARCH PROJECT

After you have assembled your research team, how do you ensure that your project will follow a smooth and efficient path? Here are some steps you can take to establish and organize your projects:

1. *Get the client's request in writing.* This applies whether your client is an in-house supervisor or an outside company. When the client places the questions down on paper, he or she is forced to think clearly and will more likely spell out the details of the project. Once you have the request in writing, pass out topics of the request to all team members.

2. *Hold a first meeting.* At an initial meeting, all team members can discuss the project. That approach will ensure that everyone hears the same problem and project objectives.

3. *Hold end-of-day meetings.* To keep tight reign on the project and to make sure everyone is remaining focused on the project's objectives, hold individual meetings at the end of the day to review progress and redesign part of the strategy, if necessary.

4. *Begin your library and field research at the same time.* Do not wait. This may seem like a strange way to go about intelligence gathering. Your first reaction might be: "Well, can't we learn what we need to know from either the field or the library research? Why do both at the same time?" The answer lies in the nature of the work. The library work and the field work will offer you different results. Limiting yourself to just library research can severely restrict your view of the company, leaving you little insight as to other avenues to pursue and people to contact.

   Just as damaging to your project's success would be an attitude that all you need to do is interview a few choice experts and then you will have your answer. After spending ten hours on the phone, you might find that a single news article would have answered the question, if only you had looked for it in the first place.

   > If there is any common problem in getting industry analyses underway, it is that researchers tend to spend too much time looking for published sources and using the library before they begin to tap field sources. . . . Published sources have a variety of limitations: timeliness, level of aggregation, depth, and so on. Although it is important to gain some basic understanding of the industry to maximize the value of field interviews, the researcher should not

exhaust all published sources before getting into the field. On the contrary, clinical and library research should proceed simultaneously. They tend to feed on each other, especially if the researcher is aggressive in asking every field source to suggest published material about the industry. Field sources tend to be more efficient because they get to the issues, without the wasted time of reading useless documents. Interviews also sometimes help the researcher identify the issues. This may come, to some extent, at the expense of objectivity.°

5. *Use one depository for literature.* Any literature you collect should go into one common filing folder or bin. When researchers get the notion that they can begin accumulating literature in their own personal files, you will begin seeing duplication and wasted effort.

6. *Keep track of the experts.* Once you have found contacts who prove to be valuable sources of information, don't lose those people. Maintain a list of key contacts and later, after the project has ended, enter their names onto a central list.

7. *Use a single outline.* Before starting, make sure everyone involved uses the same outline and understands the questions to be answered.

CONTROLLING TIME

Time is the ultimate enemy of good intelligence. Time, not money, can cause an analysis to fail. Almost everyone has access to the resources described in this book, either via telephone or modem or by visiting a library. The much more menacing problem lies in how the project manager, analyst, or business executive plans for the time it takes to gather information and analyze it. I have saved this section for the end of the chapter because time is probably the most important and most often overlooked obstacle to gaining viable intelligence.

A CURE for Meeting Deadlines

Each step in an intelligence assignment can lead you down many possible research paths, a number of which will head you in the wrong direction. The best way for you to stay on track is to form a close alliance with the client. Because you can never be sure where your ultimate answer will come from, you and the client need to become educated each step along the way. The CURE approach helps you form that relationship.

*C*heck back with the client, to stay focused. You need to constantly feed your findings to the client, who may adjust his or her thinking because of the feedback you are providing. In one project in the oil valve industry, our client was certain that some sort of magic bullet was continuing to propel a competitor's sales upward despite poor overall industry performance. Because our analysts constantly fed the latest data to the client, we discovered that an original assumption was wrong. The competitor had diverted its marketing efforts to northern California and was now chalking up sizable sales of its valves to

---

°Michael E. Porter, *Competitive Strategy* (New York: Free Press, 1980), p. 371.

the agricultural industry in the form of valves for irrigation equipment. Had we not fed the client a constant stream of findings, we would have wasted many weeks of fruitless investigation on the wrong market and the wrong region of the country.

You must view the client as an experienced scientist with a hypothesis that is based on years of dealings with the market. At the same time, the hypothesis is based on history, not necessarily on the current state of affairs. By gathering data and analyzing the results, you are testing the hypothesis. In the end, you may prove that theory right *or* wrong. This analyst-to-client feedback gives the entire intelligence process a check on reality.

Understand your own time investment. Use time sheets, as any independent consultant would, to keep track of your time. You need not have many categories; three or four will do: Literature Review; Interviewing; Client Contact; Analysis and Report Writing. Only by tracking and comparing time spent from project to project will you truly be able to gauge your usage of time and where it needs to be spent. In addition, this investment in record keeping will allow you to better estimate the time you need to spend when the next project rolls along.

Refine the request. Do not accept a fiat if you can help it. It is for your benefit and that of the client that you refine the questions being asked. Always try to ask—and receive—answers to the following standard reportorial questions:

- *Who* wants the information in the organization?
- *What* do they need? What questions are critical? What will the intelligence be used for?
- *When* do they need the answer? Can a portion of the assessment be delivered earlier, rather than wait for the entire report to be finished? If so, which portion is most important?
- *Where* is the target company? In what city, state, province, or region? What locations are involved? Plant sites? Offices? Warehouses? Branch banks or service centers?
- *Why* do they need the intelligence? Is there an alternative to the desired answer? Is there a substitute answer that would be suitable?
- *How* do they want to see the analysis? Bullet charts? Graphs? A complete report, written in prose with footnotes? If time is of the essence, will a simple memo or a face-to-face meeting do?

Earn your time. The best way to use your time honestly is to begin to charge it back. By paying for your time, your client will better appreciate the value of your service. However, this works both ways. Only accept moneys for time served or billed. No services, no money; no money, no operating budget. I know a number of internal market research and intelligence operations that survive from year to year only by selling their services; that is the deal they struck with management. As a result, though, they have become market-driven service organizations that know the resources and the time they need to spend on any particular project. Their status makes them sensitive to the needs of their clients. Earning your time is healthy for both you and your clients.

Where Are the Time Stealers?

In Table 2.3, a project is broken down by task, hours per task, and hours needed to address each question. Notice the many tasks needed to answer several of the questions. Which of these items might you overlook in planning a project?

The Fudge Factor

Fudge factor. Error factor. Call it what you want. Because developing competitor or market intelligence is an art, not a science, even the best time estimate can be wrong. No matter how much planning and spreadsheet work you do before a project, inevitably you will detour into uncharted—and unplanned—territory. To compensate for the unforeseen, add a 5–10 percent cushion in your time plan.

A CHECKLIST OF OTHER PROJECT MANAGEMENT TIPS

You must answer these questions while planning and conducting any sort of analysis project:

The literature search stage

What is the minimum number of times you would bring in a librarian to help you with a project?

How much time does the librarian spend on a search?

What time do you invest guiding the librarian?

Interviewing

Which interviews take longer than others?

What should your "success ratios" be?

Why is international interviewing generally a longer process than the equivalent U.S. interview process?

Verification of rumors

What percent of the data you gather is "fact"?

How do you distinguish between fact and rumor, and what level of proof do you require to reach a certain level of satisfaction with your findings?

Presentation expectations

What level of "polish" does management expect?

Are you given enough time to provide truly finished work? Or, are your findings acceptable in raw form, as long as the analysis is well-founded?

Do you spend a great deal of time squeezing out numbers from generally qualitative data?

TABLE 2.3   Time Analysis per Task and per Question

Question	Research Request Tasks	Time
1. What territories does the company sell in?	Locate and interview distributors	10 hours
	Locate and interview OEMs	5
	Retrieve and review trade-magazine articles	5
	Locate and interview store buyers	10
	Subtotal	30 hours
2. Whom does the company sell to?	Interview competitors	5 hours
	Review annual report	2
	Review product literature	5
	Locate and retrieve press releases	3
	Locate and interview shipping companies	10
	Subtotal	25 hours
3. What are its distribution channels?	No additional time required for this question; it can be answered using the research conducted for Questions 1 and 2 above.	
4. What markets does it hope to penetrate?	Interview trade magazine editors	5 hours
	Locate and interview Wall Street analysts in this field	5
	Locate, retrieve, and review the latest analyses	5
	Locate and interview customers regarding approach sales force has taken with them	10
	Subtotal	25 hours
5. Is the company a low-cost producer?	Retrieve loan filings for equipment purchases	2 hours
	Contact machinery suppliers for automation level of plant	10
	Examine union contracts	5
	Retrieve and review town filings from tax assessors	5
	Locate and interview major suppliers	10
	Subtotal	32 hours
6. What products does it plan to release next year?	Review patent filings	10 hours
	Attend trade show and retrieve available product literature	10
	Subtotal	20 hours
7. Can the company afford to enter a price war?	Note: No additional time required for this question; it can be answered using the research conducted for Question 5 above.	
8. What is the company's advertising strategy? Where will it advertise this coming year?	Interview advertising directors for likely trade magazines	3 hours
	Review three years of historical data from Leading National Advertisers, a source of corporate advertising expenditures	5
	Interview advertising account managers from former agency	2
	Subtotal	10 hours
	Grand Total	142 hours

THE IMPORTANCE OF DEBRIEFING

Look back on any intelligence-gathering project you completed. Think of all the sources you called. They may number in the dozens or in the hundreds.

Now, ask yourself what will occur when you are asked six months down the road to research a similar company. In those six months you have undertaken other assignments; your mind has gone to other important matters. So, you begin to research this new company, and you begin thinking, "Wasn't there a source we used last time that was very effective? Yes, I think there was, except I can't remember what it was or whom to call."

If this sounds familiar, you are in very good company. Even the meticulous researcher fails to keep perfect notes. That is why you should, at the end of every project, debrief yourself and every other researcher who participated in the project.

Figure 2.4 gives a sample format you may want to use in a debriefing. A debriefing should not be a long and arduous task that consumes hours of a researcher's time.

Project title _____

Project _____ Analyst's name _____

Total billable time _____

STATISTICS

Number of telephone calls attempted _____

Number of telephone calls completed _____

Number of valuable calls _____

VALUED SOURCES

What were some of the most productive and valuable sources you used for this assignment? (You can include: data bases, newspapers, directories, certain contacts you made.)

Valued Source   Why?

_____   _____

_____   _____

_____   _____

_____   _____

_____   _____

NEW SOURCES

What were some of the new and unusual sources you could recommend for future projects (e.g., government agencies, new databases, types of directories)?

New Source   How best used?

_____   _____

_____   _____

_____   _____

_____   _____

GENERAL COMMENTS

Based on your experience with this assignment, how can future projects be more efficiently run? Was there an aspect of this assignment and the way it was carried out that was highly inefficient?

Figure 2.4   Project debriefing form.

Avoid the "Dumber and Uglier" Option

LEONARD FULD: Where and when is benchmarking a most effective management tool? Conversely, when have you seen clients misuse or mislabel the process?

PHILIP CROSBY: I am afraid of benchmarking as it is generally used. It is always possible to find someone dumber and uglier than we are. Comparing our operations to others leaves out the human relationship element.

Philip Crosby is an expert on total quality management. He has written nine books, including *Quality Is Free* and the most recent, *Completeness: Quality for the 21st Century.* He is currently Chairman of Career IV, a consulting firm in Maitland, Florida.

It should take no more than a half hour to fill out, and should tell the reader at a glance exactly what went right and what went wrong with the research.

A thorough debriefing can serve these purposes:

- Record vital research statistics, such as the number of phone calls made for a project. These collected data, when compared to data in other projects, can assist researchers in estimating the amount of time they may expect to spend on subsequent projects or how many phone calls need to be made in order to achieve success.
- Teach others which sources prove most valuable and why.
- Almost invariably, turn up one or two new sources that were found extremely worthwhile. The debriefing will bring these new gems out.
- Reveal sources or techniques that were time wasters and resulted in many unproductive hours. This kind of information should also appear on a debriefing form.

PART TWO

FIND THE BASIC AND CREATIVE SOURCES

The Intelligence Pyramid

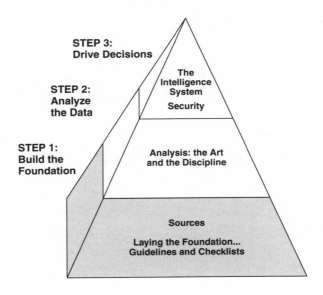

STEP 3:
Drive Decisions

The
Intelligence
System

STEP 2:
Analyze
the Data

Security

STEP 1:
Build the
Foundation

Analysis: the Art
and the Discipline

Sources

Laying the Foundation...
Guidelines and Checklists

Data sources are the lifeblood of even the most sophisticated competitive analysis. None of the analytical approaches presented in this book will do you any good unless you have the raw data. That is why I have devoted a great deal of space to sorting through and annotating thousands of company-specific sources that consultants in my firm have found useful over the years. In addition, you will read of ways to find other sources, some of which may be too specialized or unusual for this text. The global marketplace is constantly changing, as are the information channels. These chapters offer you timeless approaches that will allow you to add to your intelligence source collection for many years to come.

At times, you must overcome cultural and language barriers to locate and use these sources effectively. In the chapter on international sources, you will learn the research strategies and approaches to gaining the most information possible on a competitor, whether Japanese, German, or American.

From corrugated boxes to financial ratios, you need to know the basic and creative information sources that are available to you. The following chapters provide you with these sources and the means to find others.

3 FEDERAL, STATE, AND LOCAL SOURCES

Don't use government bureaucracy as your excuse. Just because it may be difficult to obtain information from a government office doesn't mean it's not there or not worth having. You will often find the opposite is true. To one degree or another, government offices around the world are in the business of collecting information on people and organizations. How they choose to dispense that information varies. So, rather than look at the bureaucracy and throw up your hands in dismay, embrace this end of the corporate intelligence process. Find the savvy people in your own corporation who have government contacts, know how to ask the right questions, and can interpret the documents you may ultimately receive.

FINANCIALS FROM UNCLE SAM'S LIBRARY

There are literally hundreds of published sources that offer financial histories of companies. Some simply list the income statements and balance sheets; others present full write-ups on the company along with a description of the officers and any acquisitions or mergers that may have taken place. This section brings together all the commonly known as well as some of the lesser known sources.

Public Filings—Federal, State, and Local

SEC Filings

Whenever you ask researchers where they would go to find company financials, the first question they ask is: "Do you have an SEC filing on the company?"

Since 1934, when the Securities and Exchange Commission was established, publicly traded companies have come under ever increasing scrutiny. Because corporations are accountable to the federal government, they must file highly detailed accounts of their performance.

When researching a publicly traded company, the first place you should turn for a historic analysis of the company is one of over a dozen types of SEC reports—a 10-K (annual financial report), 10-Q (a quarterly financial filing), proxy (special event report given to stockholders to vote on), or one of the lesser known filings.

Until the mid-1970s, there was only one basic way to locate and retrieve an SEC report: write to the Commission and wait two to three weeks to receive the report. Today, you have many alternatives. This chapter details your options.

Federal, State, and Local Sources

Write to the SEC. Ever so slowly, the SEC has been moving into the electronic age. For now, if you need to receive an SEC document (described below), write to (or call):

Public Reference Room
U.S. Securities and Exchange Commission
450 Fifth St., NW, Mail Stop 1-2
Washington, DC 20549-1002
202-272-7450

If you are in Washington, DC, go to the public reference room. You will be able to use research tools not available elsewhere. In particular, you can gain access to EDGAR (Electronic Data Gathering Analysis and Retrieval System). In development since 1984, it was launched in July 1992. Not all of the 10,000-plus public companies currently file electronically with the SEC and with EDGAR, but the system contains approximately 49,000 records to date. It includes annual and special interim filings, such as 10-Qs. You can only use EDGAR if you are a filing corporation, or if you visit the SEC reference room.

Other systems are also available in the SEC reference room. They are:

- *Securities Reporting System (SIRS)*. You can use this database to locate securities transactions made by company officers, directors, and owners. Each record contains the trading date, name of the owner, number of shares, price per share, SEC received date, and type of transaction (for example, stock dividend, private purchase, or open market purchase).
- *Proposed Sale of Securities Inquiry System (PSSI)*. As the title implies, this on-line system allows a search of approximately six months' securities sales data. The records typically contain the issuer's or seller's name, class of security being sold, date acquired, acquisition codes, number of securities sold, market value, and shares outstanding.
- *Proceedings & Litigation Action Display System (PLAD)*. This system offers information on public litigation involving SEC companies. A typical record contains the name, address, jurisdiction, action date, violation, and disposition. It will also identify the types of action, such as federal, state, Canadian, NASD, and stock exchange.

Regional SEC offices have limited collections available for public inspection. Their locations are as follows:

Region 1—New York and
New Jersey
New York Regional Office
75 Park Pl., 14th Floor
New York, NY 10007
212-264-1636

Region 2—Maine, New
Hampshire, Vermont,
Massachusetts, Rhode
Island, Connecticut
Boston Regional Office
73 Tremont St., Suite 600
Boston, MA 02108
617-424-5900

Region 3—Tennessee, Virgin
Islands, Puerto Rico, North
Carolina, South Carolina,
Georgia, Alabama,
Mississippi, Florida,
Louisiana east of the
Atchafalaya River
Atlanta Regional Office
3475 Lenox Rd., NE,
Suite 1000
Atlanta, GA 30326-1232
404-842-7600

Region 4—Michigan, Ohio,
Kentucky, Wisconsin,
Indiana, Iowa, Illinois,
Minnesota, Missouri

Chicago Regional Office
Northwestern Atrium Center
500 West Madison St.,
Suite 140
Chicago, IL 60661-2511
312-353-7390

Region 5—Oklahoma,
Arkansas, Texas, Louisiana
west of the Atchafalaya
River, Kansas
Fort Worth Regional Office
411 W. Seventh St., 8th Floor
Fort Worth, TX 76102
817-334-3821

Region 6—North Dakota,
South Dakota, Wyoming,
Nebraska, Colorado, New
Mexico, Utah
Denver Regional Office
1801 California St.,
Suite 4800
Denver, CO 80202-2648
303-330-6800

Salt Lake City Branch Office
500 Key Bank Tower
50 South Main St., Suite 500
Salt Lake City, UT 84144-0402
801-524-5796

Region 7—Nevada, Arizona,
California, Hawaii, Guam
Los Angeles Regional Office
5757 Wilshire Blvd.,
Suite 500 East
Los Angeles, CA 90036-3648
213-468-3098

San Francisco Branch Office
901 Market St., Suite 470
San Francisco, CA 94103
415-744-3140

Region 8—Montana, Idaho,
Washington, Oregon,
Alaska
Seattle Regional Office
3040 Jackson Federal Bldg.
915 Second Ave.
Seattle, WA 98174
206-442-7990

Region 9—Pennsylvania,
Delaware, Maryland,
Virginia, West Virginia,
District of Columbia
Philadelphia Regional Office
The Curtis Center
601 Walnut St., Suite 1005 E
Philadelphia, PA 19106
215-597-3100

For speedy service, use Disclosure. Disclosure has done what the SEC has not: it offers speedy retrieval of the full text of SEC documents in many forms, including electronic. It also offers numerous services regarding non-U.S. companies. Disclosure's services include the following:

Monitor service. Filings are tracked and reported to you daily, weekly, or monthly.

Federal and state legislation. A daily reporting service.

UCC services. Retrieval of UCC filings (see the discussion of UCCs in Chapter 12) throughout the United States.

Trademark search.

Databases and CD-ROM products.
> Compact D/'33™. A CD-ROM that contains every filing made with the SEC on or after January 1, 1990.
> Compact D/SEC®. Complete profiles of more than 10,000 public companies.

Compact D/Canada™. Financial and management information on 8,000 public, private, and crown Canadian companies.

Worldscope®. A database or a CD-ROM product; it offers data on over 10,000 international companies (U.S. and non-U.S.).

Insiderline™. A six-year database of all insider trades, as well as a daily list of significant trades.

M&A Alert™. This database contains five days of mergers and acquisitions activity, names of bidders, time of release.

Orderline™. A current awareness database that alerts you to the latest filings. The database contains an 11-year index of all SEC filings.

Various Disclosure databases are available through other database systems and networks, including Dialog and Compuserve. (See Chapter 5 for further details.) Contact:

Disclosure Corporate Headquarters
5161 River Rd.
Bethesda, MD 20816
301-951-1300; 800-638-8241

SEC Filings and What They Reveal

Most managers think of the SEC's 10-K report when they consider an SEC filing. The 10-K, the annual report filing, is probably the most often requested of all the filings. However, if you want a more complete reading on a target company, you need to be aware of the entire array of SEC reports filed by publicly traded companies. Table 3.1 lists them in their entirety.

The Weakness of Government Sources

Competitor intelligence, by definition, is timely. Government information too often is not.

If you can find your answer in time to make a business decision, then the intelligence you have gathered is invaluable. Should you miss that deadline, or provide dated information, then all your efforts could be wasted. For example, state and federal filings are usually published months or years after the fact.

Government reports are useful sources of historical data, but do not rely on them for up-to-the-minute information. Some government reports may be the only sources you have. (I am thinking of Environmental Protection Agency (EPA) or Federal Communications Commission (FCC) filings, which we will discuss later in the book.)

This is the principal rule of thumb for retrieving intelligence from government sources:

A company will only disclose what it is forced to. Nothing more.

Government sources are weakest for management background, financials on privately held corporations, change in organization structure, marketing plans, new product introductions, foreign competitors, and subsidiaries of publicly traded companies.

TABLE 3.1   Types of SEC Filings

Filing Type	Filing Period	Contents	How It Is Used
Annual Report to Shareholders	Annual.	The typical annual report offered as a document by a corporation to its investors. Not an official SEC document, but kept on file by the SEC. Often attached to the 10-K, it will contain product and market information not available through the 10-K.	Sales and product analysis by division or by market. Also, reviewing the accounting notes can provide insight on operations, inventory levels, cash flow, changes in plant and equipment, acquisitions, and divestitures.
Prospectus	Prior to registration and issuance of stock.	Often called a "red herring," this document describes the company, its products, officers, and strategic direction. Financials available.	Early warning on new competitors or new intentions by established competitors.
Proxy Statement	Annual, and for specially called meetings.	A document prepared in order to give stockholders the information necessary to cast a vote on corporate matters.	To confirm "street knowledge" of a target company's plans. By the time the proxy statement is issued, this information is fairly well known by industry insiders.
1933 Act Registration Statements: S-1, S-2, S-3, S-4, S-6, S-8, S-11, S-18, S-20; F-1, F-2, F-3, F-4, F-6; SE; N-1A, N-2, N-5, N-14	Prior to offering or trading of securities.	Part 1: The offering of securities; includes: description of securities to be registered; use of proceeds; risk factors; determination of offering price; potential dilution; distribution plan for the stock; the corporate counsel name or names of other related experts associated with stock; names of those selling the stock; related financial statements. Part 2: The expenses associated with issuing stock and financial statements.	Almost an x-ray of the company, displaying details of its management, operations, company history, and financials prior to the registration. Experts can use such documents to read between the lines and distinguish between the fluff and substance.
10-K	Annual.	A comprehensive review of company operations. Typically includes four parts: Part 1: Business description, products sold, markets,	Literally, a reference book on the company, covering the past year's activities. Most effectively used when its data are compared to those of prior years. Also,

(Continued)

TABLE 3.1   *(Continued)*

Filing Type	Filing Period	Contents	How It Is Used
		competitive issues, number of employees, cost of R&D, environmental compliance matters, list of properties, court suits, results of stockholder voting. Part 2: High–low stock prices, financial data, statement of financial condition, any change in accounting rules. Part 3: Names of directors and executive officers; their salaries or fees received above $40,000; listing of those who own more than 5% of stock. Part 4: Exhibits of financial statements.	worth comparing to "slick," company-produced annual report to determine differences or gaps in description of markets or key product areas.
10-Q	Quarterly.	Part 1: Quarterly financial statements and management review of the changes in revenue and expenses from the previous quarter. Part 2: Discussions of any legal proceedings or changes in the rights of stockholders; defaults on payments; any information related to stockholders' meeting.	The first place to find discrepancies between Wall Street projections and actual financial results. May also provide details of important events that received only brief coverage in the press.
20-F	Annual.	Annual report and registration statement filed by foreign issuers of securities. Part 1: Description of business, property owned, legal proceedings, exchange controls, limitations of securities holders, taxes, financial data, management analysis, list of directors and officers, compensation of officers and directors, management transactions. Part 2: A description of securities to be registered. Part 3: Changes in securities. Part 4: Exhibits and financial statements.	Often more descriptive than filings in the country of origin. Useful for financial analysis. Note: May need a financial analyst who is familiar with overseas accounting standards when comparing to other competitor operations in the U.S. and abroad.

TABLE 3.1 *(Continued)*

Filing Type	Filing Period	Contents	How It Is Used
8-K	Unscheduled; when there is a substantial change in the corporation, of interest to stockholders.	Acquisition or divestiture of assets, change in registrant, bankruptcy, change in accountants, resignation of any directors, change in fiscal year, and related financials.	Useful for details often glossed over in the newspapers. Otherwise, far less timely than the "street knowledge" in the investment community, where word of acquisition or divestiture is known far in advance.
10-C	Unscheduled; similar to the 8-K, but for over-the-counter traded companies.	Similar to the above.	Similar to the above.
13-D	Upon acquisition of 5% or more of a class of stock. Filing must be made within 10 working days.	Contents include: identity and background of individual filing the statement; source and amount of funds; why the transaction was made; contracts signed. All agreements or contracts are attached as exhibits.	Trace major stock shifts. The analyst may be able to trace an unstated acquisition strategy by comparing 13-D information to other acquisition patterns of the purchaser.
14D-1; 14D-9	Tender offer.	Background information on the offer, including past contacts or any negotiations with the target company; purpose of tender offer; persons to be compensated; financial statements of certain bidders. Attachments include any agreements, contracts, or other legal or tax opinions on file.	Discover reason for rejection or acceptance of tender offer. Once again, details in this report need to be analyzed by someone familiar with accounting rules and legal aspects, who can appreciate the subtleties.
13E-3	Filed whenever a company goes private.	Class of the security, background of the buyers, past transactions, terms and conditions of the agreement, source of the funds, purpose and fairness of the transaction, appraisal of the property, financial information.	An after-the-fact document packed with details about the company that are worth saving for the years ahead. The reason for the buyout, for example, may indicate strategic direction in the years to come.

(Continued)

TABLE 3.1   *(Continued)*

Filing Type	Filing Period	Contents	How It Is Used
13E-4	Tender offer from issuing company to buy back its own stock.	Similar to the above.	Similar to the above.
13-G	Annual.	Filing by people or institutions that own 5% or more of equity. The document typically contains: name of stock owner, and number and type of shares owned.	Useful in understanding the power of key managers and investment consortia.
6-K	Unscheduled; at time foreign stock is publicly traded in the U.S.	Financial information and other information that may have been reported to stockholders in issuer's country of origin.	May provide insight on company's home market and strategy; allows for additional financial analysis between annual report issues.

Government sources are best used for plant size (square footage), environmentally regulated production processes, publicly traded corporations, and general historical data on an industry.

Always do your homework and never overlook the obvious sources; that includes government sources. They may supply you with only 10 percent of your valuable intelligence, but that may be the 10 percent you could not find anywhere else.

STATE YOUR CASE: STATE CORPORATE FILINGS

All 50 states require corporations to file annual reports and other financially related documents, but very few of these filings will do you, as a researcher, any good. Most are no more than a yearly registration form. All they ask for is name, address, and names of officers. For such a monumentally auspicious name—Annual Report—they deliver very little.

Fear not: there are the exceptions that make every rule. A number of states do require that their incorporated companies file far more than just the company's name and address.

Figure 3.1 gives an example of a state annual report form.

Fuld & Company surveyed each state for the reports each requires. This information appears in the state corporate filings list, later in this section. Where a state's Office of Corporations did not request data other than name and address in response to the survey, or did not offer an adequate explanation of its forms, no description is given in the list. Where states demand a lengthier report from resident companies, we have listed the report's name and features.

C4—12/91   **MONTANA ANNUAL CORPORATION REPORT**

In compliance with Section 35-1-1104, MCA, as a profit corporation, Section 35-2-904, MCA, as a nonprofit corporation, and Section 35-4-209, MCA, as a Professional Service corporation, the undersigned corporation submits the following report:

Name of Corporation: _____

_____

Registered Agent: _____

Street Address of
Registered Office: { _____

_____

Mailing Address: (if different) _____

City, State, Zip: _____

If there is any change in the registered agent or registered office location, please complete a statement of change form and send an additional $5.00 filing fee. (A box number may be added without the form or fee.)

1. **State of Incorporation:** _____

2. **Address of Principal Office** in state of incorporation *(only foreign corporation only must complete)*

_____

_____

3. **Brief Description** of business in which corporation is actually engaged: _____

_____

4. Names and addresses (street name and number) of **Principal Officers** of corporation.

President: _____

_____

_____

Vice-President: _____

_____

Secretary: _____

_____

Treasurer: _____

_____

Other: _____

_____

_____

RETURN TO:
Mike Cooney
Secretary of State
State Capitol Room 225
Helena, MT   59620

Secretary of State's use only

Filing Fee $_____
Prior to April 15 - $10.00
After April 15 - $20.00
After September 1 - $30.00

Figure 3.1   Montana annual corporation report.

5. Names and addresses (street name and number) of Directors of corporation. Nonprofit corporations are required to have a minimum of three directors.

_____   _____

_____   _____

_____   _____

_____   _____

_____   _____

_____   _____

6. **Shares** (profit corporations only must complete) State total shares authorized and total issued. Itemize both by class and series, if any. Attach schedule, if needed.

Authorized	Issued	Class	Series	Par Value

7. **Shareholders** (professional service corporations only must complete)
I certify that all shareholders are duly licensed or otherwise legally authorized to render the same professional service as the corporation and that none has any interest in any other Professional Service Corporation. I further certify that all the shareholders, not less than one-half the directors, and all the officers other than the secretary and treasurer of the corporation are qualified persons with respect to the corporation. The name, address and number of shares of each shareholder are:

Name	Address	Shares

(attach schedule, if needed)

8. **Property Statement** (foreign corporations only must complete)

Value of property owned by Corporation: $_____(in Montana) $_____(everywhere)

Gross receipts received during previous year: $_____(in Montana) $_____(everywhere)

9. **Nonprofit Corporations** only must complete. This corporation _____ Has Members   _____ Has No Members

10. By my signature below, I an official of the above corporation do state that I signed this report in behalf of the corporation and that the statements herein contained are true, under the penalty of false swearing.

_____   x_____
        Exact Name of Corporation   Signature of Officer or Chairman of Board

_____ _____   _____
    Date   Title   Printed Name of Official Signing

For informational purposes only, each nonprofit corporation will need to designate on the 1995 Annual Report whether it is a Public Benefit Corporation, a Mutual Benefit Corporation or a Religious Corporation.

Figure 3.1   *(Continued)*

Should you need further details about the forms and reporting requirements, contact the appropriate office mentioned on the list. Generally speaking, states have the following types of offices, each containing the type of information indicated:

Corporations Office. Most state corporate offices require resident companies to file these documents, which can be found in the corporations office:

Articles of incorporation;

Amendments to articles;

Consolidation notices;

Merger announcements;

Corporate name changes;

Franchiser filings.

Occupational Safety Office. This office can be useful when you need to find out the types of machinery and processes that operate in a plant. This office will record state inspections and reports of dangerous machinery.

State Securities Office. This office acts as a state SEC, requiring each company offering a certain amount of stock within the state to file a prospectus.

Uniform Commercial Code Office. This office will be described in some detail in Chapter 11. Its primary duty is to record all commercial loans within the state. The UCC office maintains records that contain the borrower's name, the loan's purpose, and its maturity date.

Environment Office. Because there are many classes of environmental filings in each state and varying levels of monitoring the environment within the state, I recommend contacting this office for information on which filing is appropriate for you to retrieve. The Environment Office can also discuss which industries are monitored and what legislation may be pending that could increase the reporting requirements.

Labor Relations Office. This office will help to define labor relations and safety laws in the state. It also typically maintains statistics and employment trends for regions and local areas.

A Note of Warning for Competitors

Certain states are attempting to limit the information that competitors can retrieve from corporate archives. Rhode Island, for example, will not allow a competitor to view a Rhode Island-based company's annual or financial filings if that information is being used for competitive purposes. This may or may not be a trend. You should check with the respective corporate filings offices listed below to learn of any restrictions expected in the near future.

Economic Development Offices: Intelligence Listening Posts

State and county Economic Development Offices try to seek out and attract new businesses to their regions. Often, they publish their own bulletins to advertise new initiatives to corporations and other interested parties.

The following excerpt appeared in a newsletter, "From the State Capitals: Economic Development" (published by Wakeman/Walworth, Inc., 300 North Washington Street, Alexandria, VA 22314). It demonstrates that economic development offices are worth contacting because of their knowledge of future business activity in a state:

Oregon, Washington Vie for Steel Mill Site

Two sites in Cowlitz County, Washington, and two in Oregon are under consideration for a new steel plant that would create about 500 jobs.

The $400 million plant would be built under a proposed joint venture between Oregon Steel Mills, Inc., of Portland, Ore., and Nucor Corp. of Charlotte, N.C., Nucor Chairman F. Kenneth Iverson said. The mill would make sheet steel from scrap metal for distribution on the West Coast.

"The odds are pretty good we will sign a letter of intent, probably within the next two months," Iverson said. (*From the State Capitals: Economic Development,* November 23, 1992, p. 1)

State Bureaucracy: Streamlined and Online

Nearly one-half of the states have either started or are about to start an online corporate filings retrieval system. All you need is your modem and a password. However, there are some barriers to overcome:

- You will have to sign on to each system separately.
- The language and approach are somewhat different for each state, which means you need to learn another "language" each time you search.
- You receive only a portion of or highlights from the filings, not the full image. For example, a state corporate database record may yield the number of shares outstanding, the names of officers, the date, and the amount covered by UCC filings. You may even be able to retrieve some of the documents through online requests.

These barriers notwithstanding, such online systems are the wave of the future for state governments and they will only improve over time. I recommend using these systems if you need to quickly pinpoint corporate activity—even if you don't see the actual filing. Sometimes, simply noticing that a competitor may have filed with the state can forewarn you of future activity in that state. For example, it may indicate a new sales or manufacturing initiative.

For further information regarding an online system, contact the Secretary of State's Office for each state. The following states offer some level of direct online access:

Alaska	Illinois	Oklahoma
Arizona	Iowa	Oregon
California	Nebraska	Pennsylvania
Colorado	Nevada	South Carolina
Connecticut	New York	Utah
Georgia	North Carolina	West Virginia
Idaho		

ALABAMA

Securities Filings
Security Commissioner
770 Washington St., Suite 570
Montgomery, AL 36130
205-242-2984

UCC Filings
Secretary of State
UCC Div.
P.O. Box 5616
Montgomery, AL 36130-5616
205-242-5231

Corporate Filings
Secretary of State
Corporate Div.
P.O. Box 5616
Montgomery, AL 36130-5616
205-242-5324

Occupational Safety Filings
Labor Dept.
1789 Cong. W.L.
   Dickinson Dr.
Montgomery, AL 36130
205-242-3460

Environment
Environmental Management
1751 Cong. W.L.
   Dickinson Dr.
Montgomery, AL 36130
205-271-7700

Labor & Industrial Relations
Industrial Relations
649 Monroe St.
Montgomery, AL 36131
205-242-8055

ALASKA

Annual Report
Primary, secondary, and
   tertiary SIC codes
Authorized shares and par
   value
Issued shares: class, series,
   and par value
Names and addresses of
   officers and directors

Names, addresses, and nature
   of relationship between
   corporate and alien
   affiliates
Name and address of person
   having direct ownership or
   control of at least 50% of
   any class of shares

Securities Filings
Dept. of Commerce &
   Economic Dev.
Securities Div.
P.O. Box 110800
Juneau, AK 99811-0800

UCC Filings
Dept. of Administration
UCC Div.
3601 C St., Suite 1140-A
Anchorage, AK 99503
907-762-2102

Corporate Filings
Dept. of Commerce &
   Economic Dev.
Corporation Div.
P.O. Box 110800
Juneau, AK 99811-0800
907-465-2500

Occupational Safety Filings
Div. of Occupational Safety &
   Health
Dept. of Labor
P.O. Box 21149
Juneau, AK 99802-1149
907-465-2700

Environment
Dept. of Environmental
   Conservation
410 Willouhby Ave.,
   Suite 105
Juneau, AK 99810-1795
907-465-5000

*Labor & Industrial
   Relations*
Dept. of Administration
Labor Relations Div.
P.O. Box C
Juneau, AK 99811
907-465-4404

ARIZONA

Annual Report
Aggregate number of shares
Number authorized, class
   series, and par value

Merger/Consolidation
Names of stockholders who
   own at least 20% of stock

Securities Filings
Corporation Commission
Securities Div.
1200 W. Washington St.
Phoenix, AZ 85007
602-542-4242

Occupational Safety Filings
Industrial Commission
OSHA Div.
800 W. Washington St.
Phoenix, AZ 85007
602-542-5795

UCC Filings
Secretary of State
UCC Div.
1700 W. Washington St.
West Wing
Phoenix, AZ 85007
602-542-6178

Corporate Filings
Corporation Commission
Corporations Div.
1200 W. Washington St.
Phoenix, AZ 85007
602-542-3026

Environment
ADEQ
3033 N. Central Ave.
Phoenix, AZ 85012
602-207-2300

Labor & Industrial Relations
Industrial Commission
Labor Div.
800 W. Washington St.
Phoenix, AZ 85007
602-542-4515

ARKANSAS

Annual Report
Corporate officers
Balance sheet
Shares of stock authorized
  and outstanding
Value of Arkansas assets
Contact or key officer name

Securities Filings
Securities Div.
Heritage West Bldg.
201 E. Markham St.,
  Suite 300
Little Rock, AR 77201
501-324-9260

UCC Filings
Secretary of State
UCC Div.
256 State Capitol Bldg.
Little Rock, AR 72201
501-682-5078

Occupational Safety Filings
Dept. of Labor
Security Div.
10421 W. Markham St.
Little Rock, AR 72205
501-682-4500

Corporate Filings
Secretary of State
Corporation Div.
256 State Capitol Bldg.
Little Rock, AR 72201
501-682-3409

Environment
Dept. of Pollution Control
P.O. Box 8910
Little Rock, AR 72219
501-682-8913

Labor & Industrial Relations
Labor & Standards
Dept. of Labor
10421 W. Markham St.
Little Rock, AR 72205
501-682-4500

CALIFORNIA

Securities Filings
Secretary of State
Corporations Div.
3700 Wilshire Blvd.,
  Suite 600
Los Angeles, CA 90010-2901
213-736-3481

UCC Filings
Secretary of State
UCC Div.
1230 J St.
Sacramento, CA 95814
916-445-8061

Corporate Filings
Secretary of State
Corporate Filing Div.
1230 J St.
Sacramento, CA 95814
916-445-0620

*Occupational Safety &
  Health*
Occupational Safety &
  Health Div.
Industrial Relations Dept.
395 Oyster Point Blvd.
San Francisco, CA 94101
415-703-4590

Environment
EPA Dept.
P.O. Box 2815
Sacramento, CA 95812
916-445-3846

Labor & Industrial Relations
Industrial Relations Div.
395 Oyster Point Blvd.
San Francisco, CA 94101
415-703-4590

COLORADO

Annual Report
Federal employer ID number
Issued and authorized shares,
  par value
Names and addresses of
  directors

Securities Filings
State Securities Div.
1550 Lincoln St., Suite 420
Denver, CO 80203
303-894-2320

UCC Filings
Secretary of State
Commercial Recordings Div.
1560 Broadway St., Suite 200
Denver, CO 80202
303-894-2200

Corporate Filings
Secretary of State
State Dept.
Corporations Office
1560 Broadway St., Suite 200
Denver, CO 80202
303-894-2251

Environment
Natural Resources Dept.
1313 Sherman St., Room 718
Denver, CO 80203
303-866-3311

Labor & Industrial Relations
Labor Div.
1120 Lincoln St., 13th Floor
Denver, CO 80203
303-894-7541

CONNECTICUT

Securities Filings
Banking Dept.
Securities Div.
44 Capitol Ave.
Hartford, CT 06106
203-566-4560

UCC Filings
Secretary of State
UCC Conversion Services
30 Trinity St.
Hartford, CT 06106
203-566-2448

Corporate Filings
Secretary of State
Commercial Recording Div.
30 Trinity St.
Hartford, CT 06106
203-566-8570

*Occupational Safety
   Filings*
Labor Dept.
200 Folly Brook Blvd.
Wethersfield, CT 06109
203-566-4550

Environment
EPA Dept.
165 Capitol Ave.
Hartford, CT 06106
203-566-5599

*Labor & Industrial
   Relations*
Labor Dept.
Labor Relations Board
200 Folly Brook Blvd.
Wethersfield, CT 06109
203-566-4398

DELAWARE

Securities Filings
Office of the Securities
   Commission
State Office Bldg.
820 N. French St., 8th Floor
Wilmington, DE 19801
302-577-2515

UCC Filings
Secretary of State
UCC Div.
P.O. Box 793
Dover, DE 19903
302-739-4279

Corporate Filings
Secretary of State
Corporations Div.
P.O. Box 898
Dover, DE 19903
302-739-3073

Occupational Safety Filings
Div. of Industrial Affairs
820 N. French St.
Wilmington, DE 19801
302-577-2884

Environment
Natural Resources &
   Environmental Control
   Dept.
89 Kings Hwy.
P.O. Box 1401
Dover, DE 19903
302-739-4403

Labor & Industrial Relations
Dept. of Labor
Secretary of Labor
820 N. French St.
Wilmington, DE 19801
302-739-4403

War Story:
Delaware—The Little Switzerland of the United States

The little state of Delaware has long held a strong position as one of the more competitive states in attracting corporations by providing many perquisites for companies incorporating there. Almost half the Fortune 500 companies register in Delaware because of its tax breaks and minimal reporting standards.

As part of a campaign to sell the state's advantages to overseas companies considering a U.S. base, Delaware issued a brochure that contained the following passages: "We Protect You From Politics . . . By incorporating secretly, in the event of an emergency in your home country, such as insurrection or invasion by a hostile power, your company can temporarily or permanently move its domicile and be protected by the laws of The State of Delaware . . . ."[*]

Among the advantages corporations accrue as a result of filing here (and the reason state filings offer frustratingly little to the corporate researcher examining a Delaware corporation):

- The board of directors does not have to be disclosed in any filing.
- Companies can change by-laws without stockholder approval.
- Anonymous ownership of corporations is allowed.

---

[*]L.J. Davis, "Delaware Inc.," *The New York Times Magazine,* June 5, 1988, p. 28.

FLORIDA

Annual Report
Federal employer ID number
Date of incorporation
Date of last report

Securities Filings
Office of Comptroller
Div. of Securities
PL-22 Capitol Bldg.
Tallahassee, FL 32399-0350
904-488-9805

UCC Filings
Secretary of State
UCC Div.
P.O. Box 5588
Tallahassee, FL 32314
904-487-6845

Corporate Filings
Secretary of State
Corporations Div.
409 E. Gaines St.
P.O. Box 6327
Tallahassee, FL 32314
904-487-6000

Environment
Environmental Regulations
  Dept.
Div. of Environmental
  Programs
2600 Blairstone Rd.
Tallahassee, FL 32399-2400
904-488-4805

Labor & Industrial Relations
Labor & Employment
  Security
2012 Capitol Circle SE
Hartman Bldg.
Tallahassee, FL 32399-2152
904-488-8641

GEORGIA

Annual Report
Incorporation date
Date of last report

Securities Filings
Secretary of State
Securities Div.
2 Martin Luther King Dr., SE,
  Suite 315
West Tower
Atlanta, GA 30334
404-656-2894

UCC Filings
Secretary of State
Securities Div.
2 Martin Luther King Dr., SE,
  Suite 315
West Tower
Atlanta, GA 30334
404-656-2894
(Must be checked county by
county; call this office for
further information.)

Corporate Filings
Secretary of State
Corporations Div.
2 Martin Luther King Dr., SE,
  Suite 315
West Tower
Atlanta, GA 30334
404-656-2817

Occupational Safety Filings
U.S. Dept. of Labor
1375 Peachtree St., NE,
  Suite 587
Atlanta, GA 30367
404-347-3573

Environment
Natural Resources Dept.
Environmental Protection Div.
205 Butler St., SE, Suite 1252
Atlanta, GA 30334
404-656-4713

Labor & Industrial Relations
Labor Board
101 Marietta St., NW,
  Suite 2400
Atlanta, GA 30303
404-331-2896

HAWAII

Annual Report
Stock—paid-in-capital
Authorized stock par value
  and par share

Securities Filings
Business Registration Div.
Dept. of Regulatory Agencies
P.O. Box 40
Honolulu, HI 96810
808-586-2737

UCC Filings
Bureau of Conveyance
P.O. Box 2867
Honolulu, HI 96803
808-587-0134

Corporate Filings
Business Registration Div.
Dept. of Regulatory Agencies
P.O. Box 40
Honolulu, HI 96810
808-586-2727

Occupational Safety Filings
Dept. of Labor & Industrial
  Relations
Dept. of Safety & Health
830 Punchbowl St.
Honolulu, HI 96813
808-586-9100

Environment
Environmental Quality
  Control
550 Halekauwila St.,
  Room 301
Honolulu, HI 96813
808-586-4185

Labor & Industrial Relations
Labor & Industrial Relations
830 Punchbowl St.
Honolulu, HI 96813
808-586-8851

IDAHO

Annual Report
Federal employer ID number
Corporate number
Names and addresses of
    directors and officers

Securities Filings
Securities Div.
Dept. of Finance
700 W. State St.
Boise, ID 83720
208-334-3684

UCC Filings
Secretary of State
UCC Div.
State House, Room 203
Boise, ID 83720
208-334-3191

Corporate Filings
Secretary of State
Corporation Div.
State House, Room 203
Boise, ID 83720
208-334-2300

Occupational Safety Filings
Industrial Commission
State House
317 Main St.
Boise, ID 83720
208-334-6000

Environment
Health & Welfare Dept.
Environment Div.
1410 N. Hilton
Boise, ID 83706
208-334-5840

Labor & Industrial Relations
Labor & Industrial Services
    Dept.
State House
277 N. 6th
Boise, ID 83720
208-334-3950

ILLINOIS

Annual Report
Officers' names and home
    addresses
Number of shares authorized
    and outstanding
Stated capital and paid-in
    surplus
Value of property in and out
    of Illinois
Gross amount of business
    transacted by corporation
    elsewhere
Gross amount of business
    transacted by corporation
    in Illinois
Location of principal places
    of business in each state
    where authorized, and
    amount of business
    transacted in each state

Articles of Merger/
Consolidation
Plan of merger/consolidation
Number of shares outstanding,
    assignation of class entitled
    to vote, number of shares of
    such class
Number of shares additional
    in treasury
Number of shares for and
    against merger/consolidation
Amount of paid-in-capital
    before and after merger or
    consolidation
Estimated value of all Illinois
    property owned by
    corporation for the
    following year

Securities Filings
Secretary of State
Securities Div.
900 S. Spring St.
Springfield, IL 62704
217-782-2256

UCC Filings
Secretary of State
UCC Div.
P.O. Box 19276
Springfield, IL 62794
217-785-3285

Corporate Filings
Secretary of State
Business Services Div.
328 Hollett Bldg.,
    2nd & Edwards St.
Springfield, IL 62756
217-782-6963

Occupational Safety Filings
OSHA
230 S. Dearborn, Room 3244
Chicago, IL 60604
312-353-2220

Environment
EPA
P.O. Box 19276
Springfield, IL 62794
217-782-3397

Labor & Industrial Relations
Dept. of Labor
160 N. LaSalle
Chicago, IL 60604
312-793-2804

INDIANA

Corporate Report
Number of shares authorized
    and outstanding with par
    value, no par value, par
    value per share, series
Share dividend

Articles of Merger (two
    companies into one)
Manner of adoption and vote
Statement of changes in
    authorized stock

Articles of Merger (subsidiary
    into parent)
Plan of merger
Shares outstanding

Securities Filings
Secretary of State
Securities Div.
302 W. Washington St.,
    Room E111
Indianapolis, IN 46206
317-232-6681

UCC Filings
Secretary of State
UCC Div.
302 W. Washington St.,
    Room E-018
Indianapolis, IN 46206
317-232-6393

Corporate Filings
Secretary of State
Corporation Div.
302 W. Washington St.,
    Room E-018
Indianapolis, IN 46204
317-232-6576

Occupational Safety Filings
Labor Dept.
OSHA Compliance
402 W. Washington St.,
    Room W195
Indianapolis, IN 46204
317-232-3325

Environment
Environmental Management
105 S. Meridian St.
P.O. Box 6015
Indianapolis, IN 46206-6015
317-232-8162

Labor & Industrial Relations
Labor Dept.
Div. of Employment Standards
402 W. Washington St.,
    Room W195
Indianapolis, IN 46204
317-232-2673

IOWA

Annual Report
Directors' names and addresses
Stock authorized and issued

Annual Report (foreign)
Directors' names and addresses
Stock authorized and issued

*Articles of Merger/
    Consolidation*
No standard form, must be
    drawn up from Code of
    Iowa, referring to the
    appropriate chapter of
    incorporation

Securities Filings
Iowa Securities Bureau
Zuchs State Office Bldg.,
    2nd Floor
Des Moines, IA 50319
515-281-4441

UCC Filings
Secretary of State
UCC Div.
1300 Walnut St.
Hoover Bldg.
Des Moines, IA 50319
515-281-6560

Corporate Filings
Secretary of State
Corp. Div.
1300 Walnut St.
Hoover Bldg., 2nd Floor
Des Moines, IA 50319
515-281-5204

Occupational Safety Filings
Bureau of Labor
1000 E. Grand Ave.
Des Moines, IA 50319
515-281-3606

Environment
Natural Resources Dept.
Wallace State Office Bldg.
900 E. Grand St.
Des Moines, IA 50319
515-281-5385

Labor & Industrial Relations
Bureau of Labor
Industrial Commission
1000 E. Grand Ave.
Des Moines, IA 50319
515-281-5934

KANSAS

Annual Report (domestic or
    foreign corporation)
Balance sheet
Capital account at beginning
    of year
Ordinary income
Losses incurred
Withdrawals and distributions
Capital account at end of year
Ownership, location, and
    value of farming land
    owned in Kansas

Limited Partnership
    (domestic or foreign)
Balance sheet
Capital account at beginning
    of year
Capital contribution during
    year
Income or loss
Withdrawals and distribution
Capital account at year-end
Location, value, and ownership
    of agricultural property

*Articles of Merger/
    Consolidation*
No standard form

Securities Filings
Securities Commission
618 S. Kansas Ave., 2nd Floor
Topeka, KS 66603-3804
913-296-3307

UCC Filings
Secretary of State
UCC Div.
Capitol Bldg.
300 S.W. 10th St., 2nd Floor
Topeka, KS 66612
913-296-3650

Corporate Filings
Secretary of State
Corporations Div.
Capitol Bldg.
300 S.W. 10th St., 2nd Floor
Topeka, KS 66612
913-296-4564

Occupational Safety Filings
Dept. of Human Resources
Industrial Safety Div.
512 S.W. 6th St.
Topeka, KS 66603-3174
913-296-7475

Environment
Health & Environment Dept.
Environment Div.
Forbes Field Bldg., Room 740
Topeka, KS 66620
913-296-1535

Labor & Industrial Relations
Human Resources Dept.
Employment Standards Div.
512 S.W. 6th St.
Topeka, KS 66603
913-296-3094

KENTUCKY

Securities Filings
Financial Institutions
Div. of Security
477 Versailles Rd.
Frankfort, KY 40601
502-564-2181

UCC Filings
Secretary of State
UCC Div.
P.O. Box 718
Frankfort, KY 40602-0718
502-564-2848

Corporate Filings
Secretary of State
Corporations Div.
P.O. Box 718
Frankfort, KY 40602-0718
502-564-2848

Occupational Safety Filings
Labor Cabinet
1049 US-127 South
Frankfort, KY 40601
502-564-6895

Environment
Environmental Protection
   Dept.
Fort Boone Plaza
18 Reilly Rd.
Frankfort, KY 40601
502-564-2150

Labor & Industrial Relations
Labor Cabinet
Employee Standards
Mediation Div.
1049 US-127 South
Frankfort, KY 40601
502-564-2784

LOUISIANA

Securities Filings
Securities Commission
1100 Poidaras St., Suite 225
New Orleans, LA 70163
504-568-5515

UCC Filings
Secretary of State
UCC Div.
3851 Essen Lane
Baton Rouge, LA 70809
504-922-1314

Corporate Filings
Secretary of State
Corporations Div.
3851 Essen Lane
Baton Rouge, LA 70809
504-925-4704

Occupational Safety Filings
Dept. of Labor
1001 N. 23rd St.
P.O. Box 94094
Baton Rouge, LA 70804-9094
504-342-9601

Environment
Environmental Quality Dept.
7290 Blue Bonnet Rd.
Baton Rouge, LA 70804
504-765-0741

Labor & Industrial Relations
Dept. of Labor
1001 N. 23rd St.
P.O. Box 94094
Baton Rouge, LA 70804-9094
504-342-7666

MAINE

Articles of Merger (Maine
   corporation into Maine
   corporation)
Plan of merger
Number of shares outstanding,
   number entitled to vote,
   number voted for and
   against in each corporation
Designation of and number of
   shares in each class,
   number voted for and
   against in each corporation
Designation of class, number
   of shares outstanding
   before and after merger

Articles of Merger (Maine
   subsidiary into Maine
   parent company)
Number of shares outstanding,
   designation of class, and
   percentage of shares owned
   by surviving parent
Date of mailing of merger
   plan to shareholders

Articles of Merger (domestic
   and foreign companies)
Plan of merger
Number of shares outstanding,
   number entitled to vote,
   number voted for and
   against in each corporation
Designation of and number of
   shares in each class,
   number voted for and
   against in each corporation
Designation of class, number
   of shares outstanding
   before and after merger

Articles of Merger (parent–
   subsidiary merger of
   domestic and foreign
   corporations)

Plan of merger

Number of shares outstanding, number entitled to vote, number voted for and against in each corporation

Designation of and number of shares in each class, number voted for and against in each corporation

Securities Filings
Professional & Financial
  Regulations Dept.
State House Station 121
Augusta, ME 04333

UCC Filings
Secretary of State
UCC Div.
State House Station 101
Augusta, ME 04333
207-287-4177

Corporate Filings
Secretary of State
Corporate Div.
State House Station 101
Augusta, ME 04333
207-287-4190

Occupational Safety Filings
Bureau of Labor
Labor Standards Bureau
State House Station 45
Augusta, ME 04333
207-624-6400

Environment
Environmental Protection
State House Station 17
Augusta, ME 04333
207-287-7688

Labor & Industrial Relations
Labor Relations Board
Labor Dept.
State House Station 90
Augusta, ME 04333
207-287-2015

MARYLAND

Annual Report
Names and addresses of officers

Total cost, depreciation rate, and book value of furniture, fixtures, and equipment

Value of physical inventory at cost or market value

Value of raw materials and supplies

Ships, vessels, floating equipment, and water craft

Livestock

Motor vehicles

Tools, machinery, and equipment for manufacturing and other purposes

Supplies and tangible personal property

Securities Filings
Attorney General's Office
Securities Div.
200 St. Paul Place
Baltimore, MD 21202-2020
410-576-6360

UCC Filings
Assessments & Taxation Dept.
Commercial Code Div.
301 W. Preston St., Room 809
Baltimore, MD 21201-2395
410-225-1340

Corporate Filings
Assessments & Taxation Dept.
Corporate Div.
301 W. Preston St.
Baltimore, MD 21201-2395
410-225-1340

Occupational Safety Filings
Licensing & Regulation Dept.
Labor & Industry Div.
OSHA Section
501 St. Paul Place
Baltimore, MD 21202
410-333-4180

Environment
Dept. of the Environment
2500 Broening Hwy.
Baltimore, MD 21224
410-631-3084

Labor & Industrial Relations
Div. of Labor & Industry
501 St. Paul Place
Baltimore, MD 21202
410-333-4180

MASSACHUSETTS

Annual Report
Federal corporate ID number

Class of stock—number authorized and number of outstanding shares

Articles of Merger
Total number of shares authorized, par value and dollar amount

Description of each class of stock, with preferences, voting power, qualifications, and special privileges

Names, residence and post office addresses of officers

Stockholders' meeting date

Securities Filings
Secretary of State
Securities Div.
1 Ashburton Place, 17th Floor
Boston, MA 02108
671-727-3548

UCC Filings
Secretary of State
UCC Div.
1 Ashburton Place, 17th Floor
Boston, MA 02108
617-727-9640

Corporate Filings
Secretary of State
Corporations Div.
1 Ashburton Place, 17th Floor
Boston, MA 02108
617-727-2853

Occupational Safety Filings
Dept. of Labor & Industries
OSHA Div.
100 Cambridge St., 11th Floor
Boston, MA 02202
617-727-3593

Environment
Dept. of the Environment
1 Winter St., 3rd Floor
Boston, MA 02108
617-292-5856

Labor & Industrial Relations
Labor Relations Commission
100 Cambridge St.,
    Room 1604
Boston, MA 02212
617-727-3509

MICHIGAN

Annual Report
Names of parent and
    subsidiary corporations
Type of stock, shares
    authorized and outstanding,
    amount subscribed, amount
    paid-in
Balance sheet
Officers' names and addresses

Securities Filings
Commerce Dept.
Securities Div.
6546 Mercantile Way
P.O. Box 30222
Lansing, MI 48909
517-334-6200

UCC Filings
Dept. of State
UCC Section
P.O. Box 30197
Lansing, MI 48909-7697
517-322-1495

Corporate Filings
Commerce Dept.
Corporations & Securities
    Bureau
6546 Mercantile Way
P.O. Box 30222
Lansing, MI 48909
517-334-6302

Occupational Safety Filings
Dept. of Labor
Safety & Regulation Bureau
P.O. Box 30016
Lansing, MI 48909
517-322-1296

Environment
Natural Resources Dept.
Environmental Protection
    Dept.
P.O. Box 30028
Lansing, MI 48909
517-373-7917

Labor & Industrial Relations
Bureau of Safety & Regulation
Wage/Hour Div.
P.O. Box 30015
Lansing, MI 48909
517-322-1825

MINNESOTA

Annual Report (foreign)
Names, titles, and addresses
    of officers and directors
Net income

Merger (no form; a merger
    plan must be filed with the
    state)
Names of corporations to
    merge
Terms and conditions of
    merger
Value of property before and
    after merger

Securities Filings
Dept. of Commerce
Securities Div.
133 E. 7th St.
St. Paul, MN 55101
612-296-6848

UCC Filings
Secretary of State
UCC Div.
180 State Office Bldg.
100 Constitution Ave.
St. Paul, MN 55155
612-296-2434

Corporate Filings
Secretary of State
Corporations Div.
180 State Office Bldg.
St. Paul, MN 55155
612-296-9215

Occupational Safety Filings
Dept. of Labor & Industry
OSHA Unit
443 Lafayette Rd.
St. Paul, MN 55155-4304
612-296-4532

Environment
Pollution Control Agency
520 Lafayette Rd.
St. Paul, MN 55155
612-296-7301

Labor & Industrial Relations
Dept. of Labor & Industry
Labor Standards Unit
443 Lafayette Rd.
St. Paul, MN 55155-4304

MISSISSIPPI

Annual Report (domestic and
    foreign)
Names and addresses of
    directors and officers
Aggregate number of shares
    authorized, by class, par
    value, no par value, and
    series within class
Aggregate number of issued
    shares, by class, par value,
    no par value, and series
    within class
Amount of stated capital

*Articles of Merger/
    Consolidation* (domestic
    and foreign)
Plan of merger/consolidation
Total number of shares
    outstanding, designation of
    class entitled to vote, and
    number of shares of such
    class for each corporation
    and within each class

Articles of Merger (subsidiary into parent)
Class, number of shares outstanding, and number of shares owned by parent
Date plan of merger mailed to stockholders

Securities Filings
Secretary of State
Securities Div.
P.O. Box 136
Jackson, MS 39205
601-359-1350

UCC Filings
Secretary of State
UCC Div.
P.O. Box 136
Jackson, MS 39205
601-359-1350

Corporate Filings
Secretary of State
Corporations Div.
P.O. Box 136
Jackson, MS 39205
601-359-1350

Occupational Safety Filings
Mississippi Health Dept.
OSHA Div.
2906 N. State St., Room 201
Jackson, MS 39216
601-987-3981

Environment
Pollution Control Bureau
P.O. Box 10385
Jackson, MS 39289-0385

Labor & Industrial Relations
Employment Security
    Commission
P.O. Box 1699
Jackson, MS 39215
601-354-8711

MISSOURI

Articles of Merger
    (parent–subsidiary merger)

How outstanding shares are exchanged for shares of surviving company
Articles of Merger (domestic corporations—to be filed by attorney)
Date of shareholders' meeting and number of shares voted for and against merger
Plan for exchange of shares

Securities Filings
Secretary of State
Securities Div.
P.O. Box 1276
Jefferson City, MO 65102

UCC Filings
Secretary of State
UCC Div.
P.O. Box 1159
Jefferson City, MO 65102

Corporate Filings
Secretary of State
Corporate Div.
P.O. Box 778
Jefferson City, MO 65102

Occupational Safety Filings
Div. of Labor Standards
Labor & Industrial Relations
3315 W. Truman Blvd.
Jefferson City, MO 65109

Environment
Dept. of Natural Resources
Environmental Quality Div.
P.O. Box 176
Jefferson City, MO 65102
314-751-4810

Labor & Industrial Relations
Labor & Industrial Relations
    Commission
3315 W. Truman Blvd.
Jefferson City, MO 65109
314-751-2461

MONTANA

Annual Report
Authorized and issued stock class, series of stock
Names and addresses of officers and directors
Property location and value (only for foreign corporations)

Articles of Merger/ Consolidation
Use Montana Code Annotated for guidelines

Securities Filings
State Auditor's Office
Securities Div.
P.O. Box 4009
Helena, MT 59604
406-444-5236

UCC Filings
Secretary of State
UCC Div.
State Capitol Bldg.
Helena, MT 59620
406-444-3665

Corporate Filings
Secretary of State
Corporations Div.
State Capitol Bldg.
Helena, MT 59620
406-444-3665

Occupational Safety Filings
Dept. of Labor & Industry
Safety Bureau
P.O. Box 1728
Helena, MT 59624
406-444-6401

Environment
Dept. of Health & Environmental Sciences
Cogswell Bldg.
P.O. Box 200901
Helena, MT 59620-0901
406-444-2544

Labor & Industrial Relations
Dept. of Labor & Industry
P.O. Box 1728
Helena, MT 59624-1728

NEBRASKA

Annual Report (foreign and
  domestic)
Value of property owned and
  used by corporation in state

*Articles of Merger/
  Consolidation*
No standard form; use
  Nebraska Book of Statutes
  as guideline

Securities Filings
Dept. of Banking & Finance
Securities Div.
1200 N St., The Atrium,
  Suite 311
Lincoln, NE 68508
402-471-2171

UCC Filings
Secretary of State
UCC Div.
P.O. Box 95104
Lincoln, NE 68509-4608
402-471-4080

Corporate Filings
Secretary of State
Corporations Div.
P.O. Box 94608
Lincoln, NE 68509-4608

Occupational Safety Filings
Dept. of Labor
Safety Div.
P.O. Box 95024
Lincoln, NE 68509
402-471-2239

Environment
Dept. of Environmental
  Control
P.O. Box 98922
Lincoln, NE 68509-8922
402-471-2186

Labor & Industrial Relations
Dept. of Labor
P.O. Box 95024
Lincoln, NE 68509
402-471-9000

NEVADA

Securities Filings
Secretary of State
Securities Div.
Capitol Complex
Carson City, NV 89710
702-486-4400

UCC Filings
Secretary of State
UCC Div.
Capitol Complex
Carson City, NV 89710
702-687-5298

Corporate Filings
Secretary of State
Corporations Div.
Capitol Complex
Carson City, NV 89710
702-687-5105

Occupational Safety Filings
Dept. of Occupational Safety
  & Health
4600 Kietzke Lane
Bldg. F, Suite 153
Reno, NV 89502
702-688-1380

Environment
Dept. of Conservation &
  Natural Resources
Environmental Protection Div.
333 W. Nye Lane
Carson City, NV 89710
702-687-4670

Labor & Industrial Relations
Labor Commission
1445 Hot Springs Rd.,
  Suite 108
Carson City, NV 89710
702-687-4850

NEW HAMPSHIRE

Annual Report
Names and addresses of
  officers and directors
Articles of Consolidation
  (domestic and foreign)
Plan of consolidation
Number of shares outstanding

Articles of Merger (foreign
  subsidiary into domestic
  parent)
Plan of merger
Number of shares outstanding
Number of shares owned by
  surviving company

Articles of Merger (domestic
  subsidiary into foreign
  parent)
Plan of merger
Number of shares outstanding
Number of shares owned by
  surviving company

Merger (foreign and domestic
  companies)
Plan of merger
Number of shares outstanding
Number of shares owned by
  surviving company

Merger (domestic into
  domestic)
Plan of merger
Number of shares outstanding

Merger (two domestic
  companies)
Plan of merger
Number of shares outstanding

Securities Filings
Secretary of State
Securities Div.
State House Annex, 4th Floor
Concord, NH 03301
603-271-1463

UCC Filings
Secretary of State
UCC Div.
State House, Room 204
Concord, NH 03301
603-271-3276

Corporate Filings
Secretary of State
Corporations Div.
State House, Room 204
Concord, NH 03301
603-271-3244

Occupational Safety Filings
Occupational Safety
6 Hazen Dr.
Concord, NH 03301
603-271-2024

Environment
Environmental Services Dept.
P.O. Box 95
Concord, NH 03301
603-271-3503

Labor & Industrial Relations
Dept. of Labor
95 Pleasant St.
Concord, NH 03301
603-271-3171

NEW JERSEY

Securities Filings
New Jersey Bureau of
    Securities
153 Halsey St.
Newark, NJ 07101
201-504-3600

UCC Filings
Secretary of State
UCC Div.
125 State St., CN 300
Trenton, NJ 08625-0300
609-530-6400

Corporate Filings
Secretary of State
Corporations Div.
125 W. State St., CN 300
Trenton, NJ 08625
609-530-6400

Occupational Safety Filings
Occupational Health & Safety
Consultation Office
Plaza 4 Yard Ave.
Trenton, NJ 08625
609-292-0404

Environment
Environmental Protection &
    Energy Dept.
401 E. State St., CN 402
Trenton, NJ 08625-0402
609-292-2885

Labor & Industrial Relations
Dept. of Labor
Wage & Hour Compliance
    Office
P.O. Box CN 389
Trenton, NJ 08625-0389
609-292-7860

NEW MEXICO

Annual Report
Officers' names and addresses
Next annual meeting date
Balance sheet
Capital stock

Securities Filings
Dept. of Licensing &
    Regulations
Securities Div.
P.O. Box 25101
Santa Fe, NM 87504
505-827-7140

UCC Filings
Secretary of State
UCC Div.
State Capitol Bldg., Room 420
Santa Fe, NM 87503
505-827-3610

Corporate Filings
State Corporation Commission
P.O. Drawer 1269
Santa Fe, NM 87503
505-827-4529

Occupational Safety Filings
Dept. of the Environment
Occupational Health & Safety
    Bureau
P.O. Box 26110
Santa Fe, NM 87502
505-827-2879

Environment
Dept. of the Environment
P.O. Box 26110
Santa Fe, NM 87502
505-827-2850

Labor & Industrial Relations
Labor Dept.
Labor & Industrial Div.
1596 Pacheco St.
Santa Fe, NM 87501
505-827-6875

NEW YORK

Securities Filings
State Attorney General
Bureau of Securities
120 Broadway
New York, NY 10271
212-416-8200

UCC Filings
Secretary of State
UCC Div.
162 Washington Ave.
Albany, NY 12231
518-474-4763

Corporate Filings
Secretary of State
Corporations & State Records
162 Washington Ave.
Albany, NY 12231
518-474-6200

Occupational Safety Filings
Dept. of Labor
OSHA Div.
State Campus, Bldg. 12
Albany, NY 12231
518-474-4763

Environment
Environmental Conservation
    Dept.
50 Wolf Rd.
Albany, NY 12233
518-457-3446

Labor & Industrial Relations
Dept. of Labor
Research & Statistics
State Campus, Bldg. 12
Albany, NY 12233
518-457-6181

NORTH CAROLINA

Annual Report
No reports required

Merger (domestic company
  with domestic)
Number of shares outstanding,
  class, number of shares to
  vote
Number voted for and against
  merger

Securities Filings
Secretary of State
Securities Div.
300 N. Salisbury St.
Raleigh, NC 27603
919-733-4161

UCC Filings
Secretary of State
UCC Div.
300 N. Salisbury St.
Raleigh, NC 27603
919-733-4161

Corporate Filings
Secretary of State
Corporations Div.
300 N. Salisbury St.
Raleigh, NC 27603
919-733-4161

Occupational Safety Filings
Dept. of Labor
OSHA Div.
2 W. Edenton St.
Raleigh, NC 27601
919-733-2385

Environment
Dept. of Environment
Health & Natural Resources
512 N. Salisbury St.
Raleigh, NC 27611
919-733-4984

Labor & Industrial Relations
Dept. of Labor
2 W. Edenton St.
Raleigh, NC 27601
919-733-7166

NORTH DAKOTA

Securities Filings
Securities Dept.
State Capitol
600 E Blvd.
Bismarck, ND 58505-0500
701-224-2910

UCC Filings
Secretary of State
UCC Div.
600 E Blvd.
Bismarck, ND 58505-0500
701-224-2900

Corporate Filings
Secretary of State
Corporations Div.
600 E Blvd.
Bismarck, ND 58505-0500
701-224-2900

Occupational Safety Filings
Dept. of Safety
Workers' Compensation
  Bureau
4007 N. State St.
Bismarck, ND 58501
701-224-3800

Environment
Dept. of Health
Environmental Health
1200 Missouri Ave.
P.O. Box 5520
Bismarck, ND 58502-5520
701-224-5150

Labor & Industrial Relations
Dept. of Labor
600 E Blvd.
Bismarck, ND 58505-0500
701-224-2660

OHIO

Annual Report (foreign
  companies)
Book value of assets

*Articles of Merger/
  Consolidation*
No standard form. Agreement
  drafted according to Ohio
  Revised Code

Securities Filings
Dept. of Commerce
Securities Div.
77 S. High St., 23rd Floor
Columbus, OH 43266-0544
614-644-7381

UCC Filings
Secretary of State
UCC Div.
30 E. Broad St., 14th Floor
Columbus, OH 43266-0418
614-466-3623

Corporate Filings
Secretary of State
Corporations Div.
30 E. Broad St., 14th Floor
Columbus, OH 43266-0418
614-466-1145

Occupational Safety Filings
Dept. of Industrial Relations
2323 W. 5th Ave.
P.O. Box 825
Columbus, OH 43266-0576
614-644-2223

Environment
EPA
1800 Watermark St.
Columbus, OH 43266-0149
614-644-2782

Labor & Industrial Relations
Dept. of Industrial Relations
2323 W. 5th Ave.
P.O. Box 825
Columbus, OH 43266-0576
614-644-2223

OKLAHOMA

Annual Affidavit (foreign companies)
Minimum amount of capital now invested in state

Statement of Merger/ Consolidation (domestic and foreign)
Class, number, and series of shares outstanding
Names and addresses of principal officers

Articles of Merger/ Consolidation into Oklahoma Corporation
Aggregate number of shares
Class, number, series authorized, and par value of authorized shares
Amount of stated capital
Class and number of authorized shares, and consolidation received for new corporation
Number of directors in surviving corporation
Provisions limiting shareholders to acquiring additional shares
Provisions not consistent with law and regulation of affairs of corporation
Number of shares outstanding, number entitled to vote, class of designated shares of each consistent corporation
Names and addresses of directors and officers
Names, addresses, and percent of stock held by directors and others

Securities Filings
Dept. of Securities
621 N. Robinson St., Room 400
Oklahoma City, OK 73102
405-235-0230

UCC Filings
County Clerk—UCC Filings
County Courthouse
320 Robert Kerr Ave., Room 105
Oklahoma City, OK 73102
405-236-2727

Corporate Filings
Secretary of State
Corporation Records Div.
101 State Capitol Bldg..
Oklahoma City, OK 73105
405-521-3911

Occupational Safety Filings
Dept. of Labor
OSHA Div.
4001 N. Lincoln Blvd.
Oklahoma City, OK 73105
405-528-1500

Environment
Dept. of Health
Environmental Health Services
1000 N.E. 10th St.
Oklahoma City, OK 73117-1299
405-271-8056

Labor & Industrial Relations
Dept. of Labor
Wage & Hour Div.
4001 N. Lincoln Blvd.
Oklahoma City, OK 73105
405-528-1500

OREGON

Articles of Merger
Number of votes cast for and against

Securities Filings
Dept. of Insurance & Finance
Corp. Securities Section
21 Labor & Industries Bldg.
Salem, OR 97310
503-378-4387

UCC Filings
Secretary of State
UCC Div.
State Capitol, Room 41
Salem, OR 97310-0722
503-378-4146

Corporate Filings
State Corporations
158 12th St., N.E.
Salem, OR 97310
503-378-4166

Occupational Safety Filings
Dept. of Insurance & Finance
OSHA Div.
21 Labor & Industries Bldg.
Salem, OR 97310
503-378-3272

Environment
Dept. of Environmental Quality
811 S.W. 6th Ave.
Portland, OR 97204
503-229-5395

Labor & Industrial Relations
Labor & Industries Bureau
800 N.E. Oregon
P.O. Box 32
Portland, OR 97232
503-731-4200

PENNSYLVANIA

Securities Filings
Securities Commission
1010 N. 7th St., 2nd Floor
Harrisburg, PA 17102
717-787-6828

UCC Filings
Dept. of State
UCC Bureau
308 N. Office Bldg.
Harrisburg, PA 17120
717-787-8712

Corporate Filings
Dept. of State
Corporations Bureau
308 N. Office Bldg.
Harrisburg, PA 17102
717-787-1978

Occupational Safety Filings
Dept. of Labor & Industry
Occupational & Industrial
    Safety Bureau
Labor & Industry Bldg.,
    Room 1518
Harrisburg, PA 17120
717-787-3323

Environment
Dept. of Environmental
    Resources
P.O. Box 2063
Harrisburg, PA 17105-2063
717-787-2814

Labor & Industrial Relations
Dept. of Labor & Industry
Labor Relations Board
Labor & Industry Bldg.
Harrisburg, PA 17120
717-787-1091

RHODE ISLAND

Securities Filings
Dept. of Business Regulation
Securities Div.
233 Richmond St.
Providence, RI 02903
401-277-3048

UCC Filings
Secretary of State
UCC Div.
100 N. Main St.
Providence, RI 02903
401-277-3040

Corporate Filings
Secretary of State
Corporations Div.
100 N. Main St.
Providence, RI 02903
401-277-3040

Occupational Safety Filings
Dept. of Labor
Occupational Safety Div.
220 Elmwood Ave.
Providence, RI 02907
401-457-1877

Environment
Dept. of Environmental Mgmt.
9 Hayes St.
Providence, RI 02908
401-277-2771

Labor & Industrial Relations
Dept. of Labor
Labor Relations Board
220 Elmwood Ave.
Providence, RI 02907
401-457-1820

SOUTH CAROLINA

Annual Report
Names and addresses, percent
    of stock held by directors
    and others

Securities Filings
Secretary of State
Securities Div.
P.O. Box 11350
Columbia, SC 29211
803-734-2158

UCC Filings
Secretary of State
UCC Div.
P.O. Box 11350
Columbia, SC 29211
803-734-2175

Corporate Filings
Secretary of State
Corporations Div.
P.O. Box 11350
Columbia, SC 29211
803-734-2158

Occupational Safety Filings
Dept. of Labor
OSHA Div.
P.O. Box 11329
Columbia, SC 29211
803-734-9599

Environment
Dept. of Health &
    Environmental Control
2600 Bull St.
Columbia, SC 29201
803-734-5360

Labor & Industrial Relations
Dept. of Labor
Labor Mgmt. Services
P.O. Box 11329
Columbia, SC 29211
803-734-9601

SOUTH DAKOTA

Annual Report (domestic or
    foreign)
Names and addresses of
    officers and directors
Number of shares issued and
    stated value of capital

*Articles of Merger/
    Consolidation*
No standard form—must be
    formulated by attorney

Securities Filings
Dept. of Commerce &
    Regulation
Securities Div.
118 W. Capitol Ave.
Pierre, SD 57501-2017
605-773-4823

UCC Filings
Secretary of State
UCC Div.
500 E. Capitol Ave.,
    Suite 204
Pierre, SD 57501-5077
605-773-4845

Corporate Filings
Secretary of State
Corporations Div.
500 E. Capitol Ave.,
    Suite 204
Pierre, SD 57501-5077
605-773-4845

Occupational Safety Filings
Dept. of Health
Vital Records
523 E. Capitol Ave.
Pierre, SD 57501
605-773-4961

Environment
Dept. of Environment &
  Natural Resources
523 E. Capitol Ave.
Pierre, SD 57501-3181
605-773-3351

Labor & Industrial Relations
Dept. of Labor
Labor & Mgmt.
700 Governors Dr.
Pierre, SD 57501
605-773-3681

TENNESSEE

Securities Filings
Dept. of Commerce &
  Insurance
Securities Div.
500 James Robinson Plaza
Nashville, TN 37243-0565
615-741-2947

UCC Filings
Secretary of State
UCC Div.
James K. Polk Bldg.,
  Suite 1800
Nashville, TN 37243-0306
615-741-3276

Corporate Filings
Secretary of State
Corporations Div.
James K. Polk Bldg.,
  Suite 1800
Nashville, TN 37243-0306
615-741-0529

Occupational Safety Filings
Dept. of Labor
Occupational Safety Div.
501 Union Bldg., 3rd Floor
Nashville, TN 37243
615-741-2793

Environment
Environmental Bureau
Dept. of Environment &
  Conservation
15th L&C Tower
401 Church St.
Nashville, TN 37243-0453
615-532-0109

Labor & Industrial Relations
Dept. of Labor
Commissioners Office
501 Union Bldg., 3rd Floor
Nashville, TN 37243
615-741-2582

TEXAS

Securities Filings
Securities Board
221 W. 6th, Suite 700
Austin, TX 78701
512-474-2233

UCC Filings
Secretary of State
UCC Div.
1019 Brazos
Austin, TX 78701
512-475-2700

Corporate Filings
Secretary of State
Corporation Div.
1019 Brazos
Austin, TX 78701
512-463-5586

Occupational Safety Filings
Dept. of Health
Occupational Safety Div.
1100 W. 49th St.
Austin, TX 78756
512-458-7287

Environment
Dept. of Health
Environmental Health
1100 W. 49th St.
Austin, TX 78756
512-834-6640

Labor & Industrial Relations
U.S. Dept. of Labor
Wage & Hour Div.
300 E. 8th St., Room 578
Austin, TX 78701
512-482-5638

UTAH

Securities Filings
Dept. of Commerce
Securities Div.
P.O. Box 45808
Salt Lake City, UT 84145
801-530-6600

UCC Filings
Dept. of Commerce
UCC Div.
P.O. Box 45808
Salt Lake City, UT 84145
801-530-6027

Corporate Filings
Dept. of Commerce
Corporations Div.
P.O. Box 45801
Salt Lake City, UT 84145-0801
801-530-6027

Occupational Safety Filings
Industrial Commission
OSHA Div.
P.O. Box 146650
Salt Lake City, UT 84114-6650
801-530-6901

Environment
Dept. of Health
Environmental Health Div.
P.O. Box 16990
Salt Lake City, UT 84116-0990
801-538-6113

Labor & Industrial Relations
Industrial Commission
Labor Div.
P.O. Box 146650
Salt Lake City, UT 84114-6650
801-530-6921

VERMONT

Annual Report
Names and addresses of
  officers and directors
Number of shares authorized
  and issued

Securities Filings
Dept. of Banking, Insurance
  & Securities
89 Main St., Drawer 20
Montpelier, VT 05620-3101
802-828-3301

UCC Filings
Secretary of State
UCC Div.
Howard Bldg.
State & Main Sts., 3rd Floor
Montpelier, VT 05620
802-828-2388

Corporate Filings
Secretary of State
Corporations Div.
Howard Bldg.
State & Main Sts., 3rd Floor
Montpelier, VT 05620
802-828-2371

Occupational Safety Filings
Dept. of Labor & Industry
National Life Ins. Bldg.,
  Door 20
Montpelier, VT 05620
802-828-2765

Environment
Natural Resources Agency
Dept. of Environmental
  Conservation
103 S. Main St.
Waterbury, VT 05671-0401
802-244-8755

Labor & Industrial Relations
Labor Relations Board
13 Baldwin St.
Montpelier, VT 05633-6101
802-828-2700

VIRGINIA

Securities Filings
State Corporation Commission
Securities Div.
1300 E. Main St.
Richmond, VA 23219
804-786-7751

UCC Filings
State Corporation Commission
UCC Div.
1300 E. Main St.
Richmond, VA 23219
804-371-9189

Corporate Filings
State Corporation Commission
1300 E. Main St.
Richmond, VA 23219
804-371-9672

Occupational Safety Filings
Dept. of Labor & Industry
Occupational Safety &
  Enforcement Div.
13 S. 13th St.
Richmond, VA 23219
804-786-2391

Environment
Office of Natural Resources
P.O. Box 1475
Richmond, VA 23212
804-786-0044

Labor & Industrial Relations
Dept. of Labor & Industry
State Labor Law Div.
13 S. 13th St.
Richmond, VA 23219
804-786-2386

WASHINGTON

*Articles of Merger/
  Consolidation*
No standard form—must send
  articles and plan of merger
  to Secretary of State

Securities Filings
Dept. of Licensing
Securities Div.
P.O. Box 9033
Olympia, WA 98507-9033
206-753-6928

UCC Filings
Dept. of Licensing
UCC Div.
P.O. Box 9660
Olympia, WA 98507-9660
206-753-2523

Corporate Filings
Secretary of State
Corporations Div.
P.O. Box 40234
Olympia, WA 98504-0234
206-753-2896

Occupational Safety Filings
Div. of Industrial Safety &
  Health
Safety Compliance Section
P.O. Box 44600
Olympia, WA 98504-4600
206-956-5800

Environment
Dept. of Ecology
P.O. Box 47600
Olympia, WA 98504-7600
206-459-6168

Labor & Industrial Relations
Dept. of Labor & Industries
Director
P.O. Box 44001
Olympia, WA 98504-4001
206-956-4213

WEST VIRGINIA

Securities Filings
State Auditor's Office
Securities Div.
State Capitol Bldg.,
  Room W118
Charleston, WV 25305
304-558-2257

UCC Filings
Secretary of State
UCC Div.
1900 Canal Blvd., E,
    Room 139W
Charleston, WV 25305-0770
304-345-4000

Corporate Filings
Secretary of State
Corporations Div.
1900 Canal Blvd., E,
    Room 139W
Charleston, WV 25305-0770
304-345-4000

Occupational Safety Filings
Div. of Labor
Safety & Boiler Div.
Capitol Complex Bldg. 3,
    Room 319
Charleston, WV 25305
304-558-7890

Environment
Div. of Natural Resources
1900 Canal Blvd., E,
    Room 669
Charleston, WV 25305
304-558-2754

Labor & Industrial Relations
Div. of Labor
Wage & Hour Div.
Capitol Complex Bldg. 3,
    Room 319
Charleston, WV 25305
304-558-2257

WISCONSIN

Annual Report (foreign)
Directors' names and
    addresses
Authorized and issued stock,
    par value of stock
Number of Wisconsin
    shareholders

List of states and countries
    where company is licensed
    to do business
Proportion of capital
    represented in Wisconsin
    as of last fiscal year
Use for par stock and no par
    stock

Securities Filings
Commissioner of Securities
P.O. Box 1768
Madison, WI 53701
608-266-3431

UCC Filings
Secretary of State
UCC Div.
P.O. Box 7847
Madison, WI 53707
608-266-3087

Corporate Filings
Secretary of State
Corporations Div.
P.O. Box 7847
Madison, WI 53707
608-266-3590

Occupational Safety Filings
Dept. of Regulations &
    Licensing
P.O. Box 8126
Madison, WI 53708
608-266-5434

Environment
Dept. of Natural Resources
Environmental Quality Div.
P.O. Box 7921
Madison, WI 53707
608-266-1099

Labor & Industrial Relations
Labor & Industry Review
    Commission
P.O. Box 8126
Madison, WI 53708
608-266-9850

WYOMING

Annual Report
Directors' names and
    addresses
Nature of assets and dollar
    value

Securities Filings
Secretary of State
Securities Div.
Capitol Bldg.
Cheyenne, WY 82002
307-777-7370

UCC Filings
Secretary of State
UCC Div.
Capitol Bldg.
Cheyenne, WY 82002
307-777-5372

Corporate Filings
Secretary of State
Corporations Div.
Capitol Bldg.
Cheyenne, WY 82002
307-777-7311

Occupational Safety Filings
Dept. of Occupational Health
    & Safety
Herschler Bldg., 2nd Floor
Cheyenne, WY 82002
307-777-7705

Environment
Dept. of Environmental
    Quality
Herschler Bldg., 4th Floor
Cheyenne, WY 82002
307-777-7938

Labor & Industrial Relations
Dept. of Labor & Statistics
U.S. West Bldg.
6101 Yellowstone Rd.,
    Room 259C
Cheyenne, WY 82002
307-777-7261

CURRENT INDUSTRIAL REPORTS: YOUR GUIDE
TO INDUSTRY SIZE AND MARKET SHARE

For years, the U.S. Department of Commerce has published detailed industry analyses. As the order booklet states:

> The Current Industrial Reports of the Bureau of the Census present timely data on the production, inventories, and orders of approximately 5,000 products, which represents 40 percent of all U. S. manufacturing.

How can you use these reports for specific company profiles?

> You can determine market share. These booklets supply the number of companies and the amount their industry produces. If you have an idea of your target company's production, you can estimate market share for the firm.

> You can better understand which are the strongest selling products for a particular industry segment.

> Because the Current Industrial Reports track historical production information for an industry, you can see whether your target is following general industry trends.

> The reports use standard industry terminology and offer reasonably detailed breakdowns of each industry by major product groupings.

Some of the charts you would typically find in a Current Industrial Report are:

1. Shipments summary—shipments by year for the past five or six years.
2. Shipments by specified type of product—shipments by month for the past three or four years, according to product type.
3. Shipments by number and value shipped.
4. Shipments, exports, imports, apparent consumption, by quantity and value.
5. Product description, by specification.

The Current Industrial Reports appear monthly, quarterly, or yearly, depending on the industry studied. The industries covered are listed in Table 3.2 in alphabetical order. The code number appearing next to each report title is the report's series number. To order, simply ask for the report by its series number.

TABLE 3.2 Current Industrial Reports

Food
Confectionery: 1989 (MA-20D)
Confectionery: 1990 (MA-20D)
Fats and Oils: Oilseed Crushings (MQ-20J)
Fats and Oils: Production, Consumption, and Stocks (MQ-20K)
Flour Milling Products (M20A)

Textile Mill Products
Apparel: 1989 (MA-23A)
Broadwoven Fabrics (Gray) (MQ-22T)

(Continued)

TABLE 3.2   *(Continued)*

Carpet and Rugs: 1989 (MQ-22Q)
Carpet and Rugs: 1990 (MQ-22Q)
Consumption on the Cotton System and Stocks (MQ-22P)
Consumption on the Woolen System and Worsted Combing (MQ-22D)
Finished Broadwoven Fabric Production: 1987 (M22S)
Gloves and Mittens: 1989 (MA-23D)
Gloves and Mittens: 1990 (MA-23D)
Knit Fabric Production: 1989 (MA-22K)
Knit Fabric Production: 1990 (MA-22K)
Narrow Fabrics: 188 (MA-22G)
Selected Apparel (MQ-23A)
Sheets, Pillowcases, and Towels (MQ-23X)
Spun Yarn Production: 1989 (M22F.2)
Spun Yarn Production: 1990 (M22F.2)
Stocks of Wool and Related Fibers: 1987 (MA-22M)
Textured Yarn Production: 1989 (MA-22F.1)
Textured Yarn Production: 1990 (MA-22F.1)

Wood, Paper, and Related Products

Lumber Production and Mill Stocks: 189 (M-24T)
Office Furniture: 1989 (MA-25H)
Office Furniture: 1990 (MA-25H)
Plywood, Waferboard and Oriented-Strand Board: 1989 (MA-24F)
Pulp, Paper, and Board: 1989 (MA-26A)
Softwood Plywood: 1988 (MA-24H)

Chemicals and Petroleum Products

Fertilizer Materials (MQ-28B)
Fertilizer Materials: 1989 (MQ-28B)
Fertilizer Materials: 1990 (MQ-28B)
Footwear: 1989 (MA-31A)
Footwear: 1990 (MA-31A)
Industrial Gases (MQ-28C)
Inorganic Chemicals (MQ-28A)
Inorganic Chemicals: 1989 (M28A)
Inorganic Chemicals: 1990 (M28A)
Paint, Varnish and Lacquer (MQ-28F)
Pharmaceutical Preparations, Except Biologicals: 1990 (MA-28G)
Pharmaceutical Preparations, Except Biologicals: 1989 (MA-28G)
Plastics Bottles: 188 (MA-30E)
Rubber Mechanical Goods: 1989 (MA-30C)
Rubber Mechanical Goods: 1990 (MA-30C)
Rubber: Production, Shipments and Stocks: 1989 (MA-30A)

Glass, Clay, and Related Products

Clay Construction Products (MQ-32D)
Consumer, Scientific, Technical, and Industrial Glassware: 1990 (MA32E)
Consumer, Scientific, Technical, and Industrial Glassware: 1989 (MA32E)
Flat Glass (MQ-32C)
Glass Containers (M32G)
Glass Fibers: 1989 (MA-32J)
Refractories: 1989 (MA-32C)
Refractories: 1990 (MA-32C)

TABLE 3.2 *(Continued)*

Primary Metals

Aluminum Ingot and Mill Products M33D; previously, M33-2
Insulated Wire and Cable: 1989 (MA-33L)
Inventories of Steel Producing Mills (M33J)
Iron and Steel Castings: 1989 (MA-33A)
Nonferrous Castings: 1989 (M33E)
Steel Mill Products: 1989 (M-33B)

Intermediate Metal Products

Closures for Containers (MQ-34H)
Plumbing: Fixtures (MQ-34E)
Selected Heating Equipment: 1989 (MA-34N)
Steel Shipping Drums and Pails (MQ-34K)

Machinery and Equipment

Antifriction Bearings: 1989 (MA-35Q)
Computers and Office and Accounting Machines: 1989 (MA-35R)
Construction Machinery (MQ-35D)
Construction Machinery: 1989 (MA-35D)
Construction Machinery: 1990 (MA-35D)
Farm Machinery and Lawn and Garden Equipment: 1989 (MA-35A)
Fluid Power Products, Including Aerospace: 1989 (MA-35N)
Internal Combustion Engines: 1989 (M-35L)
Metalworking Machinery (MQ-35W)
Mining Machinery and Mineral Processing Equipment: 1989 (MA-35F)
Pumps and Compressors: 1988 (M35P)
Pumps and Compressors: 1989 (M-35P)
Refrigeration, Air-Conditioning and Warm Air Heating Equipment: 99 (MA-35M)
Robots (Shipments): 1989 (MA-35X)
Selected Industrial Air Pollution Control Equipment: 1989 (MA-35J)
Vending Machines (Coin Operated) 1989 (MA-35U)

Electrical and Electronics

Aerospace Industry: 1989 (MA-37D)
Civil Aircraft and Aircraft Engines (M37G)
Communication Equipment, Including Telephone, Telegraph and Other Electronic Systems
    and Equipment: 1989 (MA-36P)
Electric Lamps (M36D)
Electric Lamps (MQ-36B)
Electric Lighting Fixtures: 1989 (MA-36L)
Fluorescent Lamp Ballasts (MQ-36C)
Major Household Appliances: 1989 (MA-36K)

Miscellaneous

Motors and Generators: 1989 (MA-36H)
Pens, Pencils and Marking Devices: 1986 (MA-39A)
Pollution Abatement Costs and Expenditures: 198 (MA-200)
Radio and Television Receivers, Phonographs, and Related Equipment: 1989 (MA-36M)
Selected Instruments and Related Products: 1989 (MA-38B)
Switchgear, Switchboard Apparatus, Relays, and Industrial Controls: 1989 (MA-36A)
Titanium Mill Products, Ingot and Castings (ITA-991)
Truck Trailers (M37L)
Wiring Devices and Supplies: 1989 (MA-36K)

To order a Current Industrial Report, contact:

Customer Services
Bureau of the Census
Washington, DC 20233-8300
Telephone: 301-763-7662
Fax orders: 301-763-5550

As of this printing, the reports range in cost from $1 to $3.75—a nominal amount to spend for the details these reports offer on each market.

HOW TO RETRIEVE GOVERNMENT DOCUMENTS—THE EASY AND SMART WAY

Only a handful of countries around the globe have an explicit information access law; arguably, the most use of such a law is in the United States. In 1990, administering the Freedom of Information Act (FOIA) cost the U.S. government $83 million and generated 491,299 requests (*Access Reports*, Lynchburg, Virginia). Other countries with a policy similar to FOIA include: Australia, Canada, England, France, Holland, Hungary, New Zealand, Singapore, and Sweden.

War Story: The FOIA Shell Game

A financial services client had to assess the long-term strategy for a competitor, a vendor to the U.S. government. A large part of that assessment included the need to examine reviews of the vendor's/competitor's service record with the government.

Prior to contacting Fuld & Company, the client had used its law firm to request all documents from the General Services Administration (GSA), the agency managing the overall contract. Little turned up. The client only received a handful of papers, with much of the important information blacked-out.

In conversation, the client stated that there were actually as many as a dozen government agencies being serviced through this contract and that it was only managed by the GSA. We then decided to petition each of the agencies, first locating the Information Officer in each. We sent a separate FOIA letter to each agency. The response was overwhelming. We received hundreds of pages of documentation detailing the competitor's performance for each agency.

Lesson: Learn whom to contact under the FOIA before sending out a blanket letter. The Federal Government is a multi-faceted, complex organization with a rule book. That rule book, however, is interpreted and used in many different ways. You must try to learn how a particular agency works and how the information flows within a government branch before you can locate the keepers of the informational flame.

The analyst who hopes to find a great deal of information through FOIA needs to know where to place a request. There are many branch offices for each agency. The head office in Washington, DC, is not necessarily the best or first place to go.

Retrieval Rules

1. *Avoid contacting the agencies directly, unless you have excess time (perhaps weeks or months).* You may call the agencies themselves, but this is often a prolonged process. The agencies may be hard to find. Once found, they may be slow to respond to a request.

2. *Use a document retrieval firm located either in Washington, DC, or in the regions where you are examining federal archive files.* Many document retrieval firms are located in Washington, DC, and near other federal document storage centers around the country. Unless you know your way around the many filings offices, these service providers are highly recommended. A few are listed below.

Prentice-Hall Legal & Financial Services
500 Central Ave.
P.O. Box 1110
Albany, NY 12201-1110
518-458-8111;
   800-USA-INFO

The Data Communications Company
1990 M St., NW, Suite 640
Washington, DC 20036
202-833-1654

The Public Record Research Library
4653 S. Lakeshore Dr., Suite 3
Tempe, AZ 85282
800-929-3810

3. *Use databases, such as the Congressional Information Service (CIS).* (See Chapter 5.) CIS will abstract and cite Congressional hearings and other federal documents. Disclosure, a service mentioned earlier in this chapter, has a number of online and CD-ROM services for SEC information retrieval.

4. *Locate federal document centers, which are in most major cities.* Check your telephone directory for listings under "U.S. Government." These centers store tens of thousands of federal reports. Some are housed in major public or university libraries.

Whenever you make a FOIA request, your name is immediately placed on file with the agency as requesting government filings on the particular target company. Should that target company ask to look at the information about them in the files, the target will be able to see your name. Remember, freedom of information works both ways: If you have access to the competitor's file, the competitor has the same right to examine its own files. In the normal course of events, your competitor may expect you to submit a FOIA request on its files. This is not a trump card, as they say in the game of bridge. However, if you are interested in acquiring a company and do not want to reveal your interest too early, you may want to use a third party—an independent research vendor, or consultant—to retrieve the documents. Figure 3.2 is an example of a Freedom of Information Act form letter.

Name/Title of Addressee   Date
Name of Agency
Address of Agency
City, State, Zip Code

RE: Freedom of Information Act Request

Dear _____:

Under the provisions of the Freedom of Information Act, 5 U.S.C. 552, I am requesting access to *[identify the records as clearly and specifically as possible]*.

If there are any fees for retrieving or copying the records I have requested, please supply the records without informing me, and bill me accordingly, unless the fees exceed $_____.

If any part of this request is denied, please cite the specific exemptions by which you justify your refusal to release the information, and inform me of the appeal procedures available to me under the law.

I would appreciate your handling this request as quickly as possible, and I look forward to hearing from you within 10 days, as the law requires.

Sincerely,

[Signature]
Name
Address
City, State, Zip Code

Figure 3.2   Freedom of Information Act request letter.

The Art of State Filings

Many state capitals have copy services located near their archives. These are private services, much like the retrieval centers mentioned above. Your best bet in locating one is to call one of the larger law firms in town. They will usually know of services that retrieve court documents or other state and municipal filings.

In addition, most state corporate filing offices (such as the ones listed in the "State Your Case" section earlier in this chapter) will copy documents and send them for a small fee.

THE ULTIMATE ARCHIVE: YOUR TOWN

Proximity searching has its own intelligence rule: The closer you can get to the target company, the more likely you will find the information. This rule certainly should direct you to the steps of City Hall.

The typical city hall or townhall is divided into a number of offices. The names may differ slightly from town to town, and the offices may report to different departments, but in the end they offer the same basic functions and services. These are the standard offices and the functions they perform:

Assessors Office

This office keeps track of all property in the town. It is responsible for maintaining the following:

Tax maps. These maps break up the town into blocks and lots. Each block is coded. Once you have the code, you can go to the tax list that states the property's assessed value. In many town halls, you can only find the plant's assessed value if you know the code.

Commitment lists. Another term for these are tax rolls or rosters. Cambridge, Massachusetts, Fuld & Company's home town, offers computerized printouts of its properties, sorted alphabetically by lot number and alphabetically by street address. There are separate lists for business real and personal property, individual real and personal property, and tax-exempt property (e.g., churches and schools). Note that "personal" property is anything other than real estate (land or buildings), regardless of whether it is owned by a corporation or an individual. Each entry on the commitment list contains: (1) the name and address of the owner; (2) the assessed value of the property and equipment; and (3) the taxes assessed. There is also an auto excise tax list containing the names of car owners, their registration number, type of car, and tax amount.

The critical information to be gained from these forms and printouts includes: (1) the value of the plant, property, and equipment; (2) the names of neighboring plants or property; (3) the property tax liability/expense; and (4) the type of zoning (residential, commercial, industrial) for the area studied.

Building Inspection Office

The filings usually held by this office include:

Building plans. These are literally maps or floor plans of a new building or a standing structure. These maps do not indicate the building's contents, merely its shell, stairways, exits, and so on.

Inspection permits. Whether or not the building is used for a restaurant or factory, it receives both an initial and a yearly inspection. The initial inspection permit will contain the name of the contractor who constructed the building, a terrific lead. The contractor will likely know the building owner's initial and future intentions for the building—more important if the company you are examining is a manufacturing, rather than a service company.

Certificates of Inspection. These certificates will state the number of stories in the building and the employee capacity for the structure, floor by floor.

Some town offices have microfilmed their files of floor plans; others have not. For this reason, you may have to go to the town hall and literally hand-sketch the plan. On rare occasions, the inspection office will send the oversized blueprint to an outside print shop for duplication, ship you the copy, and charge you the amount involved.

If you are an astute, knowledgeable analyst, you will be able to develop some valuable intelligence from the floor plan alone. For example, the configuration of a factory or plant can tell you whether the target company is using one, long, continuous process or a stop-and-start batch approach. Sometimes, the machinery footings (literally, the foot marks where the heavy machines and equipment are positioned) can disclose the name and model number of the machine. By understanding the capacity and limitations of machinery, you may be able to use the floor plans to assess the target company's capacity, productivity, and room for expansion, among other detailed findings.

Town Development Board or Planning Office

Every town with a population of 50,000 or more has an entitlement grant to establish a town planning office. Towns smaller than 50,000 will often receive their planning and development direction from the state.

These offices do not have long-standing files, unlike the offices mentioned above. But they do have a good sense of the town's direction, in terms of its real estate and industrial development.

Typically, the planning office would keep on file:

HUD (Housing and Urban Development) grants. These grants lay out the town's development plans. A grant application, usually hundreds of pages long, contains maps and descriptions of the areas to be developed.

Financial assistance applications. Should a company request funding from the town or the state, the planning office would often keep this application on file. Loan applications may also be kept on file at the state's office of economic development.

Special studies. The planning office may have conducted special studies of businesses in the town. In these studies, background data on a particular business or group of businesses may have been compiled.

War Story: If You Don't Like the Competitor . . . Sewer

An automotive parts supplier ended up revealing a great deal about its long-term plans when it asked for concessions to build its plant in one town. The company wanted the town to pay for new sewer, water, and utility lines to be built from the main road into its facility. The town zoning and development boards needed detailed plans in return. It received them, and kept them on file.

We retrieved the documents within two months of their filing. Once we turned past the floor plan and construction section, we noticed an entire page clearly stating the company's short- and long-term market intentions: it would use the plant to serve its current customer, one of the large auto companies. However, within the next five years, it would expand its product line and sell to another auto manufacturer, a key customer of our client.

This seemingly innocuous filing opened up a number of strategic doors for our client, and allowed invaluable early warning of a competitor's next move.

Aside from revealing some specifics on your target company's financing, the planning office may have information on the company's overall expansion plans, especially as these plans affect the town.

FINAL ADVICE ON GOVERNMENT DOCUMENTS

Always mine and mind the experts. There are nearly as many government filings as there are stars in the sky. It frequently takes an expert to understand their full meaning or to find the salient points within the blacked-out, scribbled-on, poorly photocopied paper. You need an expert because he or she can:

Identify the 10 critical pages out of a 1,000-page filing in a government archive;

Determine the hidden words that have been blacked out, and ascertain how and why they are critical in the analysis;

Read between the lines to understand what the company is *not* saying and how that silence may "announce" a change.

Your government filing experts would include:

Accountants (CPAs) who can estimate the depreciation and debt-servicing requirements and can understand the significance of various financial information;

Engineers who know the machinery and how that machinery can perform;

Plant managers who appreciate the complexities of determining plant capacity, efficiencies, and so on;

Scientists who can read scientific papers and see trends in R&D.

Remember, no single individual has all the expertise to interpret and assess the full value of information contained in a government document. Tap into the technical expertise around you when you are reviewing a filing.

4 CORPORATE INTELLIGENCE IN PRINT

"Dear Mr. Fudd," the computer-generated direct mail letter began. Either I had become a Looney Tunes cartoon character, or someone had made a mistake. Silly as this example may be, it speaks loudly to the corporate researcher who needs to know which corporation to research. Directories help you to get basic facts straight— a company's name, address, and ownership. In this global communications era, you need to know that Owens-Illinois is different from Owens-Corning and that Boehringer Ingelheim is not the same as Boehringer Mannheim. Periodicals offer important updates in technology, techniques, and theory. Their editors and writers may be useful contacts for interviews or expert advice. Special issues and buyers' guides deliver new and vital information on an industry and indicate that the publisher, whether by design or circumstance, has become a center of industry information and contacts.

Do you remember a time when you were doing some specialized research and you *knew* that you had seen an annual issue or special directory that had exactly the information you wanted but you could not recall where it was? This chapter organizes for you the basic directories, periodicals, newspapers, and other printed sources that every researcher should have access to when beginning to look into an industry or a company.

I have divided the listed materials into three main categories: (1) financial publications, (2) investments—manuals, services, and general publications, and (3) general industry information. Some of these publications produce special issues offering data and lists that truly cannot be found elsewhere in the same detail. Information on sales, a ranking of companies in an industry, a brief company history or description, news updates and analyses, explanations of why a company has been included or dropped from an issue, identifications of product lines, and discussions of company trends are just a handful of their benefits.

Special issues of magazines that are published in North America and that in some way contain company-specific information are listed in this chapter. Where possible, the topic and month of publication of a special issue that is repeated annually are given. Where a publication has a range of special issues or frequently produces one-time comprehensive studies of a particular segment of an industry, the notation (SI) appears after the title. At your library or by contacting the publication at the address given on the masthead, you should be able to determine whether a special issue on the topic that is of interest was published recently enough to be of value in your research.

This chapter is just the beginning of your homework, but never overlook its value. You need to have the essentials firmly in hand before you can engage in more sophisticated sleuthing techniques to unearth corporate information.

FINANCIAL PUBLICATIONS

Periodicals and Annuals

Barron's (Dow Jones). A weekly business newspaper, published by the same people who bring you *The Wall Street Journal.* I would recommend *Barron's* for your library shelf. It often has far meatier articles than does the *Journal,* and it covers all industries. Its company profiles are among the best written and most valuable around, and its Quarterly Mutual Fund Record is a standard source. Written for educated businesspeople, *Barron's* explores its subjects in depth, assuming that its readers are already familiar with the superficial news—as might be provided in the *Journal.* It regularly offers stock and bond prices and Mutual Funds and Annual Reports Roundups.

Credit Card Management (Faulkner & Gray). A key monthly magazine for any analyst who needs to learn about the subtle aspects of the credit card industry. Corporate strategies, technology, and marketing are typical topics.

The Economist (SI) (The Economist Newspaper, N.A.). A truly international business magazine, with articles organized by region of the world rather than by business subject. This gives the reader a sense of the publisher's outlook. Special annual issues cover regions or countries, as well as important world business topics such as computers and automobiles. *The Economist* has a number of editions, including a North American edition.

FW [formerly *Financial World*] (SI) (Financial World Partners). This monthly offers popular articles written for senior managers and investors plus a number of summaries of stock prices and sales. The annual issues include: Mutual Fund Review, International Issue, and Midyear Forecast. Among other special issues is one on the Fastest Growing 500 companies, which measures the performance of these companies for the past ten years. A CEO of the Year is named annually.

The Journal of Commerce (SI) (Journal of Commerce). A daily newspaper that covers in great depth imports–exports and overall production news. It considers itself a global newspaper and gives its readers far more detail on shipping and import trends than would *The Wall Street Journal* or *Fortune* magazine, for example. Examples of some annual issues are: Bonus Distribution; Chemicals: Trade & Transport; Coal: Transportation & Distribution; Free-Shipping Zones. The *Journal of Commerce* is also the publisher of PIERS (Port Import Export Reporting Service), a critical database for analysts needing to assess a company's imports or exports.

The New York Times (The New York Times Company). A business reporter from the *Times* once confided to me that *The Wall Street Journal* is now considered the newspaper of record for the business community. Although this appears to be the case, based on circulation figures alone, the *Times* is still one of this country's great dailies. With this greatness comes considerable in-depth reporting on corporations. This paper is well worth some daily attention before beginning any interviewing. Researching your target company and doing your homework in intelligence gathering means retrieving earlier news articles, available in many libraries. In addition to stock prices, the newspaper will publish company earnings statements, management changes, acquisitions, mergers, and plant openings.

Wall Street Journal (Dow Jones). Last only alphabetically, this newspaper is recognized as the preeminent business information source in the country. There are often glaring gaps in its coverage but, considering its nationwide scope, it supplies more consistently accurate corporate intelligence than any other single paper today. Its concentration is on publicly held companies. Each issue contains earnings reports, stock prices, news of management changes, and so on. Each week, there are special sections on marketing, technology, and advertising. The *Journal* is often the business news trendsetter. When an article appears in the *Journal,* you will often find other newspapers and radio stations soon reporting on the same subject. If your office subscribes to no other newspaper or reference source, it should at least order the *Journal.* Because the *Journal* is so well indexed by so many databases and manual library indexes, it can be considered a reference work in itself.

Directories

Corporate Directory of U.S. Public Companies (Gale Research, Inc.). An annual listing of approximately 10,000 publicly traded corporations, their executives' names, and their subsidiaries. Some financials are included.

Directory of Companies Filing Annual Reports with the Securities and Exchange Commission (Securities and Exchange Commission). Although not beautifully packaged, this is a relatively inexpensive guide to all the companies whose stock is traded in the United States—from the penny stocks to the blue chips.

Directory of Corporate Affiliations (National Register Publishing Company). I have found this annual an excellent reference work. It not only has a superb cross-index of subsidiaries and their parent corporations, but it also lists the name and address of each subsidiary and, for most subsidiaries, the sales and product line. In addition, it contains the names of key executives for each subsidiary or affiliate of the company. National Register also publishes an international version.

Million Dollar Directory (Dun's Marketing Services). Someone who is asked to locate information on a company will often head straight for this directory. While not by any means the most comprehensive general directory, it does take advantage of the data contained in the Dun & Bradstreet credit reporting system. The details here—such as sales, and number of employees (on a plant or office level)—few directories can match.

A recommendation to any corporate researcher: Although D&B produces somewhat high-priced reference books, they are often one of a kind. D&B is constantly spinning off new texts from its database of over 8 million companies in the United States alone, and hundreds of thousands overseas.

National Yellow Pages (published by most of the regional Bell operating companies). After the court-ordered divestiture of AT&T, the various Bell operating companies began a heated competition with regional and local Yellow Pages publishers. One of the quiet research benefits of this rivalry is the *National Yellow Pages*. Although these issues go by slightly different names, depending on which organization publishes them, they all list a cross-section of U.S. companies by industry served. To locate the name, address, and telephone of a company somewhere in the United States, this wonderful resource is where you can begin. This is the poor businessperson's reference book, generally selling for approximately $30 to $40.

Nelson's Directory of Investment Research (Nelson Publications). A two-volume work that becomes critical if you need to analyze publicly traded corporations on an international scale. This is a directory of "watchers." Its focus is a listing of the financial analysts who review the performance of these corporations and their respective industries. It cross-indexes the analysts both by the companies they cover and the industry they serve. I have seen this book expand from a very fat one-volume work to a two-volume edition that includes the analysts who cover 5,000 U.S. and 4,000 other international corporations. Because many of the analysts listed are U.S.-based, their reports are written in English, even if covering a Japanese or a French corporation.

Remember the rule: Whenever money is exchanged, so is information. These analysts want to encourage purchase and sale of stock, and are more than happy to give you as much information as you need to do so. Whether you are considering a U.S. or a Japanese company, Wall Street or Tokyo is more than happy to give you that information.)

Thomson Bank Directory (Thomson Financial Publishing). This three-volume work contains information on approximately 15,000 U.S. banks and 45,000 of their branches, as well as 60,000 non-U.S. banks.

Standard Directory of Advertisers (National Register Company). On the surface, this is a book meant only for the advertising industry. But in fact, it is an excellent reference tool for general business research. The book has a roster of thousands of companies. Each entry lists the company, its advertising agency, the products, and the media used. The *Directory* comes with a complementary

Geographic and Trademark volume, from which you can cross-check a company by its location or its product trademark names.

Standard & Poor's Register of Corporations, Directors and Executives (McGraw-Hill). There are three volumes in this excellent set. Although it contains only half of the companies mentioned in D&B's *Million Dollar Directory*, the companies it does cover are covered well—with excellent indexing. The heart of the book, volume one, is an alphabetical listing of all the companies in the text. Each entry contains name, address, officers, directors, sales (where available), number of employees (also where available), and stock exchange. The other volumes index the text by geographical area and industry. It also has a parent–subsidiary directory, where the researcher can quickly spot who owns whom. The second volume offers brief biographies of many of the key executives mentioned in volume one, under their company name. A relatively inexpensive set as reference works go, and well worth the money.

Thomas Register of American Manufacturers (Thomas Publishing Co.). Probably the least expensive and one of the most effective corporate directories. Twenty-six volumes long, it lists manufacturers' products and services by product. Companies are indexed by products. The product index itself serves two very important purposes: (1) it uses standard industry terminology, which will make looking up your group that much easier, and (2) the fact that Thomas uses industry lingo makes the text a de facto dictionary. The company advertisements, interspersed throughout the set, will quickly tell you how competitors are marketing their products and the extent of their product line. The last few volumes in the set are samples of company catalogs. Again, this will serve as a means to gauge the competition's product line. Another index, on yellow paper, has an extensive trademark listing. Although not a true trademark register, it does cover thousands of commonly used manufacturer's trademarks. In addition to presenting name, address, and telephone number, the register offers an estimate of asset size. If you are competing in or selling to the manufacturing industries, you need to add this set of volumes to your library shelf.

INVESTMENTS—MANUALS, SERVICES, AND GENERAL PUBLICATIONS

Bond Guide (Standard & Poor's/McGraw-Hill). A simple but fairly comprehensive listing of bond prices for American corporate bonds (including convertibles). Some Canadian bonds are also listed.

Capital Adjustments (Maxwell MacMillan Professional and Business Reference Publishing). A two-volume, loose-leaf reference book that contains listings of stock splits, stock dividends, mergers, and their effect on capitalization.

Daily Stock Price Record (Standard & Poor's/McGraw-Hill). One of the only sources that lists a company's stock prices as they appeared during each day of trading (high, low, and closing prices). This collection comes in three sets: (1) NY Stock Exchange, (2) Over The Counter, and (3) American Stock Exchange. Companies are alphabetically listed. All stock splits, dividends, and trading halts are indicated. This is a quarterly compilation and is bound in hard cover.

Donoghue's Mutual Funds Almanac (The Donoghue Organization). An annual guide that lists over 1,500 open- and closed-end funds.

Institutional Investor (Institutional Investor Inc.). A listing of the 300 leading investment institutions. The ranking is based on investment assets, and appears in August.

Money (Time/Warner). This popular consumer magazine offers annual reviews of stocks and mutual funds.

Moody's Bond Survey (Moody's Investor Service). The *Survey* offers investors recommendations to buy or sell bonds. It also tracks and discusses trends in the marketplace.

Moody's Dividend Record (Moody's Investors Service). Along with the equivalent Standard & Poor's volume, this is an excellent source of dividend declarations and payments. The semiweekly volumes are also compiled into an annual volume.

Moody's Handbook of Common Stocks (Moody's Investors Service). Offers a financial profile of 1,000 commonly traded stocks over a 10-year span.

Moody's International Manual (Moody's Investors Service). It is important to see this directory as part of a set of Moody's investment manuals. The publisher offers biweekly news reports as part of the overall subscription service. The *International Manual* includes financial and managerial information on approximately 3,000 companies around the globe.

Moody's Investors Manuals—Transportation, Public Utilities, Municipal and Government, OTC, Industrial, Bank and Finance (Moody's Investors Service). A highly recommended set of books for any research library. When you do not have an annual report or a 10-K handy, these are the best substitutes. Each entry includes a company history, a history of acquisitions, principal businesses, income statement, balance sheet, stock price history (yearly), officers, directors, and subsidiaries and their locations. Expanded report entries include a five- to ten-year financial history, rather than the normal two-year comparison.

There are a couple of other sections to make note of. One set of blue pages tell you whether a company dropped out of the Moody's listing because it was acquired. This section also records corporate name changes. Another blue section offers a ten-year price range of stocks and bonds.

Should you need back issues, Moody's offers these volumes on microfiche.

Moody's Municipals and Governments Manual (Moody's Investors Service). Moody's has long been associated with municipal bonds and their ratings. This text can be considered the best possible starting point for exploring a bond's history.

National Stock Summary (National Quotation Bureau). For over-the-counter stock not mentioned in any of the standard investment reference texts, this would be the source you would turn to. For the unusual or little-traded OTC issue, this summary is the last word. The citations are brief, only mentioning the stock's bid and offered prices for the past six months and the dealer who traded the stock. Once you know the primary dealer's name, call this person up; he or she could be an excellent source of intelligence on the company.

Pension World (SI) (Argus Press Holdings, Inc.). This monthly reports on legislative and management changes in the investment world. During the year, a number of special issues are particularly useful in the area of competitive analysis.

Security Owner's Stock Guide (Standard & Poor's/McGraw-Hill). A compact book that reviews 5,000 common and preferred stocks. Each entry discusses a company's earnings, dividends, stock price, and S&P rating.

Standard & Poor's Dividend Record (Standard & Poor's/McGraw-Hill). Serves the same purpose as the Moody's dividend report listed above, and is organized in a similar fashion.

Standard & Poor's Outlook (Standard & Poor's/McGraw-Hill). Follows publicly traded companies and offers buy or sell recommendations.

Standard & Poor's Stock Reports (Standard & Poor's/McGraw-Hill). There is a separate set for each of the major trading groups—AMEX, NYSE, and OTC. The reports, in loose-leaf notebooks, are concise and printed on two pages. Each report contains a stock performance chart and a summary of the company's financial history. These reports are updated regularly, and should there be a major change in the company's position, new pages are issued to replace the older reports.

Trusts and Estates (SI) (Communications Channels). A monthly periodical designed to inform attorneys, trust and investment officers of banks, underwriters, and anyone else involved in long-term investments and estates. Its special issues typically include an annual forecast, a National Trust Conference issue, and a list of the most popular stocks held by U.S. common trust funds.

Value Line Investment Survey (Value Line, Inc.). This is an excellent review of a select number of publicly traded companies. Each report is one page long and is packed with data. In addition to clearly presenting (in chart form) a company's ten-year stock performance and financial history, the review includes recent management changes, product developments, and any other critical information needed by the investor. New reports are published weekly. The reports appear in three parts: (1) Summary & Index; (2) Selection and Opinion; and (3) Ratings & Reports, including industry analyses.

Wiesenberger Investment Companies Services (Wiesenberger Services). A crucial source for the researcher who needs to find out about the companies that invest in other companies. What makes these investment firms tick? This source profiles major U.S. and Canadian investment companies and mutual funds.

GENERAL INDUSTRY INFORMATION

Advertising

Advertising Age (SI) (Crain Communications, Inc.). *Advertising Age*'s annual September issue, *100 Leading National Advertisers*, summarizes the past year's advertising campaigns for the 100 largest U.S. advertisers. The issue also cites the advertising agency of record and the account executives responsible for handling each account. Each synopsis offers some projections on future advertising activity and breaks down the past year's expenditures by medium. Cable Annual Report, (Advertising) Agency Issue, and Ad Age International are among the special issues each year.

Adweek (SI) (A/S/M Communications, Inc.). Like *Advertising Age,* this is a weekly publication. Some special issues address issues of the moment, such as the top 100 national agencies ranked by billings; others are annuals.

Aerospace

Aviation Ground Equipment Market (SI) (Jane's Information Group). Suppliers of maintenance equipment can become critical information sources on competitive activity in the aerospace industry. This monthly periodical focuses on these suppliers.

Aviation Week & Space Technology (SI) (McGraw-Hill, Inc.). This key industry magazine offers detailed analyses of the forces shaping this market. Those in the industry often call the publication "Aviation Leak" because of the frequency of its news-breaking stories. Coverage of government contracts reveals the contractors assigned, the value of the contracts, and particular contractors' R&D expenditures. Quarterly issues contain income and operating information for passenger airlines, number of passengers carried by leading companies, and miles-traveled statistics by airline and by aircraft type.

Flight International (SI) (Reed Business Publishing Group). This weekly offers detailed international information on new products and market developments. In past years, the magazine has offered special issues on current aircraft (listed by manufacturer), manufacturers of turbine engines for the commercial and military sectors, and missile production (by manufacturer).

Jane's Defense Weekly (SI) (Jane's Information Group). The Jane's group of publications inventories just about every piece of military and aerospace equipment manufactured anywhere in the world. *Defense Weekly* concentrates on companies that produce military products. Special issues have a regional focus or may concentrate on particular business sectors and manufacturers.

Agriculture

Agri Marketing (SI) (Century Hallmark). The November advertising issue— called Companies, Services, Agencies, Print, Broadcast, Associations—reports on the leading farm and agricultural equipment advertisers, the type of advertising they conduct, and their agencies. The issue covers both U.S. and Canadian companies.

Air Travel

Air Transport World (Penton Publishing Co.). This periodical publishes a number of annual issues that involve analysis of specific companies in the airline industry. These issues' topics are:

Airline Marketing. Appears in June and tracks the past year's airline advertising dollars by company.

IATA Annual Statistics. Usually in October, this issue prints the International Air Transport Association's statistics for the past two years. The data cover market share of member airlines, and rank order the airlines based on their revenue.

Maintenance and Engineering. This issue, covering over 60 airlines worldwide, appears in July. The issue discusses airlines' current and planned maintenance expenditures.

Quarterly Tables. A quarterly analysis of U.S. airlines, including revenues, expenses, and other financial data.

Business and Commercial Aviation (McGraw-Hill). Each September, this magazine reviews the salaries for the airline industry.

Flight International (Reed Publishing Group). An annual review, in the January issue, of commercial aviation's accident reports. Carriers and dates of the events are listed.

Apparel and Clothing

Footwear News (Fairchild Publications). This is the most comprehensive newspaper in the industry. A number of magazines cover general industry statistics; this newspaper reports in depth on specific companies and industry events. Two special annual issues (in December and July) discuss and report financial information on the industry.

Appliances

Appliance (SI) (Dana Chase Publications). A solid source for information on production trends, new model innovations, and general industry statistics. Annual Appliance Industry Forecasts, Annual Materials Forecast, Annual Statistical Review, and Annual Review on Consumer Electronics are among its special issues.

Appliance Manufacturer (SI) (Corcoran Communications). A monthly magazine offering manufacturing and design topics similar to those in *Appliance,* cited above.

Automobiles

Automotive Industries (SI) (Chilton Book Co.). A monthly publication that covers the manufacturing and production side of the automobile industry. Its special issues center around technology and overall business performance. An Annual Industry Report Card is compiled.

Automotive News (Crain Communications). This monthly, one of the two or three leading publications in the automobile industry, offers sales and market share statistics for each automobile manufacturer. Market Data Book, usually published in April or May, offers extensive financial market information on the companies and the industry in general.

Jobber Retailer Topics (SI) (Bill Communications). This monthly magazine offers information on the distribution side of the automotive parts and equipment business. Emphasis is on a how-to approach to running and operating machining and production facilities.

Ward's Auto World (SI) (Ward's Communications). One of the most important and often quoted publications in the industry. Its special issues are packed with statistics.

Banking

ABA Banking Journal (SI) (American Bankers Association). One of the major banking journals, this monthly is geared to banks' senior management.

American Banker (Thomson Co.). Considered one of the major industry sources, this publication appears daily, except on weekends and holidays. It is written for a senior-level audience in the banking and finance industries. Its news departments cover the following subjects: lending, money markets, legislation, operations and technology, marketing, mortgages and thrifts, investment management, mergers, international banking, and personnel promotions. Its special issues cumulatively form a reference shelf on the banking and finance industries:

> *Bank Holding Companies.* The companies are ranked by the deposit size. This issue appears in April.
>
> *Correspondent Banking.* This December issue ranks correspondent banks' deposit size.
>
> *Finance Companies.* This issue ranks almost 300 finance companies and offers a summary balance sheet for the 100 leading companies. Included in the list, usually appearing in June, are captive and independent finance companies.
>
> *First 5,000 Banks.* This is a 5,000-bank listing and includes abbreviated financials of the largest commercial banks in the United States. The issue appears in June.
>
> *Largest Commercial Banks.* These February and August issues rank the 300 largest commercial banks.
>
> *Largest Credit Unions.* Appearing in May, this issue offers a ranked list of the 100 largest credit unions. Ranking is by asset size.
>
> *Largest Mortgage Companies.* In an October issue, a list is given of the 300 largest mortgage companies, with accompanying financials.
>
> *Largest Mutual Savings Banks.* A ranking of the 100 largest mutual savings banks appears in a January issue.
>
> *Largest Savings Banks.* This August issue ranks the 100 largest U.S. mutual savings banks, as well as the 300 largest savings banks, worldwide.
>
> *Largest World Banks.* With deposit and other financial information, this July listing offers a ranking of the 500 largest banks in the world.

Bank Management (Faulkner & Gray, Inc.). This monthly magazine contains articles on management issues. Less up-to-the-minute than *American Banker,* but it explores in some depth current business topics of interest to senior management. Its articles cover operations, control, finance, strategy and planning, productivity, human resource management, accounting, tax, audit, security, mergers and acquisitions, bank performance, and automation.

Bank Marketing Magazine (Bank Marketing Association). As the title implies, this magazine concentrates on advertising and marketing topics as they concern retail, trust, and personal banking. For the intelligence analyst trying to understand how banks market their products, this magazine offers many information springboards and many names of industry experts. Regular features include: Service Quality, Marketing News, Retail Banking, Community Banks, Research, People, New Products/Services, Faculty Corner, Branch Marketing, Reader Viewpoint; Marketing Management, and Trust Marketing.

Bank Technology News (SI) (Faulkner & Gray). This monthly magazine offers unusual insight into modern banking and banking competition. So much of the modern banking world hinges on the technology infrastructure that knowledge of specific systems and methods of operation can yield a great deal of competitor knowledge. Each issue of this magazine contains these features: Technology Information Series, Trends Analysis, and Product Update. Special issues discuss specific systems suppliers and related software.

Bankers Monthly (Hanover Publishing). Each May, this periodical offers an abbreviated balance sheet for more than 50 finance companies.

Banking—Regional Magazines. A number of regional banking magazines are notable. Each of the following covers banking issues from a local standpoint:

> *Arkansas Banker* (Arkansas Banking Association).
>
> *Bank News* (Bank News). A 13-state banking publication circulated in Arkansas, Colorado, Illinois, Iowa, Kansas, Minnesota, Missouri, Nebraska, New Mexico, Oklahoma, Texas, Wisconsin, and Wyoming. The February and March issues offer complete financial profiles on a variety of regional banks.
>
> *Bankers Digest* (Bankers Digest). A magazine that reports on banking in the Southwestern part of the United States.
>
> *The Florida Mortgage Broker* (The Florida Association of Mortgage Brokers).
>
> *Hossier Banker* (Indiana Bankers Association).
>
> *Illinois Bank News* (Illinois Bankers Association).
>
> *Illinois Banker* (Illinois Bankers Association).
>
> *Northwestern Financial Review* (Northwestern Financial Review Communications, Inc.). This biweekly covers the financial services industry in the upper Midwest.
>
> *Tennessee Banker* (Tennessee Bankers Association).
>
> *Texas Banking* (Texas Bankers Association).
>
> *Banking Software Review* (International Computer Programs, Inc.). A quarterly publication that, as the title implies, covers various aspects of the software and systems supplied to the banking industry.

Beverages

Beverage Industry (SI) (Advanstar Communications). One of the better industry magazines for in-depth reporting on the companies active in this sector. Its Annual Manual, which appears in September, offers market shares, as well as a host of tables on the overall industry. Among its special issues is an annual study of manufacturers and brands of soft drinks, including market share and overall sales.

Beverage World (SI) (Keller International Publishing). Another widely read publication in this industry, reporting on specific products and companies. The June issue details the major companies that manufacture bottles and cans. The July issue ranks the top U.S. beverage producers. Other special issues typically focus on marketing, merchandising, distribution/delivery, and the Annual *Beverage World* Wall Street Roundtable.

Modern Brewery Age (Business Journals). An annual Blue Book offers brewery sales and production. The February issue presents market and company production information.

Wines and Vines (Hiaring Company). The annual marketing issue (appearing in September) describes the wine industry and discusses specific production information. The January issue focuses on champagne and its producers.

Broadcasting

Broadcasting (SI) (Cahners Publishing Co.). This magazine aims to inform the owners and managers of television and radio broadcasting companies; it does not discuss specific programs. The topics a reader would typically find include: advertising, programming, technology, journalism issues, finance, and systems operations.

Television Digest with Consumer Electronics (Warren Publishing, Inc.). A magazine for the broadcast and cable industries. Its annual Fact Book contains a detailed listing of broadcasting and cable systems, names of key personnel, manufacturers and suppliers of broadcast equipment, and consultants and associations that serve the industry.

Building and Construction

Building Design and Construction (SI) (Cahners Publishing Co.). This is a magazine for engineers, architects, and contractors. Articles often cover new technology and innovations in building technology and construction. An Annual Directory of Building Products is among its special issues.

Dodge Construction News (SI) (McGraw-Hill). This daily publication covers overall news on the construction industry. It devotes various issues to equipment and materials suppliers, technology developments, and new products.

Electrical Contractor (SI) (National Electrical Contractors Association). This magazine deals with nitty-gritty issues, such as news of new products, equipment, contracting company management issues, electrical modernization, and maintenance work. Special issues cover topics such as industrial construction, building code changes, and service and maintenance.

Offshore (Penn Well Publishing Co.). Each November, an issue reports on offshore oil well construction worldwide. Data on construction in progress, construction planned, platform locations, and expected completion dates are included.

Oil and Gas Journal (Penn Well Publishing Co.). In October and May of each year, special issues appear on the planned and current construction of wells, refineries, and pipelines in the petroleum industry.

Pipe Line Industry (Gulf Publishing Co.). This January issue presents the pipeline construction for over 200 companies. The list is extremely detailed. Aside from naming names, it presents construction costs and gives a description of the project.

Professional Building and Remodeler (Cahners Publishing Co.). The July issue lists approximately 400 leading home construction contractors in the United States. Sales, company description and address, and ranking by sales are presented for each company.

Building Materials

American Glass Review (Doctorow Communications). Appearing each February, this issue lists manufacturers of flat glass and other glass products. In addition to telephone numbers and addresses, it states the brand names or trademark names the glass is sold under.

Floor Covering News (Altron). Each January, leaders in the Canadian floor covering market present their opinions on the market.

Pit and Quarry (Advanstar Communications). This magazine reports on industry trends and is aimed at those who manage or buy equipment. Twice each year, the magazine offers revenue information on the leading cement and concrete companies in the United States.

Business—General

Business Week (SI) (McGraw-Hill). Arguably, the leading weekly for U.S. industry, this magazine reports on business around the world but its focus is very much the United States. Weekly sections include Business Outlook, International Outlook, Finance, Technology, Information Processing, and Legal Affairs. It is well known for some of its special issues. Many managers keep the R&D Scoreboard issue on hand as a reference tool. The Corporate Scoreboard issue reviews hundreds of companies, quarter by quarter, examining their sales and earnings for the prior period. A Bank Scoreboard on the 200 leading U.S. banks is published in April.

The Financial Post (Financial Post Datagroup). In June, the *Post* compiles and publishes a ranking of Canada's 500 largest companies. Unlike the Fortune 500, which are industrial companies exclusively, the Post 500 companies include service, financial, real estate, and industrial concerns in the same list.

Forbes (Forbes). This magazine publishes its own Forbes 500 list, similar to the *Fortune* list. Special issues are highly regarded as sources. Scorecard on Capital and Labor, in May, ranks companies by number of employees, by sales, and by assets. The September issue ranks and analyzes U.S. mutual funds. A sweeping review of American industry, published in January, describes the state of various industries, reporting on trends and major shifts. A chart for each industry lists the leading companies and gives a concise and easy-to-read financial summary of the past year's performance. The April issue examines the 100 leading bank holding companies' assets, deposits, loans, loan losses, and similar relevant data. *Forbes* also publishes these two standards for business research:

> *Annual Directory Issue* (Forbes). The 500 leading companies are divided in this issue into five lists and ranked by sales, profits, assets, and market value. The alphabetical listing contains number of employees, headquarters, and stock exchange on which a particular company is traded.

> *Annual Report on American Industry* (Forbes). Probably the best single compendium on a broad selection of industries, this annual issue is for the researcher who needs a thumbnail sketch on an industry and the companies within it. Usually appearing in January, the issue lists over 1,000 companies (publicly traded) with $450 million or more in sales. The issue covers 46 industries and offers 5 years' financial data for each company. Financial data include: income, dividends, sales, and stock price.

Fortune (SI) (Time, Inc.). Often held up as one of the icons of American industry, *Fortune* offers mostly feature articles on a wide variety of topics. The famous Fortune 500 is the parent list that begat all other corporate listings. Companies (all publicly traded) are ranked by sales. Income statement, dividends, assets, number of employees, growth rate, and sales are given for each entry. The Second 500 Largest, the Fortune Global 500, and the Fortune Service 500 are among the sequels covered in other special issues.

Inc. (SI) (Goldhirsh Group). Geared to medium and small-size companies, this periodical offers advice along with case stories to help managers deal with issues ranging from employee benefits to sales tools. It is well known for the Inc. 500, the 100 Fastest Growing Companies in the United States, and the 500 Fastest Growing Private Companies—all presented in special issues.

Chemicals

Chemical & Engineering News (SI) (American Chemical Society). This well-known magazine within the chemical industry aims to cover technical and industry news for general management. Each year it names the top 100 chemicals producers.

Chemical Engineering (McGraw-Hill). A twice-yearly report on plant and equipment construction and installation for chemical plants in the United States, Mexico, and Canada. Plant addresses and expected capacities are given.

Chemical Week (SI) (McGraw-Hill). Considered one of the leaders in covering the chemicals processing industry, this magazine offers lengthy, in-depth articles on a variety of subjects. A recent world forecast issue and an Asia Pacific report covered international developments in this industry.

Computers and Data Processing

Byte (McGraw-Hill). A leader among the personal computer magazines, *Byte* offers detailed product reviews for both software and hardware. Because of the fast changing nature of the personal computer business worldwide, this magazine generally does not offer annual special issues. Examples of the some of the topics covered routinely are: spreadsheets, new chips, business graphics, and high-end CAD packages.

Computerworld (SI) (International Data Group). This remains one of the leading news sources for the computer industry—software or hardware. It covers all areas of the spectrum, from personal computers to large system architecture. Special issues include an annual forecast issue.

Datamation (SI) (Cahners Publishing Co.). One of the key magazines in the data processing and computer industry, *Datamation* offers important surveys on the technology, the work force, and employment trends. One of its special issues is: Ranking and Profiles of the Top 100 IS Companies Worldwide.

PC Magazine (Ziff-Davis Publishing). This biweekly has become one of the widest read computer industry publications, among both professionals and amateurs. It was ranked the ninth largest magazine in ad revenue in the United States in 1992. A typical issue may contain as many as 500 pages, much of it advertising. Each issue concentrates on a specific hardware or software product group or topic.

PC Week (SI) (Ziff-Davis Publishing). This magazine is known for its extensive coverage of the personal computer market. Its special issues often concentrate on new products. It also previews major trade shows, such as Networld, COMDEX, and PC Expo.

Drugs and Cosmetics

Drug and Cosmetic Industry (Advanstar Communications). This magazine is written for the manufacturers and marketers of cosmetics, toiletries, and over-the-counter pharmaceuticals. An annual issue is, in effect, a buyer's guide to suppliers of manufacturing and processing machinery in the drug industry. The July issue presents a ranking and profiles of the leading U.S. producers of various cosmetic products.

Drug Topics (SI) (Medical Economics Publication). This magazine reports on the pharmaceutical industry from the viewpoint of the pharmacist, buyer, or chain store executive.

Medical Marketing & Media (SI) (CPS Communications). This magazine primarily covers the marketing of pharmaceuticals in the United States. It is directed toward marketing and sales managers, and offers periodic surveys of industry trends. One of its best known special issues is an annual issue on the most widely prescribed drugs of the past year. Approximately 200 drugs are listed, along with their brand names.

Pharmaceutical Technology (Aster Publishing Corp.). The fall issues offer summary information on the latest industry trade shows.

Electrical Equipment and Power

Electrical World (SI) (McGraw-Hill). This monthly magazine for the utility industry offers articles on marketing, management, and operations. Annual special issues include a statistical report, a buyers' guide, and an Electrical Utility Executive Forum.

Power Engineering (SI) (Penn Well Publishing Co.). A monthly periodical for engineering and management at power-generating facilities. The special issues here are very practical for understanding the growth of the market.

Public Power (SI) (American Public Power Association). This bimonthly directs its editorial content to local public utilities. Among its special issues is an annual statistical issue and directory.

Public Utilities Fortnightly (SI) (Public Utilities Reports). Considered an influential monthly for executives of gas, electric, and telecommunications companies, this magazine covers regulatory and market issues critical to company management.

Electronics

Electronic Business (SI) (Cahners Publishing Company). In the scant two decades that this publication has been around, it has established itself as a major supplier of industry statistics and corporate news. Each year, it selects the *Electronic Business 100*, ranked by sales. The January issue offers a monthly listing of trade shows and industry conferences throughout the coming year.

Electronic Engineering Times (SI) (CMP Publications Co.). This weekly is designed to inform engineers, technical managers, and industry consultants. Special issues include a mid-year forecast and an annual salary and opinion survey.

Electronic News (International Group). A popular magazine for the electronics industry; covers a wide number of topics and conducts surveys throughout the year.

Electronics (SI) (Penton Publishing). This monthly review of global and U.S. events is directed toward corporate management and operations, particularly at original equipment manufacturers.

Engineering

Engineering Times (SI) (National Society of Professional Engineers). A monthly magazine for engineers and the issues they experience in common. Engineering applications of computer technology receives special emphasis.

Engineering News Record (ENR) (SI) (McGraw-Hill). A "bible" for this field, this weekly newspaper covers a spectrum of topics for the engineering community. Special issues name top performers in a wide range of functions.

Food Processing

Candy Industry (SI) (Advanstar Comunications). A monthly directed to management and operations personnel in the confectionery industry. Annual special focus on chocolate and on equipment purchasing.

Food Engineering (SI) (Chilton Co.). A wonderful magazine for describing plant engineering and state-of-the-art technology. Annual special issues name a company and a marketer of the year, report on the top 15 marketers and the 50 top European producers, and make R&D predictions.

Food Processing (Putnam). This magazine offers the leading 100 food-processing companies in the United States, ranked by sales. The issue usually appears in December.

Food Product Design (Weeks Publishing Co.). A monthly that deals with the formulation and design issues in the retail and food service markets. Issues are dedicated to specific topics, such as sweeteners, fat replacement systems, microwave development, and so on.

Restaurant Hospitality (Penton Publishing). The January issue lists the companies supplying the restaurant industry.

Snack Food (SI) (Advanstar Communications). Each June, this magazine publishes State of the Snack Food Industries Report, one of the only reviews of the snack food market. It not only offers general market statistics, but also presents, in many categories, market share by company, and dollar sales by manufacturer. Other annual special issues touch on site selection and packaging, offer a buyers' guide, and name the top 100 snack companies.

Gas (Natural)

Oil and Gas Journal (SI) (Penn Well Publishing Co.). This journal has a number of detailed, company-specific issues. Among them are:

> *Gas Processing Report.* The July issue offers statistics on facilities, production, and consumption.

> *Pipelines Economic Report.* Published in November, offers both an industry-wide and a company-by-company review of the market, with new pipeline construction and company revenues.

Pipeline and Gas Journal (Oildom Publishing Co.). Every quarter, this magazine reports on oil and gas company financial statements. The October issue reports on pipeline construction worldwide.

Healthcare

HealthCare Executive (The American College of Healthcare Executives). This bimonthly magazine is geared for executives of hospitals, long-term care facilities, or managed care organizations. Each issue concentrates on one topic; recent examples include technology, physicians and the healthcare system, and productivity.

Modern Healthcare (SI) (Crain Communications). This weekly is a major popular journal for the healthcare industry. Special issues focus on current concerns and include several annual surveys.

Hotels and Restaurants

Lodging Hospitality (SI) (Penton Publishing). A monthly magazine covering a wide variety of topics for hospitality management. Special issues include an annual outlook for the industry and an annual franchising issue.

Restaurant Business (Bill Communications). A general magazine for those who manage restaurants. Each monthly issue concentrates on one topic.

Restaurants and Institutions (SI) (Cahners Publishing Co.). An invaluable reference tool for an analyst just beginning to understand the food service industry. A number of special issues cover topics such as the R&I 400 and R&I Growth Chains.

Restaurant Hospitality (Penton Publishing). A monthly magazine that covers the restaurant industry in detail. It ranks the leading 500 independent restaurants each year, and offers sales and employment information.

Insurance

Best's Review (SI) (A. M. Best Co.). The Best series of trade magazines on the insurance industry is the epitome of the industry bible. *Best's Review* is the major monthly for agents, brokers, and management in property and casualty insurance. There are many special issues. The key publications for corporate research are:

> *Best's Insurance Reports: Life–Health* (A. M. Best). This volume, covering U.S. and Canadian health and life insurance companies, contains income statement and balance sheet data, company histories, and information on new businesses.

> *Best's Insurance Reports: Property–Casualty* (A. M. Best). This text examines the other side of the insurance coin: property and liability. It treats stock companies and mutual companies in the same manner as does the Life–Health manual listed above. Companies covered are located in the United States and Canada.

> *Business Insurance.* Edited for risk insurance and reinsurance executives, this weekly covers news on underwriting, new policies, financial performance, and regulatory developments.

National Underwriter (National Underwriter Co.). Among its special issues are:

> *Leading Life and Health Insurance Companies.* A ranking based on sales volume of the leaders, appearing in a May or a June issue.

Year-End Analysis of Property and Casualty Companies. This analysis of insurers usually appears in January.

Pensions & Investments (SI) (Crain Communications). This biweekly magazine reports the latest news and trends in the investment markets. Special issues include an annual performance report.

Iron, Steel, and Other Metals

American Machinist (SI) (Penton Publishing). A monthly written for corporate management and production managers in the durable goods and metalworking industries. Special issues include an annual buyers' guide.

American Metal Market (SI) (Capital Cities/ABC). This daily newspaper is "the *Wall Street Journal* of the metals industry." Its coverage includes pricing information and features and analyses that span the international market.

New Steel (SI) (Chilton Co.). This is one of the leading magazines in the metals industry. Special issues are packed with statistics and pricing data.

Machinery

Construction Equipment (SI) (Cahners Publishing Co.). This magazine closely examines management and operation of construction machinery. Among the special issues are an annual specifications guide and a buyers' guide.

Gas Turbine World (Pequot Publishing). This magazine publishes an annual handbook that contains order and installation information on gas turbines. In addition to company listings, it contains the numbers of machines installed and the installation sites.

Mining

Engineering and Mining Journal (SI) (Maclean Hunter Publishing). A monthly magazine covering the global metals and nonmetals mining and processing industries.

Mining Magazine (SI) (Mining Journal Ltd.). An internationally focused publication written for senior and technical management. Special issues include an annual survey of operating mines.

Skillings' Mining Review (Skillings Mining Review). Annual review of iron ore production, categorized by company and site.

Packaging and Containers

Boxboard Containers (SI) (Maclean Hunter Publishing). A monthly for executives in the box and container industry. Corrugated boxes and containers are an important intelligence barometer. Box manufacturers often feel an economic downturn or upswing as much as six months to one year ahead of the rest of the economy. Their competitive picture may be a clue to an industry's economic position.

Food & Drug Packaging (SI) (Advanstar Communications). This magazine concentrates on new packaging ideas and innovations, which can foreshadow product repositioning or changes in distribution. The type of plastic used can indicate ongoing recycling issues.

Packaging Digest (SI) (Delta Communications). A monthly magazine directed to those who design various forms of packaging.

Paper

Paperboard Packaging (SI) (Advanstar Communications). A monthly magazine for the converting industry.

Presstime (Newspaper Association of America). Both the May and November issues report on newsprint plants' expansion plans and capacity.

Pulp and Paper (Miller Freeman Publications). A key source for information on the paper industry, this magazine contains some of the most frequently published and detailed data about paper companies. Among its special issues are:

> *Capital Expenditures.* Each January, the magazine offers a listing of plant construction and expansion.

> *Company Profiles.* Usually appearing in the June issue are charts describing the leading U.S. and Canadian companies.

> *Foreign Leaders.* The October issue presents production and sales information on the 25 foreign leaders in the paper industry.

> *Quarterly Summaries.* Each quarter, this publication presents tables of sales and earnings for the leading U.S. and Canadian manufacturers.

Petroleum

Fuel Oil & Oil Heat Magazine (Industry Publications). A monthly periodical for owners and managers of local oil heat companies. It publishes an annual issue on service management analysis.

National Petroleum News (Hunter Publishing). Each quarter, the magazine lists the earnings for over 20 petroleum companies.

Ocean Industry (Gulf Publishing Co.). The October and March issues have detailed listings of current and planned offshore wells and drilling platforms. The September issue is a worldwide directory of offshore drilling rigs, identifying the actual ships and vessels used in the exploration and drilling.

Offshore (Penn Well Publishing Co.). This periodical offers detailed lists of activities within the industry. Special issues are:

> *Deepwater Wells.* The June issue contains a directory of deepwater wells throughout the world.

> *Marine Pipeline Report.* This listing of pipeline projects, current and planned, appears in July.

Oil and Gas Journal (Penn Well Publishing Co.). A number of special issues are published on a regular basis:

> *Capital Expenditures.* The February issue discusses actual outlays and planned capital expenditures for over 25 companies in the United States.
>
> *Gas Processing.* The July issue offers worldwide capacity data on gas and petroleum plants.
>
> *Pipeline Projects.* Each January, an issue lists the amount of pipeline under construction or planned.
>
> *Refinery Report.* The March issue presents refinery capacities and operating information.
>
> *Worldwide Issue.* This issue, usually appearing at the end of December, offers production statistics as well as company-specific information.

Pipeline and Gas Journal (Oildom Publishing Co.). Quarterly issues present financial data on approximately 100 oil and gas companies.

Platt's Oil and Petroleum Directories and Special Publications (McGraw-Hill). The series of Platt's publications and services offers the researcher details on pricing and legislation. Here is a sample list: *Platt's Bunkerwire/Gaswire* (telexing services on marine fuel prices/liquefied petroleum gas prices); *Platt's OHA Digest; Platt's Oilgrams* (on various topics); *Platt's Oil Marketing Bulletin; Platt's Oil Price Handbook.*

World Oil (SI) (Gulf Publishing Co.). A monthly that offers an extensive review of the petroleum industry, both domestic and worldwide.

Photography

Photo Marketing (SI) (The Photo Marketing Association). A monthly written for individuals needing to track the photo industry's trends. Special issues offer market studies and survey findings.

Photographic Trade News PTN (PTN Publishing). A semimonthly that contains news and industry trend reports and is directly aimed at the photo finisher and retailer. PTN's other publications offer special reports on major industry trade shows.

Plastics

Modern Plastics (SI) (McGraw-Hill). A monthly directed at plastics manufacturers and consumers. Concentration is on new technologies, trends, and materials in the industry.

Plastics News (SI) (Crain Communications). A general news weekly for the plastics industry. Some special issues are of particular interest to the analyst seeking corporate statistics and rankings.

Plastics World (SI) (Cahners Publishing Co.). A monthly written for technical managers and engineers. Special issues include a Yellow Pages for the plastics industry.

Publishing

Editor & Publisher (SI) (Editor & Publisher). Each week, this periodical offers statistics, features, and news articles covering the wide range of publishing news. Special issues include an E&P Market Guide.

Folio: The Magazine for Magazine Management (SI) (Cowles Business Media). A monthly designed for magazine manufacturing and business managers. Paper supply, circulation, expenses, and ad sales are typical topics.

Print Impressions (SI) (North American Publishing Co.). This monthly, geared to printing management and supervisory personnel, regularly reports on market events and trends. One of its special issues is titled PI 500: Who's Who and Ranking of Top Companies.

Publishers Weekly (SI) (Cahners Publishing Co.). This is an important and widely read publication for book sellers and book producers. Special issues preview the Frankfurt Book Fair and name the best books of the year in several categories of publication.

Railroads

Progressive Railroading (SI) (Murphy-Richter Publishing). This monthly magazine offers many valuable operational statistics. The special issues include an annual purchasing survey and annual issues on the coal and rail transit industries.

Railway Age (SI) (Simmons-Boardman Publishing). A monthly that deals with subjects of interest to railroad management, from traffic and technology to labor and finance. The most important of its special issues is the Outlook issue, which forecasts the year ahead.

Retailing

Automotive News (Crain Communications). Semiannually, this monthly publication reviews imported car sales and ranks the market leaders. Each quarter, it reviews the number of dealerships, by manufacturer.

Convenience Store News (SI) (BMT Publications). A general magazine for owners, managers, and franchisees of convenience stores. Published 16 times per year, this publication covers industry trends and offers results of marketing studies.

Discount Merchandiser (SI) (McFadden Holdings/Schwartz Publications). This monthly covers virtually all aspects of discount store operations and marketing, and overall industry trends. New technology advances are often discussed.

Discount Store News (Lebhar-Friedman). A September issue offers a ranking and discussion of the leading 100 discount store chains in the United States.

Drug Store News (SI) (Lebhar-Friedman). A biweekly that offers features and industry trends for the retail drug chain. Special annual issues include a state-of-the-industry report and a consumer brand preference study.

Caveat Analyst: Don't Believe Every Nugget of Wisdom!

LEONARD FULD: To the business analyst who reads magazines, such as *Fortune*, what advice can you give on how to avoid misinterpreting information by placing either too much or too little importance on the material?

RICHARD TEITELBAUM: Don't believe each and every nugget of wisdom you read courtesy of the fourth estate. No, it's not that the nation's business press is a lying pack of poison-quilled scriveners. (Well, not all of us, in any case.) The fact is, the business analyst is often looking for one thing from an article in a magazine or newspaper; readers are looking for quite another. Therein lies the rub.

One column in *Fortune* shows how people can misinterpret what gets into print. Every once in a great while, a reader would write to *Fortune* to complain that a small company featured in the magazine's "Companies to Watch" column had gotten pummeled in the stock market. The fact is, the column in no way purported to be a hot stock-tip sheet. It focused on marketing, manufacturing, and management strategies for small businesses. For stock picks, all an investor had to do was flip to the Personal Investing section.

Think, therefore: what is the purpose of this article? If the article's focus is on what a great job XYZ Company is doing in its total quality management push, don't read that as an endorsement of how great a marketing job it does in the spigot business—even if the spigot business is cited as the place where total quality management works best.

Try to corroborate what you read in the different publications. The *Wall Street Journal, Fortune, Business Week,* and *Forbes* typically try to avoid taking identical slants on the same stories. But respectable trade journals, databases, and local newspapers can help you build your confidence in what you're reading.

Be careful of the rush job. If an article runs for five pages but quotes only two securities analysts, beware. The journalist who has been given a reasonable amount of time to work his craft will have drawn on a variety of sources to bolster his case. Look for quotes from outside industry consultants, reactions from competitors—named or unnamed—and maybe even a customer. That shows that the journalist has put in the time to give you the real lowdown. Take note too of poetic overkill: there's nothing more tempting for a journalist—whether touting or trashing a company—than to go overboard.

Lastly, check the corrections listed in a publication's subsequent issue before committing yourself to any numbers: 13% sounds an awful lot like 30% over the telephone and if we're talking about market share or profit forecast, it's best to know about the error before you pass on your information to the chief.

Richard Teitelbaum is a writer-reporter for *Fortune* magazine.

Drug Topics (Medical Economics Co.). In December or January, this magazine forecasts the expected performance of leading drug chains and reviews the past year.

Progressive Grocer (SI) (Maclean Hunter Media). This monthly reviews specific product categories and analyzes current data.

Stores (SI) (NRF Enterprises). Published monthly for senior executives in head-quarters operations of larger chain and department stores. The top 100 department stores and the top 100 specialty stores are among the subjects of special issues.

Supermarket Business (SI) (FM Business Publications). A monthly directed to-ward senior managers of supermarkets. Annual special issues address the con-cerns of each department found in a typical supermarket.

Supermarket News (Fairchild Publications). Once a year, usually in August, this newspaper profiles major supermarket chains in almost two dozen metropolitan areas.

Rubber

Modern Tire Dealer (SI) (Bill Communications). This magazine focuses on wholesale and retail aspects of tire sales and is written for independent dealers. Information on markets and trends is a key feature.

Rubber & Plastics News (SI) (Crain Communications). This weekly is geared for rubber and plastic products manufacturers.

Rubber World (Lippincott & Peto). A monthly written for technical and scien-tific managers involved in producing natural and synthetic rubber and rubber-related products. Special issues may concentrate on subjects such as testing and analysis, machinery and equipment, adhesives and sealants, or blends and alloys.

State Business Publications

In general, almost every state and region throughout the United States has its own local area business journal. Call the library in any town in a targeted state or region, and ask the reference librarian to help you locate the magazine for that area. This section lists a number of these regional and state sources.

California Business (California Business News). Two special issues are of inter-est to the corporate researcher: (1) California's 100 Fastest Growing Companies and (2) California's 500. These list the 100 fastest-growing California companies (names of corporate officers and revenue for the past two years are included), and the 500 leading California companies, ranked by revenue produced.

Canadian Business (CB Media). This magazine issues a special edition each July: Canada's Top 500 Companies. Similar to the *Fortune* 500, these are Cana-dian companies.

Colorado Business (Wiesener Publishing). This company publishes a list of the top 300 companies in the Rocky Mountain West, ranked by assets, revenues, and earnings. There is also an alphabetical listing.

New Jersey Business (New Jersey Business and Industry Association). The May issue lists the leading 100 firms in the state, by employment size.

Telecommunications

Cablevision (SI) (Capital Cities Media). A biweekly publication directed to cable systems management. Among the special issues are a national consumer survey and a year-end summary and forecast.

CED (SI) (Capital Cities/ABC). This monthly journal deals with cable technology.

Telephony (SI) (Intertec Publishing). This weekly is one of the leading publications covering the telecommunications industry. It presents, once a month, the stock prices and earnings reports on the leading telephone companies—one of its many features of interest. A plethora of telecommunications newsletters have sprung up since divestiture, but this remains a major publication.

Telephone Engineer & Management (SI) (Advanstar). A bimonthly written for engineers, designers, and other telecommunications professionals. One of its special issues is an annual review and forecast.

Tobacco

Tobacco International Magazine (SI) (Lockwood Trade Journal). A biweekly publication geared to tobacco company middle- to senior-level management. Special issues include an annual directory and buyers' guide.

Tobacco Reporter (SI) (Specialized Agricultural Publications). In this monthly, articles address many parts of the tobacco industry, including leaf dealers, processors, and equipment suppliers.

Transportation (Trucking Fleets)

Fleet Owner (SI) (Intertec). This monthly is written for managers and owners of truck and bus fleets, but analysts can gain insight as to how these companies function.

The Private Carrier (SI) (Private Carrier Conference). This monthly, directed to nontransportation companies, provides details on how these companies employ trucks in shipping their products.

Wood and Lumber

Forest Industries (SI) (Miller Freeman). Published ten times a year, this magazine offers articles and market analysis for loggers as well as for those who manufacture lumber products such as plywood.

5 USING DATABASES FOR CORPORATE INTELLIGENCE

Electronic databases are wonderful intelligence tools—just realize their limitations. In particular, you must understand that instant information doesn't necessarily mean current information. That you can receive immediate feedback after pressing the Return key only tells you that database has something to offer. What the computer does not tell you is that most information is not yet in electronic form—nor will it likely be within your lifetime. What the lightning-fast response also fails to tell you is the information you are "instantly" receiving may be months or years old. What databases can do is save you time and give you a breadth of knowledge about an issue or a competitor. They give you information, not intelligence. Intelligence requires analysis and the gathering of primary, first hand information. Can you do without databases? No, not in today's fast-paced, international market. Use them. They are an important means to an end, but not the end itself.

Until the mid-1980s, the ever-expanding electronic information industry still heavily favored the vendor, not the user. The seller of online database time held the lion's share of computing power, and the user, very little. Now, a decade later, it's clear that technology's relatively high cost and limited capacity have given way to affordable access, powerful but inexpensive personal computers, and friendlier search tools. Their availability and ease-of-use have in many ways turned the information/intelligence world upside down. For instance, the analyst can now carry and control entire archives containing tens of thousands of records.

THE TECHNOLOGY

In several specific ways, technology has evolved to improve your ability to develop more accurate and more timely intelligence on your marketplace. Here are the key "tools" that are available.

CD-ROMs

These miniature disks contain whole libraries of books and records. They give the individual researcher the storage capacity that once resided in mainframe computers whose data could only be accessed through long-distance telephone. CD-ROMs give you instant access and full freedom to roam through gobs of historical data. Today's timesharing database providers (such as those offered on Dialog) now have to maintain more timely data on their system. In the near future, nearly every database producer will be publishing its historical data on CD-ROMs. This technology has not trickled down to a larger segment of the corporate population, partly because of the relatively high costs of the disks and the still incompatible software interfaces needed to gain access to data on the CD-ROM. This can be expected to change as the costs drop and software publishers adopt a de facto search-and-retrieval standard.

Electronic Bulletin Boards

These high-tech communication forums give you one of the most powerful message carriers imaginable. You no longer need to know who the critical expert is or where he or she is located. Type your request into one of the low-cost systems available through Prodigy, America On-line, CompuServe, or Internet, and the electronically-savvy expert might just find you.

Acknowledgment of Low-Tech Delivery

A number of database publishers have long understood that there is a greater need for their information than is being realized. Ironically, the barrier to greater usage is the computer terminal itself. Not everyone finds the keyboard easy or natural to use. Many managers still prefer to rely on pieces of paper rather than stare into a cathode ray tube. In recognition of this fact, companies such as WestLaw, a publisher of legal texts and databases, offer a companion service that delivers the on-screen data to the client via fax. WestLaw calls its product Westfax. Individual, Inc., a Cambridge, Massachusetts, company whose service is searching and organizing electronically published news on certain markets, will fax their own customized newsletters to clients. Individual can also transmit its reports directly to clients who can receive them on an E-mail system.

Storage and Retrieval of Images

Publishers now have the technology to store and deliver images, but copyright law has prohibited the information industry from routinely delivering images along with the traditional text. Over the next few years, individual court cases and legislative activity should resolve the many legal issues involved. I believe that the economics of the marketplace and consumer demand will require more electronic transmission, not less. If images become as widely distributed as text, not only will the corporate researcher be able to examine the corporate statistics, but photos, floor plans, and product illustrations will be available for review.

Virtual Libraries

The library of tomorrow may be electronic. Since the early 1980s, libraries have built numerous networks, linking their catalogs with one another. The next big step, which has already begun, will place the actual texts online. How might this help you, as a competitive analyst? If you need to know about a new technology or process, you will be able to sit down at your computer terminal and pull up an arcane Ph.D. dissertation or a conference paper—in full. By going straight to the original source documents, you will see the information unfiltered and unedited.

SECTION I: HOW TO USE DATABASES FOR INTELLIGENCE

Database: A Definition

A database is a collection or pool of information that is recorded, indexed, and stored on a computer. It functions as a computerized reference book.

Using a computerized index as your research tool, you have an almost unlimited ability to find the information you are looking for—if you know and understand how a database works. A decade ago, the majority of my communications audience had not yet worked directly with electronic databases. Today, even elementary school students can walk into small community libraries and use CD-ROM indexes of news articles and their library's own card catalog. Researchers are no longer limited by hard-copy index cards with fixed terms. An electronic database permits access to any stored terms. The computer program will search throughout the database's records—from title, to author, to abstract, to index terms—to find the words that a researcher has requested.

A database does not need a fixed index. In practice, bibliographic databases—that is, databases that house abstracts of articles—allow a search under any term; the program will do the rest of the work. If the term exists in the database, the program will match up all records that contain the term.

How a Database Can Help You with Corporate Research

Because a database is so flexible, and because you can scan any portion of a database record, there is little chance that you will miss a company name or product, if filed. A database search can help answer the following questions:

1. What articles were written about this market?
2. What companies are associated with this product group?
3. What patents have been filed for this technology?
4. What are the major magazines or texts in this industry?
5. What are the chances that I will find something in print on the target company?
6. How many companies are in the same industry as the target company?
7. Who are the reporters studying this industry?

8. How can I be updated on industry and company events without having to constantly request the information?

9. How can I compile a list of the leading experts in the industry and the key institutions they are associated with?

Database Limitations

Instant information does not mean current information. The data that spew out of your terminal with lightning speed may not be current. If you need current data on the competition, a database may not be your perfect solution. Too often, a database may contain information that is a month or even a year old.

When gathering corporate information through a database, here are some of the limitations you should be aware of:

1. *The age of a periodical.* By the time an article citation appears in a database, the original material and information in that article may be a year old. When an article is submitted to a magazine (especially a scholarly journal), six months to a year may pass before the article is printed. In addition, once the database supplier receives the journal or magazine article, another one or two months may go by before the article is entered into the database.

2. *Database selectivity.* Even when a database states that it indexes articles from a certain magazine, be careful! Because database suppliers have limited space and limited time in which to enter the abstracted articles, they often do not include the entire issue of the magazine. Bibliographic databases commonly omit advertisements, events calendars, editorials, personnel announcements, help-wanted advertisements, charts, graphs, photographs, and stock prices.

3. *Priority lists.* Sometimes, when a database supplier sees that news articles from different periodicals and newspapers duplicate one another, only one of the articles will be entered into the database. The result is loss of sources of information. Each reporter interviews different sources. When a database supplier chooses only one of the articles for its database, you are seeing only part of the picture.

4. *A missed update cycle.* This occurs most often in financially oriented databases. Suppose a database is updated once each month. If a company's reporting period ends in the week following the monthly update, the database will not report the latest financials for another three weeks. A researcher needing up-to-the-minute competitor financial reports cannot rely on such a database for absolutely current information.

How a Database System Works

If you directly conduct electronic searches, this section is addressed to you. If you manage searchers, you should understand how and why a searcher can access so many databases, and how those databases need to be used. Often, an "expectation gap" exists between the searcher and the manager who is requesting the information. The manager may have high expectations, but the searcher, not knowing exactly what the client wants or needs, may be unable to deliver the goods. Be aware of the reality of databases: how they are built, and what they can and cannot do.

A database supplier is a kind of publisher. Instead of printing the product on paper, the supplier places it on an electronic medium (a disk or a tape). When requested, the tape is sent or electronically transmitted to the distributor or vendor, who is in turn linked to a telecommunications network. The vendor, such as Dialog, Nexis, or CompuServe, has created a common search language so that a librarian can search more than one database from any number of suppliers.

Database vendors charge the user according to the time spent on the system. Some services require an additional subscription fee; others allow users to pay as they go. In other words, a user pays only for the time spent on the system.

Many services, such as Dialog or Nexis, strongly urge or require a user to attend one of their training sessions before using the system. The sessions cost approximately $100–$200, but usually pay for themselves in the free search time given by the service to attendees. By all means, sign up. The time you will inevitably waste on the computer system will translate into lost dollars that could have been better spent attending the service's training seminar.

To find an appropriate database, contact some relevant vendors listed in this chapter, and request information on their respective systems. Next, call or visit your local library or library school. Speak to the person who does the searching in the reference section. Ask about the pros and cons of each database system or vendor you have selected, and get an opinion on which system will best meet your needs and your budget.

Database Searching Tips

Databases are black boxes as far as intelligence gathering is concerned. They may have a lot of data, but you may not know how the data are stored or indexed. Here are some database searching lessons that I have learned in the course of my research. Not all of these tips apply to all the databases you may use; I present them here as general rules of thumb.

1. *Find out how much of a periodical a database abstracts.* As I mentioned earlier, most bibliographical databases do not abstract events calendars, editorials, or product announcements. If you use one database often, call or write the supplier and ask what material is included and excluded from the publications indexed.
2. *Get a publications list.* Each database supplier should be able to send you a list of indexed publications.
3. *Look for a company field.* If a database has designated a special field just to list the company or companies mentioned in the records, that database is geared to collecting and indexing company information. (Every database uses fields: they are the categories of information in a database record. For example, an article title is given a field; the publication date is given a field; and so on, for each major category.

    Figures 5.1 through 5.3 are printouts of the information provided by three databases in response to requests.
4. *Avoid four-digit SIC codes.* Any database that only uses four digits to identify an industry can possibly lead the searcher in the wrong direction or, even worse, give misleading information.

File 18:PTS F&S INDEX(R) 1980–1993/AugW2
(c) 1993 Predicasts

Set Items Description

—— ——— —————

1/5/1
03462211
Schering Seeks Ruling In Patent Dispute With Genentech Inc.
Wall Street Journal 3 Star, Eastern (Princeton, NJ) Edition June 25, 1992
p. B4
ISSN: 0043-0080 PROMT: YES

Schering-Plough: Seeks court ruling in Genentech's cancer drug patent suit
Genentech: Schering-Plough seeks court ruling in this co's patent suit

COMPANY:
    Schering-Plough
    Genentech

PRODUCT: Anticancer Drugs (2834140)
EVENT: Patents & Copyrights (37)
COUNTRY: United States (1USA)

Figure 5.1   Example of access to company field via Funk & Scott (F&S) index.

Market share based on a four-digit SIC code can be entirely wrong. For example, a company manufacturing microchips may have a large share of the market in its specific industry (13 percent), but it may have a far smaller share (0.1 percent) when compared to the entire electronics industry.

A database that allows the searcher to define an industry with a seven-digit SIC grouping is a far better source. Note the PTS F&S database printout (Figure 5.1) carries a seven-digit definition of the product, anticancer drugs.

5. *Collect synonyms.* The industry you are searching may have more than one name. Use the industry dictionaries and speak to a few analysts and experts to make sure you are searching under all possible categories.

6. *Have the database help you search for synonyms.* Database systems such as Dialog and Nexis allow you to print out the index terms that most closely resemble the ones you are using. Let's say you are using the ABI/Inform database on the Dialog system. You want to search for articles on General Motors marketing programs, but you aren't sure how ABI/Inform classifies the term "marketing" and what other terms it may use to index articles.

You take the word "marketing" and ask the Dialog system to pull out other terms that are close to "marketing." The resulting printout includes "marketing research" and "marketing strategy," which should be used when doing a thorough search on GM's marketing programs.

7. *Buy the database thesaurus.* Buy the thesaurus for any database you use often. Many suppliers will not only give you a thesaurus free but will also include search tips to help you through their database. A quick scan of the thesaurus will tell you the scope of the database. For instance, does the database

File 132:S&P Daily News 1985-85-93SEP 7
   (COPR. 1993 STANDARD & POORS CORP.)

6/5/3
1185822
GENERAL MOTORS CORP. (U.S.) 930830
   Sells Shareholdings of Group Lotus plc and Lotus Cars USA Units to Bugatti Intl. S.A.H.-
   Aug. 27, 1993, General Motors Corp. (GM) announced it signed a contract for the
immediate sale of its entire shareholding in Group Lotus plc and Lotus Cars USA to
Bugatti International S.A.H. GM added that Bugatti will acquire the entire Lotus
operation, including the Engineering Consulting and Cars businesses, as well as Lotus'
assets in the U.S.
   (Standard & Poor's News)

SIC Code: 3711
Event: Mergers & Acquisitions (M&A)

Ticker: GM   CUSIP: 370442   Company No: 00002854

File 132:S&P Daily News 1985-85-93SEP 7
   (COPR. 1993 STANDARD & POORS CORP.)

6/5/37
1156880
GENERAL MOTORS CORP. (U.S.) 930317

   Division Enters into Agreement to Manufacture and Deliver Locomotive Engines-

   Mar. 16, 1993, Burlington Northern Inc. announced that it will acquire 350 SD70M-AC
locomotive engines for more than $675,000,000 from Electro-Motive, a division of General
Motors Corp. Of these 4000-horsepower engines, eight will be delivered in 1993 with
between 60 and 100 locomotives to be delivered each year from 1994 through 1997. Most of
the locomotives will be used in coal service.
   (Standard & Poor's News)

Figure 5.2 Example of access to company field via Standard & Poor's system.

concentrate more on management issues than on new product announcements? Most thesauri cost under $50.

8. *Look for both a primary and a secondary industry.* When searching, keep in
   mind that the database may have listed your targeted company or companies under another industry. When examining companies in an industry, prepare to
   gather more than just one or two industry categories. For example, to find companies that manufacture personal computers, you would want to search not only
   under "personal computers" but also under "home computers," "microcomput-
   ers," "transportable computers," "portable computers," and so on.

9. *Ask yourself whether you need historical data or current data.* Some databases
   are better and more comprehensive suppliers of historical information than of
   information that may be only three months old. The database supplier tells you
   in its descriptive literature how often the database is updated.

10. *If you have already found an ideal article, use it for your search.* Find out
    which database indexes that magazine or newspaper, punch in the exact title,
    and print out the record that appears—with the index terms used. By printing
    it out with the index terms, you will know how that supplier indexes the articles

File 155:MEDLINE 1966-1993/OCT (9310W4)
  Set Items Description
  ___ ____ _____

  5/5/3
08045175   92183175
  Role of superficial femoral artery puncture in the development of pseudoaneurysm and
arteriovenous fistula complicating percutaneous transfemoral cardiac catheterization.
  Kim D; Orron DE; Skillman JJ; Kent KC; Porter DH; Schlam BW; Carrozza J; Reis GJ;
Baim DS
  Charles A. Dana Research Institute, Beth Israel Hospital, Harvard Medical School,
Boston, Massachusetts 02215.
  Cathet Cardiovasc Diagn Feb *1992*, 25 (2) p91-7, ISSN 0098-6569 Journal Code: CQZ
  Languages: ENGLISH
  Document type: JOURNAL ARTICLE
  JOURNAL ANNOUNCEMENT: 9206
  Subfile: INDEX MEDICUS
  Of 13,203 transfemoral diagnostic and therapeutic cardiac catheterization procedures
performed between January 1, 1980 and December 31, 1990, 73 (0.55%) were complicated
by pseudoaneurysm (PA) formation, and 15 (0.11%) by arteriovenous fistulas (AVF). The
rate of PA increased progressively from 0.44% (1980–1987), to 0.59% (1987–1989), to
0.92% (1990), with no corresponding change in the incidence of AVF. The rising incidence
of PA complicating transfemoral cardiac catheterization was associated closely with the
use of larger diameter catheters and aggressive antiocoagulation during coronary
interventions, but findings during surgical repair suggested that puncture of the
superficial femoral (SFA), rather than the common femoral artery (CFA), was an
important avoidable cause of some PA and AVF. A technique for fluoroscopic localization of
the puncture site to avoid inadvertent SFA puncture and the associated increased risk of
complication is proposed.
  Tags: Human
  Descriptors: Aneurysm—Radiography—RA; *Arteriovenous Fistula—Radiography—RA;
*Femoral Artery—Injuries—IN; *Heart *Catheterization*—*Instrumentation*—IS;
Aneurysm—Surgery—SU; Arteriovenous Fistula—Surgery—SU; *Femoral* *Artery*
—*Radiography*—RA; Heart Catheterization—Adverse Effects—AE; Retrospective
Studies; Risk Factors

Figure 5.3   Example of MEDLINE access to medical journal article, used here to locate
experts in catheterization.

you are looking for. Next, punch those same index terms back into the database,
and you will receive all other articles that pertain to your industry and companies. In the example shown in Figure 5.1, the researcher needed all articles on
the Schering–Plough/Genentech patent dispute. The first request was for articles that mentioned Schering–Plough and Genentech together.

11. *Limit you company search by financial size.* In databases that track company
    financials, you can often limit your search. For instance, you can limit the
    search to companies with sales between $50 million and $100 million.

12. *The number of times a magazine or periodical appears on a search will indicate
    its interest in and knowledge of the industry.* Although a search may not yield
    an article that answers your question, it can indicate which magazine, editor, or
    author may be the best to interview.

General industry and product lines: _____

1. Synonyms for product type, technology, or industry:
   a. _____
   b. _____
   c. _____
   d. _____
   e. _____
2. How current must the information be? (e.g., within the past month, year, etc.)
   _____
3. Are you looking for a database that offers primarily:
   _____ narrative   _____ statistics
4. What is the primary industry you are searching for?
   _____
5. What is the secondary industry that might be appropriate?
   _____
6. Do you have an ideal article that fairly well represents the information you are looking
   for? Can you supply the following about it?
   Title: _____
   Publication: _____
   Date the article appeared: _____
7. If you were unable to find an ideal article, what would be the title of the ideal article as
   you would imagine it? (Write in this imagined title below.)
   _____
   _____
   _____

Figure 5.4   Database search form.

The form shown in Figure 5.4 provides the categories and questions you should
address when searching a database for information about a corporation.

SDI: An Executive Reminder Service at Bargain Basement Prices

Librarians and information professionals first coined the term Selective Dissemination of Information (SDI). Most managers, when they first heard "SDI," associated it
with the Strategic Defense Initiative, the formal name of the "Star Wars" high-tech
military initiative during President Reagan's years in office. In recent years, database
services have begun calling the service "Current Awareness"—a much friendlier title.

SDI is simple to use. You (or your librarian) enter a search strategy that you
wish to pursue on a regular basis. Let's say that each month you want to track GM's
plans for its minivans and the marketing strategy for those vans. You select the appropriate database (such as PTS PROMT) and send that search strategy to the Dialog
system computer for storage in the SDI section. Every time Dialog downloads new
data onto the PTS PROMT database, Dialog would first pass the data by your search.
Any time your search matches information contained in one of PTS PROMT's

records, the system copies the record onto your personal electronic file. Depending on the PTS PROMT weekly update cycle, Dialog would send you the results of the SDI search. Most systems allow you to receive the printout either in paper form, via the regular mail, or electronically, by depositing the report in your electronic mail box. If you opt for the latter choice, you need only sign on to your account and download the information to your desktop computer.

Current Awareness is a wonderful tool because it reminds you automatically. As your workday becomes overrun with one to-do task after another, it becomes too easy to push off—and eventually forget—old tasks in favor of new ones. The thought of going to your library or computer terminal to conduct a laborious search can become yet another overwhelming task. Yet, you must monitor your competition meticulously and frequently. With that mandate in mind, SDI represents due diligence. After all, Murphy's law would state: "A competitor company will take advantage of a market opportunity just when you do not expect it to do so."

A final point: SDI can actually save you money. Because many vendors run their customers' SDI searches in batch mode in the middle of the night, when the system has low usage, you receive the savings.

Locating Experts through Databases

Technical experts in highly specialized areas are difficult to locate. Word of mouth may be helpful in finding leads (and perhaps just the right contact), but you may waste a lot of time on fruitless hunches.

Databases can help, provided they are used judiciously. Any bibliographic database will list articles and their respective authors. However, in some instances, these authors are free-lance or ghost writers for company senior officers—they are not the authors. Technical or scientific databases, where ghosting is almost nonexistent, are better for locating experts. Select a database and let it create a directory of experts for you.

In the example shown in Figure 5.3 an expert on cardiac catheters was located through MEDLINE, the National Library of Medicine database, which lists all authors of medical journal articles.

Choosing a Database System

Today's vendors offer a vast array of databases at highly competitive rates. Gone are the high subscription fees and much of the exclusivity that used to mark the database market. Dialog, Nexis, and Orbit, among other systems, carry many similar or closely matching databases. Yet, there are differences. Some professional searchers prefer one system's search language over another. Some systems specialize; others may encompass only technical sources or may contain databases that cover certain geographic regions. NewsNet, for example, only contains newsletters in full text. Dow Jones stresses its daily news feeds.

Despite the numerous vendors that have come and gone over the years, Dialog remains the leader in overall user friendliness and technical depth. Its selection of databases is among the largest under a one-system umbrella.

The following list of database vendors is divided into two sections: (1) traditional vendors and (2) electronic bulletin board (E-mail) systems. These are all North

American vendors. For information on leading overseas vendors, see Section III of this chapter.

Traditional Vendors

BRS Information Technologies
8000 Westpark Dr.
McLean, VA 22102
703-442-0900, 800-289-4277;
    Fax: 703-893-0906.

Favors education/general library market; contains over 120 databases with emphasis on healthcare, science, social science, and medicine. Offers a low-price, off-hours subset: BRS/After Dark.

DataTimes Corporation
1400 Quail Springs Pkwy.
Parkway Plaza, Suite 450
Oklahoma City, OK 73134
405-751-6400, 800-642-2525

Specializes in offering local news sources; offers over 80 news sources online, most in full text.

Dialog Information Services
3460 Hillview Ave.
 Palo Alto, CA 94304
415-858-3785, 800-334-2564;
    Fax: 415-858-7069

An assortment of 400+ technical and business databases. Features Dialindex (subject search), Dialnet (transmission and reception at 9600 baud), and a newsletter database competitive with NewsNet. Recently acquired VuText (local news coverage) and Data-Star, a European vendor ("Dialog of Europe").

Dow Jones News Retrieval
Dow Jones & Company, Inc.
P.O. Box 300
Princeton, NJ 08543-0300
609-520-4000

Covers current world and national news with special focus on business. Carries *The Wall Street Journal* and stock quotes.

DRI/McGraw-Hill
24 Hartwell Ave.
Lexington, MA 02173
617-863-5100

Packages and massages government-generated data on a global scale. Owns and distributes the Dodge series of construction databases.

GE Information Services
401 N. Washington St.
Rockville, MD 20850
301-340-4572, 800-638-9636;
    Fax: 301-294-5501

Specializes in delivering currency, gross national product, and overall economic data.

Mead Data Central, Inc.
943 Springboro Pike
P.O. Box 933
Dayton, OH 45401-9964
513-865-6800, 800-227-4908

Owns Nexis (general news, specialty trade magazines) and Lexis (online access to latest legal and legislative changes). Has acquired Crain's Detroit Business and The Courier-Journal of Louisville, Kentucky.

NewsNet, Inc.
945 Haverford Rd.
Bryn Mawr, PA 19010
215-527-8030, 800-345-1301;
    Fax: 215-527-0338

Offers online, full-text newsletters in financial services, healthcare, computers and technology, defense, environment, and other areas. Allows automatic scanning of latest news.

ORBIT Search Service
8000 Westpark Dr.
McLean, VA 22102
703-442-0900, 800-456-7248;
  Fax: 893-4632

Offers Chemical Abstracts, U.S. Patents Abstracts, RINGDOC, and World Patents Index.

QL Systems Ltd.
901 St. Andrew's Tower
275 Sparks Street
Ottawa, ON, Canada K1R 7X9
613-238-3499; Fax: 613-548-4260

Covers Canadian business and maritime law.

Quotron Systems, Inc.
12731 W. Jefferson Blvd.
P.O. Box 66914
Los Angeles, CA 90066
213-827-4600

Offers stock quote data via Australian Sharewatch, CurrencyWatch, Markets Charts, Munifacts, and S&P MarketScope.

West Publishing Co. (WESTLAW)
610 Operman Dr.
P.O. Box 64526
St. Paul, MN 55164-0526
612-228-2500

Provides online legal data and WestFax delivery.

Electronic Bulletin Board Systems

Each of the following electronic networks can expand your knowledge and information reach. These networks put you in touch with experts or those who can find experts. Using an electronic mail (E-mail) system, however, is not a surefire way of locating your information. E-mail can be quirky and indirect. You may come up empty if no one happens to read your message or the importance of it goes unrealized. On the other hand, there are people out there, "techno-hobbyists," who may have the answer you seek. Electronic systems tend to be expensive, but, overall, the cost for seeking information is relatively low. At a minimum, you will be rewarded with some interesting electronic chatter—and you may find your intelligence gem.

America On-line, Inc.
8619 Westwood Center Dr.
Vienna, VA 22182
703-448-8700, 800-227-6364

Offers exchanges on such bulletin boards as the Independent Investors Forum.

CompuServe Information Service
5000 Arlington Centre Blvd.
P.O. Box 20212
Columbus, OH 43220
614-457-8600, 800-848-8990

Offers a wide variety of forums, on topics such as artificial intelligence, astronomy, aviation, broadcasting, computers, consumer electronics, digital research, foreign languages, graphics support, investing, military science, photography, space, sports, students, and travel.

Internet. A collection of computer networks with shared software standards; not one centralized E-mail system. Allows access from one E-mail or database system to others in the same network via a password. Users must sign on to Delphi (800-365-4636), World (Software Tool & Die, 617-739-0202), CompuServe (see above), or another access provider within the Internet system.

Prodigy Services Company—PRODIGY
445 Hamilton Ave.
White Plains, NY 10601
914-993-8000

A Sears–IBM joint venture; popularly marketed E-mail and information services system with millions of subscribers.

SECTION II: A GENERAL LISTING OF U.S. AND INTERNATIONAL DATABASES

Databases for the Corporate Researcher

This section lists only databases that offer some form of corporate information; general economic data or market-trend information may be present but are not the basis for inclusion here. The list is by no means exhaustive. There are over 5,000 publicly available databases, some of which are produced for certain industries or for segments within an industry. To explore the many other possible online and CD-ROM electronic information resources, I refer you to the two-volume *Gale Directory of Databases* (Gale Research). Volume 1 covers online sources; volume 2 reviews CD-ROM products. Gale has provided excellent indexes that allow research by publisher, by industry topic, or by title.

The following list contains the database name, the name of the supplier, a description of the corporate information offered, and advice on how best to use the database in your company research.

ABI/Inform (UMI Data Courier). A business database that indexes feature articles from over 800 journals, and offers full text for 100 articles. Abstracts (usually 100 words) make it ideal for free text searching. Recommended for reviewing how the largest companies are handling total quality, benchmarking, reengineering, and other management trends.

Accounting & Tax Database (UMI Data Courier). Reviews articles from over 1,000 publications, 200 of which are specialty accounting journals. Abstracts are up to 150 words; some articles are full text.

Active Well On-Line (Magellan On-Line Services). Industry-specific; examines companies on an operational level and publishes details on well testing, volumes, total depth, and final status of each well site.

American Banker Full Text (American Banker). Indexes articles that appear in *American Banker.* Recommend using the index terms to gain wider access to the information pool.

APIPAT (Central Abstracting and Indexing Service of the American Petroleum Institute). Similar to APLIT in subject matter, but concentrates on patents issued by the United States, Belgium, Canada, France, Germany, Great Britain, Holland, Japan, and South Africa.

APLIT (Central Abstracting and Indexing Service of the American Petroleum Institute). Covers research and events in the petrochemical industry. Recommended for leads to R&D information on the industry.

AT&T 800 Toll-Free Directory (AT&T 800 Service). Complete listing of 800 telephone numbers available throughout the AT&T system. Cross-indexed by subject.

Automotive News (Crain Communications, Inc.). Full-text online version of the weekly newspaper by the same name; detailed articles and analyses of car production, sales and marketing news, legal and other issues.

A. M. Best Databases (A. M. Best Company). Insurance industry statistics and general news. Databases include:

- *BestLink:* Balance sheet and profit-and-loss data on over 4,400 U.S. insurance companies; information on over 900 international insurers.
- *Best's Insurance Reports—Life/Health:* Full text version of *Best's Insurance Reports—Life/Health.* Financial analysis and ratings of U.S insurers.
- *Best's Insurance Reports—Property/Casualty:* Similar to the above, but covers Property/Casualty.

BHRA Fluid Engineering (BHRA Fluid Engineering). Presents patent information on the field, and corporate/university affiliations of the authors or patent holders appearing in the database. Can be used to generate lists of experts in certain specialties.

Billboard Information Network (Billboard Publications). Provides market and sales statistics culled from over 600 radio stations and dance clubs. Reports on retail sales of approximately 600 dealers.

BIOSIS Previews (BioSciences Information Service). Reviews over 9,000 journals, institutional reports, and other research literature in the fields of biology and medicine. Contains well over 3 million records.

Current Biotechnology Abstracts (Royal Society of Chemistry). Designed for scientists, but valuable for studying the field of biotechnology and genetic engineering, including patents. Represents major journals and conference proceedings from around the world.

Books in Print (R. R. Bowker). Contains 1.8 million currently available books from over 22,000 U.S. publishers, plus book reviews from selected journals.

Business Software Database (Information Sources, Inc.). Contains name, address, product description, and specifications for over 40,000 software firms and products.

CA Search (Chemical Abstracts Service). Contains over 16 million entries on the chemical industry, including patents, journal articles, monographs, and conference proceedings. Access by patent number, country, journal name, or institution.

Chemical Industry Notes (Chemical Abstracts Service). Specializes in chemical business magazines and journals. Articles describe plant capacity and product information.

CIS (Congressional Information Service). Indexes congressional working papers, including hearings, committee reports, and documents published as a result of special investigations. Valuable source on companies in highly regulated industries, or industries under investigation. Gives brief abstract, reference date, and number; original documents available on microfiche via library subscribers.

Compendex (Engineering Information). Computerized version of *Engineering Index.* Identifies companies or experts specializing in certain areas of engineering. Offers names and organizations of authors; abstracts, index of over 4,500 journals; over 1 million entries.

Comp-U-Store (Comp-U-Card of America). Set up for at-home shopping. Can be used to locate "street" prices for thousands of products. Offerings priced well below standard list prices.

Conference Papers Index (Cambridge Scientific Abstracts). Index of scientific and technical papers from over 150 meetings each year. For each paper, gives author's name and affiliated institution, as well as the address and ordering price of paper.

DAAS/Drilling Activity Analysis System (Petroleum Information Corporation). Detailed records on oil and gas wells: data on site, depth and class of well, and potential yield.

Datapro Software Directory (Datapro). Contains over 27,000 software packages. Recommended for locating competing packages in a specific application area.

Datastream Company Accounts (Datastream International). Deals directly with financials from international companies: 500 unquoted and all U.K. stock exchange companies; 300 Canadian, 281 French, 122 German, 59 Dutch, 50 Hong Kong, 50 Swiss, 1,300 Japanese.

D&B—Dun's Market Identifiers (Dun's Marketing Services). Offers over 6.6 million records, most of which contain some financial data. Useful to locate a large company's subsidiary or plant and office sites, city-by-city; identify the function of specific offices and their size, measured either by number of employees or by sales. Indexed with D&B's expanded industrial classification codes.

D&B Million Dollar Directory (Dun's Marketing Services). Similar to the above, but includes only companies whose net worth is over $500,000. Over 160,000 entries.

D&B International Dun's Market Identifiers (Dun's Marketing Services). Contains over 200,000 records from 90 countries, reports sales in both U.S. and local currencies. Access through Dialog.

D&B—Dun's Electronic Business Directory (Dun's Marketing Services). Over 8.4 million records detailing products and services of about 60 percent of U.S. businesses. Access by name, location, and SIC code.

Disclosure Database (Disclosure Incorporated). Contains summaries of 10-K, 10-Q, 10-C, 8-K, and 20-F corporate SEC filings. Over 12,400 public companies on file. Abstracts contain Disclosure order number.

Dodge Construction Analysis System (McGraw-Hill, Inc.). Contains approximately 4 million monthly time series for construction projects of more than 200 structural types. Retrieves project-level data: county, structure type, ownership, type of construction, story height, framing cost, and builder type.

DRI International Auto (McGraw-Hill Data Products Division). Details automobile production by country and by model and make of car. Approximately 1,500 time series. Countries covered include: Argentina, Austria, Australia, Belgium, Brazil, Denmark, Finland, France, Germany, Greece, India, Ireland, Italy, Japan, Korea, Mexico, the Netherlands, New Zealand, Norway, Portugal,

South Africa, Spain, Sweden, Switzerland and the United Kingdom. Exports listed by destination.

DRI U.S. and Canadian Equities (DRI/McGraw-Hill). Lists daily time series of current and historical prices, dividends, and fundamental financial information for more than 45,000 equity issues listed on NYSE, American Stock Exchange, OTC, and Toronto and Montreal exchanges.

EI Engineering Meetings (Engineering Information, Inc.). Contains over 622,000 citations covering more than 2,000 engineering meetings and conferences. Includes civil, environmental, geological, mining, petroleum, and other engineering disciplines.

Encyclopedia of Associations (Gale Research Co.). Contains over 90,000 records; access by industry, subject area, or free text.

Energy Data Base (Newport Associates, Ltd.). Company-specific reports, including financials, on more than 500 oil companies in 15 regions of the world. Gives details on acreage, volume of reserves, net wells drilled, net daily oil production, and net cash flow.

Environmental Compliance Update (High Tech Publishing Co.). Full text of newsletter covering business compliance with environmental standards.

Excerpta Medica—EMBASE (Elsevier Science Publishers B. V.). Along with MEDLINE, can be used as an international medical science directory of experts in particular fields.

Federal Index (National Standards Association). Abstracts and indexes information on federal rulings and legislation from the *Congressional Record, Federal Register,* and *Washington Post.* Under "Contract Awards," records winners of certain contracts. Valuable when examining companies that rely on government contracts for business.

Federal Register Abstracts (National Standards Association). Corresponds to the *Federal Register* print version; covers notices of hearings and proposed legislation.

Financial Post Securities (Financial Post Datagroup). Weekly and daily time series of Canadian stock exchange data (daily volume; high, low, and closing prices) for over 3,800 securities.

Financial Times Fulltext (FT Business Enterprises Ltd.). Premier international source for industrial trends and information on competitors. Roughly 400,000 records as of this printing. Articles known for depth and broad global outlook.

Financial Times Currency and Share Index Databank (The WEFA Group). Tracks 1,100 time series of daily and end-of-month data on international exchange rates.

Financial Times Mergers and Acquisitions International/Financial Times Mergers and Acquisitions News (FT Business Enterprises Ltd.). Equipped to track the many mergers and acquisitions that take place each year.

Findex (Cambridge Information Group). Excellent for locating market studies and research reports in the United States, Europe, and other international markets. Abstracts describe contents and objectives of each study. Over 12,000 reports on file.

Foods Adlibra (Foods Adlibra Publications). Covers food trade and technical journals: patents, new product announcements, and studies on the food industry and its products.

The Globe and Mail On-line (Globe Information Services). Full-text edition of the *Globe and Mail,* a Canadian newspaper. Updated each day. A superb source of Canadian business and general news.

GPO Monthly Catalog/GPO Publications File (Government Printing Office). Two files on documents and reports available through the Government Printing Office; some are abstracted. Originating agency and cost given for each item.

Harvard Business Review (John Wiley & Sons, Inc.). All the articles from 1971 to the present, with fulltext of articles from 1976 to the present. HBR is a superb source of management and strategic information on companies, and is often a bellwether of corporate trends. Many terms and concepts introduced by HBR become the CorpSpeak of major corporations.

Industry Trends & Analysis (Arthur D. Little Resources). Indexes, abstracts, and selected full text of research studies published by Arthur D. Little. Reports cover chemicals and materials, pharmaceuticals, healthcare, biotechnology, food, environmental management, telecommunications, and other topics.

INSPEC (Institution of Electrical Engineers). A huge database of international citations from journals and conference proceedings in physics, electrotechnology, computers, and control. Lists and discusses patents. An excellent source of experts worldwide and of companies or institutions responsible for the most active R&D efforts in particular fields.

Insurance Abstracts (University Microfilms Intl.). Covers over 100 publications. An excellent source for the latest news on the industry.

International Pharmaceutical Abstracts (American Society of Hospital Pharmacists). Allows discovery of which companies are using which types of drugs and how they are experimenting with them, but information is likely to be somewhat dated by the time an article reaches the database. Lists the corporate source and the names of individuals who wrote each article.

INVESTEXT (Thomson Financial Services). Popular for its continued acquisition of stock analyst reports of publicly traded companies around the globe. Contains over 320,000 reports on over 14,000 companies in 53 industries. Although in fulltext form, a Table of Contents simplifies identifying and selecting desired portions.

ISMEC (Cambridge Scientific Abstracts). Concentrates on journals from the fields of mechanical engineering and production. Useful for assembling a list of experts in these fields.

Kompass Directories. A valuable online addition to any other standard international reference books. Each online database corresponds to the text version. The complete set yields well over a million references to businesses around the globe.

> *Kompass Asia/Pacific* (Kompass International Management Corporation). Includes over 260,000 Asia/Pacific Rim companies based in Japan, Korea, Hong Kong, Taiwan, China, Singapore, Malaysia, Thailand, Indonesia, Philippines, Brunei/Daussalem, India, Australia, and New Zealand.

> *Kompass Canada* (Kompass Canada Publishers). Lists over 35,000 Canadian companies.

> *Kompass Europe* (Reed Information Services Ltd.) Lists over 421,000 companies in Belgium, Denmark, France, Germany, Italy, Luxembourg, the Netherlands, Norway, Spain, Sweden, Switzerland, and the United Kingdom.

> *Kompass France* (Kompass France S.A.). A listing of more than 171,000 French companies.

> *Kompass Israel* (Kompass Israel Ltd.). A listing of more than 5,000 companies.

> *Kompass UK* (Reed Information Services Ltd.). Lists over 155,000 companies and the trade names used.

LC MARC (U. S. Library of Congress). A listing, beginning with 1968, of all books cataloged by the Library of Congress; section headings point to volumes on companies.

Legal Resource Index (Information Access Co.) Covers topical news items that have appeared in law journals and law newspapers published since 1980. Offers easy-to-understand reports on court cases and litigation that are often sources of information.

Magazine Index (Information Access Co.). A source equivalent to *Readers' Guide to Periodical Literature,* but by a different publisher and in database form. Covers over 400 publications; good for a quick review of company activities as reported in the general press.

Management Contents (Management Contents). Similar to ABI/Inform; reviews management and business literature, citing feature articles in business management and administration.

Marquis Who's Who (Marquis Who's Who). Online version of the classic biographical directory. Contains over 80,000 records, including CEOs of many Fortune 500 companies.

MEDLINE (U.S. National Library of Medicine). Begins in 1966 (fairly old by database standards) and has over 7 million records of medical literature throughout the world. Considered the preeminent medical database. Can provide an accurate worldwide list of experts in extremely narrow disciplines.

Mergers and Corporate Transactions Database (Securities Data Company, Inc.). Covers 35,000 transactions. Records contain the names and locations of parent companies for both the acquiring and acquired firms, plus financial data and dates of the transactions.

METADEX—Metals Abstracts/Alloys Index (ASM International). A specialty database; highly useful when exploring the field of metallurgy. Citations contain corporate affiliation, author's name, and a fairly detailed abstract. Also abstracts certain industry patents.

Microcomputer Index (Learned Information, Inc.). Covers many popular and some lesser known microcomputer publications. Software and hardware reviews. Emphasizes popular more than technical literature.

National Newspaper Index (Information Access Co.). National, not local news source. Coverage now includes PR Newswire (a press release database), Japan Economic Newswire, and Reuters Information Services Financial Report, as well as its original sources, such as *The New York Times, The Wall Street Journal, The Washington Post*, and *The Christian Science Monitor.*

Newsbeat (ADP Brokerage Information Services Group). Carries the latest business news stories; draws from Dow Jones News. Allows identification of the most critical stories by a security or stock exchange code, as well as by general topic.

Newspaper Abstracts (UMI/Data Courier). A useful regional newspaper database; some duplication of coverage in other sources, such as *The New York Times* and *The Wall Street Journal.*

Newsearch (Information Access Co.). Updated daily to include articles that have appeared in legal, popular, and trade literature. Citations are spun off monthly into the National Newspaper Index, Magazine Index, Legal Resource Index, Management Contents, and Trade and Industry Index. The big advantage of this database is its timeliness.

NTIS (National Technical Information Service). A branch of the U.S. Department of Commerce; records any government-sponsored research. All information is declassified and tends to be old news. Some historical value for learning which corporations have historically had a relationship with the federal government in a research area.

Paperchem (The Institute of Paper Science and Technology). Unmatched for its extensive coverage of the paper and pulp industry since 1968. Abstracts articles from approximately 1,000 periodicals written in 20 languages.

Patdata (BRS) (Information Technologies). Specializes in abstracting utility patent filings only. Begins with patents issued in 1971.

Permit Data On-Line (Magellan On-Line Services). Records, within days of issuance of an oil well drilling permit, the well operator, the operator's address, and the well depth. Can be used effectively by both competitors and equipment suppliers to determine activity in a region.

PESTDOC (Derwent Publications). One of the series of Derwent patent and research databases. Concentrates on the scientific and patent literature for the pesticide and herbicide industries; lists corporate source and author. (*Note:* A person conducting a search on a Derwent database should have some knowledge of chemistry or chemical structure and nomenclature. Otherwise, he or she is liable to miss crucial citations. The ORBIT system, which offers the Derwent patent database, offers special training classes in their use.)

People Finder (Information America). Contains 111 million names of individuals in the United States. Each record typically lists: name, address, telephone number, date of birth, family members, and, sometimes, names of neighbors. Useful for learning the backgrounds of executives.

PIERS Exports/PIERS Imports (Journal of Commerce, Inc.). Provides specific, unadulterated import/export data, by company. The PIERS Imports file contains nearly 4 million records taken from ships' manifests filed at U.S. ports. The Exports file contains more than 5.3 million records. Each record indicates the exporter or importer, the weight and quantity of the shipment, the port of loading or discharge, and the name of the ship. Covers only products going to or from U.S. ports, not airport shipments. Recently began tracking shipments to and from Mexico. Can be used to identify suppliers, determine a competitor's shipments by country (identify new markets), understand intracompany distribution (or, transfer pricing approaches), and locate new customers. (*Note:* A third-party customs broker can act as shipper or recipient of record, disguising the actual producer or buyer.)

PTS PREDICASTS (Information Access/Predicasts). Considered by most corporate librarians to be the best first source of published corporate information. SIC (Standard Industrial Code) seven-digit indexing allows probing into highly specific product areas.

> *PTS Annual Reports Abstracts.* A fairly new entry for Predicasts; offers annual report summaries for 3,000 publicly held U.S. companies.

> *PTS F&S Indexes.* Over 2 million citations from over 5,000 publications worldwide. Heavily indexed to include all companies mentioned. Abstracts many product announcements and contract award articles.

> *PTS International Forecasts.* Over 700,000 citations; offers forecasts in tabular format.

> *PTS PROMT.* Selects articles from thousands of publications in the F&S indexes, and supplies large abstracts. File contains over 3 million records and offers both fulltext and abstracts of articles. Abstracts are concise and reflect the most salient points within even long technical articles.

> *PTS U.S. Forecasts.* Covers industry forecasts for the United States in tabular form, much like the International Forecasts database.

> *PTS United States Time Series.* Similar to the F&S International Forecasts, but covers specific product groups in the United States.

Reuters Textline (Reuters Information Services Ltd.). One of the most sweeping global news sources. Contains over 5 million citations drawn from 2,000 publications worldwide. Online thesaurus provided.

RINGDOC (Derwent Publications). An important intelligence tool on pharmaceuticals. Contains over 1.2 million citations and abstracts; corresponds to

RINGDOC Abstracts Journal. Highly specific and technical; not for the novice searcher.

Robotics (Bowker A&I Publishing). Contains more than 12,000 citations and abstracts on the business and technical aspects of this field.

SAE (SAE International). Covers more than 50,000 citations of technical papers presented at various Society of Automotive Engineers conferences. Papers include the latest technological innovations in aerospace, automotive, and vehicle industries.

Scisearch (Institute for Scientific Information). With over 11 million records in science and technology, claims to have covered over 90 percent of the world literature in these fields. Cross-indexed to other articles by listed authors. Can be used to identify experts and companies' R&D efforts.

Spectrum Ownership Profiles On-line (CDA Investment Technologies). Reviews companies' major stockholders and institutional investors.

Smithsonian Science Information Exchange (NTIS). Cites current scientific research projects undertaken through government or private sponsorship. Indexed by sponsoring organization, by the institution performing the work, and by the dollar size of the project.

Standard & Poor's Corporate Descriptions plus News (Standard & Poor's Corporation). Offers financial profiles on 12,000 publicly traded companies. Allows searching and sorting by a wide range of dollar and industry categories.

Standard & Poor's News and News Daily (Standard & Poor's Corporation). Offers, in abstract or full text, press and earnings announcements of over 10,000 publicly held companies. Source for quarterly earnings reports, information on plant expansion and personnel, new product announcements, stock splits, and dividend reports.

Standard & Poor's Register (Standard & Poor's Corporation). Online version of S&P directory. Lists addresses, executive officers, and sales of over 45,000 companies.

Telegen (Bowker A&I Publishing). Concentrates on genetic engineering and biotechnology. Can be used to identify experts.

Textile Technology Digest (Institute of Textile Technology). Covers products and processes in the textile industry.

Textline Company Look-Up (Reuters Information Services Ltd.). Covers recent mergers and acquisitions worldwide. Updated weekly; references companies' former and present names.

Trade & Industry Index/Trade & Industry ASAP (Information Access Co.). Together, these two sister databases include over five million articles from a worldwide selection of business and industry publications. Useful for overviews of an industry, as well as identifying key competitors. Contains the full text of most articles indexed. The ASAP version contains full text of press releases from Kyodo News International and PR Newswire.

Trademarkscan (Thomson & Thomson). Supplements consultation with patent and trademark attorney. Provides initial sweep of many available trademarks already on file. Components are:

- *Trademarkscan—Federal.* Contains over 1.2 million trademarks; identifies all trademarks registered to one company.
- *Trademarkscan—State.* Contains 500,000 trademarks; can be used to identify marketing activity of smaller, regional firms.
- *Trademarkscan—U.K.* Over 680,000 records; can be used to learn how multinationals sell and market their goods, and to track the trademark registration–sales initiative relationship.
- *Trademarkscan—Canada.* Approximately 450,000 records on file; similar to the above versions.

Tulsa (Petroleum Abstracts). Specializes in petroleum exploration and production. Covers geology, patents, geophysics as it relates to petroleum exploration, drilling, well logging, well completion, oil and gas production, reservoir studies, and storage. Approximately 500,000 records.

Ulrich's International Periodicals Directory (R. R. Bowker). Online version of periodical directory. Locates trade magazines or newsletters in a wide variety of industries and disciplines.

U.S. Patents (Derwent Publications). Contains approximately 1.4 million citations and abstracts on U.S. patents.

Value Line DataFile (Value Line Publishing). Summarizes over 1,800 companies, offers 80 industry profiles. Time series data on sales, earnings, and dividend forecasts inclusive from 1955 to the present; quarterly data beginning in 1963.

VETDOC—Veterinary Literature Documentation (Derwent Publications Ltd.). Highly specialized coverage of veterinary medicine, drugs, and corporations involved in research.

Ward's Infobank (Ward's Communications). Statistical; contains 13,800 weekly, monthly, quarterly, and annual data on supply and demand of U.S. and Canadian cars and trucks. Useful for examining shifts in the auto market.

World Aluminum Abstracts (ASM International). Concentrates on the aluminum industry: publications, conference proceedings, government reports, and dissertations.

World Bank of Technology (Dvorkovitz & Associates). Contains more than 15,000 existing inventions and items of technology available for licensing; divided into 50 subject categories.

World Patents Index (Derwent). Lists over 7 million patents from 31 patent-issuing authorities, including U.S. Patent Office and counterparts in Europe, People's Republic of China, Argentina, and Brazil. Statistics generated can be used for competitive technology forecasting.

World Textiles (Elsevier/Geo Abstracts). Covers textile industry worldwide; source for R&D information and names of experts.

SECTION III: EUROPEAN AND ASIA/PACIFIC RIM DATABASES

A wide assortment of databases is available if you need to tap into the global market. This section focuses on databases that provide company-specific information. Because a number of these databases originate in Europe and Asia and are published in German, French, or other languages, you may need a translator to guide you through the business and technical nomenclature.

Topical coverage is as follows:

Europe: European Community, Europe—General, France, Germany, Italy, and United Kingdom.

Asia/Pacific Rim: Asia/Pacific Rim—General, People's Republic of China, Japan, Singapore, and Taiwan.

Europe

European Community

Celex. On F. T. Profile, Eurobases, and Data-Star. Bibliography and text updated every 4 to 8 weeks in English, Dutch, French, German, and Italian. Full text and abstracts of EC laws, treaties, preparatory documents, and related information. Contains a file on member states' implementation of directives.

Eurcom. On Lexis (Mead Data Central, Inc.). Full text; two files containing cases and EC decisions.

Euristote. On Echo. Bibliographic references, updated quarterly in all EC languages. Contains 16,000 citations with abstracts regarding current and completed research on EC. Offers information on more than 6,000 subject experts.

Eurodicautom. On Echo. Updated monthly in all official EC languages, except Greek. Contains 525,000 translations of terms and phrases used in EC.

Euroloc. On EPRC Ltd. Periodically updated in English. Contains information on government subsidies available to manufacturers in EC industries.

Euroscope. On InfoTrade N. V., FT Profile, and Lexis (Mead Data Central, Inc.). Full text, updated daily; contains reports on EC activities.

I'M-GUIDE. On Echo. Online resource for reviewing over 3,000 databases and CD-ROM sources produced or available in Europe. Consultants indexed by specialty.

Info 92. On Eurobases (Commission of European Communities (CEC)). Updated in Danish, Dutch, English, French, German, Italian, Portuguese, and Spanish, as information becomes available. Contains info on the completion of the internal EC market.

Investext (Thomson Financial Networks). On Dialog and Thomson Financial Networks. Full text, updated weekly. Contains EC investment and advisory reports from various stock brokerage firms, including: Shearson Lehman Brothers, PaineWebber Inc., Smith Barney, Harris Upham, Prudential Bache, and Morgan Stanley.

Rapid. On Eurobases (Commission of European Communities (CEC)). Full text, updated daily. Contains press release material from the EC Spokesman's Service.

SCAD. On Eurobases (Commission of European Communities (CEC)). Updated weekly in English, French, and German. Contains over 100,000 citations to articles, publications, and documents covering the EC.

Spearhead. On F. T. Profile and Data-Star. Full text, updated monthly in English. Summarizes measures and legislative changes in 1992 rules.

Europe—General

Company information means that company name, address, phone, fax and telex number, type of business, products or services, number of employees, parents and subsidiaries, and names and position of top executives are given. When additional company information, especially financial data, is provided, it will be noted. These databases are written in English unless otherwise indicated.

ABC Europe Production Europex. On Data-Star and FIZ Technik. Two reference databases updated quarterly: EURE in English and EURD in German. Contain company information, plus association memberships, sales representatives, banks, and capital, on over 149,000 exporting manufacturing firms in 32 countries.

Datastream. On Datastream International Ltd. Ten databases, both full text and numeric, updated daily in English, French, and German: (1) Company Accounts, (2) Company Shareholdings, (3) Stock Market Performance and Measurement, (4) Economic and Industrial Indicators, (5) Exchange Rates, (6) Commodities, (7) Share Indexes, (8) International and Company News, (9) Financial Futures, and (10) Fixed Income Securities. Covers companies and industries in the United States, United Kingdom, France, Germany, Hong Kong, The Netherlands, Switzerland, Japan, and Canada.

D&B—European: Dun's Market Identifiers. On Dialog. Updated quarterly. Contains company directory information on over 1.5 million European companies.

Delphes. On G. Cam Serveur, Dialog, and Data-Star. Updated weekly. Contains 480,000 citations to literature on French and international economics, markets, products, and companies.

Dow Jones International News. On Dow Jones News/Retrieval. Full text, updated daily. Contains business, financial, and economic news, analyses, commentaries, and statistics on international events that affect business, plus news on 6,000 firms worldwide and developments in international stock, bond, currency, precious metals, and petroleum markets.

Dunsprint Worldwide. On Dun & Bradstreet Europe Ltd. Updated continuously. Contains D&B Business Information Reports on 16 million companies: company information, financial data for three years, P&Ls, dividends, retained earnings, stock issues, projected sales, company payment history, and credit ratings.

ECLATX. On Questel. Updated monthly. Contains all codes classified in the European Patent Office.

European Patents Register (EPAT). On European Patent Office and Questel.

Updated weekly in English, French, and German. Contains bibliographic and legal status information on over 300,000 European patent applications, plus 100,000 patents dating from 1978.

Extel International Financial Cards. On Dialog, Data-Star, Mead Data Central, Inc., and FT Profile. Updated weekly. Covers 7,500 UK listed firms, Unlisted Securities Market, Third Market companies, international and unquoted UK firms. Contents include: registration information and registrars; all known offices; organizational data, including subsidiaries and joint ventures; share capital data; dividend information; price history; P&Ls and balance sheets over five years; summaries of all text statements; UK stock exchange classification; CUSIP number; SEDOL number.

Extel International News Cards. On Dialog, Data-Star, Mead Data Central, Inc., and FT Profile. Equivalent to compilation of one week's news about firms covered in Extel International Financial Cards. Includes all companies on primary, secondary, and tertiary markets of the London Stock Exchange, 2,000 unquoted U.K. companies, and 2,500 non-U.K. firms.

Financial Times Abstracts. On Dialog, Data-Star, and FT Profile. Updated daily on Data-Star, weekly on Dialog. Contains about 396,000 citations to company and business information published in the *Financial Times.*

Foreign Trade and ECON Abstracts. On RCC-IVEV Information Services (EVPA). Updated monthly. Written in English with titles in original language. Contains 210,000 abstracted citations to literature on economics, trade, markets, and management.

Global Report. On Globe Information Services—Info Globe On-line and Citicorp Database Services. Seven

continuously updated full text and alphanumeric databases: (1) Foreign Exchange, (2) Country Reports, (3) Money Markets, (4) Bonds, (5) Companies, (6) Industries, and (7) News. Contain worldwide business and financial information.

Infomat International Business. On Data-Star (EBUS), Gesellschaft fur Betriebswirtschaft liche Information mbH, and Dialog. Updated weekly. Contains over 900,000 summaries of business news from more than 600 worldwide publications. Business sectors include automobile, transportation, science and technology, electronics and engineering, chemicals, health care and pharmaceuticals, financial services, and information technology and telecommunications. Sources include newspapers, bank reports, economics and business journals, and trade and professional magazines.

Investext. On Dialog, Data-Star, and others. Updated weekly. Contains over 320,000 analysts' reports on companies and industries in Australia, Canada, Europe, Japan, and the United States: capital expenditures, earnings analyses, debt structure, profit and loss, production and shipment estimates (on 2,600 European firms), as well as industry overviews and statistics.

Kompass Europe. On Dialog and Kompass On-line (Reed Information Services Ltd.).

McCarthy Press Cuttings Service. On FT Profile. Updated daily in Dutch, English, French, German, and Spanish. Contains over 900,000 articles on companies and industries from over 70 newspapers and business periodicals worldwide.

McGraw-Hill Publications On-Line. On Dialog, Mead Data Central, Inc., and Dow Jones News/Retrieval. Updated daily. Covers business and financial news stories—mergers, acquisitions, takeovers, stock prices and exchanges, and economic indicators—from McGraw-Hill news sources.

Moody's Corporate News— International. On Dialog. Updated weekly. Contains business news and financial information on 5,000 public and private firms in 100 countries. Includes manufacturers, financial institutions, investment trusts, public utilities, and shipping companies.

Newsline. On Reuters Information Services. Updated daily. Contains headlines and citations to the current week's news items in 38 U.K., French, German, and Swiss daily, Sunday, and financial papers. Covers business, economics, and the EC. (More complete text available 4 to 7 days later on Reuters Textline.)

PAIS International (Public Affairs Information Service). On Data-Star, Dialog, and others. Updated quarterly in English, French, German, Italian, Portuguese, and Spanish. Contains about 385,000 citations to literature on economics, business, finance, banking, government, court decisions, statistics, political science, and international relations.

PIERS (Port Import Export Reporting Service). On Journal of Commerce Inc.

PTS F&S Indexes. On Data-Star, Dialog, and others.

PTS Promt. On Dialog, Data-Star, Nexis (Mead Data Central, Inc.), Questel, FT Profile, and others.

PTS U.S. Forecasts and PTS International Forecasts. On Data-Star (PTFC) and Dialog. Updated monthly. Contains citations and data from business, financial, and trade publications.

Reuters Country Reports. On Reuters Ltd. Updated daily. Contains news and analyses of business and political conditions around the world, plus daily reports on banking, finance, stock exchange, industry, agriculture, etc., activities within 190 countries. Provides biographies of leading political and business figures.

Reuters Textline. On Dialog and Data-Star.

Tradstat (World Trade Statistics Database). On Data-Star. Updated daily. Contains over 50 million time series on imports and exports of 65,000 commodities and products among 16 major trading countries. Reports on products and commodities include: reporting country, value of shipment, weights, alternative volume unit, price, month, and cumulative year-to-date figures. Data come from customs offices and national statistical organizations.

Worldscope. On Lexis, Bridge Information Systems, Inc., FactSet Data Systems, Inc., and Dow Jones News/ Retrieval. Updated monthly. Contains financial profiles and stock performance data for more than 10,000 of the world's largest corporations. Includes: key officers; number of shareholders and common shares; listing exchanges; net income; sales and asset figures in US dollars; operating summary; balance sheets for four years; sources and uses of funds; growth rates; financial ratios; international business summary; stock data for most widely traded issue available to foreign investors; and accounting practices.

WPI (World Patents Index). On Dialog, Orbit Search Service, and Questel. See description in Section II.

France

France has the most accessible videotex market in the world. Its unique integrated telephone–computer system, Minitel, is found in many French homes. If you are in France, basic company information can be obtained by simply dialing the Registre at 36-29-11-11, and typing in, on the computer keyboard, the name of the company you are researching. More detailed information regarding companies, including their current activities and financial status, can be obtained by dialing the Greffe du Tribunal (see Chapter 7). You can then be connected directly with the city court where your target company is registered. Numerous databases can be accessed through this system. The databases listed below are written in French unless otherwise indicated.

Agora. On G.CAM Serveur and Questel. Updated daily in English and French. Contains over 350,000 news items on French and international economics, financial developments, the EC, industries, agriculture, energy, business negotiations, and enterprises. Includes AECO.

BODACC (Bulletin Officiel des Annonces Civiles et Commerciales). On Questel and G.CAM Serveur. Updated daily. Contains over 1.2 million announcements regarding mergers, acquisitions, reorganizations, and liquidations, taken from the printed *BODACC*.

Delphes. On G.Cam Serveur, Dialog, and Data-Star. Updated weekly. Contains 480,000 citations, from French and international periodicals, on French and international economics, markets, industrial and service sectors, products, and companies.

Dun & Bradstreet France. On Data-Star. Updated periodically. Contains company information on 220,000 French companies with more than ten employees; includes import/export volume.

Essor. On Questel. Updated annually. Contains company information on 160,000 French firms, including turnover statistics, middle management executives, and legal and administrative information.

FPAT. On Questel. Updated weekly. Contains references to 847,000 French patents.

FIRMEXPORT/FIRMIMPORT. On G.CAM Serveur and Data-Star. Updated weekly. Contains company information on 37,000 firms involved in international trade; gives company location and size, names of principals, products.

INPI Société 3. On O. R. Télématique. Updated periodically. Contains 1.9 million time series of balance sheet data, taken from the INPI, on 470,000 French firms.

Noriane. On Questel and FIZ Technik. Updated monthly in French and English. Contains 60,000 citations to French and international industrial standards, building specifications, technical documents, and EC regulations.

Qui Décide en France. On G.CAM Serveur. Updated every two months. Contains company information on 90,000 firms.

Téléfirm. On G.Cam Serveur and Data-Star. Updated weekly. Contains company information, which comes from the Chambres de Commerce et d'Industrie de Paris, on 1.4 million French firms.

Transin. On Questel. Primarily in English, with some records in French, German, Italian, and Spanish. Contains 3,500 descriptions of requests or offers for transferable technologies, including new products, processes, and techniques.

Germany

These databases are written in German unless otherwise indicated.

ABC der Deutschen Wirtschaft. On Data-Star and FIZ Technik. Two databases updated quarterly, one in English (ABCE) and one in German (ABCD). Contain company information on 80,000 German manufacturing companies, including sales representatives and banks.

BDI German Industry. On Data-Star (BDIE), FIZ Technik (BDID and BDIE), and GENIOS Wirtschaftsdatenbanken. Two databases updated annually, one in English (BDIE) and one in German (BDID). Contain company information on 22,000 German manufacturers, including financial data such as capital and sales volume.

Creditreform-Online. On Bertelsmann InformationsService, Data-Star, GENIOS Wirtschaftsdatenbanken, and others. Updated daily (quarterly on Data-Star). Contains credit information on over 1.7 million joint stock and individual trading companies in Germany. Financial data include income, obligations, property and equipment, warehouse stocks, loan payment records, and credit ratings.

Firmen-Info-Bank (FIB). On AZ Bertelsmann GmbH and Bertelsmann InformationsService. Updated quarterly. Contains company information, including financial data, on 50,000 German firms with minimum of DM 20 million in sales.

Hoppenstedt Germany. On Data-Star (HOPE), Dialog, GENIOS Wirtschaftsdatenbanken, FT Profile, and Gesellschaft fur Betriebswirtschaft lichte Information. Updated quarterly. Contains company information, including financial data, bank accounts, and associations, on 50,000 German companies (and their branches) with a minimum of 20 employees and DM 2 million in sales.

WER LIEFERT WAS? On Bertelsmann InformationsService GmbH (DWLW and EWLW), Data-Star (WLWE), FIZ Technik (WLWD and WLWE), and GENIOS Wirtschaftsdatenbanken. Two databases updated quarterly, one in English (Who Supplies What?) (WLWE) and one in German (WLWD). Contain company information on 105,000 German, 12,000 Austrian, and 13,000 Swiss manufacturers and service companies.

Italy

These databases are written in Italian unless otherwise indicated.

Dati Anagrafici di Imprese Italiane. On GIANO and Sistema Informatico della Confindustria. Information put out by Confindustria, the Italian business and industry federation, is updated twice a month on member firms, and annually for nonmember firms. Contains company information on over

350,000 Italian firms, but separate files of member and nonmember firms are available.

Dati Anagrafici di Imprese Lombarde. On SIRIO. Updated periodically. Contains company information, including legal and banking representatives, trademarks, and patents, on 14,000 firms located in the Lombardy region.

Indici dei Bollettini Busarl (SIBB). On CERVED. Updated twice a month. Contains references to public reports filed by 250,000 joint-stock and limited-liability companies in Italy, gathered from journal indexes of Italian regional Chambers of Commerce.

Pagine Gialle Electroniche. On SARITEL S.p.A. Updated twice a month,

on same schedule as Italian Yellow Pages. Contains 250,000 advertisements and mailing information on over 1.8 million firms.

Sistema Archivio Bilanci Riclassificati (Sabri). On CERVED. Updated annually. Contains balance sheet data for the top 35,000 Italian joint-stock and limited-liability firms.

Sistema Ditte Operanti con L'Estero (SDOE). On CERVED. Updated monthly. Contains company information, including turnover and growth figures and import and export data, on 70,000 Italian companies that trade internationally.

United Kingdom

Examiner. On Extel Financial Ltd. Several files; updated periodically: Company News has information on leading U.K. and international companies; Foreign Exchange and Money Markets has exchange and deposit rates; Securities-U.K. has full market reports; and Miscellaneous covers major news stories.

Exstat. On Interactive Data Corp., Nihon Keizai Shimbun America, Inc. Updated weekly. Contains historical and current financial data on over 3,000 U.K., European, Australian, and Japanese firms, including P&Ls, assets, earnings, and dividends.

Extel International Financial Cards. See Europe—General listing.

Extel International News Cards. See Europe—General listing.

ICC British Company Financial Datasheets. On Dialog, Data-Star, and ICC Information Group Ltd. Updated

weekly. Provides company information and financial data on more than 1.2 million companies in the U.K.

ICC International Business Research. On Dialog. Updated weekly. Contains three subfiles that provide stockbroker research reports, company accounts, and industry reports.

ICC Key Notes Market Research. On Data-Star, ICC Information Group Ltd., and FT Profile. Updated periodically. Contains reports covering companies and trends in over 220 industries.

ICC Stockbroker Research Reports. On Data-Star, ICC Information Group Ltd., and FT Profile. Updated weekly. Contains 17,000 U.K. stockbrokers' analyses of trends in the securities industry, plus financial data on companies.

Jordan Company Information. On Data-Star, ESA-IRS, Jordan & Sons

Ltd., and FT Profile. Updated weekly. Contains company information on 2.5 million public and private U.K. firms, including financial statements, income reports, outstanding charges, mortgages, evaluations of key personnel, and directors and shareholders of newly registered companies.

Jordan's Shareholder Service. On ESA-IRS and Jordan & Sons Ltd. Updated monthly. Contains information from annual reports to shareholders of 2,000 publicly quoted and Unlisted Securities Market firms.

Key British Enterprises Financial Performance. On Data-Star. Updated monthly. Contains company information on the top 25,000 U.K. firms as determined by annual sales. Includes Companies Registration Office number of each firm.

Kompass UK. On Dialog, Kompass On-line (Reed Information Services Ltd.). Updated quarterly. Contains company information on 155,000 U.K. firms, including financial data.

MSI Market Report Series. On FT Profile. Updated periodically. Contains over 150 market reports providing in-depth analyses of individual industries.

Asia/Pacific Rim

Asia/Pacific Rim—General

Asian Economic News. On NewsNet, Inc. Updated weekly on NewsNet. Covers economic news in Far East, excluding Japan; World Bank and IMF loans to newly industrializing countries; overseas relief aid; labor and trade conditions; and weather catastrophes. For ASEAN, covers country reports, trade policy, debts, and loans. Sources include Kyodo news staff in South Korea, China, Taiwan, Thailand, Philippines, Hong Kong, Singapore, and Malaysia; TV news; and Asia-Pacific newspapers.

Asia-Pacific. On Dialog. Updated biweekly. Covers business, economics, and industry in PAC RIM nations, East Asia, Southeast Asia, Indian subcontinent, Middle East, Australia, and Pacific Islands. Sources include U.S. and international newspapers, conference proceedings, press releases, and monographs. Gives information on corporate finances, joint ventures, diversification, operations, new products, key executives, and strategic planning. Over 1,800 companies indexed by company name, location, parent company, number of subsidiaries, joint ventures, and stock holdings.

Asian Political News. On NewsNet, Inc., PTS Newsletter Database (Data-Star). Updated weekly in English. News articles dealing with political issues. Source: Kyodo news-gathering staff in Asia.

Asian Wall Street Journal, The. On Dow Jones News/Retrieval. Updated weekly. Citations and abstracts excerpted from the daily edition published in Tokyo. Covers business and financial news.

Country Report Services. On Data-Star, NewsNet, and Nexis (Mead Data Central). Updated monthly in English. Contains full text of reports covering economic and political conditions for 130 countries. Includes sociodemographic data, import/export data, annual economic indicators, GDP, per-capita income, real growth rates, unemployment rates, inflation rates, capital investment, and national accounts. Provides an Economic Performance Profile, indicating each country's position relative to the others.

Datastream. See Europe—General listing.

Dow Jones International News. See Europe—General listing.

DRI Asian Forecast. On DRI/ McGraw-Hill; Information Plus. Updated quarterly. Contains annual historical and forecast time series on economics of 11 Asian countries. Covers GDP by type of expenditures, inflation rates, income, population, trade, balance of payments, industrial production, foreign debt, money supply, and currency exchange rates. Forecasts are linked to DRI projections for other world economies. Sources include IMF International Financial Statistics.

DRI International Cost Forecasting. On DRI/McGraw-Hill. Updated quarterly. Covers projections of commodity-specific price indexes and industry-specific wages for selected developed and emerging economies. Approximately 1,800 time series. Includes: Japan, South Korea, and Taiwan.

Dunsprint Worldwide. See Europe—General listing.

East Asia Express Contacts. On News-Net, Dialog, and Data-Star. Updated daily on Dialog and weekly on Data-Star. Full text, in English, of *East Asia Express,* a newsletter containing business news on East Asian countries and their foreign trading partners. Includes business, economic, and financial news. Reports on contracts to foreign companies and updates reports of contract opportunities.

East Asian Executive Reports. On Nexis and Lexis (Mead Data Central, Inc.). Updated monthly. Contains full text of journal covering financial, legal,

and practical aspects of conducting business in 15 East Asian countries. Includes advertising, arbitration, banking, franchising, government contracting, insurance, leasing, taxation, and technology transfer for agriculture, communications, mining, and so on.

Financial Times Abstracts. See Europe—General listing.

Findex. On Dialog.

Foreign Trade and Econ Abstracts. See Europe—General listing.

Global Report. See Europe—General listing.

Infomat International Business. See Europe—General listing.

INPADOC Data Base (IDB). On Dialog, Orbit Search Service, and STN International. Updated weekly. Contains over 19 million citations to all patents issued in 56 countries and by the European Patent Office and the World Intellectual Property Organization. Titles in original languages.

International On-Line Database (INTLINE). On WEFA Group. Updated daily in English. Contains international macroeconomic data. Covers national incomes, product accounts, industrial production, business surveys, labor and wages, consumer and wholesale prices, stocks, deliveries, retail and wholesale trade, money and banking, interest and exchange rates, foreign trade, government finance, and balance of payments.

Investext. See Europe—General listing.

Kompass Asia/Pacific. On Dialog.

Monthly Asia. On WEFA Group. Updated twice a week. Covers 900 monthly time series of economic data on Asian countries: inflation, exchange rates, balance of payments, financial indicators, exports, imports, trade balances, employment indicators, and industrial production. Transformations and forecasts are available.

Moody's Corporate News— International. See Europe—General listing.

PAIS International (Public Affairs Information Service). See Europe— General listing.

PIERS (Port Import Export Reporting Service). See Europe—General listing.

PTS F&S Indexes. See Europe— General listing.

PTS Newsletter Database. On Data-Star (PTFC) and Dialog. Updated daily. Contains full text of articles from over 500 business and trade newsletters covering 40 industry areas. A menu-access version provides easy retrieval of the latest issue of a newsletter.

PTS Promt. See Europe—General listing.

PTS U.S. Forecasts and PTS International Forecasts. See Europe—General listing.

Reuters Country Reports. See Europe —General listing.

Reuters Textline. On Data-Star and Dialog. Contains articles in English from *Bangkok Post, BBC Monitoring Service: Far East, Singapore's Business Times, Japan Economic Journal, JIJI Press Newswire, Korea Economic Daily, Reuters News Service, South*

China Morning Post, and *Xinhua News Agency.* Abstracts from *Asian Wall Street Journal, Malaysia's Business Times,* and *Malaysian Business.*

Southeast Asia High Tech Review. On Data-Star and Dialog. Updated monthly in English. Contains full text of *Southeast Asia High Tech Review,* a monthly newsletter on high-tech industries in southeast Asia.

Taiwan On-Line Business Data Services. On F.B.R. Data Base Inc. Updated daily in English. Contains five files of Asian business and corporate information: (1) Newscan—headlines and citations from over 70 Chinese-language newspapers and periodicals, covering Taiwan, Hong Kong, South Korea, and the People's Republic of China; (2) Directory of Companies— information on 40,000 Taiwanese firms with identification information; (3) Corporate Reports—financial information on 20,000 of Taiwan's largest corporations; (4) Company Product/Technology—data on Taiwan's manufacturing industry; (5) Importers—lists of Taiwanese agents for overseas suppliers.

Tradstat (World Trade Statistics Database). See Europe—General listing.

Worldscope. See Europe—General listing.

WPI (World Patents Index). See Europe—General listing.

People's Republic of China

China Information Bulletin Service. On G-Search Corp. Updated daily in Japanese. Contains summaries of major articles from newspapers published in the People's Republic of China (PRC).

CHINALAW. On WESTLAW (West Publishing Company). Updated periodically in English. Contains national and provincial laws and regulations governing foreign business activity in the

PRC. Covers 143 national, municipal, provincial, and other legislative bodies, including National People's Congress, State Council, and similar governing organizations.

The Free China Journal. On Data-Times. Updated twice a week in English. Contains full text of news items, feature articles, and editorials from newspaper of the same name.

Xinhua English Language and Service. On NewsNet, Inc. Updated daily. Full text, in English, of English-language news reports from the Kinhua (New China) News Agency, the national news agency of the PRC. Covers political, economic, and cultural affairs in China, as well as other international news relating to China.

Chinese Patent Abstracts. On Orbit and Dialog. Updated every two weeks. Contains patent abstracts produced by the Chinese Patent Office. Gives details of patent applications published under the patent law of the PRC. English-language abstracts are included for all applications filed by Chinese applicants. Information about equivalent non-Chinese patent publications (patent families) is also included. Searchable by inventor name or patent assignee. Almost 50,000 patents on file.

Japan

AERA Database. On G-Search Corp. and Nikkei Telecom. Updated with about 50 articles a week. Contains current national and international news and social events. Text is in Japanese. Originates from *AERA*, a magazine.

Asahi Shimbun On-Line Database. On COM-NET (Asahi on-line database), Nexis (Mead Data Central), and FT Profile. Updated daily. Preliminary reports, in Japanese, of articles scheduled to appear in the newspaper's evening edition.

Asia-Pacific. See Asia/Pacific Rim— General listing.

COSMOS 1. On COSMOSNET (Teikoku Databank, Ltd.). Provides financial data on 260,000 small- and medium-size companies in terms of financial reliability, discovering potential clients, and conducting management analysis through company comparisons. Sources from 80 branch offices.

COSMOS 2. On COSMOSNET (Teikoku Databank, Ltd.). Gives company and executive information from corporate financial reports, balance sheets, P&Ls, and data gathered through 80 branch offices. Lists 950,000 firms.

COSMOS 3. On COSMOSNET (Teikoku Databank, Ltd.). Japanese directory containing personal data on 550,000 executives and other important figures in Japan. Includes address, date of birth, official post, education, family, and employment history.

Company Credit Reports (CCR). On COSMOSNET (Teikoku Databank, Ltd.). Contains company profiles and credit information, in Japanese, on 220,000 firms in Tokyo area. Includes name, address, phone, year founded, principal activities, number of employees, branch locations, suppliers and customers, company history, credit ratings, outstanding loans, liaabilities, sales, and P&L. Gives textual analyses of company's sales prospects and operations.

DRI Japanese Forecast. On DRI/McGraw-Hill. Updated five times a year. Covers the Japanese economy; wages and unemployment; trade; demographics; interest rates; business profits and investment; money supply; stock prices; exchange rates; wholesale and consumer price indexes; and housing starts. Sources include DRI Japanese Model, IMF International Financial Statistics Data Bank, and NIKKEI Macro Economics Statistical Data Bank.

Japan Computer Industry Scan. On NewsNet, Inc. Updated daily (weekly on NewsNet). Contains new developments in Japanese computer industry, including R&D, market share, licensing agreements with non-Japanese manufacturers, and the Japanese market for U.S. computer products. Includes charts.

Japan Consumer Electronics Scan. On NewsNet, Inc. Updated daily (weekly on NewsNet). Covers new electronics products from Japan: price availability, and target markets.

Japan Economic Daily (JED). On Dow Jones News/Retrieval. Updated daily in English. Contains newswire items on Japanese and Far East Asian business, industry, economics, and finance. Includes developments in high tech, government policies, summaries of Tokyo Stock Exchange activity, commodity prices, and exchange rates. Gives weekly schedule of meetings, conferences, and government hearings, and monthly compilation of economic indicators.

Japan Economic Newswire Plus. On Dialog and Nexis (Mead Data Central, Inc.). Updated daily. Contains news stories and feature articles covering politics and socioeconomic issues in Japan and other Pacific Rim countries. Includes information on Tokyo Stock Exchange, commodities listings, corporate financial results, government statements and notices of tariff/duty revisions, commercial code variations, and government procurement and bidding information. Covers automobile, electronics, energy, high tech, robotics, defense, and manufacturing industries.

Japan Energy Scan. On NewsNet, Inc. Updated daily (weekly on NewsNet). Contains text of weekly newsletter of same name.

Japan/Marc. On University of Tsukuba Science Information Processing Center. Updated weekly in English and Japanese (Kanji, Romanji, Kana). Books, periodicals, and other Japanese and Western materials received by the Library. Over 265,000 records.

Japan Policy and Politics. On NewsNet, Inc. Covers Japan's government, laws, regulations, and politics.

Japan Semiconductor Scan. On NewsNet, Inc. Updated quarterly. Covers present trends in semiconductors, as well as U.S.–Japan competitive news. Includes policy discussions presented by various trade associations, and analyses of market share data.

Japan Telecommunications Scan. On NewsNet, Inc. Updated daily or weekly, depending on the specific database. Contains news on Nippon Telegraph and Telephone (NTT) activities in Japanese telecommunications, technological research, development of equipment, contract awards, and policy statements.

Japan Weekly Monitor. On NewsNet, Inc. Updated weekly. Covers summary data and analyses of Tokyo Stock Exchange and Tokyo foreign exchange market activities; news of U.S. and Japanese trade and government relations; and information on trends and the U.S.–Japanese economy. Includes yen/dollar activities, daily spot quotations, and trade stats.

Japanese Aviation News: WING. On NewsNet, Inc. Updated weekly. Covers commercial aviation, traffic stats, industrial news, scientific news, and concerns of aviation and aerospace industries in Japan.

Japanese Economic Situation (NICO). On GSi-ECO. Updated biweekly. Contains 400 monthly and quarterly time series of macroeconomic Japanese data, including (of particular note to the intelligence analyst) industry production, inventories and shipments, labor and unemployment, household income, public finance, external trade, balance of payments, and overseas investments.

JAPINFO (Japanese Information on Scientific and Technical Information). On Data-Star and FIZ Technik. Updated monthly in English. Contains over 50,000 citations to scientific and technical literature published in Japan. Covers automotive engineering, aviation and space technology, biology, biotechnology, chemistry, communications, electronics, energy, engineering, environment, food and agriculture, information systems, medicine, refrigeration and heating, robotics, textiles, and transportation. Sources: over 80 institutions and organizations, journals, and symposia.

JAPIO. On Dialog, Orbit On-line, and Questel. Updated monthly in English. Most comprehensive English-language database on Japanese patents. Covers over 4 million patent applications (not patents) recorded since 1976. Includes title, inventor, patent holder, application date and number, patent number,

publication date, Japanese Classification Number, and International Patent Classification System code. Also includes Derwent patent and priority numbers.

JETRO-ACE. On G-Search Corp. Updated weekly in Japanese. Provides summaries of economic and trade condition reports on approximately 100 countries, as issued by JETRO overseas offices.

JICST File on Current Science and Technology Research in Japan. On JICST (Japanese Information Center of Science and Technology) On-line Information System. Directory updated annually in Japanese. Covers current scientific and technical research projects conducted by public labs and research organizations in Japan.

JICST File on Medical Science in Japan. On JICST (Japanese Information Center of Science and Technology) On-line Information System. Updated monthly in Japanese. Covers Japanese medical science and related subjects. Contains over 1.2 million citations. Entries include author, address, titles, titles of secondary sources, volumes and issue numbers, pages, publication date, number of cited references, report number, language, type of source, number of tables and figures.

JICST File on Science and Technology. On JICST (Japanese Information Center of Science and Technology) On-line Information System. Updated monthly in Japanese. Covers Japanese and foreign chemistry and chemical industries; earth science, mining, and metallurgy; electronics and electrical engineering; management science; civil, mechanical, nuclear, and systems engineering; architecture; energy; life sciences; and pure and applied physics. Contains more than 6 million citations concerning international science and technology.

JICST File on Science, Technology, and Medicine in Japan. On STN International and JICST (Japanese Information Center of Science and Technology) Online Information System. Updated monthly in English. Over 1 million citations, with abstracts. Covers Japanese scientific and technical literature in most scientific disciplines. Sources: 4,500 journals and serials, conference proceedings, and technical reports.

Jiji Press Ticker Service. On NewsNet and Nexis (Mead Data Central, Inc.). Continuously updated. Covers Japanese politics, economics, and industry activities. Sources include Jiji Press Wire Service.

Jiji Securities Data Service (JSD). On GE Information Services (GEIS). Provides current information on 1,600 stocks listed on the Tokyo Stock Exchange and the New York and American Stock Exchanges.

JIP/Areal Marketing Database (JIP/AMD). On JIPNET (Japan Information Processing Service Co., Ltd.). Text, in Japanese, provides Japanese demographic information. Includes data ranging from economics, agriculture, and product consumption to leisure activities.

Kyodo News Service. On NewsNet, Data-Star, and Delphi. Updated daily. Covers political, economic, and trade news that affects Japan. Includes Pacific Basin news, trade talk issues from the Japanese vantage point, and Japanese life-style and feature articles.

Legal Precedents Regarding Intellectual Property Rights. On G-Search Corp. Updated monthly in Japanese. Contains text of 6,000 legal precedents concerning intellectual property rights. Includes information on laws

pertaining to patents, design, actual use, marketing, copyright, and similar topics.

Market-Search. On G-Search Corp. Updated daily in Japanese. Provides marketing information on all Japanese industries.

NEEDS Databases. NEEDS (Nikkei Economic Electronic Databank System—Nihon Keizai Shimbun, Inc.) maintains the following databases:

- *NEEDS—Company.* On NEEDS. Updated monthly in Japanese. Contains financial data on 17,000 public and private Japanese firms. Includes name, address, numbers, date established, SIC code, key executives' names, corporate income, sales volume, and major shareholders.

- *NEEDS—Economy.* On DRI/McGraw-Hill and NEEDS. Updated monthly. Contains 11,000 monthly, quarterly, semiannual, and annual time series on the economic, demographic, and financial indicators of the Japanese economy.

- *NEEDS—Energy.* On NEEDS. Updated monthly in Japanese and English. Covers energy usage.

- *NEEDS—IR: IEE File.* On NEEDS. Updated weekly in Japanese. Contains 50,000 citations to articles covering energy and energy-related topics in 60 leading newspapers and journals worldwide.

- *NEEDS—IR: Joint File.* On NEEDS. Updated monthly in Japanese. Contains 100,000 citations to Japanese literature on business, economics, and management. Covers management, industrial, and general business journals and reports.

- *NEEDS—IR: Nikkei File.* On NEEDS. Updated daily in Japanese. Contains over 600,000 citations, with some abstracts, to articles from four daily newspapers: (1) *Japan Economic Daily,* (2) *NIKKEI Industrial Daily,* (3) *NIKKEI Marketing Journal,* and (4) *Chemical Daily News;* and six monthly journals: (1) *NIKKEI Business,* (2) *NIKKEI Computer,* (3) *NIKKEI Electronics,* (4) *NIKKEI Mechanical,* (5) *NIKKEI Architecture,* and (6) *NIKKEI Medical.*

New Era: Japan. On NewsNet, Inc. Updated biweekly. Provides current information on the Japanese telecommunications industry, including research and development, equipment, systems applications, database developments, and detailed procurement needs of Japanese firms.

Nikkan Kogyo File on New Technology and Products in Japan. On JICST (Japan Information Center of Science and Technology) On-line Information System. Updated biweekly in Japanese. Contains articles from the *Nikkan Kogyo Shimbun* (Industrial Daily News) on new products and technologies. Covers biotechnology, energy, engineering, science, and ocean and space science and technology.

Nikkei Shimbun News Database. On NEEDS. Updated weekly in Japanese. Contains full text of *Nikkei Shimbun, Nikkei Kinyui Shimbun, Nikkei Ryutsu Shimbun,* and *Nikkei Sangyo Shimbun*—newspapers covering business, financial, and industrial news.

Nikkei Telecom II Japan News & Retrieval Data. On NEEDS. Continuously updated in English. Covers the economy, stocks and bonds, corporate financial data, and related news publications of Japan. Serves as English-language equivalent to NEEDS. Includes current and historical data, and categorizes text into various sections and files. Excellent database for the analyst conducting a retrospective.

Nikkei Weekly. On Nexis and NEEDS. Updated weekly. Contains full text of English-language weekly version of *Nihon Keizai Shimbun,* a daily economics newspaper.

Nomura Research Database. On Quotron Systems, Inc. Updated weekly. Gives information on over 1,000 companies listed on Tokyo Stock Exchange. Includes company profiles, summary financial data, sales, and other financial analyses.

NRI/E Japan Economic & Business Database. On Interactive Data Corporation and The WEFA Group. Updated continuously. Covers Japan's economy and business, including economic outlook, national accounts, national income statistics, foreign trade and balance of payments, labor, money and banking, production and shipments by specific industries, stocks and bonds, interest rates, and general economic forecasts and reviews. Sources: Japanese government agencies and trade associations, such as the Ministry of International Trade and Industry, the Ministry of Finance, and the Bank of Japan.

NTT Topics. On NewsNet, Inc. Updated weekly. Reports on the activities of the Nippon Telegraph & Telephone Public Corporation of Japan (NTT). Covers the latest technological developments and marketing in the telecommunications and electronics field.

PATOLIS (Patent On-Line Information Service). On Japan Patent Information Organization (JAPIO). Updated monthly in Japanese (except for IN-PADOC). Contains citations to all patents issued since 1955 and patent applications issued since 1979, plus references to trademark applications since 1902.

Techno-Search. On G-Search Corp. Updated weekly in Japanese. Contains titles and abstracts of articles appearing in five major Japanese industrial and engineering newspapers. Includes information on new products, R&D developments, and marketing trends in Japanese industries, including the chemical and computer industries.

Teikoku Databank: Japanese Companies. On Dialog and Nikkei Telecom. Updated monthly. Contains profiles of over 158,000 Japanese firms with overseas dealings. Gives CEO's name, address, and phone; Japanese SIC number; number of employees; banking relationships; credit ratings; sales ranking; declared income; and sales, profits, and dividends for latest reporting period.

Tokyo Financial Wire (TFW). On Lexis (Mead Data Central, Inc.). Updated daily. Contains full text on over 31,000 Japanese financial, economic, industrial, and corporate news articles. Covers news on the Tokyo stock, bond, foreign exchange, and money markets, plus general business news.

Sources: Japanese business and financial newspapers.

TSR-BIGS. On NIFTY-Serve (NIFTY Corp.). Updated monthly in Japanese. Contains corporate data on 500,000 companies located in Japan. Includes firm name, geographical codes, categories of business, stockholders, information on suppliers and customers, volume of business, profits, stock exchanges, corporate income, and other corporate news.

TSR-Fines. On Tokyo Shoko Research Ltd. (TSR). Updated monthly in Japanese. Provides financial data on 50,000 Japanese corporations. Organized into five financial statements, including balance sheets, P&Ls, use of profits. Information on three successive financial reporting periods are assembled for comparisons.

Yomiuri Shimbun. On G-Search Corp. and NIFTY-Serve (NIFTY Corp.). Updated weekly in Japanese. Gives articles from *Yomiuri Shimbun,* one of Japan's leading national dailies.

Singapore

STOCK EXCHANGE OF SINGAPORE.
Reuters Information Service Inc./
    Data Services Div.
Exchange Tower, Suite 1900
2 First Canadian Place
Toronto, ON, Canada M5X 1E3
416-364-5361

    Updated stock data and Singapore/Kuala Lumpur indexes daily; other

indexes weekly. Gives 400 time series for stocks traded on Singapore exchange; daily trading data; indexes for Singapore and other Asian exchanges, including the *Straits Times* index, *Business Times* index, and stock exchange composite indexes for the Hong Kong, Taiwan, New Zealand, Tokyo, Manila, Bangkok, and Kuala Lumpur exchanges.

Taiwan

Free China Journal, The. On Data-Times. Updated twice a week. Contains news items, feature articles, and editorials from the newspaper of the same name. Covers domestic and international trends and developments.

Taiwan On-Line Business Data Services. See Asia/Pacific Rim—General listing.

Negotiate in a Vortex: The Japanese Approach

LEONARD FULD: Before negotiating with a Japanese company, what kind of competitive analysis must a non-Japanese conduct?

IKUKO ATSUMI: There are two important points you must note:

One, Japanese companies function in an organic and holistic way. The non-Japanese negotiator must therefore understand how his counterpart thinks, as much as the negotiator must know the numbers. It is important to try to harmonize, to understand your Japanese counterpart.

Two, Japanese, in general, take a vortex-style approach to carrying out business. They start from the big picture, gradually moving to a more focused point; and, they do so in a circular manner. Because negotiations should be backed up by thorough research, I recommend assigning a non-Japanese (or a totally bilingual Japanese) to undertake the necessary initial homework in this vortex style.

This vortex-style approach means you must begin with analyzing the industry, including government policies. Next, identify the rank and positioning of the leading competitor, while at the same time checking the competitor's horizontal and vertical *keiretsu* relations and strategic alliances. In addition, you need to examine the following about the company: its future vision (5-year action plan; 10-year goals); *Torishimari-yaku* (the board of directors); and the president.

Study these individuals from every angle—capability, personality, attitude toward your country, business affiliations and networks they may have, and number of years before expected retirement.

If you analyze the entire picture—the financial statements, the products, and the people—with this understanding, you will feel the company as a "living creature" allowing you to compete or work alongside with this company on a long-term basis.

Ikuko Atsumi is President of Intercultural Business Center, Inc., in Framingham, Massachusetts, a training and consulting firm offering customized seminars on doing business in all Asian countries. She formerly served as Associate Professor at Aoyama Gakuin University in Japan, as well as having founded a magazine for Japanese women.

The Future of Databases:
Going Where No Byte Has Gone Before

LEONARD FULD: How do you see the role of the global database producer changing in the coming years with regard to the demand for more specific and more timely corporate information? Do you see database alliances increasing?

PAUL OWEN: The role of the global database producer is changing as we move through the 1990s. Driven by new technologies and increased expectations, new groups of information users are evolving, resulting in rapid change and expansion of the information industry. Search software and interfaces are also evolving in response to these needs, as are delivery systems that provide true "desktop access." The evolution provides both challenges and opportunities for the information industry, which is turning to increased alliances to meet user needs.

During the 1980s, the vast majority of competitor intelligence, product, and market information passed through information professionals such as librarians and on-line specialists. Today, through the direction of top management or Chief Information Officers (CIOs), companies are seeking ways to more broadly distribute important information directly to those who use it. Despite major penetration into major corporations in the '80s, most decision makers are still unaware of the vast information resources available to them through electronic products.

A primary role of the global database producer will be to serve these new and existing markets with critical, timely, and comprehensive information—the type of information that drives informed business decision making. These new end-user needs are function-dependent and focused, placing new demands on information providers.

One such critical application is the sifting of vast amounts of information to identify the few critical pearls of information that answer competitive intelligence questions, all delivered to the electronic mailbox of the business executive.

Alliances among publishers, database providers, search software designers, and database environment providers will increase to meet these needs. We will see linkages among these players to deliver intelligence, not just data, directly to end-users.

Global database producers will provide better, not more, information. Value-added will be accomplished via managed information integration both in individual organizations and through alliances. The information industry will make its valuable content the bulk of the traffic on the information superhighway as information users seek ways to increase productivity and profits.

Paul Owen is Vice President of Corporate Sales and Marketing for the Information Access Company, a major producer of databases for business use, including the Predicasts series of databases.

6 INTERNATIONAL INTELLIGENCE
Research Strategies and Sources

Why do so many businesspeople and journalists still think "foreign" when talking about overseas competitors? Nothing in business is truly foreign anymore. It's "international." Foreign means apart from, separate. Foreign means Us versus Them. If you think "foreign," then you create information barriers—barriers that will make it nearly impossible to track international competition. If you want to develop intelligence on your competition, think about one big market, not another solar system.

This chapter is addressed primarily to readers in the United States, my home country. Readers in other countries can substitute their own home country's name with equal validity. The principles that guide the advice are the same, worldwide.

Here is a scary piece of trivia.

As late as the mid-1980s, only an estimated 7 percent of the 10,000 technical titles published each year in Japan were ever translated, abstracted, or indexed by Western nations.* This means that, although much critical intelligence is being made available through the Japanese themselves, most European and American companies are not taking advantage of the 10,000 or so intelligence opportunities that present themselves each year.

Contrast this fact to conversations I have had with managers at Japanese firms, who attest that staff in their home offices translate virtually all significant English-language business and technical documents for management.

---

*Directory of Japanese Technical Resources in the United States, National Technical Information Service, U.S. Department of Commerce, 1988.

It would be misleading to state that translating documents is all you need do to develop the necessary intelligence on your overseas markets and competition. It is not. But it is a necessary first step—one of many you need to take. This chapter will introduce you to both the basic and the more advanced approaches to developing intelligence on your international competition. These techniques evolved from those used around the globe by my firm for its clients.

The moment you step outside your country to conduct research on another company, you will find many unforeseen language, cultural, and information barriers. To conserve both your time and your budget, you need to follow a commonsense set of information-gathering steps. This chapter discusses each of these steps:

1. Tapping into U.S.-based resources;
2. Overcoming cultural and language barriers;
3. Intelligence maps: Country-specific research strategies and sources.

Inevitably, addresses and telephone numbers for sources listed in this chapter will change over the years. Contact the consulate or embassy for the country in question, and ask for the commercial attaché or information officer. That person should be able to help you track down most of the government offices, as well as many of the publishers listed. You will also find many of the magazines listed in *Ulrich's International Periodical Directory* (R.R. Bowker).

TAPPING INTO U.S.-BASED RESOURCES

In-House Listening Posts

The cardinal rule of international corporate intelligence research is:

The best international intelligence resource is your own organization.

The vast majority of the intelligence you need is probably available from within your own company. Even if your firm does not have offices outside your home-office country, you may still have contacts worldwide through your trade representatives, affiliates, and suppliers. All these groups are extensions of your organization.

Let's take an inventory of some of these home-grown listening posts:

Acquisitions and mergers	Information systems
Advertising	Legal
Credit	Library
Customer service	Marketing
Distribution	Purchasing
Engineering	R&D
Finance	Real estate
Human resources	Sales

Consider these listening posts in three-dimensional, not two-dimensional terms. For example, a salesperson may know a great deal about a particular competitor or a specific technology. But that same salesperson also knows about that competitor by region or by country. Your organization, particularly if it is globally based, has all three informational dimensions: it is (1) competitor-specific, (2) product- or technology-specific, and (3) specific by region or by country.

An International Intelligence Audit

To truly understand the international intelligence resources your company possesses, you need to conduct an *intelligence audit*—an inventory of your company experts and the information resources they have available, which are not cataloged in your company library. In a sense, the audit takes your corporate telephone directory and reindexes it by expertise and knowledge rather than by department. (The auditing process is described in greater detail in Chapter 13 and in *Monitoring the Competition: Find Out What's Really Going On Over There* (Leonard M. Fuld, Wiley, 1988).)

Auditing is a relatively simple process, and you do not have to do it all at once. Take one department or one regional office at a time. Enter the information onto a simple database management program, such as Dbase®, Paradox®, or any number of similar programs.

Tracking Targets' Operations through U.S. Locations

When an overseas, multinational company conducts business in the United States, it leaves information trails. By following the prime intelligence rule, ("Wherever money is exchanged, so is information"), you can follow a target's trail of informational bread crumbs. Be ready to react if it:

- *Enters the United States* and begins promoting its products or services in the business press;
- *Researches the U.S. market* and begins to contact trade associations, advertising agencies, and market research houses;
- *Needs to hire personnel,* through placement of notices in help-wanted ads, with headhunters, and at university recruitment offices;
- *Establishes supplier–distributor relationships;*
- *Exports or imports products* to or from the United States, and the shipping manifests are reported on by firms such as PIERS (see Chapter 11).

The U.S. Government

The federal government has assigned a number of agencies to monitor international companies. Government reports, and the analysts who produce them, can offer you worldwide industry, commodity, and country-specific information, as well as some critical analyses. They can also provide valuable background information on international markets, culture, and governments.

A key source of information is the Securities and Exchange Commission (SEC). At its public reference room in Washington, DC, the SEC maintains company filings, annual reports, and other communications with stockholders of non-U.S. corporations doing business in the United States. If companies trade stock, they must file documents with the SEC. The types of filings and their contents are described in Chapter 3.

The full weight of the U.S. government on international trade originates from the International Trade Administration (ITA), a subagency of the U.S. Department of Commerce. The ITA researches and investigates the impact of imports on U.S. commerce. Although the ITA does not investigate individual companies per se, it does look at a wide variety of industries, commodities, and countries. If your industry has been investigated, there might be information on your target company, but you will have to go in person to the ITA in Washington to review the investigation reports.

The ITA also carries out competitive investigations to measure how competitive U.S. companies are in a particular industry; these cases are called "332 cases." The Unfair Import Investigations Division hears and investigates cases that involve patent infringement and unfair trade practices. These are called "337 cases."

The ITA's country desks in Washington, DC, assist exporters with everything from trade exhibitions and free legal counseling to finding an international banker or freight forwarder. District Export Councils, comprised of experienced American exporters, conduct seminars and counsel exporters on international trade.

ITA country desks can be contacted as follows:

Asia/Pacific Rim		Europe	
ASEAN Desk	202-482-3875	Europe—General	202-482-5638
China	202-482-3583	Belgium/Luxembourg	202-482-5401
Hong Kong	202-482-2462	Denmark	202-482-3254
Indonesia	202-482-3875	France	202-482-8008
Japan	202-482-4527	Germany	202-482-2434/2435
Korea	202-482-4958	Greece	202-482-3945
Malaysia	202-482-3875	Ireland	202-482-4104
Singapore	202-482-3875	Italy	202-482-2177
Taiwan	202-482-4957	Netherlands	202-482-5401
Thailand	202-482-3875	Portugal	202-482-3945
		Spain	202-482-4508
		United Kingdom	202-482-3748

The ITA also offers the following fee-based export marketing services:

Custom import and export statistics. The ITA will customize reports based on U.S. Department of Commerce export/import data, organizing them commodity-by-country or country-by-commodity.

Comparison shopping service. The ITA will answer some basic market and competitive questions on an overseas market's distributors, agents, and sales channels. The fee for this service starts at $500.

World Traders Data Report (WTDR). These are ITA versions of Dun & Bradstreet reports. They are confidential and custom-prepared on non-U.S. companies. Information on the company's reputation, credit references, operations, payment history, trade information, product lines, number of employees, capitalization, sales volume, and key officers can be requested. Each report costs $100. Reports may take up to 90 days to reach you after ordering.

Department of State

The State Department collects information on companies and industries worldwide as part of its development of foreign policy. You may find the country desks to be of the greatest value. Included below are the Asia/Pacific and European desks.

Asia/Pacific Rim		Europe	
China	202-647-6300/6796	Belgium/Luxembourg	202-647-6071
Hong Kong	202-647-9141	Denmark	202-647-5669
Indonesia	202-647-3276	France	202-647-2633
Japan	202-647-2912	Germany	202-647-2005
Korea	202-647-7717	Greece	202-647-6113
Malaysia	202-647-3276/9	Ireland	202-647-6585
Singapore	202-647-3276/8	Italy	202-647-2453
Taiwan	202-647-7711	Netherlands	202-647-6557
Thailand	202-647-7108	Portugal/Spain	202-647-1412
		United Kingdom	202-647-6587

Overseas Private Investment Corporation (OPIC)

This is a matchmaking organization whose job is to promote U.S. investment overseas, particularly in developing countries. It sponsors investment missions, a perfect opportunity for U.S. businesspeople to develop overseas contacts in specific industries. OPIC can be reached at 202-336-8400.

Securities Analysts and Banks

Securities analysts produce rafts of reports on thousands of companies. Be aware, however, that the quality of these reports will vary and that their focus is on finances and stock prices. They may not use much ink writing about the inner workings of a plant, or the technology of a new product. This is where securities analysts' reports usually end and your own research begins. An excellent reference book, *Nelson's Directory of Investment Research* (Nelson Publications), indexes the analysts who cover U.S. and non-U.S. companies. The directory contains the names of nearly 5,000 analysts, covering 60 industry groups. The leading European and Japanese securities firms are well represented.

Most major international banks have U.S. offices in New York City, the financial hub for worldwide business activity. These banks have libraries that house collections of annual reports and other corporate information not available elsewhere.

Some overseas banks serve dual roles—stockbroker as well as financier. German banks, for example, serve in both capacities.

Trade Shows and Conferences

Only a select number of the truly international trade shows are held in the United States. But there are many other shows attended by those who serve specific regional markets. Participants at these shows may never enter the U.S. markets, but their products compete with yours overseas. Refer to Chapter 12 for further information on the strategy of attending a trade show.

Alert your overseas offices to plan appropriately for trade shows. Among the most popular cities for these events are: New York, Chicago, Tokyo, Frankfurt, Hanover, Milan, and Paris.

Business and Trade Groups

Numerous trade groups, throughout the world, promote their own economic interests. For that reason, they are more than happy to provide you with useful information about their markets and the companies in those markets.

The primary source for information on these groups is the *Encyclopedia of Associations* (Gale Research, Inc.). It cross-indexes the trade groups by subject as well as by region.

The following groups may be helpful in assessing your overseas markets and competitors:

European–American Chamber of Commerce

International Monetary Fund (IMF)

Small Business Foundation of America, Inc.

World Trade Centers Association (WTCA)

There are over 100 world trade centers around the globe, in over 40 countries. Their job is to promote trade by helping users locate other companies overseas. WTCA has established an E-mail bulletin board, known as NETWORK, that allows queries to be answered by any of the other world trade centers worldwide.

Chambers of Commerce

Some international chambers of commerce are nothing more than a post office box; others are large organizations with significant information resources. The Italian American Chamber of Commerce, for instance, distributes the CERVED database to the U.S. market. CERVED (see Chapter 5) offers highly specific company data on millions of Italian corporations. For addresses and telephone numbers, refer to *World Chamber of Commerce Directory* (see Chapter 12).

Embassies and Consulates

Embassies and consulates may be the official representatives of their respective countries, but don't always expect them to be knowledgeable on specific markets or companies. They should always be one of your first stops, however, no matter how little information may be provided. Even if the official you speak to does not have the answer, he or she may be able to refer you to another, more valuable source.

Here are some basic tips for obtaining information on overseas markets or competitors from embassies and consulates:

- Try to speak with a native from the country you are investigating, rather than an American employee of the consulate.
- Ask for the commercial or trade division. Inquire whether there is an export board or service or a trade development authority within the consulate. Each country works differently; some have separate industrial development divisions.

- Seek out middle- and lower-level staff; they are usually more responsive to inquiries and don't mind fishing around for your requested information.
- If they are long-term staff members, they can provide a valuable historical perspective and have probably developed an extensive network of contacts and referrals.
- If you are having difficulty getting information from a local consulate, try a consulate at a different location.

Universities

Universities have become the hub for much of the cultural and informational interchange among the United States, Europe, and the Pacific Rim countries. They have formed conferences, received grants for commercial and technical research, sent their professors abroad to study at corporate research institutes and think tanks, and created translation centers. Some of the better known of these programs are listed below.

The Center for Japan–U.S. Business and Economic Studies, New York University. The center is one of the first university-based organizations to focus on understanding the entire spectrum of business and economic relationships between Japan and the United States. It conducts research and offers courses, lectures, conferences, seminars, and publications.

Center for Japanese Studies and East Asian Business Program, University of Michigan. Provides a range of services and training regarding Japan and China, and is involved in transmitting available information to the American business community. The East Asia Business Program was established in 1985 as a joint venture of the Center for Japanese Studies, the Center for Chinese Studies, and the School of Business Administration. Its objective is to strengthen the capacity of American business to compete in and collaborate with the countries in East Asia. Its programs for management and labor promote better understanding of East Asia and offer the specific knowledge needed to cope with current business problems and opportunities.

George Mason University. Conducts programs that focus on changing the current infrastructure for acquiring and disseminating information so that more effective communication and utilization of Japanese technical information can be achieved.

Japan Engineering Leadership Program, The College of Engineering, University of Wisconsin—Madison. Offers courses in Japanese technology, in both the classroom setting and via audiographic teleconferencing. The audiographic course can provide training and education in Japanese technical vocabulary and a variety of engineering courses via home or worksite delivery. To receive a taped demonstration contact: Thomas W. Smith, Director.

Minda de Gunzberg Center for European Studies, Harvard University. Academics across the country have formed an organization dealing specifically with the European Community. Five years old and 600 members strong, this association publishes a newsletter and presents conferences. Contact: Center for European Community Studies, George Mason University, 4400 University Drive, Fairfax, VA 22030.

University of Rhode Island—Pacific-Basin Capital Market Research Center. The PACAP Research Center serves the securities industry and academia through three major programs: (1) PACAP Databases Program, which creates, maintains, and distributes capital market databases for 11 nations in the Pacific Rim; (2) PACAP Finance Conference Program, which provides an international forum among global communities of business, government, and academia to exchange research ideas and findings; (3) PACAP Research, Education, and Training Program, which promotes academic research and teaching programs.

Accounting Firms

Large American accounting firms have extensive networks of offices around the world. Some that do not have offices have, instead, a corresponding relationship with other firms in various countries. Smaller firms can benefit from the vast pool of information available through these accounting firms.

Libraries

Aside from those located in consulates and embassies, there are libraries maintained by international trade associations. (Libraries and library systems are discussed within the country sections later in this chapter.) The Library of Congress should be your first stop for international secondary information such as industry statistics and relatively rare trade journals and newsletters. It has very deep collections covering most areas of the world. Most of these collections are not strictly for business research, but they are likely to have a book or periodical you will not be able to find without traveling to the country of origin. Contact: U.S. Library of Congress, Washington, DC 20540; 202-707-5000.

OVERCOMING CULTURAL AND LANGUAGE BARRIERS

The First Steps

Intelligence is a product resulting from interpretation. I have seen American, Japanese, and European managers view the same case or business situation and come up with different conclusions. They all had the same information; the major difference was how they applied their culturally laden experience to the case.

When you have defined your intelligence needs and have determined what information you already have, what you need to know, and why you need to know it, you are ready to take your next steps. Each step of the process requires acknowledgment and understanding of the cultural contexts that affect competitive advantage.

1. *Gathering information.* The business, economic, and social culture of the particular Asian, Latin American, or European company, industry, or country you are investigating will affect your strategy for gathering data.
2. *Analyzing information in context.* Each piece of data gathered must be analyzed through a *cultural filter* in order to create *accurate intelligence.* The facts alone, out of context, are of little value.

3. *Applying intelligence to plot a strategy for competitive advantage.* Developing a successful competitive strategy based on intelligence requires extensive knowledge of the culture that is shaping the competitor's "personality." A good competitive strategy takes into account the actions and counteractions of all the players involved, not just one's own activities. To recognize and predict what your competitors can do, you must develop insight into how their culture shapes their approach to business negotiations.

Cultural Filters: Vital for Success

Corporate and regional cultures overlay the entire process of business intelligence. In order to gather, analyze, and plan strategy effectively, you must see your competitor in the correct cultural light. To do that, you need to don glasses fitted with special cultural filters. Assess the components that create your competitor's competitive advantage—either domestically or globally—by familiarizing yourself with the cultures within and surrounding the target company. Cultural intelligence is essential for the delivery of accurate business intelligence, and the components of cultural intelligence are:

- The national culture;
- The location of the facility;
- Regional differences;
- The overall economic climate;
- The national government's culture;
- The industry's culture;
- The company's corporate culture;
- Departments' culture within the company.

The ease with which you gather, analyze, and apply intelligence depends on how well you understand each of these cultural differences and its effect on competitive advantage. Conversely, by being unfamiliar with a region's or a company's culture, you may misunderstand and misinterpret the signals sent out by your overseas competitor or customer.

Language: A Major Barrier

Language can be a barrier in your search for foreign competitor intelligence, but it is NOT an insurmountable barrier. Here are some suggestions for overcoming language barriers:

- *Use your competitors' own weak spots.* Follow this rule: Wherever money is exchanged, so is information. Your suppliers and distributors come in contact with your competitors' people every day. Retrieve your competitors' literature, attend conferences they attend, and speak to their customers—who are also likely to be your customers.
- *Use local universities.* Business school professors, who often act as global consultants, may have a great deal of information on your global competitors. Hire international students to translate for you on specific projects.

- *Use your own employees.* Look for employees who speak another language, have lived abroad, or may even have worked for your competitors.
- *Use ethnic clubs.* Local expatriate groups usually will have members who speak their native language.
- *Use translation services.* The American Translation Association offers a series of publications, including a newsletter that contains translation service advertisements and a list of U.S. translators categorized by area of interest. The Federation of Translators, the American Translation Association's international affiliate, can refer you to translators based abroad.

Cross-Cultural Information

Publications and training tools are useful resources for dealing more effectively with international projects. Here is an alphabetical list of cultural information sources.

American Graduate School of International Management. Dedicated to international business training; offers a Master of International Management degree. Provides research services and in-house training for business executives.

American Society for Personnel Administration (ASPA) International. A special chapter of ASPA, devoted to human resource management; exists for those interested or involved in multinational organizations. Sponsors meetings and seminars on global human resource topics and publishes *Resource,* a monthly newsletter.

Copeland Griggs Productions. Offers cross-cultural films and training tools. Publishes *Going International: How to Make Friends and Deal Effectively in the Global Market Place,* an in-depth guide to negotiating, communicating, marketing, and managing abroad.

David M. Kennedy International Center. Offers programs on intercultural understanding and publishes *Culturegrams* describing the customs of 81 countries.

Economist Group, The. The *Economist Business Traveller's Guides,* a series of comprehensive handbooks, offer information to business executives traveling in major countries around the world.

Intercultural Business Center, Inc. Offers a wide variety of business training programs on the Asia/Pacific Rim region. Trainers, all experts, have practiced or lived in these regions. Courses, including relocation courses for various countries, are presented publicly and in-house. Training program titles include: Technology Transfer; Legal and Tax Systems; How To Merge Japanese and American Style Management.

Intercultural Communication Institute. Offers seminars and workshops designed to meet the needs of professionals for intercultural and multicultural education, training, business, counseling, and consulting.

International Cultural Enterprises, Inc. Produces audio tape guides for doing business in Indonesia, Japan, Korea, Malaysia, Singapore, and Thailand.

Reuters Information Services Inc. The Reuters Country Reports database provides detailed reports on the business, economy, and local customs of 50 countries. Contact the "Help Desk."

SIETAR International. The International Society for Intercultural Education, Training and Research offers publications on cross-cultural relations and intercultural communications, including a bimonthly newsletter and a quarterly, *The International Journal of Intercultural Relations.*

SRI International. SRI publishes a Business Customs and Protocol Series, a collection of business protocol guides for 16 countries.

Facts on File Publications. The Global Guide to International Business, edited by David Hoopes, lists 3,000 service organizations and agencies that provide different types of international business information.

The Institute of International Education. Assists with exchange programs and scholarships. Has a large information center, and publishes books on international topics and guides for U.S. students wishing to study abroad.

The Intercultural Press. Offers publications on international and cross-cultural subjects. *Interacts* and *Updates* are two series that provide practical, country-specific business and cultural information.

U.S. Department of State, Foreign Service Institute. Prepares personnel for foreign service and can share information on how to establish cross-cultural training in your firm. Publishes in-depth *Area Studies* and concise *Post Reports* on countries where there is a U.S. Embassy.

Cross-Cultural Communication Tips

You will never find the perfect cultural road map for every negotiation, business dealing, or contact. But if you follow some of these tips, gleaned from our consultants' experiences in the international arena, you will markedly improve your chances of finding the information you are looking for.

- *Rehearse.* You'll never get a second chance to make a first impression even by phone, so develop an interview strategy for your first contact. Rehearse your introduction so that it is culturally acceptable. Solicit feedback on your performance from cultural sources. Learn to pronounce names and countries properly.
- *Pace your speech.* Learn to speak English (or whatever your language of business might be) at the right pitch for each person. Don't speak too slowly or in a condescending tone, but don't speak too fast either.
- *Avoid idioms.* Don't use idioms, slang, or obscure industry-specific jargon.
- *Be polite and patient.* Be extremely polite and considerate. Ask if this is a good time for your contacts to talk; if not, make an appointment to call back.
- *Use tact.* Never get too personal too fast. Use tact and diplomacy at all times.
- *Respect age and position.* Try to determine the age of the person you are addressing; generally, the older the person is (regardless of rank), the more formal and respectful you should be.
- *Know the job responsibility.* Make sure you are addressing your requests and questions to the right person. Job titles may not be the same as in your home country. Ferret out actual job responsibilities to be certain that your contact has access to the information you need.

- *Do not appear overeager.* If you want your contact to be forthcoming, be prepared to be so yourself, but avoid appearing overeager, anxious, or pushy.
- *Be culturally tolerant.* Be aware of differing cultural tolerances for small talk, hypocrisy, corruption, and so on.
- *Read between the lines.* Observe how your contact may be communicating messages through body language or behavior, rather than simply through conversation.
- *Restate questions.* Check and double-check, by restating questions, to be sure that the messages you are sending out are the ones being received. All communication is subject to distortion. Keep checking your own cultural biases and the effects that long-distance communications will have on your ability to understand your counterparts' reactions.
- *Appreciate class distinctions.* Remember the importance of the class system in some countries. Critical information is generally exchanged only between equals, so try to describe yourself as a peer.
- *Act humble.* Be self-deprecating—if necessary, pretend not to understand—to encourage your contact to further explain things.
- *Use open-ended questions.* Phrase your questions so as not to reveal your predisposition; otherwise, your contact may tell you what he or she thinks you want to hear instead of the truth.
- *Ask for referrals.* Encourage recommendation of other sources and ask whether you should use your contact's name when calling those sources. Ask whether your number or name might be passed along to "So-and-So" first. It is always better to be introduced via a mutual contact.
- *Offer translations.* If information is coming to you in writing, offer to have the translation done on your end. This allows the comfort of communicating in the home-country language; generally, more information will be supplied.
- *Account for time zones.* Take time zones into account when dialing overseas.
- *Prime your contact.* Try to establish contact without needing something in return. Write an introductory letter and send information on your company to prime your contact for your call at a later date.
- *Arrange a meeting.* Try to arrange some face-to-face time, either on a trip by your contact to your home country in the future, or as part of an itinerary you have planned when you go abroad.

INTELLIGENCE MAPS: DEVELOPING INTERNATIONAL RESEARCH STRATEGIES

Like the immutable laws of gravity, there are also laws guiding the flow of information across countries and continents. By recognizing these laws, you can begin to find ways to overcome them—or even use them to your advantage. They are:

1. *The Ripple Effect Law: Information is most available at its source and becomes less available the farther it travels away from that source.* Every business transaction generates an information ripple that emanates outward to the public at large. The information ripple will tend to weaken as it moves outward, breaks

up, scatters, and eventually comes to a stop. As the information reaches various barriers and holes, it becomes trapped and loses direction. So too, news of business transactions taking place overseas will be lost unless you can find a way to capture them early.

2. *The Intelligence Antennas Law: Each country or region has a set of intelligence antennas that act as information magnets and are superior in picking up and absorbing information in that country or region.* There are thousands of potential intelligence antennas. They vary from country to country and culture to culture because of the form of government, legislated regulations, cultural leanings, technology, and other factors. You will likely only need to use five or six to hone in on a particular competitor in any one country. Consider intelligence antennas as starting points that will lead you to the next step, then the next contact, and, ultimately, the desired information. These are the basic categories of intelligence antennas:

   - *Analysts:* Stock and industry specialists;
   - *Associations:* Trade and professional organizations;
   - *Banks:* Commercial or merchant banks, investment bankers, independent financiers;
   - *External traders:* Businesspeople located outside the country being examined—industry representatives, suppliers, or distributors who come into contact with the target company in that country, or the target company's competitors within its own boundaries;
   - *Government:* Federal, state, regional, or provincial offices;
   - *Internal traders:* General businesspeople located and operating inside the country being examined—competitors, suppliers, distributors, unions, employees, importers, exporters, and so on;
   - *Publications:* Newspapers, magazines, newsletters, databases, books.

What Is an Intelligence Map?

An intelligence map is a country's information picture, a navigation chart for reaching your research strategy destination. It uses the laws of the Ripple Effect and Intelligence Antennas to help shape your international research approach. It selects the best sources from the above categories and lays them out in order of their importance or usability. In reality, an intelligence map is a list based on the informational reality of a country or region.

In Germany, for example, the commercial courts are the identified intelligence antennas. They have their pulse on German business and require companies to file disclosure documents with them. In France, publications—in particular, the Minitel database and communications system—are an intelligence antenna. In Japan, the industrial ministry, MITI, and its subsidiary agencies are fonts of business and technology information and are strong intelligence antennas. In the United States, the U.S. government, represented by agencies such as the EPA, SEC, and FCC, is rich with information about business activity. (See Chapters 3 and 11 for more details.)

There is no one right way to draw an intelligence map. Two people may draw two different maps of the same area, based on their own experiences and the markets they serve in those countries. For example, after a general intelligence map of

War Story: The Pen May Be Mightier in France

In 1986, the Gillette Corporation bought Waterman, the high-end French pen manufacturer, as part of its strategy to increase its share of the pen market and to fill in a gap in the high-end portion of that market. Part of the assignment of Fuld & Company was to see how this acquisition would change Waterman's marketing plans in the United States and Europe. To do so, we conducted a due diligence search of the press on both sides of the Atlantic Ocean. When we examined articles appearing in both the American and the French press at that time, very different pictures emerged.

- American publications discussed Waterman's image and Gillette's advertising strategy for the U.S. market, and almost entirely ignored the fact that Waterman was a French company with its plants and management overseas.
- Financial details on Waterman itself were almost entirely omitted by the U.S. press.
- French newspapers, such as *Investir* (Paris), supplied details on Waterman's gross sales, number of pens sold, net profit, and market share in France.
- When the American press published the same information—if at all—it appeared nearly six months later than in France. Most of the information about Waterman's French operations were lost to the U.S. news sources.

In reviewing why the details of Waterman's operations were not covered by the American press, we came up with a number of possible reasons: (1) The U.S. press just doesn't "get it" and neglects to report details on non-U.S. operations; (2) U.S. magazines' readership is not interested in issues so far away, and the editors simply responded to this lack of international interest by focusing on the local story—Gillette's acquisition (not Waterman's purchase); (3) the omission may have been purely a matter of economics and space. U.S. stories come first, international news comes second.

The lesson for the analyst is: Always seek competitive information from its country of origin. To expect all information to appear on a database or in your own country's business press is naive. You may receive only a small piece of the whole picture—if you receive any piece at all.

Germany is drawn for one project, a research assignment that involves looking at a German company for a pharmaceutical client may require redrawing the map to account for the "scientific intelligence antennas." The antennas are different because the focus is on a highly narrow marketplace. The German pharmaceuticals intelligence map is, in effect, a subset of the larger one.

How to Create an Intelligence Map

To draw an accurate intelligence map, you must discover where the intelligence antennas are located. Take the following steps:

1. Identify a business event or a company;
2. Call sources (securities analysts, Department of Commerce analysts, news reporters, banks, consulates) who follow business events for that country;
3. Ask these questions, paraphrased as necessary:
    - "If you had to go to Country X to find information on private company Y, what sources would you go to first?"
    - "Which sources—local newspaper, stock analyst, bank, database, or government filing—would give you the most accurate and timely information on a private company?"
    - "Which of the sources are most likely to have the information, and which are least likely? Could you rank them?"
4. Based on the answers, determine which of the sources prove to be stronger antennas and which are weaker. The stronger ones will define your intelligence map. Keep this map in mind, and you will be able to gather intelligence more quickly and more accurately.

COUNTRY-SPECIFIC RESEARCH STRATEGIES

This section reviews a set of intelligence maps that identifies the key intelligence antennas for selected countries. The sources, addresses, and telephone numbers for each antenna are given. Wherever possible, special instructions for gaining access to the various sources or agencies cited are included.

The countries covered in this section are in Western Europe, the United Kingdom, France, Germany, and Italy; and, in Asia/Pacific Rim, China and Japan.

The United Kingdom

Government	Agencies, such as the Department of Trade & Industry, Companies House, and the Regional Development Offices, make information available on both publicly traded and privately-held companies.
Business Information Services	Information services abound in the U.K. and can save time in finding both secondary sources, as well as industry experts.

British Companies—Forms and Filing Requirements

Public Limited Company (PLC). Larger companies use this legal form. A PLC must have an allotted share capital of £50,000 or more, a quarter of which must be fully paid up. PLCs can offer shares to the public and can be admitted to the Stock Exchange.

Private Limited Company (Ltd. or Co. Ltd.). The U.K. has over a million private limited companies; many are small family businesses. These companies, large or small, cannot offer shares to the public.

All companies must register the following documents at Companies House:

- Memorandum of Association—details the firm name, registered office, products and services, share capital issued and type of share, and names and addresses of directors.
- Articles of Association—the rules that govern internal affairs such as appointment and removal of directors, and procedures at company meetings.
- Annual Return—summarizes and updates changes of directors, company secretaries, products and services, and mortgages or charges against the company assets when these changes occur.
- Annual financial statements—sent to the Companies Registration Office (CRO) and to every shareholder; must include a directors' report of the firm's progress, the balance sheet, the profit and loss account, accounting policies used in document preparation, and the auditors' report on accounts.

Financial statements vary according to the size of the company. Small and medium-size companies do not have to submit full accounts. A small company that meets two out of three of the following criteria for two consecutive years does not have to reveal its turnover or profitability: (1) annual turnover does not exceed £2,000,000; (2) balance sheet total does not exceed £975,000; (3) number of employees does not exceed 50.

A medium-size company that meets two out of three of the following criteria for two consecutive years must file a full balance sheet but does not have to reveal its turnover: (1) annual turnover does not exceed £8,000,000; (2) balance sheet total does not exceed £3,900,000; (3) number of employees does not exceed 250.

Partnership. Two or more people are jointly and severally liable. Partnerships are not considered legal types and are not obligated to provide information.

Foreign companies. Companies based outside the United Kingdom must register and file, but they are not required to be audited.

Databases

See Chapter 5 for databases that originate from or provide information on the United Kingdom.

Directories

British Consultants Bureau Directory. Lists individual firms and consultants alphabetically and by field of activity.

CBD Research (available in the United States through Gale Research Inc.):

Centres and Bureaux. Lists 1,000 British centers, bureaus, and similar organizations that provide statistical data.

Directory of British Associations and Associations in Ireland. Lists 7,000 national organizations based in England, Wales, Scotland, and Ireland. Includes local and regional organizations.

The Economist. Publishes the Crawford directories:

Crawford's City Changes. A monthly that tracks changes in companies' staff and departments, structure and strategies, and personnel and clients, as well as trends and all other changes affecting London's business and financial community.

Crawford's Investment Research Index. Investor relations guide to U.K. firms. Looks at stockbroker research departments of U.K. and overseas firms in London, investor relations officers in the top U.K. companies, and financial public relations directors of major U.K. consultancies.

Crawford's Directory of City Connections. Lists and details all quoted and major unquoted companies as well as the top 1,000 major pension funds. Gives more information about contacts in the U.K. financial area than any other reference source.

Guide to Venture Capital in the UK (The Oryx Press). Provides venture capital associations, venture capital divisions of banks, and companies supplying funds for R&D. Gives a wide range of information on 250 companies and institutions supporting new products, services, or business expansions.

The Hawkes Corporate Register (Monitor Publishing Co.). A who's who in corporate Britain.

Industrial Research in the United Kingdom (Longman; available in the United States through Gale Research Inc.). Covers industrial firms, research associations and consultants, government departments and their laboratories, and universities and polytechnic schools; offers brief entries for trade and development associations, and for learned and professional associations.

Kelly's Business Directory (Kelly's Directories; also available through Reed Business Publishing). One of the leading industrial guides to British industry. Contains company information on over 84,000 U.K. businesses and importers; more than 10,000 classified product, trade, and service headings. Provides brand and trade names, product description, and name of manufacturer or U.K. distributor. Over 1,500 listings of organizations that manufacture or supply oil and gas products and services, and over 4,000 listings of worldwide exporting companies, classified by product type and indexed in French, German, and Spanish.

United Kingdom Business Finance Directory (Graham & Trotman; available in the United States through Gale Research Inc.). Profiles more than 1,500 institutions. Gives complete contact information, corporate association memberships, investment management contact names, location of branch offices, key financial services offered, and capital lending criteria.

UK Kompass (Reed Business Publishing). In-depth information on British industrial firms, products, and services.

Books and Other Published Sources

Books

European Company Information: EEC Countries (London Business School Information Service).

Guide to Company Information in Great Britain (ICC Information Group Ltd.).

Her Majesty's Stationery Office (HMSO). Similar to the U.S. Government Printing Office, HMSO remains the central government publishing house for the United Kingdom. Many of its publications are made available in the United States through Berman-Unipub (Lanham, Maryland).

Invest in the UK (CommuniCorp., London House).

Legal Industrial Espionage, 2d ed. (Eurofi PLC).

The Touche Ross Guide to the Regulation of Banks in the UK (Eurostudy Publishing Company Ltd.). Comes in three sections and is a one-stop reference tool for understanding changes in U.K. banking. Eurostudy also publishes a variety of business reports.

London Daily Newspapers

Daily Express   *Financial Times*
Daily Mail   *The Guardian*
Daily Mirror   *The Independent*
Daily Telegraph   *The Times*
Evening Standard   *Times of London*

Weekly Newspapers

The Mail on Sunday   *Sunday Mirror*
The Observer   *Sunday Post*
Sunday Express   *Sunday Telegraph*
Sunday Mail   *Sunday Times*

Regional Newspapers

Belfast Telegraph   *Glasgow Daily Review*
Birmingham Post & Mail   *Manchester Evening News*
Bristol Evening Post   *The Scotsman*

Periodicals

Barclays Review (Barclays Bank)

Business Traveller (Perry Publications (Holdings) PLC)

Director (Director Publications Ltd.)

Doing Business in Europe (VP, CCH Additions Ltd.)

International Management (McGraw-Hill International Publishing)

International Marketing Review (M C B University Press Ltd.)

Lloyds Bank Review (Lloyds Bank Ltd.)

London Commerce (London Chamber of Commerce)

Management Decision (M C B University Press Ltd.)

Management Today (Management Publications Ltd.)

Market Research Europe (Euromonitor Publications Ltd.)

Market Research Society Journal (Market Research Society)

Marketing (Marketing Publications Ltd.)

Marketing in Europe (Economist Intelligence Unit)

Marketing Week (Centaur Publications Ltd.)

Quarterly Review of Marketing (Marketing House Publishers Ltd.)

Retail Business (Economist
  Intelligence Unit)

Sales & Marketing Management
  (I.S.E. Publications Ltd.)

Trade & Industry (Her Majesty's
  Stationery Office)

U.K. Specialists in the United States

The British-American Chambers of Commerce.
New York: 212-889-0680
San Francisco: 415-296-8645
Santa Monica: 213-394-4977

British Embassy, Washington, DC: 202-462-1340.

British Information Service (Invest in Britain Bureau (IBB)). This service's general reference library is open to researchers. Government documents and statistics are available, as are trade directories, but little company-specific information is available. A good place to gather information on distribution and supply networks, potential partners, and regional and economic factors.

ITA U.K. Country Desk. (See listing in Chapter 5.)

Commercial Departments of British Consulates General. Assist British manufacturers exporting to the United States; also help U.S. companies locate appropriate British resources, and are potential sources of leads.

Atlanta:
  404-524-8823; Fax: 404-524-3153
Boston:
  617-248-9555; Fax: 617-248-9578
Chicago:
  312-346-1810; Fax: 312-346-7021
Cleveland:
  216-621-7674; Fax: 216-621-2615
Dallas:
  214-637-3600; Fax: 214-634-9408
Houston:
  713-659-6270; Fax: 713-659-7094

Los Angeles:
  310-477-3322; Fax: 310-575-1450
Miami:
  305-374-1522; Fax: 305-374-8196
NY Trade Development:
  212-245-0495
San Francisco:
  415-981-3030; Fax: 415-434-2018
Seattle:
  206-622-9255; Fax: 206-622-4728
Washington, DC:
  202-462-1340; Fax: 202-898-4255

U.S. Representatives in the United Kingdom

American Chamber of Commerce

American Consulates. The United States and Foreign Commercial Service (US&FCS), which operates under the ITA, offers customized programs, business advice and information, counseling services, and marketing and promotional help. Contact the American Consulates General (dialing sequence is for calls originating from the United States):

London: 011-44-71-499-9000
Belfast: 011-44-232-128-239
Edinburgh: 011-44-31-556-8315

American Embassy, London

Companies House

All companies must register with the Companies Registration Office (CRO), better known as Companies House. The range of documents provided by this agency, which operates under the Department of Trade and Industry (DTI), includes: annual returns, accounts, memorandum of association, articles of association, mortgage register, liquidators/receivers statement of account, and appointment of liquidator.

Offices are located in each U.K. country, and information held at Companies House can be obtained by contacting the office in the region where the target company is registered. Information will be sent promptly. Microfiche costs £4; photocopies are £5.50. Information can be faxed to you if you keep a deposit account of £200.

Government Offices

Department of Trade and Industry (DTI). The DTI, like the U.S. Department of Commerce, offers many good sources of information. The DTI is also a valuable resource for the latest European Community information. These are the specialized DTI offices:

Central Statistical Office (and Publications Centre). The government's official statistical office for business; publisher of the *Business Monitor Series,* which provides data on various industry sectors, based on company filings. Helpful in evaluating your company's progress and comparing it to the rest of your industry. Figures give total sales, imports and exports, and operating ratios.

Export Market Information Centre. Provides information on the size, share, and structure of overseas markets for products, industries and services; the general economic background of countries; and information on multinational companies. The Centre has its own database, BOTIS (British Overseas Trade Information System), which contains information on products, markets, overseas agents, distributors, and importers. Statistics, market research reports, and directories are also available. The Centre also offers the Export Intelligence Service, a special service to subscribers; its computerized system is designed to give advance warning about trade and product opportunities.

Export Marketing Research Scheme. Provides free professional advice and can put you in touch with a professional export marketing research adviser.

Fairs and Promotions Branch. Contact this office to find out about the timing and location of trade fairs that may be of interest.

Health & Safety Executive (Library and Information Services). This agency, which sets health and safety standards in the workplace, produces numerous reports.

Monopolies & Mergers Commission. Produces reports and can sometimes provide information on firms that have been involved with the commission during mergers.

Business Information Services/Libraries

Business information services, usually attached to U.K. universities and libraries, are valuable sources of information. They provide online searches, annual reports, market research reports, Extel cards, McCarthy press clippings, credit ratings, and numerous business publications. Charges for their services range from £40 to £65.

Libraries are also reliable resources for business information; even small reference libraries have basic business directories. Local libraries can be especially effective suppliers of information on local businesses.

A number of business information services can be reached by telephone (dialing sequence is for calls originating from the United States):

The British Library Business Information Service. 011-44-71-323-7457; Fax: 011-44-71-323-7453. The U.K. national library service for the provision of business information. The British Library's particular strength is the provision of worldwide information on companies, markets, and products, with an emphasis on the U.K. and continental Europe. Resources include: online databases; published market research reports; trade magazines and industry newsletters; company reports; company product literature and in-house magazines; trade directories; and business magazines. Statistical material and government publications can be obtained via the library's contacts with other U.K. organizations.

London Business School Information Service. 011-44-71-723-3404. In addition to research services, the London Business School offers seminars on business information and publishes a number of good guides to business and economic information in the European Community.

Manchester Business School Business Information Service. 011-44-61-275-6502; Fax: 011-44-61-273-7732.

Science Reference & Information Service (British Library). 011-44-71-323-7926; Fax: 011-44-71-323-7930. Provides patent information for the past ten years. Ask for the British Patent Desk.

University of Warwick Business Information Service. 011-44-203-523251; Fax: 011-44-203-524211.

Regional Development Organizations/Science Parks

Regional Development Organizations (RDOs) are semipublic organizations that have a wealth of information about business in their area. Contact the RDO in the region where your target company is located. The RDOs have established a regional database system from which you will be able to get general and company-specific information. Here's a list of some development organizations:

Devon & Cornwall Development Bureau. 011-44-752-793379; Fax: 011-44-752-788660.

Industrial Development Board for Northern Ireland. 011-44-232-233233; Fax: 011-44-232-231328.

Northern Development Company (NDC). 011-44-91-261-0026; Fax: 011-44-91-232-9069.

Scottish Development Agency. 011-44-41-248-2700; Fax: 011-44-41-221-5129.

Wales Investment Location (WINVEST). 011-44-222-223666; Fax: 011-44-222-223243.

Welsh Development International. 011-44-222-223666; Fax: 011-44-222-223243.

Yorkshire and Humberside Development Association. 011-44-532-439222; Fax: 011-44-532-431088.

For a more complete list of contacts and information, order *Invest in the UK* (CommuniCorp) by phoning 011-44-71-938-2222.

Science parks are usually attached to U.K. universities and are designed to encourage the flow of information between the corporate and academic worlds. Every country in the United Kingdom contains at least one science park. For further information, contact the U.K. Science Park Association at 011-44-21-308-8815.

Chambers of Commerce

British Chambers of Commerce have no governmental power; their main activity is to lobby the government. They are nonprofit organizations, and companies voluntarily join. The chambers are independent and actually compete with each other in trying to promote business within their own areas.

Association of British Chambers of Commerce. Provides practical information and possible contacts.

London Chamber of Commerce and Industry. Offers a good library of periodicals and government documents. Publishes *London Commerce* as well as *The London Chamber of Commerce and Industry Directory* (Guardian Publications Ltd.).

Trade Associations

Association of Certified Accountants

British Export Houses Association

British Standards Institute

Business Cooperation Network

Confederation of British Industries (CBI). This independent political organization publishes an information packet on the EC, *Europe Sans Frontieres,* plus surveys and reports on British business.

Export Buying Offices Association (EXBO)

Institute of Chartered Accountants

Institute of Directors (IOD). Publishes *Director.*

Institute of Freight Forwarders Ltd.

The Institute of Marketing. The leading professional marketing body in Europe. Provides marketing consultancy services and produces several publications, including *Marketing Week.*

Market Research Society. Publisher of the *International Directory of Market Research Organizations.*

Banks/Stock Exchanges

London is considered the financial capital of the world. Its stock exchange has the longest listing of securities. (Dialing sequence below is for calls originating from the United States.)

International Stock Exchange 011-44-71-588-2355; 011-44-232-21094; 011-44-41-221-7060.

Securities and Investments Board 011-44-71-638-1240.

Bank of England 011-44-71-601-4444. Provides information on the British economy and publishes the Bank of England quarterly bulletin.

Bank of Scotland 011-44-31-243-5769; Fax: 011-44-31-243-5660; in New York, 212-490-8030; Fax: 212-557-9460.

Barclays Bank 011-44-71-283-8989; in New York, 212-412-4000.

Lloyds Bank. In London, 011-44-71-356-1470; Fax: 011-44-71-929-1669; in New York, 212-607-4300; Fax: 212-607-4917.

Midland Bank. 011-44-71-260-8412; Fax: 011-44-71-260-7436; in New York, 212-969-7060.

Royal Bank of Scotland. 011-44-31-556-8555; Fax: 011-44-31-557-6565; in New York, 212-269-1700; Fax: 212-269-8929.

France

Commercial Courts (Greffe du Tribunal)	These local courts will maintain financial filings on companies of all sizes, whether their stock is traded or not.
Databases	France has a wide variety of databases and the means to access them. The Minitel system allows the viewer to scan literally thousands of these databases and business-related bulletin boards at relatively low cost.
Chamber of Commerce and Industry	Supplies both industry, market, and company information upon request.

French Companies—Forms and Filing Requirements

Entreprise Unipersonnelle à Responsabilité Limité (EURL), a new type of French company, is popular with overseas investors because it requires only one shareholder.

Groupement d'Interêt Economiques (GIE) is a joint venture.

Société Anonyme (SA) is like a corporation. It can issue shares to the public, has a share capital of FF 250,000 or more, and must be held by at least seven shareholders. An SA is run by either a board of directors that elects a chairman (*president*) or a supervisory council that appoints a management committee (*directoire*). SAs can be public or private, quoted or unquoted.

Société en Nom Collectif (SNC) is a general partnership where partners are jointly and severally liable.

Société à Responsabilité Limité (SARL) is a limited liability company with minimum share capital limited to FF 50,000. There is a minimum of two shareholders and no board of directors.

All companies must be on record at the Registre du Commerce and must file a legal form, balance sheet, judicial history, registration certification, social security history, and official reports. All filed information is available to the public at the Registre and at the local courts. Only businesses that exceed a certain size in terms of sales, assets, and number of employees are required to submit financial statements for audit, and the size of the company determines the amount of financial data that must be revealed. The smaller the firm, the less information is required. Small firms are those with a balance sheet total of less than FF 1.5 million, turnover of less than FF 3 million, and fewer than 10 employees. Medium-size companies have a balance sheet total of less than FF 10 million, turnover of less than FF 20 million, and fewer than 50 employees.

Bulletin Officiel des Annonces Civiles et Commerciales announces the incorporation of a new business and periodically publishes financials, depending on the size of the company. Company announcements published in the *Bulletin* are available online on the BODACC database. (See Chapter 5.)

There are no filing requirements for foreign firms.

Databases

For a description of Minitel, France's integrated telephone–computer system, see Chapter 5, Section III, "France."

Directories

DAFSA (Société de Documentation et d'Analyses Financieres). 011-33-1-40-60-40-60. The DAFSA publications are among France's leading directories:

L'Annuaire Bancaire. Gives detailed accounts of foreign and French banks operating in France.

L'Annuaire des Liaisons Financieres. A two-volume directory of corporate links and shareholders; specifies the capital holdings that link over 60,000 French and foreign firms. Lists corporate address, direct and indirect shareholders, and direct and indirect ownership of other companies. Can be found on the Adelien database.

L'Annuaire des Sociétés et des Administrateurs. "Sociétés," the first volume of this two-volume set, covers 950 French companies and others quoted on the Bourse or foreign stock exchanges. It gives corporate address, phone, legal status, date of establishment, registration place and number, nominal capital, principal shareholders, senior management, subsidiaries, activities, number of employees, profit and loss data, and major changes in capital structure, dividends paid, face value of shares, and market high and low. The second volume, "Administrateurs," covers 15,000 individuals, including their positions and their addresses (some home addresses appear, rather than work addresses).

France 30,000 (Dun & Bradstreet Information Services). Two volumes cover companies in manufacturing, wholesale and retail commerce, services, public utilities, banks, and insurance. Volume One gives corporate address, phone, CEO, department number (the principal unit of local government administration in France), Dun's number, sales, and number of employees, and contains an alphabetical index to trade names and a geographical index to secondary establishments. Volume Two indicates whether a company is quoted on the Bourse, the company's nominal capital, its legal form (most are SAs), sales, and main SIC code and name of activity. Percentage of sales derived from exports, and principal shareholders (nationality and percentage of holdings) are sometimes listed.

French Company Handbook (International Herald Tribune, Books Division). Gives detailed historical and financial profiles of the top 100 French companies, using American accounting terminology: revenues, operating income, cash flow, net income, balance sheet figures for working capital, equity investment, total assets, long-term debt, and stockholders' equity. Overseas activities and foreign subsidiaries as well as research developments and business strategies are summarized. Phoned orders can be charged to a credit card.

Kompass France (available through Reed Business Publishing). Covers over 50,000 companies in four volumes. Gives addresses, phone numbers, bankers, number of employees, nominal capital, sales, senior management, products exported, and activity codes.

Newspapers and Periodicals

Paris Daily Newspapers

International Herald Tribune (news in English)

La Tribune de l'Economie (economic and financial)

Le Monde (independent)

Le Figaro (news)

Les Echos (economic and financial)

Periodicals

French American Commerce

Le Nouvel Economiste

Le Point

L'Expansion

L'Express

L'Usine Nouvelle

Valeurs Actuelles

French Specialists in the United States

Alliance Francaise. In Washington, DC, 202-234-7911; in Boston, MA, 617-523-4423. Promotes cultural events and teaches French culture and language.

French-American Chamber of Commerce, New York. 212-371-4466. Provides networking opportunities.

French-American Foundation, New York. 212-288-4400; Fax: 212-288-4769. Promotes bilateral exchanges between France and the United States. Most programs are academic in nature.

French Embassy, Washington, DC. 202-944-6000.

> *Press and Information Service* (202-944-6066), located at the French Embassy, publishes a bimonthly newsletter, written in English, that summarizes articles from major French papers and from *France Magazine.*

No subscriptions are taken over the phone. Also distributes newsletters from other branches of the Embassy such as *French Advances in Science & Technology*.

French Trade Office, New York. 212-307-8800. Special information is available on exporting, 212-264-0623; investing, 212-757-9340; and cultural affairs, 212-439-1400.

Invest in France Agency (formerly, DATAR) is the government agency responsible for assisting non-French investors. Four offices in the United States provide information on grants, loans, tax exemptions, and credits:

New York: 212-757-9340; Fax: 212-245-1568

Chicago: 312-661-1640; Fax: 312-661-0623

Houston: 713-266-9772; Fax: 713-266-9884

Los Angeles: 310-785-9735; Fax: 310-785-9213

The agency publishes a newsletter, *France: Industrial Investment File*.

ITA Country Desk—France. In Washington, DC, 202-482-6008.

Available company information includes names and addresses of French suppliers and trade associations. A research library is open to the public and offers both French and American publications, statistics, directories, and market studies, and French subsidiaries in the United States. Offices are located in:

Atlanta: 404-522-4843

Chicago: 312-661-1880

Detroit: 313-567-0510

Houston: 713-266-7595

Los Angeles: 213-879-1847

Miami: 305-372-9798

Washington: 202-944-6300

Promosalons, Arlington, VA. 703-522-5000. Contact this company for information on trade shows in France.

Minitel Services Company, New York. 212-399-0800. This joint venture company offers over 100 domestic services and provides, through its computerized network, the capability to consult with 13,000 services offered in France.

The Minitel system is the most advanced videotex system in the world. Available services now include access to:

Bottin Enterprises, which contains information on 300,000 French companies;

CDPME, which gives information on companies up for sale or takeover;

Euridile, which lists 1,700,000 companies recorded in the business registry;

Kompass France, which lists 89,000 companies in the industrial service sector;

Telefirm, which indexes 800,000 French companies listed at the Registre.

Numerous other databases contain French banking and stock market data, economic and trade statistics, business news, and much more.

EC information can also be obtained through services like: European standards and community programs; and Eurobase, which provides information (in English) on Eureka, one of the EC's R&D programs.

U.S. Representatives in France

Telephone dialing sequence is for calls originating in the United States.

American Chamber of Commerce, Paris. 011-33-1-47-23-80-26. *American Chamber of Commerce in France Yearbook* (latest edition) contains trade figures, useful tips, and addresses for doing business in France. It has a complete listing of Franco-American organizations in France.

American Embassy, Paris. 011-33-1-42-96-12-02. This source can help you make contacts at the Chambers of Commerce, banks, and trade associations.

United States and Foreign Commercial Service (US&FCS). This agency, which operates under the ITA, offers marketing and promotion, information, and counseling services. Its "Gold Key Service" offers customized programs. Headquarters is at the American Embassy; regional offices are in:

Bordeaux: 011-33-56-52-65-95   Nice: 011-33-93-88-89-55

Lyon: 011-33-78-24-68-49   Strasbourg: 011-33-88-35-31-04

Marseille: 011-33-91-54-92-00

Courts and Government Offices

Greffe du Tribunal de Commerce de Paris. 011-33-1-44-41-5454.

Registre National du Commerce. 011-33-1-46-92-58-00.

These government bodies are central repositories of company information. All French companies must register the following: status (legal form), balance sheet, judicial history, registration certificate, social security history, and official reports. A copy of these records is kept at the Registre and another at the Greffe du Tribunal de Commerce.

You can get the legal form, balance sheet, and registration certificate by writing to the Registre. However, you must request the information in French, and you must pay before you receive any information. This will all take about three weeks. If you go in person, the cost is less, but you cannot get a balance sheet.

For more detailed financial information, contact the Greffe du Tribunal (local court) in the *département* where the company you are investigating is registered. France has 95 départements (jurisdictional areas somewhat similar to U.S. counties). Company information is filed in these local courts throughout France. The courts hold more information than the Registre; they should even have company yearly budgets on file. But you must know which court to contact. The letterhead of your target company should contain registration information. If you contact the Greffe du Tribunal de Commerce at the correct location, the court will do the search for you. Remember, obtaining and understanding information from these repositories requires speaking, reading, and writing French. The search will cost about FF 250 and it will take about 48 hours to get the information. You can send a check in the mail.

If you are in France, the Minitel system can give you information from the Registre and from the local courts. Dial the Registre at 36-29-11-11, and type in the target company's name to receive the balance sheet, registration certificate, and legal form. Dial the Greffe du Tribunal at 43-29-06-75, and type in the company's name to receive more detailed and timely financial information.

Delegation à l'Amenagement du Territoire et à l'Action Regionale (DATAR). DATAR recently changed its name to Invest in France Agency (France's Industrial Development Agency). 011-33-1-40-65-12-34; Fax: 011-33-1-43-06-99-01.

Institut National de la Proprieté Industrielle (INPI). 011-33-1-42-94-52-52. Provides patent and trademark information.

Institut National de la Statistique et Des Etudes Economiques (INSEE). 011-33-1-45-40-12-12. Publishes statistical booklets and information, but not company-specific information. Began to publish economic forecasts in English in 1990.

Ministere de l'Economie des Finances et du Budget. 011-44-1-42-61-33-04. Provides economic, financial, and budgetary information on various government and business sectors to the public through booklets known as "Les Notes Bleues."

Business Information Services

Société de Documentation et d'Analyses Financieres (DAFSA). 011-33-1-44-37-26-26. Provides data and analyses of companies, banks, and other institutions in France and Europe. DAFSA can give you in-depth company profiles on both listed and unlisted companies, as well as ad-hoc reports. Available services include:

- *Adelien.* Database that contains information on over 60,000 French firms and foreign firms; shows direct, indirect, and crossed share holdings.
- *Les Dossiers DAFSA.* Analysis of trading data on 1,200 French public firms.
- *Les Fiches Banque.* Analyses of principal French and foreign banks with details on management, shareholders, minority holdings, and market performance.
- *Les Fiches Informations Internationales.* Financial information, in English, on the top 800 multinational companies, including summaries of four years' financial statements.

DAFSA also provides customized company information. Some staff members speak English, and the agency can deliver information in English.

Chamber of Commerce and Industry

Chambre de Commerce et d'Industrie de Paris (CCIP) (Paris Chamber of Commerce and Industry). 011-33-1-45-08-36-01; Fax: 011-33-1-42-08-38-51. The Chambre de Commerce is not part of the government but is under the "guardianship" of the Ministry of Commerce. Every French company must pay a small percentage of turnover to a central pool of funds that supports the units of the Chambre. The presidents of French companies are in charge of contributing money; thus, they have the right to participate in the election of the directors of the Chambre in their region. The relationship between the local chambres and French companies is significant. The local chambres manage business parks and industrial zones, and provide research, analysis, information, and technical assistance. They will conduct simple research for FF 300, or more extensive research, including clipping newspaper and magazine articles for the past two years, for FF 337. Research generally takes three days. They also supply market analysis of products. There is at least one Chambre in each of the 95 *départments* (units of local government administration). Each one contains a center of documentation and a library; both are open to the public. The Chambre also publishes business books and manages the top business schools, such as Ecole Superieur de Commerce de Paris (ESCP) and Ecole Européenne des Affaires (EAP).

Contact the main office listed above to obtain the address, phone, and fax for any of the local chambres.

For more regional information about development, the economy, or the advantages of setting up businesses in specific areas of France, contact the following regional offices:

Côte d'Azur Development. 011-33-93-92-42-42; Fax: 011-33-93-80-05-76.

Grenoble Isere Development. 011-33-76-70-97-97; Fax: 011-33-76-48-07-03.

Nord Pas-de-Calais Development. 011-33-20-63-0405; Fax: 011-33-20-55-39-15.

Banks/Stock Exchanges

Banque de France. 011-33-1-42-92-36-10.

Banque Nationale de Paris SA. 011-33-1-42-44-45-46.

Commission des Operations de Bourse (COB). 011-33-1-40-58-65-65. The COB is the stock exchange association—the French equivalent of the SEC. It has information on both public and private quoted companies. The COB's main purposes are to make information on quoted companies available and to make sure that these companies publish specific information. To visit the Documentation Center, you must call the appointment office and set up a time. You can also phone to request that company information be sent to you free. Legal form of the company; annual reports for the past five years; magazine and newspaper articles, and other financial information are kept on file.

Palais de la Bourse (Paris Stock Exchange). 011-33-1-49-27-10-00; Fax: 011-33-1-49-27-14-33. Banks hold a significant amount of information in France, but company-specific information is almost impossible to obtain from the outside. You will need to develop French banking connections. As an alternate, the Banque de France does publish industry studies.

Germany

Local Courts	The Handelsregister logs the existence and status of German companies.
Chamber of Commerce and Industry	Local chambers have company-specific information, as well as details on credit history.
Trade Associations	Highly influential and knowledgeable about the industries they serve.
Banks	Since banks also serve as stock brokers, the banks themselves become information repositories for all publicly-trade corporations.

German Companies—Forms and Filing Requirements

Aktiengesellschaft (AG), or corporation, was a legal form of incorporation traditionally reserved for very large companies, but more medium-size companies are now using it. Minimum capital is DM 100,000. An AG can be either public or private, and is managed by an executive board (*Vorstand*) that operates under a supervisory board (*Aufsichtsrat*). The purpose of the boards is to provide for the owners safeguards similar to those offered by the separation of the responsibilities of a chairman from those of a CEO. Only an AG's shares can be traded on the stock exchange.

Einzelkaufmann is a sole trader.

Gesellschaft des burgerlichen Rechtes GbR/BGB-Gesellschaft is a civil law partnership; these companies are typically law firms.

Gesellschaft mit beschrankter Haftung (GmbH), or private limited liability company, requires minimum capital of DM 50,000, of which half must be paid up. A GmbH is the more common type of company; most family businesses and foreign subsidiaries are GmbHs. This type of firm is run by "registered managers." If there are more than 2,000 employees, a management board is required. Shareholders are not limited, but shares can only be transferred with the consent of the other shareholders.

Kommanditgesellschaft auf Aktien (KGaA) is a limited partnership by shares. At least one partner must carry unlimited liability. If one of the partners is a limited liability company, the partnership becomes a *GmbH & Co. KG.*

Offene Handelsgesellschaft (OHG) is a general partnership based on a partnership agreement where the partnership is a self-accounting unit.

Zweigniederlassung is a branch of a foreign corporation.

Laws governing German business enterprises are derived from the *Handelsgesetzbuch* (Commercial Code), which applies in part or whole to all businesses. Basic facts about every business enterprise must be entered in the commercial register, but there is no centralized registry. All obligatory documents are filed with the trade registry at the local court (*Amtsgericht*) responsible for the district where the company has its main headquarters. Registration documents contain: company name, commercial purpose, amount of initial capital and confirmation that the minimum share capital has been paid, date when the articles of association were signed, and names of the business managers, partners, or sole owners.

All registered companies must join the local Chamber of Commerce and Industry (*Industrie-und-Handelskammer*). There are 69 Chambers; they represent local companies in negotiations with the state and federal governments.

AGs are required to maintain accounting records and have their annual statements audited. Quoted companies must give the stock exchange and the banks copies of their accounts, auditor's report, and executive and supervisory board reports. Quoted or not, AGs must publish their profit and loss account in at least one German newspaper and file the auditor's report at the local trade registry.

GmbHs have had to file more detailed records since 1987, but these requirements have not yet been strictly enforced. The new auditing requirements depend on size criteria, not legal form. Only small companies escape auditing.

Small companies are those that do not exceed two of the following three criteria: (1) balance sheet total = DM 3.9 million; (2) annual sales revenue = DM 8.0 million; (3) number of employees = 50.

Medium-size companies are those that do not exceed two of the following three criteria: (1) balance sheet total = DM 15.5 million; (2) annual sales revenue = DM 32.0 million; (3) number of employees = 250.

Private businesses and partnerships that meet two of the following three criteria have auditing and publication requirements: (1) balance sheet total = more than DM 125 million; (2) annual sales revenue = DM 250 million; (3) number of employees = 5,000.

Foreign companies must register and generally follow the same registration rules.

Databases

Business databases are written in German unless otherwise indicated. (See Chapter 5.)

Directories

Verlag Hoppenstedt. 01-49-61-513801. Source of the following publications:

Deutsch-Amerikanische Geschaftsbeziehungen (German American Business Contacts). The first of two listings is an alphabetical roster of towns, with the names of the companies that are based in them. Address, phone, CEO, SIC code, number of employees, nominal capital, sales, and name and address of American partner are given. The second listing indicates American associate companies: address, phone, and name of the German company with which they are connected. There is also a list by SIC code of parents and German associates.

Die Nicht Notierten Deutschen Aktiengesellschaften. This two-volume work contains the same information as *Handbuch der Deutschen Aktiengesellschaften,* but covers the leading unquoted German AGs and provides balance sheets and profit and loss statements.

Handbuch der Deutschen Aktiengesellschaften. Covers quoted, and some unquoted, German and foreign companies listed on German exchanges. Contains a list of companies that have ceased trading, have liquidated, or have changed their legal status. Gives address, phone, bankers, senior management, activities, year established, major shareholders, owners, subsidiaries, capital and dividend history, year-end date, profit and loss statements, and summaries and balance sheets.

Handbuch der Gross-unternehmen. Covers 22,000 companies with 100 or more employees, capital over DM 500,000, or a turnover exceeding DM 10 million; banks with balance sheets of over DM 500 million; and insurance companies with premiums of over DM 50 million. Two volumes, arranged by town of registration, give phone, bank, legal form, year established, managing directors, supervisory board and senior managers, main shareholders, nominal capital, number of employees, sales, trade association memberships, branches, and subsidiaries. Firms are also listed according to their line of business as classified by the Federal Statistical Office. Classifications are printed in German, French, and English.

Mittelstandische Unternehmen. Covers 21,000 medium-size companies, listed by town, that employ between 20 and 100 people or whose sales are between DM 2 million and DM 10 million. Gives address, phone, industry code and activities, bankers, date established, number of employees, nominal capital, and senior management.

Saling Aktienfuehrer. Covers 509 German AGs and 203 foreign corporations that trade on the German stock exchanges. Gives address, phone, executive and supervisory boards, year established, number of employees, year-end date, locations of plants, capital, history, major shareholders (and percentage of holdings), share price, dividend, summary balance sheets, and profit and loss statements.

Kompass Deutschland (Kompass Deutschland Verlag Vertriebsges GmbH; available in the United States through Reed Publishing). Covers 36,000 manufacturers who employ over 20 employees. Gives address, phone, bankers, number of employees, and senior management. Some also include sales, year established, capital, parent company, and place of export. Product index is in German, English, and French.

Taschenbuche des Offentlichen Lebens (Paperback Covering Public Life) (Festlian Verlag, Bonn). Lists trade associations, Chambers of Commerce, public authorities, professional associations, embassies, and federal and state government offices.

Wer Gehort zu Wem (A Guide to Capital Links in West German Companies) (Commerzbank, Frankfurt). 011-49-69-13620. Covers 10,000 companies. Gives activity code, main shareholders, and percentage of holding. Two separate sections alphabetically list (1) shareholders and companies they're involved with, and (2) biggest foreign shareholders in German firms, arranged by country.

The Federation of German Address Book Publishers (Verband Deutscher Adressbushverleger e.V., Dusseldorf). 011-49-211-32-09-09. There are many address directories of importers, wholesalers, retailers, and organizations listed by sector and industry. Contact this organization for help in locating a directory that is of interest to you.

Newspapers and Periodicals

Major Daily Newspapers

Abendzeitung (Munich)

Augsburger Allgemeine (Augsburg)

Berliner Zeitung (Berlin)

Bild (Hamburg)

B.Z. (Berlin)

Die Rheinpfalz (Ludwigshafen)

Die Tageszeitung (Berlin)

Die Welt (Bonn)

Der Tagesspiegel (Berlin)

Express (Cologne)

Frankfurter Allgemeine Zeitung (Frankfurt)

Freiheit (Halle)

Hamburger Abendblatt (Hamburg)

Handelsblatt (Dusseldorf)

Hannoversche Allgemeine (Hannover)

Hessissche/Niedersachsische Allgemeine (Kassel)

Kolner-Stadt-Anzeiger (Cologne)

Leipzig Volkszeitung (Leipzig)

Munchner Merkur (Munich)
National-Zeitung (Berlin)
Neues Deutschland (Berlin)
Neue Westfalische (Bielefeld)
Norwest-Zeitung (Oldenburg)
Nurnberger Nachrichten (Nuremburg)
Offenbach Post (Offenbach)
Rhein-Zeitung (Koblenz)
Rheinische Post (Dusseldorf)
Ruhr Nachrichten (Dortmund)
Saechsische Zeitung (Dresden)
Suddeutsche Zeitung (Munich)
Stuttgarter Nachrichten (Stuttgart)
Sudwestpresse (Ulm)

Tribuene (Berlin)
Westdeutsche Allgemeine (Essen)
Westdeutsche Zeitung (Dusseldorf)
Westfalische Nachrichten (Munster)
Westfalische Rundschau (Dortmund)

Weekly Papers

Bayernkurier (Munich)
Bild am Sonntag (Hamburg)
Deutsches Allgemeines Sonntagsblatt
  (Hamburg)
Die Ziet (Hamburg)
Rheinischer Merkur (Koblenz)
Vorwarts (Bonn)

Periodicals

European Business Publications Inc., 203-656-2701; Fax: 203-655-8332. This company, the U.S. representative for Frankfurter Allgemeine Zeitung GmbH, publishes a monthly newsletter, *German Brief (Informationsdienste),* in English. Its up-to-date information covers all aspects of political, economic, and business developments in Germany. Country reports and other newsletters are among its other publications.

German Information Center, New York. 212-974-8830. This organization publishes a weekly newsletter, *The Week in Germany,* which summarizes, in English, important news from major German newspapers.

German News Co., Inc., New York. 212-348-5975. Subscriptions to German publications are available from this source.

German Specialists in the United States

Berlin Economic Development Corporation. In Boston, 617-556-8890; in San Francisco, 415-788-0785. This publicly funded regional development office offers advice and help for setting up business in the greater Berlin area. It can also be used as a gateway to contacts and information sources in other eastern parts of Germany.

German American Business Association, Alexandria, VA. 703-836-6120.

The German-American Chamber of Commerce.
    Chicago: 312-782-8557; Fax: 312-782-3892
    Los Angeles: 213-381-2236; Fax: 213-381-3449
    New York: 212-974-8830; Fax: 212-974-8867
    San Francisco: 415-392-2262; Fax: 415-392-1314

German Consulates.
   Atlanta: 404-659-4760
   Boston: 617-536-4414
   Chicago: 312-580-1199
   Detroit: 313-962-6526
   Houston: 713-627-7770
   Los Angeles: 213-930-2703
   New York: 212-308-8700

German Embassy, Washington, DC. 202-298-4000.

German Industry and Trade Office, Washington, DC. 202-659-4777.

German Information Center, New York. 212-974-8830.

Goethe Institute, New York. 212-439-8700. Promotes the German language and provides a broad range of cultural information.

ITA Country Desk—Germany, Washington, DC. 202-482-2434/2435. Specialist for business matters pertaining to the eastern part of Germany.

U.S. Representatives in Germany

American Chamber of Commerce, Executive Office, P.O. Box 100162, Rossmarkt 12, D-6000 Frankfurt-am-Main 1; 011-49-69-283401; Fax: 011-49-69-285632. This bilateral membership organization, with its business and social functions, helps Germans and Americans to enter each other's markets. The Chamber has a library from which import/export data and other business information are available. Regional Chamber chapters, run by local companies, are established throughout Germany. The Chamber is a good place to make business contacts, and has up-to-date information on business activities in Germany.

American Embassy, Deichmanns Aue 29, D-5300 Bonn 2; 011-49-228-339-3391. Industry specialists at the American Embassy use local credit agencies, banks, directories, and networking contacts to create company-specific World Traders Data Reports and to assist American firms. Offices of the United States and Foreign Commercial Services (US&FCS) are located at the embassies and consulates:

   Berlin: 011-49-30-819-7888
   Dusseldorf: 011-49-211-49-00-81
   Frankfurt: 011-49-69-75-305-453
   Hamburg: 011-49-40-44-1061
   Munich: 011-49-89-23011
   Stuttgart: 011-49-711-21-02-21

Courts and Court Publications

There is no central court in Germany. German companies are registered at the *Handelsregister* at local civil courts (*Amtsgericht*) located throughout the country. There are over 450 of these courts. German companies indicate on their letterhead the court at which they are registered. You can write to courts and request information, but it will be faster for you to send someone in person. AGs' and GmbHs' auditing reports should be found at the courts.

Bundesfirmenregister. Another way to find out where a target company is registered. This annual publication consists of a series of regional volumes that lists all companies registered with the local courts. Call the American Embassy and ask whether someone can look up your target company in the *Bundesfirmenregister* for you. For your own copy of the *Bundesfirmenregister,* contact: Verlagsbetriebe Walter Dorn GmbH, AM Tuev 63000, Hannover 89, FRG; 011-49-511-830351.

Bundesanzeiger (Federal Journal). All stock corporations must publish the opening and closing prices, and any changes in the status of the company or the roster of directors, in the *Bundesanzeiger,* which the public has the right to inspect. You can hire a business information service like Hamburg Institute for Economics to retrieve clippings from the *Bundesanzeiger.*

Government Offices

Federal Office for Foreign Trade Information (Bundesstelle für Aussenhandelsinformation (BfAI)). 011-49-221-20-57-1; Fax: 011-49-221-20-57-212. The official, central information agency for all foreign trade questions. It provides government information on exporting and importing, and conducts studies on foreign trade markets. BfAI publishes *The Federal Republic as a Business Partner* and has new booklets on doing business in the unified Germany.

In addition, BfAI publishes *Nachrichten für Aussenhandel (Foreign Trade News),* a daily paper, and *Aussenhandelsdienst (Foreign Trade Service),* a weekly magazine that contains *Auslandsanfragen (Foreign Inquiries),* a supplement in which foreign companies can publish requests for contacts. This supplement was created to help foreigners establish new business contacts and expand existing ties with German firms. These publications are intended for a German audience, and the contents focus on non-German markets and industries. However, because foreign firms advertise in them, they can be sources of information on what your competitors are doing in the German market. BfAI trade papers are published by Verlagsbetriebe Walter Dorn GmbH.

Federal Ministry of Economics (Ministerium für Wirtschaft). 011-49-228-6151; Fax: 011-49-228-6154436.

Finance Ministry (Haus der Ministerien). 011-49-228-6820; Fax: 011-49-228-6824420.

These two ministries provide information on investment grants in eastern Germany.

Federal Statistical Office (Statistisches Bundesamt (StaBuA)). 011-49-6121-4186511. The main government office for official statistics publications. A directory of publications can be obtained from the distributor: Verlagmetzler-Poeschel, Postfach 7, 7408 Kusterdingen, FRG.

German Standardization Institute (Deutsche Institut für Normung (DIN)).

German DIN Information Center for Technical Regulations (Deutsches Informationszentrum für Technische Regeln im DIN)

To contact these sources, call 011-49-30-26-01-600; Fax: 011-49-30-26-01-231.

Federal Office for Trade and Industry (Bundesamt für Wirtschaft (BAW)). 011-49-6196-404-1; Fax: 011-49-6196-404-212. This office supplies information on import quotas for the commercial sector and for agricultural products.

Federal Environmental Agency (Umweltbundesamt). 011-49-228-885790.

German Patent Office (Deutsches Patentamt). 011-49-89-2-19-50.

European Patent Office (Europaisches Patentamt). 011-49-89-2-39-90.

Business Information Services/Credit Agencies

Creditreform. 011-49-2131-109210; Fax: 011-49-2131-109140. This long-established credit agency will notify you within three months if there are any changes in the creditworthiness of a firm researched for you. Creditreform is online on Data-Star and Bertelsmann Information Service.

Hamburg Institute for Economics (Institut für Wirtschaftsforschung (HWWA)). 011-49-40-35621. This center has collected economic and political literature since 1908. It provides a clipping service, has annual reports on German and foreign companies, and has a periodical database retrieval service. It also publishes an economics journal, *Intereconomics*. You can go in person to the Hamburg Archive and get news clippings for free. *Bundesanzeiger (Official Gazette)*, the published version of the information at the Handelsregister, is available at the Archive.

Chamber of Commerce and Industry (Industrie-und-Handelskammer (IHK))

Deutscher Industrie-und-Handelstag (DIHT) (Association of German Chambers of Industry and Commerce), 011-49-228-104-0. This is an umbrella organization for the German Chambers of Commerce and Industry (*Industrie-und-Handelskammer (IHK)*). DIHT provides information about business in Germany and supports the German Chambers of Foreign Commerce (*Deutsche Auslandshandelskammer (AHK)*), which are located in foreign countries around the world. AHKs are set up in accordance with the host country; the German American Chamber of Commerce, in the United States, is an example of an AHK operated by the DIHT.

The IHKs are public institutions organized regionally. Membership is required for all industry, trading, and service businesses, but not mandated for professionals. Local IHKs possess company-specific information and can provide data on creditworthiness, history, and executives and board members.

By networking through the IHKs, you will find the best marketing and distribution channels, as well as any advantages your target company has within a particular region.

A complete list of IHKs in Germany follows. When calling from the United States, dial 011 before the numbers given here.

Aachen Coburg: 49-241/4380;
  Fax: 49-241-438259
Arnsberg/Southeast Westphalia:
  49-2931/87 80; Fax: 49-29-31-21427

Aschaffenburg: 49-6021/8 80-0;
  Fax: 49-6021-879 81
Augsburg/Swabia: 49-821/31 62-0;
  Fax: 49-821-3162-323

Baden-Baden/Middle Upper Rhineland:
49-7221/70 01-0

Bayreuth/Upper Franconia: 49-921/8
86-0; Fax: 49-921/127 78

Berlin: 49-30/3 15 10-0; Fax: 49-30/3
15 10-1 00

Bielefeld/East Westphalia: 49-521/5
54-0; Fax: 49-521/55 42 19

Bochum: 49-234/6 89 01-0; Fax:
49-234/689 01-0

Bonn: 49-228/22 84-0; Fax: 49-228/22
84-170

Braunschweig: 49-531/47 15-0;
Fax: 49-531/47 15-299

Bremen: 49-421/3 63 70;
Fax: 49-421/363 72 99

Bremerhaven: 49-471/9 24 60-0;
Fax: 49-471/9 24 60-90

Chemnitz: 37-71-6-823801;
Fax: 37-71-6-43018

Coburg: 49-9561/74 26-0;
Fax: 49-9561/74 26-50

Cottbus: 37-59-2-484143

Darmstadt: 49-6151/87 10;
Fax: 49-6151/87 12 81

Dillenburg: 49-2771/90 50;
Fax: 49-2771/9 05 28

Dortmund: 49-231/5 4170;
Fax: 49-231/5417-109

Dresden: 37-51-479547

Duisburg-Wesel: 49-203/28 21-0;
Fax: 49-203/2 65 33

Dusseldorf: 49-211/3 55 70;
Fax: 49-211/3 55 7401

Emden/East Friesland & Papenburg:
49-4921/89 01-0; Fax: 49-4921/89
01-33

Erfurt: 37-61-345658; Fax: 37-61-62105

Flensburg: 49-461/806-0;
Fax: 49-461/80671

Frankfurt am Main: 49-69/219 70;
Fax: 49-69/2197-424

Frankfurt am Oder: 37-30-23620

Freiburg/Southern Upper Rhineland:
49-761/38 58-0; Fax: 49-761/38
58-2 22

Friedberg: 49-6031/6 09-0;
Fax: 49-6031/6 09-1 80

Fulda: 49-661/28 40; Fax: 49-661/2 84 44

Gera: 37-70-51513; Fax: 37-70-23301

Giessen: 49-641/79 54-0; Fax: 49-641/7
59 14

Hagen: 49-2331/3 90-0; Fax: 49-2332/1
35 86

Halle: 37-46-37991

Hamburg: 49-40/36 13 80;
Fax: 49-40/36 13 84 01

Hanau: 49-6181/2 43 87/88;
Fax: 49-6181/25 85 43

Hannover-Hildesheim: 49-511/3107-0;
Fax: 49-511/3107-444

Heidelberg/Rhine & Neckar:
49-6221/90 17-0

Heidenheim: 49-7321/324-0;
Fax: 49-7321/324-169

Heilbronn/Neckar: 49-7131/96 77-0;
Fax: 49-7131/96 77-1 99

Karlsruhe/Middle Upper Rhineland:
49-721/17 40; Fax: 49-721/1 74-2 90

Kassel: 49-561/7 89 10; Fax: 49-561/7
89 12 90

Kiel: 49-431/59 04-0; Fax: 49-431/59
04-234

Koblenz: 49-261/10 60; Fax: 49-261/10
62 34

Koln (Cologne): 49-221/164 00;
Fax: 49-221/164 01 23

Konstanz/Rhine Highlands & Lake
Constance: 49-7531/28 60-0;
Fax: 49-7531/28 60-70

Krefeld/Middle Lower Rhineland:
49-2151/63 50; Fax: 49-2151/63 5138

Lahr/Schwarzwald/Southern Upper
Rhineland: 49-7821/27 03-0;
Fax: 49-7821/27 03-22

Leipzig: 37-41-71-53438;
Fax: 37-41-51030

Limburg: 49-6431/80 91-93

Lindau/Bodensee: 49-8382/40 90, 40
   95; Fax: 49-8382/40 57

Lippe-Detmold: 49-5231/76 01-0;
   Fax: 49-5231/76 01 57

Lubeck: 49-451/13 50; Fax: 49-451/13
   52 84

Ludwigshafen: 49-621/5 90 40;
   Fax: 49-621/59 04-166

Luneberg: 49-4131/7 09-0;
   Fax: 49-4131/70 91 80

Magdeburg: 37-91-33951;
   Fax: 37-91-344391

Mainz/Rhineland-Hessia: 49-6131/2
   62-0; Fax: 49-6131/2 62 69

Mannheim/Rhine & Neckar: 49-621/17
   09-0; Fax: 49-621/17 09-100

Monchengladbach: 49-2161/24 10;
   Fax: 49-2161/24 11 05

Munich/Upper Bavaria: 49-89/5116-0;
   Fax: 49-89/5116-306

Munster: 49-251/70 70; Fax: 49-251/70
   73 25

Neubrandenburg: 37-90-4101

Neuss: 49-2101/27 98-0;
   Fax: 49-2101/27 55 01

Nuremberg: 49-911/13 35-0;
   Fax: 49-911/13 35-500

Offenbach am Main: 49-69/8 20 70;
   Fax: 49-69/82 07-199

Oldenburg: 49-441/22 20-0;
   Fax: 49-441/22 20-888

Osnabruck-Emsland: 49-541/3 53-0;
   Fax: 49-541/35 3171

Passau/Lower Bavaria: 49-851/50 70;
   Fax: 49-851/50 72 80

Pforzheim/Northern Black Forest:
   49-7231/20 10; Fax: 49-7231/20 1158

Potsdam: 37-23-21591

Regensburg: 49-941/569 40;
   Fax: 49-941/942 79

Remscheid: 49-2191/230 75;
   Fax: 49-2191 230 79

Reutlingen: 49-7121/ 20 10;
   Fax: 49-7121/ 20 1181

Rostock: 37-81-37501

Saarbrucken: 49-681/95 20-0;
   Fax: 49-681/95 20-8 88

Schoppfheim/Baden/Rhine Highlands
   & Lake Constance: 49-7622/39 07-0;
   Fax: 49-7622/39 07 42

Schwerin: 37-84-78922;
   Fax: 37-84-83390

Siegen: 49-271/33 02-0; Fax: 49-271/33
   02 37

Solingen: 49-212/20 30 21;
   Fax: 49-212/20 30 25

Stade/Elbe-Weser: 49-4141/60 66-0;
   Fax: 49-4141/60 66 24

Stuttgart/Middle Neckar: 49-711/20
   05-0; Fax: 49-711/20 05-354

Suhl: 37-66-22278

Trier: 49-651/7 10 30;
   Fax: 49-651/7103-153

Ulm: 49-731/17 30; Fax: 49-731/17 3173

Villingen-Schwenningen: 49-7721/20 40

Weingarten/Lake Constance & Upper
   Swabia: 49-751/40 90

Wetzlar: 49-6441/40 08-0;
   Fax: 49-6441/40 08-33

Wiesbaden: 49-6121/15 00-0;
   Fax: 49-6121/37 72 71

Wuppertal: 49-202/24 90-0;
   Fax: 49-202/24 90-9 99

Wurzburg/Wurzburg-Schweinfurt:
   49-931/30 10; Fax: 49-931/30 1100

Regional Offices

Boblingen: 49-7031/62 01-0;
   Fax: 49-7031/62 01 50

Esslingen: 49-711/35 91 41;
   Fax: 49-711/35 97 64

Groppingen: 49-7161/6715-0;
   Fax: 49-7161/695 85

Ludwigsburg: 49-7141/12 21;
   Fax: 49-7141/12 22 35

Nurtingen: 49-7022/3 40 26;
   Fax: 49-7022/24 31

Remshalden-Grunbach: 49-7151/720
   21,22

Trade Associations

Germany has a multitude of private sector, semigovernmental, and governmental institutions and organizations. Many in the private sector have considerable influence and give advice and information. Over 80 percent of businesses belong to one or more of these trade associations, which can often provide business data and industry-specific information.

The most important associations of German manufacturers are organized under:

Federal Association of German Industry (Bundesverband der Deutschen Industrie (BDI)), 011-49-221-37-08-00; Fax: 011-49-221-37-08-73.

This private organization of firms has voluntary membership. It maintains relations between commercial enterprises and government and provides information on German products and exporters.

A directory titled *Verbande, Behorden, Organisationen der Wirtschaft* is published annually in German. It lists all the national and regional organizations in the German business world, and is available through: Hoppenstedt Wirtschaftsverlag GmbH, 011-49-61151-3800.

For information in English, get a copy of *The Federal Republic of Germany as a Business Partner,* a booklet put out by the Federal Office of Foreign Trade Information (BfAI) in Cologne. It has listings of the important industry associations with addresses and phone numbers. Among the key trade associations are:

Confederation of German Employers' Associations (Bundesvereinigung der Deutschen Arbeitgeberverbande (BDA)), 011-49-221-379-50.

Federal Office for Food & Forestry (Bundesamt für Ernahrung und Forstwirtschaft (BEF)), 011-49-69-15-64-0; Fax: 011-49-69-15-64-445.

German Retailers' Foreign Trade Association (Aussenhandelsvereinigung des Deutschen Eingelhandels e.V. (AVE)), 011-49-221-21-66-17. Deals with consumer products of all types, but especially textiles.

Working Committee of German Market Research Institutes (Arbeitskreis Deutscher Marktforschungsinstitute e.V. (ADM)), 011-49-4542-801-0. Gives addresses and advice about market research companies free of charge.

Regional associations and Friendship Clubs also provide addresses of potential business associates, institutions, lawyers, and so on. They work in close association with top-level associations in the German business community.

Banks/Stock Exchanges

Banks in Germany are authorized stockbrokers, shareholders, and depositories, and are board members of companies. They have industrial holdings and are mandatory members of German Chambers of Commerce and Industry (IHKs). Banks provide annual and quarterly reports, investment research, portfolio management, and company-specific information. They can provide you with a *Bank Information Report (Bankauskunft),* which is a company credit report; however, you must be a customer of the bank and you must notify the target of your request. These reports might not be up-to-date, so they need corroborating evidence.

With unification and the need for investment in the former eastern sector, banks are offering special loans and grants to both German and foreign companies.

Germany has a central bank owned by the federal government:

German Federal Bank (Deutsche Bundesbank), 011-49-6-95-66-1.

The *Deutsche Bundesbank* receives regular reports from other banks. Write for the *Deutsche Bundesbank Monthly Report,* which you can get in English. Topics include banking, finance, monetary policy, and global economic data.

Banks

Berliner Industriebank, 011-49-30-820030; Fax: 011-49-30-8243003.

Commerzbank AG, 011-49-69-1362-1.

Deutsche Ausgleichsbank, Bonn 011-49-228-8310; Fax: 011-49-228-831255.

Deutsche Ausgleichsbank, Berlin 011-49-30-850850; Fax: 011-49-30-85085299.

Dresdner Bank AG, 011-49-69-263-1.

Federal Association of German Banks (Bundesverband Deutscher Banken e.V.), 011-49-221-166-32-20 Press Office. Contact this association to make banking connections. It can provide general company information regarding the reputation of your target company. However, it will only give this type of information to its customers or to another bank, so you need to use your own bank as a liaison.

Stock Exchanges

Berlin: 011-49-30-31-80-1-249
Bremen: 011-49-421-32-12-82
Dusseldorf: 011-49-211-13-89-0
Frankfurt: 011-49-69-21-97-1
Hamburg: 011-49-40-36-13-02-0
Hannover: 011-49-511-32-76-61
Munich: 011-49-89-59-90-0
Stuttgart: 011-49-711-29-01-83

No federal authority regulates these exchanges. Applications for a listing must be made by a bank and supported with financial information. Companies must submit annual reports, but no other disclosures are required.

Saling Aktienfuehrer, a stock exchange guide that provides financial data on public companies, is available from the publisher, Hoppenstedt Wirtschaftsverlag GmbH, 011-49-611-51-3800; Fax: 011-49-6151-380360.

Italy

Databases	The CERVED series of databases contain detailed financial information on millions of Italian corporations.
Trade Associations	Excellent general source for local businesses and industry throughout Italy.

Italian Companies—Forms and Filing Requirements

Societa in accomandita per azioni (SapA) is an incorporated partnership. Liability for some partners is unlimited.

Societa in accomandita Semplice (SaS) is a limited partnership with liability limited to the amount of capital contribution. SaSs are rarely quoted.

Societa per Azioni (SpA), or corporation, is a joint stock company and can be quoted. It must have minimum capital of L 200 million.

Societa in nome collettivo (Snc) is a general partnership and the liability of the partners is not limited.

Societa a responsibilita limitata (Srl) is a private limited liability company with minimum capital of L 20 million.

SpAs and Srls are legal entities and must file the following documents at the Cancelleria office at the local civil court: (1) a deed of incorporation; (2) articles of association, any changes in appointments and retirements of directors and statutory auditors, and any resolution for dissolution; (3) annual financial statements, which must be published in the Chamber of Commerce's Companies' Official Bulletin (BUSARL).

SpAs' letterheads and business documents should state name, legal address, and registration numbers issued by the Registration of Enterprises and Chamber of Commerce.

Partnerships are not separate legal entities. The partnership agreement must be filed with the local Register of Enterprises, but there is no requirement for disclosure of financial statements.

Foreign companies must also register and publish in BUSARL.

The Civil Code sets out required minimum contents of the balance sheets and income statement (profit & loss) for all companies regardless of size. However, because the European Company Law—the 4th Directive—is not yet implemented in Italy, standard reporting forms are not yet used. Consolidated financial statements are not yet required by law, nor published, but the National Commission for Corporations and the Stock Exchange (CONSOB) has requested consolidated financial statements from most companies on the stock exchange. Documents are open to the public at the local courts.

Databases

The available databases are written in Italian unless otherwise indicated. See Chapter 5.

Directories

Annuario Generale Italiano (Guida Monachi). The three volumes of this work contain, respectively: (1) 100,000 listings of companies and trade/other associations, including name, address, phone, legal form, main activities, date of establishment, principal subsidiaries, branches, and agents; (2) product indexes in English, French, German, and Spanish that cross-refer to the headings in Volume One; (3) an alphabetical index of the 100,000 companies, and information on directorships and managerial posts.

Dun's 10,000: l'Annuario delle maggiori societa in Italia (D&B Marketing Services). Covers 10,000 companies. Five tables provide the following information respectively: (1) 1,000 companies by sales in 1986 and profit as a percentage of sales; (2) 1,000 companies by number of employees, sales per employee, and profit as a percentage of sales; (3) 45 leasing companies by income; (4) 90 insurance companies by gross premium; and (5) 315 banks by value of customers' accounts.

Dun's Guide (D&B Marketing Services). Covers 8,150 medium-size companies with turnovers between L 5 million to 10 million. It gives (in Italian) name, address, phone, year established, number of employees, sales, and firms' activities.

Guida deli'azioista (Databank SpA on behalf of Credito Italiano). Covers companies quoted on Italian main and second stock markets, but not those on the third market. Gives address, phone, activities, share capital, number of shares outstanding, directors' names, profit and loss information, summary balance sheets, net profit, and dividends for the past three years.

Kompass Italia (Reed Business Publishing). In three volumes, covers 30,000 companies in Italy and San Marino. Gives name, address, telephone registration place and number, senior management, banker, year established, products, plant locations, countries of export, nominal share capital, sales, and employees. Product indexes in Italian, French, English, German, and Spanish provide: Italian diplomatic, consular, and commercial offices abroad; Italian Chambers of Commerce abroad and foreign Chambers of Commerce in Italy; foreign diplomatic and trade reps in Italy; official bodies, organizations, and trade associations affiliated to the General Confederation of Italian Industry and the General Confederation of Commerce and Tourism; principal trade fairs; foreign companies and agents; and trademarks.

Newspapers and Periodicals

Newspapers

Corriera della Sera (Milan; independent)
Corriere Mercantile (Genoa; financial and political)
Il Fiorino (Rome; business)
Il Giornale (Milan; independent)
Il Matino (Naples; morning)
Il Messaggero (Rome; independent)
Il Sole 24 Ore (Milan; financial, political, economic)
Il Tempo (Rome; right-wing)
International Daily News (Rome; English daily)
Italia Oggi (Milan; financial)
La Repubblica (Rome; left-wing)
La Stampa (Turin; independent)
L'Avvisatore Marittimo (Genoa; shipping and financial)
Ore 12 (Rome)

Periodicals

Assicurazioni
Il Mondo Economico
L'Espresso
Milano Finanza

Italian Specialists in the United States

Consulate General of Italy, New York, 212-737-9100.

ITA Country Desk—Italy, Washington, DC, 202-482-2177.

Italian American Chamber of Commerce (IACC), New York, 212-279-5520. A private membership organization, but part of the network of the Union of Italian Chambers of Commerce. Provides services to the Italian government, but its first priority is to benefit Americans who are members and are doing business in Italy. IACC's computer system, CERVED, connects directly with Italy's leading business data banks and provides online information on more than 3.5 million Italian firms. You can access these databases, including SANI, SABB and SDOE, and receive current financial, corporate, and product data on every registered Italian company. The IACC also produces several trade publications, including *United States/Italy Trade Directory*.

Italian Cultural Institute, New York, 212-879-4242. Promotes academic exchanges and provides translation services.

Italian Embassy, Washington, DC, 202-328-5500.

Italian Trade Commission

Atlanta: 404-525-0660
Chicago: 312-670-4360
Los Angeles: 213-879-0950
New York: 212-980-1500

A good source of business information, and one of the first you should tap into. The National Institute for Foreign Trade in Rome oversees the Trade Commission, which is part of a worldwide trade information network. The Commission assists in the importing of Italian products and provides some of the publications of the Central Statistical Office (ISTAT) and the National Institute for Foreign Trade (ICE). Through the Commission, you can begin to make connections with Italian professionals, agents, lawyers, interpreters, and so on.

U.S. Representatives in Italy

American Chamber of Commerce in Italy (Camera di Commercio Americana in Italia), 011-39-2-869-0661; Fax: 011-39-2-805-7737. Provides information on doing business in Italy and publishes an Italian-American business directory.

American Consulates General. The United States and Foreign Commercial Service (US&FCS), which operates under the ITA, offers customized programs, business advice and information, counseling services, and marketing and promotional help. Contact the American Consulates General in Palermo, 011-39-91-343532, or Florence, 011-39-55-298276.

American Embassy, Rome, 011-39-6-467411.

Courts and Court Publications

Cancelleria Commerciale, 011-39-5436. The Cancelleria Commerciale in Milan contains an alphabetized index of all Italian companies. Very specific information can be obtained by presenting a form that contains the *numero di tribunale* of the company and a L 3,000 *Marca da Bollo* stamp. This information is only available in person from the Cancelleria Commerciale and cannot be obtained from overseas or with an incomplete request form. Photocopies of the documents may be obtained in a few days for a minimal fee. There is no publication from which to get the registered information; you must look at individual files.

Official Gazette (Ufficio Fogli Annunci Legali (FAL)). FAL documents, available at the Uffici Giudiziari, contain details of court transactions, especially companies' bankruptcy actions; it is mandatory to notify the FAL office in cases of bankruptcy. Other documents available are expropriation notices, requests for bids announced by the municipalities, and announcements of legislative assemblies.

Prefettura (Fogli Annunci Legali), 011-39-77581.

Register of Business Enterprises (Cancelleria Commerciale); local court (Tribunal Civile). All businesses must register at the local court (*tribunale civile*) in the district in which the registering company has its headquarters. When registered, a company receives an identification number (*numero di tribunale*), which is then the court's reference number for that company.

Government Offices

Institute for Assistance in the Development of Southern Italy (Instituo per l'Assistenza allo Sviluppo del Mezzogiorno (IASM)), 011-39-6-84721. IASM assists small and medium-size Italian companies by providing financial services, but is not allowed to release any company-specific information. IASM performs studies and provides information on the area's economy, however, and it publishes *Industrial Incentives in the Mezzogiornio,* describing investment in southern Italy.

Ministry of Foreign Trade (Ministero del Commercio con l'Estero), 011-39-6-5993; 011-39-6-59921 for publications. A government affiliate that works closely with the Institute of Trade in Rome and provides business promotion and development services to Italian companies. The Ministry's daily bulletin assists Italian exporters, keeping them updated on changes in prices, tax rates, EC developments, and trade issues.

Ministry of Industry, Commerce & Artisan Trade (Ministero del Industria, Commercio e Artigianato), 011-39-6-4705.

National Institute for Foreign Trade (Istituto nazionale per il Commercio Estero (ICE)), 011-39-6-59921. A government body with a worldwide network (it uses SICE, a foreign trade information system) that promotes foreign trade and provides market intelligence, export services, and promotional support. It compiles information on Italian exports, oversees the Italian Trade Commission Offices in the United States, and produces several publications. ICE can obtain names of Italian professionals, local correspondents, surveyors, and interpreters.

Chambers of Commerce

Italian Chambers of Commerce are considered government agencies. Businesses must be licensed through the local Chamber of Commerce (Camera di Commercio); there is one chamber for every province in Italy. The chambers, controlled by the Italian Ministry of Trade and Commerce, are very involved with the businesses in their area and have annual reports on companies as well as their registration documents, which reveal company name, address, incorporation date, legal form, directors and officers, nominal capital, and products or services offered. Information is available immediately upon request in person at a Chamber of Commerce office. A brief company description and list of company executives (*visura camerale*) or a more complete list (*certificato*) with detailed descriptions of individuals can be obtained. Chambers also provide Certificates of History (*Certificato Storico*) that outline the company's performance. However, there can be a three-week wait for this historical information because it is compiled manually upon request and can be several pages long.

The annual financial statements of SpAs and SrLs are published in the Chamber of Commerce's Companies' Official Bulletin (BUSARL). Through the chambers, all BUSARL documents are available: certificates of incorporation, authenticated photocopies of any company acts, or general information on the company. It takes a few days to get BUSARL documents, which are different from the registration documents.

The relationship between the chambers and Italian companies is very important. The firms pay the local chamber a mandatory fee, determined by the capital registered by the company. Companies receive a variety of business-related services from the chambers, such as information, research and analysis, and technical assistance. In metropolitan areas, the chambers may provide publications and industry studies.

CERVED Information Service, 011-39-6-780541; Fax: 011-39-6-78054299. CERVED, an SpA company founded with capital from the Italian Chambers of Commerce, provides a centralized database system that accesses all the information originating from the chambers. However, rather than calling overseas, call the Italian American Chamber of Commerce in New York (see below), which has exclusive rights to the CERVED system and can access it for you. There is a charge per database and per company.

Italian American Chamber of Commerce (IACC), New York, 212-279-5520.

Union of Italian Chambers of Commerce, Industry, Artisanship and Agriculture (Union Italiana delle Camere di Commercio, Industria, Artigianato e Agricoltura), 011-39-6-47041; Fax: 011-39-6-4744741. A government entity and the official representative of the Parliament; not a trade association. All local chambers belong to the union.

Trade Associations

Italy has many regional trade associations, which are great sources for industry information. Some of their many annual industry reports are in English.

Federation of Industry and Commerce (Confederazione Generale dell'Industria Italiana (Confindustria)), 011-39-6-59031; Fax: 011-39-6-613230. Call the Confindustria and ask to obtain *Quadriconfederalli,* which lists all the associations of industry and commerce in Italy. The Confindustria has its own database, Dati Anagrafici di Imprese Italiane, which has company information on 350,000 firms. There are separate files for members and nonmembers; the nonmember files are less extensive.

Banks/Stock Exchanges

Italy has an old-fashioned banking system that is adapted to regional environments and is somewhat inefficient, but is very profitable. The system is made up of commercial banks and special credit institutes. These banks are good sources of general economic and business information. However, credit information on Italian companies that the bank does business with is generally not available.

Banca Commerciale Italiana, SpA, 011-39-2-88501. Conducts research and publishes information on companies' finances and the stock market.

Bank of Italy (Banca d'Italia), 011-39-6-47921. The Bank of Italy is a public institution, owned by shareholders, and has several roles. It is the most important supervising body in the bank system.

Banco di Roma, SpA, 011-39-6-54451. Publishes economic reviews and provides complete banking services.

Cassa di Risparmio Delle Provincie Lombarde, 011-39-2-88661.

Mediobanca SpA, Banca di Credito Finanziario, 011-39-2-88291. Conducts research and publishes *Le Principali Societa Italiane* as well as financial and stock market information on Italian companies.

National Commission for Corporations and the Stock Exchange (Commissione Nazionale per le Societa e la Borsa (CONSOB)), 011-39-6-84771. Regulates companies quoted on Italy's ten stock exchanges; also regulates convertible bonds, unlisted securities, and insider trading. The most important exchanges are:

    Genoa: 011-39-10-2094400
    Milan: 011-39-2-85341
    Naples: 011-39-81-323232
    Rome: 011-39-6-6794541
    Turin: 011-39-11-547743

People's Republic of China

External Traders	Forming business alliances with non-Chinese businesses already doing business in China can open many bureaucratic doors and speed the information flow.
Internal Traders-Partnership Network	Identify internal Chinese businesses as partners because reliable printed information is relatively scarce and because different regions may conduct business differently.

Databases

For information on databases containing information on Asia/Pacific Rim companies, see Chapter 5.

Directories

American Firms Importing from the People's Republic of China (US–China Business Council). Covers over 2,000 companies, including more than 200 that do business directly with China's provinces. Company name, street address, and cable address; phone and telex; executives responsible for imports from China; banks, customs house brokers, and ports used; products imported; business with provinces; and total business volume are given for company entries.

China Directory of Industry, Commerce and Economic Annual (Xinhau Publishing House/Professional Book Company; available from Science Books International Inc.). Covers China's major industries. Entries list company name, address, phone and telex numbers, cable address, business description, number of employees, and names of executives. Company name and address in Chinese provided for photographic reproduction on shipping labels or postal documents. Maps and general information on China's economy, laws, and regulations are included.

Directory of Chinese Libraries (China Academic Press/Gale Research Company). In English and Chinese. Lists 500 major libraries with foreign holdings; 1,700 public libraries (with addresses); 700 college and university libraries; and 300 special libraries.

Directory of Chinese Officials and Organizations: National Level Organizations (National Technical Information Service).

Executive Guide to China (John Wiley and Sons, Inc.). List of offices of American-owned corporations in Beijing. Published in 1984.

New York–Beijing Directory (China Daily Distribution Corporation). Covers companies and organizations involved in trade between New York and Beijing. Entries include name of organization, New York and Beijing addresses, names of contacts, phone and telex numbers, and description of activities.

Official American Business and Industry (Trade with China) (Asia Systems Media, Inc.). Covers about 3,500 U.S. companies interested in trade with the People's Republic of China. English and Chinese used in text. Entries include company name, address, phone, names and titles of key personnel and contacts, description of products and services, branch office or subsidiary locations, number of employees, and financial data.

The US–China Business Services Directory (The US–China Business Council).

Newspapers and Periodicals

Beijing Review (English, French, Spanish, Japanese, and German; weekly)

Beijing Ribao (Chinese; daily)

Business China (fortnightly)

China Business Report (every two months)

China Business Review (bimonthly)

China Daily (English; daily)

China Economic News (weekly)

China Journal of Biotechnology (English)

China Market (monthly)

China Newsletter (bimonthly)

China Oil

China Offshore Oil (quarterly)

China Reconstructs (monthly)

China Trade News (monthly)

China Trade Report (monthly)

China Trade Weekly Bulletin

China's Customs Statistics (quarterly)

China's Foreign Trade (bimonthly)

Chinese Science Abstracts (English; monthly)

East Asian Executive Reports, Ltd.

FBIS Reports (Foreign Broadcast Information Service) (daily)

Guangming Ribao (Chinese; daily)

Intertrade (monthly)

Jingji Ribao (Economic Daily)

Maritime China (quarterly)

Renmin Ribao (People's Daily) (Chinese)

Shenzhen Tequ Bao (Shenzhen Special Zone Daily) (reports on special economic zones open to foreigners)

Shichang Zhoubao (Market Weekly) (Chinese; weekly)

SINO–British Trade Review (monthly)

United Nations Development Forum

Wenhiui Bao (Shanghai) (Chinese; daily)

World Economic Herald

Zhongguo Duiwai Maoyi (China's Foreign Trade) (Chinese, English, French, and Spanish; monthly)

Zhongguo Guanggao Bao (China's Advertising) (weekly)

Zhongguo Jianshe (China Reconstructs) (English, Spanish, French, Arabic, Portuguese, Chinese, and German; monthly)

U.S. Sources on China

ITA, Washington, DC: Office of Investigations, 202-482-5497; Country Desk—China, 202-482-5527.

U.S. China Business Council, Washington, DC, 202-429-0340; Fax: 202-775-4276. Formerly National Council of US/China Trade, this organization publishes *China Business Review* (monthly newsletter), *China Market Intelligence,* and *US Investment in China* (a study of 500 U.S. projects in China).

Other publications include: *A Guide to China's Trade and Investment Organizations; US–China Business Services Directory; Opportunities in China's Major Projects and ICB Reports; The Beijing Real Estate Report; China's Metals and Minerals;* and *China's Electric Power Development: Identifying Market Opportunities.* The council's business information center has publications and databases on China's economy and trade, industrial sectors, information, organizational charts, trade statistics, contracts, and details on foreign investments. From its offices in Washington and Beijing, the council provides custom market and investment research to members.

U.S. Consulate General, Guangzhou, 011-86-20-66-9900; Fax: 011-86-20-66-6409.

U.S. Department of Commerce, Washington, DC, 202-482-4811.

U.S. Embassy, Beijing, 011-86-532-3831; Fax: 011-86-1-532-3178.

U.S. Export-Import Bank, Washington, DC, 202-622-9823. Lends or guarantees credits to a foreign borrower or to an intermediary to finance U.S. exports to China. Offers China the most favorable interest rates and repayment terms allowed. Provides U.S. companies with a *Directory of Export Services in Asia,* along with credit information on foreign buyers and banks.

Chinese Representatives in the United States

China Council for the Promotion of International Trade (CCPIT) and *China Chamber of International Commerce (CCOIC),* Washington, DC, 202-244-3244; Fax: 202-244-0478. National nongovernmental organizations that promote China's foreign trade and attract and utilize foreign investment and advanced technology, they provide members with consulting/legal services and patent/trademark services; link the government with businesses; arrange foreign economic, trade, and technical exhibitions; and collect and distribute product literature and international publications on science and technology. CCOIC issues certificates of origin, documents on foreign trade, and shipping certificates. It also arranges for assessment and feasibility studies for Sino-foreign economic and technical projects, offers credit information services, and compiles and publishes periodicals on China's foreign economic and trade relations and technology.

China Daily Distribution Corp. 212-219-0130. Distributes *China Daily.*

China Institute in America, New York, 212-744-8181. Offers a wide variety of classes and lectures on Chinese language, history, art, and current events.

China National Tourist Office, New York, 212-867-0271.

China Patent and Trademark Agent (USA) Ltd., New York, 212-912-1870. Files and processes patent and trademark applications, and consults on technology and investment. An independent consulting firm; publishes *China Patents and Trademarks.*

> Head office:
> China Patent Agent (HK) Ltd.
> 22nd Floor, Great Eagle Center
> 23 Harbor Road
> Wanchei, Hong Kong

Embassy of the People's Republic of China, Washington, DC, 202-328-2520/2517.

US–China Business Council, Washington, DC, 202-429-0340. Formerly the National Council for US–China Trade, this private nonprofit organization assists members in business dealings with the PRC. It publishes the bimonthly *China Business Review.*

Government Offices

China National Import and Export Commodities Inspection Corporation (CIECIC), 011-86-1-500-3344. Foreign businesses may commission this organization to issue documentation for customs, to settle accounts, and for dispute resolution and letter-of-credit purposes.

Customs General Administration, 011-86-1-5556106. Publishes *Customs Statistical Journal* in English and provides consultants for assistance in obtaining statistical data.

Ministry of Chemical Industry, 011-86-1-446561.

Ministry of Coal Industry, 011-86-1-555891.

Ministry of Commerce, 011-86-668581.

Ministry of Electronics Industry, 011-86-1-868451.

Ministry of Foreign Affairs, 011-86-1-555831; 552190; 550257.

Ministry of Foreign Economic Relations and Trade (MOFERT), 011-86-1-512-6644. The Administrative section has five departments: (1) Import/Export, (2) Foreign Aid, (3) International Corporation, (4) Foreign Investment, and (5) International Organization Liaison. The Center for Market and Trade Development at the International Trade Research Institute of MOFERT offers advertising and market development services to foreign companies. The business section is comprised of many national-level import/export corporations. Most factories cannot sell their products directly; they must get permission from MOFERT and the ministry of the pertinent industry.

Import/export companies are the liaison between the factories and foreign buyers. The following corporations have direct investment in several factories:

China National Cereals, Oils and Foodstuffs Import and Export Corporation, 011-86-1-466-3366.

China National Electronic Technology Import and Export Corporation, 011-86-1-821-2233.

China National Light Industrial Products Import and Export Corporation, 011-86-1-512-3728.

China National Metals and Minerals Import and Export Corporation, 011-86-1-500-7722.

China National Technical Import and Export Corporation, 011-86-1-831-7733; Fax: 011-86-1-831-6696

China National Silk Import and Export Corporation, 011-86-1-512-3338.

General information and detailed written brochures on each of the factories can be provided upon written request. Many more factories belong to city and provincial-level import and export corporations.

Ministry of Light Industry, 011-86-1-556687.

Ministry of Machine Building Industry, 011-86-1-867008.

Ministry of Metallurgical Industry, 011-86-1-557031.

Ministry of Petroleum Industry, 011-86-1-444631.

Ministry of Textile Industry, 011-86-1-556831.

Patent Office of the People's Republic of China, 011-86-201-9221; 201-4447 ext. 2223.

Shanghai Patent Agency, 011-86-385-668. One of many provincial city-level patent offices.

State Administration of Commodity Inspection, 011-86-1-500-2387. Establishes relationships with foreign notary organizations—among them, the American International Group. Recognizes inspections of commodities conducted by these bodies prior to shipment to China.

State Administration for Industry and Commerce, 011-86-801-3300 ext. 211; Fax: 011-86-801-3300-2322. Foreign companies wishing to establish permanent offices in China are required to register with the appropriate Chinese authorities: MOFERT, the appropriate Ministry of Industry, the city-level government, and the State Administration for Industry and Commerce, which functions under the direct supervision of the State Council. There are six departments: (1) Enterprise Registration, (2) Economic Contract Management, (3) Market Management (monitors the price of the small, private, free-market businesses), (4) Private Enterprises, (5) Advertisement Management, and (6) Economic Policy Inspection. Information is in Chinese and English.

State Statistical Bureau, 011-86-1-868521. Produces the *Statistical Yearbook of China* and provides statistics in 24 languages.

Trademark Registration Bureau, State Administration for Industry and Commerce, 011-86-801-3300 ext. 324.

Trading and Trade Promotion Corporations

Beijing Economic Development Corporation, 011-86-1-753680.

Beijing Exhibition Center, 011-86-1-890611.

Beijing Exhibition Service, 011-86-1-890541 ext. 487.

Beijing Import and Export Control Committee, 011-86-1-556106.

China Council for the Promotion of International Trade, 011-86-8013866. National nongovernmental economic and trade organization composed of social dignitaries and representatives of enterprises and organizations in China. Aims to promote China's foreign trade, attract capital, introduce advanced foreign technology, and foster various forms of economic and technical cooperation.

Encourages foreign trade and economic cooperation; sponsors and arranges Chinese exhibitions abroad and foreign exhibitions in China; helps foreigners to apply for patent rights and trademark registration in China; promotes foreign investment and organizes technical exchanges with other countries; provides legal services; and publishes trade periodicals including *Directory of Chinese Foreign Trade.* Divisions include:

Patent Agency: 011-86-801-3376

Trademark Agency: 011-86-801-0208

Department of Legal Affairs: 011-86-866118

China Trade Promotion Review: 011-86-4081892

Economic Information Department: 011-86-867229

Foreign Affairs: 011-86-866572

Liaison Department: 011-86-867504
    Division of the Americas and Oceania Affairs, 011-86-8012867/
    8013344/8011320; Fax: 011-86-8011370

China Export Commodities Fair (CECF), 011-86-677000. Organized by the Ministry of Foreign Economic Relations and Trade, CECF operates two trade fairs a year, in the spring and fall.

China National Technical Import Corporation, 011-86-890931. Imports plant components and equipment, acquires modern technology and know-how from abroad, undertakes co-production and joint venture, and engages in technical consultation and updating of existing enterprises.

Foreign Exchange Control Bureau, 011-86-1-3338521.

Foreign Trade Bureau, 011-86-1-5554808. Several independent trade companies form the Bureau. For more information, see Ministry of Foreign Economic Relations and Trade (MOFERT), under "Government Offices."

Guangdong Exhibition Service Company, 011-86-20-75793.

Guangdong Foreign Trade Development Corporation, 011-86-20-776-299; Fax: 011-86-20-766-025, 755-815. A provincial-level import/export comprehensive trade company. Handles imports and exports according to the need of domestic enterprises, including products of light industry, metallurgical and mining equipment, textiles, chemicals, medical equipment, and so on. Provides contacts between domestic enterprises and foreign clients, and offers information on local factories (location, energy resource, technological assessment, raw materials, factory equipment, and so on). Has more than ten branch companies and offices inside China. One branch company, Yueshang Development Ltd., is in Hong Kong, and another is in Macao. Information is written in Chinese.

Permanent Hall for Negotiation and Exhibition of Xinjiang Export, 011-86-20-62290.

Shanghai International Trust and Service Corporation, 011-86-21-332-1025, 6650; 011-86-21-320-7412. This provincial import/export company handles mail order and foreign trade; arranges export, customs, and deliveries for overseas Chinese; and drafts contracts. It provides foreign companies with information on enterprises in Shanghai and on export and import products. Information is in both English and Chinese.

Shanghai Trade and Transportation Company (formerly Shanghai Foreign Trade Bureau), 011-86-21-321-0718.

Shanghai Overseas Enterprise Corporation (formerly Shanghai Foreign Trade Corporation), 011-86-21-321-6965; Fax: 011-86-21-323-4701. These provincial-level import/export companies provide foreign trade information for Chinese enterprises in many industries, including chemical, medicine, medical equipment, fashion, and textile. The corporation has several representative offices overseas, in Japan, Hong Kong, the United States, Germany, and Switzerland. Written information is in both Chinese and English.

Associations and Federations

All China Federation of Industry and Commerce, 011-86-1-501-6677; Fax: 011-86-1-512-2631. Like an American Chamber of Commerce, this federation consists of industrialists and business professionals. It has 500,000 members and 100,000 enterprises, including joint ventures and foreign-owned companies. Services include: international and domestic business information and consulting; investment information on environmental projects; and arrangements for visits to Chinese companies. It publishes the newspaper *Industry and Commerce Times* and the magazine *Chinese Industry and Commerce;* both are written in Chinese. The federation provides information in both English and Chinese.

Chinese People's Association for Friendship with Foreign Countries, 011-86-541010.

Shanghai Federation of Industry and Commerce, 011-86-21-433-5795. Shanghai is the leading industrial city. This federation, comprised of industrialists and businesspeople who are members of several democratic parties in China, provides services to the industrial and commercial sectors, including information on investment, trade, and partners for joint ventures. Members include more than 4,600 state-owned, collective and private enterprises. For foreign companies, it provides written information about Shanghai enterprises and arranges visits to local companies. It has contacts with a wide range of industries.

Departments include: Liaison (external relations); Economic Consultancy for Domestic Enterprises; and Economic Research on Policy in China. Information is in both English and Chinese.

Banks

Bank of China (State Bank), 011-86-1-668941. In New York: 212-935-3101; Fax: 212-593-1831.

Bank of China Trust Company and Consultancy Department, 011-86-1-6543431 ext. 339.

Bank of Communications (Commercial Bank), 011-86-21-213400.

Central Bank, People's Bank of China, 011-86-1-653431.

In China, There Are Facts—and Then There Are Facts

LEONARD FULD: Do you need different kinds of intelligence when deciding to enter or work within the Chinese market, versus the Japanese market?

DENIS SIMON: Working in the Chinese market requires a very different approach with respect to information gathering and processing. This different approach is necessitated by two factors.

- First, the Chinese business environment continues to be in flux as a result of the rapid changes taking place throughout the economy. As one Chinese expert has remarked, "Everything you hear in China is true, but none of it is reliable." Foreign firms cannot simply count on what they hear in one location in China also being true in another part of the country. Different locations interpret central government directives in different ways, depending on their own interests and situational factors.
- Second, information availability is affected by the fact that, aside from government classified information and information open to the public, there is a third, somewhat amorphous category of information called *neibu* (domestic use only) which, in essence, shuts out from foreign companies a substantial amount of useful and necessary commercial information.

Unlike the Japanese business environment, where there is a plethora of books, magazines, newspapers, and government publications dealing with all sorts of economic and related topics, the Chinese information environment is not very transparent. This requires firms doing business in China to seek out and form a "partnership network" that can be used to open up doors to needed information. Such a network can help to surface information that, in general, may be beyond the easy reach of the foreign firm seeking to understand why a specific problem has arisen or what changes are likely to occur in the business environment as a result of the ongoing economic reforms and associated political jockeying taking place in the PRC.

Dr. Denis F. Simon is Director of the Center for Technology and International Affairs at the Fletcher School of Law and Diplomacy of Tufts University. He is a lecturer and writer on the problems of technology development in both China and the East Asian newly industrialized nations. He is a consultant to several major corporations as well as to international organizations such as the U.N., the World Bank, and the Office of Technology Assessment of the U.S. Congress.

China International Trust and Investment Corporation (CITIC), 011-86-1-500-2255; Fax: 011-86-1-500-1535. Responsible to the State Council, it raises funds abroad for investment in China and engages in joint investment ventures in China and abroad. CITIC is an important and powerful enterprise.

Hong Kong and Shanghai Banking Corporation (Hong Kong), 011-86-21-216030; 218383.

Industrial and Commercial Bank of China, 011-86-1-868901. Handles industrial and commercial credit.

Midland Bank Group, 011-86-1-504410.

People's Bank of China, 011-86-863907.

Standard Chartered Bank, 011-86-21-214245.

The World Bank, 202-477-1234. Publishes studies of the Chinese economy.

Japan

Government	The Japanese government publishes a great deal on its country's technology and business activity, through JETRO, JICST, Patent Office, and other agencies. Much of the government's data pool is increasingly becoming available on-line.
Publications	Japan is arguably the most literate and published culture in the world. There are many on-line, as well as published information sources available that report on company financials, patent filings, and general business activity.
University Network	Universities supply the raw talent for and are in constant touch with Japanese industry.
Internal Traders	Personal networks that include Japanese banks, industry suppliers, distributors and other industry specialists, are important if you are going to understand the competition. These contacts have critical information not available elsewhere.

Databases

See Chapter 5 for listings of databases on Japanese companies.

Directories

Consumer Japan (Euromonitor Publications). Compiles information needed to plan business strategies in Japan: market data on consumer products sold in Japan; stats on market details; profiles on 75 major Japanese manufacturers and 35 retailers; and lists of information sources such as government agencies.

Dentsu Japan Marketing/Advertising Yearbook (Dentsu Incorporated). Offers data on the Japanese market, including economic background, recent statistics, details on corporate marketing, advertising expenditures and volume, dynamic activities in sales promotion, and sports and cultural event promotion. Includes recent trends in TV, hi-definition TV, electronic library technology, and newspaper and magazine publishing.

Diamond's Japan Business Directory (Diamond Lead Co., Ltd.). Entries identify over 1,000 Japanese companies listed on the Tokyo Stock Exchange: banks, communications companies, department stores, insurance companies, investment houses, manufacturers, service industries, transportation and utility companies. Includes name, address, phone, directors, and officials for each listed company.

Directory of Japan Affiliated Companies in the USA and Canada (JETRO). Over 8,200 listings, arranged alphabetically by state or province. Includes company name, address, phone, CEO, type of business, year established, products, services, and parent company.

Directory of Japanese Databases (National Technical Information Service (NTIS)). Details 43 Japanese databases accessible from the United States, giving producer's name, address and phone, and produces the research report *Tapping Japan's Database Resources: An American Strategy.*

Directory of Japanese Technical Reports (National Technical Information Service (NTIS)). Complete bibliographic citations of new information available through NTIS.

Directory of Japanese Technical Resources in the United States (National Technical Information Service (NTIS)). Lists over 250 commercial services, government agencies, and libraries that acquire, translate, or disseminate Japanese technical information. Gives background articles about accessing Japanese technical resources, and cites translations of Japanese technical documents that are available through NTIS.

Economic World Directory of Japanese Companies in the USA (Economic Salon, Ltd.). Includes 600 listings giving firm name, address, phone, type of business, financial data, and names of executives. Includes similar data on parent company in Japan.

Guide to Science and Technology in Japan (Longman Group UK Ltd.; available in the United States through Gale Research Co.). Covers education, industrial research, agriculture, medicine, life sciences, biotechnology, energy, aerospace, aviation, railways, electronics, earthquake and disaster prevention, environmental protection, earth sciences, marine science, defense. Profiles learned and professional societies and associations, Tsukuba Science City information sources, and international scientific and technological cooperative projects. Includes directory of major research establishments.

Industrial Goods Distribution in Japan (Dodwell & Co. Ltd.). Analyzes Japan's industrial goods distribution system. Includes economic overview; recommendations for execs involved in Japanese industrial goods distribution. Gives a comprehensive look at important characteristics of Japan's trading companies' distribution systems.

Industrial Groupings in Japan (Dodwell Marketing Consultants/International Publications Service). Covers 16 major industrial groupings in Japan. Lists firm name, affiliates, subsidiaries, line of business, number of employees, and financial data such as gross sales, net income, and capitalization.

Japan Company Handbook (Toyo Keizai Inc.). A classified list of public companies in Japan, their products, net worth, officers, branches, capital, stockholders, share price, principal business lines, and so on.

Japan Directory (Japan Press, Ltd.). Guide for establishing business contacts in Japan. Covers leading foreign and Japanese business firms, banks, industrial associations, embassies, consulates, government agencies, clubs, port authorities, schools, hotels, restaurants, and stores. Includes address, phone, year of establishment, and key personnel. Provides home address and phone of foreign residents in Japan.

Japan Trade Directory (JETRO; available in the United States through Gale Research Co.). Information on 3,000 Japanese companies by prefecture location, 18,000 products and services, and advertising data. Lists firms with address, phone, and directors, and indicates whether firm is wholesaler or distributor. Covers trade and industrial associations and features a trade name index.

Japan Yellow Pages (Japan Yellow Pages Ltd./Croner Publications, Inc.). Comprehensive guide to Japanese manufacturers and traders, with 25,000 listings under 800 product/service/professions categories.

Japan's High Technology: An Annotated Guide to English-Language Information Sources (Oryx Press). Identifies over 500 directories, online databases, abstracting and indexing tools, newsletters, translation guides, and other sources on Japanese high tech. Gives complete bibliographic information.

Retail Distribution in Japan (Dodwell & Co. Ltd.). Details Japanese retail system covering: socioeconomic changes, system characteristics and recent developments, distributions channels for imported products, business practices, and technological developments. Includes directory of 530 retailers, wholesalers, and importers.

Second Section Firms (Toyo Keizai, Inc.). A companion to *Japan Company Handbook* (see above). Gives information on products, net worth, officers, branches, capital, stockholders, share price, and principal lines of business.

Selling Japan (JETRO/International Publications Service). Comprehensive data on all aspects of the Japanese marketplace.

Structure of Japanese Electronics Industry (formerly Key Players in the Japanese Electronics Industry) (Dodwell & Co. Ltd.). Examines Japan's electronics industry in Japan and in the world market. Analyzes market trends by major product groups, using annual reports of specific companies. Includes market shares and product data for 40 major products; a directory of nine giants and 320 other major electronics firms; relevant statistics; and trade associations.

Newspapers and Periodicals

Asahi Evening News (English)
Asahi Shimbun
Chemical Daily News
Japan Economic Daily

Japan Economic Journal (English version of *Nihon Keizai Shimbun;* weekly)

Japan Times, The (English; weekly)

Nihon Keizai Shimbun (financial, businesslike)

Nikkan Kogyo Shimbun (respected, technical)

NIKKEI Industrial Daily

NIKKEI Marketing Journal

Wall Street Journal

Periodicals

Business Japan

Business Tokyo

The East

Economic Eye (quarterly)

High Technology Business

Industrial News Weekly

Infomediary: The Journal of Information Brokerage and Consultancy

Japan Automotive News

Japan Commerce & Industry

Japan Economic Journal, The

Japan Economic Review

Japan Industrial & Technological Bulletin, The

Japan Letter

Japan Publications Guide

Japan Petroleum & Energy Weekly

Japan Quarterly, The

Japan Steel Journal

Journal of Japanese Trade and Industry (bimonthly)

Look Japan

Mechanical Engineering (ASME)

NIKKEI Architecture

NIKKEI Business

NIKKEI Computer

NIKKEI Electronics

NIKKEI Mechanical

NIKKEI Medical

Science (AAAS)

Speaking of Japan (monthly)

Spectrum (IEEE)

Tokyo Business Today (formerly *Oriental Economist*) (monthly)

Tokyo Journal

Tokyo Keizai Shinposha

Tokyo Weekender

Venture Japan: The Journal of Global Strategic Alliances

Newsletters

Asahi Shimbun Japan Access (Asahi Shimbun). A weekly briefing published 50 times a year, in English, by one of Japan's leading newspapers. Encourages understanding of Japanese concerns, customs, and culture. Reports on business, politics, finance, and social and cultural issues. Edited in Tokyo; printed and distributed in the United States.

Biotechnology in Japan News Service (Japan Pacific Associates). A monthly newsletter that has been covering Japanese biotechnology and R&D developments in the field in Japan since 1982.

C2C Currents: Japan and *C2C Abstracts: Japan* (Scan C2C, Inc.). *Currents* is a monthly that provides English bibliographic citations of articles recently published in Japanese journals. *Abstracts*, also a monthly publication, contains English abstracts or summaries of Japanese articles.

Daily Japan Digest. This newsletter, faxed daily, ensures receiving the most timely information that appears in the Japanese press. News items are under a variety of headings, such as Top of the News: Foreign Relations; Foreign Investment: Banking & Finance; Business; Economy; Electronics: Automotive, Trade; Labor; and Transport.

U.S.–Japan/Japan–U.S. News Views (Ranko International). A free monthly newsletter covering a variety of business, economic, and social topics, in both English and Japanese.

U.S. Sources on Japan

U.S. Government

ITA Country Desk—Japan, 202-482-2425/4527.

Joint Economic Committee of the U.S. Congress (Joint Economic Committee's Publications Department), 202-224-5321. Conducted a study called Global Economic & Technological Change: Japan & Asia/Pacific (July 1992) that provides a comprehensive examination of Japan's economic success and its implications for the United States. This committee regularly produces reports on China, Eastern Europe and the former Soviet Union.

National Technical Information Service (NTIS), 703-487-4650; Fax: 703-321-8547. Part of the Department of Commerce, this agency provides online and published sources of Japanese technical and scientific information as well as U.S. government assessments of Japanese research and product development. NTIS has access to Japanese directories and lists of experts in Japan, and can directly access JOIS, the database of the Japan Information Center for Science & Technology (JICST), for about $100 an hour plus telecommunications costs. JICST is Japan's central organization of information for the advancement of science and technology. However, most information in the JICST database is written in Japanese, and about 40 percent of the material originates from sources outside of Japan.

Japan Technology Program (JTP); Japanese Technical Literature Program; NTIS/JICST Online Information System (JOIS) Coordinator, 703-487-4819; Fax: 703-321-8199. JTP facilitates the use of Japanese information, sponsors programs and seminars on tracking scientific and technical information in Japan, and produces the *Japan Technical Literature Bulletin.* The bulletin reports on recent happenings in Japan's scientific, technological, and R&D communities, and gives English abstracts of Japanese technical literature and government laboratory newsletters.

JTP works closely with NTIS to inform the public on: how to use Japanese information, what information is available, and how to obtain it. In conjunction with NTIS, JTP obtains and abstracts Japanese scientific and technical documents and provides information on scientific and technical developments in Japan. It offers these Japanese directories:

Directory of Japanese Databases, which details 43 Japanese databases accessible from the United States; gives producers' names, addresses, and phone numbers, and issues the research report *Tapping Japan's Database Resources: An American Strategy.*

Directory of Japanese Technical Reports, which gives complete bibliographic citations of new information available through NTIS. *Directory of Japanese Technical Resources in the United States,* which lists over 250 commercial services, government agencies, and libraries that acquire, translate, or disseminate Japanese technical information. Includes background articles about accessing Japanese technical resources, and citations of Japanese technical documents, translated into English in 1990 and 1991, that are available through NTIS.

Besides commissioning and publishing literature, the Japanese Technical Literature offices act as liaisons with other government agencies and departments interested in acquiring and disseminating Japanese technical literature.

State Department Japan Desk, 202-647-3152.

U.S. Organizations and Associations

American Association for the Advancement of Science (AAAS), Directorate for International Programs, 202-326-6400. The AAAS publication *Science* frequently provides information on science and technology in Japan and the Pacific Rim.

American Chemical Society (ACS), Chemical Abstracts Service, 614-447-3600. The ACS database, Scientific & Technical Network (STN), provides access to the database of Japan Information Center for Science and Technology (JICST). It also produces several publications that cover Japanese chemical literature, including patents and current serial titles.

American Electronics Association, 408-987-4200. Publishes a market entry handbook for U.S. software companies, *Soft Landing in Japan.* Written by representatives of U.S. software companies located in Japan, the handbook covers marketing, sources of assistance, technical orientation, distribution, legal issues, staffing, and product support. Case histories of companies such as Lotus, Comshare, and Oracle are featured.

Asia-Pacific Council of American Chambers of Commerce (APCAC), 202-659-6000.

Asia Society. Offers special programs and publications dealing with economic and public affairs issues.

CHI Research/Computer Horizons, Inc., 609-546-0600; Fax: 609-546-9633. Provides indicator services in technology and science, which assess national, corporate, and institutional R&D performance. The assessments of patent and paper production are indicators predicting amount of R&D activity, and nature and subject of trends. CHI has its own patent database, offers online research, and publishes reports on technology and science. Along with Venture Economics, Inc., it publishes *The Japan Technology 50,* an analysis of the technological strength of Japan's major corporations.

Japan Pacific Associates, 415-322-8441; Fax: 415-322-8454. A management consulting firm specializing in working with CEOs of entrepreneurial, advanced technology companies in both Japan and the United States. Publishes a newsletter, *Biotechnology in Japan News Service,* and *Biotechnology in Japan Yearbook.*

Japan Society, 617-451-0726. Offers cultural programs, a business forum, and language classes. It has a library and provides public information and referrals on local Japanese resources, translation, employment, and interpreter services. The business forum has speaker and "how-to-do-business" programs plus a weekly clipping service of articles on Japan from selected U.S. newspapers.

National Science Foundation US–Japan Program, 703-306-1710. Collects, translates, and disseminates Japanese technical literature. Sponsors joint research in various scientific and technical fields, and organizes research stays at Japanese university, government, and corporate laboratories.

SCAN C2C, Inc., 301-949-81-1; Fax: 301-942-0434. Provides C2C OnCall, a service that allows clients to tailor their Japanese competitive intelligence needs. SCAN C2C's Document Delivery Service offers retrieval and photocopies of original articles from Japanese journals; SCAN C2C offers continual or ad hoc monitoring of Japanese databases. Translations can be either abstracts or full text. Custom research delivers conference papers and government reports.

Society of Manufacturing Engineers (SME), 313-271-1500. A member group of IEEE; sponsors seminars, workshops, and conferences. Has a reputation for being good at disseminating technical information, and has a large technical library that provides reference services.

Technology Transfer Society, 317-262-5022; Fax: 371-262-5044. Acts as an information outlet for a variety of published materials dealing with the transfer of technology. Publishes the monthly newsletter *T-Squared* and the quarterly *Journal of Technology Transfer.* Produces a directory that lists members alphabetically and by area of expertise. Distributes other publications, such as *Science in Japan: Japanese Labs Open to US Researchers,* at a discount to its members.

US–Japan Business Council, 202-728-0068. This organization of U.S. business leaders, formerly known as the Advisory Council on Japan/US Economic Relations, desires to facilitate bilateral business relations. Sponsors an annual Japan–U.S. business conference with its counterpart, the Japan–U.S. Economic Council.

U.S. University Programs

California

University of California, Los Angeles, 310-825-1323. The Oriental Library holds no Western materials, but has over 120,000 Japanese volumes as well as Chinese and Korean works.

Hawaii

Japan-America Institute of Management Science (JAIMS), 808-395-2314. JAIMS and the University of Hawaii are working together to make Hawaii the center of international business in the Pacific. JAIMS seeks to develop and enhance cross-cultural communication through management education and training. JAIMS offers seminars and research and education programs, and has developed Computer Assisted Language Learning (CALL) software for businesspeople interested in learning Japanese, as well as a line of audio cassette tapes for conversational Japanese. The College of Business Administration provides interdisciplinary programs and information/consulting services to public and private sector organizations.

Illinois

Asean Library, University of Illinois at Urbana, 217-333-1501; Fax: 217-244-2047.

Maryland

Japan Technical Information & Evaluation Service (J-TIES), University of Maryland, 301-405-3685. Prepares abstracts and summaries, and provides technical analysis. Monitors and summarizes national conventions, conferences, and other meetings of Japanese technical societies.

Massachusetts

MIT Japan Program, 617-253-2839; Fax: 617-258-7432. The program was founded to promote closer ties among scientists, engineers, and industrial managers in the United States and Japan. The largest and most comprehensive center of applied Japanese studies in the United States, it offers both education and research. A pioneering interdisciplinary program to investigate the Japanese technology process generates 10 to 12 new research papers annually. Lists of papers are available, and copies can be ordered for a nominal fee. Research includes collaborative R&D, technology management, and the internationalization of R&D. Projects have included: (1) a study of the aerospace technology and industrial policy in Japan; (2) development of interactive software to simulate cross-cultural negotiations with the Japanese; (3) management of R&D in the computer industry; and (4) study of East–West economic relations, encompassing security, export controls, and technology.

Michigan

Center for Japanese Studies & Far Asian Business Program, University of Michigan, 313-764-6307. Provides a range of services and training regarding Japan and China, and is involved in informing the American business community about available information.

New York

The Center for Japan–U.S. Business and Economic Studies, Leonard N. Stern School of Business, New York University, 212-998-0750; Fax: 212-995-4219. One of the first university-based organizations to focus on understanding the entire spectrum of business and economic relationships between Japan and the United States. Conducts research and offers courses, lectures, conferences, seminars, and publications.

North Carolina

North Carolina State University, 919-515-3450. The Honors Internship Program provides students with an opportunity to work in Japan, in affiliates and subsidiaries of U.S. corporations.

Virginia

George Mason University, 703-993-1000. Programs focus on changing the current infrastructure for acquiring and disseminating information so that more effective communication and utilization of Japanese technical information can be achieved.

Wisconsin

Japan Engineering Leadership Program, College of Engineering, University of Wisconsin—Madison, 608-263-2191. Offers courses in technical Japanese, in both the classroom setting and via audiographic teleconferencing. The audiographic course can provide training and education, at a worksite, in technical Japanese and a variety of engineering courses.

Japanese Representatives in the United States

Banks in New York:

Asahi Bank, 212-432-6400; Fax: 212-432-1135.

Dai-Ichi Kangyo Bank, Ltd. (DKB), 212-466-5200. Publishes *DKB Economic Report,* a monthly publication that focuses on economic and financial outlooks, industrial trends, major economic indicators, and special DKB topics.

Fuji Bank, 212-898-2000.

Import/Export Bank of Japan, 212-888-9500; Fax: 212-888-9503.

Industrial Bank of Japan (IBJ), 212-557-3500.

Japan Development Bank, 212-949-7550; Fax: 212-949-7558. Japan's government financial organization; develops Japanese domestic investment, and issues bonds.

Long-Term Credit Bank of Japan (LTBJ), 212-335-4400.

Japan Economic Institute of America (JEI), 202-296-5633. A small research and information group that operates under the Foreign Ministry. Publishes *JEI Report* and *Japan–US Business Report,* which offer careful analyses of business, economic, and political developments between the United States and Japan. *JEI Report* is a two-part publication issued weekly: *JEI Report A* studies a relevant aspect of the Japanese economy or Japan–U.S. economic and political relations. *JEI Report B,* a companion publication written in newsletter style, contains up-to-the-minute, concise news analysis and contains facts, names, and dates regarding the news items. This office does not provide any type of Japanese contact lists.

Japan Embassy, Washington, DC, 202-939-6700.

> *Embassy Branches*
> Anchorage: 907-279-8428
> Atlanta: 404-892-2700
> Boston: 617-973-9772
> Chicago: 312-280-0400
> Honolulu: 808-536-2226
> Houston: 713-652-2977
> Kansas City: 816-471-0111
> Los Angeles: 213-624-8305
> New Orleans: 504-529-2101
> New York: 212-371-8222
> Portland: 503-221-1811
> San Francisco: 415-921-8000
> Seattle: 206-682-9107

Japan External Trade Organization (JETRO), 212-997-0400; Fax: 212-997-0464. This is the New York office of this nonprofit government organization, which is affiliated with the Ministry of International Trade and Industry (MITI). For a detailed description of JETRO, see the "Government Offices" section later in this chapter. JETRO's branches in the United States are located in:

> Atlanta: 404-681-0600
> Chicago: 312-527-9000
> Dallas: 214-651-0839
> Denver: 303-629-0404
> Houston: 713-759-9595
> Los Angeles: 213-624-8855
> San Francisco: 415-392-1333

Japan Information Center for Science & Technology (JICST), Washington, DC, 202-872-6371; Fax: 202-872-6372. This is JICST's U.S. office. Its Selective Dissemination of Information (SDI) service provides information available from JICST's Tokyo headquarters on about 180 subjects. Literature searches and photocopying of full-text articles are other available services. See the "Government Offices" section, later in this chapter, for details.

Japan National Tourist Organization, 212-757-5640; Fax: 212-307-6754.

Japan Productivity Center, 703-838-0414; Fax: 703-838-0419. A small U.S. office of the Center, which is headquartered in Tokyo. It organizes study groups for Japanese businessmen coming to the United States and for U.S. business people going to Japan.

Manufactured Imports Promotion Organization (MIPRO), Washington, DC, 202-659-3729; Fax: 202-887-5159. A nonprofit organization supported by the Ministry of International Trade and Industry (MITI). Its goal is to foster expansion of Japan's manufactured imports. MIPRO sponsors exhibitions in Japan and publishes helpful business guides that focus on marketing, selling, and distributing in Japan. It also provides the names and addresses of Japanese representatives who work in various industries.

U.S. Representatives in Japan

American Center Library, 011-81-33-436-0901.

American Chamber of Commerce of Japan, 011-81-33-433-5381; Fax: 011-81-33-463-1446. Promotes the development of commerce between Japan and the United States. Special committees work with the Japan Direct Marketing Association and the Japan Chamber of Commerce and Industry. The American Chamber collects and disseminates statistical and commercial information to members. Its "Breakfast Program" introduces Americans to Japanese business leaders and keeps Americans informed on business trends and issues in the Japanese marketplace. It publishes *The ACCJ Journal; The American Chamber of Commerce in Japan—Directory of Members*, which includes addresses and phone/fax numbers for the 1,400 members; *The ACCJ Newsletter*, which lists business leads, industry parks, and calendars of events, and reports on the activities of various committees; and White Papers and special studies.

American Consulates
Okinawa City: 011-81-92-751-9331
10 Kano-cho, 6 chome, Ikuta, Kobe: 011-81-978-331-9679
254 Nishihara, Urasoe City, Okinawa 901-21: 011-81-98-876-42118
Sankei Bldg., 27 Umeda-cho, Kita-ku, Osaka: 011-81-6-341-2754
21296 Gusu Kuma, Urasoe, Naha: 011-81-988-77-8142
1 Nishi, 13 chome, Kita 1-jo, Chuo-ku, Sapporo: 011-81-11-221-5121

American Electronics Association, 011-81-33-237-7195; Fax: 011-81-33-237-1237. The Japanese office of the association that publishes *Soft Landing in Japan,* a market entry handbook for U.S. software companies. Written by representatives of U.S. software companies located in Japan, it covers the market, sources of assistance, technical orientation, distribution, legal issues, staffing, marketing, and product support, and gives selected case histories.

U.S. Export Development Office (EDO) (also known as U.S. Trade Center), 011-81-33-987-2441. Responsible for trade promotion; works with the ITA on exhibitions, trade missions, and fairs. It is of general help to U.S. businesspeople.

Additional Overseas Source

The British Library, 011-44-71-323-7924/5; Fax: 011-44-71-323-7965/7495. The library has a unit devoted to researching the Japanese. Services include: online searching, including direct searches of Japanese databases; market intelligence and information; document retrieval; language help; and referral to other information sources. The library has more than 3,500 Japanese scientific, technological, and commercial journals; more than 9,000,000 Japanese patents and virtually all Japanese industrial property publications; market and industry surveys; company and trade information; and conference reports. It also offers a range of publications and seminars on how to seek information on Japanese science, technology, and industry. It publishes a directory, *Japanese Business Publications in English.*

Government Offices

Japan External Trade Organization (JETRO), 011-81-33-582-5511; Fax: 011-81-33-589-3419. Publications: 011-81-33-582-5184; Fax: 011-81-33-587-2485. This nonprofit government organization promotes trade and economic relations, provides up-to-date information on the Japanese market, offers free personalized consulting services, and organizes trade missions and trade shows. JETRO has acted as an intelligence agency, gathering information for the Japanese about the United States, but now also provides ways for U.S. business professionals to gather information on Japan. A roster of market research firms and consultancy services can be obtained from JETRO.

In addition to its computerized database service and a network of experts, JETRO produces a video series on how to do business in specific Japanese industry sectors and publishes in-depth industry reports.

JETRO publishes a variety of booklets and magazines, such as *New Technology Japan.* Its major business directories include *The Directory of Japan Affiliated Companies in the USA and Canada; The Japan Trade Directory; Nippon Business Facts and Figures; A Directory of Sources of Information and Business Services;* and *Selling in Japan.*

Japan Federation of Prefectural Trade Promotion Agencies, 011-81-33-213-6870. Oversees internal trading between prefectures in Japan. All information provided is in Japanese.

Japan Foreign Trade Council, Inc., 011-81-33-435-5952. A very closed council; the only way to access information is to be a true insider.

Japan Information Center for Science and Technology (JICST), 011-81-33-581-6790; Fax: 011-81-3593-3980. JICST operates under the control of the Science and Technology Agency in the Office of the Prime Minister. As the central organization for information activities on the advancement of science and technology, the center collects and disseminates technical literature, sponsors R&D projects, and offers assistance to information users. JICST has a collection of 14,000 journals, but only half of these are of Japanese origin. JICST makes its information available online through the JOIS database. Business researchers can access JOIS through NTIS. (See "U.S. Information Sources," earlier in this chapter.)

Japan International Science and Technology Exchange Center, 011-81-33-288-0970; Fax: 011-81-33-288-0980; in Washington, DC, 202-939-6700. Established in November 1990, the center assists foreign researchers by introducing them to research opportunities in public and private Japanese research laboratories. It supports and promotes study activities and helps researchers to adapt to living in Japan. It also provides information about science and technology trends in Japan and overseas.

Japan Patent Office—Japan Patent Information Organization (JAPIO), 011-81-33-503-6181; Fax: 011-81-33-580-7164. JAPIO operates under the Patent Office, managing and disseminating patent information. It produces PATOLIS, the most comprehensive database for patent information in Japan, JAPIO, the most comprehensive database for Japanese patents in the English language.

The Patent Office started using an "Electronic Patent Application System" or "Paperless Patent Application System" on December 1, 1990. Japan had been criticized for having a slow patent processing system, and the Structural Impediment Initiatives have mandated that Japan reduce processing time from the current average of three years to two years. (In the United States, it takes about 18 months.) Japan is the most prolific nation in the world in generating patents, holding 40 percent of the world's total patents. The new system works online or through floppy disks. The large-scale computer network handles the entire patent examination process. The system is open and is connected to external databases as well as to the internal patent office databases. Online applications will be accepted through ISDN (Integrated System for Digital Network) and PPXIP (Packet Information Exchange Network System), which sends the application directly into the database in the Patent Office. However, a Japanese lawyer must prepare the electronic input.

Japan Productivity Center, 011-81-33-409-1111; Fax: 011-81-33-409-1986. Produces, in English, statistical publications that show the rate of productivity for industry. Its small U.S. office organizes study missions.

Manufactured Imports Promotion Organization (MIPRO), 011-81-33-988-2791; Fax: 011-81-33-988-1629. This nonprofit organization, supported by

MITI, sponsors trade exhibitions in the World Import Mart in Tokyo. MIPRO has an office in the United States and publishes several business booklets.

Ministry of Finance, 011-81-33-581-4111. Organization Division, Security Bureau. Compiles financial data on traded companies.

Ministry of Foreign Affairs, 011-81-33-580-3311. Oversees embassies and consulates around the world.

Ministry of Post and Telecommunications, 011-81-33-504-4411.

Government Research Laboratories

Government reports, newsletters, and company technical reports (called *giho*) can be obtained from government/corporate groups by faxing the publication departments of government research laboratories. Below is a list of the necessary *fax numbers:*

Building Research Institute: 011-81-298-64-2989

Communications Research Laboratory: 011-81-423-27-7458

Electronic Navigation Research Institute: 011-81-422-41-3169

Electrotechnical Laboratory: 011-81-298-55-1729

Fermentation Research Institute: 011-81-298-54-6009

Fire Research Institute: 011-81-422-42-7719

Forestry and Forest Products Research Institute: 011-81-298-74-3720

Geological Survey of Japan: 011-81-298-54-3571

GIDH-Hokkaido: 011-81-11-854-4676

Government Industrial Research Institute (GIRI):

    GIRI-Chugoku: 011-81-823-73-3284

    GIRI-Kyushu: 011-81-942-83-0850

    GIRI-Nagoya: 011-81-52-916-2802

    GIRI-Osaka: 011-81-727-51-6945

    GIRI-Shikoku: 011-81-878-67-8234

    GIRI-Tohoku: 011-81-22-236-6839

Hydrographic Department, Maritime Safety Agency: 011-81-3-3542-7174, 3545-2885

Industrial Product Research Institute: 011-81-298-54-6618

Institute of Agricultural Machinery (IAM) Bio-oriented Technology Research Advancement Institution (BRAIN): 011-81-48-651-9655

Institute of Physical and Chemical Research, The (Riken): 011-81-484-62-4608

Institute of Public Health: 011-81-3-3446-4314

Institute for Sea Training: 011-81-3-3580-4492

Japan Atomic Energy Research Institute: 011-81-33-3580-6107

Japan Chemical Analysis Center: 011-81-434-23-5326

Japan Information Center of Science and Technology (JICST): 011-81-33-593-3375

Japan Key Technology Center (KTC): 011-81-33-3505-6830

Japan Marine Science and Technology Center: 011-81-468-66-3061

Japan Sewage Works Agency: 011-81-484-21-7542

Marine Technical College: 011-81-797-32-7904

Mechanical Engineering Laboratory: 011-81-298-54-2513

Meteorological Research Institute: 011-81-298-51-1449

National Aerospace Laboratory: 011-81-422-48-5888

National Cancer Center: 011-81-3-3545-3567

National Cardiovascular Center Research Institute: 011-81-6-833-9865

National Chemical Laboratory for Industry: 011-81-298-55-1397

National Children's Medical Research Center: 011-81-3-3414-3208

National Food Research Institute: 011-81-298-38-7996

National Institute of Agrobiological Resources: 011-81-298-38-7408

National Institute of Agro-Environmental Sciences: 011-81-298-38-8199

National Institute of Animal Health: 011-81-298-38-7880

National Institute for Environmental Studies: 011-81-298-51-4732

National Institute of Health, The: 011-81-3-3446-6286

National Institute of Health and Nutrition, The: 011-81-3-3202-3278

National Institute of Health Services Management: 011-81-3-3202-6853

National Institute of Hygienic Sciences: 011-81-3-3707-6950

National Institute of Industrial Health: 011-81-44-865-6116

National Institute of Mental Health, NCNP: 011-81-473-71-2900, 72-1858

National Institute of Neuroscience, NCNP: 011-81-423-44-6745

National Institute for Research in Inorganic Materials: 011-81-298-52-7449

National Institute of Science and Technology Policy: 011-81-33-503-3996

National Research Institute of Agricultural Economics: 011-81-3-3940-0232

National Research Institute of Agricultural Engineering: 011-81-298-38-7609

National Research Institute of Aquaculture: 011-81-5996-6-1962

National Research Institute of Far Seas Fisheries: 011-81-543-35-9642

National Research Institute of Fisheries Science: 011-81-3-3533-5693

National Research Institute for Metals: 011-81-33-3792-3337

National Research Institute for Pollution and Resources: 011-81-298-54-3049

National Research Laboratory of Metrology: 011-81-298-54-4135

National Space Development Agency of Japan: 011-81-33-436-2928

NHK (Japan Broadcasting Corporation) Science & Technical Research Laboratories: 011-81-3-3417-5536

Nippon Institute for Biological Science: 011-81-428-31-6166

Osaka Bioscience Institute: 011-81-6-872-4818

Port and Harbor Research Institute: 011-81-466-42-9265

Power Reactor and Nuclear Fuel Development Corporation: 011-81-3-3583-6386

Public Works Research Institute: 011-81-298-64-2840

Railway Technical Research Institute: 011-81-425-73-7356

Remote Sensing Technology Center of Japan: 011-81-33-3403-1766

Research Development Corporation of Japan (JRDC): 011-81-33-581-1486

Research Institute of Industrial Safety: 011-81-3-3452-6565

Research Institute for Polymers and Textiles: 011-81-298-54-6233

Ship Research Institute: 011-81-422-41-3026

Traffic Safety and Nuisance Research Institute: 011-81-422-41-3233, 3232

Tropical Agriculture Research Center: 011-81-298-38-6316

Independent Research Institutes

Asahi Research Center, 011-81-33-507-2406; Fax: 011-81-33-50400537.

Fujitsu Research Institute, 011-81-43-299-3104; Fax: 011-81-43-299-3070.

Mitsubishi Research Institute in Tokyo, 011-81-33-270-9211; Fax: 011-81-33-279-1308.

Nomura Research, 011-81-03-211-1811; Fax: 011-81-03-278-0420.

Chambers of Commerce and Industry

Japan Chamber of Commerce and Industry, 011-81-33-283-7825. Publishes the *Standard Trade Index of Japan.*

Kobe Chamber of Commerce and Industry, 011-81-78-251-1001.

Nagoya Chamber of Commerce and Industry, 011-81-52-221-7211.

Naha Chamber of Commerce and Industry, 011-81-68-3758.

Osaka Chamber of Commerce and Industry, 011-81-6-944-6215.

Tokyo Chamber of Commerce and Industry, 011-81-33-283-7500.

Yokohama Chamber of Commerce and Industry, 011-81-45-671-7400.

Trade Associations

Communications Industry Association of Japan, 011-81-33-231-3156; Fax: 011-81-33-246-0495. Focuses on communication media makers like the telecommunications industry, and provides research and information for members.

Consumer Product Safety Association, 011-81-33-582-6231; Fax: 011-81-33-586-1545. Inspects consumer products, including products from the United States, and has information available in English

Council of All-Japan Exporters' Association, 011-81-33-431-9507; Fax: 011-81-33-436-6455.

Hokkaido Northern Regions Economic Exchange Association, Hokkaido Economic Federation, 011-81-221-6166.

Industry Club of Japan, 011-81-33-281-1711; Fax: 011-81-33-281-1797.

Information Science and Technology Association (INFOSTA), 011-81-33-813-3791; Fax: 011-81-33-813-3793. Has a "Japan Information Desk Service" set up for Western businesspeople seeking information sources and service organizations. It gives advice on technological and professional services in Japan.

International Medical Information Center (IMIC), 011-81-33-353-1538; Fax: 011-81-33-357-0073. Nonprofit organization developed from the information section of the Faculty of Medicine at Keio University to provide medical information.

Japan Association of Corporate Executives, 011-81-33-211-1271.

You Need a Personal Intelligence Network in Japan

LEONARD FULD: When American or European companies assess their Japanese competitors, what are their two or three most common information-gathering mistakes? How would you recommend that non-Japanese companies gather information on their Japanese counterparts?

BUNDO YAMADA:

The Barriers

When American and European companies collect information about their Japanese competitors, the following problems arise:

1. It is not easy to access core information through typical American or European research methodologies. Because disclosure of corporate information through the published literature in Japan is not adequate, you need both expertise and Japanese business experience to extract the necessary details from the limited published materials.

2. Because employees have loyalty and a familylike relation to their company, it is rather difficult to obtain inside information about the company, or information that may be damaging to the company.

3. Because the cost of translation is high, there is no incentive for Japanese companies to translate their corporate documents into foreign languages unless translating those documents will be profitable to the company. It is also often the case that nuances of the Japanese language are not translated correctly.

4. Because American and European companies may not fully understand the particular importance of human networks in Japan, they can miss the opportunity to collect accurate information without costing a lot. Valuable information can be obtained through close friends.

The Potential Solutions

The following points concern ways to collect unbiased information about Japanese corporations:

1. Japanese "main banks" maintain accurate information about their clients,[1] markets, and industries. If a company has a business relationship with a Japanese bank, it is possible to use the bank as a trustworthy source of information.

2. Another good method is to request a research firm with a high reputation, to do research.

3. With the exception of highly specialized information, industrial associations and government agencies generally can provide detailed and accurate objective information.

4. It is best to establish a network with research firms or individual specialists to exchange information. If, through the continuous exchange of information, trust and friendship are established, then the personal networks will exert real power to obtain hard-to-get information.

---

[1] In Japan, some banks have strong ties to corporations and handle the majority of those corporations' transactions. Such banks are called "main banks."

Bundo Yamada is President of the Fujitsu Research Institute, a research and consulting firm in Tokyo, Japan.

Japan Association for International Chemical Information (JAICI), 011-81-33-816-3462; Fax: 011-81-33-816-7826. Abstracts Japanese chemical patents, translates Japanese patents and articles, and publishes *Kagaku Shoho*, which contains the abstracts.

Japan Commercial Arbitration Association, 011-81-33-214-0641.

Japan Database Industry Association (DINA) and *Japan Information Processing Development Center (JIPDEC)*, 011-81-33-432-9381/9385; Fax: 011-81-33-432-9289. This nonprofit, neutral organization has a patronage membership from various industry sectors. JIPDEC constantly gathers and analyzes information processing data and publishes timely reports that reflect the current situation in information processing around the world. It conducts surveys and studies on specific issues and problems, and will conduct them on a contract basis. JIPDEC receives researchers from abroad and works on the exchange of information. It publishes, in English, *Informatization White Papers*, and *Japan Computer Quarterly*.

Japan Federation of Smaller Enterprise Organizations (JFSEO), 011-81-33-668-2481; Fax: 011-81-33-3668-2957. Provides valuable information and seminars for small companies, and offers publications in English.

Japan Institute for Social and Economic Affairs (Keizai Koho Center), 011-81-33-201-1415; Fax: 011-81-33-201-1418. This nonprofit, independent organization works with Keidanren (The Federation of Economic Organizations, one of Japan's major business organizations) providing information on the economy. It publishes, in English, *Speaking of Japan*, which provides texts of recent speeches; *Economic Eye*, a quarterly journal in which articles are selected from major Japanese periodicals; and *Japan 199X*, a pocket-size compendium of statistics that compares Japan's economic society to those of other countries. It also provides directories of information: *Japan Information Resources in the US* and *Japan Periodicals*. Its library is open to the public. The center offers seminars, education and exchange programs, and lectures for the purpose of creating and supporting a stimulating business environment. The center conducts research and analysis of trends in domestic and international economics, and works with overseas research institutes. It distributes its publications in the United States via OSC America.

Japan Pharmaceutical Information Center (JAPIC), 011-81-33-546-1811; Fax: 011-81-33-546-1814. Produces a database with information on all aspects of drug regulation and clinical use, but provides no information in English.

Banks/Stock Exchanges

Dai-Ichi Kangyo Bank, Ltd. (DKB), 011-81-33-596-1111. Publishes the *DKB Economic Report*, a monthly newsletter containing industrial trends, financial outlooks, and economic indicators.

Fuji Bank, 011-81-33-216-2211.

Industrial Bank of Japan, 011-81-33-214-1111.

Latin America: An Information Openness

LEONARD FULD: When a United States, European, or Asia, Pacific Rim company is considering competing in the Latin American market, what intelligence is crucial for it to develop, and how should it begin its research and analysis?

JOSÉ SALIBI: When a United States, European, or Asia Pacific company is considering competing in the Latin American market, I recommend that they begin their research and analysis by talking to key people in the industry (including competitors, customers, and suppliers) in the country they are targeting. Written information is usually not accurate in Latin American countries. Public and company libraries are usually not efficient. Information provided by the media is not very strong since journalists in Latin American countries are not as informed as their United States and European counterparts.

   The positive point about talking to key people in the industry is that people in Latin America tend to talk a great deal (more than they should). Their sense of discretion is not very high and they might provide researchers with amazing information. I highly recommend that researchers belong to Latin American industry associations, participate in trade shows, and seek help from their country of origin's Chamber of Commerce.

José Salibi is a senior partner with HSM Cultura & Desenvolvimento, a Brazilian conference organization that has introduced some of the world's foremost business thinkers, including, Michael Porter and Peter Drucker, to Brazilian business executives.

Japan Development Bank, 011-81-33-270-3211; International Dept.; 011-81-33-245-0439. Japan's government financial organization; develops Japanese domestic investment, and issues bonds.

Mitsubishi Bank, 011-81-33-240-1111.

Sumitomo Bank, 011-81-6-227-2111.

Osaka Securities Exchange, 011-81-6-229-8643.

7

ADDITIONAL VALUABLE SOURCES AND CONCEPTS—AND WAYS TO APPLY THEM

> Inventiveness and decision-producing intelligence go hand-in-hand. The successful analyst or seeker of competitive information knows how to go beyond the standard news magazines and databases. It is very much a lust for information that drives the truly great analysts to find and use sources such as the ones suggested in this chapter.

A number of basic intelligence sources do not fit neatly into any of the previous categories. Typically, they are not magazines or other reference sources that could be considered conventional.

For example, in my competitor intelligence seminars, I always ask the audience, which primarily consists of marketing executives and business planners, if they have ever heard of *The Wall Street Transcript*. At best, only half of the audience ever acknowledges having heard of the newspaper. It is a basic source, one every intelligence gatherer should know about; yet few do.

Other basic sources and methods to be discussed here include:

How to find a patent filing;

What a business school case study offers;

A tip on finding regional data;

Where to find management biographies;

The usefulness of state business directories.

WHAT DID THE CEO SAY? ASK THE *TRANSCRIPT*

The Wall Street Transcript is published weekly by:

> The Wall Street Transcript Corporation
> 99 Wall Street
> New York, NY 10025
> 212-747-9500

Each issue contains analysts' reports, roundtable discussions of industries (Figure 7.1), quarterly earnings reports of publicly held companies, and transcripts of speeches made before groups of analysts.

The *Transcript* essentially takes company press releases and analysts' news reports and publishes them with little or no editing. Speeches made before financial societies and business roundtable discussions are published in their entirety. Each issue is a couple of hundred pages long and is indexed by company or industry. Cumulative indexes appear monthly, quarterly, semiannually and annually, and are a prime source for updates on company trends.

THE PATENT HUNT

Before beginning to read about this subject, you must know the difference between a patent and a trade secret. Understanding the definitions will help you to realize the significance of a patent in determining a company's technical and strategic direction. Figure 7.2 compares their characteristics.

Chase the Patent, Not the Trade Secret

James Pooley, in his book *Trade Secrets: A Guide to Protecting Proprietary Business Information* (AMACOM, New York, 1989), describes a trade secret as "commercially useful" and "proprietary." In general terms, Pooley defines these phrases as follows:

> Generally speaking, proprietary information is simply "commercially useful" ideas. We are not concerned here with novelty or obviousness; considerations which arise with patents. However, if you expect anything to be "proprietary," whether it is technological data or customer information, it must at least be generally known. The phrase "commercially useful" is used here to mean eliminating information of academic interest only . . . .

A patent, on the other hand, tells the world what your invention is and how it works. Strictly defined, a patent is a government-issued certificate that secures for the owner the right to exclude others from making, using, or selling the claimed invention for up to 17 years for a utility patent and 14 years for a design patent.

An important point for you to understand is that trying to determine a competitor's trade secret may be a waste of time and is potentially illegal. You can assign your company's scientists to reverse engineer a competitor's product, but you may not want to conduct interviews to piece the answer together for fear of breaching various confidentiality agreements. Besides, while you are spending your time and

Property & Casualty Insurance

A TWST Roundtable Discussion

MODERATOR:

Richard A. Holman - Editor & Publisher

PARTICIPANTS:

William W. Dyer, Jr. - Century Shares Trust
Herbert E. Goodfriend - Prudential-Bache Securities
David Seifer - Donaldson Lufkin & Jenrette Securities

INDUSTRY PERFORMANCE

(PN401/01) TWST: Herb, we'll start with you. First the easy ones, what's been driving these stocks? Why have they performed the way they did over the last year?

Mr. Goodfriend: The word "driving", Richard, is somewhat of an overstatement, unless you consider driving downward as well as upward.

TWST: Sure.

Mr. Goodfriend: After a brief, buoyant period at 1989 year-end, which anticipated a prompt, V-shaped recovery in commercial pricing that didn't materialize and the expectation that interest rates would come down sharply -- which has also not materialized to the degree expected -- what we've seen is, first, a period of relative stabilization in pricing, and then renewed price cutting in several of the major lines of commercial underwriting. There have been some areas that have firmed. Those are the specialty lines that are not the center of the bell curve; and at the same time, we've had more controversy and fluidity in the personal lines side of the ledger. We've also had some more storms and some more hurricanes, and I guess, relatively, we've had greater interest in other groups because, in fact, the market decided not to turn defensive during this period of time. In addition, you had great concern over the balance sheet, not merely junk bonds, but those companies that were deeply involved in other securities that might have too much water in them. Perhaps they were associated with other organizations that might have had real estate, mortgage, and other problems on the asset side--or a mismatching.

Finally we have the fear that as we look at the economy over the balance of this year and the R-word has not materialized (recession) to the degree that some economists expected that then portfolio managers will say, "What's the sense of going into defensive stocks at a time when the industry really hasn't shown vigorous turnabout?" So I think the driving force has been on the downside side, virtually since year-end.

TWST: Dave, how do you see it?

Mr. Seifer: I would add that in 1989 when the stocks were performing well, you had a sluggish economy, lower interest rates, lower inflation, and the perception of improving fundamentals. This year, we lost lower interest rates. Inflation certainly has not come down the way it was thought. Fundamentals haven't improved yet. After a very fine year of stock performance in 1989, investors have taken profits. They have gone from an overweighted to an average or even underweighted position, and 1990 is an average-to-below-average relative performance year. Until there is some catalyst from either fundamentals, inflation or interest rates or an economy that slows down, I think that the group will stay average-to-below-average.

TWST: You mentioned three catalysts: fundamentals, interest rates and inflation rates. Not the same direction for all of them, though?

Mr. Seifer: No. We need a definite improvement in fundamentals and, as Herb alluded to, that is coming slowly.

TWST: Well, which way would interest rates and inflation head?

Mr. Seifer: Downward. Lower inflation and lower interest rates are plus factors for financial services stocks.

(Continued on Page 97,992)

Figure 7.1   Sample opening page from a *Wall Street Transcript* roundtable discussion.

PATENT v. TRADE SECRET

	Patent	Trade Secret
SUBJECT MATTER	• Specific and limited by statute (machines, articles of manufacture, processes, and compositions of matter)	• Applies to broad range of intellectual property and business information
REQUIREMENTS	• Must be useful • Must be novel • Must not be obvious	• Must be potentially useful • Must not be generally known • Need not be novel or obvious
DEFINITION	• Defined strictly by language of the "claims"	• Often difficult to define with equal precision, but can be as broad as the "equities" of a particular case require
DISCLOSURE	• Required	• Any disclosure must be limited and controlled
PROTECTION	• Defined by narrow but specific statute • Monopoly granted	• Varies, depending on circumstances and court; based on many theories • Protection only against "unfair" users: none against those who independently discover or reverse-engineer
DURATION	• 17 years from issuance	• Potentially unlimited
EXPENSE	• Procuring • Policing infringement	• Protecting from unauthorized disclosure or use
RISK	• Invalidity	• Independent discovery or inadvertent disclosure
MARKETABILITY	• Licensing easier	• Licensing more difficult, and requires policing of licensee security measures

Figure 7.2　A comparison of patent information and trade secrets. (Reprinted with permission from James Pooley, *Trade Secrets: A Guide to Protecting Proprietary Business Information*, AMACOM, New York, 1989.)

energy pursuing the technology of a competitor's trade secret, a third competitor may leapfrog both you and your target.

In *Top Secret Recipes: Creating Kitchen Clones of America's Favorite Brand-Name Foods* (Plume, 1993), Todd Wilbur demonstrates how he has reproduced in his kitchen many popular foods manufactured through trade secret recipes. Among his conquests are a reproduction of a Hostess Twinkie and a Kentucky Fried Chicken recipe. His research made for an amusing article in *USA Today* (July 13, 1993, page 6D), but how to make these new discoveries into successful mass-marketed products was not discussed.

Winning the day with any product depends on distribution, pricing strategy, technology, cost of production, and a host of other competitive issues, most of which can be learned through solid business intelligence techniques.

Analyzing patents is one of the intelligence techniques that can make the difference between a successful and an unsuccessful competitive analysis.

Understanding Patents

The number and importance of patents are increasing at a rapid rate, worldwide. According to Derwent, producer of one of largest global patent databases (World Patents Index), in 1980 its system contained 2,036,030 patent records. Contrast this to July 1994, when it contained 6,735,379, and you clearly see the dramatic growth in just under fifteen years. Derwent expects its World Patents Index to break the 7,000,000 record mark by late 1994 or early 1995. As further proof the patent's increasing technical and strategic clout, approximately one-quarter of all scientific or technical publications produced each year originate in patent offices around the world.

In the United States, there are three major patent categories:

1. Utility patents: These patents are issued for a process or a machine.
2. Design patents: The Patent Office defines this group as a "new, original ornamental design for an article of manufacture."
3. Plant patents: These patents are granted to anyone who has invented or discovered and "asexually reproduced any distinct and new variety of plant."

Many corporations—among them, probably, are some of your competitors—publicly announce patent filings to demonstrate their competitive strength or prowess. Their managements see patents as part of their strategic portfolio of assets, and they want their stockholders to understand that fact. Here are sample announcements:

> With thousands of patents in force worldwide, IBM Technology Products is an innovative presence in the industry and the first to develop and produce four consecutive generations of memory chips.—IBM 1992 Annual Report, page 28

> Corning owns more than 120 U.S. patents today for cellular-ceramic materials, products and processes, a mark of the advances in technology since the original substrate of the 1970s.—Corning Incorporated Annual Report 1992, page 5

Just counting or reviewing the number of patents filed is not enough. Many companies will file patents on technologies or products they have little or no intention of ever using. They might file to block a competitor's move, or to eventually license out the process to another firm that has the wherewithal or position to act on that process or product. Analyze a competitor's patents as an entity, not piecemeal. Patents are just one piece of the competitive puzzle.

Approaches to Analyzing Patents

Companies use almost as many ways to analyze patents as there are patents. However, all these analytical methods can be grouped into two general types:

1. *Experts' review.* Patents are often meaningless to amateurs or even to technologists who are not well versed in a particular process. Yet, when a group of true experts convenes, they will have the ability to quickly sort and discriminate among the densely written filings.

2. *Patent analysis model.* Companies such as CHI Research, Inc. (Haddon Heights, New Jersey, 609-546-0600) and Battelle Memorial Institute (Columbus, Ohio, 614-424-6424), have created large databases of patents filed worldwide. The models allow analysts to examine the strategic and tactical implications of patents that are filed globally. Francis Narin, president of CHI, told the European Patent Office's Information User's meeting, in September 1991, that CHI's computer model and database can be used for: Competitor strengths assessments; R&D productivity assessments; merger and acquisition target identification; long-term investment strategies; due diligence and technology valuation; cross-licensing negotiation support; and industry and regional economics.

The Wealth of Patent Resources

Before you can use any model, you need to find the patents themselves. There are now many avenues for a search.

One warning, though, before you start. Successful patent research often requires (1) technical knowledge of the process or product and (2) database search skills. Do not discount the need for database skills. Do not begin a serious patent search without first finding a skilled research or information service that has the right technical knowledge.

Once you have the search capability, there will be no shortage of information pools just waiting to be tapped. You should be aware that:

- There are more than 65 federally sponsored patent depository libraries (see Table 7.1). Each depository library houses a minimum 20-year backfile of patents.
- The Patent and Trademark Depository Library Program (PTDLP) has made CD-ROM disks available in the depository libraries, giving researchers a speedy information tool.
- The number of privately run or government-sponsored global databases has multiplied. Instant online access to literally millions of patent filings is now possible without ever having to leave your office. A list of these databases follows later in this chapter.

How to Search for Patents

To conduct a patent search, whether online or manually, you need to understand the cataloging structure. The following list describes how to search for patents, using this filing protocol.

1. If the number of the patent is known, then look the number up in the *Official Gazette of the United States Patent and Trademark Office.* This is published weekly and is organized numerically by patent number. The abstract of the patent in the *Official Gazette* includes the following information:
   a. Patent number.
   b. Inventor's name and address.
   c. Assignee (person/corporation that has the right to use the patent).

TABLE 7.1   Patent and Trademark Depository Libraries (PEDDLE)

State	Name and Telephone of Library
Alabama	Auburn University Libraries, 205-844-1747
	Birmingham Public Library, 205-226-3680
Alaska	Anchorage: Z.J. Loussac Public Libraries, 907-261-2916
Arizona	Temp: Noble Library, Arizona State University, 602-965-7607
California	Los Angeles: Public Library, 213-612-3273
	Sacramento: California State Library, 916-322-4572
	San Diego: Public Library, 619-236-5813
	Sunnyvale: Patent Information Clearinghouse, 408-730-7290
Colorado	Denver Public Library, 303-640-8874
Connecticut	New Haven: Science Park Library, 203-786-5447
Delaware	Newark: University of Delaware Library, 302-451-2965
District of Columbia	Washington: Howard University Libraries, 202-636-5060
Florida	Fort Lauderdale: Broward County Main Library, 305-357-7444
	Miami–Dade Public Library, 305-375-2665
	Orlando: University of Central Florida Libraries, 407-275-2562
	Tampa: Campus Library, University of Central Florida, 813-974-2726
Georgia	Atlanta: Price Gilbert Memorial Library, Georgia Institute of Technology, 404-894-4508
Hawaii	Honolulu: Hawaii State Public Library System, 808-586-3477
Idaho	Moscow: University of Idaho Library, 208-885-6235
Illinois	Chicago Public Library, 312-269-2865
	Springfield: Illinois State Library, 217-782-5659
Indiana	Indianapolis–Marion County Public Library, 317-269-1741
	West Lafayette: Purdue University Libraries, 317-494-2873
Iowa	Des Moines: State Library of Iowa, 515-281-4118
Kansas	Wichita: Ablah Library, Wichita State University, 316-689-3155
Kentucky	Louisville: Free Public Library, 502-561-8617
Louisiana	Baton Rouge: Troy H. Middleton Library, Louisiana State University, 504-388-2570
Maryland	College Park: Engineering and Physical Sciences Library, University of Maryland, 301-454-3037
Massachusetts	Amherst: Physical Sciences Library, University of Massachusetts, 413-545-1370
	Boston Public Library, 617-536-5400 ext. 2657
Michigan	Ann Arbor: Engineering Transportation Library, University of Michigan, 313-764-7494
	Detroit Free Library, 313-833-1450
Minnesota	Minneapolis Public Library Infoline, 612-372-6633
Missouri	Kansas City: Linda Hall Library, 816-363-4600
	St. Louis Public Library, 314-241-2288
Montana	Butte: Montana College of Mineral Science and Technology Library, 406-496-4281
Nebraska	Lincoln: University of Nebraska—Lincoln, Engineering Library, 402-472-3411

(Continued)

TABLE 7.1 *(Continued)*

State	Name and Telephone of Library
Nevada	Reno: University of Nevada Library, 702-784-6579
New Hampshire	Durham: University of New Hampshire Library, 603-862-1777
New Jersey	Newark Public Library, 201-733-7782
	Piscataway: Library of Science & Medicine, Rutgers University, 201-932-2895
New Mexico	Albuquerque: University of New Mexico Library, 201-932-2895
New York	Albany: New York State Library, 518-473-4636
	Buffalo and Erie County Public Library, 716-858-7101
	New York Public Library (The Research Libraries), 212-714-8529
North Carolina	Raleigh: D. H. Hill Library, N. C. State University, 919-737-3280
North Dakota	Grand Forks: Chester Fritz Library, University of North Dakota, 701-777-4888
Ohio	Cincinnati & Hamilton County, Public Library of, 513-369-6936
	Cleveland Public Library, 216-623-2870
	Columbus: Ohio State University Libraries, 614-292-6175
	Toledo/Lucas County Public Library, 419-259-5212
Oklahoma	Stillwater: Oklahoma State University Library, 405-744-7086
Oregon	Salem: Oregon State Library, 503-378-4239
Pennsylvania	Philadelphia, The Free Library of, 215-686-5331
	Pittsburgh, Carnegie Library of, 412-622-3138
	University Park: Pate Library, Pennsylvania State University, 814-865-4861
Rhode Island	Providence Public Library, 401-455-8027
South Carolina	Charleston: Medical University of South Carolina Library, 803-792-2371
Tennessee	Memphis & Shelby County Public Library and Information Center, 901-725-8876
	Nashville: Stevenson Science Library, Vanderbilt University, 615-322-2775
Texas	Austin: McKinney Engineering Library, University of Texas, 512-471-1610
	College Station: Sterling C. Evans Library, Texas A&M University, 409-845-2551
	Dallas Public Library, 214-670-1468
	Houston: The Fondren Library, Rice University, 713-527-8101 ext. 2587
Utah	Salt Lake City: Marriott Library, University of Utah, 801-581-8394
Virginia	Richmond: James Branch Cabell Library, Virginia Commonwealth University, 804-367-1104
Washington	Seattle: Engineering Library, University of Washington, 206-543-0740
West Virginia	Morgantown, Evansdale Library, West Virginia University, 304-293-4510
Wisconsin	Madison: Kurt F. Wendt Library, University of Wisconsin—Madison, 608-262-6845
	Milwaukee Public Library, 414-278-3247

    d. International classification number.

    e. United States class and subclass number.

    f. Number of claims against patent.

    g. Abstract of patent.

2. An example is shown in Figure 7.3. If the inventor or assignee of the patent is known, then go to the *Index of Patents, Part I: List of Patentees,* an alphabetical list. A segment of the list is shown in Figure 7.4. There is also an index of assignees. Under each assignee's name is the patent number.

3. If neither the patent number nor the inventor is known, then the search must be conducted by subject.

    a. Go to the *Index of Classification,* which is arranged by subject (Figure 7.5 shows sample entries). Choose the term that best represents the subject matter of interest.

    b. Once the pertinent class and subclass are determined, then the *Manual of Classification* should be checked. The *Manual* contains the entire classification schedule under each class (for an example, see Figure 7.6) and will help determine the best subclass to use.

    c. The final check of the class and subclass is Classification Definitions. This is a series of detailed definitions that illustrate the kind of subject matter that can be found in each class and subclass.

    d. Once the correct class and subclass are obtained, then the *Official Gazette* can be used. At the back of each weekly issue is an index ("Classification of Patents") by class and subclass with each patent number under that particular subject. At the end of this index is a table entitled "List of Patent, Design, Plant Patent, Reissue and Defense Publication Numbers Appearing in the *Official Gazette.*" This is a guide to the particular issue containing the specific patent number.

    e. If there is no number under the class or subclass, then no patent was issued. If you cannot find the patent, then you have chosen the wrong class or subclass. Check the *Index of Classification* again.

4. After the patent abstract is found, the patent can be ordered by contacting:

    U.S. Department of Commerce
    U.S. Patent and Trademark Office
    Washington, DC 20231
    703-557-4636; Fax 703-557-4636

The Patent Office also publishes a booklet, *General Information Concerning Patents,* which can help you in your patent search.

5. There are 38 libraries nationwide that maintain a patent depository. They are open to the public and provide technical staff for assistance. Table 7.1 lists these libraries.

A Database That Is Patently Obvious

When using databases, I have discovered that a number of them index and track patent information in their fields. Only a handful of databases solely monitor patents; another 20-odd databases incidentally watch for new patent filings, although they are

Re. 31,019
STRINGLESS ELECTRONIC MUSICAL INSTRUMENT
Fred J. Evangelista, 14 Linda La., Severna Park, Md. 21146
Original No. 4,177,705, dated Dec. 11, 1979, Ser. No. 973,801,
    Dec. 28, 1978. Application for reissue Jun. 25, 1980, Ser.
    No. 162,777
Int. Cl.³ G10H 1/00 1/02
U.S. Cl. 84—1.16   20 Claims

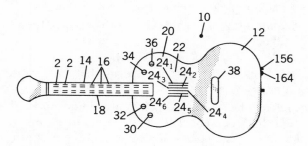

1. In an electronic musical instrument for simulating a stringed
instrument having a [body portion adapted to carry] tone generating means [and a neck portion adapted to carry a finger-board
assembly coupled to said tone generator means] and being op-
erable to vary the tonal output thereof, the improvement comprising.

  tone generator means including an electrical oscillator circuit
    [for each fundamental frequency desired to be simulated and]
    including switch operated circuit means [operable from said
    fingerboard assembly] for selectively changing [the] tonal
    [output] frequency [of said oscillator circuit]:
  [a respective] *an* output amplifier circuit coupled to said os-
    cillator circuit and being energized in accordance with the
    operative state of a player actuated switch device; and
  said player actuated switch device [consisting of] *comprising* a
    relatively thin [flexible blade-type] switch actuator member
    [mounted on edge in a substantially upright position on the
    outer surface of said body portion adjacent said fingerboard
    assembly,] *having a pair of sides and* being adapted [thereby]
    to be deflected bi-directionally [transverse] *transversely* [to
    said upright position] when strummed, struck, picked or
    plucked or bowed by a player, and at least one pair of elec-
    trical switch contacts located on each side of said actuator
    [element] *member*, wherein deflection of said actuator [ele-
    ment] *member* in either direction operates one of said pair
    of switch contacts to energize said output amplifier circuit.

Figure 7.3 Example of patent abstract from
*Official Gazette of the U.S. Patent and Trade-
mark Office.*

Sweat Buddy, Inc.: *See*—
>   Black, Henry C.; and Black, Ella J., 4,224,712, Cl. 15-209.00R.

Sweat, C. Downing, Jr.: *See*—
>   Hebert, Chris J.; Hollister, Ralph T.; and Sweat, C. Downing, Jr., 4,220,170, Cl. 134-167.00R.

Sweat, George B.; and Warren, Alvin E. Tree climbing apparatus. 4,230,203, 10-28-80, Cl. 182-134.000.

Sweda International, Inc.: *See*—
>   Goldstein, Amnon; Swett, Robert W.; and Greenwood, David L., 4,189,217. Cl. 354-7.000.
>   Markkanen, Carl O.; Benson, William G.; and Goldstein, Amnon, 4,208,009, Cl. 235-475.000.

Swedo, Raymond J.; and Marvel, Carl S., to University Patents, Inc. Biphenylene polymers and resins and the production thereof. 4,197,393, 4-8-80, Cl. 528-173.000.

Sweeney, Kevin M., to Simulaids, Inc. Disposable protective sleeve, having a pneumatic action, for a rigid splint board or the like. 4,182,320, 1-8-80, Cl. 128-89.00R.

Sweeney, Lawrence J., to Franklin Steel Company. Drive cap. 4,190,118, 2-26-80, Cl. 173-130.000.

Sweeney, Michael T.: *See*—
>   Moore, William T.; and Sweeney, Michael T., 4,234,240, Cl. 350-6.100.

Sweeney, Patrick E.; and Critcher, John J., to United States of America, Army. Directional fuze selector apparatus for artillery delivered mines. 4,205,609, 6-3-80, Cl. 102-8.000.

Sweeney, Ralph B.; and Verdouw, Albert J., to General Motors Corporation. Mount assembly for porous transition panel at annular combustor outlet. 4,191,011, 3-4-80, Cl. 60-39.320.

Sweeney, Richard F.; and Sukornick, Bernard F., to Allied Chemical Corporation. Process for producing halogenated hydrocarbons. 4,192,822, 3-11-80, Cl. 260-653.000.

Sweeney, Richard F.: *See*—
>   Lockyer, George D., Jr.; Burd, Dennis E.; Sweeney, Richard F.; Sukornick, Bernard; and Ulmer, Harry E., 4,187,386, Cl. 585-367.000.

Figure 7.4   Example of list of patentees.

Button . . . . 24 90+
Abrading cleaning shields 51 265
    Design . . . . D2 405+
Apparel, design . . . . D2 449+
Art collection . . . . 425 801°
Attaching
    Processes 2 265
    Sewing machine . . . . . 112 104+
Bell buttons mechanical 116 172
Collar or cuff 24 101
Design . . . . D2 405+
    Lapel . . . . D11 95+
Eyelet and rivet setting 227 55+
Fabric 24 92
Fastener making 29 4
Fasteners . . . . 24 90+
Feeder 227 31
    Sewing machine 112 113
Fluorescent and
    phosphorescent 250 462
Hinged leaf . . . . 24 97+
Hole (See buttonhole) . . 24 202
    Cutters . . . . 30 118+
    Marking guides 33 190
Hook D2 378.2
Loop 24 202.1
Making 79
Making, metal 29 4
Metallic . . . . 79 3+
Pearl & composition . . . 79 6+
Setting machine 227 55
Shank buttons 79 2
Strap or cable button . . . 24 114.5
Switch . . . . 200 329+
Telegraph key 178 110
Whip 231 6
Work supports 79 18
Buttoner 24 40
Design, shoe D2 378.3
Machine for shoes 12 58.3
Buttonhole 24 202
Cutting . . . . 83 905°
    Hand tool 30 118
Marker 33 190
Sewing machines . . . . . . 112 65+
    Processes and seams . . 112 264
Shoe closures 36 52
Stitch machine 112 157
Workholder in making 269

Figure 7.5 Example of subject classification.

```
      CLASS 9  BOATS, BUOYS AND AQUATIC DEVICES
1.1        BOATS, BOAT COMPONENTS OR ATTACHMENTS
1.2        . Wheeled landing or launching aid
1.3        . Circular
1.4        . Canoes or kayaks
1.5        . With protective covers or shields
1.6        . Boarding aids
1.7        . Deck or gunwale attachments
3          . Lifeboats
4 R        . . Inclosed
4 A        . . . . Even keel
5          . Hunting
2 R        . Sectional and folding
2 C        . . . Collapsible
2 F        . . . Foldable
2 S        . . . Sectional
2 A        . . . Inflatable
6 R        . Hull construction
6 M        . . . Metal
6 P        . . . Plastic
6 W        . . . Wood
6.5        . . Formers and framers
7          . Seats and foot supports
8 R        BUOYS
8 P        . . Offshore platform
8.3 R      . Illuminating
8.3 E      . . . Electrical
8.5        . Oil distributors
9          . Wreck indicating
10         . Safes
11 R       LIFE RAFTS
11 A       . . Inflatable
12         . Ship parts and furniture
13         . Mattress
14         LIFE-SAVING APPARATUS
15         RAFTING AND BOOMING
16         . Timber couplings
30         LIFE CRAFT HANDLING
31         . Conveying from storage position to launching position
```

Figure 7.6 Example of class and subclass listing.

not called patent databases. (See Table 7.2.) For a more complete description of a particular database, see Chapter 5.

Grasping Intellectual Property

Patents clearly identify an area of intellectual property. But with computer software now driving the growth of industries, the limits that define intellectual property are constantly being tested. What makes this area of law particularly difficult to define is its international aspect. Aside from the services of a good attorney and the resources

TABLE 7.2   Database Sources for Patent Filings

Database	Publisher	Description
Aluminum Industry Abstracts	ASM International	Aluminum patents and literature
APTIC	U.S. Environmental Protection Agency	Antipollution patents
BNA Patent, Trademark & Copyright Journal	Bureau of National Affairs	U.S. federal and state court decisions pertaining to patents and trademarks
CA Search	Chemical Abstracts Service	Patent specification: chemistry
CAB Abstracts	CAB International	Agricultural patents and biological information
Claims/Citation	IFI Plenum Data	Patent references cited during patent examining process
Claims/U.S. Patent Abstracts	IFI/Plenum Data Co.	Engineering, chemistry, and mechanical patents
Claims/Uniterm	IFI/Plenum Data Co.	All U.S. chemical and chemically related patents
Energy Science & Technology	U.S. Department of Energy	Patents for energy
FLUIDEX	Elsevier Science Publishers	British patents in fluid engineering
Food Science and Technology Abstracts	International food information service	Includes food patents
Foods Adlibra	Foods Adlibra Publications	Patents in food industry
INPADOC/Family and Legal Status	European Patent Office	References to patents for 56 countries
INSPEC	IEEE	Electronics, physics, computers, electrical and information technology patents
Japio	Japan Patent Information Organization (JAPIO)	Abstracts of Japanese patents
LEXIS Federal Patent, Trademark & Copyright Library	Mead Data Central	Patent, trademark, and copyright case court decisions
LEXIS United Kingdom & Commonwealth Legal Libraries	Mead Data Central	U.K. statutes on patent law
LEXPAT	Mead Data Central	Complete text for over 1 million U.S. patents
MARPAT	Chemical Abstracts Service	Graphic representations of generic structures since 1988
Metadex	ASM International	Metallurgical patents
Paperchem	Institute of Paper Chemistry	Pulp and paper technology patents

TABLE 7.2 *(Continued)*

Database	Publisher	Description
Telegen	Bowker A&I Publishing	Genetic engineering and biotechnical patents
Trademarkscan	Thomson & Thomson	Information on trademarks in the U.S. (federal and state), and the U.K.
Water Resources	U.S. Geological Survey	Patents for conservation, engineering, and water control
Weldasearch	The Welding Institute	Patents (mostly British) for plastics and metal welding
WESTLAW Intellectual Property Library	West Publishing	Full text of federal court decisions and statutes on intellectual property law
World Patents Index	Derwent Publications	Abstracts of chemical, electrical, mechanical, and general patents—international coverage
World-Surface Coating Abstracts	Paint Research Association	Patents for all aspects of paint and surface coatings

of the U.S. Patent and Trademark Office, other federal agencies may be of help. Here is a list of relevant government offices and their possible uses:

Copyright Office
U.S. Library of Congress
Washington, DC 20559
202-479-0700

Information on international copyright law; issues publications, such as *Copyright Basics* and *International Copyright Relations of the United States.*

U.S. Customs Service
Intellectual Property Rights Branch
1301 Constitution Ave., N.W.
Washington, DC 20229
202-566-6956

Regulations on the limits of exporting or importing intellectual property.

International Trade Administration
U.S. Department of Commerce
14th St. and Constitution Ave., N.W.
Washington, DC 20230
Domestic: 202-377-4767;
International: 202-377-8300

Knowledge of how other companies may complete licensing agreements and of limits imposed on exporting intellectual property.

Office of the U.S. Trade Representative
Executive Office of the President
600 17th St., N.W.
Washington, DC 20506
202-395-3230

Publishes the Annual Report of the President on the Trade Agreements Program. A useful source for gauging new markets and potential competitive licensing opportunities.

THE VALUE OF BUSINESS SCHOOL CASES

Business school cases are often overlooked as a source of company information. Within an average maximum of 30 pages, business school cases examine a company's management, operations, marketing strategies, and business failures and successes. A researcher can find answers to several of the following questions in a typical business school case:

What is the industry structure?

Who are the chief industry players?

What are the company's income and current assets?

Who reports to whom in the organization?

How does the company market its products?

How has the company dealt with past management or business problems?

Although any particular case could be out-of-date, it might provide your research with a starting point. An old organization chart may not represent the current management structure, but it is a beginning. Your first interviews can be focused on how and where the organization has changed since the study first appeared.

Business school cases also tend to offer a good deal of general industry data, including overall sales and competitor position in the market.

One caveat—Even when you find a case that seems to directly answer a question you may have about a corporation, beware! Many companies agree to submit to a university researcher's questions only after it is agreed that the actual case report will disguise many of the names and the financials discussed. The case's overall thrust may remain accurate, but it may obscure many of the details.

Another drawback is that the information contained in a case may be simply too dated to use.

Some case studies are available only to business school students and are restricted to certain classes. However, you can buy hundreds of cases over the counter. As of this printing, a Harvard Business School case study costs $5.

The Harvard Business School is the leading promoter of the case study method and has one of the largest collections of case studies in the world. Abstracts and indexes are available in a softbound catalog—itself a good reference source.

To extend its line of case studies, Harvard Business School now offers computer software for analyzing the cases, videos that supplement the cases, and books that give further background or readings. To order a case study, related materials, or a catalog, call or write:

The Harvard Business School Publishing Corporation
Operations Department
Boston, MA 02163
617-495-6117

As interest in the case method grew, the European Case Clearing House (ECCH) was formed. It has begun to harvest the many individual cases originating from a wide assortment of institutions, including: INSEAD, the United Nations Development Programme, and a number of United Kingdom business schools. To order any case materials, contact:

ECCH at Cranfield Ltd.
Cranfield Institute of Technology,   *or*   ECCH at Babson Ltd.,
Cranfield,   Babson College
Beds MK43 OAL   Babson Park
United Kingdom   Wellesley, MA 02157 USA
011-0234-750903; Fax: 0234-751125   617-239-5884/6; Fax: 617-239-5885

GO GLOBAL, THINK LOCAL

I once saw this phrase on a bumper sticker. It was referring to the environment, but I think it aptly describes where the analyst ought to go to find the most timely and most detailed information. Local magazines, newspapers, newsletters, and other community media must speak directly to their readerships. Their news will have regional interest, especially if it hits personal or public budgets.

One of the easiest ways to find good local sources is to ask the information operator for the phone number of the town's library. The reference librarian can give you the names of local publications.

Do not expect databases to have all the local news sources. Online services have made great strides, but a very large proportion of local news sources are not likely to appear on an electronic source for many years—if ever. Therefore, for detailed information, plant-by-plant and office-by-office, go local.

War Story: DECing the Queen Elizabeth

In the late 1980s, Digital Equipment Corporation (DEC) sponsored its annual high-tech bash, DEC World, in its home-base city of Boston. Thousands of corporate information systems managers from all over the world converged on the area. Attendance overran all the hotel capacity in the city of Boston and 30 miles into the suburbs. DEC even had to hire the *Queen Elizabeth II*, the largest ocean liner in the world, to accommodate the extra traffic.

The Boston Globe, Boston's largest newspaper, offered dozens of articles during the two-week extravaganza. Staff writers discussed new products and technologies and speculated on DEC's strategies. Try finding highly detailed articles like these in *The Wall Street Journal* or *The Chicago Tribune*. For the duration of the meeting, the best source for understanding DEC came from its own backyard.

MANAGEMENT BIOGRAPHIES IN PRINT

For packaged biographies on managers or executives in companies or industries you are examining, here are some biographical directories you might find useful:

Bio-Base: A Master Index to Biographies in 500 Biographical Dictionaries (Gale Research Co.). Contains an estimated 4 million citations of biographical directories and dictionaries. Each entry contains the person's name, the date of birth or death, and the publication in which the biography appears.

Biography & Genealogy Index (Gale Research Company). A guide to other biographical reference books.

International Who's Who of the Arab World (International Who's Who of the Arab World). Lists approximately 3,500 biographies.

Leaders in Electronics (McGraw-Hill). A key text for researching prominent individuals in the electronics industry.

Leading German Industrialists (Leitende Manner der Wirtschaft) (Verlag Hoppestedt). Lists over 43,000 Germans who are involved in German business or in the economy in general.

Marquis Who's Who (Marquis Who's Who). Considered the seminal biographical work. Offers *Who's Who in America, Who's Who in the East, Who's Who in the West, Who's Who in the South and Southwest,* and *Who's Who in Finance and Industry.* These reference books contain hundreds of thousands of capsule biographies. In addition, Marquis offers a *Directory of Medical Specialists.*

New York Times Biographical File (Mead Data Central). A service, not a single reference work; provides online biographies.

Standard & Poor's Directory of Corporations (Standard & Poor's Corporation). Volume 3 of this three-volume work offers brief biographies of the senior executives mentioned in its corporate listings.

Trustees of Wealth (Gale Research). Ordinarily thought of as a fund-raiser's biographical reference tool, but actually much more. Contains thousands of biographies of foundation trustees who are often directors and senior executives with major U.S. corporations. An invaluable tool for researching corporate executives. Each entry lists office address, business affiliations, title, year of birth, employment history, and educational background.

Additional Tips

Most biographies are never labeled as such. You will find biographies published in less formal ways, in bits and pieces. Here are some possible sources of biographical information on the individuals you need to analyze. (See Chapter 12 for ways to use these biographies in profiling management thinking and decision making.)

Corporate press releases. Companies will announce personnel promotions through press releases. These are often sent to the promoted executive's hometown newspaper for publication.

Using Intelligence Fiercely

LEONARD FULD: Since you were affiliated with Toshiba, how would you say the Japanese use intelligence—perhaps differently or more seriously than their Western counterparts?

JOHN REHFELD: While I was at Toshiba America Laptop Computer Business in the late 1980s, there was a great deal of intelligence required about the distribution channel.

During that stage of the PC business, the distribution channel had a lot of power over the manufacturers. Manufacturers were finding any creative way they could to gain mine share and shell space from the channel. This included Spiffs, promotions, market development fund, special discounts, special return policies.

There is a great deal of competitive advantage to be gained if you could outmaneuver other manufacturers within the channel to gain the mine share and shell space. We gather this information by talking to the channel, figuring out street price and reversing back channel margins to figure out how much money was going to the channel, talking to the stores, talking to former employees.

We would hold off-site business development sessions with a major channel member such as consumer distributors Ingram Micro and Mirasel, and one-tier stores such as Computerland and MicroAge. We would do this in an attempt to get close to the channel and determine what incentive we could give to get more help.

Since then, the manufacturers and the brand identity have gained more power relative to the channel, and this whole special discounting phenomenon has somewhat stabilized.

I believe that Japanese companies study their competition much more carefully than American companies. They tend to really identify one or two key competitors, label them as the "enemy" among their employees, and study everything they can to compete against them. This is especially true in Japan where companies like NEC and Toshiba will be very fierce competitors. In fact, Michael Porter, in this book *Competitive Advantage of Nations,* identified the fierce competitiveness among Japanese companies as a competitive advantage for the global market.

John E. Rehfeld was president and COO of Seiko Instruments USA, Inc. and continues to serve on its board of directors. In addition, he was Vice President and General Manager of Toshiba America's Information Systems Division, where he developed major markets for its laptop computers. He is currently President and CEO of Etak, Inc., a California-based multimedia software and content company.

Why Developing Countries Need Intelligence, and Why Industrial Countries Need to Understand This Need

LEONARD FULD: Are industrial countries, like the United States, underusing their information resources when entering developing countries? Have developing countries increasingly been using information resources, such as computer databases available from Western Europe, Japan, and the United States, in order to better assess their home market or overseas competition?

F. MITHAT KÜLÜR: Attracting foreign investment is increasingly viewed by developing countries as a sustainable means of upgrading their technological capabilities and industrial production base.

Changes in the global political balances, broad dissatisfaction with the pace of development under protected, state sector motivated industrial policies, and reductions in multi- and bilateral financial assistance have fueled this tendency to accept foreign private investors as a source of capital for building up assets and employment opportunities. Local companies are increasingly encouraged to forge partnerships with foreign counterparts as a means of acquiring know-how and technology, access to new markets, and modern management principles.

This change in attitude has signaled shifts in the policies of developing country governments toward greater liberalization. Previous defensive stances portraying foreign investments as neo-imperialism have undergone complete transformation. Today, governments of developing countries grope with the challenge of attracting companies from the industrialized world to locate at their shores. As the competition between developing countries to attract investors intensifies, the conditions for the foreign investors in these countries become increasingly welcoming. This new epoch has given rise to intelligence needs for both the developing countries and corporations of the industrialized world.

For the developing countries, the issues involve identifying foreign corporations that are deciding where to locate a foreign operation or may opt for a foreign location if approached with an attractive offer. Development agencies or other government and semigovernment investment promotion centers, or private organizations involved in attracting foreign investments into their countries, are looking for the companies ready to invest overseas so that they can target them. And the enticement involves: knowing whom in each company to approach; knowing the strategic rationale behind the company's decision to invest overseas so that the conditions available in the country and incentives can be packaged accordingly; knowing which location the company is contemplating and what incentives have been offered by these competitors so that a winning bid can be prepared; as well as getting the timing and mode of approach and presentation just right to achieve maximum impact on the decision.

These agencies also need to be attuned to the competition/alliance strategies of a potential investor to devise the best means of inserting themselves as complementary partners. If Thailand knows that the competitor of X is contemplating a major investment in the Philippines, knows the strategic impulse behind the plan, and knows the incentives and site benefits offered by the Philippines, Thailand can formulate a proposal customized for X with Thailand as the ideal location.

F. Mithat Külür is an Industrial Development Officer with the United Nations Industrial Development Organization and organized the 1991 experts meeting on technoindustrial intelligence in Vienna, Austria.

Credit reports. The Dun & Bradstreet credit reports (see Chapter 9) frequently summarize senior executives' biographies and will include some uncommon items, such as family ties to the company, and work history.

Home-town newspapers. Although small, these papers often profile successful executives among the leading personalities in their town.

Speakers' bureaus. Senior managers and consultants will sometimes book their speaking engagements through a speakers' bureau. Find out, through your professional associations or Chamber of Commerce, which speakers' bureaus handle certain types of experts. They may have resumes or biographies of their speakers available to send to you.

Trade and professional associations. Some of these groups publish membership directories; others summarize members' or speakers' careers in program announcements for their conferences.

University alumni relations/development offices. The fund-raising arms of colleges and universities keep track of and recruit successful alumni. In the process, these groups generate press releases or articles for the university house organ or alumni magazine.

STATE INDUSTRY DIRECTORIES: FOCUSING ON YOUR MARKET

National company directories, such as *Standard & Poor's Corporate Directory* or *Dun & Bradstreet's Million Dollar Directory,* will take you a long way toward finding information on national firms, but they will fall short on local, smaller companies. State directories can then come to the rescue. They are published by either the state government or by private publishers. A typical entry in a state industry directory appears very similar to an entry in the Dun's or S&P sources. It contains company name and address, telephone number, product or service, estimated sales, number of employees, and names of senior officers.

One of the largest publishers of state industry directories is Harris Publishing Company. From its powerful set of combinations, you can select either an individual state directory or regional editions. Harris also offers the directories on CD-ROM, a more efficient way to search the text. The CD-ROM capability may help you to quickly identify strategic patterns by noting, for example, where suppliers are located in relation to their customers.

To order materials from Harris Publishing, write or call:

Harris Publishing Company
2057 Aurora Rd.
Twinsburg, OH 44087-1999
216-425-9000, 800-888-5900; Fax: 216-425-7150

To find out whether a state government offers an industry directory, contact the Secretary of State or the Office of Corporations.

8 CREATING CREATIVE SOURCES

Watching and listening. These are among your best techniques for developing intelligence. The size of the trade show booth, the number of trucks pulling away from the loading docks, the types of services being "bundled together"—all are reflections of corporate activity. They are the true generators of intelligence.

HOW TO CREATE YOUR OWN CREATIVE INTELLIGENCE SOURCES

This book lists thousands of sources, yet no book can hope to list all the available sources. Each industry has its own pet research gems; some are unique to one industry. In this chapter, I take you through the "creative sourcing" process—that is, help you identify creative sources in your industry, when the ones suggested in this book do not apply or are not appropriate.

To introduce you to the process, let me show you the sources other industries have used successfully in tracking down bits of corporate intelligence. Table 8.1 lists various creative techniques or sources and the industries in which they are used.

WHAT YOU NEED TO LOCATE CREATIVE SOURCES

The executives who first told me about the techniques and sources listed in Table 8.1 did not go through great philosophical probings to identify these sources. They came across them through their experiences or heard of them from their colleagues.

What do *you* need, to identify creative sources that work in your industry or to profile the company you are investigating? By following the steps listed below, you will be able to identify formerly unknown sources:

TABLE 8.1 Selected Industry Techniques and Intelligence Gained

Industry	Technique	What Is Learned
Consulting	Staying outside a plant and watching the personnel enter and leave	Number of employees
Petroleum	Counting the number of links being sunk down a well shaft	Depth of the well
Packaging	Observing whether a shipping truck is single- or double-axled	Single axle indicates a lighter load; double axle indicates a heavier load
Consumer electronics	Trade show analysis (see "Trade Shows: Open Season on Competitors" in Chapter 11)	The marketing strategy and new products being offered
Retailing	Counting the number of stores listed in the Yellow Pages	Competitor's market share or, at least, its store locations

1. *Understand exactly what you are looking for.* This may sound like an insipid or even ridiculous statement. Yet, unless you can pinpoint your research goals, you will be unable to identify the necessary sources.

For example, when you look for "marketing strategy," are you looking for the number of stores the company will open within the next five years, or are you trying to determine its intended pricing structure? By defining the question, you save valuable research time and begin zeroing in on sources that directly address the question.

The consultant in Table 8.1, for instance, did not want to merely know the plant size. He actually wanted to know the number of employees and he successfully addressed that question.

2. *Determine the number of answers you want.* Each answer will likely require a different source. Suppose you want to find out a company's number of employees *and* the compensation it pays its sales force. They are two very different intelligence problems. The number of employees can be approximated with a simple plant sighting, a count of the people walking in and out. Determining compensation level may require your interviewing industry executive search firms, unions, or a competitor's compensation officer.

3. *Find a proxy.* This is a key point to understand. Once you have defined your questions, you have to ask yourself: "Is there another source that will give me the same or similar information?"

Finding a proxy is one of the most important ideas in this entire book. You have to remain loose and open to all possible sources. Don't put on research blinders and think, for example, that only a newspaper article will have your answer and that if there is no article available you should give up. Quite the contrary!

Let's look at some examples of research proxies.

1. You need company assets, and the balance sheet is not available because the target is a privately held company. Try a UCC filing.
2. You need the volume shipped, and bills of lading are not publicly available. Try analyzing the outgoing corrugated boxes to estimate the product content per box and the number of boxes shipped.

THE BEST WAYS TO FIND CREATIVE SOURCES

Speak to your own people who work in the area you are investigating. If you want to know how to find out the volume shipped, go first to your company's shipping department and ask: "If you had to find out our competitor's shipping volume and you did not have their bills of lading, what other sources would you use?"

Two important ideas to note here are:

1. *These individuals are almost never market researchers.* In fact, they are anybody but researchers. Your creative sources by definition are new and unusual. These are sources the researchers themselves must find. But they are not necessarily sources the researchers are directly acquainted with.

2. *The best people to approach for ideas for creative sources are the people who deal with the day-to-day operation of the business—from the ground level.* Shippers, production people, product managers, salespersons, service technicians, and programmers don't do research, but they do understand how their company operates.

Listening to the Silence: The Need for Content and Patent Analysis

LEONARD FULD: Can you describe how content analysis can be used as a predictive tool on a very specific product or competitive level? Describe the reasons why content analysis complements patent analysis, particularly when it comes to assessing future technologies and competitive strategy.

DICK KLAVANS:

Content Analysis

Here is how and where content analysis—a statistical analysis of the occurrence and words and phrases throughout a collection of literature—can help you assess future technologies and competitive strategies.

Content analysis is more effective in assessing competitive intentions but is less effective in assessing capabilities. Conversely, patent analysis can pick up capabilities but is weak in identifying intentions. Both have limitations that are discussed below.

Identifying Intentions with Content Analysis: Content analysis (and related techniques that try to identify underlying meanings from the words used by a competitor's executives or managers) can help to clarify a competitor's intentions. Words are a mirror of the corporate personality. If the text is appropriately selected, an informed analysis can "decode" the words and provide insights into corporate directions and priorities. The effectiveness of content analysis is sensitive to two factors: (1) the source of the text, and (2) the framework for identifying themes.

(Continued)

- **Source:** Content analysis of a top executive's speeches (or other documents for public consumption) are more suspect if a speech writer is involved. It's much better if the document is closer to unguarded speech.
- **Framework:** Content analysis should start with the identification of a framework that includes the possible themes that are expected to appear.

Patent Analysis

Identifying Capabilities with Patent Analysis: Patent analysis (and related techniques that focus on the scientific and technical "outcomes" of an R&D lab) help to clarify a competitor's capability. Patents are particularly useful when secrecy is *not* pervasive (such as in the pharmaceutical industry). A firm with a stream of interconnected patents is indicative of a firm with an underlying ability to develop a particular technology. However, patent analysis is also sensitive to problems of source and framework.

- **Source:** Each country has its own patent system. Focusing on the U. S. patent data is sufficient if the inventive capabilities of the firm are in the United States, but can be seriously misleading for estimating the capabilities of global firms with significant R&D outside the United States. Focusing on patents can also be misleading if the purpose of the analysis is to estimate scientific capabilities.
- **Framework:** Patent analysis should also start with the identification of a framework that includes the possible technological capabilities that are expected to appear. Without this step in the analysis, it will be impossible to "listen to the silence"—e.g., observe that the firm is studiously avoiding patenting in a specific area. As mentioned above, silence in an expected area is a critical finding. It usually indicates a vulnerable capability.

Dick Klavans is President of the Society of Competitive Intelligence Professionals and Vice President of the Center for Research Planning (CRP) in Haverford, Pennsylvania, a firm that specializes in content analysis.

A clever shipper would tell you about the corrugated boxes as a source. Another might suggest that you estimate the number of products per truckload and find a way to estimate the number of trucks that leave the plant per month. You can check on the number of trucks by simply counting them from a distance, or by speaking to the truck leasing company that the competitor uses. The leasing firm might also give you an idea of how often the competitor uses the firm's trucks.

But let's say you are new to an industry and you are investigating a company that is outside your area of expertise. To locate those creative sources, you will have to find key individuals who might know a good number of sources or alternate sources. Here are some individuals, in a few selected industries, who might supply you with ideas for excellent creative proxies:

Banking: Product managers, tellers

Software: Buyers, programmers

Chemicals: Production managers, salespeople, shippers

Insurance: Brokers, salespeople

Packaged foods: Food brokers, packagers

To get the person to think of a creative source for you, never ask the entire question. Ask your question in parts. The entire question could create a mental block. For example, don't ask a shipper, "What is Company X's sales volume?" Instead, ask:

Do you know how much of the product Company X fits in one truckload?

Do you know how many trucks Company X ships out in one week?

Are its sales seasonal? If so, when does Company X ship more and when does it ship less? Is it currently in a slow or a busy season?

With that approach, you break down your major question (Company X's sales) into its components:

$$\text{Products sold} = (\text{Products/truckload}) \times (\text{Number of truckloads})$$

The last question above takes into account anomalies in sales and seasonal fluctuations.

Reality will often dictate that one shipper may not be able to answer all of your questions. You may have to go to a number of shippers, or other industry sources, to derive a reliable estimate of Company X's sales.

9 BUILDING A FINANCIAL STATEMENT

"It's amazing," a new analyst would say to me. "How can you possibly divine out the profit and loss statement or balance sheet from a privately held company, or from a small subsidiary of a large conglomerate?"

What the beginner does not realize is that (1) the estimate comes from a combination of good data and a knowledge of the manufacturing or service process under examination; and (2) most of these financials are "best guesses." These best-guess financials often accurately interpret the critical financial factors and the impact they have on the corporation, but they would not pass an accountant's audit. They are not expected to. Their purpose is to provide enough insight to make an informed decision.

HOW TO ESTIMATE A FINANCIAL STATEMENT

Financial statements are the bugaboos of intelligence gathering. They are difficult to derive. Unless a competitor literally hands a statement over to you, you can never be totally sure the financials you have assembled are correct.

This chapter will help you make the best out of a difficult situation. You have already seen how and where you can purchase state and SEC filings. Never overlook these financials sources (remember your homework). But what happens when public filings are not available, when no one ever required that the particular privately held corporation file a statement in the first place? Or, a stickier problem, what if you have to derive the financials of a company that is a subsidiary of a publicly held corporation? You will find the parent company's financials, but probably not those of its subsidiaries.

You can use three major sources to derive company financials in cases where they are not revealed in public filings or news articles: (1) credit reports, (2) financial ratios, and (3) expert interviews (sources of production costs).

War Story: A Shattering Piece of Information

Hunting for a glass manufacturer's estimated sales figures, Fuld & Company made sure to do our homework first: we ordered a credit report on the company.

At first glance, the report gave us our answer: the company reported $15 million in sales each year. Yet, when we read a little further into the report, we discovered that the company had switched from being just an import office for a foreign manufacturer to building its own plant.

After making a few inquiries, we discovered that the company was actually generating sales on the order of $30 million, or twice what the credit report stated. We also learned that the reason for this jump in revenue was the new plant itself, and that one year ago, before the plant was built, the company's sales were actually $15 million.

What we saw was a credit report that was updated to the extent that it reported the new plant. Unfortunately, the other half of the report was not changed to match this new information.

In truth, you should use all three of these sources in conjunction with one another. Each alone is weak and needs corroboration. Together, these sources will either corroborate or disprove each other. In the end, you will be able to make a stronger case for the final income statement or balance sheet you eventually draft.

CREDIT REPORTS

Credit reports are the lazy way to garner information on the competition. As the expression goes: You get what you pay for. If a credit report costs you $20 or $30, that is exactly the amount of intelligence you will be getting—$20 or $30 worth. Yet, it is still a source you should turn to first.

Credit reporting agencies are either independent services, such as Dun & Bradstreet (D&B), or are in some way affiliated with a trade group, such as the Lumbermen's Credit Association. The depth and quality may differ markedly between one credit agency and another. One credit report may offer extensive financial information; another may present no more than a vague and broadly defined rating code.

To order a credit report, you may only need to phone the credit agency of your choice and order the report. In other instances, as with D&B, customers must pay in advance for their estimated usage.

At their best, credit reports offer the following when you are in search of corporate intelligence:

Basic information—name, address, standard industrial classification, age of firm, and parent–subsidiary relationship.

Financials—usually, this means sales or net worth figures. Where public filings are available, these reports may cite their financial data.

General purpose of business.

Reports of financial difficulty or court cases outstanding.

Payment record.

But take note. Most credit reports are designed for purchasing agents, not for researchers, that is, they concentrate on payment record, not on the choice marketing or plant data you need.

When ordering a report, here are some drawbacks to be aware of:

- Credit reports concentrate on payment record and debt, not on income or operating expenses.
- Credit services often cover a broad range of companies. They become a jack-of-all-trades, lacking a specialty or insight into any one field. This mass production system may cause a particular service to overlook or omit potentially valuable data.
- Little investigation is carried out by the services' researchers, aside from a review of the available public filings (SEC, state, UCC).
- Because of its established update cycles, a credit agency may miss the latest income statement issued by a company. The current company financials may then not be reflected in the credit report until one year later.
- Credit reports contain little background information on the company's principals and their corporate affiliations.
- Credit reports are not designed to supply marketing, planning, production, or sales information, except in the most general terms.
- Instead of admitting there is no information, credit reports will often substitute pat phrases such as "trend up" or "premises neat and clean." This is noninformation or nonintelligence.
- Credit services have little to offer on small, privately held companies.

The credit services below were chosen because of their nationwide coverage. Other, local services may serve one region or town, and were not included here. To find the credit agencies in your area, look in the Yellow Pages under the heading "Credit Reporting Agencies."

To see how to develop a full financial or cost analysis, using these and other tools in the book, see the *Mule Glue* cost analysis case in Chapter 12.

Dun & Bradstreet Information Services
One Diamond Hill Rd.
Murray Hill, NJ 07974-0027
908-665-5000

Background. The D&B U.S. credit reports database has 10.3 million records as part of its overall database of 18 million records. D&B's international database contains 13.7 million records of companies in 210 countries. Because of differences in the availability of information outside the United States (often, far less is available), the buyer needs to expect inconsistencies and omissions in the depth and breadth of the data published in the international D&B reports.

Major Purpose. The D&B system allows analysts to dip into its rich data pool in any number of ways. The result is different products, each with a different application. There are aspects of each application that an intelligence analyst can use to better understand a target company, but it must be remembered that these are credit reports, not intelligence reports. As such, *they are not intelligence sources, but rather sources that lead you to intelligence.* This applies to all credit reports, not just those of D&B.

Report categories. Overall categories included in D&B reports include: Dun's number (identification number), summary, payments, finance, banking/banking relationships, history, operations, special events, and public filings.

Among the D&B reports you should consider retrieving are the following:

Business Information Report (Credit Report). Aside from changing the name of this report, D&B has enhanced certain sections of it over the years. In particular, I have found many more UCC filings listed. These are indicators of equipment purchases or size of company assets. In addition, D&B has cleverly found new ways to link its information between files, as in the creation of the Family Tree Service, described below.

Payment Analysis Report. When you start a financial analysis of a target company, you may not know how the company compares to its competition or other firms in its class. D&B takes its vast collection of financial data from available credit reports and compares them in aggregate form—by industry classification—to your chosen company. The discovery that a company has made a profit or incurred a loss is significant. You may learn far more and your analysis will have a greater "comfort level" by running this type of financial comparison.

Family Tree Service. In almost 20 years of training analysts, I have seen the neophytes often stumble or take long research detours because they could not link one company to another, or because they failed to find the company altogether. A name change, an acquisition, or a divestiture creates an aura of stealth around corporations. D&B's Family Tree Service reports on corporate relationships and on links between corporations and their subsidiaries—or even intercompanies affiliates—where each company may own a piece of the other. In this age of strategic alliances, knowledge of corporate affiliations can help you to understand potential strategic direction.

Lumbermen's Credit Association
111 West Jackson Blvd.
Chicago, IL 60604
312-427-0733

Background. A credit reporting agency specializing in the lumber and woodworking industries. Its major product, the Red Book, contains credit ratings on lumber operators, intermediate distributors, remanufacturing consumers, and any other entity that buys lumber, dimension, veneer, or plywood for manufacturing purposes.

Major purpose. Credit reference guide for the lumber industry.

Report Categories. Name, address, business classification, and credit rating (including financial strength, paying habits) are supplied. Ratings are extremely general. More details may be obtained from the credit agency.

Fidelifacts
50 Broadway
New York, NY 10004
212-248-5619; 800-678-0007

Background. Fidelifacts is an investigative credit reporting firm. Reports are issued on a case-by-case basis. Investigators review a wide variety of sources, including other credit reports, online databases, state motor vehicle bureaus, UCC statements, tax liens, mortgages and deeds, liens, court records, and various regulatory agency filings. In addition, they will conduct interviews.

Major purpose. Reports are used for a wide variety of consumer loan and criminal investigations. Most important for the corporate analyst or strategist, the reports help management investigate the principals before any corporate acquisition. Asset searches, a person's background and credentials, and any criminal activity may be included.

Report categories. A typical report will contain the following categories of information: credit history, criminal records, motor vehicle search, employment history, education, military records, and references.

Produce Reporter Company
845 E. Geneva Rd.
Carol Stream, IL 60188-3520
708-668-3500, Fax: 708-668-0303

Background. Instead of individual credit reports, this service issues a semiannual Blue Book that covers 16,000 produce industry companies, including: growers/shippers, distributors, brokers, buying brokers, terminal receivers/jobbers, chain stores, merchants, importers, exporters, chippers, and canners. Six regular supplements and weekly updates are also issued.

Listing coverage. In addition to company name and address, each listing contains names of key personnel, summarized operating facts, business classification, and volume and commodities handled.

Sporting Goods Industries Clearing House (parent: Credit Exchange, Inc.)
28 East Jackson Blvd., Suite 720
Chicago, IL 60604

Background. Established to determine credit and reliability of sports clubs and pros as consumers of sporting goods.

Major purpose. Assembles reports for manufacturers and retailers, who in turn sell to sports clubs and sports pros (primarily on the golf and tennis circuits). The report information is gleaned from the subjects themselves.

Report categories. Antecedent history, employment history, payment record, other pertinent financial data, and reports of delinquent payment are researched and reported.

TRW Business Credit Services
3110 Central Ave.
Riverside, CA 92506
800-527-9663; Fax: 909-276-9442

Background. With over 2.5 million credit reports on file, TRW is smaller than Dun & Bradstreet. The coverage includes both public and private companies in most U.S. service and manufacturing industries. The service is available through TRW or through other information systems, such as Dialog.

Major purpose. To provide business credit reports to commercial customers. TRW is most useful to vendors and customers.

Report categories. Account status (including the last sale date recorded, payment terms, high credit, account balance, and status of payment), affiliated bank, product line description, sales, employment, parent name, bankruptcy, and tax and legal history are investigated for the report.

The Ratio Test

To see whether companies with known financials had ratios that matched those given by a book containing ratios for this industry, Fuld & Company took seven manufacturers of office computing and accounting machines with known financials. (These companies were all publicly traded, and filed annual reports with the SEC.)

Results: Our test group differed considerably from the so-called industry average. For example, our group posted an average of 3.3 for the current ratio. The average current ratio presented by the book was 2.1.

The net assets/net worth figure was even worse. The book offered 36.5 percent and our group averaged 60.8 percent.

The average ratios given by the financial ratio chart are compared with the test results in Table 9.1.

TABLE 9.1 Comparison of Test Group with Industry Average

	Quick Ratio	Current Ratio	Net Assets/ Net Worth (%)	Return on Equity (%)
Textbook average	1.0	2.1	36.5	17.4
Test group average	1.8	3.3	60.8	10.0
Ratios for test group companies:				
Standard Register	2.4	3.3	53.1	15.1
Analog Devices	1.8	4.3	106.0	6.5
Digital Equipment	2.3	4.2	30.0	13.0
Technitrol	2.1	3.5	23.6	11.0
Safeguard Scientific	1.6	2.3	63.0	1.0
Lundy Electronics	1.7	3.3	57.0	8.4
National Semiconductor	0.8	1.8	93.0	15.7

The Ratio Rule

Test the ratios you want to use before you apply them! If you can, conduct a test similar to the one described above. Find a group of companies that seem similar in size and industry grouping to your target company, and run their financials against the ratios. If the results are close, then you know you most likely have a set of usable ratios. If not, find a new table of ratios or do not use this technique. (Your target company may be so unique that it will not fit into any industry grouping.)

FINANCIAL RATIOS

Bankers use this tool every day. They apply industry financial ratios to companies seeking loans from their bank to see, for example, whether a company's debt picture is above average. A banker may also want to look at a firm's current asset/current liability ratio (also known as "current ratio").

These ratios tell the banker whether a company is a good risk for a loan, both from a short- and long-term perspective. You can use this same tool to help piece together a target company's balance sheet or income statement. Here is an example of how you can employ a financial ratio to derive a firm's fiscal picture:

The Murf and Turf grass-seeding company has assets totaling approximately $100,000. You need to find out its total liabilities.

In an industry guide, you find that the standard current assets/current liabilities ratio for this industry is 2:1 (total assets are two times the total liabilities).

Using the formula of 2.0 = current assets/current liabilities, you plug in the one value you know, which is the current assets figure. Simple algebra will then tell you that the total current liabilities amount to $50,000 (assuming that the ratio you were given was correct in the first place).

Theoretically, you might need only three of Murf and Turf's financial figures (let's say current assets, gross revenue, and cost of goods sold) to derive the entire income statement and balance sheet.

Later in this chapter, I list books that contain lists of financial ratios for various industries and company sizes. Be aware that these ratios can be a dangerously misleading tool. The big question you must always ask before using a set of ratios is: Does this set of ratios accurately portray my target company's true financial picture?

Drawbacks

Industry groups—banks and trade associations included—will compile financial averages so that those in the industry can compare their company to others in the industry. Usually, two major problems are inherent in the use of such ratios:

1. *The ratios don't represent your target company's industry.* Murf and Turf is a grass-seeding and lawn-care company. Yet the only ratios you can find describe agriculture and farming. Agriculture is the larger and more general industry heading. Should its ratios happen to match with your target company's ratios, it

---

War Story: Ballparking a Number

Our researchers have frequently encountered this situation: We are given an assignment to estimate a company's income statement. All we have to start out with is the company's credit report and a few press clippings.

In one case, the company happened to have been a manufacturer of small household hardware supplies. The credit report gave an overall sales figure of $25 million. The credit report did not, however, offer any other financial information.

The researcher identified a set of financial ratios that the company would fit into. She plugged the $25 million into the sales-related ratios and derived such items as assets, expenses, and so on. Yet the researcher could not rely on an extrapolated set of numbers—all of which were based on one speculative sales figure.

By speaking to a plant manager at a competing firm, she discovered that her long-term assets figure was too high, and lowered it accordingly. When she interviewed the public utilities, she received more accurate numbers for the company's power consumption. By speaking to a local union, she found out that the salary figure should be raised (the figure she derived from the ratios was more representative of a nonunion shop).

At the end of the battery of interviews, the researcher was able to assemble a fairly accurate financial picture of the company. But to do this she used the financial ratios as a springboard for discussion, a way to prompt the experts to offer their best guesses on the corporation's income and expenses.

---

would be purely coincidental. Lesson: Make sure that the ratios you use belong to your industry.

2. *The ratios reflect companies that are much larger or much smaller than your target company.* Murf and Turf may be ten times larger than its nearest competitor. But the ratios you are using are based on a group of companies far smaller than Murf and Turf. The proportions between the smaller and larger companies will not match—and again, if they do, it would be coincidental. Lesson: Make sure the companies you use have the same asset size as your target company's.

Where to Find Your Ratios

Speak to the trade association that represents your target company's industry. Go to your local banker, who will have textbooks that contain hundreds of industry ratios. "Sources of Business Ratios," later in this chapter, lists some of the more basic sources.

ANALYZING WITH RATIOS: WHAT TO WATCH OUT FOR

Anyone can play with the numbers, but only an astute analyst can turn those numbers into insights. You must use the ratios for yet another perspective on your competitor.

Compare what you learn from the numbers with the information supplied from interviews and other sources. What are some of the questions you should ask during the analytical process? How can ratios help place in perspective everything you have learned so far? These are some of the analytical guideposts to watch for:

Ability to Pay Current Obligations. The position of a banker who needs to determine a client's ability to handle debt is very similar to that of the competitive analyst. Both must grasp the financial reality of the company. Both need to take into account other industry factors and norms not measured by pure ratios. Three traditional measures are used here.

1. *Current ratio.* The current ratio is the result of current assets divided by current liabilities. Bankers and analysts use this ratio to understand a company's ability to pay short-term obligations—its liquidity. A company is generally judged "liquid" if its current ratio is 2:1 (there are some differences by industry). As an example:

$$\text{Current ratio} = \frac{\text{Current assets}}{\text{Current liabilities}} = \frac{\$250,000}{\$125,000} = 2.0$$

This 2:1 ratio is a fairly conservative number and may not reflect the particular industry you are examining, where the ratio may be closer to 1.5:1. Just using the 2:1 relationship, a banker would say that this company is a safe bet. What the banker is saying is that at least 50 percent of the current assets can be converted into cash reasonably fast.

   Advice: As an intelligence analyst, however, you need to go beyond these numbers and identify the specific assets. Using such sources as UCC filings (see Chapter 11), credit reports, and interviews with suppliers (to determine payment history and overall reliability), you will soon discover whether a state of liquidity exists or whether the numbers are below industry norms, indicating limits in the competitor's ability to pay or to take chances with aggressive pricing, hiring, or marketing campaigns.

2. *Acid-test ratio (quick ratio).* The current ratio becomes the acid-test ratio by eliminating any noncash assets, such as inventory. The acid test assumes that, because inventory is not cash and could take weeks or months to be converted into cash, it is not truly a liquid asset.

$$\text{Acid-test ratio} = \frac{\text{Cash} + \text{Accounts receivable}}{\text{Total current liabilities}} = \frac{\$125,000}{\$125,000} = 1.0$$

The typical ratio is 1:1. Anything below 1.0 may be considered financially precarious.

   Advice: You can draw several inferences from the quick ratio. For example:

   - A high quick ratio could indicate a very conservative, risk-averse competitor that is unwilling to leverage cash resources.
   - On the other hand, a high quick ratio could signal that the competitor is poised to mount a competitive challenge—perhaps one that is already rumored in the industry.

To draw any final conclusions, you need to combine experts' comments with the quick ratios you have compiled. Gather other evidence of activity or inactivity before allowing the ratios themselves to lead you to a decision.

3. *Debt-to-equity ratio.* This ratio compares total liabilities to stockholders' equity. In effect, it measures indebtedness and solvency.

$$\text{Debt/equity ratio} = \frac{\text{Total liabilities}}{\text{Total stockholders' equity}} = \frac{\$400,000}{\$325,000} = 1.23$$

Advice: You may be able to determine stockholders' equity from annual reports, regulatory filings (such as Securities and Exchange Commission filings), credit reports, and some state or provincial government filings (see Chapter 3), but the level of indebtedness is not absolute. The "normal" debt-to-equity ratio is somewhere about 1:0. The above example shows 1:23 and would indicate a company with slightly more leverage than a banker might feel comfortable with. As an analyst, ask these questions: What is a standard industry level of debt? Is this resulting number a normal outcome, or does it indicate a company in trouble? One way to find out is to consult the *Robert Morris Associates Annual Statement Studies,* which lists ratios for actual companies in hundreds of industries.

Profitability/Return on Investment. The two basic measures here are return on equity (ROE) and return on assets (ROA). These would become critical if your company were to acquire another firm or to begin its due diligence work for a joint venture or alliance. As a potential investor or acquirer, you need to know the relative return you can expect from your investment.

$$\text{Return on equity} = \frac{\text{Net income}}{\text{Total stockholders' equity}} = \frac{\$200,000}{\$1,000,000} = 20 \text{ percent}$$

A 20 percent return is considered a healthy return on equity for most companies. Always compare your findings with industry averages before you draw a conclusion about your target company's standings.

Return on Assets. This ratio helps determine how much profit a company is able to generate from each dollar of assets on its balance sheet. The before-tax ROA ratio is calculated as follows:

$$\text{ROA (before taxes)} = \frac{\begin{array}{c}\text{Operating earnings}\\\text{before interest/taxes}\end{array}}{\text{Total assets}} = \frac{\$350,000}{\$2,000,000} = 17.5 \text{ percent}$$

If you think of the ratio in terms of dollars and cents, this company earned 17.5 cents for every dollar of assets. One way to make use of this ratio is to compare it to your own ROA; another use would be in an acquisition analysis, to compare it to members of an industry peer group.

Let's take ROA analysis a step further. If the same company can earn 17.5 cents on each dollar of assets, it can earn 17.5 cents on assets supported by borrowed funds. If the borrowed funds only cost the company 8 percent on average (taking into account zero-interest trade payables, equipment loans, lines of credit, mortgages, and so on), then it has the ability to generate healthy 9.5 percent returns on leveraged

What Ratios Can't Tell You: Biotech Example

Based on the return-on-equity (ROE) formula, the biotechnology industry should not exist today. The biotechnology industry has spawned hundreds of start-up companies over the past decade. Many of them are still not profitable, yet they continue to receive funding through stockholders or venture capitalists.

Biotech is a great example of why intelligence analysts should understand and use ratios, but at the same time not get lost in their simplicity.

With some biotech companies, you would be investing in their *future* products and income, their future ROE. A current ROE would look disastrous. Therefore, when analyzing this ROE, you need to understand far more than just the strict ratio. You must technically review the future product portfolio and the income it may generate. For example, if the FDA has just approved a new genetically engineered healthcare treatment in a much needed treatment area, the future ROE may be immense, even though, right now, it's in the basement.

If I were a banker doing the analysis, I might tell the biotech company that it is currently a big risk and a loan is probably out of the question. If I were a stockholder, ready to speculate, or a large pharmaceutical house wanting to diversify for future growth, I might place my money on the table by purchasing shares or supplying venture capital.

Aside from pure ratio analysis, you need a partial mix of Wall Street financial wisdom, scientific analysis, and personality profiling. You need an analysis team that is strong in technical and general business expertise. The scientist, accountant, and business analyst may each come up with a totally different view, and none of them may be accurate. Together, they have a far better chance of understanding the whole picture, financial and otherwise. This team needs to answer a variety of interrelated questions, such as:

- What is the current ROE? What might it be five years from now, when the approved drugs or treatment have been fully tested and placed on the market? (Projected cash flow is the key at this stage.)
- How deep should this start-up's pockets be? What additional money will it need to pump into R&D, testing, and, ultimately, marketing and selling? Will it become a money pit?
- Who manages the company? How successful have the managers been with past start-ups?
- Are the patents and treatments technically unique? Are they likely to maintain a market edge, or will they be superseded by a more potent medication or treatment?

Lesson: The investment answers will come from a variety of areas of expertise, including financial analysis. Financial ratios often prescribe the normal operating boundaries for a company, assuming that the company operates under normal conditions. They are a useful tool, but not an exclusive one. Analysis done piecemeal, or by only looking at one aspect of the question (such as making a buying decision based purely on examining the company's financial ratios), is asking for trouble. Lack of time is no excuse here. To gain the proper perspective, you must spend the time and add layers of expertise and interpretation to any ratio analysis.

assets. In other words, the amount the company earns on borrowed funds is greater than the amount it pays in interest expense. This is called financial leverage, and it is very important to prospective investors, acquirers, or shareholders in a company.

Bear in mind that extraordinary gains or losses, heavily depreciated fixed assets, or a high level of intangible assets (for example, goodwill) can distort the ROA figure. Always remember to analyze the ratio in the proper context, taking into account the company's unique business dynamics and those of the industry in general.

Appreciating Depreciation

Depreciation is an accounting approach to spreading the cost of a fixed asset, such as plant or office machinery, over an estimated useful life. To an analyst, understanding and interpreting a company's depreciation numbers can explain a great deal about its manufacturing process or approach to business. As you will read in the *Mule Glue* case (Chapter 12), a great deal of the client's cost difference can lie in its penchant for buying bigger and more expensive machines, which increases the depreciation number. A competitor, producing nearly the same amount of product, would be able to sell its units at a far lower cost. Analyzing a competitor's depreciation numbers can also shed light on its overall spending and investment philosophy. The competitor might be thrifty in every way; the client, on the other hand, might want only the best and shiniest equipment—and be forced to pay for it.

Understanding depreciation, therefore, offers insight into a company's operations but not the entire answer.

When deciding to depreciate assets, all companies must choose from among three depreciation methods:

1. *Straight-line method.* This approach assumes that the asset steadily declines in value, at the same rate each year. An asset—say, a photocopier—worth $10,000 and stated as having a 10-year life span, depreciates at 10 percent per year. Each year, it declines in value by $1,000. After 10 years, it is worth $0 and is taken off the books.

2. *Double-declining-balance method.* This is an accelerated means of depreciating assets. For example, if an asset has a 10-year life and would have been depreciated at 10 percent per year for 10 years in a straight-line depreciation, the double-declining approach would apply a rate of 20 percent. After 5 years, the asset, effectively, would be worth nothing.

3. *Sum-of-the-year's-digits method.* The approach here is more complicated than the double-declining-balance approach, but offers similar results. It, too, accelerates depreciation.

Always consult with your accountant before applying any depreciation figures to your analysis. The accountant, who knows accounting rules and regulations, will be able to tell you what depreciation standards your target company has been using.

FINDING FINANCIALS: GO TO THE EXPERTS

As you were reading through the previous section, which explained the pros and cons of financial ratios, you might have caught yourself saying, "He talks about plugging two or three values into the ratios and coming out with a financial statement. But what I need to know is, how did he come up with those two or three numbers in the first place?"

A good question. Earlier chapters have shown that you can get some financial data from various publications and financial filings. Other sources of company financials are the many experts available, and they are not necessarily accountants or nuclear physicists. They are individuals who are close to the company or the community in which the company is located.

Let's start by taking an ordinary income statement and examining each line item. Who would be the best source for this kind of information? Who would know, for example, about a company's labor costs? Based on our experience, we then place alongside each statement category the most likely sources for information on that category:

Sales: Commercial credit agencies, competitor's sales force, independent representatives, distributors, competitors

Cost of goods sold: Product stripdown engineers (e.g., Underwriters Laboratories)

Raw materials: Department of Commerce, suppliers, distributors

Direct labor: Bureau of Labor Statistics

Indirect labor: Industry directories, unions, state filings

Supplies: Banks, local suppliers, industry studies, industry directories

Heat, light, and power: State power commission, utilities companies

Repairs: Industry analysts, unions, competitors (regional)

Property taxes: Commercial realtors, assessors, town records

Maintenance: Unions, trade associations, competitors, contractors

Insurance: Local insurers, state rate commissions

Rent: Commercial realtors, assessors

Loans: Banks

R&D: Trade reporters, trade associations, directors of R&D

Advertising: Advertisers, advertising account executives, advertising departments of newspapers

Modifying the Ratios through Interviews

No ratio will be the perfect equation of a target company's balance sheet or income statement. You will need to adjust the numbers you arrive at.

Interviewing the experts will tell you whether your numbers are out of line or on the money. Interviewing is an excellent means of adjusting the inventory numbers you may have derived (although, in the same industry, one company's inventory may be totally different from its competitors').

Table 9.2 uses the Murf and Turf example from earlier in the chapter and carries it through to adjusted ratios.

TABLE 9.2   Steps in Uncovering Financial Data Using Ratios

	Step 1	Step 2	Step 3	Step 4
	Known data	Industry ratios	Financial data derived through ratios	Final result: data adjusted based on interviews
Current assets	$100,000			$100,000
Current ratio		2:1		5:3
Current liabilities	—		$50,000	$60,000

SOURCES OF BUSINESS RATIOS

The following pamphlets and books list financial operating ratios for a wide variety of both service and manufacturing industries. In certain instances, industry trade associations compile statistics and ratios; in other cases, the data may have been gleaned from banks, government agencies, or credit services.

A tip: When you are looking for ratios on a particular industry that is not in the list below, call the major trade association for that particular industry. Chances are good that it has compiled and collected financial data from its member companies. Although the financials themselves might be proprietary, the ratios derived from those figures are available to the public.

General (including manufacturing)

Annual Statement Studies (Robert Morris Associates)

Cost of Doing Business: Corporations (Dun & Bradstreet)

Industry Norms and Key Business Ratios (Dun & Bradstreet)

IRS Corporate Financial Ratios (Off-the-Shelf Publications)

Quarterly Financial Report for Manufacturing, Mining and Trade Corporations (U.S. Federal Trade Commission and the Securities and Exchange Commission)

Banks

Bank Operating Statistics (Federal Deposit Insurance Corporation)

Financial Statements and Operating Ratios for the Mortgage Banking Industry (Mortgage Bankers Association of America, Economics and Education Department)

Department Stores

Financial and Operating Results of Department and Specialty Stores (National Retail Federation Financial Executive Division)

Discount Stores

Mass Retailer's Merchandising Report (International Mass Retail Association)

Drug Stores

NWDA Operating Survey (National Wholesale Druggists' Association)

Finance Companies

Analysis of Year End Composite Ratios of Installment Sales Finance and Small Loan Companies (Journal of Commercial Bank Lending, Robert Morris Associates)

Food Stores

Annual Financial Review (Food Marketing Institute)

Financial Ratios (National Grocers Association)

Operating Results of Independent Supermarkets (Food Marketing Institute)

Restaurants

Restaurant Industry Operations Report (National Restaurant Association)

10 LET YOUR FINGERS DO THE STALKING

Using Yellow Pages and City Directories

"Prodigy and NYNEX plan to put some 1.7 million business listings from 300 Yellow Page books in NYNEX's territory onto Prodigy's online database service . . . ," states the Reuters news wire. In the very near future, we are likely to see all Yellow Pages available in electronic form. This possibility only highlights the fact that if a business has a phone, it is listed somewhere. Telephone books, therefore, are the most complete set of corporate directories available—and probably the least expensive. Want to know what competitor activity is taking place elsewhere? Scan the Yellow Pages.

The Yellow Pages and city directories are two very potent corporate intelligence-gathering tools. Each can reveal a company's neighbors, the size of the market, and background information.

They are very different, yet in many ways very much alike. Table 10.1 illustrates their similarities and differences.

THE YELLOW PAGES

A Yellow Pages directory is probably one of the most effective and least expensive intelligence-gathering tools you can buy for your corporate library. Before a corporate library begins considering any other reference texts, it should make sure its collection of Yellow Pages covers every geographical area in which its company operates.

How can you use this potent intelligence tool?

TABLE 10.1   Comparison of Yellow Pages and City Directories

Features	Yellow Pages	City Directories
Contents	Company names, addresses, telephone numbers, and advertisements.	Company and individual names, addresses, and telephone numbers, as well as biographical background on business owners and residents.
Indexing	Lists companies by product or service category only; no alphabetical or telephone listing.	Lists companies and private residences by street, alphabetically by name, and numerically by owner's telephone number.
Number of volumes	One volume for each major metropolitan area. May include many towns, as, for example, the Greater Boston Yellow Pages, or one borough, as in New York City.	Usually, each city directory contains only one city, and does not include adjacent towns in its listing.
Availability	There is a listing for almost every city in the United States.	City directories are usually published only for the larger U.S. cities. There are thousands of Yellow Pages; there are hundreds of city directories.

- *To locate the number of competitors in a particular market.* For example, under the heading Discount Stores, you can locate all Kmart stores in that trading area.
- *To define a realistic trading area.* If you are based on the East Coast and are asked to research a company in the Midwest, how are you to know what a realistic trading area is for that target company? The greater metropolitan Yellow Pages for your target's city will provide a map for that trading area. Figure 10.1 shows an example for the Greater Boston area.
- *To locate suppliers and distributors.* Let's say you have to locate suppliers for a glass company. You already know that, in the glass industry, suppliers of sand, coal, and scrap are situated near the manufacturing plants. The Yellow Pages will provide you with a comprehensive list of these suppliers—some of whom most likely deal with the target company.
- *To retrieve marketing and product line information.* Take a close look at your typical Yellow Pages display advertisement. It is a highly informative document, almost resembling a miniature D&B credit report. It may list, aside from the company's name and address, its product line, the year it was established, and the marketing message and image it wishes to project to its customers.
- *To determine industry size.* Just run your finger down a Yellow Pages column for any category, and you will have a good idea of industry size in the region (that is, the number of companies and competitors in the market).
- *To understand industry terminology and check your search.* Whenever you begin searching an industry for competitors, suppliers, or any related companies, you want to make sure you have not left out any categories. Unknown to many users, most Yellow Pages now have a fairly thorough cross-index in the back of each volume. This ensures that you will not overlook a crucial category or industry heading.

If you didn't have the NYNEX Business To Business Directory, this is what you'd be missing.

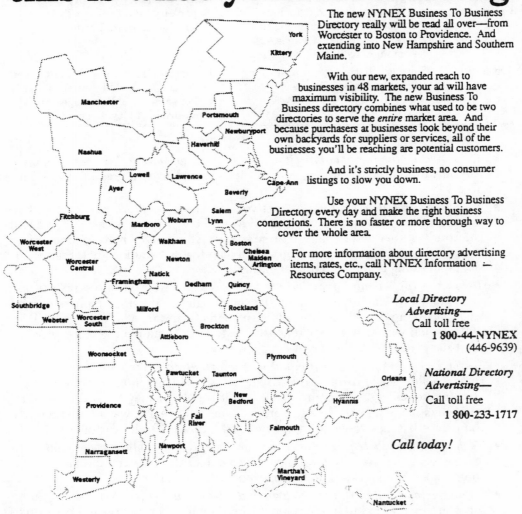

The new NYNEX Business To Business Directory really will be read all over—from Worcester to Boston to Providence. And extending into New Hampshire and Southern Maine.

With our new, expanded reach to businesses in 48 markets, your ad will have maximum visibility. The new Business To Business directory combines what used to be two directories to serve the *entire* market area. And because purchasers at businesses look beyond their own backyards for suppliers or services, all of the businesses you'll be reaching are potential customers.

And it's strictly business, no consumer listings to slow you down.

Use your NYNEX Business To Business Directory every day and make the right business connections. There is no faster or more thorough way to cover the whole area.

For more information about directory advertising items, rates, etc., call NYNEX Information Resources Company.

Local Directory Advertising—
Call toll free
1 800-44-NYNEX
(446-9639)

National Directory Advertising—
Call toll free
1 800-233-1717

Call today!

Figure 10.1 Map of area covered by Greater Boston Area Yellow Pages. This defines an actual—not artificial—trading area.

For example, for a complete list of department stores in the area, you may look under the category of Department Stores. But when you check the index in the back of the Yellow Pages, you discover that you should also be looking under Discount Stores to make your list truly complete.

How to Order the Yellow Pages

On the first few pages of your local Yellow Pages will be the address and phone number of your local telephone business office. Call to find out the specific order requirements. You may discover, for instance, that if your toll calls to the metropolitan area you are interested in exceed a certain dollar volume, you may be able to receive that Yellow Pages edition at no charge. Otherwise, each edition may cost you about $10–30.

The Difference between the Business-to-Business and Consumer Yellow Pages

The Business-to-Business Yellow Pages may cover a larger trading area—50 miles instead of 35 miles, for instance. But it will also eliminate any of the consumer listings, such as retail stores or dry cleaners. Conversely, the Consumer Yellow Pages will eliminate strictly industrial categories. Your best bet, if your area still prints it, is the general metropolitan area Yellow Pages, which includes both the Consumer and the Business-to-Business editions. The general metropolitan Yellow Pages is becoming a rare commodity as the various telephone companies continue to further divide their market segments, catering to each group with a specialized edition.

Yellow Pages in Other Forms

The need for better and easier business data has spawned electronic versions of the traditional Yellow Pages and print directories. The electronic versions listed below are not a substitute for the printed versions (for example, they do not have the graphics), but they do offer easy access and a sort capability. You can avoid tediously sorting through dozens of metropolitan Yellow Pages listings to compile a list of suppliers, distributors, or competitors. The following sources allow you to cross-reference your request by industry category, company size, and region.

A caveat: No single data source is perfect or complete. Be aware that most electronic phone directories cannot be as current as the actual phone books. If you need to be absolutely sure of the names you've collected, you may want to spot check or research the names from the original source directories.

The high prices for the CD-ROM products are probably out of the range of the individual researcher. Visit your local business school library or other special library. If it does not have one of the following databases, it can probably refer you to another special library that does.

SilverPlatter Directories (SilverPlatter). This CD-ROM set from one of the first CD-ROM publishers contains approximately 100 million U.S. residential and business addresses, phone numbers, and industry categories. The database, one of the largest available, is updated every six months.

Business Lists-On-Disc (American Business Information, Inc.). Compiled from over 4,800 Yellow Pages, this business database covers over 9.3 million businesses. The records contain name, address, phone number, sales, number of employees, and size of Yellow Pages advertisement. The searcher can sort the lists using either Standard Industrial Classification (SIC) codes or the traditional Yellow Pages headings. Approximately 50,000 of the listings contain more detailed business profiles.

Dun's Business Locator™ (Dun & Bradstreet Information Services). Contains over 10 million business listings. You can cross-index your search by zip code, SIC code, and U.S. parent company. The records are not nearly as complete as the full credit report. For an in-depth record, you need to tap into the D&B credit information files (see Chapter 9).

SLEUTHING YOUR COMPETITION WITH CITY DIRECTORIES

The telephone book listed the private security consulting agency run by McCord. There was no answer. They checked the local "criss-cross" directories which list phone numbers by street addresses. There was no answer at either McCord's home or his business. The address of McCord Associates, 414 Hungerford Drive, Rockville, Maryland, is a large office building, and the cross-reference directory for Rockville lists the tenants. The reporters divided the names and began calling them at home. One attorney recalled that a teenage girl who had worked part-time for him the previous summer knew McCord, or perhaps it was the girl's father who knew him. The attorney could only remember the girl's last name—Westall or something like that. They contacted five persons with similar last names before Woodward finally reached Harlan A. Westrell, who said he knew McCord. (Carl Bernstein and Bob Woodward, *All the President's Men*, Warner Books, 1975, p. 21.)

Woodward and Bernstein used a city directory (also known as a criss-cross directory) to help crack the Watergate case. Detectives and just plain savvy researchers have employed these invaluable reference tools for a variety of reasons.

Although not as current as a Yellow Pages might be, city directories can do things Yellow Pages were never designed for. For instance, suppose you want to find out about a company and need to interview some neighboring companies or residents within blocks of the establishment. The city directory will have a section that lists the neighboring buildings and their occupants, street by street.

Should you need to track down a company by its telephone number, most city directories list residents by their phone numbers. (See Figure 10.2.)

Fuld & Co. has found that a city directory can quickly give a researcher an idea of a town's layout and the target company's location. It answers questions like these: Is the target in a commercial or a residential section of town? Who are some of the target company's neighbors? Is there a stationery store nearby that may deal with the target company and its employees on a daily basis? Those in and around the target company may very well be able to tell the researcher if, for example, the target has begun hiring more employees or is laying off the present work force.

One caveat with regard to city directories: They tend to be somewhat dated; many times, phone numbers and addresses have been changed. But, for the most part,

NUMERICAL TELEPHONE DIRECTORY
BLUE PAGES

This Directory takes the "mystery" out of blind numbers. It lists telephone numbers in numercial sequence, making it easy to "decode" blind phone numbers in classified ads—especially valuable for real estate agencies, used car dealers, etc.

dial code

numbers in sequence

name of telephone subscriber

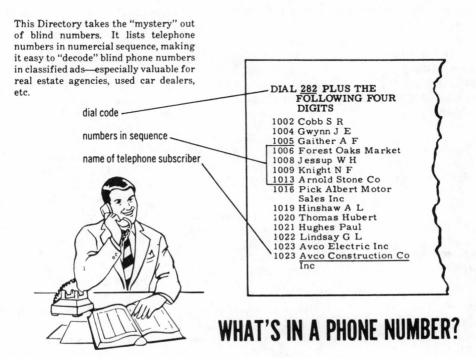

DIAL **282** PLUS THE
FOLLOWING FOUR
DIGITS

1002 Cobb S R
1004 Gwynn J E
1005 Gaither A F
1006 Forest Oaks Market
1008 Jessup W H
1009 Knight N F
1013 Arnold Stone Co
1016 Pick Albert Motor
     Sales Inc
1019 Hinshaw A L
1020 Thomas Hubert
1021 Hughes Paul
1022 Lindsay G L
1023 Avco Electric Inc
1023 Avco Construction Co
     Inc

WHAT'S IN A PHONE NUMBER?

ABOUT THE FIRM:
Who called me? When your call back message gives a telephone number only—or includes a common surname such as Jones, Smith, Brown, etc.—this Numerical Telephone Directory will assist in determining correct firm name. Make use of both Alphabetical and Street Guide information to establish names of officers, owners or partners, products and services, and correct address. Properly identify firm and caller and have needed records, file or correspondence on hand before returning call.

ABOUT THE INDIVIDUAL:
Who called me? When only a telephone number is known, this Numerical Telephone Directory will assist in determining the name of the subscriber—with this information combined with other sections of your City Directory you may quickly establish such information as wife's name, place of employment, job title, home address, business address and telephone number.

Figure 10.2 Extract from Reverse Telephone Section of R. L. Polk City Directory (Boston). (Published with permission of R. L. Polk & Co.)

corporations' addresses and phone numbers do not change quite so fast. Even directories that are years old have a good deal of usable information.

City directories vary widely in price, based on the size of the city or town and the individual publisher. They may cost as little as $25 or as much as $400. Write the publisher for the price and ordering information.

A number of well-known city directory publishers cover all sizes of cities and towns. Here is a list of the more popular publishers, some of whom have been around for decades:

Bresser's Cross-Index
   Directory Company
684 West Baltimore St.
Detroit, MI 48202
313-874-0570

City Publishing Company
118 South Eighth St.
Independence, KS 67301
316-331-2650

Cole Publications
901 Bond St.
Lincoln, NE 68521
402-475-4591

Criss-Cross, Inc.
P.O. Box 720230
Oklahoma City, OK 73172
405-359-6414

Dickman Directories
6145 Columbus Pike
Delaware, OH 43015
614-548-6130

Haines and Company
8050 Freedom Ave., NW
North Canton, OH 44720
216-494-9111

Hill-Donnelly Corporation
2602 South Mac Dill Avenue
P.O. Box 14417
Tampa, FL 33690
813-837-1009

Marc Publishing Company
600 Germantown Pike
Lafayette Hill, PA 19444
215-834-8585

Metropolitan Cross-Reference
   Directory
2 Ripley Ave.
Toronto, M6S 3N9
Ontario, Canada
416-763-5515

R. L. Polk & Company
2001 Elm Hill Pike
P.O. Box 1340
Nashville, TN 37202
615-889-3350

Stewart Directories
302 West Chesapeake Ave.
Baltimore, MD 21204
301-823-4780

Woodard Directory Company
8609 Cheltenham Court
Louisville, KY 40222
502-425-1054

Data You Can Extract from the Directories Themselves

Even before you venture outside the directory, the book itself contains a wealth of data about your target. In certain instances, you will find a company's officers and corporate size indicated.

To give you a better idea of what information is covered and how it differs from section to section, here is a description of a typical directory's contents:

1. The alphabetical section will typically contain in each listing the occupant's name and address, his or her occupation, age, surname cross-reference, spouse's name, corporation's officers, corporation's products, distinction between corporation and partnership, and business owner's name. (See Figure 10.3.)

2. Aside from name and address, the street listing section repeats everything you will find in the alphabetical section, but offers the information on a street-by-street basis. (See Figure 10.4.)

3. The telephone section lists a town's occupants by their telephone numbers; no other information about the occupants is given in this section. For more details, you will have to turn to the alphabetical section in the front of the directory.

ALPHABETICAL DIRECTORY
WHITE PAGES

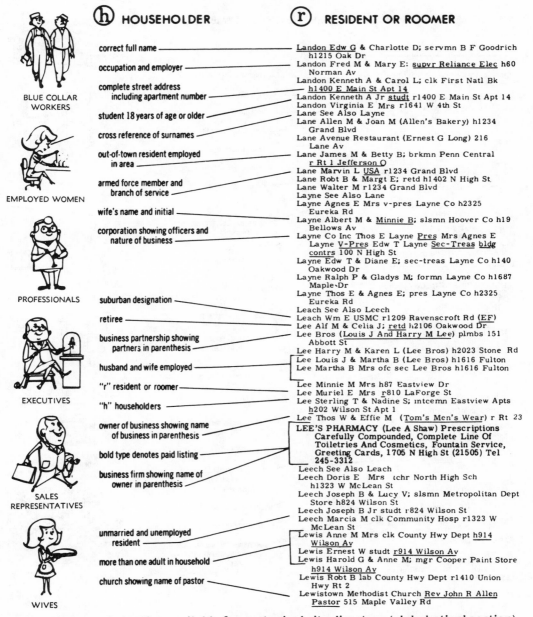

ⓗ HOUSEHOLDER

BLUE COLLAR WORKERS

EMPLOYED WOMEN

PROFESSIONALS

EXECUTIVES

SALES REPRESENTATIVES

WIVES

correct full name

occupation and employer

complete street address including apartment number

student 18 years of age or older

cross reference of surnames

out-of-town resident employed in area

armed force member and branch of service

wife's name and initial

corporation showing officers and nature of business

suburban designation

retiree

business partnership showing partners in parenthesis

husband and wife employed

"r" resident or roomer

"h" householders

owner of business showing name of business in parenthesis

bold type denotes paid listing

business firm showing name of owner in parenthesis

unmarried and unemployed resident

more than one adult in household

church showing name of pastor

ⓡ RESIDENT OR ROOMER

Landon Edw G & Charlotte D; servmn B F Goodrich h1215 Oak Dr
Landon Fred M & Mary E; supvr Reliance Elec h60 Norman Av
Landon Kenneth A & Carol L; clk First Natl Bk h1400 E Main St Apt 14
Landon Kenneth A Jr studt r1400 E Main St Apt 14
Landon Virginia E Mrs r1641 W 4th St
Lane See Also Layne
Lane Allen M & Joan M (Allen's Bakery) h1234 Grand Blvd
Lane Avenue Restaurant (Ernest G Long) 216 Lane Av
Lane James M & Betty B; brkmn Penn Central r Rt 1 Jefferson O
Lane Marvin L USA r1234 Grand Blvd
Lane Robt B & Margt E; retd h1402 N High St
Lane Walter M r1234 Grand Blvd
Layne See Also Lane
Layne Agnes E Mrs v-pres Layne Co h2325 Eureka Rd
Layne Albert M & Minnie B; slsmn Hoover Co h19 Bellows Av
Layne Co Inc Thos E Layne Pres Mrs Agnes E Layne V-Pres Edw T Layne Sec-Treas bldg contrs 100 N High St
Layne Edw T & Diane E; sec-treas Layne Co h140 Oakwood Dr
Layne Ralph P & Gladys M; formn Layne Co h1687 Maple Dr
Layne Thos E & Agnes E; pres Layne Co h2325 Eureka Rd
Leach See Also Leech
Leach Wm E USMC r1209 Ravenscroft Rd (EF)
Lee Alf M & Celia J; retd h2106 Oakwood Dr
Lee Bros (Louis J And Harry M Lee) plmbs 151 Abbott St
Lee Harry M & Karen L (Lee Bros) h2023 Stone Rd
Lee Louis J & Martha B (Lee Bros) h1616 Fulton
Lee Martha B Mrs ofc sec Lee Bros h1616 Fulton
Lee Minnie M Mrs h87 Eastview Dr
Lee Muriel E Mrs r810 LaForge St
Lee Sterling T & Nadine S; mtcemn Eastview Apts h202 Wilson St Apt 1
Lee Thos W & Effie M (Tom's Men's Wear) r Rt 23

LEE'S PHARMACY (Lee A Shaw) Prescriptions Carefully Compounded, Complete Line Of Toiletries And Cosmetics, Fountain Service, Greeting Cards, 1705 N High St (21505) Tel 245-3312

Leech See Also Leach
Leech Doris E Mrs tchr North High Sch h1323 W McLean St
Leech Joseph B & Lucy V; slsmn Metropolitan Dept Store h824 Wilson St
Leech Joseph B Jr studt r824 Wilson St
Leech Marcia M clk Community Hosp r1323 W McLean St
Lewis Anne M Mrs clk County Hwy Dept h914 Wilson Av
Lewis Ernest W studt r914 Wilson Av
Lewis Harold G & Anne M; mgr Cooper Paint Store h914 Wilson Av
Lewis Robt B lab County Hwy Dept r1410 Union Hwy Rt 2
Lewistown Methodist Church Rev John R Allen Pastor 515 Maple Valley Rd

Figure 10.3 Information available from a typical city directory (alphabetical section).

STREET DIRECTORY
GREEN PAGES

⊚ HOMEOWNER SYMBOL   ★ NEW NEIGHBOR SYMBOL

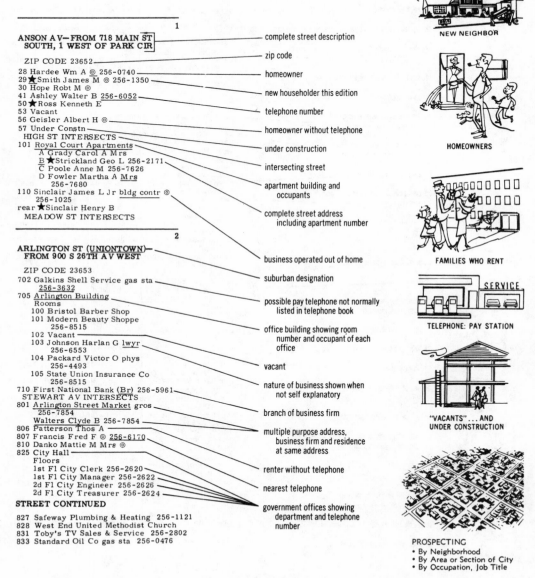

1

ANSON A V—FROM 718 MAIN ST
SOUTH, 1 WEST OF PARK CIR   ——— complete street description

   ZIP CODE 23652   ——————————— zip code
28 Hardee Wm A ⊚ 256-0740 ——————— homeowner
29 ★Smith James M ⊚ 256-1350 ————
30 Hope Robt M ⊚
41 Ashley Walter B 256-6052 ————— new householder this edition
50 ★Ross Kenneth E
53 Vacant   ————————————————— telephone number
56 Geisler Albert H ⊚ ——————————— homeowner without telephone
57 Under Constn ——————
   HIGH ST INTERSECTS ————————— under construction
101 Royal Court Apartments —————
     A Grady Carol A Mrs
     B ★Strickland Geo L 256-2171 —— intersecting street
     C Poole Anne M 256-7626
     D Fowler Martha A Mrs
       256-7680   ————————————— apartment building and
110 Sinclair James L Jr bldg contr ⊚   occupants
     256-1025
rear ★Sinclair Henry B   ————————— complete street address
   MEADOW ST INTERSECTS   including apartment number

2

ARLINGTON ST (UNIONTOWN)—
FROM 900 S 26TH A V WEST

   ZIP CODE 23653
702 Galkins Shell Service gas sta ——— business operated out of home
   256-3632   ————————————————— suburban designation
705 Arlington Building ————————
   Rooms
    100 Bristol Barber Shop   —————— possible pay telephone not normally
    101 Modern Beauty Shoppe   listed in telephone book
       256-8515
    102 Vacant ———————————————— office building showing room
    103 Johnson Harlan G lwyr   number and occupant of each
       256-6553   office
    104 Packard Victor O phys
       256-4493   ————————————— vacant
    105 State Union Insurance Co
       256-8515   ————————————— nature of business shown when
710 First National Bank (Br) 256-5961   not self explanatory
   STEWART A V INTERSECTS
801 Arlington Street Market gros ——— branch of business firm
    256-7854
    Walters Clyde B 256-7854
806 Patterson Thos A ————————— multiple purpose address,
807 Francis Fred F ⊚ 256-6170   business firm and residence
810 Danko Mattie M Mrs ⊚   at same address
825 City Hall ————————————
   Floors
    1st Fl City Clerk 256-2620 ————— renter without telephone
    1st Fl City Manager 256-2622
    2d Fl City Engineer 256-2626 ———— nearest telephone
    2d Fl City Treasurer 256-2624 ————
STREET CONTINUED
                                       government offices showing
827 Safeway Plumbing & Heating 256-1121   department and telephone
828 West End United Methodist Church   number
831 Toby's TV Sales & Service 256-2802
833 Standard Oil Co gas sta 256-0476

NEW NEIGHBOR

HOMEOWNERS

FAMILIES WHO RENT

SERVICE

TELEPHONE: PAY STATION

"VACANTS"... AND
UNDER CONSTRUCTION

PROSPECTING
• By Neighborhood
• By Area or Section of City
• By Occupation, Job Title

Figure 10.4   Sample page of a street directory—the street-by-street listing.

11 ADDITIONAL CREATIVE SOURCES THAT WILL PAY OFF

> There is no lack of information sources for developing
> intelligence. Any time you find yourself stumped and
> believe you've hit an information cul-de-sac, don't be-
> lieve it. Take a breath and ask yourself, "Who else may
> need the same information?" Usually, you will come up
> with an answer. If that doesn't work, talk over your
> problem with a few experts and ask them where they
> would go for the information. In our diverse business
> world, someone will have what you need and will be
> happy to help you.

When I talk about creative sources, I mean sources that are not ordinarily used for intelligence gathering, but may very well answer the specific questions you may have on your competitor's activities or plans. A glance at the sources and techniques described in this chapter will tell you that their origins are from many sectors, including universities, government, and trade groups.

In addition, I have included a number of techniques and intelligence-gathering tips that apply to specific industries.

R&D: THE UNIVERSITY CONNECTION

Aside from company financials or plant capacity, locating "inside information" about a competitor's research and development activities can be one of the most difficult intelligence tasks. Yet there are ways to gain entry into the R&D labyrinth.

The University Liaison Office

Through a liaison office, you can locate a university scientist who may be involved in the R&D work you need to know about. Many high-technology universities, such as the Massachusetts Institute of Technology, have corporate liaison offices that act as go-betweens and coordinators for university research department/corporate R&D activities.

A liaison office serves an administrative function in making sure that no university researcher falls into a conflict-of-interest situation. They also encourage corporations to grant universities funds to carry out R&D research under corporate sponsorship.

At the many universities that do not have liaison offices, you should head straight for the public relations office. It should be able to steer you to the researcher you need to contact.

The Company University

When you spot a major corporation located in a small town, you are likely to find a university nearby.

Much like company towns, there are also company universities—educational institutions located in and around major corporations and in many ways dominated by these corporations. After all, when a company supplies a good portion of the student body and funding to a university, the university develops a dependency and, in many instances, a mutually rewarding relationship.

One way this relationship shows up is through a university's research facilities. Corporations frequently enter into joint ventures with nearby universities.

Perhaps all you will have to do is pull out the Yellow Pages for the town where the company is located and contact the list of universities in that town. But sleuthing is not always that simple. Many companies offer grants to universities quite a distance away from their plant. If you strike out after contacting all of the local institutions, try the next tip.

Tips in Technical Literature

By conducting a simple literature search, you can find most of the experts in a field. These experts in turn can either give you information on a particular company's R&D activities or direct you to the people who are involved at other universities or research institutions.

The key to conducting this type of search is to understand that the articles you turn up will probably be severely out-of-date, at least by fast-moving corporate standards. This means you will find articles that are older than six months—often years old.

Your aim is not to examine the articles; in fact, you do not even have to read much more than the abstracts. Your best bet is to contact the researchers listed in the bibliographic references. These experts—not the articles—will be up-to-date on the R&D occurring in the corporate world.

Many of the technical databases cited in Chapter 5 list the scientist, the institution, and the area of expertise. Databases such as Compendex, MEDLINE, and CA Search are some of the key technical databases for locating experts in a particular field. If you want to find an expert in femoral catheters, for instance, enter the MEDLINE (National Library of Medicine) database. You will find an appropriate article's title, the author (or researcher), and the institution he or she is affiliated with.

NEWSLETTERS THAT TAP INTO THE R&D PIPELINE

When the university route fails you, there is still another way to tap into the vast scientific rumor mill. Industry newsletters cater to research scientists and venture capitalists. Some are nothing more than high-tech gossip sheets; others are detailed scientific journals.

A call to the editors of a newsletter that represents your R&D area can provide you with numerous industry contacts that may eventually lead you to your target company.

Note, however, that editors protect their contacts and are not likely to give out names wholesale. If you want a name, you will have to offer something in return. You should expect to offer the editor a new piece of industry gossip or a new name to contact. Remember, acquiring a piece of intelligence is just like any business transaction—you must give something to receive something.

R&D newsletters are endless. Here is a list of some popular ones in a variety of fields.

Biotechnology

Applied Genetics News (Business Communications Co., Inc.). New developments in agriculture, livestock, foods, healthcare, chemicals, and waste treatment.

Biotechnology Investment Opportunities (High Tech Publishing Co.). Examines how trends in the market may have an impact on biotech R&D.

Genetic Technology News (Technical Insights, Inc.). Forecasts and examines emerging products in the pharmaceutical, food, and energy industries.

Japan Report: Biotechnology (News Media International, Japan). R&D and new-product information in the segment of Japan's biotechnology industry relating to pharmaceuticals, food processing, and brewing.

Chemicals

Electronic Chemicals News (Chemical Week Associates). Discusses R&D at corporations and research centers involved in chemicals and materials for the electronics industry.

Computers and Electronics

Data Storage Report (Jonas Press Publishing Co.). News and technology trends for all types of information storage devices and systems.

Datatrends Report on DEC and IBM (DataTrends Publications, Inc.). Reports on DEC's and IBM's latest developments, marketing strategies, and products.

Fujitsu Weekly (Digitized Information). Reports on Fujitsu's new developments, including R&D, marketing plans, new products and services.

Hitachi Weekly (Digitized Information). Reports on Hitachi's new developments, including R&D, marketing plans, new products and services.

Imaging News (Telecom Publishing Group). New strategies, products, R&D in the imaging field.

Imaging Update (Worldwide Videotex). News on R&D hardware and software for the computer graphics and imaging fields.

NTT Weekly (Digitized Information). Reports on NTT's new developments, including R&D, marketing plans, new products and services.

Toshiba Weekly (Digitized Information). Reports on Toshiba's new developments, including R&D, marketing plans, new products and services, plus exports and pricing trends.

UNIX Update (Worldwide Videotex). News on UNIX R&D, as well as on products and marketing strategies.

Instrumentation

NDT Update (NDT Update). Reports on new developments in nondestructive testing (NDT), as well as business trends and new technologies.

Sensor Review (IFS Publications). Reviews patent applications, development and licensing of sensor-based technologies and products.

Materials

Advanced Ceramics Report (Elsevier Advanced Technology). New products and processes for high-performance ceramics.

Advanced Coatings & Surface Technology (Technical Insights, Inc.). Reviews products and processes being developed, regarding substrates.

Biomedical Materials (Elsevier Advanced Technology). R&D news on applications of materials for medical purposes. Materials typically covered are ceramics, polymers, and composites.

Diamond and Structural Carbon News (Business Communications Co., Inc.). New developments in carbon structural materials, including carbon fibers and industrial diamonds.

High-Tech Materials Alert (Technical Insights, Inc.). Covers new developments in alloys, metallic whiskers, ceramics, and graphite.

Japanese New Materials Advanced Alloys and Metals (News Media International, Japan). Reports on advanced materials developments across a wide assortment of industries.

Optical Materials & Engineering News (Business Communications Co., Inc.). Reports on optical materials worldwide and includes details on R&D funding.

Pharmaceuticals/Medical

Cancer Weekly (Charles W. Henderson). A wide-ranging review of everything related to cancer research and therapies, including university research, government laboratories, FDA approvals.

The Genesis Report/DX (The Genesis Group Associates, Inc.). Latest information on diagnostic medicine, including information on new products, R&D, and business strategies.

Medical Research Funding News (Faulkner & Gray, Inc.). Reports on legislation, government policy issues, and technology developments that may affect medical research; latest NIH grants listed.

R&D (General)

Innovation (A.G. Publications, Ltd.). Reports on R&D and science/technology industry in Israel and discusses potential uses of research.

Innovators Digest (Merton Allen Associates). Summary reports on developments in science, engineering, technology, and manufacturing.

Inside R&D (Technical Insights, Inc.). A general R&D news summary for a wide variety of industries and markets.

NTIS Alert, Foreign Technology (U.S. Department of Commerce, National Technical Information Service). Summary reports of developments in science and technology worldwide.

Technology Access Report (University R&D Opportunities). Gleans information on the latest research taking place within universities, independent laboratories, and medical centers; reviews possible licensing and cooperative agreements.

Telecommunications

AIN Report (Phillips Business Information, Inc.). Reports on the development and marketing of advanced information networks (AINs).

EDI News (Phillips Business Information, Inc.). Covers electronic data interchange (EDI) developments and new technologies.

ISDN News (Phillips Business Information, Inc.). Reviews integrated services digital networks (ISDN), new technologies, products, contract awards, and joint ventures.

Voice Technology News (Phillips Business Information, Inc.). Reviews the latest technologies and product developments, as well as market changes.

Other R&D Sources

A number of directories and publications regularly list leading research centers and research contracts (government, nonprofit, and corporate). Some of these sources are:

Directory of American Research & Technology (R. R. Bowker/Reed Reference Publishing). A directory of industrial and corporate R&D facilities. The listings cover an estimated 10,000 facilities and present information on the personnel and the specialties of each facility.

Directory of Research and Development Contractors (Government Data Publications). A federal government magazine that lists the latest contracts and who the awardees are. The announcements also appear in an annual directory.

Research Centers Directory (Gale Research Co.). A well-indexed directory, listing university and nonprofit research institutions throughout the United States.

FAXING FOR INTELLIGENCE

Many countries have established foreign trade offices that will supply company information on a per-inquiry basis. Some overseas trade offices have extensive files or databases of manufacturing plants within their border, to the point where they can supply you with plant capacity, sales, and number of employees.

If you do not know where to fax for this information, refer to Chapter 6 or contact:

U.S. Department of Commerce
International Trade Administration (ITA)
Public Affairs Office
14th St. & Constitution Ave., N.W.
Washington, DC 20230
202-482-3808

The ITA maintains lists of trade missions and overseas chambers of commerce.

Foreign consulates based in the United States, or in any country, are a good second source. See the consulates listed throughout Chapter 6. When calling a consulate or embassy, ask for the information officer. If the consulate does not have the information or names you are seeking, it can tell you where to call, write, or fax.

UNIFORM COMMERCIAL CODES

Ever wonder how some service company discovered that you just bought a photo-copier or a new computer and would like to sell you parts or supplies for the new equipment?

If you took out a commercial loan to purchase the equipment, your bank probably filed a Uniform Commercial Code (UCC) form that stated what you bought and for how much. The bank is then required to file a copy of the form with the secretary of state's office in the state capital.

To discover what company took out a loan for which piece of equipment, you need only go down to the state house office and review the latest UCC filings.

War Story: Wood It Not Be for the UCC

When researching a wood stove manufacturer, the investigator was trying to locate one of the manufacturer's equipment suppliers. At the bottom of a Dun & Bradstreet credit report was a list of UCC filings. One of these UCC listings indicated that the wood stove company had purchased a furnace for the plant.

When called, the furnace supplier indicated that his was the major piece of casting equipment in the plant. He was able to offer us capacity and production information specifically relating to that one wood stove manufacturer.

UCCs are a prime source of reviewing a company's latest additions to plant assets. This is the source used by Dun & Bradstreet, as well as by other credit and investigative agencies, to help uncover plant assets.

The form itself may vary from state to state. To find out how a particular state files its UCCs, write or call the UCC Filings Office in the state in question.

In recording the type of loan and its limitations, the UCC may involve a number of forms:

Original financing statement

Continuation of original financing statement

Amendment to financing statement

Partial release of collateral

Assignment of financing statement

Subordination.

A sample of one type of UCC form (used in the Commonwealth of Massachusetts) is reproduced in Figure 11.1.

Uniform Commercial Code — FINANCING STATEMENT — Form UCC-1

IMPORTANT — Read instructions on back before filling out form

This FINANCING STATEMENT is presented to a filing officer for filing pursuant to the Uniform Commercial Code.

4. ☐ Filed for record in the real estate records.	5. ☐ Debtor is a Transmitting Utility	6. No. of Additional Sheets Presented:
1. Debtor(s) (Last Name First) and address(es)	2. Secured Party(ies) and address(es)	3. For Filing Officer (Date, Time, Number, and Filing Office)
The Company, Inc. 50 Main Street Cambridge, MA 02138	First Bank 150 Broadway Boston, MA 02110	

7. This financing statement covers the following types (or items) of property:

Ten (10) high-speed video display terminals, one (1) Central Processing Unit, Data General 100 with 512 KB memory, two (2) high -speed controllers, two (2) hard disk drives, one (1) high-speed laser printer, one (1) data base management package of software.

Purchase# A1325d   Purchase Date 10/8/84

Filed With Boston City Clerk

☒ Products of Collateral are also covered.

Whichever is Applicable (See Instruction Number 9)	The Company, Inc. By: /s/ John Smith, Partner Signature(s) of Debtor (Or Assignor)	First Bank By: /s/ Officer, Asst.VP Signature(s) of Secured Party (Or Assignee)

Filing Officer Copy — Alphabetical
STANDARD FORM — UNIFORM COMMERCIAL CODE — FORM UCC-1   Rev. Jan. 1980   *Forms may be purchased from Hobbs & Warren, Inc., Boston, Mass. 02101*

Figure 11.1 Uniform Commercial Code form (for Massachusetts).

For quick retrieval of UCC filings on annual state corporate forms, I recommend you call the UCC Network in Sacramento, CA (916-929-4311). This company can provide a UCC from any state in a matter of days. The service is quick and inexpensive.

INDUSTRIAL DEVELOPMENT: THE BOND THAT EYES

More often than not, government filings are next to useless for finding timely and detailed competitor information. One of the few exceptions is the industrial development bond.

Anytime a company requires government funding to finance its operations, it immediately opens itself up to scrutiny. When the company decides it wants state funding, it must file forms with the state agency that administers the funding, usually the state development authority located in the state's capital. In contrast to the ordinarily skimpy commercial credit reports, the financial information revealed in a state funding application can be most enlightening.

In a recent case, Fuld & Company was asked to trace a rumor in the furniture industry. The rumor concerned a small company's buying out the product line of a much larger concern—a company ten times its size. The question before us: How could a David-like company manage to swing the deal, buying out a Goliath of a plant? One way might be through state financing.

Fuld & Company contacted the state capital to find out whether the company had filed for financial assistance with the state. We found a seven-page document that not only verified the rumor, but also told us the magnitude of the loan and provided background on the smaller, more obscure of the two companies. Among the pieces of intelligence the application supplied were:

Date the company was established

Number of employees, by specialty

Listing of owners (with birthdates, titles, and percent of ownership)

Lawyer's name

Principal bank

Information on expected construction

Value of plant and equipment

Salaries of senior officers

To locate corporate financial assistance applications, follow these steps:

1. Call the state capital.
2. Ask for the Industrial Development Authority.
3. Pose your question to the administrator or librarian. This person will know the file or docket number, and will either send you a copy of the application or tell you where you can find a copy.

TRADE SHOWS: OPEN SEASON ON COMPETITORS

Trade shows are vital sources of competitor information. Ironically, as hard as a competitor will try to mask its marketing strategies during the course of a year, it will try

---

War Story: The Japanese Snoop and Scoop

The Japanese have long been aggressive in their pursuit of trade show data. Japanese companies will swoop down on industrial trade shows, cameras in hand. They will then proceed to scoop every piece of literature into their satchels, and to photograph every booth. They return to their offices and pore over their finds, picking through the material to discover new products and marketing strategies.

---

just as hard to reveal as much as possible about a new product while attending a trade show.

Trade shows are notorious for talkative salespeople, piles of literature, and lots of real-life products to see, examine, and try out. It is also the best place to gather a quick and fairly accurate idea of the market, its dynamism, growth prospects, and trends.

INTELLIGENCE SHOPPING AT TRADE SHOWS

Bag your competitor's strategy, instead of a few glossy brochures.

"I just heard one of our key suppliers talking to a competitor. Do you think he's selling to them, too?" said the store buyer into his cellular phone, as he continued to walk around the trade show in the northern section of Chicago's cavernous McCormick Place.

A few minutes later, one of his counterparts, located in one of McCormick Place's southern halls, called him back.

Trade Show Information Exchanges

The Trade Show Bureau surveyed trade show attendees to ask them what actions they took at the last trade show they attended. This was their response:[1]

   95%   Asked for literature to be sent.
   95%   Saw and talked with current suppliers.
   94%   Compared similar products.
   77%   Found at least one new supplier.
   76%   Asked for a price quotation.
   51%   Requested a sales representative be sent to my company.
   26%   Signed a purchase order.

---

[1]The Power of Trade Shows: Fact Sheet #3, Trade Show Bureau, Copyright 1992.

"There's definitely something going on here. I just spotted that same supplier and the competitor's buyer sitting down to lunch. They're talking business for sure. There were lots of papers being passed across the table, and I saw the competitor sign a few of them. This certainly changes our thinking . . ."

Trade shows have become far more than just shopping expeditions for most savvy companies. They are fertile ground for learning a competitor's strategy, a customer's marketing goals and overall industry shifts. You need to go to a trade show armed with questions and a plan for getting the answers.

"We have found that 75% of attendees go to shows with a preset agenda," stated E. Jane Lorimer, President of the Trade Show Bureau, a nonprofit educational and research organization. "It used to be that lots of people came to trade shows to socialize. No more. Now fewer people may go, but those that do attend bring with them buying power. People go with an agenda."

Companies, such as The Wiz, Best Buy, Circuit City and Sears, will send 20-person teams with a variety of expertise to the semi-annual Consumer Electronics Show. Team members will fan out through the Consumer Electronics Show with specific informational objectives in mind. Some may only examine technology; others will go expressly looking for operational information, merchandising strategies of competitors, or international market interests.

If there is a cardinal rule to explain why trade shows generate so much strategic intelligence, it is this: "Wherever money is exchanged, so is information." Because almost everyone at today's trade show—attendee and exhibitor alike—is there to close a sale or begin a business relationship, a great deal of information is exchanged. There is probably more business transacted and more information exchanged at an industry trade show than during any other yearly event or activity.

"Almost 66% of all consumer electronics store buying takes place in and around the two yearly Consumer Electronics Shows," says Sam Lippman, Electronic Industries Association Staff Vice President in charge of running the CES extravaganzas. To enhance the competitive information exchange, Lippman's crew has installed a network of computer terminals, called Electronic Product Locators, throughout the show that help prospective buyers (and competitors) learn who is selling what products.

HOW CAN YOU PREPARE FOR THE INTELLIGENCE?

Using a trade show to develop intelligence is fairly straightforward. All it takes is some preplanning, common sense and determination.

Target the key shows. Your strategic planning, market research group, or whoever is responsible for competitive assessments, needs to identify the critical shows throughout the world. The major trade shows constantly rotate around the world, from Chicago, to Tokyo, to Paris, and so on. Recognize, too, that some of the best shows are the smaller regional ones.

How do you identify the shows? Your local business school library will probably have one of a number of directories listing when and where shows are to be held. Your best resource is the industry trade magazines. Typically, the magazine's events calendar will list all the shows for the next few months, in chronological or regional order. Note these locations and, if you cannot attend, assign sales and marketing people from your company's local offices to attend.

Form a "Vertical Buying Team." Many companies have assembled task forces, consisting of managers from different functional areas (technical, sales, operations and marketing). These teams have mapped out in advance the shows they expect to attend during the year. They then visit each show, examining only those booths or seminars that meet their strategic objectives. This is called vertical buying. Instead of trying to take in the entire show, the team targets aspects of the show that tie into its highly specific strategic intelligence needs. For example, a company that has decided it needs to improve its warehousing and distribution system will visit the Machine Tools Show to examine the latest innovations in robotics; next, they target COMDEX for software and systems used for inventory control, and so on.

Identify your internal experts ahead of time. You want to assemble your most experienced and technically knowledgeable people at a trade show. The way to do this is through an intelligence audit of the experts in your company. The expertise you should look for can range from competitor-specific knowledge to understanding a particular chemical process. There is so much information flying around a trade show floor that only a multifunctional team can hope to capture it successfully.

Hold a pre-show meeting. A few days before the show, the team leader needs to assign trade show or conference attendees specific objectives. Hand out a checklist of what they need to look for. Include in the list key competitors and expected product or service announcements, and a map of the show floor with the key booths marked.

Debrief during the show. Constantly test your questions and hunches against trade show reality by bringing your team back to a specific booth or hotel room near the show floor where everyone can compare notes. "We held debriefing sessions at each show," recalled Anthony Lorenc, a Manager of New Business at AT&T's Network Cable Systems. "In some instances, we would learn what was wrong with our products and, in nearly the same breath, how we could improve them. We also used these debriefings to pool leads that needed to be followed up on. These sessions also helped us disprove some potentially resource-draining rumors. A rumor might have AT&T escalating its effort in a certain product area. Instead, disproving the rumor saved us from wasting time and resources."

Go to off-the-floor networking meetings. Some of the most vital conference or trade show information will come from informal, pick-up meetings that may occur after a speaker has ended a talk. It is at these meetings that you will (as I have) bump into the CEO or VP of Marketing for a large corporation. Often participants in such a meeting will take the opportunity to ask some very frank and pointed questions, the answers to which you do not want to miss.

Make communications easy. Too often all that a company has to show for its attendance is trade show literature, some formal memos, and expense reports. In order to act upon the significant pieces of news and intelligence your team develops from one of these shows, make sure team members are allowed to express themselves easily and freely. Arm your staff with cellular phones, especially at the larger shows where you need to spread your team out geographically. You need them to stay in touch regularly.

"I have even seen some of these teams," says Lorimer of the Trade Show Bureau, "take laptop computers to a show in order to write a quick memo, which they then modem directly to their offices—all this while the show is taking place."

Hold a post-show analysis and meeting. Pull your team together at your offices once the show has ended. Find various public forums to report your conclusions. Identify major sales or staff meetings and ask the meeting chairperson to place you on his or her agenda.

Also try to avoid writing lengthy reports. "Many times we did not write formal reports after returning from a show," says AT&T's Lorenc. "Instead, we had immediate face-to-face meetings with product managers. Nowadays, we use AT&T electronic mail to deliver the response."

ASSEMBLE A PRE-SHOW STRATEGY KIT

This is far less intimidating than it may sound. Each member of your vertical buying or intelligence team should receive an information packet describing current industry news, as well as thumbnail sketches of key companies, whether they be competitors, customers or suppliers. You can make this a fairly simple job by using widely available library sources. Examples of what you might include in a trade show intelligence packet are:

- Copies of competitors' advertisements
- Online news reports of your competitors that your librarian can supply by searching such database systems as Dow Jones, Nexis, or Dialog
- Pre-show planner and directory
- Marked-up map of the trade show floor, identifying each of the targeted booths your team will approach
- Telephone numbers of key "information" staff back at your office for team members to call if they have questions

Trade shows have become serious business. Those companies that have taken these expositions seriously are the ones that not only look for product, but also look for—and use—the intelligence found there.

A TRADE SHOW INTELLIGENCE CHECKLIST*

There are a myriad number of questions you could ask and relatively little time in which to ask them in a show that lasts only two or three days. The following is a checklist of information points you should note when attending a trade show:

Target Company Booth (Competitors, Customers or Suppliers)
　　　Size and location
　　　Number of people manning booth

---

*Source: Fuld & Company, Cambridge, MA.

Level of seniority among exhibitors
Amount of off-the-floor networking
Level of activity at hospitality suite
Back wall advertising slogans
New product displays
Types of literature given out
Themes or slogans used
Price sheets and stated terms
Attendee interest level

Show Seminars

Topics and themes
Level of attendance
Identify which meetings target companies attend
Note questions asked and who asks them

Product Demonstrations

Note questions asked
Product features
Availability and release date
Bundling and pricing options
Level and sophistication of demonstrator

Target Company's Technology

Identify technology changes
Note bundling of technology into product or service
Target company's emphasis (or lack) on technology
Leading edge or old technology
System efficiency

A Listing of Trade Show Directories

Your library will likely have at least one of the following trade show directories. You will find most of these reference books will list trade shows and dates three or four years in advance.

Exposition Trade Shows & Fairs Directory (American Business Directories, Inc.). An annual that contains the name, address, telephone, and owner of the trade show.

International Exhibitors Association—Membership Directory & Product Service Guide (International Exhibitors Association). Contains approximately 1,500 members' corporate name, address, phone number, and contact name.

Trade Shows & Exhibits Schedule (Bill Communications). This reference book contains the show name, the sponsoring organization (always worth a phone call to better understand the makeup of the booths and any last-minute competitors who may be attending), dates of upcoming shows, expected attendance, and a brief description of the show's theme.

Trade Shows Worldwide (Gale Research Co.). Covers more than 5,700 trade shows worldwide, as well as listing over 4,600 trade show organizations. In addition, it indexes and lists over 700 convention centers and over 40 exhibit builders worldwide. Alongside these core lists are names of publications, consultants, and trade associations that serve the trade show and convention markets.

BUYER'S GUIDES

Are you looking for a list of purchasing agents in an industry? Or trying to find a group of companies that purchase a certain brand of oil supply equipment? Do you need a comprehensive list of manufacturers of a certain type of electronic component?

Buy a buyer's guide. These guides are compiled with the industry's readers in mind. Let's say you come up short in your initial attempt to locate experts on a company you are investigating. These buyer's guides will offer names of competitors, suppliers, distributors, and so on.

Leafing through a buyer's guide should be your next step, after you have listed your assignment's objectives and retrieved your articles. The guide may supply you with the first real expert names to call.

When asked to define a buyer's guide, most people think of a trade magazine's special issue that they have seen at one time or another. Listed in the back of the magazine are names of companies that are in some way important to the magazine (advertisers) or to the industry (suppliers, manufacturers, distributors). Almost every trade magazine will have one special issue during the year that serves as a buyer's guide. You can purchase these buyer's guides separately from the publisher, or as part of a subscription. One recommendation: The buyer's guide may cost as much to nonsubscribers as the entire magazine's subscription. If you subscribe, you will probably get the buyer's guide free. If you feel you will use the magazine to any extent, subscribe.

The Granddaddy of Buyer's Guides: The Thomas Register

This is a 16-volume, hardbound set of books the width of the Encyclopaedia Britannica. It lists companies from literally thousands of industries. Although not as comprehensive as a telephone directory, the Thomas Register is frequently called the bible of buyer's guides.

Not only does it list a vast number of companies, but it also indexes their names by industry group. Another feature is the brand or trade name directory in the Register's Yellow Pages. Companies' brand names are listed in alphabetical order—a real time-saver when you have the brand name but do not know which company manufactured the product. Finally, the Register's company advertising and catalog summaries will give you a good idea of a particular company's product line and marketing strategy. Besides the company name, these display ads announce the product line and to whom the company wants to pitch its products.

Sweet's General Building & Renovation Catalog File (McGraw-Hill), or simply "*Sweet's*," as it is known in the construction trade, is a guide similar to the Thomas

Register. It contains information on over 2,100 manufacturers and includes over 19,000 pages of listings and product information. Sweet's has gone high-tech in recent years, offering its product on CD-ROM.

Trade Association Membership Lists: Buyer's Guides of Another Sort

When you cannot find a buyer's guide that represents the industry you are interested in, or the Thomas Register does not fit the bill, then a trade association might have a membership list that will meet your need.

Often these lists are free or are sold at a nominal charge. Some associations do have restrictions regarding whom they can sell to.

The best source for locating the association that suits your project requirements is Gale Publishing Company's Encyclopedia of Associations. A three-volume reference work, it contains names of literally thousands of organizations. All associations in the Encyclopedia are indexed by title, city, state, and subject.

HELP-WANTED ADS AS AN INTELLIGENCE SOURCE

Help-wanted ads and the newspapers that publish them are invaluable sources of competitor information.

Aside from the company itself, there are three major sources of information about company employment: (1) state employment offices, (2) local classified and display advertisements, and (3) the staff of the classified advertising departments at local newspapers. Properly utilized, the last two are particularly valuable sources of competitor information.

State employment offices. These offices are frequently given a contract by a local company to seek out people to fill a specified number of slots. One example: A large conglomerate had just opened a new plant in a relatively small town. The local state employment office was given the exclusive contract to fill all production positions. Because of its unique position, it knew the plant's expected employment capacity, its start-up plans, and the breakdown of the types of individuals the company was looking for.

Newspaper classified advertising departments. In cities where there may be only one major newspaper, the classified advertising department often will be aware of the current hiring picture for a large local company, or can tell you who might be responsible for hiring. The classified's sales staff can steer you to the more active personnel agencies in town, which are likely sources of information on competitor hiring practices.

Help-wanted or display advertising. These ads are a company's way of selling itself to prospective employees. In part, the advertisements are a come-on, giving the reader more fluff than substance. But the advertisements can also disclose whether a competitor is shifting direction or expanding a division or product group.

These tips on classifieds suggest that the business analyst can track competitor movement in specific regions in great detail and at minimum expense through the

---

War Story: A Source of Backwoods Intelligence

Fuld & Company was given a fairly difficult assignment of determining exactly how many blue- and white-collar employees a tobacco plant was going to employ over the next six months, and the expectations for employment for the next five years. The plant was located in a small Southern town that had one newspaper and no other major company dominating the town.

Here was the problem: The plant was not yet open. It was a very small portion of a multinational conglomerate. Public filings were of no use.

The fact that it was a small town with only one newspaper, we discovered, worked to our advantage. We called the local newspaper, but instead of asking for the editor, we requested the classified ads department. The woman there told us that she was aware of the new plant and knew it was hiring. She also told us that the newspaper was not carrying any help-wanted advertising for the plant (at which time our hopes fell).

Then she told us a bit of good news: The local state employment office had the contract to hire for the plant. We called the state office, as she suggested, and the manager there told us all the current as well as projected hiring figures for the plant. Had we wanted to, we could have gone down to the office and actually reviewed the job descriptions that were posted.

---

help-wanted advertising pages. Where else would a researcher be able to discover intelligence on hiring trends, and disclosures on plant value or marketing strategy?

Help-Wanted Advertisements: An Exercise

Let's look at a typical display ad placed by an employer in a Sunday newspaper. In this case, the employer is McDonnell Douglas. This one advertisement (see Figure 11.2) reveals more information than you will find in a press release or other trade news.

In practice, that is what a classified advertisement is: a press release. The McDonnell Douglas help-wanted ad reveals the following:

1. *Plant assets.* "Our commitment began with a new sixty-five million dollar Microelectronics Center now being built. . . ."

2. *Projected product line.* ". . . to produce custom designed electronics circuits and radiation detectors for use by our other divisions. . . ."

3. *Type of employee.* The ad lists only technical people, those with electrical engineering degrees or the like. More important, it also lists their specialties—a significant piece of information. For example: "Detector Testing Engineer: A BS/MS. EE. Minimum of two years' experience in in-process and final testing of HgCdTe photovoltaic detectors and focal plane arrays is needed. Automated test experience desirable."

DETECTOR SPECIALISTS
MAKE A COMMITMENT WITH US

McDonnell Douglas, a recognized leader in the Aerospace Industry, has made a commitment to excellence in the field of Microelectronics, and we're looking for the best Microelectronics and Detector Specialists to help us.

Our commitment began with a new sixty five million dollar Microelectronics Center now being built to produce custom-designed electronics circuits and radiation detectors for use by our other divisions and in military applications.

This has created many excellent opportunities for Scientists and Engineers in the field of Silicon Technology, Mercury Cadmium Telluride Photovoltaic Detectors, Focal Plane Arrays, Hybrid Design and Development.

If you're looking to be the best in your field, we're looking for the best people we can find for the following openings:

MANAGER, DETECTOR DEVELOPMENT
A PHD in EE or Physics as well as a minimum of five years infrared detector experience is desired. Should have supervisory skills, a background in semiconductor device development, and customer related experience.

MANAGER, FOCAL PLANE ARRAY DEVELOPMENT
A PHD in EE or Physics with five or more years experience in semiconductor device development. Should have supervisory experience, be familiar with automatic focal plane testing and customer related experience.

DETECTOR FABRICATION ENGINEERS
A BS/MS, EE or Physics. Minimum two years experience in HgCdTe device processing, including one or more of the following: photolithography, implantation, suface passivation and metallization.

DETECTOR TESTING ENGINEER
A BS/MS, EE. Minimum of two years experience in in process and final testing of HgCdTe photovoltaic detectors and focal plane arrays is needed. Automated test experience desirable.

SEMICONDUCTOR DEVICE SPECIALIST
A PHD (or equivalent) in EE or Physics with a minimum of three years experience in design, modeling and simulation of electronic devices in narrow gap materials.

So if you're ready to work with the best, send your resume to:

Manager, Professional Employment
McDonnell Douglas Corporation
P.O. Box 516 • Department 62-06
St. Louis, Missouri 63166

MCDONNELL DOUGLAS
MICROELECTRONICS CENTER

An Equal Opportunity Employer • U.S. Citizenship Required

Figure 11.2 Display advertisement example.

How to Use Classified Ads Effectively

Now that you know what classified or display help-wanted advertising can do for you, how do you manage to use these ads in a way that will reveal competitor activity?

1. Locate the competitor's plants or service locations that you want to watch.
2. Through the Ayer's guide to newspapers and magazines (a source discussed later in the book), find the newspapers located within a 50-mile radius of the towns where the plants are situated.
3. Either subscribe to all the newspapers or hire a news clipping service to clip all the ads pertaining to your competitor.

One-shot attempts at locating an intelligence-packed ad will often yield poor results. This technique works best when you are able to monitor the classified ads over a period of time. You will spot hiring trends, details on product shifts, and changes in marketing strategy.

SHOPPING FOR INTELLIGENCE AT THE MALL

Every shopping mall has a real estate developer associated with it, as well as a manager or managing office. Both of these sources can tell you a good deal about a mall's tenants.

When interviewing a mall's manager, we have been able to uncover a target company's square footage costs, current square footage, expansion plans, and lease arrangements.

Locating mall management offices is easy; the phone number will be listed in the Yellow Pages or White Pages. The number usually belongs to the mall's management office or real estate developer.

LOCATING DOMESTIC AND OVERSEAS SUPPLIERS THROUGH THE FCC

The Federal Communications Commission (FCC) exists, in part, to protect the public. This is particularly true regarding management of telecommunications and use of radio waves and their potentially harmful emissions. The FCC requires that manufacturers identify source suppliers and present schematics of the products sold. The filings that demand some of this information are: 730 (Part 68 Registration) for telecommunications equipment, and 731 for other types of electronic products, such as personal computers (under Part 15/18 Registration).

What makes these reports so powerful for competitive analysis is their completeness. Not only will they identify the U.S. assembler or marketer of the equipment, but they will go one step further by identifying the original manufacturer or manufacturers of the entire product or the many component parts.

For telecommunications equipment, those who file under the Part 68 class of telecommunications products include manufacturers, refurbishers of telephone equipment, private labelers, and assemblers of equipment. The equipment represented under Part 68 is:

Adjunct components used with one- and two-line telephones

Adjunct devices for digital service applications

Adjuncts and components used with generic host systems

Adjuncts used with MF & PF systems

Alarm dialing systems

Analog concentrators

Answering machines

Call diverters

Conferencing bridges

Consoles used with Centrex systems

Conversation recorders

Credit card terminal equipment

Data modems

Data protective circuitry used on analog networks

Data terminals having unique one-of-a-kind modems

Directly connected paging equipment

Equipment providing CSU functions including encoded analog content

Equipment providing CSU functions and not encoded analog content

Facsimile machines/computer cards

Fully protected key telephone systems

Fully protected multifunction systems

Fully protected PBXs

Key system for analog data applications

Least-cost routing equipment

Limited-use terminal devices

Local area data channel modems

Modular hybrid telephone systems

Modular key telephone systems

Modular PBX systems

Monitoring equipment

Multifunction ancillary devices

Multifunction data devices including dialing modems

Multifunction telephones

Multiplexers or channel banks connecting to registered CSUs

Music-on-hold adjuncts

Nondialing speakerphones

Number display (caller ID) devices

On-premises data-over-voice equipment

Other miscellaneous applications

Privately owned coin phones with instrument-implemented features

Refurbished grandfathered unprotected KTS

Refurbished unprotected PBX

Repertory dialers

Single or two-line telephone

Single or two-line phone with "system" features

Small call distributors

Special use device

Specialty adapters

Stand-alone ringers, chimes, bells, ring relays, ring detectors, visual test equipment

Toll restrictors

Totally protected hybrid systems

Totally protected key systems

Totally protected PBX systems

Totally protective circuitry for analog voice band applications

Traffic recorders

Unprotected KTS

Unprotected PBX

Voice mail systems

Wireless (Cordless) telephones

A typical entry when filing 730 for telecommunications equipment will have the following categories:

1. Name of applicant
2. Code of applicant (an ID number)

War Story: Telecommunications Equipment

A manufacturer who had been in the telephone equipment business for the past five years had recently spotted two new competitors in his line of products. Because of the frenzied growth of this newly deregulated market, the manufacturer was not able to make the right connections to determine whom these two competitors were buying their products from.

The manufacturer only knew that they were importing the equipment from Taiwan and South Korea. And he only knew that because he turned the equipment on its side and read the label "Made in Taiwan."

Now he needed to know more. He had already tried to contact his independent reps for information as to their source of supply. He had also contacted the companies he imported from, to see whether they knew who might be producing the equipment. No luck. There are hundreds of electronics manufacturers, small and large, in the Far East. He was searching for a microchip in a haystack.

Our experience with the telecommunications industry told us to turn first to the Federal Communications Commission. The FCC's Telephone Equipment List gave us our answer, including the name, address, and piece of equipment produced by the foreign supplier.

---

3. Code for manufacturer of equipment
4. File number for this entry
5 Code for equipment category
6. Code for network address signaling
7. File number for tracking entry through registration
8. Description of the equipment
9. Description of type of jack necessary

All applications under Part 68 are disclosed prior to acceptance and have to be approved by the FCC for use as a telecommunications product.

Ordering Part 68 Registrations

The forms are kept on file with the FCC at the address given below. Historical data are kept on file at the National Technical Information Service (NTIS). For more information, contact:

Federal Communications Commission
25 M St., N.W.
Washington, DC 20554
202-634-1833

If you would like faster access to some of the data on file, you can subscribe to an online service provided by:

Interactive Systems, Inc.
1777 N. Kent St.
Arlington, VA 22209
703-838-1901

The FCC Can Be Your P.A.L.

The latest information on Part 15/18 filings can be obtained by calling the FCC at 301-725-1585. This branch of the FCC has, since 1990, provided an electronic bulletin board service that is free to the public. The bulletin board is called P.A.L. (Public Access Line).

The Equipment Authorization Branch is the organization that has spearheaded the P.A.L. project since its beginning, in 1986. Its purpose is to provide access to pending and granted equipment authorization data. P.A.L. is available, at no charge, through a public phone number. All you need is a 1200-baud modem. The menu of information available through P.A.L. includes:

Access Equipment Authorization Database (with grantee names and addresses)

Applying for an Equipment Authorization

Other Commission Activities and Procedures

Operational Information on the FCC Laboratory

Public Notices

P.A.L.'s direct access telephone number is 301-725-1072. The communications protocol for linking your computer to the P.A.L. system is: 8 bits, no parity, two stop bits. In order to access the records, the user must know the FCC Identifier of the equipment covered in the pending application. If the application has already been approved, then you will find this ID number on the equipment's label.

For more information on the P.A.L. system, contact:

Federal Communications Commission
Authorization and Evaluation Division
7435 Oakland Mills Rd.
Columbia, MD 21046
301-725-1585

OUR EFFLUENT SOCIETY: ENVIRONMENTAL IMPACT STATEMENTS, A BACK-DOOR APPROACH TO COMPANY INTELLIGENCE

Speak to experienced researchers in the chemical and pharmaceutical industries and they will tell you how valuable environmental impact statements are. As the title implies, companies that are planning to build plants or change production processes that might in some way affect the environment must file with a local—and possibly a federal—agency.

These are just some of the questions an environmental impact statement can answer:

1. What is the projected plant size?
2. What type of process will be used?

3. Approximately how many people will be employed (which you can learn through the number of parking spaces reported)?

4. What will the project cost the company?

5. How many production sites will be created?

Experienced industry researchers will also tell you that the state or local environmental filings are more frequently filed and are often more detailed than the federal forms.

Some states require more than just one filing per project. For instance, in Massachusetts, a company first has to file an Environmental Notification Form (ENF) before filing an impact statement. This notification is placed on public record with the state environmental agency. The notification will then allow state authorities to determine whether further examination of the project is required.

Throughout this chapter, I will use the Massachusetts system as an example of state requirements and the type of corporate information that these forms may reveal. Understand, though, that Massachusetts may be somewhat typical but may not include all categories or rules that other states have. Yet I believe that even a brief glance at the Massachusetts reporting requirements will make you aware of just how extensive—and how revealing—these impact or notification statements are.

The Massachusetts Environmental Notification Form (ENF) is intended to provide the Secretary of Environmental Affairs and the general public with relatively early notification that projects are being planned that may or may not have significant impacts on the environment. The purpose of the ENF is to identify general types of impacts from a project as best one can without having to perform final design or detailed analysis. The ENF is intended to identify those projects that may have significant impact potential, and if so, to identify which types of impacts are significant and which are not. Through this process, the scope of any further environmental studies can be limited simply to those issues of concern, and the project proponent need not investigate those factors that are not at issue.

The process to be followed is fairly straightforward. The project proponent should fill out the ENF as accurately and completely as possible, given the preliminary state of project development. Then there will be a public review process and a determination by the Secretary as to whether an Environmental Impact Report (EIR) will be required, and if so, what topics should be covered. The Secretary will use information submitted by the project proponent in Section I-D., "Scoping," as the initial basis for determining the scope of an EIR and which alternative should be studied.

The ENF itself is not meant to be a comprehensive environmental analysis of the project. In most cases, a best professional estimate based on available data, practice, and information will suffice. More detailed information on specific items may be requested during the review of the ENF to help in performing a satisfactory environmental evaluation. The degree of accuracy will vary from project to project.

The sequence of procedures that proponents are advised to follow is:

1. Begin preparation of the ENF at a relatively early stage of project development.

2. Determine likely state permits and financial assistance.

3. Consult with affected agencies and assemble information useful in completing the ENF and finding out whether the project may be exempt from the MEPA (Massachusetts Environmental Protection Agency) process.

4. Publish the intent to submit an ENF in a newspaper of local circulation in each community affected by the proposed project or in a newspaper of regional or statewide circulation if an affected community is not served by a local publication. The notice should be published no more than 30 days before submitting the ENF.

5. Complete the ENF and submit it, with original USGS (U.S. Geological Survey) or other map.

What You Can Learn from a Notification Form

To see it is to believe it: there is a wealth of plant information in one of these statements. To offer a sample, here are a number of categories the state environmental board requires of companies filing for notification:

Project name.

Project address.

Project's commencement date.

Cost of project.

Description of project.

Short- and long-term impacts (the environmental categories, such as inland wetlands, air pollution, and noise).

Listing of equivalent federal environmental filings also required.

Requests for financial assistance and the agencies from which aid will be requested.

Total acreage likely to be affected by the project.

Description of the building or processing plant.

Number of parking spaces.

Estimated traffic to and from the site.

Accompanying drawings of plant and access roads.

Explanation of the pollutants produced.

Estimated daily water consumption.

Detailed description of type and nature of air and noise pollution generated.

To order a filing, you can call or write your state's environmental office, or the office of water or air pollution.

CORRUGATED BOXES: A SOURCE OF PRODUCTION DATA

"Just let me find the competitor's box supplier and I can find the number of units that the competitor is shipping at any particular season." These are the words of a Canadian packaging manufacturer who understands that over 95 percent of all products manufactured today ultimately wind up being placed in corrugated boxes of some type. His suggestion is to simply locate the box supplier and through it identify the number of boxes shipped.

Sounds like a simple solution, right? In truth, it is—but execution of this research technique requires additional insight into the box manufacturing industry.

Lesson 1. Not all box manufacturers are alike. Some are better sources than others.

Box manufacturers fall into two categories: (1) the conglomerate box producer and (2) the independent box supplier. The conglomerate producer is also a major paper manufacturer and has hundreds of other product lines besides corrugated boxes. The independent supplier buys prepared corrugated paper from a conglomerate paper manufacturer, then cuts, bends, and glues it together to form a box.

The conglomerate is not likely to know or care much about a particular client's seasonal box needs—especially those of a small purchaser of boxes. A conglomerate must maintain expensive corrugation machinery. Because of this additional overhead, salespeople are only interested in selling bulk orders. They are neither interested in, nor do they watch for, small orders. They also do not monitor seasonal usage on the part of clients.

The independents, on the other hand, do not generally own these expensive corrugation machines. They can, therefore, offer services to the needs of smaller clients or special orders. These independents know when their clients need boxes and how many. They can often gauge seasonal demands, because such orders are part of their business.

Lesson 2. One easy way to locate the competitor's box manufacturer is simply to examine the box itself. The supplier will make sure to place its imprint on one of the outside walls of the box. An example is given in Figure 11.3.

War Story: Know Thy Brothel

After hearing how corrugated boxes could be used to trace a company's shipments or sales, one executive who attended an Fuld & Company intelligence-gathering seminar came up with this anecdote that closely resembles the case of the corrugated box.

He said that the IRS had been trying to uncover a particular brothel's yearly sales, without success. Internal Revenue agents apparently did not want to plant themselves outside the house of ill repute, counting the number of customers parading in and out. Too time-consuming.

They chose another, creative intelligence-gathering technique. They asked themselves: What does every brothel need . . . aside from talent? The answer was simple—towels, of course. The agents managed to locate the company supplying the towels to the institution in question. By learning the number of towels used by the brothel, the IRS then estimated sales for this tax evader.

Corrugated boxes are only one source of production data. But the lesson that the corrugated box teaches is universal: Locate a company's source of supply and you will likely determine that company's sales.

PO #0625-004

11¼X8¾X4

**COMPLIES WITH SPEC.
PPP-B-636I**

Figure 11.3 Corrugated box supplier imprint.

Lesson 3. Most companies will use more than one box supplier. The researcher will then have to locate a competitor's entire list of box suppliers in order to track all shipment data.

The following are names of some of the box industry's leading directories and trade groups. Both can be used to trace a company's immediate box supplier. Remember, because of shipping costs involved in a low-cost item such as cardboard boxes, a competitor's suppliers will likely be located in the same region as the shipping point of origin.

Association of Independent
 Corrugator Converters
P.O. Box 25708
Alexandria, VA 22313

Containerization &
 Intermodal Institute
P.O. Box 1593
North Caldwell, NJ 07007

Lockwood's Directory of
 Paper and Allied Trades
Vance Publishing Corp.
133 E. 58 St.
New York, NY 10022

National Paperbox &
 Packaging Association
1201 E. Abingdon Dr.,
 Suite 203
Alexandria, VA 22314

Pacific Coast Paper Box
 Manufacturer's Association
2301 Vernon Ave.
P.O. Box 60957
Los Angeles, CA 90060

Paper, Film & Foil Converter
 —Annual Directory and
 Buyer's Guide
Maclean-Hunter Publishing
 Corp.
300 W. Adams St.
Chicago, IL 60606

Source of Supply/Buyer's
 Guide
Advertisers & Publishers
 Service
300 N. Prospect Ave.
Park Ridge, IL 60068

COMMERCIAL BANKING AND THE WITHDRAWAL OF INFORMATION

Once you can identify the groups that are common across many industries, your actual intelligence gathering can begin. Although its products are different from those of a typical manufacturer, banking, like any other industry, has its distributors, wholesalers, and end-users or consumers:

Industry	Manufacturer	Distributor	End-user
Lumber	Sawmill	Lumber outlet	Builder
Banking software	Software producer	Licensee bank	Corporation

By understanding how your target industry is structured, you have a far better chance of locating information on your target company. Banking, like lumber, has a set industry structure. The structures themselves may be different, but studying each separately reveals distinct patterns. By following these patterns, you will uncover your intelligence.

A Trusted Banking Source

Pension and trust banking has become a highly dynamic and fiercely competitive industry. Fortunately for the corporate researcher, a source has come to the rescue: *Money Market Directory* (Money Market Directories, P.O. Box 1608, Charlottesville, VA 22902; 800-446-2810).

Whenever you are doing competitor research, you run into the same basic questions: Who is the supplier? Who are the customers or end-users? How much are the customers buying from the suppliers? These are the very questions *Money Market Directory* answers. The *Directory* contains the names of independent pension fund managers, their corporate clients, and the size of the accounts managed. This is one of the few sources in any industry that actually supplies a competitor's customers.

Taking Stock at Meetings

There is no better way to get first-hand information on a publicly held company than to become a shareholder and attend stockholders' meetings, or to attend security

---

War Story: In Pensions Do We Trust

Many large corporations have their pension fund investments managed by an outside commercial bank or independent pension fund consulting firm. Our client, though, wanted to know what particular features interested a competitor's clients and what features, among the client's present offering, were worth building on in future marketing efforts.

After paging through the *Money Market Directory*, we located the competitor's customers. Next, we designed a questionnaire and polled these corporate customers. As long as we kept the questionnaire short, respondents were certainly willing to talk.

Finding the right person to speak to was fairly easy; the person most responsible for working with the pension fund was likely located in the company treasurer's or controller's office.

analysts' meetings, which are held all around the country. Each type of meeting is different, but the benefits are very much related.

Stockholders' Meetings. By purchasing stock, you have bought your ticket of admission to these annual meetings. A good portion of the meeting is scripted, but questions from concerned stockholders in the audience can bring out information not contained in the press packet. Company representatives will discuss the latest company products, key personnel changes, company financials, and stockholders' questions.

By attending a stockholders' meeting, you will receive information a day ahead of its appearing in the press. Also, when you are a shareholder in a small, over-the-counter company, you will be privy to meetings and information that may never reach the press.

Security Analysts' Meetings. These meetings are opportunities for the president and CEO of small and large companies to "strut their stuff" in front of security analysts from different parts of the country. Some of the small and relatively young companies will be looking for analysts to recommend their stock to potential investors through the research reports and newsletters they publish. This public relations gambit can prove to be a windfall for you if you are willing to be patient and listen. The CEOs will typically mingle during the latter part of the meeting, and during these informal chats, you can ask pointed questions or listen as others do so. Fuld & Company analysts who have attended are constantly surprised at how open and informal the company heads are with new product plans or overall strategy in the context of these meetings. Figure 11.4 shows a recent calendar of events and pertinent organizational information for a chapter of the Society of Security Analysts. The benefits of membership will be comparable in any other chapters nationwide.

UNDERSTANDING THE SOFTWARE INDUSTRY

A software company is a far more elusive target than a large manufacturing concern, bank, or insurance company:

- A software company may operate out of a garage. Once the owner buys the microcomputer, let's say, he or she does not have to contact anyone until the product is finished or ready for market.
- There are still no official, proven, or established distribution channels in the software industry.
- A software company, unlike a manufacturing plant, does not depend on a flowing river for its power or for disposing of waste.
- As a rule, no one software company dominates an entire market. There are exceptions, of course. Lotus® 1-2-3® controlled the spreadsheet market until a number of contenders entered, such as Microsoft's Excel®, Quatro™, and others, and ate into Lotus's market share. In most software product categories, there are no longer concentrations of markets.

Here are some tips on how we have successfully uncovered detailed intelligence on software companies:

♣ March 1994

Calendar of Events

New York Society of Security Analysts

71 BROADWAY / 2nd FLOOR — LUNCHEON & OTHER MEETINGS

Key to symbols

✎ See details inside   ✉ Registration required; see separate brochure for details   ☎ Teleconference available; call *(800) 424-2149* by 11:00 am for reservations.   📖 **Education courses:** Refer to individual course brochures or call for registration information.

Monday	Tuesday	Wednesday	Thursday	Friday
Committee Members: All information to be included in the April *Calendar of Events* must be received in NYSSA's office by March 4. To submit meeting information, please call (212) 344-8450.	**1** ☎**Pall Corporation** *Maurice G. Hardy, Pres & CEO* *Katharine Plourde, Chair* *5:30 pm:* 📖Level I Review	**2** ☎**Burlington Coat Factory** *Monroe G. Milstein, Chairman* *Kathleen Dieter, Chair* *5:30 pm:* 📖Level II Review	**3** ☎**United Dominion Realty Trust** *John P. McCann, President* *Jeffrey A. Helton, Chair* *5:30 pm:* 📖Level I Review	**4** ✉**Emerging Markets: Investment Opportunities in Greece** *(8:30 am - 4:35 pm)* *see brochure*
7 *5:30 pm:* 📖Level III Review	**8** ☎**SBS Engineering, Inc.** *Christopher J. Amenson, President* *George N. Robinson, Chair* ✎**Emerging Markets — Pension Fund Investing** *Edwin Ehrlich* *William Hayes, Chair* *5:30 pm:* 📖Level I Review	**9** ☎**Praxair, Inc.** *H. William Lichtenberger, Chr* *Theodore Semegran, Chair* **Market Technicians Association** *Monthly Meeting (4:30 pm) Pamela King, Chair* *5:30 pm:* 📖Level II Review	**10** ☎**Bay View Federal Bank** *John E. Brubaker, President* *Janet Yuen, Chair* ✎**401k Market: Opportunities and Issues** *Theodore Benna* *Vincent C. Catalano, Chr* *5:30 pm:* 📖Level I Review	**11**
14 ✉**Current Japanese Economic & Political Environment** *(8:00 am - 2:00 pm)* *Gordon R. Schonfeld, Chair* *see brochure* *5:30 pm:* 📖Level III Review	**15** *5:30 pm:* 📖Level I Review	**16** ☎**H. J. Heinz Company** *Dr. J.F. O'Reilly, Chr & CEO* *Roy D. Burry, Chair* *5:30 pm:* 📖Level II Review	**17** 📖**Intensive Four-Day CFA Review Course** *8am-6pm* *Dr. Robert J. Stalla, CFA, Instructor* *5:30 pm:* 📖Level I Review	**18** 📖**Intensive Four-Day CFA Review Course** *8am-6pm* *Dr. Robert J. Stalla, CFA, Instructor* *Course continues through Sunday, March 20*
21 ☀ (no snowman symbol) **First Day of Spring (Sunday 3/20)** *5:30 pm:* 📖Level III Review	**22** ☎**Wallace Computer Services, Inc.** *Robert J. Cronin, President* *Kenneth C. Bohringer, Chair* **United Dominion Industries** *William R. Holland, Chairman* *Cornelius V V Sewell, Jr., Chair* *5:30 pm:* 📖Level I Review	**23** ☎**Brown-Forman Corporation** *Owsley Brown II, President* *Roy D. Burry, Chair* **Guilford Mills** *Charles A. Hayes, Chairman* *Arthur E. Lichtendorf, Chair* *5:30 pm:* 📖Level II Review	**24** Except where otherwise noted: all meetings listed are luncheon presentations beginning with a buffet at *11:30 am,* followed by a *12:30 pm* presentation, and are held at NYSSA's headquarters, 71 Broadway, 2nd floor. Advance reservations are not taken; regular meeting fees ($12 members/$24 non-members) are collected at the door. *5:30 pm:* 📖Level I Review	**25**
28 *5:30 pm:* 📖Level III Review	**29** ☎**Rollins, Inc.** *Gene L. Smith, CFO* *Kathleen Dieter, Chair* *5:30 pm:* 📖Level I Review	**30** ☎**American Stores Company** *Victor L. Lund, President* *Janet J. Mangano, Chair* *5:30 pm:* 📖Level II Review	**31** ☎**Regeneron Pharmaceuticals** *Fredric D. Price, CFO* *Franklin M. Berger, Chair* *5:30 pm:* 📖Level I Review	ℭ **Important Numbers:** NYSSA: (212) 344-8450 *or* (800) 248-0108 Fax: (212) 809-6439 Darome: (800) 424-2149 Jobline: (804) 980-3688

Published by **The New York Society of Security Analysts, Inc.** 71 Broadway, New York 10006 • (212) 344-8450 • Fax (212) 809-6439

Editor: Judith Zatz

Founded in 1937 Incorporated September 5, 1940 Under Laws of the State of New York Charter Member of Federation

Figure 11.4 Sample calendar of events, Society of Security Analysts, New York chapter.

War Story: The Growth of a Company

A client that was about to release a major software product needed to know how another company with a similar product was managing to grow so successfully. What could we find out about the competitor's organization structure?

The first and most obvious source was the competitor's software manual, which listed all the authors. After a check of some computer clubs and local consulting firms, we managed to get further biographical background on some of the authors as well as some key executives within the firm.

The national trade press had given a lot of coverage to this type of software and had included a number of in-depth interviews with the target company's executives.

The result: We were able to construct a company organization chart and growth plans.

---

1. *End-user/computer clubs.* Software companies, especially the newer ones, have to convince the computer elite that their product is superior and well worth an investment. We have used computer clubs to find current clients or companies where the product is being test-marketed.

To find the computer club in your area, contact a local college and ask for its computer science department. Someone there will know where and when the local club branch will meet and when your particular piece of software will be discussed. Meeting attendees are end-users who can tell the interviewer the product's features, pricing, and pluses and minuses.

2. *The press.* Just before a product is released, software companies and their ad agencies love to innundate the trade press with press releases and photographs of the product and its packaging. Unlike other industries, the computer (and especially the microcomputer) industry has hundreds of magazines and newsletters, many of which are not content with just reprinting press releases. Instead, they will conduct lengthy interviews with a firm's principals. To locate a particular interview, you can turn to any number of indexes, some computerized (naturally!) and others in text form.

3. *The software manual.* The manual itself contains the authors' names and details on the product's purpose and features. Rarely does a company in any other industry offer the end-user such a detailed view of its product.

4. *Local computer stores.* Retail stores located near the software supplier probably know the creators of the software and some details about the company's organization and future product releases.

5. *Trade shows.* Like any other thriving industry, the software industry has latched onto the trade show as a means to display its product and gain visibility. Events calendars of upcoming trade shows are published in magazines such as *Byte* and *Computerworld.* Your local computer club will also keep you posted.

A PRESCRIPTION FOR PHARMACEUTICAL RESEARCH

The pharmaceutical industry prides itself on its secrecy and its ability to market and make lots of money on commodity-type products. In reality, though, the pharmaceutical industry is not as secretive as it would like to believe. Like any industry, its activities leave traces. This section will help you find those traces.

Before listing the recommended sources, let's look at why the pharmaceutical industry is not a closed shop. Virtually every business transaction results in information being passed along about the parties involved. The pharmaceutical industry is no exception to this rule. Let's examine what happens to a drug company when it begins to manufacture and market a product—who is approached and contacted outside the company.

Advertising agencies. Some companies have their own in-house agencies, but most others will contract with outside agencies. Look for these agencies to proudly announce their new client in the local and national advertising trade press, such as *Advertising Age*.

Contract packagers. Drug companies will often have outside companies do their packaging. Packagers will know well in advance when a new product may enter the market. They produce the labels and bottles; they are also important

---

War Story: A Drug's Future Shipments

The future is probably the hardest piece of intelligence to develop. One client had requested that we pinpoint a competitor's intended shipping plans for a new product that was months or even a year away from introduction. Specifically, the client wanted to know which plant would be supplying the product and what the initial shipments would look like.

First, we consulted the FDA. They would only say what was already public knowledge. They could tell us that the drug was under review. The FDA would not tell us about the company's advertising plans (although they could release papers on the target company's advertising for other products already released). The FDA could not legally release information prior to the approval date.

Next, we consulted a number of other sources for names of experts to contact. Among the sources we referred to were the *Physicians' Desk Reference*, *Wall Street Transcript*, *Directory of Contract Packagers*, and *National Wholesale Druggists' Association Membership Directory*.

After spending a number of days on the telephone talking with wholesalers, potential suppliers, competing companies, and Wall Street analysts, we managed to compile an accurate picture of the company and its shipping plans. Specifically, we identified the plant that was going to ship the raw material, we identified the competitor's plant that was going to package the product, and we received estimates of expected shipments as well as the product pricing.

sources of marketing shifts. That is, they will often know, by seeing the change in its packaging, that a drug company is changing its marketing stance.

FDA (Food and Drug Administration). This federal authority regulates the drug industry and has on file applications for new products and historical filings on past products and product approvals.

Managed Care Organizations (MCO). These are the new powerhouses in the healthcare community, especially in the United States. One class of MCO is the Health Maintenance Organization (HMO). MCOs are a growing segment, with new patients signing up every day. This fact also makes the HMO a large buying group of medical and pharmaceutical products. The pharmaceutical houses no longer cater exclusively to the neighborhood pharmacy, but have increasingly concentrated their sales and marketing efforts on these MCOs. You will inevitably find a great deal of new product and new product testing information here. Increasingly over the next decade, as MCOs tighten up their formularies—the lists of permitted drugs and devices they will cover under their insurance plans—all the pharmaceutical firms will be jockeying for position on these formulary lists. MCOs are becoming significant intelligence barometers.

Retailers. Buyers for major drugstore chains are more likely to know about a manufacturer's marketing and pricing plans than would a small single-store pharmacy. A manufacturer's salesperson may have approached the buyer weeks or months before a pricing or marketing change was announced to the public and the press.

Wall Street analysts. These observers may admittedly not know much about a company's detailed manufacturing operations, but they will understand the marketing signals a company is sending out to its investors. We have used these analysts to confirm shipping and pricing information about a new product.

Aside from these major sources, there are knowledgeable marketing and production executives within each pharmaceutical house who must keep up on the industry and have heard or have verified for themselves the rumors about a particular product. Whether they legally can or are willing to release this information is another matter. The issue of friendliness may be a problem. Strict FDA and antitrust guidelines may prohibit their speaking to anyone outside their own company.

What sources are available to help you uncover the experts who can tell you about a drug and a competitor's activities regarding the drug? Here are descriptions of those sources.

Directory of Contract Packagers & Their Facilities (Institute of Packaging Professionals). Lists over 200 packagers nationwide, indexing them by the industry they serve (for example, food, pharmaceuticals, chemical specialties, consumer goods, military, and shipping). A typical entry lists the manufacturer's services, equipment used, status of quality and control testing, shipping and receiving licensing, and type of warehousing.

Drug Facts & Comparisons (Facts and Comparisons, Inc.). A valuable reference source for locating drug information by therapeutic class; allows you to compare drugs in the same class. From a competitive analysis standpoint, this text offers a number of important features: (1) it presents a quick reference of relative costs of similar drugs; (2) it lists products by dosage form and strength, again providing an easy form of comparison; (3) its monthly update sheets keep you informed of drugs under investigation or those recently approved.

Freedom of Information Office or Dockets Management Branch (Park Building, 12420 Parklawn Dr., Room 123, Rockville, MD 20857; 301-443-7542). The FDA offers a number of key pieces of information under the Freedom of Information Act (FOIA). The FDA cannot disclose approval of any drug prematurely (that is, before the appropriate hearing committee has made it official), but it offers other information that could be useful to a competitor. Examples of filings that are available include:

> *Drug Master File (DMF).* DMFs provide information that becomes part of a generic drug application. DMFs are referenced in an application to the Office of Generic Drugs at the FDA. The DMF lists all suppliers used by a pharmaceutical company to produce specific generic products. Knowledge of key suppliers can help you identify when a competitor might start increasing production, or whether it is using a supplier who may be low cost, thereby giving the competitor margins greater than yours.

> *510(k) Filing.* The Center for Devices and Radiological Health (CDRH), a unit of the FDA, ensures the safety and effectiveness of medical devices. Companies producing medical devices that are considered noncritical and similar to products manufactured prior to 1976, according to the law, must file premarket notification that describes in detail the product and its specifications. This is called a 510(k) filing. You can obtain these filings under the FOIA. Devices that the FDA considers life-supporting are filed under another form, the PMA (Pre-Market Approval), which is not available under the FOIA.

Medical & Healthcare Marketplace Guide (Investment Dealers' Digest). A wonderfully detailed reference work, profiling over 5,500 medical devices and pharmaceutical companies. Each profile presents the company history, any merger or acquisition activity, product categories, parent–subsidiary relationships, and parent–subsidiary addresses. Helps orient the analyst by giving all the right corporation names and relationships. In this industry, a simple misspelling may lead you to analyze the wrong company—one whose name is very similar to that of your target.

National Wholesale Druggists' Association Membership & Executive Directory (National Wholesale Druggists' Association). Wholesalers may be one step removed from the retailing end of the drug industry, but they are also a step closer to the manufacturing operations and may be an excellent source of rumored information. They may also help place your hunches in perspective, and tell you how accurate your shipping and pricing information might be.

Physicians' Desk Reference (PDR) (Medical Economics Publishing). This reference on nearly 3,000 products is one of the bibles of the drug industry. It is equivalent to a Thomas Register for pharmaceuticals, only far more detailed. Its sections include:

Manufacturers' Index
Product Name Index
Product Category Index
Generic and Chemical Index
Product Identification

Product Information Section
Discontinued Products
Diagnostic Product Information
Poison Control Centers
Key to Controlled Substances Categories

FINDING MANAGEMENT OUT: GETTING INFORMATION ABOUT A COMPANY'S OFFICERS

Here are two statements:

1. Management background can be one of the most difficult segments of corporate information to uncover.
2. Management background is fairly easy to locate.

These statements seem to contradict each other. It is the second statement that holds true for the researcher who knows where to look. Aside from the standard Who's Who directories that list prominent officials and national leaders, there is a wealth of additional information about those in the business community.

Where else can you turn to uncover an individual's background?

Town newspaper and hometown releases. You have seen the press announcements—for example, "Mr. Smith has been promoted to Vice President of Marketing." These announcements are usually accompanied by a photograph. Whenever a corporation announces a major employee promotion, it sends out what is called a hometown release, a press release geared to the executive's local town paper. Without knowing that any news item was ever published, you can often call a local newspaper and ask the editor when and if a news release had ever appeared about Mr. Smith. More frequently than you would expect, the paper will have published an announcement and can send you a clipping. These clippings can contain the executive's new title, experience with the company, and possibly some mention of the person's family.

Newspaper morgues. Larger city newspapers will have established newspaper clipping files, called morgues, where they have stored tens of thousands of news articles. Even if you cannot find the person you are looking for mentioned in a morgue article, you may find the name of a relative who can provide a lead to your prospect.

Family businesses are prime candidates for the morgue. These concerns are usually civic-minded and receive a good deal of press over the years.

Because most morgues are designed for use by in-house news staff only, you may have to receive permission to use the files.

Town halls. The municipal town hall will have on file real estate records that report the value of an individual's house. Voter registry will have information on a person's age. Most of this information is available to you with just a telephone call.

Universities. Universities are proud of their graduates and make it their business to publicize their alumni stars. You can find alumni information in a number of university sources:

Biographies. Many universities have compiled extensive biographies on their graduates—especially the wealthier or more prominent alumni. You can probably find these bios in either the alumni relations or public relations office.

Faculty. Should you be able to find out what school or division your subject attended while at the university, you may possibly locate a faculty member who knows him or her and can provide some background on the former student.

Yearbooks. Every alumni relations office or university public relations office has a historical collection of yearbooks that can provide name, address, and other biographical information.

POWER COMPANIES: AN UNDERUTILIZED SOURCE

Here is another intelligence gem. Public utilities are probably the best single source for locating the number of homes in a state or region that are using a particular appliance. Most market penetration studies are national in scope. Utilities allow you to examine usage on a local level. You can then use these data to determine a company's market share on a local level.

For years, utilities have collected information on their customers to determine power consumption and usage.

Power companies need to know what appliances are being plugged in and how many of them are out there. The data they collect are publicly available. Most utilities conduct these surveys yearly, but there is no prescribed pattern. In addition, the information collected will vary widely from utility to utility. This makes the data difficult to compile for a national study, but it can provide crucial information for a company needing to know exactly how many products (dishwashers, for example) are being used in a geographic area.

How do utilities collect their information? In many areas, they take a sample of their user population and conduct face-to-face interviews.

To find out where and when a utility has completed a consumer study, contact its public relations or public information department.

CUSTOMS HOUSE BROKERS: IMPORTING COMPANY INFORMATION

Intermediaries abound in everyday business transactions. A customs broker is one of these go-betweens. Anytime an intermediary is involved in the purchase or sale of a product, you have another intelligence source, another possible conduit of information about a competitor.

What are customs brokers and how do they work? You will find them listed in the Yellow Pages in any major port city or any city with an international airport.

War Story: How Many Dishwashers in North Carolina?

We had to locate the number of dishwashers operating in North Carolina.

After reviewing all of the merchandise and trade magazines, we were only able to come up with national sales figures on the number of dishwashers sold. We could not find state-by-state or regional data.

A Southern electric utility company had recently completed an appliance survey. The object of the study was to learn the penetration, or number of households, that use various electrical appliances. The survey covered only residential customers, not commercial or industrial users.

The result: The study identified the percent of homes that used each category of appliance.

Companies hire brokers to check their goods in, once they arrive at their U.S. destination. By federal law, companies must have a broker represent them for any shipment worth $250 or more.

Once the brokers have paid the import duties (they have 10 days' grace after the merchandise arrives in port), they then notify the receiving company's traffic manager, who arranges for pickup.

There is no easy way to identify any one customs broker with a particular company. Brokers are known to keep their customer list secret. The brokerage business is highly competitive, and brokers are often out of their offices, soliciting clients. Their offices frequently are at airports or dock areas.

Once you have located the right broker, though, you have found an expert on import trends for a particular product. The broker may also know quite a bit about an individual company's latest product line long before the details reach the trade press or the merchants.

Aside from the Yellow Pages, you can locate brokers through their national association: National Customs Brokers Forwarders Association of America (NCBFAA), One World Trade Center 1153, New York, NY 10048; 212-432-0050.

PIERS: A UNIQUE SOURCE ON EXPORTS AND IMPORTS

In addition to customs house brokers, you can now determine specific shipping data through *The Journal of Commerce* PIERS (Port Import Export Reporting Service) database. The PIERS organization extracts data from ship manifests from 47 U.S. ports. PIERS does not take in airport shipments. The level and specificity of the data can be extraordinary. Only when the shipper or consignee is represented by a customs house broker are the data disguised; otherwise, the database reveals both the shipper and the consignee, as well as quantity shipped, date shipped, date arrived, port of origin, and port of arrival.

My firm has used this resource to help determine manufacturing start-ups by tracking the import of supplies. We have also been able to analyze a plant's utilization of its capacity and the plant's output, based on use of materials. PIERS itself suggests some of the following uses for its data:

- Seasonal patterns of exports/imports.
- Rank importers/exporters by volume by month.
- Track cargo movements of one particular exporter/importer.
- Determine trade routes by compressing data into aggregate form.
- Examine port market shares.
- Uncover gaps in a competitor's service to particular markets.
- Analyze inland flow of products.

As a PIERS customer, you can either turn to the PIERS organization directly for help, or you can tap into the service online. If you prefer to go online, I recommend you use their custom search service first. This database can be difficult to understand and manipulate the first time through. Plus, as a beginner, you may miss many creative search strategies that the experienced PIERS staff can suggest. For additional information on the PIERS database, see Chapter 5 or contact: *The Journal of Commerce*, Two World Trade Center, 27th Floor, New York, NY 10048; 212-837-7000, 800-952-3839.

CHAMBERS OF COMMERCE: UBIQUITOUS INTELLIGENCE GATHERERS

You can look at a Chamber of Commerce in two ways:

1. It is merely a booster organization for local businesses.
2. It is a superb research organization that possesses a good deal of information on local businesses. The information is often unpublished (remember that public information does not always mean published information), but is cataloged by the Chamber.

The latter viewpoint makes a Chamber of Commerce a terrific regional intelligence source. Not only does it often have on file the name of the company you are looking for, but it may also have the name of the owners, the number of employees, and other details, such as the company's reputation, history, and participation in civic activities.

Chambers range in size from a desk-drawer operation to a large business with an enormous staff. There is a Chamber of Commerce in just about every business community in the United States. To give you an idea of just how many that means, there are approximately 100 in Alabama, 200 in New York State, and 50 in West Virginia.

You can find Chambers of Commerce in any number of different ways; the Yellow Pages are just one means to locate them. The best directory, for both domestic and foreign Chambers and Consulates, is *Johnson's World Wide Chamber of Commerce Directory*. This superb book offers:

American Chambers of Commerce in foreign countries.

Canadian Chambers of Commerce.

Foreign Chambers of Commerce throughout the world.

Foreign Embassies and Consulates in the United States.

U.S. Consulates, Embassies, and Foreign Service posts throughout the world. Foreign Consular offices in the United States.

You can order the directory by writing:

World Chamber of Commerce Directory
World Chamber of Commerce Directory, Inc.
P.O. Box 1029
Loveland, CO 80539
303-663-3231; Fax: 303-663-6187

ACQUIRING ACQUISITION INTELLIGENCE

One of the most difficult searches involves information on a merger or acquisition. Unless two publicly held companies are merging, you will find little information. In many states, privately held corporations are not required to file extensive statements detailing a recent merger. If a company is not publicly traded, the SEC cannot demand that the company file reports. Without these sources, how do you go about tracking down intelligence on a competitor that may have recently acquired another corporation?

Unlike stock and bond trading, there is no one source that tracks this type of corporate activity. Yet there are sources you can turn to for information. A 1982 study, "The Acquisition Search: How Major Corporations Locate and Assess Acquisition Candidates" (Fuld & Company, formerly Information Data Search, Cambridge, MA), discovered that those experienced in the merger and acquisition business rely on news articles and indexes only half of the time. The best source for the latest acquisition news is the Old Boy network—a group of executives who are in touch with the industry and actively take an interest in its corporate changes.

Investment bankers are an excellent channel for tapping into this Old Boy network. Investment banking houses have established files that profile acquirable companies and, conversely, which companies other companies like to acquire. In other words, the investment banking community has profiled the major acquiring companies and their targets.

Don't misunderstand their knowledge or importance, though. They are financial gadflies, deal makers. By their own admission, they know a little about a lot of companies. They are not technocrats who know about a machine's inner workings; their job is to keep their financial fingers on the pulse of the corporate community.

Some of the best sources of your industry's merger and acquisition news may be right in your own company. Almost half of those responding to a recent survey claimed that they prefer to call up a company contact to get the lowdown on a company's status.

In the dozen years since my firm's 1982 study, my discussions with senior managers in charge of their company's acquisitions have only served to reinforce the study's statements. Today there are more resources, including online databases and CD-ROM products, but the Old Boy network is still very much alive. The reference books or electronic tools help you screen more finely and faster than before. Based on the study's findings and on interviews with acquisition executives, here are my recommendations to find details on an acquisition:

1. First review the literature and the news articles. Many times, you will find that the acquisition you heard about was already cited in an article. The directories in the next section specialize in catching this type of news.
2. Through your company's bank, your company's financial officers, or your stockbroker, locate a helpful investment banker. If this banker doesn't know much about your industry, he or she will know a colleague who does.
3. Contact your company's controller, treasurer, or financial vice-president.

Merger and Acquisition News Sources and Directories

Business and Acquisition Newsletter (Newsletters International, Inc.). A monthly publication that announces companies that want to buy or sell other entities, products, or patents.

Capital Adjustments (Maxwell Macmillan Professional & Business Publications). A loose-leaf series of books that track, among other subjects, worthless securities.

Capital Changes Reports (Commerce Clearing House). A five-volume work that offers the financial history of a company. A typical report will trace a company's stock splits, dividends, exchange of securities, and mergers and consolidations.

Directory of Obsolete Securities (Financial Information, Inc.). A boon for the researcher in search of a lost company. Tells in a very concise way whether a company has changed its name, merged, was acquired, dissolved, liquidated, reorganized, went bankrupt, or in some other way changed its corporate status.

European Deal Review (Off-the-Shelf Publications, Inc.). A quarterly summary of merger and acquisition activity in Europe.

F&S Directory of Corporate Change (Information Access Corporation/Predicasts). A spinoff from Predicasts' bibliographic database. Divided into three sections: (1) an alphabetical index of companies, (2) companies listed by their Standard Industrial Classification (SIC), and (3) a section that lists all the name changes. Although this index may not cover every merger and acquisition that has occurred, if the announcement went public you can be fairly sure that this text has picked it up. Also available on an online database.

Media Mergers and Acquisitions (Paul Kagan Associates, Inc.). A specialty newsletter that concentrates on M&A activity within the media.

Mergers & Acquisitions Report: America's M&A Weekly (Dealer's Digest, Inc.). Includes a detailed listing of new offers and completed deals, and news on offers that have fallen through.

Mergers and Acquisitions: The Journal of Corporate Venture (MLR Publishing). A quarterly periodical that, besides publishing statistics on recent merger and acquisition activity, also presents a roster of the latest reported mergers and acquisitions.

Moody's Investment Manuals and CD-ROM Products (Moody's Investors Services). The Moody's name is one of the best known in business research

The Truth about Rumors

LEONARD M. FULD: What percentage of the rumors you first hear in pharmaceuticals end up as fact?

WAYNE ROSENKRANS: Rumors tend to become fact, if you wait long enough. It is also true that rumors rarely occur in isolation. Often, there are a number of other signals, sometimes subtle, which begin to appear coincident with the rumor. An example was the failure . . . of Synergen's sepsis drug, Antril, to show efficacy in its pivotal trials. The analyst community, which is very twitchy in pharmaceuticals, had begun to buzz with a low level of negativity in regard to the Antril trials. These early twitchings were "laid to rest" as being due to attempts at profit taking, yet the internal rumors persisted. Ultimately, the rumors were proven correct. Antril failed to show efficacy—and hence FDA approval was declined.

There are two principal categories of rumors in my experience: (1) those dealing with the appearance of an unexpected competitor, and (2) those dealing with the demise of a competitor compound or company. It should be stressed that the pharma industry, perhaps more than any other industry, is heavily research dependent (witness the average 12 to 24 percent of pharma sales devoted to R & D). Hence, many rumors arise from scientists speaking to each other at congresses, and so on. Often, scientific conclusions are drawn, even before the company has made a conscious decision to progress or kill a project, which will manifest themselves as a rumor.

In the pharma industry, therefore, it pays to listen to the rumor mill. Often, the question is not is the rumor true, but when will it bear out. The "intelligent" analyst, with her or his antennae well tuned, will probably have begun reading the peripheral signals mentioned earlier, before the rumor appears, which will give it context. Action then depends on the strategic importance of that context. A high-priority context should elicit a "storm warning" of potential change in the environment followed by periodic updates and a final resolution, "Go to DEFCON1, or stand down." Lower-priority contexts should be placed on a significant watch mode until some form of resolution is apparent which can then be communicated.

Dr. Wayne Rosenkrans is currently Associate Director of Strategic Intelligence for SmithKline Beecham's R&D group.

and investment, both for bond rating and investment information services. Each Moody's Investment Manual contains a section that lists all recent mergers and acquisitions, as well as name changes. More recently, the CD-ROM products, Moody's Company Data™ and Moody's International Company Data™, offer monthly updates on corporate changes, particularly merger and acquisition news.

A number of other significant databases cover the merger and acquisition scene. Because they are online (or available through CD-ROM), you may have the chance to manipulate the data for further, customized analysis. The databases and their publishers are:

FT Mergers and Acquisitions
FT Profile
Sunbury House
79 Staines Rd., W. Sunbury
Thames PW167UD U.K.
011-44-932-761444

*IDD M&A Transactions and Text
   Enhanced MLR Database*
IDD Information Services
Two World Trade Center
New York, NY 10048
212-323-9109

M&A Filings
Prentice-Hall Online
Prentice-Hall Legal and Financial
   Services
1090 Vermont Ave., N.W., Suite 430
Washington, DC 20005
202-408-3120

Securities Data Company
1180 Raymond Blvd.
Newark, NJ 07102
201-622-3100

PART THREE

ANALYSIS: THE ART AND THE DISCIPLINE

The Intelligence Pyramid

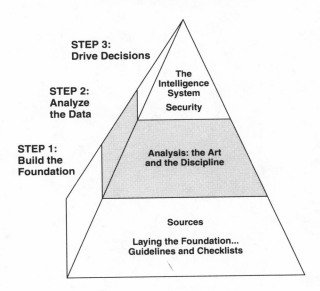

Analysis is both an art and a discipline. I have met successful business-people who, in the blink of an eye, can assimilate and analyze large amounts of information. They intuitively understand the analysis process and have disciplined themselves to constantly analyze the information they receive. What appears to observers as a lightning-quick computation often is the result of an internal analytical engine, constantly churning away inside the individual.

The techniques and cases presented in this Part examine this blink-of-an-eye event and expand on it. I will take you through the thought process of a seasoned analyst or astute businessperson when assessing a competitive situation. The next few pages describe how to sort and select input, what analytical framework to apply to a particular issue, and what you must understand before you make your next important decision.

357

12 A PRACTICAL APPROACH TO ANALYSIS

Analytical Techniques and Cases

I wish I could find another word to use instead of analysis, which seems to make many businesspeople break out in hives. The very thought of analysis conjures up an intimidating array of equations, regression analyses, and other statistical goodies. Analysis is really the application of common sense and experience to raw information. You need analysis in order to develop competitor and market intelligence, but you don't necessarily need a PhD to develop it. Some of the greatest entrepreneurs in modern business—Bill Gates of Microsoft, Ray Kroc of McDonald's—analyzed their competition constantly (and successfully) without ever taking a course in business analysis. What they could do well was pick out the most valuable insights and act on them.

Information is the manager's main "capital," and it is he who must decide what information he needs and how to use it.—Peter Drucker[1]

For this capital to produce healthy returns, the manager must convert it into intelligence. Analysis is the means to do so. The analysis need not be complicated, only complete and accurate.

There is no model or single way to analyze a company or a competitive environment. Most of the time, analysis is simply a process of winnowing the good from the useless information and finding a framework in which to add value to that good information. Ultimately, analysis is only "good" if you can make use of it and act on it.

This chapter takes a practical, real-world approach to analysis. It assumes that most managers do not have a great deal of time or resources and that these same

---

[1]Peter Drucker, *The Changing World of the Executive* (New York: Times Books, 1985), p. 37.

managers possess the ability to analyze without necessarily remembering the intricacies of their college statistics courses. Using this rationale, the chapter is divided into the following sections:

Section I: Learn to Read the Tea Leaves;

Section II: Know When to Analyze: The Moment of Change;

Section III: Find the Right Framework and Analysis Tool.

Each section is illustrated with actual (disguised) cases from a variety of industries worldwide.

SECTION I: LEARN TO READ THE TEA LEAVES

Intelligence is a process of focus. To make solid business decisions, you must: (1) focus on your market (sometimes easier said than done); (2) identify which of the many market forces is most important so you can concentrate your time and effort; and (3) understand which strategy your target company is pursuing and bring all your information-gathering and analysis efforts to bear on that strategy.

Once again, time is most critical here, and you need to spend it wisely. You cannot afford to waste time exploring the wrong market, the wrong competitor, or the wrong strategy. To do so is to pursue the wrong market path and face potential failure. This chapter will give you the ability and the tools to focus your intelligence efforts.

The Tools

The tools for competitive analysis are all around us. The raw analytical material starts with the intelligence resources that exist at our fingertips—news articles, broadcast news, trade shows, industry gossip, and internal reports from sales and R&D units. The problem is that, here and there, we spot a piece of the intelligence picture, but we do not see the entire panorama.

Sometimes, by carefully reviewing the news and applying your industry experience, you can read between the lines. For instance, instead of reading each article in isolation as it appears in your daily newspaper or trade journal, you should make it a habit to clip out articles of interest on your market and your competition and save them in a file. Then, every week or so, pull out the most recent clippings and read them together. This process of comparing and contrasting information can point out new competitive initiatives. This contrast-and-compare activity is a form of analysis.

As examples of elements of the big picture, I have selected two *Wall Street Journal* articles. By themselves, they spawn questions and even suggest some answers. I have highlighted words or phrases (in bold type) that begin to hint at analytical concepts and "hot" buttons. From an in-depth examination, let's see how we can determine aspects of competitive analysis and, ultimately, competitive strategy.

Time Warner's New Leadership Trims Business Connections from Ross Era

Time Warner Inc.'s chairman and chief executive, Gerald M. Levin, has quietly begun to dismantle some controversial business ties that marked the **freewheeling corporate culture** of his predecessor, the late Steven J. Ross.

Barely two months after Mr. Ross died . . . Mr. Levin is sharply paring back Time Warner's business relationship with Oded "Ed" Aboodi, who was among the late executive's most trusted advisers as well as a personal friend.

[Sources] say Mr. Levin is also attempting to **remodel the sprawling entertainment and media company's culture to reflect his own more disciplined and conventional corporate style.**

In addition to revising such arrangements, Mr. Levin has also overseen a restructuring of the Time Warner board . . . . (Source: *Wall Street Journal,* February 25, 1993, p. A3. Emphasis added.)

Questions

1. What is the predominant issue that seems to be gripping Time Warner?
2. How many changes are being made here both of a short-term and long-term nature?

Possible Analysis

- Time Warner will become more focused on particular markets and move away from being "all things to all people" in the entertainment business. This new focus may result in a series of divestitures.
- Management structure and decision making will change and will be a reflection of the new CEO, Gerald Levin. It is likely that more financial controls will be in place and that decisions will be made in a more fiscally conservative manner.

Microsoft Loses Bid for a Trademark on the Word "Windows" for PC Software

The U.S. Patent & Trademark Office has rejected a bid by Microsoft Corp. to gain a **trademark on the word "Window"** when used to describe personal-computer software products.

Microsoft's efforts to win control over the term Windows has raised hackles among some software and computer companies, who see the campaign as part of a pattern of Microsoft attempts to overpower smaller rivals.

"It hurts our ability to compete if Microsoft owns the name of Windows," said Heidi Sinclair, Vice President, Corporate Strategy, at Borland International. . . .

"It's hard to prevail against a company the size of Microsoft," said Ed Anson, a software developer in Andover, Mass., who sold his trademarked Hyper-Windows name to Microsoft last year for less than $10,000. (Source: *Wall Street Journal,* February 25, 1993, p. B8. Emphasis added.)

Questions

1. Can you think of other industries where trademarks and/or patents become barriers against competition?
2. How would you position Microsoft in its industry? Is it a customer, supplier, or competitor? How many roles is it playing? In which of these roles is it the strongest?

3. Is there an overall weakness in Microsoft's overall strategy? How would you begin to find that out?

Possible Analysis

- By identifying other industries where trademarks or patents are barriers, we might be able to determine how long Microsoft can maintain a competitive edge, either in pricing or in profits it could generate from product line extensions.

- Microsoft seems to be both competitor and supplier. However, it appears to be strengthening its role as a critical sole-source supplier, because everyone has to write software to the Microsoft Windows specifications. Even though it may have lost exclusive rights to the Windows trademark, it has achieved a competitive advantage other operating system competitors will be hard pressed to beat.

- Even Microsoft cannot be everything to everybody. Where is it weakest? In which software categories does it fall short? Utility software? Database software? Industry-specialized categories? It cannot have differentiated itself in each of the many customer niches.

These articles have generated questions and identified some of the competitive forces that players in those markets must face. When you understand the competitive forces but still have questions, you need an analytical model, a way of thinking about your competition and the industry. Your analytical model will serve as a framework from which to develop intelligence on your competitors, suppliers, customers, or any other players in your market.

SECTION II: KNOW WHEN TO ANALYZE: THE MOMENT OF CHANGE

When, not *What,* to analyze is often the single most frustrating problem facing managers. With thousands of potential sources and dozens of techniques available, the analyst needs to reach for the intelligence jugular, to find and analyze the most critical information in a timely fashion. The Moment of Change can alert analysts to key analytical opportunities. I define it as follows:

> The Moment of Change is a time when a major event takes place. That event could come from within the company or from without. Any such event will generate a great deal of information on a target company and, often, on other affected subsidiary or affiliate operations. The analyst does not have to witness the Moment, just be able to recognize it at a later date.

The Moment of Change is related to the most basic of intelligence rules: "Wherever money is exchanged, so is information." The rule implies being aware of every business transaction or finding some way to locate a transaction in order to find the necessary information, even after the fact. Because the Moment is a major, sometimes traumatic shift, it will generate not a mere trickle, but rather a shower of information. Corporate divestiture, acquisition, and bankruptcy are examples of upheavals of the status quo that will generate important competitive information. You need to begin your analysis during these specific Moments of Change.

If you think of your competition as having erected information barriers around itself, remember that the Moment of Change creates a rift in the wall. This opening may be just wide enough for you to view the inner workings of a competitor's, customer's, or supplier's strategy.

The Manville Moment: An Informational Explosion

From 1974 to 1982, Manville Corporation had settled over 4,100 lawsuits related to its asbestos products. But with a backlog of over 17,000 lawsuits still pending, the company decided to declare bankruptcy. Its declaration of bankruptcy forced Manville to disclose untold amounts of information the court demanded of it—in part to inform existing creditors. The filings literally filled an entire room in the New York City federal court building where the hearings were being held.

Why even bother monitoring Manville, a company now in bankruptcy? Because bankruptcy does not necessarily mean future liquidation. In fact, many bankrupt companies emerge from bankruptcy far leaner and most cost-efficient than their existing competition. Consider the condition of American Airlines—the largest U.S. carrier in the early 1990s. Because American had accumulated so much debt and overhead in its 1980s expansion program, the company found it increasingly difficult to compete against TWA and other airlines that have once again become solvent. These far smaller, reconstituted airlines could now offer price-competitive deals to consumers while still making a profit, something American found difficult to accomplish.

A bankrupt company in the United States must reveal everything about its current and future plans. Even when a company, such as Manville, is crippled and in Chapter 11, as a competitor you should still know its cost of operations and other strategic details. You may also want to buy one of its profitable business units.

Bankruptcy was a true moment of change for Manville. Using a number of business news databases from the Dialog system as barometers, Figure 12.1 was created. From the moment of bankruptcy, information about Manville grew by orders of magnitude. From fewer than 100 citations per year in 1980, the news ballooned to approximately 1,000 citations by 1984. Although concerned mostly with the lawsuits, many of the business journals and local papers also explored Manville's other, nonasbestos operations, including its forest products, fiberglass, and mining businesses. With each painful step Manville took to finally emerge from bankruptcy in 1988, it needed to report to the world—mainly through the courts—its every move.

For example, Manville had to explain to the Environmental Protection Agency (EPA) when and how it was going to increase its paper production following the bankruptcy declaration. A February 1986 letter on file with the EPA and with the federal bankruptcy court makes very clear how Manville had to reveal and explain far more in its environmental filings than it might otherwise have done in its pre-bankruptcy filing period:

> As explained in the forms, since mid-1981 our company went into bankruptcy and drastically downsized. We have been slowly rebuilding. Production equipment, shut down in mid-1981, has been coming back on as the market will allow. Some of it has come on and had to go back down due to lack of orders. We have now returned all paper machines to service except machines 3 and 4. During this time, we have had to become more efficient. We had a maximum production of 2,142 T/D [tons per day] in 1980 (April) and followed this in March of 1981 with a maximum of 2,138 T/D with all 7 machines. . . . The sum of maximum production for all paper machines in 1985 would be 2,225. . . . Although we have gone through traumatic economic times I

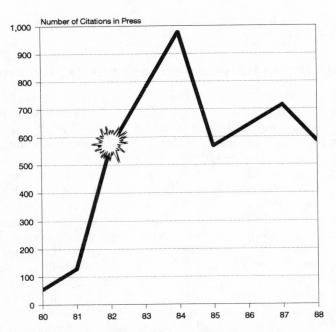

Figure 12.1 The Manville bankruptcy: How a moment of change often equates to an information explosion. (Dialog News Databases)

believe this data states the fact that production for our West Monroe pulp and paper mill is 2,200 air dry tons/day. . .

In compiling Table 12.1, I have speculated what information was typically available before and after the Manville bankruptcy declaration. The table illustrates how a Moment of Change can offer rich analytical opportunities based on competitors' current and future plans.

Other Moments to Watch For

Some Moments of Change result from a company's own fortunes or failures. In other instances, government or society creates a major change through legislation or through a labeling of what is acceptable and what is not. I place these other Moments of Change into three categories: (1) regulatory change, (2) privatization of industry, and (3) acquisition and divestiture.

Regulatory Change

Governments are constantly changing industry regulations, sometimes loosening, sometimes tightening up the ways companies can operate within certain markets. As an example, in 1987, the French government relaxed the regulation governing synthetic sweeteners. Food companies of all sorts suddenly released scores of new low-calorie drinks and foods. Table 12.2 shows the rupture in the competitive information wall that can result from such a Moment of Change.

Changes in environmental regulations can create tremendous manufacturing upheavals that may push the informational doors on a manufacturing facility wide

TABLE 12.1 Analytical Opportunities Before vs. During Manville's Bankruptcy Declaration

Intelligence Sources	Pre-Bankruptcy	During Bankruptcy
Government Filings (Federal, State, Local)	• New plant construction • Standard financial filings • Environmental compliance data • Quarterly and annual financial reports	• New plant construction • Frequent financial reports to courts, with in-depth accounting of subsidiary operations formerly undisclosed • Detailed description of plant expansions or closures that may be linked to payment of debts to creditors • Explanation of new investments or acquisitions to courts, as well as to SEC • Advance notices of all corporate restructuring • Disclosure of trade secret or process information used to describe liability or explain value of assets for creditors
Press	• Standard earnings reports • Change of officers, promotions • New marketing and product initiatives	• Detailed financial review of individual operations, on a plant-by-plant, region-by-region basis • Close examination of all officer promotions, along with assessment of why the company chose them and what strategic direction this may indicate • Courtroom reports of legal proceedings, with analysis of long-term prospects for the company
Suppliers/Distributors	• Reports of possible shift in payment times or on-time delivery of product	• Understanding the level of debt: detailed listing of creditors and amounts owed • Assessment of future manufacturing and distribution strategy: plans filed for change in distribution system and suppliers used
Competitors	• Standard market share assessments • Reports from competitor's sales force on sales tactics used	• Knowledge of Manville's new business strategy based on information picked up from former Manville customers • Understanding of internal Manville operations based on nonconfidential information garnered from newly hired former Manville employees • Review of Manville's new advertising and trade show promotion will indicate new direction and long-term strategy

TABLE 12.2   Effects of a Regulatory Change

Activity Generated from the Moment of Change	Strategy Revealed
Equipment and raw materials suppliers contacted by manufacturers	Food producers redesigned their product lines, extending existing product categories and adding new ones.
Press announcements	
Meetings with chain store buyers in advance—focus groups	
Pharmaceutical and food agencies may require advance approval and regulatory filings—some of which may be made public	
Ad agencies test market concepts among consumers	New advertising strategies were devised.
Test markets started with advance products placed on store shelves	
Printers, media buyers contacted to produce and distribute ads	
Package design firms contacted at least six months in advance to prepare designs and layout	Packaging changes took place.

open. This is particularly true in the United States and in the European Community countries, where regulations are becoming increasingly stringent.

In one European study on the detergent industry, which we completed a few years ago, the German "Green Dot Program" allowed us to examine in great depth the companies competing in the German market. The Green Dot program required manufacturers to reclaim and recycle all the packaging in which their products were sold. Not only are these expensive guidelines for manufacturers to maintain, but they generate a lot of industry and competitive information. Although the Green Dot program began as a voluntary effort, before long companies had to adhere to these new standards or German retailers would not stock their products. Partly because of its strict environmental laws, Germany has become the packaging bellwether for the rest of Western Europe and, to some degree, for the United States. By tracking competitive activity in the German market, we were better able to anticipate how our client's competitors would behave in France or in the United States.

In another study, this time U.S.-based, we needed to assess the manufacturing costs and process of an industrial adhesives plant located in Maryland. A subtle, but critical, change in a pollution law made all the difference here. In 1991, the Maryland Department of Environmental Protection (DEP) decided to treat methylene chloride as a toxic substance. Plants in Maryland had to file a detailed abatement plan with the Maryland DEP—not the federal EPA. The plan filed for this particular plant detailed capital investment in new manufacturing technology needed to reduce emissions. By analyzing the reported chemical changes in the adhesives formulation and the output of each production line, we were able to determine that the competitor planned to make a major change in its adhesive, one that could possibly weaken its bond strength—and its competitive position.

The client was able to take advantage of this analysis. Management turned some of the findings over to its sales force, who contacted accounts they had been able to penetrate, alerting them to the possibility of a change in the performance of the competitor's products. The rest of the analysis allowed management to apply the intelligence to long-term strategy.

The most difficult aspect at this time is not finding the information, but making sense out of it. Because the market opportunity is so great and the Moment is so potentially dramatic, many companies enter the fray. It is not clear which of them will stay in the market and which will fall out. Experienced analysis is needed to determine the right answer. Intelligence Case 2, on timelining, later in the chapter, will indicate how to analyze the large amounts of information generated in a pharmaceutical Moment of Change.

Privatization of Industry

In the past ten years, governments around the world have begun to divest their nationally owned companies at a rapid rate. This act of privatization is a Moment of Change. Along with the airline industry, telecommunications has experienced widespread privatization around the globe. The privatization of government-run telecommunications companies is followed by foreign market competition and overseas investments on the part of other telecommunications companies. Whenever a privatization is announced, the international business and trade press is filled with accounts of AT&T, NTT, British Telecom, Northern Telecom, and others bidding for part of the contract to upgrade the system in question.

As of this writing, the following countries have recently announced privatization of their telecommunications systems: Argentina, Australia, Chile, Hong Kong, Mexico, New Zealand, the United Kingdom, and Venezuela. Privatizations still planned (Moments yet to come) include: Brazil, Costa Rica, Honduras, Indonesia, Ireland, Kenya, Nigeria, South Korea, Sudan, Sweden, and Taiwan.

War Story: The Generic Moment

The explosion of generic drugs worldwide is a subject my firm has studied for a number of clients over the past decade. Whenever a drug loses patent protection, the innovator company is extraordinarily vulnerable to severe market share loss as soon as a generic version is approved and launched. Dramatic sales volume swings can occur with the marketing of a new generic drug. The first company to launch a generic competitor usually achieves quick penetration of the total product segment. Typically, the first and second companies to enter with a particular generic will capture 90 percent of the market almost overnight. In addition, demand is increasing for generics because of healthcare economics; governments throughout the world have introduced legislation to increase the use of less expensive generic substitutes.

Although the patent holder may try various strategies to offset sales loss upon expiration, few of these strategies have succeeded. A few years prior to a patent's expected expiration, the competitive forces line up in an effort to become the first in line with the generic version.

At the expiration date—the Moment of Change—these forces are unleashed, along with a great deal of information. Table 12.3 summarizes the Moment's effects.

TABLE 12.3 From Patent Drug to Generic—A Pharmaceutical Moment

Possible Strategies	Changes and Activity	Information Released
Patent holder may quickly move to create its own generic version	• Incorporate a new company or subsidiary • Create product identity and packaging changes • Contact suppliers and renegotiate terms of contract and amounts of raw chemical	• Publicly available documents resulting from filings with government regulatory agencies • Possible dosage changes indicated by packaging type • Possible over-the-counter switch indicated by more consumer-oriented packaging change, new consumer education program • Import/export data may reveal existence of other sources of supply and activity
Joint ventures formed	• Negotiations between patent holder and potential generics houses or distributors	• Some alliances announced in advance as "propaganda" to intimidate less worthy opponents
Generics houses gear up for new market	• Plant construction is reported • Managed care and government agencies are asked to list the generic product on their formularies	• Machinery suppliers contacted • Contacts made with generics companies, their sales forces or distributors • New hires with either previous-product or market experience • Contacts made with state formularies and HMOs
Raw chemical suppliers enter the market	• Machinery purchased from equipment suppliers • Plant expansion takes place	• Equipment suppliers discuss the market with other potential customers • In the United States, Drug Master Files are submitted with the ANDA (Abbreviated New Drug Application) to the FDA—publicly available • Surrounding communities are informed of company's plans

Acquisition and Divestiture

Any time a company spins off a subsidiary—whether a public or a private corporation—that well-planned separation is a Moment of Change. Information spills out into the street when the old work force is cut or trimmed and former employees are walking the streets. The SEC oversees the transaction when publicly traded companies are involved. With privately held companies, the home-town press is likely to pick up on the story. Virtually the same information spillage occurs with an acquisition.

The following excerpt from a press announcement describes Mobil Oil's divestiture of its polystyrene resins unit to BASF. The announcement offers strong hints for followup on both Mobil (the seller) and BASF (the buyer).

Mobil Gains from *Polystyrene* Sale

In its third quarter, Mobil Corp. (Fairfax, VA) will post an $80 million profit from the sale, completed early this month, of its polystyrene resins business to BASF. The transaction marks BASF's entry into the North American solid polystyrene resins market (*CW,* Jan. 22, p. 6), giving the world's second-largest solid polystyrene producer the number-two spot in North America. Previously, BASF had only expandable polystyrene resin capacity in the U.S.

The polystyrene resin operations have capacity for more than 620 million lbs/ year, with manufacturing plants in Joliet, IL; Santa Ana, CA; and Holyoke, MA. The Joliet plant includes a 120-million lbs/year expansion of high-impact polystyrene capacity, which came onstream a year ago. Research and development functions are also included in the sale. BASF has offered jobs to the unit's 288 employees. Mobil Chemical will continue to operate its polystyrene fabricating businesses, which are unaffected by the sale. (Source: *Chemical Week,* July 15, 1992, p. 7.)

Can you imagine what you could do with all the environmental, ownership, and business operations information if you could assemble a team of industry experts to analyze all the information resulting from this dramatic change within Mobil and BASF? If you were with another chemical company, you would need to look no further than your own company and its engineers, scientists, salespeople, and strategists.

SECTION III: FIND THE RIGHT FRAMEWORK AND ANALYSIS TOOL

Before you can conduct a cost analysis, management assessment, or any other kind of analysis, you have to know the key areas to analyze. You do not have enough time to analyze every aspect of a company. By heading in the wrong analytical direction, you may waste a great deal of precious time and come to the wrong conclusions.

Michael E. Porter, in his book *Competitive Strategy* (The Free Press, 1980), outlines the three basic strategies a company may pursue:

1. *Low cost.* A company's goal is to achieve overall cost leadership in an industry. The low-cost competitor may be able to undercut pricing of other players and still sustain healthy profits.
2. *Differentiation.* A company chooses to create a unique product or service that may allow it to charge higher prices or gain market share in a specific niche.

3. *Focus.* A company has chosen to limit its product or service to a particular buyer segment or geographic market.

Your competitor may have assumed one or two of these strategic directions, but not likely all three, according to Porter. If you can determine which of the three operating strategies your competitor is pursuing, you can then begin to apply the right framework for information collection and analysis.

Porter provides a list of the skills and resources a company would require in order to pursue each of the three strategies. To this list, I have added the business transactions that occur as a result of each strategic activity (see Tables 12.4 and 12.5). If you take this analysis to the next step and apply the cardinal intelligence rule of "Wherever money is exchanged, so is information," you will discover that each of these transactions may generate valuable pieces of competitive information that can then be analyzed.

Strategy option 3, focus, is a combination of differentiation and low-cost. It takes the strategy to an exclusively local or a market segment level.

A fruit and vegetable store located near my home is a perfect example of a focused strategy. Located just down the street from a large supermarket, it manages to attract customers from many blocks away—and from the far larger and lower-priced supermarket. It has accomplished this feat by focusing on what its customers want: high-quality fruits and vegetables. The store's owners make sure that they display only the shiniest, unmarred products, in contrast to the bruised and battered produce sold in the neighboring supermarket. This emphasis on focus has allowed the owners to charge a premium for their products. Yet, the customers keep coming.

The small store has fared well as a result of its focus strategy. It may have limited its revenue by deciding to remain small, but it has remained a thriving business, despite the formidable competitor down the street.

Companies often telegraph their strategies; it's how they execute them that's a mystery. Companies freely communicate their strategies to the market—through their customers and suppliers, and in their annual reports. Comparing and contrasting various strategic pronouncements will help you understand how each firm wants to position itself. The difficulty lies in assessing how a company will achieve the announced strategic goals. The Intelligence Cases, later in the chapter, will illustrate how to use various analysis tools to uncover possible company strategies and predict how a company might execute its chosen strategy.

For the moment, compare the following excerpts from the Digital Equipment Corporation (DEC) and Hasbro 1992 annual reports:

Digital Equipment Corporation:

. . . We will do whatever it takes to plan, design, implement, manage, and maintain the systems our customers need for their success. Those systems can be anything from a local area PC network for a five-person office to a system for automating an entire factory or a network linking all the generating stations on a national power grid. . . .

Hasbro, Inc.:

Our products must be affordable for the families and children who buy them. Around the world, 80% of all the products we sell retail for less than $20 or its local equivalent. . . .

TABLE 12.4 Strategy Option 1: Low Cost

Skills and Resources Required	Possible Activities	Resulting Information
Sustained capital investment	• New machinery purchased • Contract engineering firms hired • Service contracts issued	Cost of investment Depreciation Level of automation Equipment type and capacity
Process engineering skills	• Hiring and recruitment of trained personnel • Internal training programs • Information systems and technology introduced or upgraded	Number of shifts—employment levels Speed and efficiency of process—manufacturing, inventory, distribution, or customer service
Continuous improvement	• Union negotiations • Training programs throughout company	Labor rates Number of shifts Downtime levels
Ease and flexibility in manufacturing	• Contact packaging suppliers • Have sole source suppliers redesign components to meet specifications • Reconfigure plant machinery and purchase new machinery • Upgrade software and information systems	Manufacturing process Efficiency levels of manpower and machinery Production yield Utilization of capacity New product roll-outs
Low-cost distribution	• Purchase or rent warehouse space • Review installation and economics of order/inventory system	Customer logistics Delivery times and service levels

TABLE 12.5 Strategy Option 2: Differentiation

Skills and Resources Required	Possible Activities	Resulting Information
Strong marketing abilities	• Use of direct mail • Shift in advertising—placement and theme • Sales force hiring and training programs	• New regional or industry segment strategies • Redeployment of sales force into new markets or service areas
Product engineering	• Time from patent filing to production shortened • Staffing and hiring levels of development team	• New products and/or line extensions • Introduction of new technologies
Creative flair	• Unusual corporate alliances or trading relationships formed • Reposition product or service at trade shows • Possible promotion of VIP programs or other "convenience" programs for customers	• Decision to license products or process, rather than rely on internal resources—as a result, allowing competitor to extend market reach • Ability to identify new customer niches or product applications
Basic research	• Hiring in a new technology • Corporate-sponsored university research programs • Published papers and pronouncements; talks at technical and scientific societies	• Long-term market shifts • Insight on direction of R&D
Quality or technology leadership	• Software and systems suppliers, and intermediate equipment suppliers	• X-ray of technology and organization infrastructure necessary to push competitor to next strategic level
Ability to draw skills from other businesses	• Promotion of key staff—press releases • Movement of personnel • Customer exposure to new product, service, or sales teams	• Use of internal resources • Ability to innovate

A changing world requires that we not be captive to any country for production. We are global manufacturers, producing our products regionally in Europe and Asia. However, we are also the only major toy company that manufactures in the United States approximately 50% of its products sold there. . . .

Retail partnerships are critical. We are working more closely every day with our retailers by making more use of retail sales information, managing in-store promotions, increasing our use of computer-to-computer technology and by managing just-in-time inventory programs.

The DEC excerpt profiles a company that has no single, coherent strategic direction. According to its own statement, it wishes to compete in the PC networking market against some very low-cost, effective competition. After years of expansion and hiring, DEC will have a difficult time competing in certain low-cost arenas.

It also wants to differentiate itself as a systems consulting house—a very high-priced, high-value business. But can it truly compete against an Andersen Consulting, or an EDS? These are independent firms, not tied down to a particular product line—unlike DEC, which manufactures product. DEC, from this excerpt, appears to want to serve everyone in every market. However, it cannot be a low-cost leader at the same time.

This was a 1992 report, discussing 1991 activity. Since the report was issued, DEC has trimmed its operations and arguably has become more efficient. But DEC may still be pursuing too many strategies all at once—and fulfilling none of them successfully.

Hasbro, on the other hand, is making a clear statement that it is low-cost and is pursuing this strategy aggressively through its manufacturing operations, information technology, and product positioning and pricing. Hasbro is an easier company to analyze because it has directed analytical focus to the cost issue.

If you were to analyze Hasbro's operations and long-term plans, your next step would be to build an analytical framework based on cost. Intelligence Case 1, later in the chapter, will give you some practice.

Some Notes of Caution

Analysis is more an issue of time than of money. For that reason, you rarely have a chance to redo a poorly done analysis. When you have a firm grasp of your analytical objectives, be sure you are not using bad data. Conversely, if you have good data, don't plug them into a less-than-satisfactory analytical model or framework. Both are common problems, and both can be prevented if you take a few precautionary steps.

1. *Make the data reliable.* By following the guidelines and sources listed throughout this book, you will be swimming in information. Your biggest challenge will therefore be determining what information is most reliable or most useful to you.

I recommend adopting a basic 3/2/1 (highest to lowest) rating system for tagging all the data or information sources you gather. Such systems are used by government intelligence agencies to sift through their thousands of bits of information each day and week. Your ratings can be as simple as:

3 = fact (needs at least two sources to verify)

2 = somewhat reliable (has at least one source for the information)

1 = rumor (received conflicting information or information that the source was hesitant to support)

This approach will force you to use the most reliable information first; there will be less need to double-check your findings.

There is also a second, hidden benefit. Assume you continue to tag all your information and keep track of it throughout your investigation or for many months. By going back occasionally to review those pieces of information you rated as 1, you may find that a consistent percentage become facts over time. This may tell you to pay closer attention to rumors, or at least rumors of a certain type. It may also indicate how fast competitive information travels in your industry, and how far in advance you should be preparing for a competitor's moves. By tagging and tracking your ratings, you may create a reliable forecasting tool to add to your analytical tool kit.

2. *Maintain due diligence.* As a general rule of intelligence analysis, you need to surround yourself, each day, with market and competitor information. Remember, competitor information may be very elusive, remaining visible for a split second and then disappearing. You need to be there to catch it.

In earlier chapters, I discussed many inexpensive, easily accessible sources that will give you the capability of keeping a close and constant watch on your market. The list below pulls together the key groups of sources and gives suggestions for using them as monitoring tools:

- *Commercial databases.* Online databases offer a quick way to review the market, the competition, and overall business conditions. Create SDIs (see Chapter 5) that can automatically scan and report on your subjects of special interest.

- *Specialty trade publications.* Develop a list of a half-dozen industry magazines and newsletters that you actually *read* on a regular basis. Occasionally, rotate this reading list, thereby exposing yourself to new perspectives on the same subject. Employ your staff—those located in your offices as well as worldwide—to scan their newspapers and local trade press. Give them a "stop list" of company names and key issues that have first priority, and have them ship their clippings back to you or to your designated network of product managers and analysts.

- *News clippings.* Hire a news clipping service, such as Burrelle's Press Clipping Service (75 East Northfield Road, Livingston, NJ 07039, 800-631-1160). Online databases are increasing their local news coverage, but they still do not cover even a small fraction of all the local newspapers and journals. Clipping services are often far more complete and more timely. The drawback here is the time you must spend sorting through the piles of clippings you receive. Still, news clipping services remain a potent intelligence tool and a good complement to any online searches you perform. News or press clipping services are located throughout the world. Look in your Yellow Pages or call your local library's reference desk for one located near your town or near your competitor's town.

- *Help-wanted advertisements.* In the cities where your competitors have offices, give your sales force a stop list of companies to monitor in the local help-wanted Sunday supplements. Doing this is far more cost-effective than using a clipping service; you generally know the cities in which your competition has a plant or a facility. This activity offers a side benefit: it keeps the people who clip ads alert to changes or competitive activity and encourages conversations between the home office and the field.

- *Published studies.* Keep track of published studies sold by such companies as Frost & Sullivan and other producers of off-the-shelf market reports. Findex— a database available on the Dialog system, and a published directory—indexes thousands of these reports. Many of them will be too general and possibly too dated for your needs, and you will likely need to do additional analysis before making a business decision. Still, these studies often provide a good overview of market dynamics and the key players.

- *Wall Street reports.* Contact the security analysts who track your market and write reports on it. Make sure you are on their mailing lists, and subscribe to their report series, if necessary. I have found analyst reports to be variable in quality and depth. A tip from my clients: order reports on your own firm and examine the accuracy and veracity of their contents. If the reports pass muster, then you probably have a reliable analyst. If not, go elsewhere. I refer you to *Nelson's Directory of Investment Research* (see Chapter 4) and to Chapter 6 for security analyst resources in Europe and in Asia/Pacific Rim.

- *Trade shows and product literature.* Plan out your trade shows from an information-gathering perspective. Make sure you know who from your company will attend, and assign each person specific goals. See Chapter 11 for more details.

- *Public filings.* Create a checklist of government filings you need to receive each quarter or each year. Locate or borrow whatever expertise you need to interpret the information contained in those filings.

- *Advertisements.* Employ your firm's advertising agency to send to you your competitor's advertising tear sheets or ad clips. These can be as valuable as a straightforward news article. Track advertising expenditures through such services as Leading National Advertisers (see Chapter 2).

- *Personal contacts.* This last item is by no means the least important. Work hard to maintain an experts contact list—inside and outside your company—to help you interpret subtle market signals. Many experts are right inside your own firm. A client of ours has a saying that goes something like this: "An expert is anyone who lives more than 100 miles from our company." Fight this myth and begin to tap into sources of expertise close to home.

For more information on competitor monitoring and intelligence programs, I refer you to my earlier book *Monitoring the Competition* (John Wiley & Sons, 1988).

Real World Analysis: The Next Step

The remainder of this chapter consists of six disguised cases handled by Fuld & Company and representing a wide range of competitive issues. Each case has three major divisions:

1. Case discussion—the major problems or questions the client had, and a background discussion of the industry and competition.

2. Analytical framework—how the case was approached and why we used that approach.

3. Case analysis—the findings and the analysis as presented to the client.

INTELLIGENCE CASE 1:

Cost Analysis		
Case Discussion	Analytical Framework	Case Analysis

The Problem. The client was suffering from severe price competition originating from a relatively new competitor. Some managers began to rationalize away the threat, suspecting that the competitor had a "magic bullet" that gave it the ability to buy raw material at far lower prices. Others thought the competitor actually may have built a far more cost-efficient operation. The questions remained: Was price the cause or just the symptom? Could the competitor truly have built a more efficient manufacturing system? Or, was the competitor no more efficient than the client but simply decided to enter into a price war to gain market share?

The Process. This case is derived from a project Fuld & Company completed in 1992 for a client in the food industry. Even though the case has been disguised in order to shield the client's identity, the case write-up is quite faithful to details of the actual study.

At first, it may seem odd that a food industry analysis can be disguised as a glue manufacturing case, but in fact most production processes are startlingly similar. When they are broken down step by step, even service industry processes bear a close resemblance to manufacturing operations.

Products and services are "made" using one of three techniques:

1. *By continuous process.* Examples include the manufacture of wire or the continuous process of long-distance telephone service.
2. *In batches.* Examples include the production of soup, or the selection of targets for a credit card promotional package.
3. *By assembly.* Examples include the manufacture of a car or claims processing at an insurance company.

It makes little difference whether the process output is high-strength glue, as in this case, or a credit card promotion. One lesson of this case is that the costs of producing almost all goods and services can be understood in terms of these three techniques.

Case Background

Anaerobic adhesives began to appear in the mid-1970s under trade names like "Crazy Glue" and "Super Glue." Cleveland Adhesives developed the first anaerobic product in 1976 and called it "Elephant Glue." Its advertising showed an elephant in a harness, suspended in the air by the glue bond between the harness and a 1-inch-in-diameter cylinder dangling from a huge crane.

Elephant Glue was sold in very small foil tubes for a very high price. Cleveland had the market to itself for about two years before other companies figured out how to handle the three temperature-sensitive components needed to make anaerobic adhesives. The competitors were similar to Cleveland—established adhesives firms that built sales by adding distribution and line extensions, not by competing on price.

By 1981, consumers could buy anaerobic adhesives in stores that handled hardware, drugs, housewares, mass market merchandise, auto parts, plumbing supplies, hobby supplies, and similar products.

Prices moved up with inflation, and margins stayed high. Elephant Glue held the bulk of the market by virtue of its strong brand name recognition and its 19 different formulations.

In 1985, a start-up entered the field. Ozark Glue Works, operating from a plant in Cape Girardeau, Missouri, sold its "Mule Glue" product to the distribution channels for a flat 10 percent less than the prices charged by Cleveland and its long-time competitors. At first, Ozark had quality problems, and distributors and stores were cautious about offering the product. Nevertheless, Ozark began to take market share by virtue of Mule Glue's low price. By the middle of 1987, quality improved but the price stayed low. A 1988 *Consumers Report* rated Ozark Original Mule Glue formulation as a Best Buy.

By 1990, Mule Glue had cut sharply into Elephant Glue's share, largely by targeting mass merchandiser outlets such as Wal-Mart and Home Depot. Mule Glue Works was still priced 10 percent under Cleveland's prices. Cleveland's parent company, Agglomerated Industries, was unhappy with the situation, but neither Cleveland nor the parent company wanted to cut prices on Elephant Glue. Before deciding on a strategy, Cleveland wanted to learn how Ozark Glue Works was maintaining such a low price.

Management's Questions

The steady loss in business and in market share caused Cleveland's managers to distrust their own knowledge of the market. Their questions demonstrated completely different interpretations of what might actually be going on. Here are some of the questions they were asked to address:

- Is it possible that Ozark's costs are lower, or is the company just determined to build market share? To what end?
- What costs could be lower at Ozark?
- What would have to be different for those costs to be lower?

Case Discussion	Analytical Framework	Case Analysis

By comparing Cleveland's detailed profit and loss statement with that of Ozark, the competitor, we found an analytical framework—a Side-by-Side P&L. This framework allowed us to accomplish three goals:

1. *Understand Cost.* Because all the managers' questions concerned cost, we needed an analytical framework in which to develop the necessary intelligence on costs and the related manufacturing processes. We also needed a framework in which the client's own data would fit. The framework had to show us where and how the competitor used its raw materials or controlled its costs differently. We chose the structure of the profit and loss statement as the analytical model.

2. *Determine the Manufacturing Process Used.* The Side-by-Side P&L is wonderful for opening a window on a manufacturing process because it forces the analyst to understand the underpinnings of costs—quantity of raw materials used,

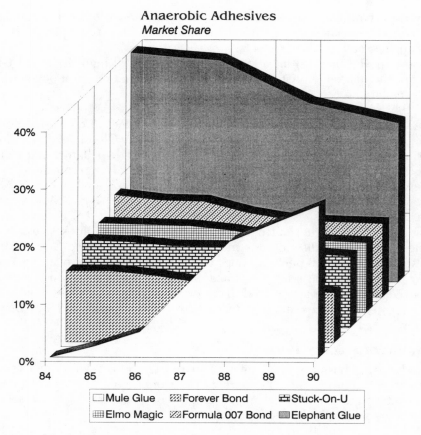

Figure 12.2 Changes in market share.

types of machinery and depreciation rates, packaging quantity and output, as well as process methods used.

3. *Stick to the Facts.* The Side-by-Side P&L gave us the structure we needed for in-depth examination of the client's own facilities and cost position. Anytime you begin dealing with cost or pricing issues, you are touching a politically sensitive area—an area open to a great deal of rationalizing and very little fact finding. The profit and loss statement demands cold, hard data. In some cases, the analyst or business manager may know the target company's total revenue and its bottom line, but none of the detailed line items in between. Without understanding the specific costs, you cannot truly explain how the target company achieved its profitability.

Case Discussion	Analytical Framework	Case Analysis

Saving Time: Pinpointing the Critical Factors

Although the P&L gave us the structure we needed, it threatened to derail us by demanding we fill in each informational gap. How could we gain an understanding of the critical swing factors that could either raise or lower Ozark's costs dramatically, compared to those of Cleveland?

Within its own cost structure, our client helped us identify three cost elements that would become critical to the focus of our work: (1) Material costs, (2) Plant and equipment, and (3) Administrative costs. These are represented in Figure 12.3.

The All-Important Plant Tour

The client walked us through its plant, identifying each step of the manufacturing process and how the raw materials were used. This tour may seem like a mundane exercise, but it is a vitally important first step for *any* analyst who needs a firm grasp of (1) how a product is transformed from raw materials to work in progress, to finished goods, and (2) what machinery is required to bring about this transformation.

In the course of seeing the product and the process, our project manager was able to create lists of questions that related to specific process steps. Our team's ability to ask highly specific questions added to the sophistication and accuracy of our analysis.

The First Stab

We started with Cleveland's own expanded P&L, filled in with data. We cloned it for an Ozark P&L and filled in the scant information that was available. (See Figure 12.4.) We then approached Cleveland's purchasing and R&D managers and asked them to fill in the blanks and to evaluate the information we had gleaned on Ozark's raw materials and packaging.

Filling in the Gaps

We had to constantly review our numbers. Each time we received a new piece of data, there was a good chance that one of the supposed constants would prove variable.

Table 12.6 summarizes the major pieces of information collected and the information sources used. Some of the plant components mentioned in the table can be identified in the floor plan of Ozark, shown in Figure 12.5.

By corroborating the findings and feeding the intelligence to management, we ultimately developed a reasonable representation of what the 1990 Ozark P&L should have looked like. (See Figure 12.6.)

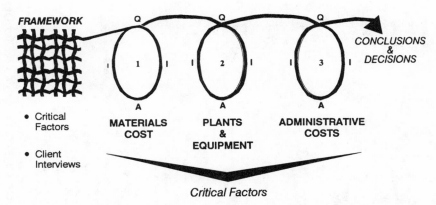

Figure 12.3 Critical factors in cost analysis.

ELEPHANT GLUE DIV. P&L for 1990 / OZARK GLUE WORKS P&L for 1990

	Elephant Units	Elephant Dollars	% of Sales		Ozark Units	Ozark $/Unit	Ozark Dollars	Sources
Sales	5,920,000	$74,296,000		Sales	5,684,058	$11.30	$64,201,435	Internal
Raw Materials	Pounds			**Raw Materials**	Pounds	Cost/Lb		
Acrylic	3,552,000	$9,768,000	13.1%	Acrylic	3,410,435	$2.83	$9,660,057	Suppliers, truckers & traffic dept.
Methylene chloride	1,657,600	$2,436,672	3.3%	Methylene chloride	1,591,536	$1.51	$2,409,745	
Catalyst	414,400	$12,059,040	16.2%	Catalyst	397,884	$30.63	$12,186,293	
Additives	296,000	$94,720	0.1%	Additives	284,203	$0.31	$89,126	
Scrap (2%)		$485,274	0.7%	Scrap			$121,280	Equipment mfg
Total Raw Materials Costs		$24,843,706	33.4%	**Total Raw Materials Costs**			$24,466,501	
Labor	Hours			**Labor**	Hours	Rate/Hr		
Plant direct (12/shift)	110,822	$1,612,466	2.2%	Plant direct	42,525	$10.76	$457,569	Article from local paper, internal estimates
Plant indirect	12,480	$199,742	0.3%	Plant indirect	4,673	$11.84	$55,311	
Cleanup	38,938	$566,542	0.8%	Cleanup	5,047	$10.76	$54,305	
Packaging	98,509	$1,433,303	1.9%	Packaging	94,443	$10.76	$1,016,205	
Total Labor Costs	260,749	$3,812,053	5.1%	**Total Labor Costs**	146,688		$1,583,390	
Packaging	Quantity			**Packaging**	Quantity	Cost		
Tubes	94,720,000	$8,524,800	11.5%	Tubes	90,944,928	$0.10	$9,094,493	Internal estimates
Blister packs	94,720,000	$15,155,200	20.4%	Blister packs	90,944,928	$0.16	$14,551,188	
Cartons	657,778	$690,667	0.9%	Cartons	631,562	$1.01	$637,878	
Total Packaging Materials		$24,370,667	32.8%	**Total Packaging Materials**			$24,283,559	
Waste disposal (gallons/yr)	68,750	$281,250	0.4%	Waste disposal (gallons/yr)	7,500		$25,364	State DEP
Energy (Mfg)		$264,160	0.4%	Energy (Mfg)			$22,736	Internal est.
Cost of Goods Sold		$53,591,837	72.1%	**Cost of Goods Sold**			$50,381,550	
Gross Margin		$20,704,163	27.9%	**Gross Margin**			$13,819,885	
Sales, Gen'l & Admin.				**Sales, Gen'l & Admin.**				
Sales staff 7 @ $78K each	$1,000/wk/salesper	$546,000	0.7%	Sales staff			$330,000	Customers; internal est.
Advertising		$2,878,007	3.9%	Advertising			$1,663,070	Ad agency
Other selling expenses		$350,000	0.5%	Other selling expenses			$150,000	Internal est.
Depreciation		$6,643,020	8.9%	Depreciation			$3,675,430	Compilation
Other admin. staff (24 @ $38,750 avg.)		$930,000	1.3%	Other admin. staff			$697,500	Internal est.
Other admin.		$456,080	0.6%	Other admin.			$365,000	Internal est.
Total SG&A		$11,801,107	15.9%	**Total SG&A**			$6,881,000	
Operating Profit		$8,903,056	12.0%	**Operating Profit**			$6,938,885	
Corporate charges (2% of sales)		$1,485,920	2.0%	Corporate charges			$0	
Pre-tax Profit		$7,417,136	10.0%	**Pre-tax Profit**			$6,938,885	

Figure 12.4 Completed P&L for Ozark. Cost differences appeared throughout Ozark's operations. There was no magic bullet.

TABLE 12.6 Analysis of P&L Categories and Sources Used

P&L Category	Information Gathered (Excerpts)	Source
Materials Cost	Chemical makeup is roughly the same.	Cleveland R&D Director
	Costs Ozark roughly 3% more per pound than Cleveland to get the two liquid components and about 5.25% more per pound for the catalyst.	Cleveland Purchasing
	Cleveland makes 19 different formulations; any change in formulation requires 2 hours for cleaning out the vats, only 30 minutes for the same formulation.	Cleveland Manufacturing
	Not likely that Ozark can consistently buy low by anticipating price fluctuations in the soy market.	Hoboken Soy Catalyst Company, key supplier
	Ozark switched to slightly heavier gauge tube in 1987. Estimate is that it is 10% more expensive than Cleveland's.	Supplier
	Output is approximately 5.5 million pounds of finished product.	Local newspaper article
	In 1990, added 80,000 square feet to storage.	Local newspaper article
Labor	Cleveland: With 19 products to juggle, downtime from cleaning cuts into operating hours. Vats operate at 74% of the available time. The plant runs 3 shifts, 5 days per week.	Cleveland Manufacturing
	Average Ozark plant employee earns $10.76 per hour. There are 73 workers altogether in 2 shifts. (Labor costs are considerably lower than those of Cleveland.)	Local newspaper article
	Downtime for Ozark's injection molding machinery, the key element in the adhesives process, is 45 minutes—less than half that of Cleveland's downtime.	LaPointe Machine Corporation
	Altogether, Ozark's estimated downtime based on the above information is 1 hour out of 16 to 18 hours per day—or under 10%.	Cleveland Manufacturing
Machinery	Credit report indicates timely bill payment (indicates positive cash flow), plus a number of UCC filings showing leased equipment.	D&B Credit Report
	Ozark recently built a large freezer. Could they be saving money by receiving large bulk deliveries of the frozen catalyst from a Mexican supplier who only ships orders for 10 or more containers?	Cleveland Management
	No new vats purchased since stepping up production in 1987.	Vat supplier

(Continued)

TABLE 12.6 *(Continued)*

P&L Category	Information Gathered (Excerpts)	Source
	No new vacuum pumps purchased recently, perhaps indicating a different batch process.	Vacuum pump distributors in Memphis and St. Louis
	Company recently leased 5 large injection molding machines made by LaPointe Machine Corporation for a total cost of $1.62 million.	UCC state filings
	Machines were customized; equipment brochures indicate an efficient cleaning process that would allow for fast turnaround.	LaPointe Machine Corporation
	The original plant was built in 1985 for $2.04 million; 1987 renovations cost $1.75 million. The new addition cost $2.64 million. The subcontractor on record is: Steam Engineering Corporation, Memphis, TN.	Local building inspection and permitting offices
Waste Disposal	Trucking waste $186/barrel for Ozark and $225 for Cleveland.	Cleveland CEO
	Improper cure happens 2% of the time at Cleveland.	Cleveland Manufacturing
	Copy of Ozark's filings with the Missouri Environmental Protection Agency showed a relatively low level of cleaning solvent usage, only about 7,500 gallons a year. This confirms other information about little downtime between batches.	State of Missouri Department of Environmental Protection
Energy	Ozark uses coal-fired cogeneration unit to make steam and is selling electricity back to the local utility. Its energy costs therefore appear to be relatively low.	Southern Missouri Electric & Gas
	Because Ozark uses cogeneration, energy probably costs Ozark 4 tenths of a cent per pound of product.	Steam Engineering Corporation
Miscellaneous	Ozark spends less on advertising than Cleveland because it uses mostly cooperative promotions with home centers and mass merchandisers.	Cleveland's Advertising Agency
	Administrative salaries for Ozark likely less than 75% those of Cleveland.	Cleveland's Controller
	Depreciation charges estimated based on accounting rules in effect at time Ozark made investments.	Cleveland Controller

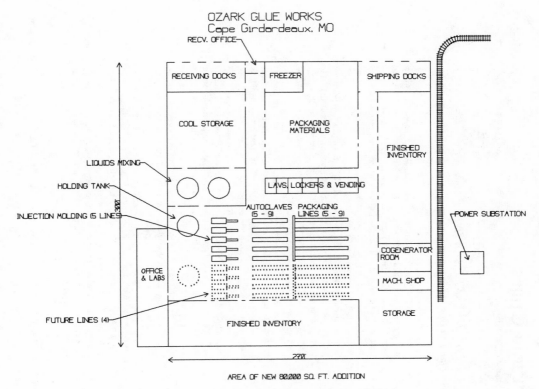

Figure 12.5 Floor plan of Ozark Glue Works.

The Intelligence and the Implications

With the profit and loss statement completed, the negative gaps stood out clearly (see Figure 12.7). Not only were we able to deliver a full report, complete with all the supporting documents, but the analysis was conclusive: Cleveland had to make some fundamental changes in the way it does business, or it would continue to suffer severe losses.

These were the highlights of our analysis.

- Ozark has a different manufacturing process, one that is difficult and expensive to duplicate. The process gives it a substantial cost advantage.
- Ozark has other advantages: its labor costs are lower than Cleveland's, and its selling costs are lower because of its focus on the mass market and home center markets.
- The competitor has positioned itself as the low-cost, low-price leader, and it can sustain that strategy.

Cleveland's concern over raw materials prices was a false assumption, a misdiagnosis of the situation. The true problem for Cleveland lies in its existing infrastructure, which will take time to shed. Manufacturing will have to make some immediate changes in its process, to try to reduce downtime. Management will have to examine

Cape Girardeau Times

All the News that Fits, We Print

Final Edition

Newsstand: $.35
Home delivery: $.30

Weather: Mild, breezy
Monday, April 26, 1990

OZARK GLUE WORKS EXPANDS AGAIN IN EAST CAPE IND. PARK

Company Credits Unique Incentive Plan and Good Glue for its Success

By Edna Buchanan, Business Reporter

Bob Gresham, president of Ozark Glue Works, announced today that his firm would add 80,000 square feet to its plant in the East Cape Industrial Park. Gresham said that the company, which makes the Mule Glue line of high strength adhesives, needed the extra space for more storage. At the same time, the company will renovate one section of its original plant, which was built in 1984.

Gresham, who hails from Paducah, KY, founded Ozark with his partner, Mel Carter, after working as a sales manager for National Glue Corp. Carter was the plant manager for National's glue works in St. Louis. The two say they decided to start their own business when an idea they had for a new product was rejected by National.

The two entrepreneurs credited Cape Girardeau-area employees for part of their success. The company Introduced a unique incentive plan late last year, and the employees have responded by contributing numerous suggestions on how to cut downtime and waste in the plant. The employees get a fairly low base wage, said Carter, but they share the savings of any suggestions that work. As a result, the average plant employee makes $10.76 an hour, with maintenance workers getting a small premium. There are 73 workers in the highly automated plant, which will make about 5-1/2 million pounds of high-strength adhesives in 1990. Ozark operates 2 shifts. Most of its output went to big chains like Wal-Mart, but Gresham said he hoped to sell more to local hardware stores by selling to cooperatives like True-Value.

Ozark is known locally as being a good place to work, and it also has a reputation for watching its costs carefully. Rhoda Phillips, Ozark's office manager, jokes about the time Carter and Gresham took the bus to Shreveport, LA, to visit a plant that was making some special machinery for Ozark. "They couldn't get a direct flight anyway, and the airfare really boggled their minds, so they took an eight hour bus ride across Arkansas and saved themselves about

SCHOOL BOARD PROPOSES $1.2 MILLION BOND ISSUE FOR NEW HIGH SCHOOL GYM

by William Bennett, Special Reporter

The Cape Girardeau City School board voted 6-3 last night to ask the voters' approval for a $1.2 million bond issue to build a new high school gym. The vote, which came at the end of an acrimonious 3-1/2 hour meeting, is sure to create controversy, warned Mary Morrison, chairperson of We Oppose New Taxes (WONT). Morrison, who is rumored to be considering a run for School Board, said she would take WONT's case to the voters, and she promised, "We'll give this one a rough ride for sure."

Figure 12.6 Local newspaper article reveals more than labor costs. See the article's last paragraph to understand how Ozark's management lives a low-cost philosophy.

COST IMPACT - PER POUND	ELEPHANT GLUE	MULE GLUE	ACTUAL GAPS
Cost of Materials (per Pound)	$4.197	$4.304	$0.108
Cost of Downtime	$0.096	$0.010	($0.086)
Cost of Labor not incl. Downtime	$0.548	$0.269	($0.279)
Packaging Materials	$4.117	$4.272	$0.156
Waste Disposal	$0.048	$0.004	($0.043)
Energy	$0.048	$0.004	($0.044)
Admin Costs			
Salaries	$0.308	$0.207	($0.101)
Advertising	$0.486	$0.293	($0.193)
Depeciation	$1.122	$0.647	($0.476)
Other G&A	$0.077	$0.064	($0.013)
Corporate Charges	$0.251	$0.000	($0.251)
ACTUAL COST GAP			**($1.223)**
PROFIT IMPACT OF THE GAPS			**($7,239,378)**

Figure 12.7   Elephant Glue versus Mule Glue: The gaps per unit.

the overhead costs and labor structure to determine where and when it may have to trim its labor force or reinvest in machinery.

What Cleveland Should Do

In the long term, Cleveland had these options:

- *Buy the competitor.* This would be an appropriate solution, but not necessarily the best. There is no certainty that someone else would not come up with a new, less costly process in the interim. Such an innovation—not unheard of—would devalue the potential acquisition.
- *Begin to write off its existing machinery and go over to Ozark's process technology.* This possibility is far more likely for Cleveland than outright acquisition.
- *Drop the product altogether.* Not likely. Cleveland has managed to build a brand name and distribution channels for a line of products that is still making money for it.

In the short term, Cleveland could act to:

- *Cut prices to maintain share.* This appears a necessary quick-fix in order to keep the customer base from eroding further.
- *Maintain prices at the same level in order to retain profitability.* Cleveland may want to do this selectively, but it looks unlikely that the same prices can be held across the board without losing share to Ozark.
- *Eliminate the less profitable products out of its selection of 19.* Cleveland should be able to determine which of its 19 products are best-sellers and which are marginal. If it could pare down its production to its five to ten leaders and eliminate the marginal lines, it would be able to increase production of the remaining lines, as well as decrease downtime that results from cleaning the vats whenever production switches to a new line.
- *Use cash flow, sheltered by depreciation, to develop a technology that's better/cheaper than Ozark's.*

INTELLIGENCE CASE 2:

Timelining: Forecasting New Product Introduction		
Case Discussion	Analytical Framework	Case Analysis

The Problem. A Fuld & Company pharmaceutical client had just learned that a competitor had received Federal Drug Administration (FDA) approval for the potential marketing of an over-the-counter (OTC) drug that directly competes with one of the client's own consumer OTC products. This FDA go-ahead only permits the competitor to prepare its manufacturing facilities for FDA production quality inspection, in anticipation of receiving the final FDA approval for marketing the drug, which is expected within the next year. The client needed to know exactly when and in what quantity the competitor was going to launch its product. This knowledge would give the client the ability to precisely plan a preemptive marketing strike, using pricing and advertising tactics. The danger was great: If the client missed the roll-out window, millions of dollars in market share would be lost.

Time: The Intelligence Problem

As with Intelligence Case 1, the problem usually dictates the analytical solution. In this instance, the client's concern centered around *time.* "How long," the client wanted to know, "will it take for the competitor to introduce its product?" FDA approval only signaled a warning, not the actual product launch date.

We needed to find a way to link the element of time with the release of information about the competitor. The analytical tool we used is called *timelining.*

Case Discussion	Analytical Framework	Case Analysis

The Timelining Principle is brief and simple:

> *Like history, business processes repeat themselves.*

Timelining is a way to chart the order of how companies do things, tag the information spun off from these activities, and place that information into an analytical framework.

Almost every business process follows a certain pattern, which may differ from company to company. For a company to constantly recreate or reinvent the way it does something would be very costly. As a result, business is a process of repetition.

Timelining forces the analyst to examine data in a chronological context. Instead of just random recognition—4,7,1,3,2,6,5—timelining says to watch for a pattern—1,2,3,4,5,6,7. In the real world, you gather information about competition haphazardly. You may have a competitive goal in mind, but you pick up the information where and when it's available. By doing so, you can see whether you have a pattern or only a wild assortment of information pieces. Even when you are missing some of the information—____, 2, 3, ____, 5, ____, 7—you can still see the pattern and where the information is leading you.

Figure 12.8 translates into a timeline a company's decision to release a new product. Between the first decision and the moment of product release, many events had to take place—filing of engineering reports with the town and environmental authorities, plant inspections by utilities and equipment manufacturers installing new equipment, and so on. As Figure 12.8 indicates, the information volume grows and becomes more available as the date of the plant opening approaches. "Wherever money is exchanged, so is information" once again makes clear that the more business transactions occur, the more information is available.

More important to note: To build a plant, you need to undertake certain steps, in a specific order or chronological pattern. In Figure 12.8, the steps were as follows:

1. Decision to build
2. Site selection
3. Environmental impact statement
4. Design work by an architectural engineering firm
5. Site work and construction
6. Equipment purchases
7. Equipment installation
8. Hiring

Even if you captured information relating only to steps 1, 3, 4, and 5, you could determine approximately when the plant would come on line. This is the beauty of timelining. You do not have to have every single piece of information in hand. With only a few critical pieces, once you have discovered the pattern, you have your answer.

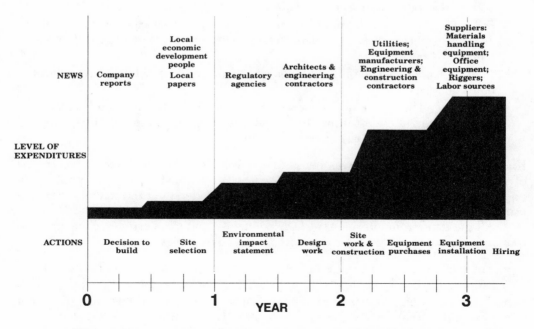

Figure 12.8 Timelining: How each step leads to additional sources.

| Case Discussion | Analytical Framework | Case Analysis |

We developed the timeline by identifying each process that was taking place. If this had been a study to examine how a banking competitor was streamlining its check processing operations, we would have met with the Information Systems staff at the client's bank, and anyone else who was involved in the technology or the personnel side of check processing. These bank employees intimately know every process step, the sequence of steps, and the length of time it takes to complete each step. They can also describe how long it would likely take to improve or completely re-engineer such a process. They know the suppliers, the equipment, and the costs.

In the pharmaceutical case, we needed to understand (1) each piece of equipment and how it worked and (2) the expertise and personnel required at each stage. The client took the project manager on a tour of one of its plants. This allowed us to visually and mentally tag each piece of equipment and its purpose. [Note: This is a useful exercise, no matter what the intelligence assignment. If your analysts or interviewers can firmly picture the manufacturing or service process in their minds, they will have far more complete and accurate interviews.]

The client also introduced us to its engineering, marketing, and production staff, who helped answer many of our more technical questions. The manufacturing details we received during these internal client interviews later helped us project the competitor's production volume up to one year into the future. Remember, the competitor's plant had not even opened yet.

Some of the process details are described as follows:

- *Chemical mixing.* Granulator is used to mix the raw chemical with additives. Granulators come in different sizes. A moderate size granulator can produce 400–600 kilograms in several hours.
- *Pill press.* The resulting mixture enters a pill press that can produce 1,000 to 3,000 pills per minute. Our client told us to expect this type of press to average 2,000 pills per minute.
- *Coating machine.* The pills may then go to a drum like machine that applies the outer coating.
- *Packaging.* This phase actually consists of a series of machine steps, including printing the ID code, filling the bottle, inserting the cotton, sealing, capping, labeling, and printing the expiration date.

Knowledge of these details was necessary as we probed for details on the timing of the expected product launch. Because the FDA must certify all production equipment for quality control, it was important to understand the machinery being used.

All the data, from interviews, FDA documents, and news articles, came in as we found them, in no particular order. Here are some examples:

- The client estimated the level of inventory a manufacturer must have in order to prepare for this kind of product roll-out.
- The number of pills expected to be packaged per bottle and how many different size bottles there would be—24 pills, 50 pills, 100 pills—were revealed.
- The plant had begun hiring for its first shift.

- Equipment manufacturers and, through interviews, the likely key equipment to be used were identified.
- The product's brand name (learned through contacting a supplier) had been chosen.
- The estimated dosage was learned from a packaging company known in the industry.
- The capacity of the granulator was determined.
- We were able to make a firm estimate of the expected production yield over the course of the start-up period before roll-out.

In the process of gathering the data, we began to piece together the pattern that was to become the final timeline. We combined the incoming data with the client's own view of the likely production process.

The next task was to organize data by time. Now that we understood the process, we had to map the sequence of events involved. Table 12.7 shows the timelining sequence for the prospective roll-out.

Before we could draw any conclusions, we had to support our pieced-together timeline with more corroborating data. We interviewed dozens of other contacts in the industry, including: packaging materials suppliers, graphic designers, corrugated box manufacturers, trucking/shipping companies, and retail buyers. As always, our interviewing approach was straightforward. The information we received was, by and large, available in small pieces. The information only became intelligence when we were able to *assemble* it, in this case using a timeline.

TABLE 12.7   Sequence of Events for Timelining Framework

Event	Reasoning
1. Refitting manufacturing plant	The manufacturer needed enough time to produce and accumulate 6 months' worth of pills, the amount required to meet the roll-out plans.
	The client's own marketing department had determined, based on other similar roll-outs, how many pills the competitor needed to distribute in order to successfully penetrate the market.
2. FDA Approval	The FDA has to approve the equipment directly involved in the drug's manufacture. We learned through various equipment suppliers that the FDA had come in and certified the necessary equipment.
3. Plant visit by packaging supplier	A purchasing person representing the client had visited a packaging supplier's plant and recalled seeing labels with the drug's name and even its dosage (an important number that allowed us to estimate the amount of raw chemical that had to be processed, and, therefore, the length of time it would take to build the necessary inventory).
4. Hiring	A training consultant, who worked with the client and many other pharmaceutical companies, was able to tell us that the competitor was hiring personnel for the first shift. Our client estimated that it would take 10 weeks for the first shift to produce up to 80 percent yield from each batch—a necessary level to achieve production efficiency. It would take another 7 weeks to train the second and third shifts. Without these additional shifts, the competitor would be unable to achieve the quantity needed to launch the product.

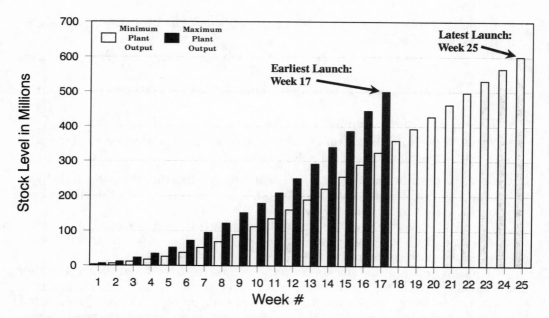

Figure 12.9   Reaching product launch stock level: Minimum and maximum lead time.

Combining our knowledge of the plant's actual FDA certification date and hiring information with the time it would take for the new employees to produce products at a certain yield rate, we were able to project how long it would take for the competitor to stockpile enough pills to launch the product. The estimated 6–7-week product launch window we supplied in our analysis (see Figure 12.9) helped the client successfully plan a preemptive strategy of flooding the market with price-cutting coupons, special institutional promotions, and so on.

The analytical framework was a timeline. The resulting intelligence was the launch date.

INTELLIGENCE CASE 3:

Future Strategy: Using the SWOT Technique		
Case Discussion	**Analytical Framework**	**Case Analysis**

The Problem. A leading competitor in the lawn mower manufacturing industry, a privately held company, appears to be making significant changes to its strategy and business approach. Through acquisitions, it has overtaken the client company (and others) to become the market share leader. Technology has not traditionally provided the competitive edge. More typically, it is a company's ability to establish efficient manufacturing and distribution capabilities. We needed to learn as much as possible about the company's future strategy, because its every gain represents a loss to our client.

Background: Market Description

Here are some of the market statistics assembled through the client and through various trade magazines:

- The total lawn mower market is dominated by four domestic manufacturers.
- The U.S. market for walk-behind and riding mowers reached an all-time high of 5.9 million units in 1987 and then steadily declined to a 1992 level of 5.15 million units. Recessionary pressures, a decline in home-building starts, and other economic factors have contributed to the downward trend, the result of which is an all-out battle for market share.
- The target competitor is Lawnsavers, a privately held company that has built market share through acquisition of two other firms.
- The mix of industry wide sales is 85 percent gas-powered products and 15 percent electric products. The mix at the client company (Green Acres) is the same, but Lawnsavers generates close to 30 percent of its sales from electric mowers.
- For the most part, electric mowers are a low-end, low-margin product. Another player, TBL, has offered a rechargeable product for two years, but, by most measures, the product has been a flop. Retailing around $350, it costs three times as much as a comparable gas-powered model.

Figure 12.10 shows the market share for all industry participants.

Case Discussion	**Analytical Framework**	**Case Analysis**

This competitive problem has a particularly broad scope. We could not limit our focus to price, or cost, or new product introduction. The client was facing all these issues and more. This kind of broad-brush problem requires a sweeping analytical tool, one that can cut across a whole host of issues in a relatively short period of time. Because so many aspects of the business had changed in a short time period, we elected to perform a top-down SWOT analysis of the competitor. SWOT stands for:

- **Strengths.** These have also become known as a company's core competencies. Among them are: proprietary technology, patents held, particular skills, resources, market position, distribution systems, and so on.
- **Weaknesses.** Poor management; heavy long-term debt; old, obsolete plant and equipment; and a reputation for poor products or services are among typical weaknesses.
- **Opportunities.** This is a synonym for favorable conditions in the overall market and the industry environment. For example, if a U.S. government plan to outlaw small gasoline engines is effected, such as those propelling lawn mowers, an opportunity for the use of electric mowers and rechargeable electrics would be created.
- **Threats.** Current and future conditions might harm a company. For example, the federal government may limit the future use of small, nonessential gasoline engines, such as those that power lawn mowers.

The Goal

The goal of a SWOT analysis is to determine where the competitor stands *relative to your own company.* The strengths and opportunities you identify for the competitor may be threats to your company. By the same token, the competitor's weaknesses and threats could present ideal opportunities for an attack at its most vulnerable points.

SWOT is not necessarily a numerical comparison—the kind found in a benchmarking analysis. Rather, it is a mostly qualitative means of measuring the direction a company is taking or is about to take in the market. There is another contrast in goals: Benchmarking examines history; SWOT reviews history in order to anticipate the future.

Case Discussion	Analytical Framework	Case Analysis

For SWOT to be an effective analysis tool, not only must it help group and sort the data, but it must also help the analyst or manager sift out the less useful pieces from the most important ones. Table 12.8 assembles samples of the data we uncovered

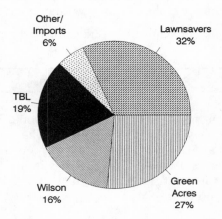

Figure 12.10   Market share for the lawnmower industry.

TABLE 12.8 SWOT Lawnmower Data

Strengths	Ratings	Data	Source
Distribution	A	Lawnsavers acquired four independent lawn equipment wholesalers/servicers in Northern California and two in the southern part of the state.	*San Francisco Chronicle*
Sales	B	Rumors of Lawnsavers' acquisition of Southeastern U.S. distributors.	Green Acres sales manager
	A	Lawnsavers has hired a key salesperson to go after the home center market.	
Management	A	New management team may prove capable of breaking into the home center and other mass markets.	West Coast sales manager
	B	New management team was assembled from senior executives of very successful Fortune 100 companies.	OPEI Newsletter
Technology	B	Possibility that Lawnsavers is developing a new, revolutionary, cordless electric mower. Such mowers have failed in the past for lack of cutting power.	Vendor
Capacity	A	The new plant can produce approximately 2,000 mowers a day, operating 3 shifts (or 500,000 mowers per year). This will certainly give them mass market capability.	Town filings; engineering firm
Weaknesses	**Ratings**		
Management	C	Old management was recently fired and replaced by new, young management team, possibly inexperienced.	OPEI Newsletter
	A	Lawnsavers owner and CEO is known as a tinkerer and will delay new product releases until he is satisfied it is free of bugs.	Former employee
Technology	B	This new battery technology is likely to create many manufacturing and service headaches. Many feel that the 4- to 6-month launch date is very optimistic. Unlikely that the Lawnsavers group can bring down costs to develop new technology to an acceptable level for Green Acres profitability guidelines.	Green Acres manufacturing manager
	B	The battery technology was licensed to Green Acres from a Swiss R&D firm for $2 million.	

(Continued)

393

TABLE 12.8 (Continued)

Weaknesses	Ratings	Data	Source
Costs	A	The new automated factory for building the Go-N-Mow cost $5.2 million, not including soft costs such as parts inventory and training. Soft costs are estimated at $1.2 million, a relatively large investment for this size firm. Total = $6.4 million. This will likely saddle them with considerable debt for such a risky venture.	Local newspaper, suppliers
Profitability	A	Gross margin for the new mowers is expected to be only $13 per mower. Parts cost is about $67; labor, about $9; technology license fee, about $5; shipping, $2.	UCC filings, suppliers, newspaper articles
	A	Cash flow appeared to be positive at far lower production level than was profitable, indicating that Lawnsavers could hold on for a long time even if not fiscally profitable—as long as it could throw off enough cash to keep operations going and allow it to achieve its apparent goal of expanding its distributor network and penetrating the home center market.	Financial analysis of sources, filings, and interviews with Green Acres management

Opportunities Ratings

	Ratings	Data	Source
Customers	A	The fastest growing outlets for lawn mowers have been the home centers.	Trade association
Competitors	A	Other competitors, such as TBL, have already offered less-than-perfect cordless mowers, but are working on newer, more effective models with longer battery life between charges.	Supplier
Trends	B	According to industry studies, all appliances, including lawn mowers, are moving toward smaller, lighter, easier-to-use devices. Overall battery technology, according to the experts, is close to achieving a number of commercial breakthroughs.	Trade magazine

Threats Ratings

	Ratings	Data	Source
Customers	A	Retailers, such as Wal-Mart, are going to continue to squeeze the whole goods companies, such as Green Acres and Lawnsavers, on price. Margins for most Lawnsavers products will shrink over next five years.	Store buyers, magazines, Green Acres salespeople

A = Highly important
B = Somewhat interesting
C = Interesting but not necessarily useful

Units	Direct Costs	Fixed Costs	Total Costs	Revenue	Profit (Loss)	Cash Flow
100,000	$ 8,300,000	$3,675,000	$11,975,000	$ 9,600,000	$(2,375,000)	$ (990,000)
200,000	16,600,000	3,675,000	20,275,000	19,200,000	(1,075,000)	310,000
300,000	24,900,000	3,675,000	28,575,000	28,800,000	225,000	1,610,000
400,000	33,200,000	3,675,000	36,875,000	38,400,000	1,525,000	2,910,000
500,000	41,500,000	3,675,000	45,175,000	48,000,000	2,825,000	4,210,000

Figure 12.11   Go-N-Mow cost and revenue summary.

during the gathering stage of the assignment. To make the data more useful, each item has been tagged with a rating code based on its importance (A to C, highest to lowest). Although subjective, the code is a quick-and-dirty means to pull out the most critical pieces.

As we sorted through the rated information on the SWOT grid (Table 12.8), these facts became clear:

- The industry is moving toward the mass market retailer, such as the large home center.
- Lawnsavers has put a mass market sales and distribution organization in place to achieve truly mass market economies.
- Lawnsaver's new management is far more aggressive than the old regime and is likely to push ahead creatively to find new customers and market niches.

By combining the financial information with the SWOT analysis, we were able to offer the client a number of reasonable and realistic options that had to be pursued immediately. Lawnsavers was banking heavily on selling enough of its new electric mowers to pay back the high investment it had made. (See Figure 12.11.) If its strategy paid off, Lawnsavers would increase market share principally at the client's expense. Could Lawnsavers bring the product to market fast enough?

Our analysis demonstrated a number of weak points in the competitor's armor. Among them was an owner who tends to slow down the release of new technology—in this case, the rechargeable mowers.

Green Acres' Competitive Response

Green Acres now knows that Lawnsaver is here to stay and will permanently hold its lead in the lawnmower market unless Green Acres takes a number of decisive actions—soon. By examining the SWOT analysis, Green Acres' management was able to see where it was most vulnerable and how it must capitalize on the potential market opportunities. Green Acres therefore decided that it needed to:

1. Aggressively develop its own rechargeable product;
2. Take advantage of Lawnsavers' tendency to tinker with products (thus delaying product release), and roll out its own rechargeable mower within the next 6 months.
3. Lower its own margins by subcontracting out an increasing portion of actual engine and chassis manufacturing. In effect, Green Acres decided to become a marketing and distribution company and move away from the notion that it was a manufacturer.

INTELLIGENCE CASE 4:

Benchmarking: Understanding and Incorporating Industry Best Practices		
Case Discussion	**Analytical Framework**	**Case Analysis**

The Problem. The client had a large, established glass bottle manufacturing operation, in which it had invested a great deal of capital and equipment. In recent years, its entrenched operations had become too costly to enable it to compete effectively on price. It was losing too many bids, and new, substitute products, such as the now-familiar plastic PET bottles, had taken huge chunks of market share away from it. The client knew it had to make a dramatic change if it was to survive. The problem confronting it was: What changes could it make for the greatest effect, in the shortest period of time, for the lowest possible cost?

The core problem for the client was one of productivity. In effect, it found itself in an economic vise. From the outside marketplace, increasing competition, alternative products, and price cuts forced it to cut into its traditionally large margins; from the inside, the company had to (1) pay relatively high industry wages to its unionized plant workers, and (2) contend with an old plant that was expensive to maintain and even more expensive to retool.

Management knew very well that it was in a difficult position. But it also realized that if it did nothing, it would continue to lose its market to other glass bottle companies or to substitutes. Because of the large amounts of money it needed to effect change (and the labor and political fallout that would result from the massive changes), the client needed to know exactly how far away from best-in-class it was. Management also expected our benchmark study to reveal which aspects of the operation it needed to upgrade and over what period of time.

Case Discussion	**Analytical Framework**	**Case Analysis**

This section offers a quick overview of benchmarking and how it works. It is a simple primer, not a detailed review of the benchmarking process. For a greater understanding of this analytical tool, I recommend the following books:

Benchmarking: A Tool for Continuous Improvement, by Kathleen H. J. Leibfried and C. J. McNair (HarperCollins, 1992).

The Benchmarking Management Guide, by Gregory H. Watson, (Productivity Press, 1993).

Benchmarking: A Practitioner's Guide for Becoming and Staying the Best of the Best, by Gerald J. Balm (Quality & Productivity Management Association, 1992).

Benchmarking: The Search for the Best Practices That Lead to Superior Performance, by Robert C. Camp (Quality Press/American Society for Quality Control, 1989).

A definition of the term is:

Benchmarking is the search for industry best practices that lead to superior performance.

The general philosophy of benchmarking—and the reason it has been embraced by many companies—is a very practical, operational bent. In essence, benchmarking forces the businessperson to:

- Know the operation;
- Know the industry leaders or competitors;
- Incorporate the best of what is learned;
- Gain superiority in the market.

The Five Steps to Successful Benchmarking

1. *Identify the benchmarks.* Pick the benchmark categories based on your best guess as to where the problems lie. You may misjudge, but that is unlikely. Undoubtedly, as soon as you begin the data gathering and benchmark comparisons, you will find out whether you have erred in selecting one benchmark or another.

What kind of benchmarks should you look for? Select such operationally descriptive categories as: number of inventory turns, promotional costs, number of service calls per appliance, response time for customer service, customer satisfaction, level of repeat business, maintenance costs, production output, or efficiency of a manufacturing process. Start by identifying areas in which you *know* you could improve.

2. *Find best-in-class.* You have a choice between selecting a best-in-class competitor or another company that is not in your industry (these are known as generics) but whose operations may have aspects you want to emulate. As anyone who has ever completed a benchmark study will tell you, there are pros and cons to each choice: Selecting a competitor to benchmark against will give you a very direct industry comparison. At the same time, the competitor may not represent the best of what is out there. Also, you cannot share information with a competitor.

Benchmarking against generic companies allows you to explore new business practices not used in your industry. As Robert C. Camp described in his book, *Benchmarking: The Search for the Best Practices That Lead to Superior Performance* (listed above), Xerox learned a great deal about ways to improve its warehousing and inventorying practices by benchmarking itself against L. L. Bean, the mail order company with a reputation of having a very efficient inventory system. Because Bean did not represent a direct competitive threat in any way, Xerox and Bean felt free to exchange information that would benefit both companies.

Look through trade journals in your industry to see whom they report on as a best-practices company and what aspects of a competitor may be best-in-class. If a competitor truly excels in a particular area, it has probably boasted about it to the press. Alone, this may not be enough to identify the company as best-in-class, but you may hear confirmation from customers or suppliers, reassuring you that you are applying the best-in-class label to the right company.

3. *Collect data.* Recommendations on data sources and information-gathering techniques can be found in other chapters of this book. As a rule, assume that data are available in some form. You just need the persistence and industry savvy to dig them out.

4. *Determine gaps.* At the end of your data collection and analysis, you will begin to compare the findings (such as yield, number of customers handled per hour, response times, and so on) with information about your company. The comparison will force you to conclude that you have either a positive or a negative gap vis-à-vis your benchmark company or operation. Benchmarking, thankfully, has little jargon, but the two terms you need to remember are *negative gaps* and *positive gaps.* Negative gaps occur where outside operations are superior to yours; positive gaps are where internal operations are superior to outside operations.

5. *Project future performance.* At this point, you have all the current intelligence on your operations and need to make some assumptions. These are your "what-if" estimates: you assume certain given conditions and add in the changes you wish to make. Because many benchmark studies involve a number of disciplines, you may require skilled individuals to work out the projections—engineers, marketers, and salespeople who can correctly and realistically project future performance.

Figure 12.12 shows how these five steps lead to benchmarking's goal.

A Real-World Caveat: Benchmarking and Politics

Even industrial giants can run aground on benchmarking . . . it's quite possible for one department to launch a benchmarking program that inadvertently undermines another . . . . (Source: *Business Week,* November 30, 1992, p. 75.)

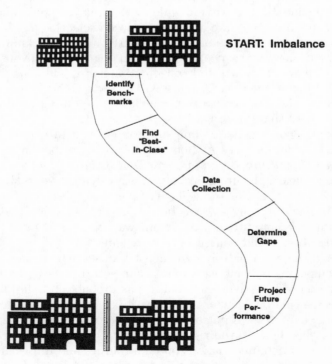

Figure 12.12   The road to benchmarking.

Benchmarking, in theory, is a beautifully simple tool that can teach your company some honest and beneficial lessons. In reality, it can become a political football. At times, the benchmark analysis is so charged with demands for dramatic operational change that some groups may have a hard time permitting the change to happen. They may feel their jobs are threatened, or their reputations are on the line. As a consequence, the conclusions may never be acted on.

Many managers who have been involved in numerous benchmark projects recommend the following:

- Receive common agreement on the benchmarking objectives beforehand.
- Work toward buy-in from all those groups who may be affected by any changes.
- Narrowly define the scope of the project. Take on one operational objective, not two or three. Examine turnaround time and quality of customer service, rather than your company's entire operations.

Case Discussion	Analytical Framework	Case Analysis

The Glass Bottle manufacturer's problem was one of productivity. As shown in Figure 12.13, the company was subject to external and internal pressures. It had completed the first two benchmarking steps. The best-in-class was identified and the operational benchmarks had been selected.

Figure 12.13 shows that the client selected benchmark categories that—if addressed—could shed some light on its productivity and on ways it might improve its output-per-worker in a relatively economical manner. Specifically, identifying optimal employment levels (the number of people needed to produce a desired yield) would provide an important manufacturing benchmark.

Step 3: Collecting the Data

Once the client had helped us identify the core problem, the categories of data became clear. The primary pieces of information we had to collect centered around three categories: (1) labor head count and costs per plant; (2) numbers of bottles produced; and (3) overall capacity and growth plans.

The information collection required over 100 interviews, visits to various government filings offices, and a review of plant floor plans. Throughout the information-gathering period, we were in touch with the client for feedback. The iterative process of feeding information back to the client once again helped us fine-tune our questions and narrow the overall scope of the research.

Available union contracts, summarized in Figure 12.14, revealed specific labor costs and staffing levels for many of the plants.

Step 4: Determining Gaps

The entire assignment involved investigating the performance measures for over 15 competitor plants in the United States. One or two of the 15 proved to be far and away the best performing operations.

The harsh reality for the client came when we presented the gap analysis, comparing one of its plants to that of the best-in-class. Figure 12.15 illustrates the massive difference between what the client thought the gap originally was and the gap we finally documented.

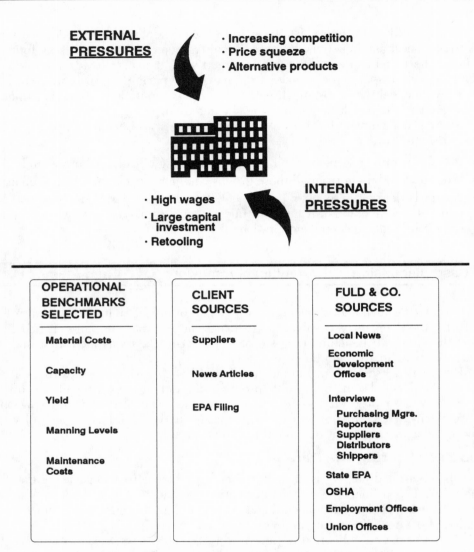

Figure 12.13   Why the client was concerned.

Step 5: Project Future Performance

The final analysis showed a huge gap between the best-in-class and the client's operations. The question the client now needed to address was how much investment would be required to achieve best-in-class status.

A performance gap (Figure 12.16) revealed how the client could hope to reach second-best-in-class status within three years (1992) by making appropriate changes in a timely fashion. If all competitive and economic conditions remained roughly the same, the client could match best-in-class by 1994 or 1995.

PRODUCTION DATA

"Approximately 200,000,000 bottles produced per year, including approximately 75,000,000 produced on weekend shifts...

...According to one union official, the plant has just about reached capacity and would need more equipment to raise production.

...The plant has been open seven days a week for the last three to four years.

(Interviews with Union Foremen & Local News Reporters)

LABOR & WAGE DATA

Number of Workers Per Shift and Wages

Task	Number	Hourly Wage
Shaping	10	12.42
Forming	3	12.25
Finishing	21	12.42
Inspection	2	11.89
Packing	4	12.32

(Union Contracts)

YIELD DATA

Precise Data...

"98% of the bottles produced are actually shipped."

"The plant's net yield is between 92 and 97 percent."

Indication of Yield...

According to a union official, there is " a lot of breakage. Four years ago we installed German equipment...tons of scrap are produced."

EPA Filings, union Documents, Interviews

Figure 12.14 Sampling of data collected.

(Measured Against Plant #1, B-I-C)

GAP	PERCEIVED	REALITY
Capacity	-20 million bottles	-320 million bottles
Yield	-8%	-18%
Output	Parity	-13 million bottles/worker

Figure 12.15   Summary of negative performance gaps.

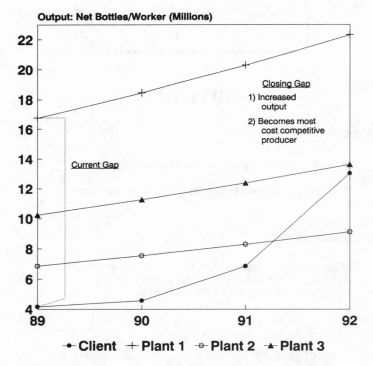

Figure 12.16   Performance gap: Output projections.

Lessons Learned

Setting large benchmarking objectives, involving extensive operations, is like commanding a battleship. A host of personnel, computer calculations, and transmitted orders are required to change the ship's course even slightly. Improving the productivity at this company would take a few years. The client needed to overcome political fallout, make tough investment decisions, and gently nudge all these changes into place over time. Small benchmark studies—which this was not—are much more like steering a small sloop. You can effect changes faster, less expensively, and with easier buy-in on the part of everyone involved.

This company's competitive dilemma was the result of overconfidence. Before the benchmark study began, the client's management reviewed internally available information on its market and its competition and concluded, "Things are not so bad." Both operations and management had placed the competition in a lesser light, underestimating the chief competitor's strength.

Marketing had long been screaming for more efficiency and productivity. Yet the numbers received from operations kept showing the company in a favorable position. Why improve?, they asked. Why fix what's not broken?

Resulting Actions

Over a one-year period, the client strove to become more competitive by bringing its manufacturing operations more in line with the competition. It did so by:

- Raising the level of automation in the key plants, through an aggressive capital investment program.
- Reducing the size of the work force.
- Renegotiating labor contracts (something it could not do before the study, because it did not have the intelligence to prove that it was at a severe cost disadvantage, a large part of which was caused by a relatively high-cost union labor force).

INTELLIGENCE CASE 5:

Inside the Manager's Mind: How to Anticipate Decisions		
Case Discussion	Analytical Framework	Case Analysis

The Problem. Knowing your competition has always meant understanding how decision makers think and act. In this disguised case, a high-technology company's management and ability to innovate were so successful that it spawned many admirers—including our client. The client, a multinational Pacific Rim company, wanted to know how this high-technology competitor was able to innovate and change direction so often and so deftly, without making many costly mistakes. It believed that by learning the lessons of this model, it could adopt some of the same style for its own technology ventures.

The Agile Competitor

HiTech is a company whose management appears driven. It always manages to ride— if not create—the latest technology wave. At the same time, it achieves an ever-growing profit margin in an industry where margins have become thin.

If an examination of HiTech is limited to pronouncements in the press, one sees only a boisterous CEO, touting his firm's latest innovation. A great deal of the company's advertising message is delivered through magazine, newspaper, and television ads. What is not seen is what truly makes HiTech tick—how management makes decisions, what steps it has to go through, and what drives the second-tier managers as well as senior management.

Our Pacific Rim client wanted to know how HiTech:

- Manages to make seemingly quick and effortless changes in product lines or product line extensions.
- Adheres to long-term goals and generally stays on track.
- Creates true empowerment with even the lowest level in the corporation. (Does this mean that HiTech is a truly decentralized corporation?)
- Ties financial controls into performance as well as into innovation.

Case Discussion	Analytical Framework	Case Analysis

Before exploring the disguised high-technology case, let's examine two other cases that make a strong argument for the need for management profiling in any competitive assessment.

The two cases involved U.S. clients that had very similar problems regarding their competition. In each instance, the competitor had managed to hold onto or grow its market share, despite the fact that it had not seen a profit for years. The cases occurred years apart, yet each client faced the same issue: How and why was the competitor in this market? Why would it put up with such market losses for so long? Did each competitor want to "buy" market share so badly that it was willing to incur tremendous losses?

1. *The Case of the Shell Game.* In the first case, a German competitor was actually playing a shell game with its overhead and its cash. The client only realized this some years later, after comparing notes with its own divisions, which had run into the same competitor in different markets. It turned out that the competitor's management had long ago made up its mind that it wanted to grab certain emerging markets from its chief rival (our client). It was willing to fund its money-losing, relatively high-tech venture with its other profitable lines. It was also willing to wait until our client finally gave up on the market and mothballed its plant. Immediately following the client's exit from the market, the rival drove up prices on its suddenly unique product. The competitor now owned the market. Only years later did the client catch on to these tactics and seek ways to anticipate the competitor's move in other mutually competitive arenas and product categories.

2. *A Need for a Foothold.* In the second case, the client was concerned that a major competitor, which appeared to be losing a great deal of money, was about to expand its capacity in an industry that had little room for expansion. Any expansion would likely create an oversupply of product and further drive prices down. The client's division was profitable, but only marginally. Why, the client asked, was this Pacific Rim competitor continuing to hammer away at a seemingly saturated marketplace?

The answer to the question lay, once again, with management thinking, not with the balance sheet. This particular Asian multinational wanted to stake out a strong position within the American market. It was willing to fund these losses for many years in order to entrench itself in this market. In subsequent analyses, it turned out that the Asian parent saw this product line as a beachhead from which it could then launch other products through the same distribution channels. Its management was looking beyond the immediate losses and seeing profit centers in the years ahead.

Caveat: Always Analyze Personalities in Context

Be warned that a management profiling model should be only one part of a larger analysis. Just as a cost or a technical analysis describes one aspect of a company, so does a management analysis. Corporations are complex organisms. To reduce an analysis to an oversimplified, one-dimensional assessment is a mistake. The process of management profiling tends to give analysts a sense that they have a crystal ball and can therefore delve into all the mysteries of competitor activity. Nothing could be farther from the truth.

As the Strategic Intelligence Index at the front of this book indicates, there are four dimensions of understanding any company, whether a competitor, a customer, a supplier, or a distributor. The dimensions are: (1) costs, (2) technology, (3) management, and (4) process. You must understand and appreciate the importance of each of these in order to develop useful, accurate intelligence.

A Profiling Framework

Managers are not born, they are made.

This statement is especially true of the key decision makers who have had years of experience either with the target company or within the industry. In either case, they are products of hard-won battles, disappointing losses, and their general education and upbringing. You are not likely to determine a manager's innermost thoughts, but you will be able to detect the general direction and inclination of that manager through a methodical profiling of his or her background and behavior.

To do so, you need to examine four facets of a management profile:

1. *Style/Culture.* This dimension explores the level of autonomy or autocracy that the manager has experienced and mirrors. In this dimension, you need to ask questions like these:

   - Does the manager require consensus to make decisions?

   - How far will the manager allow subordinates to go before stepping in and rendering a decision or countermanding their decisions?

   - Is the manager used to working effectively within larger bureaucratic organizations?

   - Does the individual tend to make snap decisions, or is he or she methodical, preferring to wait for more information?

2. *Background/Competencies.* Where a manager comes from, both in education and in experience, will tell you where and when that manager is on firm ground and where he or she may hesitate or rely on others for decisions. For this dimension, you need to explore the following questions:

   - Does the person have a great deal of training in a technical field? Or, is he or she from a general marketing or sales background?

   - Does the person have a reputation for being a "numbers cruncher," or was he or she taught by those who prefer to examine the big picture?

   - Has the individual ever designed a product or service or been involved in the drafting of that product or service? Has the individual ever filed for a patent, or worked on a lab bench?

   - Where did the person go to school? Does he or she have advanced training in a specialized field? What was the philosophy of that school, professor, or mentor?

3. *Proclivities/Orientation.* This dimension examines the bottom line for the manager. You need to ask the following questions:

   - Does the manager always need to show a profit? Or, is market share or some other gain the significant measure?

   - Does the manager seek to better organize and harmonize his or her organization and will he or she therefore work with human resources or continually work toward building a team spirit within the organization?

   - Does the individual thrive on tension, or will a harsh competitive climate slow the decision maker down?

   - Is he or she a tinkerer, always seeking to improve a particular product or service, thereby slowing down decisions? Or, does the manager leave the details up to subordinates?

4. *Past Moves.* We are all creatures of habit, and nowhere is this more evident than in the way we make decisions. If something worked well for us once, we are likely to repeat that action. It is therefore important to examine the history of a manager's decisions. This is among the most important and easiest of the profiling dimensions to discern, because it is history and others know about it.

Case Discussion	Analytical Framework	Case Analysis

For the past decade, HiTech, Inc. has proven itself nimble and decisive. Its management, starting with its CEO, is willing to make large changes to ensure future growth and profits. The client wanted to understand how HiTech could handle innovation and change so adeptly.

Some of the detailed comments and quotes gleaned from magazine articles, analyst's reports, and interviews showed how we drafted our conclusions. By placing these statements into the profiling framework (see Table 12.9), we were able to identify the why and how of HiTech's decision-making environment.

TABLE 12.9 Profiling via the Spoken and Written Word

Quotes and Citations	Summary Characteristics
Style/Culture	
"Systems integration is a service. . . . These companies should go where the business is. They ought to make this move while the going is good. . . ."	An ability to change quickly
"We used to rely upon strategic planners who were somewhat divorced from the business itself because they had no direct product-line responsibilities. Instead we eliminated this middle management position and shifted the planning responsibility directly to the production and product line people themselves. They were already shifting our business over to the smaller, more profitable devices." (*Leading Business Magazine,* 1993)	Empowering operations down the line
"We try to instill power at the individual level by putting forth a culture that values knowledge-based or experience-based power rather than something hierarchically based." Former HiTech manager	Decentralized decision making
"There will be a spontaneous team formed with content experts and market experts who will come together for a particular project or to solve a particular problem and then disband once the task is complete." HiTech manager	Sharing of time and skills
"But the CEO defines the vision, and then you have the next level of senior and to some extent middle management setting the tone, and then the worker bees are attacking the market at more of an operational and tactical level." Computer consultant	Senior management sets the long-term vision and leaves execution of strategies to managers
Background/Competencies	
"We have more architectural managers today than a few years ago . . . we tweak the products, play around with them and learn as we go along, rather than analyze it to death. If it looks like it isn't working, then we can try something else." HiTech sales manager	Engineering with a marketing bent

(Continued)

TABLE 12.9 *(Continued)*

Quotes and Citations	Summary Characteristics
"We generally hire people who have shown discipline and are results-oriented. More recently, we have been hiring sales managers who can communicate well—both in the written and spoken word." HiTech sales manager	Well spoken; good writers
Proclivities/Orientation "Very rarely in meeting with senior management do you walk away from a meeting knowing what needs to be investigated further, or what needs to be done, or who will have ownership for doing it. This same definitive style is carried all the way down through the organization. . . ." Securities analyst	Decisiveness and sense of taking responsibility
"We have a 10 percent rule, meaning that any new idea has to increase the product's performance or value by 10 percent, or it has to net out to no more than a certain cost. What we try to do is map ideas in a quantitative way." HiTech senior designer	Cost-consciousness in every aspect of the operation
"We're fairly independent. We get goals and collateral support from management that are broadly laid out, and as long as you're successful you aren't criticized for doing it differently." HiTech field sales engineer	Goal-oriented, not task-oriented
Past Moves "When you talk about innovation in the context of a company like HiTech, what you're really talking about is how they are moving forward based on decisions that they've made in the past. . . . There is a definite momentum and staying power to that innovation, which becomes an historical perspective that you really can't separate out from the company's future activities." Securities analyst	Constant drive to innovate, as indicated by repeated successes
"HiTech is a company that changes its organization quickly and often. . . . Approximately one year ago, our insight into end users came from OEMs. That was no longer adequate. As a result, we took our field force of 200, trimmed the group down to 150, and reorganized them to be more responsive to end users." HiTech regional sales manager	

The Bottom Line for HiTech: The Ability to Control Innovation

In this company, the CEO set the tone but did not control. Instead, he built an organization that thrives on innovation, as indicated by the way senior managers steer the company. At the same time, this innovation is not allowed to run away with the budget.

After compiling the various characteristics described—and corroborated from the many conversations and articles we collected—we made these general conclusions about the company's executives:

- The company has built a culture that rewards innovators without losing control over the financial aspects of managing new product development.
- Even midlevel managers can authorize projects, and division managers have even more autonomy. Very few projects require senior management approval.
- Projects that do not meet goals are abandoned without hesitation. This is not only a time-saving activity but a cost-saving one as well.
- The careers of people who are involved with discontinued projects are not hurt. This makes it easier for people to acknowledge that a project should be stopped.
- Midlevel and senior management are considered aggressive.

Competitive Response

In order to shorten its product development and sales cycle, the client knew it had to adapt many of the HiTech's innovative management methods. Almost immediately, it began to flatten the organization by very directly pushing decision-making responsibilities in research and in marketing down to the regional or product group levels of the organization. Management worked with its personnel department to build in a new bonus and salary reward system to reflect approval of this new management approach.

Lessons to Be Learned

- Management and culture analysis is a great tool. Alone, however, it is not enough; you need to compare and contrast the findings with financial, operational, and overall market analysis. Remember, company management does not just look at itself. It examines the company's financial health and that of the market conditions around it.
- People come and go. Your management profiling must track *current* management. In a fast-changing industry, you may need to revisit this analysis twice a year.
- Even individual philosophies can change. Continually track senior management's progress and pronouncements in the press, using either news clipping services or database searches.
- No single person controls the destiny of a corporation. Who else besides the CEO should be in your analysis portfolio?

INTELLIGENCE CASE 6:

Finding the Bellwether		
Case Discussion	Analytical Framework	Case Analysis

Forecasting Global Competitive Strategies

Problem. The client, a U.S.-based detergent company with an international market, was concerned about the changes in packaging and formulation strategy that were occurring in its industry. Management did not want to be left behind when major marketing initiatives occurred. They needed to know just how serious the environmental laws and market shifts were and how wide a window of opportunity actually existed to make any change. In addition, the client's market was rapidly becoming a global one. It therefore needed to take into consideration the laws, customs and practices of many unfamiliar overseas markets.

Background

Detergent packaging—or the packaging of almost any consumer product—can be a complex and strategically important issue. In a business that often counts profits by pennies rather than by dollars, investments in packaging R&D, new store displays, educating the consumer market, and test marketing the product must be weighed very carefully. Sometimes packagers are driven into making these changes because of regulatory changes; other times the driving force is the consumers or competitors themselves.

In this instance, all the major players were sensing a shift in market conditions for environmentally safe packaging. At the same time, technology was providing manufacturers with the ability to mass produce super-concentrated detergents that manufacturers might be able to sell at a premium price. The new formulations were also thought a plus for consumers, who would only have to bring home detergent weighing half or one-quarter the weight of the previous full-strength version.

The client therefore needed to anticipate the potential impact of both packaging and formulation changes. However, the client did not know where and when these changes were taking place and how long it would take them to affect its major market—the United States.

Part of the solution lay in understanding which markets were the bellwethers, providing early warning signals for the rest of the world.

Case Discussion	Analytical Framework	Case Analysis

Competitive bellwethers can tell you where and when to look for product innovation or new market opportunities. By studying these bellwether markets, you can anticipate the nature and size of the impact such innovation will have on your products and your customers.

There are four types of bellwether forces:

Regulatory. A government will change a regulation often as a result of political pressure, such as the election of a new legislature or the enactment of a series of local regulations that force the hand of national regulatory authorities. Because the wheels of government can move slowly, sometimes taking years to enact a piece of legislation, you have a long time to track and prepare for these changes.

Technology. In electronics or software, in particular, a new product category or leap-frog innovation can create and wipe out entire product groups. New technology can create new competitors and severely challenge the position of the current market leaders. As we saw earlier in this chapter, Microsoft's Windows™ program forced its DOS competitors to recreate their software that ran on DOS only and gave the Apple MacIntosh™ the first serious challenge to its operating system since its creation over a half-dozen years earlier. Intel's 486 chip almost eliminated products carrying its earlier and less powerful 386 chip in less than one year. Should some chemist invent a much dreamt about gasoline substitute that is also environmentally friendly, you will see today's gasoline products virtually disappear.

Industry Shifts (consolidations, mergers). Industry mergers or consolidations can quite suddenly change the magnitude and power of the players who are participants and suppress or kill off all johnny-come-latelies. One example of this is the acquisition of generic pharmaceutical companies by the traditional ethical drug firms. Not only do these acquisitions legitimize a former industry stepchild, but it also threatens to handicap those generic pharmaceutical firms that do not merge. Among the benefits, these mergers give the generic partners access to greater R&D resources.

Similar dramatic shifts are occurring in the data communications-telecommunications-entertainment industries. Here you have several examples: AT&T purchasing McCaw Cellular, or Southwestern Bell's expenditure of $650 million to enter the cable TV business; U.S. West's stake of 25.2 percent of Time Warner; and others still in the making.

Consumer. Shifts in consumer attitude and opinion are far more subtle bellwethers. Eating habits change over decades, but may begin in the health food stores, for example. These stores were considered out of the mainstream and began near colleges and university towns. Dried, packaged soups, such as the Ramen dried soups, are another example of consumer-driven bellwethers. The growth in the Ramen soup market may have started in Asia but soon found a strong niche in health-conscious American consumers. West coast food companies made the public aware of the Ramen soups. Traditional soup companies, such as Campbell's, eventually caught on to the trend and introduced their own version of the Japanese-styled dried soups.

Consumers can also change the way companies deal with the environment. Germany and Minnesota in the United States were among the first areas to legislate packaging changes, recycling and overall manufacturing process accountability. In almost all cases where environmental laws have changed, it started with consumer or community activism in those regions. Tracking this bellwether became critical to our client's need to understand packaging changes in the detergent market.

Bellwethers become reality when you have the . . .

Necessary conditions. You generally need more than two competitors or two geographic areas to accept these bellwethers as a true indicator of change—and not just an odd blip in the overall market picture.

Migratory patterns. You have to assume that any industry or competitive change has occurred in many forms and similar patterns before, and that those changes followed an actual migratory pattern, from region to region or country to country. In the detergent case, we learned that the German environmental movement is so strong that it very much influences packaging changes in Europe and eventually elsewhere around the globe, including the United States. Coated drink cartons, and special spouts are examples of innovations that manufacturers test in one market in the hope of mass producing at a far lower cost per unit in markets elsewhere. This was the legitimate concern the client had in the detergent business. The question was where to watch for the bellwether change (which market would give them the true reading?).

Was There a Detergent Bellwether?

The following excerpts are evidence that there were clear bellwethers forewarning manufacturers of major changes within the detergent industry around the globe (see Table 12.10).

Superconcentrated detergents, an industry innovation, were also forcing these multinational competitors to change their packaging to accommodate the more compact product. Superconcentrates were again being tested in Europe in advance of the U.S. In a sense, while these manufacturers were testing the product for the European consumer, Europe itself was being used as staging ground for entry into the U.S. market.

Among the types of packaging being tested in Europe were:

Bag-in-a-box
Ball dispensers
Gussetted plastic pouches
Coated cartons
Plastic cartons
Plastic shampoo-style bottle
Pump dispensers
Plastic pouch

Report Excerpt

As a result of our research we have concluded that among the major competitors, at least Company X will be introducing a super-concentrated liquid detergent very soon in Europe; perhaps later in the U.S. Because we know Company X is working with a shampoo-styled dispenser manufacturer and that these types of containers are used successfully by other players in the detergent market, we also believe that Company X will very likely be using a similar dispenser for its concentrated product in the U.S. market. Based on product development and marketing time needed product introduction will be within the next 18 months to two years . . .

TABLE 12.10 Detergent Bellwethers: Harbingers of Strategic Change

Regulatory Bellwether	**Environmentally-safe packaging**
	The client had begun to see some dramatic competitor packaging changes in its U.S. market. When we began to explore the market overseas, it became clear that many of these new packaging designs were first being tested in Europe. Many of these new packaging designs were first marketed in Germany, which effectively forced these changes because of newly enacted recycling laws.
	Over 30 new packaging variations were being introduced in Europe and 12 in the United States. One leading competitor alone introduced over 9 new packaging changes in Europe and only 2 in the United States. Even realizing that some of these new packages were attempts to penetrate specific markets and not to effect a sweeping packaging change, global detergent competitors were still making concerted moves toward new and more environmentally friendly packaging in Europe. From all indications, U.S. environmental agencies were preparing regulations that would follow many of those regulated and voluntary corporate programs already underway in Europe. . .
Consumer Bellwether	**Need for continued consumer education**
	Reports from sources and trade magazines stressed the need to educate the consumer about Bag-In-Box products before the concept could be fully accepted. According to a private-label detergent manufacturer which also markets a bag-in-box product, the concept was performing below expectations for all manufacturers. "Consumers, glancing at the box without reading the label, mistake it for a powdered detergent," he said. . .
Technology Bellwether	**New flexible refill pouches**
	Company D was using flexible plastic refill pouches with gussetted bases for its dishwashing liquids, calling it the "Flexi-Pak." Sources within the company implied that Company D was considering extending the Flexi-Pak concept to some of its laundry detergent products. It was still unclear which particular products would make use of the refill pouches or when the packaging innovation might be introduced. The packaging change would reduce product waste going into landfills by 75 percent, according to Company D. . .

Case Discussion	Analytical Framework	Case Analysis

Superconcentrates did indeed take the market by storm in the early 1990s; yet, the packaging changes were only partially adopted in the United States by consumers. The client was advised to move aggressively in its introduction of superconcentrates and against making dramatic changes to packaging design, since there does not seem to be a clear leader or design in this aspect of detergent marketing. Increasingly, newer, more recyclable packaging is being offered to consumers, along with the superconcentrates. At this writing Europe remains a fractured market for detergent manufacturers, with a large number of different packaging designs available in the marketplace.

The Long Term

Overall, the packaging samples and primary information gathered from countries, such as Germany, indicate that over the next twenty years

- Governments will mandate that industry reclaim all packaging.
- Manufacturers will produce more permanent packaging and sell refills, using less material.

PART FOUR

TAKE ACTION

The Intelligence Pyramid

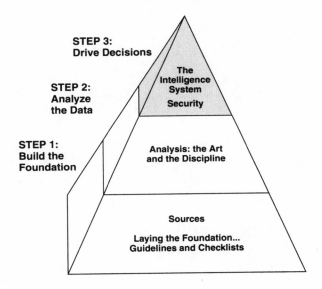

STEP 3:
Drive Decisions

STEP 2:
Analyze
the Data

STEP 1:
Build the
Foundation

The
Intelligence
System
Security

Analysis: the Art
and the Discipline

Sources

Laying the Foundation...
Guidelines and Checklists

13

HOW TO BUILD YOUR OWN INTELLIGENCE SYSTEM

A Corporate Imperative

Nathan Rothschild, the famous British merchant-banker, received early warning of Napoleon's defeat at Waterloo through a message sent by carrier pigeon from one of his correspondents on the Continent. Making it appear as if he had heard Britain would lose the war, he quickly dumped all his British-backed government securities on the market. Other investors, following Rothschild's lead, did likewise. However, as soon as Rothschild saw the market bottom out, he bought back every piece of paper at fire sale prices and made a killing. If Nathan Rothschild could receive early warning of Napoleon's defeat at Waterloo in 1815 by using nothing more than his carrier pigeon network, then the modern corporation—large or small—with lightning-fast technology at its disposal, can do the same in today's corporate battlefield. There is no excuse for competitive surprises. All any company needs is an organized network of people.

This chapter offers a step-by-step approach for building a simple, efficient intelligence system.[1] The guidelines I am proposing are based on actual cases and experiences with various clients. In most instances, the framework of a successful intelligence system is built on and around the culture of each organization. In other words, intelligence systems—despite all the potential computer-based applications this concept conjures up—are very much a human issue. Note how the following corporate stories seem to reflect this perspective.

---

[1]For a more detailed review, I refer you to Leonard M. Fuld, *Monitoring the Competition: Find Out What's Really Going On Over There* (John Wiley & Sons, New York, 1988).

417

A pallet of the competitor's ceramic product sat on the shop floor, displayed for everyone at Corning's Erwin, New York, plant to see. Until that moment, most in the facility were satisfied with Corning's equivalent product. Yet, after reviewing the competitor's sample and its characteristics, Corning realized it had to improve Corning's product to compete successfully . . . .[2]

Banc One has begun to regularly collect the direct-mail solicitations sent by its competitors to the bank's own employees. The program to date has yielded invaluable information on competitors' pricing, new products, and target markets.[3]

At Xerox evaluation begins as soon as the engineers lay eyes on a machine. . . . The engineers never try to fix a broken machine and, when available, buy a service contract. Servicemen from Kodak, for instance, will install the Kodak 150 copier at Xerox, while Xerox engineers stand by, watching every move, even photographing the process to see what's involved.[4]

At Canon Corporation we have analysts, who have been trained in British schools, to translate and interpret technical articles published in the United States and in Europe.[5]

The Kraft CMIC group has created an in-house database called RECAP (Research Capsules) that has fully indexed millions of dollars worth of research purchased or produced for the Kraft organization. RECAP is extremely flexible and allows the user to search for a report by analyst, code word, title, date, or even the purpose of the research. For the first time Kraft has a handle on the market research that was becoming buried in its organization.[6]

The best-run intelligence systems highly leverage their people resources. Some do so by incorporating a giant web of computer-based client servers; some enlist low-tech means of intelligence storage and delivery. Whatever path these successful programs have taken, they all have followed three basic steps:

1. Prepare the organization;
2. Motivate the troops;
3. Store and deliver the intelligence.

STEP 1: PREPARE THE ORGANIZATION

Intelligence systems succeed because of people, not machines and not computers. If you had to place the topic of intelligence systems in a business school curriculum, you would place it under the category of Organizational Behavior, not under Marketing, Control, or Systems. A successful intelligence system works because all employees are primed to share, communicate, and use their own hard-won market information.

---

[2]Leonard M. Fuld, "Achieving Total Quality through Intelligence," *Long Range Planning*, 25(1), pp. 109–115.
[3]Fuld, *Monitoring the Competition*, p. 28.
[4]*Democrat & Chronicle*, Rochester, NY(USA), January 29, 1984.
[5]Fuld & Company Seminar, "Intelligence Sources, Techniques & Systems."
[6]Fuld, *Monitoring the Competition*, p. 131.

Companies that keep barriers to this information flow, or think that a high-tech E-mail network will substitute for good employee communications, are mistaken.

You cannot just take a software package out of its shrink-wrapping and hope that it will organize all your information. You must find ways to share and communicate vital information; storing it comes later. If the organization does not share information, no technology will help. On the other hand, if the organization has begun to share and use its own vital intelligence, then a computer-based system may be the next step in the process.

You're Bigger Than CNN

Cable News Network (CNN) may have hundreds of affiliate stations and scores of reporters. Yet, CNN cannot compare to the multinational conglomerates of the world, with their hundreds of thousands of employees. Such large corporations—General Electric, Fujitsu, and Siemens, among a host of others—have armies of well-trained individuals who are immersed in a market. These intelligence/news-gathering experts include scientists, independent brokers, salespeople, purchasing managers, and many others. Harness this capability, for both the quantity and the quality of the industry news these internal experts can offer.

In contrast, think about the intelligence potential represented in even the smallest of companies. The people in a 20-person firm spend each business day dealing with customers, suppliers, and competitors. The reason many companies have problems establishing successful intelligence programs is not a lack of internal knowledge, but the fact that they have not yet figured out how to harness that knowledge to analyze their competition. A prime fact of intelligence gathering is: You are your own best consultancy.

Intelligence Never Travels in a Straight Line

Chances are that a vital piece of intelligence will have entered your company in many different ways and will take many different directions as it travels through the organization. A piece of news is seldom known by only one individual, and you need only try to capture that piece of intelligence once. Build a broad network of communications vehicles that can capture and speed along the critical intelligence. Like a commercial fisherman who is generally far more successful with a wide net than with 20 individual casting poles, you need to spread a wide corporate information net. Remember, you only need to capture the intelligence once. With a wide enough net, you will be able to do so. Later in this chapter, I will describe some types of electronic and manual nets you may want to consider.

Adopting a Three-Part Philosophy

In a two-year study my firm conducted in the mid-1980s, and in subsequent consultations, three immutable principles have guided any successful intelligence system or program. They are:

1. *Constancy.* You must gather information constantly, day-in, day-out, not just during the traditional strategic planning cycle. Most corporations will spend a great deal of time and money, for three months of every year, trying to understand

their competitive environment. The purpose of this yearly effort is to develop the corporate short-term and long-term plans. Your competitors won't wait till next year at the same time to compete again. They compete every day and their intelligence-savvy managers urge employees to look for and gather critical information every day.

2. *Longevity.* You must invest in the intelligence program for the long term. Six months, one year, or even two years may not be enough to prove the worth of a program. The most successful intelligence systems have taken three to five years to mature. As a result, cost becomes a major issue. The more costly the system, the more difficult it will be to maintain over the long run. From my experience, the longest-running, most successful programs have been allowed to grow and mature over many years just because they started out as relatively low-cost and low-maintenance endeavors.

3. *Involvement.* One way to simultaneously control intelligence system costs and create a broad-based system is to spread the responsibility for collection and analysis of information across the entire organization—salespeople, purchasing agents, market research, senior management. The more people see the development and use of intelligence as part of their jobs, the more readily available the intelligence will be and the more it will be used.

Creating a Ringmaster

Should the system be centralized or decentralized? This is probably the question most frequently asked by clients interested in establishing an intelligence system. It is also the most misunderstood.

Thirty years ago, when information had to be controlled from a central location, I might have advised a client to adopt a centralized system, where all files—electronic and manual—would be kept in one place. At that time, information was maintained with a library approach. Mainframes controlled the data flow, few terminals were available, E-mail was in its infancy, and the few photocopiers that existed were tightly controlled by the print shop or copy manager. In short, information had to be kept in one place in order for it to be managed and ultimately found.

Today, the information flow has reversed itself. The individual now controls the flow and—to a large extent—the storage of information. Personal computers (stand-alone or networked through client servers), personal copiers, E-mail, voice mail, and other personalized technologies allow anyone to manage his or her own information base. The corporate intelligence system must recognize this reality and build a system that leverages the dynamics of this new information age.

Because your company's experts are literally everywhere your company is—in the field, the R&D labs, the shop floor, the customer service desk—you need to coordinate the information flow, not create a bottleneck by centralizing it.

The intelligence system manager must organize the intelligence system so that it provides the company with the means to find the information already located within its own walls.

Figure 13.1 presents an organization chart and an intelligence chart. The organization chart describes a typical, vertical company structure, where employees report

Organization Chart
Traditional Corporations Create Information Barriers

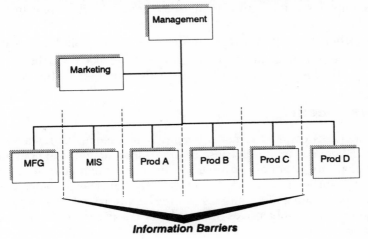

Intelligence Chart

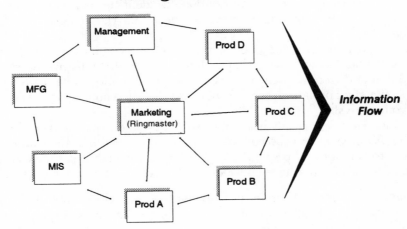

Figure 13.1 Changing information barriers into information flow.

to superiors and are responsible for subordinates. The intelligence chart describes how the same organization can remove its strict vertical barriers and create a flow of information exchange.

The great irony in many large corporations, is that by encouraging individual business unit profitability, management often ends up building information barriers. As a consequence of employee's wanting their own business unit to succeed, they will often withhold information from another business unit. Good business practice then works against good intelligence practice.

The intelligence system manager, or Ringmaster, can break down these barriers and foster healthy information exchange by:

- Creating and distributing an "Intelligence Directory" of all files and experts within the company, cross-indexing them by expertise;
- Using the company's voice mail or E-mail to distribute important information, or information requests;
- Bringing together internal experts to hash out critical competitive issues;
- Encouraging senior management to recognize intelligence contributions of subordinates—particularly if those contributions directly benefit the company.

A Needs Assessment

An intelligence needs assessment is not a luxury. It is a necessity for any company considering an intelligence system. Because of time, labor, and budget constraints, no organization can hope to gather all possible pieces of information on its market and its competition. It's neither practical nor cost-effective. Just as a company writes a strategic plan in order to apply its limited resources appropriately, so an intelligence program must determine its objectives and apply its resources in the most efficient and effective manner.

A needs assessment is a means of gauging how your organization actually handles the internal information flow. It is a three-part intelligence snapshot that (1) determines the most commonly needed information, (2) identifies widely used internal resources, and (3) locates communications channels and the vehicles people use to communicate.

When you conduct a needs assessment, use a two-person team to interview your staff. You will find—as we have—that different people listening to the same statements will detect different nuances. A two-person team allows one team member to ask the questions and probe, while the other takes detailed notes (which you will need later, for your analysis).

Your interviewing approach should use open-ended questions, offering more than yes/no or one of a few choices. You need to ask broad questions and allow the respondents to wander and perhaps stumble into areas of needs that you and your management team may not have considered. Phrase your questions in this style:

"What areas of competitor activity do you feel need close attention?" "The past five times you needed competitor information, what kinds of questions did you ask about the target companies?"

Conduct equal interviews. Interview senior managers apart from their subordinates. A senior manager's opinion will frequently squelch a subordinate's answer, even if the working relationship is fine. The senior manager may have a different—but no necessarily better—perspective on the corporation than does a subordinate; they may identify different intelligence problems. For all these reasons, schedule separate but equal interviews.

Allow enough time. Because you are using open-ended questions, each interview may take as long as two hours. Considering that your write-up time will be nearly as long as your interview, you should not schedule more than two to three interviews per day, per interview team.

To analyze your findings, use a quantitative model. Unless you quantify your findings, it becomes very difficult to reconcile all the various comments into a

---

War Story: Lost Crossing the Atlantic

Here was an intelligence accident waiting to happen. While conducting an intelligence needs assessment and audit for a multinational pharmaceuticals firm with headquarters in Europe, we discovered that the U.S. division and European group each had their own, incompatible ways of communicating. The U.S. Division had very specific and clearly identified intelligence goals. It knew its competition and competitive products. The European parent, however, had kept the U.S. division at arm's length, not always informing it about new developments and sharing little information, unless it thought that information vital to the division's markets.

The needs assessment uncovered the fact that the U.S. and European offices had incompatible communications systems. Even within the U.S. division, the R&D group used a different E-mail system than the marketing group used. In addition, the European parent company had research and marketing files that remained apart from and unknown to the U.S. division, although both entities sold versions of the same products across the globe.

Then the accident happened. In the middle of the assessment, the U.S. parent had to recall a newly reformulated medication because pharmacies and physicians had reported undesirable—and in some cases dangerous—side effects. The product recall cost the U.S. division tens of millions of dollars. Only later, after management had applied damage control, did the U.S. division discover that the European parent had experimented with the reformulation and had shelved it when there was evidence of potential negative effects. The European parent did not say anything to the U.S. division or share the files, not considering them important enough.

A number of lessons were learned here. We worked with the U.S. subsidiary, recommending ways to electronically and manually improve its communication network. But the most important lesson of benefit to the client was the realization that an intelligence system would not only improve its competitor monitoring, but would also increase the sharing and use of its own internal intelligence.

---

common scheme, a common denominator. The model we have developed allows us to quickly identify the critical areas of need, resources, and communications channels.

An Intelligence Audit

An intelligence audit is one of the simplest and most immediately rewarding steps in building an intelligence system. It literally means identifying the experts and other sources of knowledge extant throughout your organization. In effect, the intelligence audit reorganizes your company's personnel directory, listing people by expertise instead of by department.

Your intelligence audit should include these categories:

- Employees, by competitor, technical, market, or other expertise;
- Private manual files and a description of their contents;
- Independent databases maintained on nonnetwork computers;
- Collections of market studies and special books not elsewhere cataloged.

Design an inventory form that can be easily filled out by office administrators, and make the form computer-ready for entering onto a database. I recommend building a simple database management file, using a Paradox or DBase IV-type program to house and ultimately sort the data.

In audits conducted by my firm, we have amassed thousands of entries within a couple of weeks. Because we had entered the information onto an electronic database, we could quickly manipulate the data many different ways. As a result, we were able to produce an intelligence directory, cross-indexed by expertise and other topics of interest to the intelligence system's customers.

STEP 2: MOTIVATE THE TROOPS

The foundation for any intelligence system is a work force that is motivated to share and help develop intelligence. To motivate an organization, you need to accomplish two tasks:

1. Raise awareness of the key issues;
2. Provide incentives for continued contributions to the system.

Here are the issues to consider when greater motivation is your goal.

Invisible and Visible Intelligence

Companies of all sizes have most of the competitive data they need, but the data are invisible. People who have the knowledge either cannot find those who need the knowledge, or they do not know what information is important in the first place.

To make intelligence visible, an organization needs incentives and awareness, which are the keys to the intelligence system. Awareness is the more difficult to achieve.

Too often, a decision maker does not have the necessary information because the person who could give it either does not know it's important or does not know who needs it. Your company's salespeople, loan officers, plant engineers, scientists, and purchasing managers come into contact with the outside world every day. For them to do their jobs well, they need to remain focused on a series of tasks; anything else, any information not relevant to the task at hand, will likely be ignored. A successful intelligence system will help broaden this awareness of other issues that may ultimately be useful to others in the company.

There are many conventional and creative ways to raise awareness in an organization. Xerox imports the competition:

From time to time, our competitive-evaluation people arrange special demonstrations of competitive products. Not long ago, they were displayed in the main cafeteria in

Webster [NY]. Over a period of several months, some 7,000 employees—in groups of 50 at a time—were given time off from their jobs to see what the competition had to offer.[7]

Your intelligence manager must understand that people absorb information in different ways. Xerox realized that the employee lunchroom was a perfect place to exchange information. The display's sponsors understood that only so many memos describing the competitor's copies can be sent before people stop reading them.

Try these other ways of using communications tools to raise awareness:

Bulletin boards. Post news clippings of your competitors' announcements on a bulletin board near the elevator, cafeteria, or other high-traffic areas.

Newsletters. Reserve a few inches of space in various corporate newsletters and magazines to advertise competitor news and to ask others to contribute information.

Meetings. Give the people who chair key meetings (their names would be learned during your intelligence audit) flyers to announce competitive activity and to solicit responses.

Road shows. Take your intelligence message "on the road" around the company. Invite speakers from the groups before whom you are to speak to also present the reasons why an intelligence system is important. If one of "their own" is up there presenting, chances are your audience will accept the intelligence concept a lot faster.

You can become very creative in raising awareness. One client recommended that the intelligence program manager place management's latest questions about the competition in the company's airline ticket envelopes. In that way, every time someone is about to embark on a trip, he or she will be forced to see the hot issues and will think about those issues while traveling.

Where Incentives Are Important

Even in the most highly motivated organizations, you need to show your colleagues that management recognizes their contributions. Although monetary reward is often the first incentive that comes to mind, I discourage clients from this path because of the difficulty in assigning specific dollar amounts to particular pieces of information. There is also a potential for steering your company into legal gray areas. Instead, encourage your organization to provide the following types of incentives:

Feed-forward information. An intelligence program is a two-way street. Just as your salespeople are among your best information suppliers, they also need information for their jobs. The more you can voluntarily send bits and pieces of intelligence to your organization (realizing that much of it will not be immediately useful), the more cooperation you will foster in the future. Send them news clippings, copies of database searches, sample product brochures, advertising tear sheets—almost anything that might be relevant to their competitive arena. By taking this proactive stance, you are building trust and confidence among your most important intelligence suppliers.

---

[7]*Xerox World* (Xerox Corporation), Winter, 1983, p. 8.

Letters of recognition. Senior management can very easily give "'at-a-boys,'" or personal thanks to those who have contributed to the intelligence effort. A single letter of thanks from the company president will do a lot for most employees' continued efforts.

Announcements in house organs. Existing newsletters give visible recognition to specific individuals. Even if you have omitted the particulars for reasons of confidentiality, some words of public praise will benefit your overall program.

Awards. Use annual sales meetings, and similar forums, to hand out plaques and certificates to your best contributors. While attending one such meeting at a client's offices, I witnessed one salesperson receiving a plaque and beaming as the vice president of sales handed the award to him. You can bet that his colleagues in the audience were impressed enough to consider doing what he had done. That one plaque probably contributed more to motivating the organization than any speech or a thousand memos on the subject.

Mandate. This often unspoken incentive does not have to be draconian. I have seen some very gentle mandates used effectively. For instance, one general sales manager simply added three lines to his organization's trip/expense reports, requiring the person coming off a road trip to write down any competitor information that was learned. He was looking for even the smallest tidbit, and trying to train his organization to be alert for competitor activity. If the did not fill out the three lines, they were not reimbursed for their expenses.

Experiment with a combination of awareness and incentive tools until you see which ones work. Raising awareness and providing incentives is a constant process; it continues throughout the entire life of the intelligence system. Stick to the basics of why and how people are motivated, and you will often find commonsense, low-cost approaches to this key intelligence system step.

By laying down the awareness and incentive intelligence nets, you are likely to catch the intelligence you need, when you need it.

STEP 3: STORE AND DELIVER THE INTELLIGENCE

Using computer-based systems for storage and transmission of intelligence has become a very real option for many companies. But it should not be the first one. An organization just starting an intelligence program must first take care of the needs assessment, intelligence audit, and motivational issues presented above. Even after those are done, the intelligence system manager has to find out how much staff time is available to maintain a computer-based system. You may find, as many of our clients have, that because of limited human resources, it is better to concentrate on creating people networks and motivating the organization; perhaps six months or a year later, you can consider computer-based options.

How to Store Intelligence: The Three Pillars

There are three pillars supporting every successful intelligence system. They are: (1) manual files; (2) the library, and (3) computer systems.

War Story: Electronic Matchmaker Turned Deal Maker

At MTV Networks, groupware became a new weapon for the affiliate sales force. When the Viacom Inc. unit was battling last summer against rival Turner Broadcasting System Inc.'s Cartoon Channel, trying to get cable operators to carry MTV's new Comedy Central network instead, salesmen in some areas were meeting unexpected resistance. Then a saleswoman in Chicago discovered that a cable system in her territory had been offered a special two-year, rock-bottom price by Cartoon Channel.

She typed this intelligence into a groupware network that tracks most day-to-day activity of the sales force. Others noticed that another salesman in Florida had also heard something about a new, more aggressive deal from the competition. Top MTV executives were told of the tactic and were able to counterattack by changing their own pricing and terms.

Source: *The Wall Street Journal,* December 9, 1993, p. 1.

Manual Files

Whenever I ask seminar audiences how many of the participants have their own set of competitor files, almost all hands go up. These are mostly private files, maintained for a small group within a company and not shared. The major goal for the intelligence manager is to locate these files, make them more user-friendly, and build a set of files that store internally produced documents, not just those produced on the outside.

For the foreseeable future, the manual file will remain a staple for even the most sophisticated system. The contents of a manual file will mostly remain in paper form because the volume may tax the storage capacity of many systems, or some of the information is not easily scanned into electronic form, or it is simply easier to maintain the data in written form rather than in electronic form.

You can beef up your manual files to better serve the intelligence system by doing the following:

Increase the internal sources. As stated earlier, most of the intelligence you need on your market is available from within your company. Yet, most managers I have contacted describe competitor files containing information generated from outside their companies. These files are filled with annual reports, regulatory filings, product literature, database printouts, and so on. You must encourage inclusion into these files of internal sales and technical reports, memos, and notes. Try to achieve at least a 50–50 balance of internal versus external documents.

Distribute index of files. The best way of linking these manual files is to index their general contents on a computer-based system. This job can be carried out during the intelligence audit. If your company operates in a groupware environment, you can place this index on the network and make it accessible to everyone. (Note: Such an index accomplishes a number of goals in building your intelligence system. It raises awareness of available resources and it provides an incentive by making information available without any gatekeeper blocking the way.)

Maintain a two-tiered structure. Most companies have first- and second-tier companies against which they compete. Because your time, staff, and resources are limited, I recommend actively developing intelligence on the first-tier companies, usually numbering 5 to 15. Those companies are the ones on which you need to spend time and resources. For the second tier, stick with your SDI/Current Awareness searches (see Chapter 5), and other more passive means of picking up the latest news.

The Library

Your corporate library needs to augment its standard collection in order to serve an intelligence system. The intelligence system manager should note that librarians are trained indexers and catalogers. Their job is to organize information, a wonderful skill to apply to any intelligence system. Ask your corporate librarians to do the following:

Collect and store all trade show literature. You can never be sure when you will want to compare your competitor's brochure from last year with the current year's, or to assemble price sheets or photos of competitors' products. All of this ephemeral material needs to be in your library, where it will be maintained and can be found in the future.

Prepare SDI/Current Awareness reports. Your library can organize and generate the current awareness reports referred to in Chapter 5.

Store product samples. A number of food and pharmaceutical companies store and catalog competitors' packaging and labels. Some of this information is available on the companies' wide area networks (WAN).

Computer Systems

Computerizing the network of intelligence gatherers can mean quicker responses from more people. That's what AT&T did 6½ years ago when it launched an on-line computer service called AAA—Access to AT&T Analysts—to help employees learn from the hundreds of thousands of workers with specialized insight on the competitive arena. . . . Says Martin Stark, a district manager in AT&T's strategic planning department: "If you can answer a question for me in three hours that would otherwise have taken several weeks, the whole company has benefited." (Source: *Fortune,* November 2, 1992, p. 105.)

Computer-based intelligence systems work best when they foster the growth of—not supplant—people networks. Make no mistake, it is a waste of time to consider a computer-based system as a substitute for 10 experts sitting in one room or conducting a conference call to analyze a competitive situation. However, when the system manages to save *people-time* by locating intelligence quickly and by identifying experts, it has given the company possessing such a system a competitive advantage. Like Nathan Rothschild, who used state-of-the-art carrier pigeons, you have the same access to the data as anyone else. The advantage Rothschild's system provided was the speed with which he received vital intelligence. Speed is often reason enough for considering the computer-based option.

What exactly is a computer-based system? A successful computer-based intelligence system is far more than just a bundled software–hardware package. Four basic elements are required:

1. A hardware base;
2. People to collect and feed in data;
3. The software to make the data accessible;
4. People to analyze the data and turn them into intelligence.

Until a few years ago, the hardware–software elements often made such systems prohibitively expensive. In 1980, a computer-based intelligence system consisted of a central mainframe that fed information to "dumb" terminals located throughout the company. The pioneer purchasers of such systems found them expensive, difficult to customize for each user group, and hard to maintain. They were like a large, drafty mansion that looks handsome and promising from the outside, but becomes a monetary sinkhole when you start working on the inside. Early computer-based intelligence systems required many professionals to customize the package and many more to feed information into the terminals. A third group was then needed to interpret the output. The yearly out-of-pocket expense and the lack of quick results often discouraged many managers, who summarily dumped such systems.

Today, client-server architecture and relatively inexpensive—yet powerful—desktop computers have lowered the initial intelligence system cost barriers for most corporations. No longer do you have to consider a million-dollar-plus investment in a single computer. In most instances, the computers and networks are already in place. Almost every executive and manager in a large corporation has a personal computer or can gain access to one. However, intelligence system managers still must measure the investment in terms of the organization's time and, to a lesser extent, the outlay for software.

A potential stumbling block is the deceptive ease with which these systems allow you to enter data. System managers frequently see the glossy brochures and think "the package" will solve the entire system equation—which it does not.

When a computer-based intelligence system works well, it becomes an almost invisible part of the company's entire communications network. It becomes as much intertwined with the company's business operations as the fax machine and phone system. It helps flatten the corporate hierarchy by treating suppliers and users of intelligence equally, not based on rank or position. Corning's intelligence system is one such system that has become part of the information infrastructure.

> . . . Through its E-Mail system, its Information Exchange Intelligence System and its data base, Corning's intelligence program is beginning to act like an information switch box, relaying customer-related information from whatever point it entered Corning to the appropriate user of the information.[8]

To determine whether your company should develop or expand a computer-based or technology-based system, you need to examine four issues: (1) how to know whether you need a computer system; (2) types of technology; (3) using available technology; and (4) going outside.

---

[8]Fuld, "Achieving Total Quality through Intelligence," p. 112.

1. *How to know whether you need a computer system.* There is no perfect litmus test for determining whether you need a computer-based system, but there are some questions you should ask yourself. If four or more of the statements below apply to your company, you may want to consider a computer-based system:

Self-Test	Answers	
"My business . . .	Yes	No
. . . is subject to a high volume of information."	____	____
. . . is multidivisional, geographically dispersed."	____	____
. . . has a complex product mix."	____	____
. . . has many competitors."	____	____
. . . is subject to rapidly changing technology or services."	____	____
. . . has a technology-friendly culture."	____	____

Even after you have answered these questions and it appears that your answers are overwhelmingly in favor of establishing such a system, examine the costs and time involved in its maintenance.

"The key lesson," states Michael Sandman of Fuld & Company, "is to start modestly and to build slowly. Develop a network of people before trying to develop a network of computers. Have substantial resources available when the time comes to embark on a broad computerization program, and don't commit to that type of program until the competitor intelligence effort has a constituency that is pleased with the output."[9]

2. *Types of technology.* There are many ways to develop and store data—the same data—on a computer-based system. I have chosen to define these categories more along the lines of the hardware platform used (i.e., small PC-based system versus mainframe). Generally speaking, the smaller and simpler the system, the less expensive it is to develop and maintain.

PC-based. I have seen many PC-based intelligence databases that work perfectly fine and serve large numbers of people. Their drawback is a lack of information sharing. Stand-alone systems are also subject to loss of ownership; that is, the system's creator leaves the company or is transferred, and no one else has the time or the inclination to maintain it. On the other hand, today's powerful processors and storage drives can run a database and network that were reserved for large minicomputers only a few years ago.

Many network packages have been redesigned to fit onto PC-based systems. (A partial listing of some software and system vendors appears later in this chapter.)

Groupware. This new category led by Lotus Development Corporation's "Lotus Notes"™ package, is really an electronic umbrella that allows a string of computers to be tied together on a local area network (LAN) or a wide area network (WAN). This is an important innovation from the intelligence system's perspective. Anyone on that network can examine anyone else's data (provided there are no additional security codes). The Notes™ package, in particular, is easy to use and has received high marks from individuals who have incorporated it into

---

[9]"Computers and Computer Software for Competitive Intelligence," in Douglas Bernhardt, ed. *Perfectly Legal Competitor Intelligence* (Financial Times/Pitman Publishing, 1993), p. 215.

their intelligence programs. (Recent versions of Notes™ have made it even more functional and easier to use.)

Nevertheless, Notes™ is still not a turnkey system. It does require the help of information systems people to install and fine-tune the package. A host of software vendors have built database screening programs explicitly for Notes™, such as the Sandpoint Corporation's Hoover™ package. These packages work with Notes™ to scan large databases, selecting articles and records based on specific search criteria.

Large system (mainframe-based). In large corporations, there are still many mainframe-based information systems with excess capacity. Although mainframe systems usually come with equally large price tags, your company's Information Systems group may be looking for customers and will also take much of the system development headaches and time demands off your hands. In general, it appears that most intelligence systems are moving away from large systems and going toward smaller PC-based or groupware network approaches.

Voice and Electronic Mail (E-Mail). You might call these tools "intelligence system peripherals," rather than considering them the core of an intelligence program. From my experience, however, voice mail and E-mail are among the most powerful and severely underestimated weapons in your intelligence system's arsenal. Just ask any commodities trader who works for a multinational trading firm. Traders rely on E-mail to buy and sell many millions of dollars of goods every day. David Luther, former Senior Vice President—Quality at Corning, Inc., believes voice mail has opened up many communications channels at Corning and has sped up the overall information flow.

Tips for selecting the appropriate technology are in Figure 13.2.

3. *Using available technology.* Your company may have many of the necessary resources and software to begin a system. Before going outside to purchase a new software package, try to answer the following questions:

What packages and services does your information systems department offer?
Does your library already conduct Current Awareness or SDI searches?
What database management software exists in-house?

War Story: The Blind Man, The Elephant's Tail, and E-Mail

An intelligence manager for a large chemicals company has managed to build up an electronic mail routing list of over 700 colleagues located in offices around the globe. For many years, he has sent them news on the competition. In return, he asked that they reciprocate. As a result, each week he receives 20 to 30 messages. He compiles and edits all the messages he has received each month and sends the impromptu newsletter back to all 700 members of his intelligence network. Now instead of each contributor feeling like the blind man who was holding the tail of the elephant (thinking it was a snake), they see the entire beast—the entire competitive picture, that is.

INFORMATION PROFILE	VOICE MAIL	E-MAIL	GROUP-WARE	PC-BASED	LARGE SYSTEM
Small Organization	✓			✓	
Low Volume	✓	✓		✓	
High Volume	✓				✓
Few Products	✓	✓		✓	
Complex Product Mix	✓				✓
Few Competitors	✓			✓	
Many Competitors	✓				✓
Shared Markets & Competitors	✓	✓	✓		✓
Divisionally Separate Competitors	✓	✓		✓	✓
Stable Market	✓			✓	
Dynamic Market	✓	✓	✓		
Techno-Phobic	✓				
Techno-Friendly	✓	✓	✓	✓	✓

Figure 13.2   Checklist: How to select the appropriate technology.

Will a simple spreadsheet package adequately analyze your quantitative data?

Has another group already tested or begun using a groupware program? Can you tie into that system?

Does your E-mail system have a bulletin board capability?

Do you have the ability to broadcast information through your network of fax machines?

Is there an internal software/systems users group where you can learn of new applications or piggyback onto another person's software?

4. *Going outside.* Literally hundreds of database management and text management software packages are on the market. The following vendors have developed intelligence-specific applications:

Henco Software, Inc.
100 Fifth Ave.
Waltham, MA 02154
617-890-8670
(Package name: *Synchrony*™)

Lotus Development
55 Cambridge Parkway
Cambridge, MA 02142
617-577-8500
(Package name: *Lotus Notes*™)

Quest Management Systems, Inc.
580 Kirts Blvd., Suite 315
Troy, MI 48084
313-362-3770
(Package name: *Incite*™)

Sandpoint Corporation
One Canal Park
Cambridge, MA 02141
617-868-4442
(Package name: *Hoover*™)

Verity Corporation
1550 Plymouth St.
Mountain View, CA 94043
415-960-7600
(Package name: *TOPIC*™)

TIMING—REASONABLE EXPECTATIONS

The one piece of advice I offer any company that is about to start an intelligence system is: Take it slow. The best intelligence systems have taken at least three to five years to mature. It takes that amount of time to grow the internal networks and put the electronic systems in place.

As a general rule, start out the first year working with one group or business unit. Try not to take on the entire corporation. The first year will be a proving ground. You will learn where the political and organizational minefields are and how to avoid them, and how to motivate employees to contribute intelligence. Be especially vigilant for these minefields:

Technophiles vs. Technophobes. Within most large companies, there are two different cultures with respect to the use of information technology: (1) the technophiles (those who embrace and use technology) and (2) the technophobes (those for whom technology is either a giant gadget or a feared hobgoblin and who do not touch the keyboard).

Morale. Ideally, you want to establish an intelligence program (or any other program) in a company that has high morale. Conversely, in an organization where layoffs have taken place or where a company has just been bought and the acquired work force does not know where it stands, everyone will be wary and will erect many information barriers.

Staffing. You may need only one or two people dedicated to the task of intelligence management, but if the corporation cannot find those individuals and the jobs are divided up among many other people with many other jobs, the system's development will undoubtedly slow down, if not lose momentum altogether.

The solution to these problem areas begins with recognizing that they exist. Successful system designers avoid the one-size-fits-all approach. They see each organization in its own unique setting, and they shape the system accordingly.

A PLAN FOR GETTING STARTED

The first 6 to 12 months will be the most important ones for your intelligence system. This is the time when you have to establish the foundation and prepare the organization. Among your first steps should be the following:

1. *Write the mission statement.* You must clearly identify both the target audience and the goals for your intelligence system. What kind of intelligence do you expect to develop and for whom? Is your audience primarily senior management, or the sales force? Which business units will use the system?

2. *Raise awareness through bulletin boards and displays.* Find every opportunity to expose your organization to competitive information. Post news clippings and advertisements. Use displays of literature you may have come across at trade shows (see Chapter 11).

3. *Conduct the needs assessment audit.* Always take the intelligence pulse of the organization. Find out what your system users and suppliers need every day. In addition, take the opportunity, while conducting the assessment, to undertake an intelligence audit of the company. In this audit, identify privately maintained competitor files, names of internal experts, and other resources that may have an intelligence value.

4. *Provide incentives.* Find ways to offer recognition to those who provide the intelligence.

Customer Intelligence/Competitive Action

LEONARD FULD: As the packaged goods industry rapidly evolves, what types of intelligence will be most needed by brand leaders such as Quaker State or Campbell?

HERBERT BAUM: The essence of the packaged goods business in the 1990s and beyond is competitive leverage—real and/or perceived. Fast moving technology has made product parity a fact of life. You can only hold real product advantage for a short period of time. Then, your competition catches up.

This scenario is why the power of brands is so important. There is impenetrable leverage in a strong brand name. Nurture it and you will hold your leverage (vs. competition). Neglect it and your leverage will drop like a stone.

As we seek leverage beyond the power of our brand, we start with consumer intelligence. What benefits do consumers look for in our category? How can we position our product to be different from—and better than—the competition? Then, we begin working on delivering the advantage to consumers—in the product, in the package, in the price, in the marketing message.

Next, we scour the marketplace for every piece of competitive information we can get our hands on. We study their leverage. We research it versus what we're saying—to ensure we're more motivating than they are.

And finally, a comprehensive understanding of the retail environment and your customer base is absolutely essential. Know where the business potential is—and then, like a dog on a mailman's leg—go after the high-potential customers with marketing geared to their format, consistent product quality, and, above all, extraordinary customer service.

Herbert Baum is Chairman and CEO of Quaker State Corporation and former President of Campbell Soup USA.

Benchmarking: A Process of Involvement

LEONARD FULD: Where and when is benchmarking a most effective management tool?

DAVID LUTHER: Corning Incorporated has been an enthusiastic and frequent user of competitive intelligence. In fact, one of the major drivers of strategic change has been the commissioning of in-depth studies, using public information, to reveal market opportunities and competitive strengths and weaknesses. The results of these efforts have influenced decisions at the very highest level of the firm.

However, a newer and different approach to using competitor and market intelligence is now emerging that may, over time, have more impact than the studies mentioned above, and that is the use of benchmarking. Currently, virtually all descriptions of benchmarking focus on the search for the best practice and emphasize the need to pick the critical process within the organization, and understand what it does and how it does it, before seeking outside comparisons. This is very useful, and following the procedure is a key to success.

However, there are two other substantial benefits that do not get a great deal of attention. The first is the validation, or denial, of internal goals. Frequently, the goal-setting process within the firm is somewhat arbitrary, or, at best, is built on the internal experience of the firm. A good benchmarking effort can reveal whether a process is even worth pursuing by the firm. We would learn that even if we do all we say we will do, we will never be competitive, and should exit the event. That is very valuable information.

The second benefit is that the typical benchmarking effort can involve a cross-section of the organization that can be much more sensitive to briefly glimpsed marketplace advantages. A Corning team, intent on learning about training of customer service representatives, saw software in another company that was able to handle multiple orders from a single customer, when each of the orders was going to a different business. Customers are frequently impatient with a response that is incomplete simply because the data are in another part of the house. Corning's customer service representatives knew this and they knew that what they saw was valuable. Their term for this was "finding golden nuggets."

The bottom line is that this new use of competitive data helps to focus goals, helps to identify advantages that senior managers might miss, and gets the whole team involved.

David Luther is former Senior Vice President of Quality Relations at Corning, Inc. and currently president of Luther Quality Associates, a company considered a leader in implementing total quality management. He has spearheaded much of Corning's total quality and benchmarking efforts over the past decade.

5. *Decide on type and size of computer-based system.* Even for the most technologically sophisticated company, you should hold back on purchasing a software package or expanding an existing computer-based system until at least midyear in your trial period. Wait to see whether your people-based efforts have worked before turning to database development. You also need to spend time encouraging the organization to participate as contributors. I have seen some managers rush their information systems people to design a system. In the end, no one used it, because no one felt compelled to do so. Quite the opposite was true of Banc One and other companies where, at the beginning, the Ringmaster spent a great deal of time talking to the organization. Only after the organization accepts the concept and begins contributing to the program should computer-based systems be applied.

14 SECURITY: THE FLIP SIDE

Intelligence is a curious business. The more you gather competitive information and analyze it, the more you begin to realize that others may be doing the same to you. You and your competition constantly release information into the marketplace. You can never lock it all up, simply because of your need to conduct business. Yet, many companies recklessly expose far more information than they need to—critical information that they should be protecting. Are you one of them?

Can you lock up your company's market intentions? How much strategic business information can you secure?

Here is how one competitor's unintentional intelligence leak gave Hewlett-Packard a competitive advantage. A product manager at Hewlett-Packard was about to launch a new product, so he asked his company's meeting and planning department to book hotel dates for press announcements. Much to his surprise, the meeting department, after trying to arrange dates, told him his product's chief competitor had already booked space at most of the same hotels on the same dates. He then knew he had to shorten his roll-out plans for the new product by a few weeks.

The intelligence collected by Hewlett-Packard, accidental as the gathering may have been, started as another company's intelligence leak. This case should force you to ask a number of questions: Could this company have kept the information from Hewlett-Packard in the first place? Can your firm hope to stop vital competitor intelligence from leaking out? Where does—and where should—security end and decisive business action begin?

Adapted and excerpted from a presentation made by Leonard Fuld, "Competitor Intelligence: Can You Plug the Leaks?," to the American Society of Security Management and subsequently published in *Security Management* magazine, August 1989.

Most security managers are aware of the recent growth of formal corporate intelligence departments. Companies and their market research departments have taken up the task of researching their competition without planting bugs or stealing information. Marketing departments have earmarked budgets and hired analysts dedicated to uncovering competitive threats.

All this interest in competitor intelligence places an extra burden on the security manager to defend his or her company from leaks. How do you stop vital, often strategically critical information from leaving your company?

Ironically, my firm, Fuld & Company, Inc., specializes in obtaining competitive information for clients—information that security typically tries to stop me from having. Yet, I think it is fair to suggest that my business—that of intelligence gatherer—and your business of security are two sides of the same coin. In fact, the intelligence concept can, in certain cases, help you better protect your company's vital business activities.

What is a leak, and how does it relate to intelligence gathering? According to *Webster's New Collegiate Dictionary,* a leak is information that becomes known "despite efforts at concealment." By definition, therefore, leaks are pieces of information that a company tried to bottle up but could not. Can you plug some of the holes to prevent that information from leaking out in the first place?

As in the Hewlett-Packard case, most intelligence leaks are transmitted legally and ethically. In fact, some are even mandated by law. Here I include filings such as Environmental Protection Agency (EPA) notices, Securities and Exchange Commission (SEC) documents, regulatory forms, and thousands of others.

Other corporate information, while not mandated, will leak out in the course of doing business. Every handshake and business transaction can produce waves of information on a company. Some of that information is harmless; some is potentially dangerous, often giving valuable information on a competitor.

Much information will always leave your company, whether or not you have a successful security program in place. Some of these leaks include the following:

- *Gossip at a trade show.* When I think of trade shows, I have a mental picture of giant ears with little feet on them. Trade shows are gossip centers where a great deal of information is passed back and forth—some of it valuable, some of it useless. For this reason, trade shows offer the industry watcher plenty of grist for his or her intelligence mill.

  Often my firms' research assignments will take us to trade shows, where we attend seminars and take all the available literature. You can expect that your competitor also collects all available literature on your company.

- *Papers presented at a technical conference.* I know a technologist who regularly attends many scientific conferences in her field. By diligently listening to the technical experts present their papers, she can learn about a competitor's new product development efforts and overall strategic positioning. Her technical training gives her the ability to read between the lines. If a colleague at a competing company discusses a certain technology, she is able to interpret the use of that technology and the impact it may have on a competitor.

  You cannot stop these conferences from happening. Scientists and engineers need to exchange this information to grow professionally. Hence, they pass much information back and forth across the lectern.

- *Help-wanted advertisements.* Through their hiring process, companies send a lot of intelligence signals out into the marketplace. To hire employees, a company must disclose a wide range of operating details about its business. You should consider corporate help-wanted ads as nothing less than press releases. The information these ads contain includes financial information, research and development plans, organizational structure, and just about any aspect of a company.
- *Airplane discussions.* Airplanes offer a false sense of privacy. I have often heard a passenger shouting confidential information to another person in the next seat, to overcome the noise of the plane.
- *Supplier knowledge.* In certain industries, suppliers must sign confidentiality agreements. In others, suppliers are free to serve many companies and can talk about their experiences—to your company's detriment.
- *Sales pitches.* Sales presentations and the literature that accompanies them offer the intelligence gatherer a timely and specific source of new product information.
- *Company press releases.* Ask journalists about the number of press releases they receive each week, and you will see their eyeballs roll back into their heads. Most large companies publish a flurry of these releases, only to have a small number appear in print. However, for the savvy intelligence analyst, a press release may offer insight not easily obtained elsewhere. The question for the security manager is a tough one: How can you screen out the most damaging information? Or, will some of this intelligence always leak out?
- *Friendships, poker games, and off-site relationships.* Everyone, from shipping clerks to chief executives, talks about their businesses at restaurants, social clubs, and friends' houses. This chitchat can carry with it a lot of harmful information. I recall a pharmaceutical executive who told me that, although he had left one drug company a number of years ago to go to a competitor, he still meets with his buddies from the former company every Tuesday night for their weekly poker game. He told me that they always talk shop.

    Because such conversations were what originally brought members of this group together, it is natural they would want to continue talking about their industry. Harmless or not, poker games generate leaks.

Can you short-circuit these information channels? Unfortunately, many leaks are unstoppable.

No company, no matter how large and seemingly impenetrable, can block the flow of business information. Even IBM, often cited as the security manager's model company, discloses a great deal of information through its daily buying and selling. When buying desks, contracting with employment agencies, placing help-wanted ads, attending trade shows, and buying equipment for its research and development labs, IBM is forced to talk, specifically and clearly.

When any company contracts business, it has to disclose information. This is one reason why leaks occur. Can you stop these transactions? No, you cannot. You may be able to shut certain information avenues by, for example, asking suppliers to sign confidentiality agreements. But, as you might imagine, you cannot completely halt the information flow.

The implication of all this is that leaks are largely caused and transmitted by people—not exclusively by newspapers or other published sources. There are as many routes for these leaks as there are people in the company and the industry. Confidentiality agreements and stern lectures can certainly slow down—but cannot stop—the poker games and restaurant conversations.

Another reason you cannot stop most leaks is people's perceptions. Employees, in their workday world, consider most pieces of information they handle harmless. They do not worry about what they consider harmless information, especially since they have enough serious, obviously damaging information to protect. What they don't worry about, they don't watch. The information they do not watch will leave your company unquestioned and unchecked.

A skilled observer can assemble the bits and pieces of disjointed, seemingly harmless information into a larger, coherent whole. It is only when the puzzle is assembled that the information can become potentially harmful.

An example of these potentially harmless intelligence bits occurred in a project my company completed, in which a blueprint we retrieved from a town hall indicated an odd piece of machinery on the floor plan. The blueprint identified the machine by make and model number. We then called the machine's supplier, who gave us the name of the sales representative in the area. When we spoke to him, he told us the purpose of the machine and how the plant was using it.

Without the blueprint, we would not have discovered another process going on in the plant. Taken separately, both the blueprint and the sales representative had different and seemingly quite separate pieces of information. Pieced together, the information became intelligence that could give our client a competitive edge.

However, you may be able to slow down, if not stop, some of the information before it leaves your firm and causes harm. The following list is not comprehensive, but it does represent the thoughts of a professional intelligence gatherer and the advice that might be offered:

- *Review public relations documents or any other public documents your firm releases.* Almost every company needs a public relations effort to garner attention in the industry. Yet, that same effort can send into the competitive arena unnecessary information that could do your firm more harm than good.

  If possible, make sure your public relations department has its press releases screened by product managers. One security-minded president of a large aerospace company screens his key supplier's press releases as well as releases issued by his own firm.

- *Eliminate noncompliance information from filings.* Sometimes, companies file too much, thus revealing unnecessary information to the public and competitors. After we have made our proper Freedom of Information Act (FOIA) filing with a government agency to examine a particular contact file or EPA statement, we often discover that the company has overcomplied with government regulations. The outcome: We learn far more about that company's operations, cost structure, and so on, than we should.

  The federal government demands a great deal of disclosure from various companies in certain circumstances. Have your legal counsel examine those regulations carefully. Ask manufacturing personnel, or whoever is involved in submitting information for the filing, to list the data they would prefer withheld. Then, see if some of that information could be legally eliminated from the filing.

- *Start employee awareness programs.* Alert employees who attend trade shows to enter public arenas discreetly. Talking too loudly or too much is dangerous. You do not want to hamstring their sales efforts, but you must teach them to think of the cost of disclosing too much information at the wrong time.

The ultimate lesson is that you and your competitors have almost equal access to intelligence about each other. You may have intelligence leaks, but so does the company down the street. Everyone operates under the same intelligence rules.

The ultimate victor in the marketplace will be the company whose management can perform two intelligence activities well: (1) act on its competitors' leaks soonest, and (2) at the same time, slow down its own vital intelligence from quietly leaving the company.

A FORMULA FOR INTELLIGENCE LEAKS

No hard and fast rule exists that can measure the absolute number of damaging pieces of information leaving a company each day. Instead, this section offers you a barometer, a means of assessing the potential damage.

The formula reads as follows:

Calculation	Example	Rationale
Total company employees	60,000	You must include the entire company population because nearly everyone in the company is in contact with the outside world: Sales, many times each day; other staff jobs, far less each day.
25 percent of employees have frequent contact	15,000	A conservative estimate of the percentage of employees who have frequent contact with the business world each day.
Each member of the 25 percent group will make five phone calls or have five meetings with people outside the company during a typical workday	75,000 potential meetings or calls	This represents all the possible opportunities for information to leave a company through conversations. This calculation excludes all other data that may be sent via electronic means, such as fax, electronic mail, Internet, and voice mail.
Assumption: Only 1 percent of these calls can contain actual, damaging information	750 damaging calls daily	Some of these may have an immediate impact on the company; others may sit there, like time bombs, ticking away for a number of months or years before doing harm.
Number of leaks each year, assuming that there are 250 working days in the year	187,500 potentially harmful leaks, annually	This assumes that there are no overlapping leaks, carrying the same information.

Use this formula as a way to measure the negative impact your information-generating business activity can have on your business. I have seen information, buried in archives or in some conference paper presented years ago, come back to haunt the company that allowed the information to leave its offices. You might argue about the significance of the actual numbers cited above, but no matter what the final mathematical product, the resulting answer is clear: Companies must constantly strive to filter the information they allow the outside world to hear and see. Unless corporations and organizations can do so, they chance harming their own competitive initiatives, today and tomorrow.

ADDRESSES AND TELEPHONE NUMBERS OF PUBLISHERS AND SOURCES

A.M. Best Co.
Ambest Rd.
Oldwick, NJ 08858
TEL: 908-439-2200

A/S/M Communications Inc.
1515 Broadway, 37th Fl.
New York, NY 10036-6902
TEL: 212-764-7300

ADA Publishers Inc.
211 E. Chicago Ave.
Chicago, IL 60611
TEL: 312-440-2500

ADP Brokerage Information
    Services Group
2 Journal Sq. Plaza
Jersey City, NJ 07306
TEL: 201-714-3000

AG Publications Ltd.
P.O. Box 7422
Haifa 31070, Israel

ASM International
9639 Kinsman Rd.
Materials Park, OH
    44073-0002
TEL: 216-338-5151
FAX: 216-538-4634

AZ Bertelsmann GmbH
Carl-Bertelsmann-Str. 161
D-4830 Gutersloh 1, Germany
TEL: 011-49-5241 805473
FAX: 011-49-5241 76984

Advanstar Communications
7500 Old Oak Blvd.
Cleveland, OH 44130-3369
TEL: 216-243-8100
FAX: 216-891-2651

Advertisers & Publishers
    Service Inc.
6300 N. River Rd., Ste. 505
Rosemont, IL 60018
TEL: 708-823-3145

Aerospace Industries
    Association of America
1250 Eye St., NW
Washington, DC 20005-3922
TEL: 202-371-8400

Agency for International
    Development
320 21st St., NW
Washington, DC
TEL: 202-647-9137

Agricultural Products
    Inspection Office
117-2 Kwanhun-dong,
    Chongro-ku
Seoul, Korea
TEL: 011-82-2-70-4518

Air Cargo Inc.
1819 Bay Ridge Ave.
Annapolis, MD 21403
TEL: 410-280-5576

Air Science Co.
Learned Info Inc.,
    143 Old Marlton Pike
Medford, NJ 08055
TEL: 609-657-4888

All China Federation of
    Industry and Commerce
93 Beiheyan Dajie
Beijing, China
TEL: 011-86-1-501-6677
FAX: 011-86-1-512-2631

Allerton Press, Inc.
150 Fifth Ave.
New York, NY 10011
TEL: 212-294-3950
FAX: 212-463-9684

Alliance Francaise
2142 Wyoming Ave.
Washington, DC 20008
TEL: 202-234-7911
15 Ct. Sq.
Boston, MA 02108
TEL: 617-523-4423

Aluminum Association
900 19th St., NW, Ste. 300
Washington, DC 20006
TEL: 202-862-5100

America Online, Inc.
8619 Westwood Center Dr.
Vienna, VA 22182
TEL: 703-448-8700:
    800-227-6364

American Advertising
  Federation
1400 K St., NW, Ste. 1000
Washington, DC 20005-2471
TEL: 202-898-0089

American Apparel
  Contractors Association
P.O. Box 720693
Atlanta, GA 30358
TEL: 404-843-3171

American Apparel
  Manufacturers Association
2500 Wilson Blvd., Ste. 301
Arlington, VA 22201
TEL: 703-524-1864

American Association for the
  Advancement of
Science Directorate for
Intl Programs
1333 H St., NW
Washington, DC 20005
TEL: 202-326-6400

American Association of
  Advertising Agencies
666 Third Ave., 13th Fl.
New York, NY 10017
TEL: 212-682-2500

American Banker
One State St. Plaza
New York, NY 10004
TEL: 212-943-6700

American Bankers Association
1120 Connecticut Ave., NW
Washington, DC 20036
TEL: 202-663-5000

American Bureau of Metal
  Statistics
400 Plaza Dr.
P.O. Box 1405
Secaucus, NJ 07094-0405
TEL: 201-863-6900

American Business
  Information Inc.
5711 S. 86th Cir.
P.O. Box 27347
Omaha, NE 68127
TEL: 402-593-4600
FAX: 402-331-1505

American Center Library
ABC Bldg., 20603 Siba, Koen
Minato-ku, Tokyo, Japan
TEL: 011-81-33-436-0901

American Chamber of
  Commerce France
21, ave. George V
75008 Paris, France
TEL: 011-33-1-47-23-80-26

American Chamber of
  Commerce Germany
Executive Office, P.O. Box
  100162, Rossmarkt 12
D-6000 Frankfurt am Main
  1, Germany
TEL: 011-49-69-283401
FAX: 011-49-69-285632

American Chamber of
  Commerce Italy
Via Cantu 1
I-20123 Milan, Italy
TEL: 011-39-2-869-0661
FAX: 011-39-2-805-7737

American Chamber of
  Commerce Japan
Fukide Bldg. #2, 4-1-21,
  Toranomon 4-chome
Minato-ku, Tokyo 105, Japan
TEL: 011-81-33-436-0901

American Chamber of
  Commerce Korea
3rd Fl., 307 Westin Chosin
  Hotel
87 Sokang-dong Chung-ku
Seoul 100, Korea
TEL: 011-82-2-752-3061;
  753-6471
FAX: 011-82-2-755-6577

American Chemical Society
1155 Sixteenth St., NW
Washington, DC 20036
TEL: 202-872-4600
FAX: 202-872-4615

American College of
  Healthcare Executives
840 N. Lake Shore Dr.,
  Ste. 1103 W.
Chicago, IL 60611
TEL: 312-943-0544

American Consulate, Japan
5-26 Ohori
2-chome, Chuo-ku, Fukuoka,
  Japan
TEL: 011-81-92-751-9331

American Council of Life
  Insurance
1001 Pennsylvania Ave., NW
Washington, DC 20004
TEL: 202-624-2000

American Dental Trade
  Association
422 King St., W.
Alexandria, VA 22302-1597
TEL: 703-379-7755
FAX: 703-379-7755

American Electronics
  Association - Japan
Kioicho 3-3
Chiyoda-ku, Tokyo 102, Japan
TEL: 011-81-33-237-7195
FAX: 011-81-237-1237

American Electronics
  Association - U.S.
5201 Great America Pkwy.,
  Ste. 520
Santa Clara, CA 95054
TEL: 408-987-4200

American Embassy, France
2 Ave. Gabriel
Paris 75382, France
TEL: 011-33-1-42-96-12-02

American Embassy, Germany
Deichmanns Aue 29
D-5300 Bonn 2
TEL: 011-49-228-339-3391

American Embassy, Italy
Via Vittorio Veneto 119/A
00187 Rome, Italy
TEL: 011-39-6-467411

American Embassy, UK
24/31 Grosvenor Sq.
London W1A 1AE, England
TEL: 011-44-71-499-9000

American Financial Services
Association
1101 14th St., NW
Washington, DC 20005
TEL: 202-289-0400

American Graduate School of
International Management
Thunderbird Management
Center
Glendale, AZ 85306
TEL: 602-978-7115

American Health Care
Association
1201 L St., NW
Washington, DC 20005
TEL: 202-842-4444

American Hospital
Association
840 N. Lake Shore Dr.
Chicago, IL 60611
TEL: 312-280-6155
FAX: 312-280-5979

American Hotel & Motel
Association
1201 New York Ave., NW,
Ste. 600
Washington, DC 20005-3917
TEL: 202-289-3100
FAX: 202-289-3199

American Hotel Association
Directory Corp.
1201 New York Ave., NW
Washington, DC 20005
TEL: 202-289-3100

American Institute of
Aeronautics & Astronautics
(AIAA)
370 L'Enfant Promenade, SW
Washington, DC 20024-2518
TEL: 202-646-7400
FAX: 202-646-7508
ATTN: Michael Lewis, The
Aerospace Center

American Institute of CPAs
1211 Ave. of the Americas
New York, NY 10036-8775
TEL: 212-575-6200

American Iron and Steel
Institute
1101 17th St., NW, Ste. 1300
Washington, DC 20036-4700
TEL: 202-452-7100
FAX: 202-463-6573

American Machine Tool
Distributors Association
1335 Rockville Pike, Ste. 300
Rockville, MD 20852-1400
TEL: 301-738-1200
FAX: 301-738-9499

American Managed Care
Pharmacy Association
(AMCPA)
2300 9th St., S., Ste. 210
Arlington, VA 22204
TEL: 703-920-8480

American Meat Institute
1700 N. Moore St., Ste. 1600
Arlington, VA 22209-1995
TEL: 703-841-2400
FAX: 703-527-0938

American Paper Institute
260 Madison Ave.
New York, NY 10016
TEL: 212-340-0600
FAX: 212-689-2628

American Petroleum Institute
1220 L St., NW
Washington, DC 20005-4070
TEL: 202-682-8000
FAX: 202-682-8030

American Petroleum Institute
275 7th Ave., 9th Fl.
New York, NY 10001
TEL: 212-366-4040

Central Abstracting &
Information Services
American Public Power
Association
2301 M St., NW
Washington, DC 20037-1484
TEL: 202-775-8300
FAX: 202-467-2910

American Society for
Personnel Administration
ASPA/International
606 N. Washington St.
Alexandria, VA 22314
TEL: 703-548-3440

American Society of Hospital
Pharmacists
4630 Montgomery Ave.
Bethesda, MD 20814
TEL: 301-657-3000

American Textile
Manufacturers Institute
1801 K St., NW, Ste. 900
Washington, DC 20006-1301
TEL: 202-862-0500
FAX: 202-862-0570

American Trade Center,
Commercial Unit
600 Min Chuan E. Rd.
Taipei, Japan
TEL: 011-886-2-713-2571
FAX: 011-886-2-718-1482

American Translators
Association
1735 Jefferson Davis Hwy.,
Ste. 903
Arlington, VA 22202
TEL: 703-412-1500

American Warehouseman's
Association
1300 W. Higgins, Ste. 111
Park Ridge, IL 60068
TEL: 708-292-1891

American-Indonesian
Chamber of Commerce
711 Third Ave., 17th Fl.
New York, NY 10017
TEL: 212-687-4505

Appliance Manufacturers
5900 Harper Rd., Ste. 105
Solon, OH 44139
TEL: 212-349-3060

Arbeitskreis Deutscher
Marktforschungsinstitut e.V.
(ADM)
Papenkamp 2-6
D-2410 Molln, Germany
TEL: 011-49-4542-801-0

Argus Press Holdings, Inc.
6151 Powers Ferry Rd., NW
Atlanta, GA 30339-2941
TEL: 404-955-2500

Arkansas Bankers Association
221 W. 2nd St., Ste. 1027
Little Rock, AR 72201
TEL: 501-376-3741

Arthur D. Little Decisions
   Resources
17 New England Executive
   Park
Burlington, MA 01803
TEL: 617-270-1207
FAX: 617-273-3048

Asahi Research Center
Imperial Tower Bldg., 1-1-1
   Uchisaiwaicho
Chiyoda-ku, Tokyo 100, Japan
TEL: 011-81-33-507-2406
FAX: 011-81-33-279-1308

Asahi Shimbun
5-3-2 Tsukiji
Chuo-ku, Tokyo 104-11, Japan
TEL: 011-81-33-545-0131
FAX: 011-81-33-545-0239

Asahi Shimbun International
   Inc.
757 Third Ave.
New York, NY 10017
TEL: 800-666-0170
FAX: 212-755-3908

Asia Pacific Communications,
   Corp.
27 E. 61st St.
New York, NY 10021
TEL: 212-935-6727
FAX: 212-935-6755

Asia Press Company,
   Ltd./CRC Press, Inc.
2000 Corporate Blvd., NW
Boca Raton, FL 33431
TEL: 800-272-7737

Asia Society, The
725 Park Ave.
New York, NY 10021
TEL: 212-288-6400

Asia Systems Media, Inc.
2530 Corporate Pl., Ste. A111
Monterey Park, CA 91754
TEL: 213-722-1553

Asian Finance Publications,
   Ltd.
3/F Hollywood Centre,
   233 Hollywood Rd.
Hong Kong
TEL: 011-582-815-5221
FAX: 011-582-854-2794

Asian Sources Publications
   Ltd.
Reader Services Dept.,
   G.P.O. Box 8952
Hong Kong
TEL: 011 5815 5221
FAX: 011 5854 2794

Associated Equipment
   Distributors
615 W. 22nd St.
Oak Brook, IL 60521
TEL: 708-574-0650
FAX: 708-574-0132

Association for Computing
   Machinery
1515 Broadway
New York, NY 10036-9998
TEL: 212-869-7440
FAX: 212-944-1318

Association for the
   Advancement of Medical
   Instrumentation
3330 Washington Blvd.,
   Ste. 400
Arlington, VA 22201-4598
TEL: 800-332-2264

Association of British
   Chambers of Commerce
9 Tufton St.
London SW1P 3QB, England
TEL: 011-44-71-2221555

Association of Certified
   Accountants
29 Lincoln's Inn Fields
London WC2A 3EE, England
TEL: 011-44-71-242-6855

Association of Finance
   Companies
3rd Fl., Sinthorn Bldg.,
   Wireless Rd.
Bangkok 10500, Thailand
TEL: 011-66-2-2500129

Association of Home
   Appliance Manufacturers
20 N. Wacker Dr., Ste. 1500
Chicago, IL 60606
TEL: 312-984-5800

Association of Independent
   Corrugator Converters
P.O. Box 25708
Alexandria, VA 22313
TEL: 703-836-2422

Association of International
   Trading Companies
394/14 Samsen Rd.
Bangkok 10300, Thailand
TEL: 011-66-2-2800951

Association of Iron and Steel
   Engineers
3 Gateway Center, Ste. 2350
Pittsburgh, PA 15222-1004
TEL: 412-281-6323

Association of Steel
   Distributors
401 N. Michigan Ave.
Chicago, IL 60611-4267
TEL: 312-644-6610

Aster Publishing Corp.
859 Willamette St., Box 10460
Eugene, OR 97440-2460
TEL: 503-343-1200
FAX: 503-344-3514

Aussenhandelsvereinigung des
   Deutschen
Einzelhandels e.V. (AVE)
Mauritiasseinweg #1
(German Retailers' Export
   Association)
50676 Cologne, Germany
TEL: 011-49-221-21-66-17
FAX: 011-49-221-24-39-65

Automotive Information
Council
13505 Dulles Technology Dr.
Herndon, VA 22071-3415
TEL: 703-713-0700

Automotive Market Research
Council
300 Sylvan Ave., P.O. Box 1638
Englewood Cliffs, NJ 07632
TEL: 313-977-1160

Automotive Service Industry
Association
444 N. Michigan Ave.
Chicago, IL 60611-3975
TEL: 312-836-1300

Automotive Warehouse
Distributors Association
9140 Ward Pkwy.
Kansas City, MO 64114
TEL: 816-444-3500

BIOSIS
2100 Arch St.
Philadelphia, PA 19103-1399
TEL: 800-523-4806
FAX: 215-587-2016

BMT Publishing Inc.
7 Penn Plaza
New York, NY 10001-3900
TEL: 212-594-4120

BPI Communications, Inc.
49 Music Sq., W., Box 24970
Nashville, TN 37202
TEL: 615-321-4250
FAX: 615-327-1575

BRS Information Technologies
8000 Westpark Dr.
McLean, VA 22102
TEL: 703-442-0900
FAX: 703-893-4632

Banca Commerciale Italiana,
SpA
Piazza Della Scala 6
21021 Milan, Italy
TEL: 011-39-2-88501

Banca d'Italia
Via Nazionale 91
00184 Rome, Italy
TEL: 011-39-6-47921

Banco di Roma, SpA
180 Viale Tupini 180
00144 Rome, Italy
TEL: 011-39-6-5451

Bank Administration Institute
Foundation
One N. Franklin St.
Chicago, IL 60606-0943
TEL: 312-553-4600

Bank Marketing Association
1120 Connecticut Ave., NW
Washington, DC 20036
TEL: 202-663-5268
FAX: 202-828-4540

Bank News
912 Baltimore Ave.
Kansas City, MO 64105
TEL: 816-421-7941
FAX: 816-472-0397

Bank of China (State Bank)
(China)
Bank of China Bldg.
410 Fuchengmen Nei Dajie
Beijing, China
TEL: 011-86-1-668941

Bank of China (State
Bank)   (US)
410 Madison Ave.
New York, NY 10017
TEL: 212-935-3101
FAX: 212-593-1831

Bank of China Trust Company
and Consultancy
Department
17 Xijiaomin Xiang
Beijing, China
TEL: 011-86-1-6543431x339

Bank of Communications
(Commercial Bank)
200 Jiang Xi Rd.
Shanghai, China
TEL: 011-86-21-213400

Bank of England
Treadneedle St.
London EC2R 8AH, England
TEL: 011-44-71-601-4444

Bank of Korea (Central Bank
in U.S.)
767 Third Ave., 31st Fl.
New York, NY 10017
TEL: 212-759-5121

Bank of Scotland
Uberior House
Edinburgh EH1 2JF
TEL: 011-44-31-243-5769
FAX: 011-44-31-243-5660

Bank of Scotland (U.S.)
380 Madison Ave.
New York, NY 10017
TEL: 212-490-8030
FAX: 212-557-9460

Bankers Digest
6440 N. Central Expressway,
Ste. 215
Dallas, TX 75206-4191
TEL: 214-373-4544
FAX: 214-373-4545

Bankers Monthly
200 W. 57th St., 15th Fl.
New York, NY 10019-3211
TEL: 212-399-1084

Banque Nationale de Paris SA
16 Blvd. des Italiens
75009 Paris, France
TEL: 011-33-1-42-44-45-46

Banque de France
1 rue de la Vrilliere
75001 Paris, France
TEL: 011-33-1-42-92-36-10

Barclays Bank
54 Lombard St.
London EC3P 5AB, England
TEL: 011-44-71-283-8989

Barclays Bank (U.S.)
75 Wall St.
New York, NY 10265
TEL: 212-412-4000

Basin Capital Markets
Research Center
University of Rhode Island-
Pacific, College of BA
Kingston, RI 02881-0802
TEL: 401-792-5105; 5807
FAX: 401-792-4312

Battelle Memorial Institute
505 King Ave.
Columbus, OH 43201
TEL: 614-424-6424
FAX: 614-424-5263

Beijing Economic
  Development Corporation
1 Dong Dajie, Changmenwai,
  PO Box 6201
Beijing, China
TEL: 011-86-1-753680

Beijing Exhibition Center
Xizhimenwai Dajie
Beijing, China
TEL: 011-86-1-890611

Beijing Exhibition Service
Bldg. #1, Beijing Exhibition
  Ctr. W.
Beijing, China
TEL: 011-86-1-890541 x487

Beijing Import and Export
  Control Committee
People's Court Bldg.,
  Wangfujing Dajie
Nan Kou, Beijing, China
TEL: 011-86-1-556106

Berlin Economic
  Development Corp.
185 Devonshire St.
Boston, MA 02210
TEL: 617-556-8890

Berlin Economic
  Development Corp.
456 Montgomery St., Ste. 1010
San Francisco, CA 94104
TEL: 415-788-0785

Berliner Industriebank
Landeckerstrasse2
1000 Berlin 33, Germany
TEL: 011-49-30-820030
FAX: 011-49-30-8243003

Bernan-Unipub
4611-F Assembly Dr.
Lanham, MD 20706
TEL: 301-459-7666

Bertelsmann
  InformationsService GmbH
Landsberger Str. 191a
D-8000 Munich 21, Germany
TEL: 011-49-89 5795220
FAX: 011-49-89 5706693

Bethlehem Books
915 W. 13th St.
Vancouver, WA 98660
TEL: 206-695-8647

Beverage Marketing
  Corporation
850 Third Ave.
New York, NY 10022
TEL: 212-688-7640
FAX: 212-826-1255

Bill Communications, Inc.
633 3rd Ave., 32nd Fl.
New York, NY 10017-6798
TEL: 212-986-2235; 5807
FAX: 212-370-7841

Billboard Publications Inc.
1515 Broadway
New York, NY 10036
TEL: 212-764-7300

Board of Governors of the
  Federal Reserve System
Public Services - #M5138
Washington, DC 20551-0001
TEL: 202-452-3000

Bowker A&I Publishing
121 Chanlon Rd.
New Providence, NJ 07974
TEL: 908-665-6688

Bresser's Cross-Index
  Directory Company
684 W. Baltimore St.
Detroit, MI 48202
TEL: 313-874-0570

Bridge Information Systems,
  Inc.
717 Office Pkwy.
St. Louis, MO 63141
TEL: 314-432-5347
FAX: 314-432-5391

British Consulate General
126 E. 56th St., Tower 56,
  14th Fl.
New York, NY 10022
TEL: 212-265-8888

British Consultants Bureau
1 Westminster Palace Gardens
1-7 Artillery Row, London
SW1P 1RJ
TEL: 011-44-71-222-3651;
  0234

British Embassy
3100 Massachusetts Ave., NW
Washington, DC 20008
TEL: 202-462-1340

British Export Houses
  Association
16 Dartmouth St.
London SW1H 9BL, England
TEL: 011-44-71-222-5419
FAX: 011-44-71-799-2206

British Library, The
25 Southhampton Bldg.
London WC2A 1AW, England
TEL: 011-44-323-7924/5
FAX: 011-44-71-323-7965

British Standards Institute
2 Park St.
London W1A 2BS, England
TEL: 011-44-71-629-9000

British Telecommunications
  PLC -
BT Telecom Gold
Bindley Way, Apsley
Hemel Hampstead, Herts.
  HP3 9RR, England
TEL: 011-44-42 237559

Bundesamt fur Emahrung
  und Forstwirtschaft
(BEF)
(Federal Office for Food &
  Forestry)
Adickesallee 40, Postfach 18
02 03
D-6000 Frankfurt am Main
  18, Germany
TEL: 011-49-69-15-64-0
FAX: 011-49-69-15-64-445

Bundesamt fur Wirtschaft
(BAW)
(Federal Office for Trade &
Industry)
Frankfurterstrasse 29-31,
Postfach 51 71
D-6236 Eschborn 1, Germany
TEL: 011-49-6196-404-1
FAX: 011-49-6196-404-212

Bundesstelle fur
Aussenhandelsinformation
(BfAI)
Blaubach 13, Postfach 10 80 07
D-5000 Cologne 1, Germany
TEL: 011-49-221-20-57-1
FAX: 011-49-221-20-57-212

Bundesverband Deutscher
Banken e.V.
(Federal Association of
German Banks)
Mohrenstrasse 35-41, Postfach
10 02 46
D-5000 Cologne 1, Germany
TEL: 011-49-221-166-32-20

Bundesverband de Deutschen
Industrie (BDI)
(Federal Association of
German Industry)
Gustav-Heinemann-Ufer
84-88, Postfach 51 05 48
D-5000 Cologne 51, Germany
TEL: 011-49-221-37-08-00
FAX: 011-49-221-37-08-73

Bundesvereinigung de
Deutschen
Arbeitsgeberverbande (BDA)
(Confederation of German
Employers' Associations)
Gustav Heinemann-Ufer 72,
Postfach 510 508
D-5000 Cologne 51, Germany
TEL: 011-49-221-379-50

Bureau of National Affairs Inc.
1231 25th St., NW
Washington, DC 20037
TEL: 202-452-4200
FAX: 202-822-8092

Business Communications
Company, Inc.
25 Van Zant St., Ste. 13
Norwalk, CT 06855-1781
TEL: 203-853-4266
FAX: 203-853-0348

Business Journals Inc.
50 Day St., P.O. Box 5550
Norwalk, CT 06856
TEL: 203-853-6015

Business Trend Analysts, Inc.
2171 Jericho Turnpike
Comack, NY 11725
TEL: 516-462-5454
FAX: 516-462-1842

C.C. Crow Publications
Box 25749
Portland, OR 97255
TEL: 503-646-8075

CAB International (CABI)
Wallingford, Oxon, OX10
8DE, England
TEL: 044-491-32111
FAX: 04-491-33508

CDA Investment
Technologies
1355 Piccard Dr.
Rockville, MD 20850
TEL: 800-232-2285
FAX: 301-975-9600

CERVED
Via Appia Nuova, 696
1-00179 Rome, Italy
TEL: 011-39-6-780541
FAX: 011-39-6-780541

CHI Research/Computer
Horizons, Inc.
10 White Horse Pike
Haddon Heights, NJ 08035
TEL: 609-546-0600

CMA Testing and Certification
Laboratories, The
Rm. 1401-3 Yan Hing Centre
9-13 Wong chuk Yeung St.
Fo Tan, Shatin, New
Territories, China
TEL: 011-852-698-8198
FAX: 011-852-695-4177

CMP Publications Co.
600 Community Dr.
Manhasset, NY 11030
TEL: 516-365-4600

COMLINE International Corp.
Meiji Bldg., 1F
1-5-15, Jinnan, Shibuya-ku,
Tokyo 150, Japan
TEL: 011-81-33-7705506
FAX: 011-81-03-377-05501

CPS Communications Inc.
7200 W. Camino Real, Ste. 215
Boca Raton, FL 33433
TEL: 407-368-9301

CUC International/
Comp-U-Card Division
707 Summer St.
Stamford, CT 06904-2094
TEL: 203-324-9261
see also Compu Serve

CW Publishing Inc.
375 Cochituate Rd.
Framingham, MA 01701-9171
TEL: 508-879-0700

Cahners Publishing Company
275 Washington St.
Newton, MA 02158-1630
TEL: 617-964-3030

California Business News Inc.
221 Main St., Ste. 700
San Francisco, CA
90010-3594
TEL: 213-937-5820

Cambridge Information Group
7200 Wisconsin Ave.
Bethesda, MD 20814
TEL: 301-961-6750

Cambridge Scientific Abstracts
7200 Wisconsin Ave., Ste. 601
Bethesda, MD 20814
TEL: 301-961-6750

Capan Convention Bureau/
National Tourist
Organization
Rockefeller Plaza,
630 Fifth Ave.
New York, NY
TEL: 212-757-5640
FAX: 212-307-6754

Capital Cities/ABC, Inc.
825 Seventh Ave., Box 640
New York, NY 10019-6014
TEL: 212-887-8560

Cassa di Risparmio Delle
    Provincie Lombarde
Via Monte de Pieta 8
20100 Milan, Italy
TEL: 011-39-2-88661

Cassell PLC
Publishers Distr. Ctr.,
    PO Box C-831
Rutherford, NJ 07070
TEL: 201-939-6064

Centaur Publications Ltd.
50 Poland St.
London W1V 4AX, England
TEL: 011-44-71-439-4222
FAX: 011-44-71-439-9669

Center for European
    Community Studies -
George Mason University
Ste. 450, 4001 N. Fairfax Dr.
Arlington, VA 22203
TEL: 703-993-1000
FAX: 703-875-0122

Center for Japan-US Business
    & Economic Studies
New York University
44 W. 4th St., MEC Ste. 7-190
New York, NY 10012
TEL: 212-998-0750
FAX: 212-995-4219

Center for Japanese Studies &
    East Asian Business
    Program
University of Michigan,
    108 Lane Hall
Ann Arbor, MI 48109
TEL: 313-764-6307;
    313-764-0383
FAX: 313-936-2948

Center for Japanese Studies &
    Far Asian Business Programs
University of Michigan,
    108 Lane Hall
Ann Arbor, MI 48109-1290
TEL: 313-764-6307

Central Bank - People's Bank
    of China
17 Xijiaomin Xiang
Beijing, China
TEL: 011-86-1-653431

Central Statistical Office
Cardiff Rd.
Newport, Gwent NP9 1XG,
    England
TEL: 011-44-633-812973

Central Statistical Office/
    Publications Centre
P.O. Box 276
London SW8 5DT, England
TEL: 011-44-71-873-8466

Centre for European Business
    Information
Greater London Business
    Centre
Bastille Ct., #2 Paris Garden
London SE1 8ND, England
TEL: 011-44-71-261-1163

Century Hallmark
6201 W. Howard St.
Miles, IL 60714
TEL: 708-647-1200

Charles W. Henderson
P.O. Box 5528
Atlanta, GA 30307-0528
TEL: 800-633-4931;
    205-991-6920
FAX: 205-995-1588

Chemical Abstracts Service
2540 Olentangy River Rd.,
    PO Box 3012
Columbus, OH 43210-0012
TEL: 614-447-3600

Chemical Manufacturers
    Association
2501 M St., NW
Washington, DC 20037
TEL: 202-887-1100

Chemical Week Associates
888 Seventh Ave., 26th Fl.
New York, NY 10106
TEL: 212-621-4900
FAX: 212-621-4949

Chilton Book Company
One Chilton Way
Radnor, PA 19089
TEL: 215-964-4000

China Academic Press
POB 1511
137 Chaonei St., Beijing,
    China
TEL: 011-86-1-513-2862

China Chamber of
    International Commerce
    and China
4301 Connecticut Ave., NW,
    Ste. 193
Washington, DC 20008
TEL: 202-244-3244
FAX: 202-244-0478

China Council for the
    Promotion of International
    Trade (CCPIT) (US)
4301 Connecticut Ave., NW,
    Ste. 139
Washington, DC 20008
TEL: 202-244-3244
FAX: 202-244-0478

China Council for the
    Promotion of International
    Trade (China)
1 Fu Zing Men Wai St., PO
    Code 100860
Beijing, China
TEL: 011-86-8013866

China Credit Information
    Service, Ltd.
POB 22297 9F,
    30 Kuangyuan Rd., 7th Fl.
Taipei, Taiwan
TEL: 011-886-2-381-0720
FAX: 011-886-2-314-2967

China Daily Distribution Corp.
15 Mercer St.
New York, NY 10013
TEL: 212-219-0130

China Economic News
    Service (CENS)
POB 43-60 4F, 561
    Chunghsiaso Rd., Sec. 4
Taipei 10516, Taiwan
TEL: 011-886-2-765-2445
FAX: 011-886-2-762-9143

China Exhibition Agency
25A Dongsi Shitiao
Beijing, China
TEL: 011-86-1-444627

China Export Bases - Fujian
  Branch
1 Shangbin Lu
Fuzhou, China
TEL: 011-86-1-34068

China Export Bases -
  Shanghai Branch
27 Zhongshan Dong Yi Lu
Shanghai, China
TEL: 011-86-21-214617

China Export Commodities
  Fair (CECF)
Guangzhou Foreign Trade Ctr.,
  117 Lui Hua Rd.
Guangzhou, China
TEL: 011-86-677000

China External Trade
  Development Council
  (CETRA)
4/8F, No. 333 Keelung Rd.,
  Section 1
Taipei 10548, Taiwan
TEL: 011-886-2-738-2345;
  725-5200
FAX: 011-886-2-757-6653

China Institute in America
125 E. 65th St.
New York, NY 10021
TEL: 212-744-8181

China International Economic
  and Trade
Arbitration Commission
1 Fuzingmenwai
Beijing, China
TEL: 011-86-862966/8013344

China International Trust and
  Investment Corporation
  (CITIC)
19 Jiangnomenwai Dajie
Beijing, China
TEL: 011-86-1-500-2255
FAX: 011-86-1-500-1535

China National Chartering
  Corporation
  (SINOCHART)
Import Bldg., Erligou, Xijiao
Beijing, China
TEL: 011-86-1-890931

China National Technical
  Import Corporation
Erligou, Xijiao
Beijing, China
TEL: 011-86-1-890931

China National Tourist Office
60 E. 42nd St.
New York, NY 10165-0163
TEL: 212-867-0271

China Patent and Trademark
  Agent (USA) Ltd.
One World Trade Ctr.,
  Ste. 2551
New York, NY 10048
TEL: 212-912-1870

China Phone Book Company
GPO Box 11581
Hong Kong

China Productivity Center
North Rd.
Taipei, Taiwan
TEL: 011-886-2-713-7731

China Statistical Information
  and Consultancy Center
  (CTIC)
POB 443, Spring Gardens
Manchester M60 1HF,
  England
TEL: 061-228-0420

Chinese Export Commodities
  Fair
Guangzhou Foreign Trade
  Center,
Guangzhou Customs Admin.
Xi Changan Jie, Beijing,
  China
TEL: 011-86-20-556105/
  5579984

Chinese Manufacturers
  Association of Hong Kong,
  The
1/F, CMA Bldg.,
  64 Connaught Rd.
Central, Hong Kong
TEL: 011-852-541-6166
FAX: 011-852-541-4541

Chinese National Association
  of Industry & Commerce
Yu-Ming Manson
7 Roosevelt Rd., 4th Fl.,
  Section 1
Taipei, Taiwan
TEL: 011-886-2-351-2161

Chinese People's Association
  for Friendship with
  Foreign Countries
1 Tai Ji Chang St.
Beijing, China
TEL: 011-86-54010

Citicorp Database Services
88 Pine St., 16th Fl.
New York, NY 10005
TEL: 212-898-7200;
  800-842-8405
FAX: 212-742-8956

City Bank of Taipei
50 Chung Shan N. Rd.,
  Section 2
Taipei, Taiwan
TEL: 011-886-2-542-5656

City Publishing Company
118 S. Eighth St.
Independence, KS 67301
TEL: 316-331-2650

Cole Publications
901 Bond St.
Lincoln, NE 68521
TEL: 402-475-4591

College of Engineering
  University of Wisconsin -
  Madison
1500 Johnson Dr.,
  1018 Research Bldg.
Madison, WI 53706
TEL: 608-263-2191

Japan Engineering
  Leadership Program
Columbia Books, Inc.
1212 New York Ave., NW #330
Washington, DC 20850-3243
TEL: 202-898-0662

Columbia Communications Inc.
370 Lexington Ave.
New York, NY 10017
TEL: 212-532-9290

Commerzbank AG
Neue Mainzer Strasse 32-36
6000 Frankfurt 1, Germany
TEL: 011-49-69-1362-1

Commission des Operations
  de Bourse (COB)
Tour Mirabeau 39-43, Quai
  Andre Citroen
F 75739 Paris Cedex 15,
  France
TEL: 011-33-1-40-58-65-65

Commissione Nazionale per le
  Societa e la Borsa
(National Commission for
  Corporations and the Stock
  Exchange (CONSOB))
Via Isonzo 19
00184 Rome, Italy
TEL: 011-39-6-84771

Commissioner of Banking
  (Hong Kong)
Queensway Government
  Office Bldg.
66 Queensway
Central, Hong Kong
TEL: 011-852-862-2671

CommuniCorp., London House
19 Old Ct. Pl.
Kensington, London W8 4PO,
  England
TEL: 011-44-71-938-2222

Communication Channels Inc.
6255 Barfield Rd., NE
Atlanta, GA 30328
TEL: 404-256-9800

Communications Industry
  Association of Japan
Sankei Bldg., Annex 7-2,
  1-chome
Ohte-machi, Chiyoda-ku,
  Tokyo 100, Japan
TEL: 011-81-33-231-3156
FAX: 011-81-33-246-0495

Companies Registration
  Office (CRO) - Northern
  Ireland
IDB House, Chichester St.
Belfast, BT1 4JX, Northern
  Ireland
TEL: 011-44-232-234488

CompuServe Information
  Service
5000 Arlington Centre Blvd.,
  P.O. Box 20212
Columbus, OH 43220
TEL: 614-457-8600;
  800-848-8990
FAX: 614-457-0348

Computer and
  Communications Industry
  Association
666 11th St., NW, Ste. 600
Washington, DC 20001
TEL: 202-783-0070

Confederation of British
  Industries (CBI)
Centre Point,
  103 New Oxford St.
London WC1A 1DU, England
TEL: 011-44-71-379-7400
FAX: 011-44-71-240-1578

Confederazione Generale
  dell'Industria Italiana
  (Confindustria)
(Federation of Industry and
  Commerce)
Viale dell'Astronomia 30,
  Casessa Postale 10807
00144 Rome/EUR
TEL: 011-39-6-59031
FAX: 011-39-6-613230

Conference of State Bank
  Supervisors
1015 18th St., NW, Ste. 1100
Washington, DC 20036-5725
TEL: 202-296-2840

Congressional Information
  Service (CIS)
4520 East-West Hwy., Ste. 800
Bethesda, MD 20814-3389
TEL: 301-654-1550

Consulate General of Malaysia
Consul Investment,
  630 3rd Ave., 11th Fl.
New York, NY 10017
TEL: 212-687-2491/490-8450

Consulate General of Malaysia
Commercial Section,
  350 S. Figueroa St.
Ste. 400, WT Ctr.
Los Angeles, CA 90071
TEL: 213-621-2661/2686
FAX: 213-485-8617

Consulate General of Malaysia
John Hancock Ctr., Ste. 3350
875 N. Michigan Ave.
Chicago, IL 60611
TEL: 312-787-4532
FAX: 312-787-4769

Consumer Product Safety
  Association
Shimei Bldg., 4th Fl., 3-17-7,
  Roppongi
3-chome, Minato-ku,
  Tokyo 106, Japan
TEL: 011-81-33-582-6231
FAX: 011-81-33-586-1545

Containerization &
  Intermodal Institute
P.O. Box 1593
North Caldwell, NJ 07007
TEL: 201-226-0160

Corcoran Communications,
  Inc.
29100 Aurora Rd.
Solon, OH 44139
TEL: 312-472-8116

Cosmetic, Toiletry and
  Fragrance Association
11101 17th St., NW, Ste. 300
Washington, DC 20036
TEL: 202-331-1770

Cote d'Azur Development
10, rue de la Prefecture
BP 142
06003 Nice Cedex, France
TEL: 011-33-93-92-42-42
FAX: 011-33-93-80-05-76

Council of All-Japan
Exporters' Association
Kikai Shinko Kaikan Bldg.
5-8, Shibakoen 3-chome
Minato-ku, Tokyo, Japan
TEL: 011-81-33-431-9507
FAX: 011-81-33-436-6455

Council on Hotel, Restaurant
and Institutional Education
1200 17th St., NW
Washington, DC 20036
TEL: 202-333-5900

Cowles Business Media Inc.
6 River Bend Ctr.
Stamford, CT
TEL: 203-358-9900
FAX: 203-348-5792

Crain Communications Inc.
220 E. 42nd St.
New York, NY 10017-5806
TEL: 212-210-0100

Crain Communications Inc.
740 Rush St.
Chicago, IL 60611-2590
TEL: 312-649-5200

Crain Communications Inc.
1725 Merriman Rd., Ste. 300
Akron, OH 44313-5251
TEL: 216-836-9180

Crain Communications Inc.
1400 Woodbridge Ave.
Detroit, MI 48207-3187
TEL: 313-446-6000

Creditreform
Postfach 101552
D-4040 Neuss 1, Germany
TEL: 011-49-2131109210
FAX: 011-49-2131109140

Criss-Cross Inc.
P.O. Box 720230
Oklahoma City, OK 73172
TEL: 405-359-6414

Croner Publications, Inc.
34 Jericho Turnpike
Jericho, NY 11753
TEL: 718-464-0866
FAX: 718-464-5734

Cultural & Information
Section
54 Nan Hai Rd.
Taipei, Japan
TEL: 011-886-2-303-7231
FAX: 011-886-2-303-5142

Current Publications, Ltd.
GPO Box 9848
1501 Enterprise Bldg.,
228 Queen's Rd.
Central Hong Kong
TEL: 011-852-815-8396

Customs General
Administration
6 Jian Guo Men Nei Ave.
Beijing 100730, China
TEL: 011-86-1-555-6106

D-S Marketing Ltd.
Plaza Ste., 114 Jermyn St.
London SW1Y 6HJ, England
TEL: 011-44-71-930-5030;
USA: 800-221-7754
FAX: 011-44-930-2581

DAFSA
25 rue Montmartre
F-75081 Paris, Cedex 02,
France
TEL: 011-33-1-42332123

DRI/McGraw-Hill
24 Hartwell Ave.
Lexington, MA 02173
TEL: 617-863-5100

Dai-Ichi Kangyo Bank, Ltd.,
The (Japan)
1-5, Uchisaiwaicho 1-chome
Chiyoda-ku, Tokyo 100, Japan
TEL: 011-81-33-596-1111

Dai-Ichi Kangyo Bank, Ltd.,
The (U.S.)
One World Trade Center,
Ste. 4911
New York, NY 10048
TEL: 212-466-5200

Daily Japan Digest, The
205 N. Emerson St.
Arlington, VA 22203
TEL: 703-528-7570
FAX: 703-528-8123

Dana Chase Publications, Inc.
1110 Jori Blvd., CS9019
Oak Brook, IL 60522-9019
TEL: 708-990-3484

Data Base Asia Ltd.
Arion Commercial Centre,
Two Queens Rd. W.
Hong Kong

Data Resources, Data
Products Division
24 Hartwell Ave.
Lexington, MA 02173
TEL: 617-863-5100

Data Storage Report
E. Jonas McCloud,
53 Park Belmont Pl.
San Jose, CA 95136
TEL: 408-365-9494

DataTimes Corporation
Pkwy. Plaza, Ste. 450
1400 Quail Springs Pkwy.
Oklahoma City, OK 73134
TEL: 405-751-6400;
800-642-2525

DataTrends Publications Inc.
8130 Boone Blvd., Ste. 210
Vienna, VA 22182-2608
TEL: 703-760-0660
FAX: 703-760-9365

Datapro Research Corp.
600 Delran Pkwy.
Delran, NJ 08075
TEL: 800-328-2776
FAX: 609-764-2580

Datastream International Ltd.
Monmouth House,
58-64 City Rd.
London EC1Y 2AL, England
TEL: 071-250-3000
FAX: 071-253-0171

David M. Kennedy
   International Center
Brigham Young University,
   Box 24538
Provo, UT 84602-4538
TEL: 801-378-6528

Davison Publishing Company
P.O. Box 477
Ridgewood, NJ 07451
TEL: 201-445-3135

Delta Communications Inc.
N. City Front Plaza, Ste. 2300
Chicago, IL 60631-3595
TEL: 312-222-2000
FAX: 312-222-2026

Denlinger's Publishers Ltd.
P.O. Box 76
Fairfax, VA 22030
TEL: 703-830-4646

Dental Technicion Ltd.
203 King's Cross Rd.
London, England WC1

Dentsu Incorporated
1114 Ave. of the Americas
New York, NY 10036
TEL: 212-869-8318
FAX: 212-719-5028

Dentsu Incorporated - Japan
11-10 Tsukiji
1-chome, Tokyo 104, Japan
TEL: 011-3-544-5585

Department of Trade and
   Industry (DTI)
123 Victoria St., Ashtown
   House
London SW1H 6RB, England
TEL: 011-44-71-215-7877

Derwent Inc.
1313 Dolley Madison Blvd.,
   Ste. 303
McLean, VA 22101
TEL: 703-790-0400
FAX: 703-790-1426

Derwent Publications Ltd.
Rochdale House,
   128 Theobalds Rd.
London, WC1X BRP, England
TEL: 071-242-5823
FAX: 071-405-3630

Deutsche Ausgleichsbank
Wielandstrasse 4
5300 Bonn 2, Germany
TEL: 011-49-228-8310
FAX: 011-49-228-831255

Deutsche Ausgleichsbank
Niederlassung Berlin,
   Sarrazinstrasse 11-15
1000 Berlin 41, Germany
TEL: 011-49-30-850850
FAX: 011-49-30-85085299

Deutsche Bundesbank
Wilhelm Epstein Strasse 14,
   Postfach 100602
D-6000 Frankfurt-am-Main
   50, Germany
TEL: 011-49-6-95-66-1

Deutsche Institute fur
   Normung (DIN)
(German Standardization
   Institute)
Burggrafenstrasse 6,
   Postfach 11-07
D-1000 Berlin 30, Germany
TEL: 011-49-30-26-01-600
FAX: 011-49-30-26-01-231

Deutscher Industrie-und
   Handelstag (DIHT)
(Association of German
   Chambers of Industry &
   Commerce)
Adenaueralle 148,
   Postfach 14 45
D-5300 Bonn 1, Germany
TEL: 011-49-228-104-0

Deutsches Patentamt
(German Patent Office)
Zweiburckenstrasse 12
D-8000 Munich 2, Germany
TEL: 011-49-89-2-19-50

Development Bank of
   Singapore, The
6 Shenton Way, DBS Bldg.
Singapore 0106
TEL: 011-65-220-1111

Devon & Cornwall
   Development Bureau
5 Derriford Park
Derriford, Plymouth PL6 5QZ
TEL: 011-44-752-793379
FAX: 011-44-752-788660

Dialog Information Services,
   Inc.
3460 Hillview Ave.
Palo Alto, CA 94304
TEL: 415-858-3785;
   800-334-2564
FAX: 415-858-7069

Diamond Lead Co., Ltd.
4-2 Kasumigaseki
1-chome Chiyoda-ku,
   Tokyo 100, Japan
TEL: 011-81-33-504-6631
FAX: 011-81-33-502-2614

Dickman Directories
6145 Columbus Pike
Delaware, OH 43015
TEL: 614-548-6130

Digital News
41 West St., 8th Fl.
Boston, MA 02111
TEL: 617-423-9030

Digitized Information
202, 4-2, Akatsutsumi
   3-Chome, Setagaya-ku
Tokyo 156, Japan
TEL: 03 325-4660
FAX: 03 325-7540

Direct Marketing Association
   (New York)
11 W. 42nd St., 25th Fl.
New York, NY 10036
TEL: 212-768-7277
FAX: 212-768-4546

Disclosure Inc.
516 River Rd.
Bethesda, MD 20816-1584
TEL: 301-951-1300
FAX: 301-657-1962

Distilled Spirits Council of
   the U.S.
1250 Eye St., NW, Ste. 900
Washington, DC 20005
TEL: 202-682-3544

Doctorow Communications
Inc.
1033 Clifton Ave.
Clifton, NJ 07013-3641
TEL: 201-779-1600

Dodwell & Co. Ltd.
Kowa No. 35 Bldg.,
14-14 Akasaka
1-chome Minato-ku,
Tokyo 107, Japan
TEL: 011-81-3-35890207

Dodwell Marketing Consultants
CPO Box 297, Togin Bldg.
4-2 Marunouchi
1-Chome, Chiyoda-ku, Tokyo
100-91, Japan
TEL: 011-81-33-211-4451
FAX: 011-81-33-211-2145

Dow Jones & Company Inc. -
Dow Jones News/Retrieval
P.O. Box 300
Princeton, NJ 08543-0300
TEL: 609-520-4000

Dun & Bradstreet Business
Information Services
8310 Capital of Texas Hwy.,
Ste. 200
Austin, TX 78731
TEL: 800-234-3867

Dun & Bradstreet Europe Ltd.
Holmers Farm Way
High Wycombe, Bucks,
HP12 4UL, England
TEL: 0494 422000
FAX: 0494 422260

Dun & Bradstreet
Information Services
Three Sylvan Way
Parsippany, NJ 07054-3896
TEL: 201-605-6000
FAX: 201-605-6921

Dun & Bradstreet [HK], Ltd.
2/F Sun Hung Kai Centre,
30 Harbour Rd.
Wanchai, Hong Kong
TEL: 011-852-833-6555

Dun's Marketing Services
Three Sylvan Way
Parsippany, NJ 07054-3896
TEL: 800-526-0651
FAX: 201-605-6911

Dvorkovitz & Associates
P.O. Box 1748
Ormond Beach, FL 32175
TEL: 904-254-4746

E.E. Judge & Sons Inc.
P.O. Box 866
Westminster, MD 21157
TEL: 301-876-2052

ECCH - Babson College
Babson Park
Wellesley, MA 02157
TEL: 617-239-5884/6
FAX: 617-239-5885

ECCH - Cranfield Institute
of Technology
Beds MK43 OAL
United Kingdom
TEL: 0234 750903
FAX: 0234 751125

ECHO - Commission of the
European Communities
(CEC)
B.P. 2373
L-1023 Luxembourg,
Luxembourg
TEL: 011-352 34981200
FAX: 011-352 34981234
ECHO = European
Commission Host
Organization

ECRI (Emergency Care
Research Institute)
5200 Butler Pike
Plymouth Meeting, PA 19462
TEL: 215-825-6000
FAX: 215-834-1275

EDIP Publishing
Westland House, Green Ln.
Shipleybridge, Horley
Surrey, RH6 9TG, England

EPRC Ltd.
141 St. James Rd.
Glasgow G4 DLT, Scotland
TEL: 011-41 5524400
FAX: 011-41 5520775

ESA-IRS (European Space
Agency - Information
Retrieval Service)
ESRIN, Via Galileo Galilei
I-00044 Frascati (Rome), Italy
TEL: 06 9411801
FAX: 06 94180361

EUROBASES - Commission
of the European
Communities (CEC)
200, rue de la Loi
B-1049 Brussels, Belgium
TEL: 02 2950001
FAX: 02 2960624

Economic Development
Board (EDB)
250 N. Bridge Rd., #24-00,
Raffles City Tower
Singapore 0617
TEL: 011-65-336-2288
FAX: 011-65-339-6077

Economic Planning Board
(EPB)
Chungang-dong, Kwacheon-si,
Kyonggi-do
Seoul, Korea
TEL: 011-82-2-503-9144/5
FAX: 011-82-2-503-9141
Economic Ed. Div. -
011-82-2-503-9033
Fax: 011-82-2-503-9033

Economic Salon, Ltd.
60 E. 42nd St., Ste. 734
New York, NY 10165
TEL: 212-986-1588

Economist Group, The/Simon
& Schuster
200 Old Tappan Rd.
Tappan, NJ 07675
TEL: 201-767-5937

Economist Intelligence Unit
40 Duke St.
London W1A 1DW, England
TEL: 011-44-71-493-6711

Economist, The
111 W. 57th St.
New York, NY 10020-1903
TEL: 212-541-5730
FAX: 212-541-9378

Editor & Publisher Co.
11 W. 19th St., 10th Fl.
New York, NY 10011-4234
TEL: 212-675-4380

Edward N. Hayes Publishing
Co.
4229 Birch St.
Newport Beach, CA
92660-1908
TEL: 714-756-9063

Electronic Industries
Association
2001 Pennsylvania Ave., NW
Washington, DC 20006-1813
TEL: 202-457-4957

Elsevier Advanced Technology
Mayfield House,
256 Banbury Rd.
Oxford, OX2 7DH, England
TEL: 011-44-865 512242

Elsevier Science Publishers
Company Inc.
655 Ave. of the Americas
New York, NY 10010
TEL: 212-989-5800
FAX: 212-633-3990

Elsevier/Geo Abstracts
Regency House, 34 Duke St.
Norwich, NR3 3AP, England
TEL: 44-0603-626327
FAX: 44-0603-667934

Embassy of the People's
Republic of China
2300 Connecticut Ave. NW
Washington, DC 20008
TEL: 202-328-2520/2517

Engineering Information, Inc.
(Ei)
345 E. 47th St.
New York, NY 10017
TEL: 212-216-8500;
    800-221-1044

Environmental Policy Institute
218 D St., SE
Washington, DC 20003
TEL: 202-544-2600
FAX: 202-543-4710

Eurofi Plc.
Vo-tec House, Humbridge Ln.
Newbury, Berkshire RG14
    5TN, England
TEL: 011-44-635-31900

Euromonitor Publications Ltd.
87-88 Turnmill St.
London EC1M 5QU, England
TEL: 011-44-71-251-8024

Europaisches Patentamt
(European Patent Office -
    Germany)
Erhardstrasse 27
D-8000 Munich 2, Germany
TEL: 011-49-89-2-39-90

European Business
    Publications Inc.
P.O. Box 891
Daren, CT 06820
TEL: 203-656-2701
FAX: 203-655-8332

European Patent Office
    (EPO) - Austria
Vienna Suboffice,
    Schottenfeldgasse 29
Postfach 82, A 1072-Vienna,
    Austria
TEL: 011-43-1-52161201
FAX: 011-43-1-52161493

European-American Chamber
    of Commerce
40 W. 57th St., 3lst Fl.
New York, NY 10019-4092
TEL: 212-315-2196
FAX: 212-315-2183

Eurostudy Publishing
    Company Ltd. - UK
36-38 Willesden Ln.
London NW6 7SW, England
TEL: 011-44-71-328-5152
FAX: 011-44-71-625-6223

Executive Office of the
    President
600 17th St., NW
Washington, DC 20506
TEL: 202-395-3230

Export Buying Offices
    Association (EXBO)
DTI, 66 Victoria St.
London SW1H 6SW, England
TEL: 011-44-71-215-4595/3

Export Institute of Singapore
1 Maritime Sq. #10-40
World Trade Centre, Telok
    Blangah Rd.
Singapore 0409
TEL: 011-65-271-9388
FAX: 011-65-274-0770

Export Market Information
    Centre
1-19 Victoria St.
London SW1H OET, England
TEL: 011-44-71-215-5000

Export Marketing Research
    Scheme
4 Westwood House,
    Westwood Business Park
Coventry CV4 8HS, UK
TEL: 011-44-203-694484

Export-Import Bank of Korea
16-1-Yoido-dong,
    Yongdeungpo-ku
Seoul 150, Korea
TEL: 011-82-2-784-1021
CPO Box 4009, Seoul

Export-Import Bank of The
    Republic of China
8th Fl., 8 Nan Hai Rd.
Taipei, Taiwan
TEL: 011-886-2-321-0511
FAX: 011-886-2-394-0630

Extel Financial Ltd.
Fitzroy House,
    13-17 Epworth St.
London EC2A 4DL, England
TEL: 011-44-71-251-3333
FAX: 011-44-71-251-2725

F.B.R. Data Base Inc.
P.O. Box 11530
Taipei, Taiwan
TEL: 03 875 4355
FAX: 03 875 4360

F.M. Business Publishing
342 Madison Ave.
New York, NY 10173-2298
TEL: 800-776-1246

FIZ Technik
Ostbahnhofstr, 13,
    Postfach 600547
D-6000 Frankfurt 60,
    Germany
TEL: 011-49-69 43080225
FAX: 011-49-69 43080200

FT Business Enterprises Ltd.
Number One, Southwork
    Bridge
London, SE1 9HL, England
TEL: 0932 761444
FAX: 0932 781425

FT PROFILE
P.O. Box 12
Sunbury-on-thames
Middlesex TW16 7UD,
    England
TEL: 011-44-932-761444
FAX: 011-44-932 781425

FactSet Data-Systems, Inc.
One Greenwich Plaza
Greenwich, CT 06830
TEL: 203-863-1500

Facts & Comparisons Inc.
111 W. Port Plaza, Ste. 423
St. Louis, MO 63146-3098
TEL: 314-878-2515

Facts on File
460 Park Ave., S.
New York, NY 10016
TEL: 212-683-2244
FAX: 212-213-4578

Fairchild Publications
7 W. 34th St.
New York, NY 10001
TEL: 212-630-4000
FAX: 212-630-3868

Fairs and Promotions Branch
Dean Bradley House,
    52 Horseferry Rd.
London S1P 3AG, UK
TEL: 011-44-71-276-3000

Faulkner & Gray Inc.
118 S. Clinton St., Ste. 700
Chicago, IL 60661
TEL: 312-648-0261

Federal Communications
    Commission (FCC),
Authorization and Evaluation
    Division
7435 Oakland Mills Rd.
Columbia, MD 21046
TEL: 301-725-1585

Federal Deposit Insurance
    Corporation
Reading Rm. 7118,
    550 17th St., NW
Washington, DC 20429
TEL: 202-898-8563
FAX: 202-898-6985

Federal Home Loan Bank
    Board
1700 G St., NW
Washington, DC 20552
TEL: 202-377-6934

Federal Home Loan Mortgage
    Corporation
8200 Jones Branch Dr.
McLean, VA 22102
TEL: 703-903-2701
FAX: 703-903-3562

Federal Trade Commission
    (FTC)
6th & Pennsylvania Ave., NW
Washington, DC 20580
TEL: 202-326-2222
FAX: 202-326-2050

Fidelifacts
50 Broadway
New York, NY 10004
TEL: 800-678-0007

Financial Information Inc.
30 Montgomery St.
Jersey City, NJ 07302
TEL: 201-332-5400

Financial Post Datagroup, The
333 King St., E.
Toronto, Ontario,
    CN M5A 4N2
TEL: 416-350-6440
FAX: 416-350-6501

Financial Times Profile
Sunbury House,
    79 Staines Rd., W. Sunbury
Thames PW167UD U.K.
TEL: 44-932-761444

Financial World
1328 Broadway
New York, NY 10001
TEL: 212-594-5030
FAX: 212-629-0021

Florida Association of
    Mortgage Brokers
Box 13089
Tallahassee, FL 32317
TEL: 904-878-3134

Food Marketing Institute
800 Connecticut Ave., NW,
    Ste. 500
Washington, DC 20006-2701
TEL: 202-452-8444

Foods Adlibra Publications
9000 Plymouth Ave., N.
Minneapolis, MN 55427
TEL: 612-540-4759
FAX: 612-540-3166

Forbes Inc.
60 Fifth Ave.
New York, NY 10011
TEL: 212-620-2200

Foreign Exchange Control
    Bureau
17 Xijiaomin Xiang
Beijing, China
TEL: 011-86-1-3338521

Foreign Trade Bureau
190 Chaoyangmennei Dajie
Beijing, China
TEL: 011-86-1-5554808

Freedom of Information
    Office/Dockets
Management Branch
Park Bldg., 12420 Parklawn
    Dr., Rm. 123
Rockville, MD 20857
TEL: 301-443-7542

French Embassy
4101 Reservoir Rd., NW
Washington, DC 20007
TEL: 202-944-6000

French International
   Development Association
   (FRIEND)
1, Ave. Charles Floquet
75007 Paris, France
TEL: 011-33-1-40-65-12-34
FAX: 011-33-1-43-06-99-01

French Trade Office
810 Seventh Ave.
New York, NY 10019-5818
TEL: 212-307-8800

French-American Chamber of
   Commerce
509 Madison Ave., Ste. 1900
New York, NY 10022-5501
TEL: 212-371-4466

French-American Foundation
41 E. 72nd St.
New York, NY 10021
TEL: 212-288-4400
FAX: 212-288-4769

Fuji Bank
5-5 Otemachi
1-chome, Chiyoda-ku,
   Tokyo, Japan
TEL: 011-81-33-216-2211

G-Search Corporation
Hoko-kowa Bldg., 8th Fl.,
   1-2-4, Tsukiji
Chuo-ku, Tokyo 104, Japan
TEL: 03 55651480
FAX: 03 55634012

G.CAM Serveur -
   Europeenes de Donnees
1, rue du Boccador
F-75008, Paris, France
TEL: 011-33-1 47028834
FAX: 011-33-1 47201143

GE Information Services
   (GEIS)
401 N. Washington St.
Rockville, MD 20850
TEL: 301-340-4572;
   800-638-9636
FAX: 301-294-5501

GENIOS
   Wirschaftsdatenbanken
Kasernenstr. 67,
   Postfach 10 11 02
D-4000 Dusseldorf 1,
   Germany
TEL: 0211 8871524
FAX: 0211 8871520

GIANO - Sistema Informatico
   della Confindustria
Viale dell'Astronomia 30
Rome, Italy
TEL: 011-39-6-59031

GSi-ECO
4 S. rue de la Precession
F-75015 Paris, France
TEL: 011-33-1 45667-889
FAX: 011-33-1 47-344692

GTE Directories, Ltd.
23/F Fortress Tower,
   250 King's Rd., North Point
Hong Kong
TEL: 011-852-669-9888
FAX: 011-852-807-3133

Gale Research Inc.
835 Penobscot Bldg.
Detroit, MI 48226-4094
TEL: 800-223-4253;
   313-961-2242
FAX: 313-961-6083

Gardner Publications Inc.
6600 Clough Pike
Cincinnati, OH 45244
TEL: 513-231-8020

Gas Appliance Manufacturers
   Association
1901 N. Moore St., Ste. 1100
Arlington, VA 22209
TEL: 703-525-9565

General Aviation
   Manufacturers Association
   (GAMA)
1400 K St., NW, Ste. 801
Washington, DC 20005
TEL: 202-393-1500

General Electric Co. - GE
   Information Services
   (GEIS)
401 N. Washington St.
Rockville, MD 20850
TEL: 301-340-4000

General Videotex Corp.
Delphi, 1030 Mass Ave.,
   4th Fl.
Cambridge, MA 02138-5302
TEL: 617-491-3393;
   800-544-4005

Genesis Group Associates,
   Inc., The
29 Park St.
Montclair, NJ 07042
TEL: 201-509-7735
FAX: 201-509-7745

Geophysical Directory, Inc.
P.O. Box 130508
Houston, TX 77219
TEL: 713-529-8789

George Mason University
4400 University Dr.
Fairfax, VA 22030
TEL: 703-993-1000
FAX: 703-323-3849

German American Business
   Association
103 Ross Alley
Alexandria, VA 22314-3129
TEL: 703-836-6120

German American Chamber
   of Commerce
104 S. Michigan Ave., Ste. 600
Chicago, IL 60603
TEL: 312-782-8557
FAX: 312-782-3892

German Embassy
4645 Reservoir Rd., NW
Washington, DC 20007
TEL: 202-298-4000

German Industry & Trade
   Office
1627 I St., NW, Ste. 550
Washington, DC 20006
TEL: 202-659-4777

German Information Center
950 Third Ave.
New York, NY 10022
TEL: 212-888-9840

German News Company Inc.
1749 First Ave.
New York, NY 10028
TEL: 212-348-5975

Gesellschaft fur
  Biotechnologische
  Forschung mbH
Mascheroder Weg 1
D-3300 Braunschweig-
  Stockheim, Germany
TEL: 531 6181641
FAX: 531 6181515

Globe Information Services
444 Front St., W.
Toronto, Ontario, CN M5V 2S9
TEL: 416-585-5250;
  800-268-9128

Goethe Institute
1014 Fifth Ave.
New York, NY 10028
TEL: 212-439-8700

Goldhirsch Group
38 Commercial Wharf
Boston, MA 02110-3809
TEL: 617-248-8000
FAX: 617-248-8090

Gorman Publishing Company
Triangle Plaza,
  87 W. Bryn Mawr Ave.
Chicago, IL 60631
TEL: 312-693-3200
FAX: 312-693-0568

Government Institutes Inc.
Four Research Pl., Ste. 200
Rockmill, MD 20850
TEL: 301-921-2300
a branch of CETRA

Government Printing Office
N. Capital & H Sts., NW
Washington, DC 20401
TEL: 202-512-2034

Graphic Arts Technical
  Foundation
4615 Forbes Ave.
Pittsburgh, PA 15213
TEL: 412-621-6941

Greffe du Tribunal de
  Commerce de Paris
1 Quai de Corse
75181 Paris Cedex 4, France
TEL: 011-33-1-44-41-54-54

Grenoble Isere Development
1, Pl. Firmin Gautier
38028 Grenoble Cedex 1,
  France
TEL: 011-33-76-70-97-97
FAX: 011-33-76-48-07-03

Griffin Publishing Company
  Inc.
1099 Hingham St.
Rockland, MA 02190-1198
TEL: 617-878-5300

Griggs Productions
2046 Clement St.
San Francisco, CA 94121
TEL: 415-668-4200

Guangdong Exhibition
  Service Company
774 Dongfeng Wu Lu, 8th Fl.
Guangzhou, China
TEL: 011-86-20-75793

Guangdong Foreign Trade
  Development Corporation
774 Dongfeng Donglu, 8th Fl.
Guangzhou, China
TEL: 011-86-20-776-299
FAX: 011-86-20-766-025;
  755-815

Guangdong Keji Chubanshe
(Guangdong Scientific and
  Technical Press)
25 Xinji Lu, PO Box 49
Guangzhou, Guangdong, China
TEL: 011-862931

Guardian Publications Ltd.
Albany House, Hurst St.
Birmingham B5 4BD
TEL: 011-44-21-622-4011

Guida Monachi
Via Vitorchiano, 107-109
00189 Rome, Italy
TEL: 011-39-6-3288805

Gulf Publishing Company
P.O. Box 2608
Houston, TX 77252
TEL: 713-529-4301

Hachette Magazines Inc.
1633 Broadway
New York, NY 10019
TEL: 212-767-6385

Haines and Company
8050 Freedom Ave., NW
North Canton, OH 44720
TEL: 216-494-9111

Hanover Publishing
200 W. 57th St.
New York, NY 10019-3283
TEL: 212-399-1084

Harris Publishing Company
2057 Aurora Rd.
Twinsburg, OH 44087-1999
TEL: 216-425-9000;
  800-888-5900
FAX: 216-425-7150

Harvard Business School
  Publishing Corp.
Operations Dept.
Boston, MA 02163
TEL: 617-495-6117

Harvard University
27 Kirkland St.
Cambridge, MA 02138
TEL: 617-495-4303
FAX: 617-495-8509

Haus de Ministerien
(Finance Ministry)
Leipziger Strasse 5-7
O-1080 Berlin, Germany
TEL: 022-49-228-6820
FAX: 011-49-228-6824420

Health & Safety Executive
Baynards House,
  1 Chepstow Pl.
Westbourne Grove
London W2 4TF, UK
TEL: 011-44-71-221-0870

Health Industry
  Manufacturers Association
1200 G St., NW, Ste. 4000
Washington, DC 20005
TEL: 202-983-8700

Health Insurance Association
  of America
1025 Connecticut Ave., NW,
  Ste. 1200
Washington, DC 20036
TEL: 202-233-7780

Heilongjiang Scientific and
  Technical
Publishing House
28 Fenbu Jie, Nangang District
Harbin, Heilongjiang, China
TEL: 011-35613

Her Majesty's Stationery
  Office (HMSO)
Sovereign House, Botolph St.
Norwich NR3 1DN, England
TEL: 011-44-603-622-211

Hiaring Company, The
1800 Lincoln Ave.
San Rafael, CA 94901-1221
TEL: 415-453-2517

High Tech Publishing Company
P.O. Box 1923
Brattleboro, VT 05301
TEL: 803-254-3539

Hill-Donnelly Corp.
2602 S. MacDill Ave.,
  P.O. Box 14417
Tampa, FL 33690
TEL: 813-837-1009

Hitchcock Publishing Company
P.O. Box 830409
Birmingham, AL 35283-0409
TEL: 800-633-4931
FAX: 205-995-1588

Hokkaido Northern Regions
  Economic Exchange
Association
Hokkaido Economic
  Federation
Nihon Seimei Bldg., Nishi
4-chome, Kita 3-jo, Chuo-ku,
  Sapporo 060, Japan
TEL: 011-81-221-6166

Hong Kong Economic &
  Trade Office/Industrial
Promotion Office (HQ)
1150 18th St., NW, Ste. 475
Washington, DC 20036
TEL: 202-331-8947
FAX: 202-331-8958

Hong Kong Electronics
  Association
Rm. 1806-8 Beverly House
93-107 Lockhart Rd.
Wan Chai, Hong Kong
TEL: 011-852-865-6843

Hong Kong General Chamber
  of Commerce
22nd Fl., United Centre,
  95 Queensway
Hong Kong
TEL: 011-852-529-9229
FAX: 011-852-527-9843

Hong Kong Tourist Association
590 Fifth Ave.
New York, NY 10036
TEL: 212-869-5008
FAX: 212-730-2605

Hong Kong Trade
  Development Council
  (HKTDC) - U.S.
219 E. 46th St.
New York, NY 10017
TEL: 212-838-8688
FAX: 212-838-8941

Hong Kong and Shanghai
  Banking Corporation
  (Hong Kong)
POB 151, 185 Yuan Ming Lu
Shanghai, China
TEL: 011-86-21-216030/
  218383

Hongkong and Shanghai
  Banking Corporation Ltd.
  (U.S.)
USA Area Management Office
140 Broadway, 4th Fl.
New York, NY 10015
TEL: 212-658-5100

Hoppenstedt
  Wirtschaftsverlag GmbH
Havelstrasse 9, Postfach 40 06
D-6100 Darmstadt 1, Germany
TEL: 011-49-61-151-3800
FAX: 011-49-6151-380360

Hunter Publishing Ltd.
  Partnership
950 Lee St.
Des Plaines, IL 60016-6588
TEL: 312-296-0770

ICC Information Group Ltd.
Field House, 72 Oldfield Rd.
Hampton, Middlesex TW12
  2HQ, England
TEL: 011-44-81-783-1122
FAX: 011-44-81-783-0049

IDD Information Services
Two World Trade Center
New York, NY 10048
TEL: 212-323-9109

IFI/Plenum Data Company
302 Swann Ave.
Alexandria, VA 22301
TEL: 703-683-1085;
  800-368-3093
FAX: 703-683-0246

IFS Publications
35-39 High St.
Kempston, Beds MK42 7BT,
  England
TEL: 011-44-234 953605
FAX: 011-44-234 854499

INFOTRADE N.V.
A. Gossetlaan 32a
B-1720 Groot-Bijgaarden,
  Belgium
TEL: 011-32-2-4666480
FAX: 011-32-2-466970

Illinois Bankers Association
111 N. Canal
Chicago, IL 60606-7299
TEL: 312-984-1500

Importers and Exporters
  Association of Taipei
  (IEAP) (U.S.)
925 S. Atlantic Blvd., #205A
Monterey Park, CA 91754
TEL: 818-961-8636
FAX: 818-289-6662

Incentive Manufacturers
  Reps. Assn.
1555 Naperville/Wheaton Rd.,
  Ste. 103B
Naperville, IL 60563
TEL: 708-369-3466

Independent Bankers
  Association of America
1 Thomas Cir., NW, Ste. 950
Washington, DC 20005
TEL: 202-659-8111

Indiana Bankers Association
1 N. Capitol, Ste. 315
Indianapolis, IN 46204-2240
TEL: 317-236-0750
FAX: 317-236-0754

Individual Inc.
84 Sherman St.
Cambridge, MA 02140
TEL: 617-354-2230

Industrial Bank of Japan
3-3 Marunouchi
1-chome, Chiyoda-ku,
  Tokyo 100, Japan
TEL: 011-81-33-214-1111

Industrial Development
  Board for Northern Ireland
Chichester House,
  64 Chichester St.
Belfast BT1 4JX, England
TEL: 011-44-232-233233
FAX: 011-44-232-231328

Industrial and Commercial
  Bank of China
Yuetan South St.
Beijing, China
TEL: 011-86-1-868901

Industry Club of Japan
4-6 Marunouchi 1-chome
Chiyoda-ku, Tokyo, Japan
TEL: 011-81-33-281-1711
FAX: 011-81-33-281-1797

Industry Department for
  Scotland
Magnet House, 59 Waterloo St.
Glasgow G2 7BT, Scotland
TEL: 011-44-41-248-2855

Industry Department for Wales
Cathays Park
Cardiff CF1 3NQ, Wales, U.K.
TEL: 011-44-222-825-111

Industry Publications
389 Passaic Ave.
Fairfield, NJ 07004
TEL: 201-227-9219

Information Access Company/
  Predicasts Inc.
362 Lakeside Dr.
Foster City, CA 94404
TEL: 415-358-4643
FAX: 415-358-4759

Information Industry
  Association
555 New Jersey Ave., NW,
  Ste. 800
Washington, DC 20001
TEL: 202-639-8262
FAX: 202-638-4403

Information Science and
  Technology Association
  (INFOSTA)
3 Asaki Bldg.
5-7-2 Koisi Kawa, Bunkyo-ku
  Tokyo 112, Japan
TEL: 011-81-33-813-3791
FAX: 011-81-33-813-3793

Information Sources Inc.
1173 Colusa Ave.,
  P.O. Box 7848
Berkeley, CA 94707
TEL: 800-525-6220
FAX: 510-525-1568

Information Technology
  Association of America
1616 N. Fort Myer Dr.,
  Ste. 1300
Arlington, VA 22209
TEL: 703-522-5055

Instituo per l'Assistenza allo
  Sviluppo del Mezzogiorno
  (IASM)
(Institute for Assistance in
  the Development of
  Southern Italy)
Viale Pilsudski 124
00197 Rome, Italy
TEL: 011-39-6-84721

Institut National de la
  Propriete Industrielle
  (INPI)
26 bis, rue de Leningrad
75008 Paris, Cedex 08,
  France
TEL: 011-33-142-94-52-52

Institut National de la
  Statistique et Des Etudes
  Economiques (INSEE)
18, blvd. Adolphe-Pinard
75675 Paris Cedex 14, France
TEL: 011-33-1-45-40-12-12

Institut fur
  Wirtschaftsforschung
  (HWWA)
Neuer Jungfersstieg 36
D-2000 Hamburg 36,
  Germany
TEL: 011-49-40-35621

Institute for Electrical
  Engineers (IEEE)
Michael Faraday House,
  Six Hills Way
Stevenage, Herts. SG1 2AY,
  England
TEL: 0438-742837

Institute for Scientific
  Information
3501 Market St.
Philadelphia, PA 19104
TEL: 800-523-1857
FAX: 215-386-6362

Institute of Chartered
  Accountants
399 Silbury Blvd.
Central Milton Keynes MK9
  2HL
TEL: 011-44-908-248-100

Institute of Directors (IOD)
116 Pall Mall
London SW1Y 5ED, England
TEL: 011-44-71-839-1233
FAX: 011-44-71-930-1949

Institute of Food Technologists
221 N. Lasalle St.
Chicago, IL 60601
TEL: 312-782-8424

Institute of Freight
  Forwarders Ltd.
Suffield House, 9 Paradise Rd.
Richmond, Surrey TW9 1SA,
  England
TEL: 011-44-81-948-3141

Institute of International
  Education, The
809 United Nations Plaza
New York, NY 10017
TEL: 212-883-8200

Institute of Marketing, The
Moor Hall, Cookham
Maidenhead, Berkshire SL
  PQH
TEL: 011-44-62-85-24922

Institute of Packaging
  Professionals
481 Carlisle Dr.
Herndon, VA
TEL: 22070
FAX: 703-318-8970

Institute of Paper Science &
  Technology
500 Tenth St., NW
Atlanta, GA 30318
TEL: 404-853-9500
FAX: 404-853-9510

Institute of Textile Technology
P.O. Box 391
Charlottesville, VA 22902
TEL: 804-296-5511
FAX: 804-296-2957

Institution of Electrical
  Engineers
Michael Faraday House,
  Six Hills Way
Stevenage, Herts. England,
  SG1 2AY
TEL: 0438 742857
FAX: 0438 742840

Institutional Investor, Inc.
488 Madison Ave.
New York, NY 10022-5751
TEL: 212-303-3300
FAX: 212-303-3592

Instituto Nazionale per il
  Commercio Estero (ICE)
(National Institute for
  Foreign Trade)
Via Liszt 21
00144 Rome, EUR
TEL: 011-39-6-59921

Interactive Data Corporation
95 Hayden Ave.
Lexington, MA 02173-9144
TEL: 617-863-8100

Interactive Systems Inc.
1777 N. Kent St.
Arlington, VA 22209
TEL: 703-838-1901

Intercontinental Marketing
  Corp.
IPO Box 5056
Tokyo 100-31, Japan
TEL: 011-81-33-661-8373
FAX: 011-81-33-667-9646

Intercultural Business Center
  Inc.
1661 Worcester Rd., Ste. 103
Framingham, MA 01701
TEL: 508-879-3808

Intercultural Communication
  Institute
8835 SW Canyon Ln., Ste. 238
Portland, OR 97225
TEL: 503-297-4622
FAX: 503-297-4695

Intercultural Press, The
P.O. Box 700
Yarmouth, ME 04096
TEL: 207-846-5168

International Advertising
  Association
342 Madison, Ste. 2000
New York, NY 10173
TEL: 212-557-1133
FAX: 212-983-0455

International Association of
  Plastics Distributors
6333 Long, Ste. 340
Shawnee, KS 66216
TEL: 913-268-6273
FAX: 913-268-6388

International Association of
  Refrigerated Warehouses
7315 Wisconsin Ave. #1200 N.
Bethesda, MD 20814
TEL: 301-652-5674

International Bank of
  Singapore Ltd.
50 Collyer Quay #02-01,
  Overseas Union House
Singapore 0104
TEL: 011-65-223-4488

International Coffee
  Organization
22 Berners St.
London W1P 4DD, England
TEL: 011-44-71-580-8591
FAX: 011-44-71-580-6129

International Computer
  Programs Inc.
823 Westfield Blvd.
Indianapolis, IN 46220
TEL: 800-428-6179
FAX: 317-574-0571

International Cultural
  Enterprises Inc.
1241 Dartmouth Ln.
Deerfield, IL 60015
TEL: 800-626-2772

International Data Group
  (IDG)
488 Madison Ave., 6th Fl.
New York, NY 10022
TEL: 212-909-5900

International Exhibitors
  Association
5501 Backlick Rd., Ste. 200
Springfield, VA 22151
TEL: 703-941-3725
FAX: 703-941-8275

International Food
  Information Service GmbH
  (IFIS)
Melibocusstr, 52
D-6000 Frankfurt am Main
  71, Germany
TEL: 069-6690070
FAX: 069-66900710

International Herald Tribune,
  Books Division
181 Ave. Charles de Gaulle
92521 Neuilly, France
TEL: 011-33-1-46-37-94-94

International Institute of
  Synthetic Rubber Producers
2077 S. Gessner Rd., Ste. 133
Houston, TX 77063-1123
TEL: 713-783-7511

International Mass Retail
  Association
1901 Pennsylvania Ave., NW,
  10th Fl.
Washington, DC 20006
TEL: 202-861-0774

International Medical
  Information Center (IMIC)
30 Daikyo-cho
Shimjuku-ku, Tokyo 160, Japan
TEL: 011-81-33-353-1538
FAX: 011-81-33-357-0073

International Monetary Fund
  (IMF)
700 19th St., NW
Washington, DC 20431
TEL: 202-623-7000
FAX: 202-623-4661

International Publications
  Service
1900 Frost Rd., Ste. 101
Bristol, PA 19007-1598
TEL: 800-821-8312

International Rubber Study
  Group
York House, 8th Fl.,
  Empire Way
Wembley, England HA9 OPA

International Stock Exchange
  - Belfast
10 High St.
Belfast BT1 2BP
TEL: 011-44-232-21094

International Stock Exchange
  - Glasgow
P.O. Box 141, 69 St.
George's Pl., Glasgow G2 1BU
TEL: 011-44-41-221-7060

International Stock Exchange
  - London
Old Broad St.
London EC2 N1HP, England
TEL: 011-44-71-588-2355

International Trade
  Exhibitions in France Inc.
8 W. 40th St., Ste. 1505
New York, NY 10018
TEL: 703-222-5000

Intertec Publishing
55 E. Jackson
Chicago, IL 60604
TEL: 312-922-2435
FAX: 312-922-1408

Invest in Britain Bureau
  (IBB) (U.S.)
845 Third Ave.
New York, NY 10022
TEL: 212-745-0495

Invest in France
1, ave. Charles Floquet
75007 Paris, France
TEL: 011-33-1-40-65-12-34
FAX: 011-33-1-43-06-99-01

Investment Dealer's Digest Inc.
2 World Trade Center, 18th Fl.
New York, NY 10048-0638
TEL: 212-227-1200

Iron and Steel Society Inc.
410 Commonwealth Dr.
Warrendale, PA 15086-7512
TEL: 412-776-1585
FAX: 412-776-0430

Iron and Steel Society of
  AIME
Italian American Chamber of
  Commerce (IACC)
350 Fifth Ave., Ste. 3015
New York, NY 10018
TEL: 212-279-5520

Italian Cultural Institute
686 Park Ave.
New York, NY 10021
TEL: 212-879-4242

Italian Embassy
1601 Fuller St., NW
Washington, DC 20009
TEL: 202-328-5500

Jane's Information Group
Dept. DSM, 1340 Braddock
  Pl., Ste. 300
Alexandria, VA 22314
TEL: 800-321-5358
FAX: 703-836-0029

Japan Association for
  International Chemical
  Information (JAICI)
Gakkai Center Bldg.,
  2-4-16 Yayoi
Bunkyo-ku, Tokyo 113, Japan
TEL: 011-81-33-816-3462
FAX: 011-81-33-816-7826

Japan Association of
  Corporate Executives
Nippon Kogyo Club Bldg.,
  1-4-6 Marunouchi
Chiyoda-ku, Tokyo 100, Japan
TEL: 011-81-33-211-1271

Japan Chamber of Commerce
  and Industry, The
2-2, 3-chome, Marunouchi
Chiyoda-ku, Tokyo, Japan
TEL: 011-81-33-283-7825

Japan Commercial Arbitration
  Association (DINA)
3-5-8 Chibakoen
Minato-ku, Tokyo 105, Japan
TEL: 011-81-33-432-9381;
  432-9385
FAX: 011-81-33-432-9289

Japan Development Bank
  (Japan)
9-1 Otemachi
1-chome, Chiyoda-ku,
  Tokyo 100, Japan
TEL: 011-81-33-270-3211
Intl. Dept. -
  011-81-33-245-0439

Japan Development Bank
  (U.S.)
575 Fifth Ave., 28th Fl.
New York, NY 10017
TEL: 212-949-7550
FAX: 212-949-7558

Japan Economic Institute of
America (JEI)
1000 Connecticut Ave., NW,
Ste. 211
Washington, DC 20036
TEL: 202-296-5633

Japan Embassy
2520 Massachusetts Ave., NW
Washington, DC 20008
TEL: 202-939-6700

Japan External Trade
Organization (JETRO) -
Japan
2-2-5 Toranomon
2-chome, Minato-ku,
Tokyo 105, Japan
TEL: 011-81-33-582-5511
FAX: 011-81-33-589-3419
Publications:
011-81-33-582-5184
Fax: 011-81-33-587-2485

Japan External Trade
Organization (JETRO) -
U.S.
1221 Ave. of the Americas
New York, NY 10020
TEL: 212-997-0400
FAX: 212-997-0464

Japan Federation of Prefectual
Trade Promotion Agencies
Kokusai Kaunko Kaikan Bldg.
8-3 Marunouchi 1-chome
Chiyoda-ku, Tokyo 100, Japan
TEL: 011-81-33-213-6870

Japan Federation of Smaller
Enterprise Organizations
(JFSEO)
2-8-4 Nihonbashi
Kayabacho, Chuo-ku,
Tokyo 103, Japan
TEL: 011-81-33-668-2481
FAX: 011-81-3668-2957

Japan Foreign Trade Council,
Inc.
6th Fl., World Trade Centre
Bldg.
4-1 Hamamatsu-cho
2-chome, Minato-ku,
Tokyo 105, Japan
TEL: 011-81-33-435-5952

Japan Information Center for
Science and Technology
(JICST) - Japan
5-2, Nagatacho
2-chome, Chiyoda-ku,
Tokyo 100, Japan
TEL: 011-81-33-581-6790
FAX: 011-81-3593-3980

Japan Information Center for
Science and Technology
(JICST) - U.S.
1550 M St., NW
Washington, DC 20005
TEL: 202-872-6372
FAX: 202-872-6371

Japan Information Processing
Development Center
(JIPDEC)
3-5-8 Shibakoen
Minato-ku, Tokyo 105, Japan
TEL: 011-81-33-432-9381
FAX: 011-81-33-432-9289

Japan Information Processing
Service Company, Ltd.
(JIP) - JIPNET
6-7 Nihonbashi Kabuto-cho
Chuo-ku, Tokyo 105, Japan
TEL: 011-81-33-668-6171

Japan Institute for Social and
Economic Affairs (Keizai
Koho Center)
6-1 Otemachi
Chiyoda-ku, Tokyo 100, Japan
TEL: 011-81-33-201-1415
FAX: 011-81-33-201-1418

Japan International Science
and Technology Exchange
Center
Mitsuri Kojimachi Bldg.,
2-12-6 Kojimachi
Chiyoda-ku, Tokyo 102, Japan
TEL: 011-81-33-288-0970;
U.S.: 202-939-6700
FAX: 011-33-288-0980

Japan Pacific Associates
467 Hamilton Ave., Ste. 2
Palo Alto, CA 94301
TEL: 415-332-8441
FAX: 415-322-8454

Japan Patent Information
Organization (JAPIO)
Sato-Dia Bldg., 4-1-7 Tokyo,
Koto-ku
Tokyo 135, Japan
TEL: 011-81-03-569-05555
FAX: 011-81-03-569-05566

Japan Press, Ltd.
Japan Directory Div., 12-8
Kita Aoyana
2-chome Minato-ku, Tokyo
107, Japan
TEL: 011-81-33-404-5151
FAX: 011-81-33-423-2358

Japan Productivity Center -
Japan
3-1-1 Shibuya
Shibuya-ku, Tokyo 150, Japan
TEL: 011-33-409-1111
FAX: 011-81-33-409-1986

Japan Productivity Center -
U.S.
1729 King St., Ste. 100
Alexandria, VA 22314
TEL: 703-838-0414
FAX: 703-838-0419

Japan Society
Curtis Saval International
Center
22 Batterymarch St.
Boston, MA 02109
TEL: 617-451-0726

Japan Society
333 E. 47th St.
New York, NY 10017
TEL: 212-832-1155

Japan Yellow Pages Ltd.
ST Bldg., 6-9 Iidabashi
4-chome Chiyoda-ku,
Tokyo 102, Japan
TEL: 011-81-33-239-3501
FAX: 011-81-33-237-8945

John Wiley and Sons, Inc.
605 Third Ave.
New York, NY 10158
TEL: 212-850-6331

Jonas Press Publishing Company
53 Park Belmont Pl.
San Jose, CA 95136
TEL: 408-629-8249
FAX: 408-629-8249

Jordan & Sons Ltd.
Jordan House, 47 Brunswick Pl.
London N1 6EE, England
TEL: 011-44-71-253 3030
FAX: 011-44-71-251 0825

Journal of Commerce, Inc.
Two World Trade Center
New York, NY 10048-0662
TEL: 212-837-7000
FAX: 212-208-0393

K-III Information Company
Inc.
424 W. 33rd St.
New York, NY 10001
TEL: 212-714-3100
FAX: 212-695-5025

K.G. Saur
121 Chanlon Rd.
New Providence, NJ 07974
TEL: 800-521-8110
FAX: 908-665-6688

Kaohsiung Branch Office
88 Wufu 3rd Rd.
Kaohsiung, Japan
TEL: 011-886-7-251-2444/7
FAX: 011-886-7-231-8237

Kegan Paul International
11 New Fetter Ln.
London EC4P 4EE, England
TEL: 011-44-71-583-9855
FAX: 011-44-583-0701

Keller International
Publishing Corp.
150 Great Neck Rd.,
P.O. Box 781
Great Neck, NY 11021
TEL: 516-829-9210
FAX: 516-829-5414

Kelly's Directories
Windsor Ct., E. Grinstead
House
E. Grinstead, W. Sussex
RH19 1XD, England

Kennedy Publications
20 Templeton Rd.
Fitzwilliam, NH 03447
TEL: 603-585-6544
FAX: 603-585-9555

Knolls Publishing
240 Cedar Knolls Rd.
Cedar Knolls, NJ 07927-1621
TEL: 216-349-3060

Kobe Chamber of Commerce
and Industry
Kobe CIT Center Bldg.
1-14, Hamabe-dori 5-chome
Chuo-ku, Kobe 651, Japan
TEL: 011-81-78-251-1001

Kurt Salmon Associates
12 E. 49th St., Ste. 1400
New York, NY 10017
TEL: 212-319-9450

L'Expansion
482 F. Groupe Expansion,
57 ave. de Wagram
75017 Paris, France
TEL: 011-33-1-47-63-12-11

L'Usine Nouvelle
59 rue du Rocher
75008 Paris, France
TEL: 011-33-1-44-69-55-55

Law Society of Hong Kong
Swire House, Rm. 901,
Chater Rd.
Central, Hong Kong
TEL: 011-852-522-1121

Le Nouvel Economiste
22 rue de Tremoille
75008 Paris, France
TEL: 011-33-1-47-23-01-05

Le Point
22 rue de Rennes
75006 Paris, France
TEL: 011-33-1-45-44-39-00

Leading National Advertisers,
Inc.
11 W. 42nd St.
New York, NY 10036-8088
TEL: 212-789-1400
FAX: 212-789-1450

Learned Information Inc.
143 Old Marlton Pike
Medford, NJ 08055-8750
TEL: 609-654-6266
FAX: 609-654-4309

Lebhar-Friedman Inc.
425 Park Ave.
New York, NY 10022-3556
TEL: 212-756-5000

Life Insurance Association
138 Cecil St., 03-00 Cecil Ct.
Singapore 0106
TEL: 011-65-225-1122

Life Insurance Marketing &
Research Association
P.O. Box 208
Hartford, CT 06141-0208
TEL: 203-677-0033
FAX: 203-678-0187

Lippincott & Peto Inc.
1867 W. Market St., Box 5485
Akron, OH 44313-6901
TEL: 216-864-2122

Lloyds Bank
71 Lombard St.
London EC3P 3BS, England
TEL: 011-44-71-356-1470
FAX: 011-44-71-929-1669

Lloyds Bank (U.S.)
P.O. Box 2008
Peck Slip Station, NY 10038
TEL: 212-607-4300
FAX: 212-607-4917

Lockwood Trade Journal Inc.
130 W. 42nd St., 22nd Fl.
New York, NY 10036
TEL: 212-391-2060

London Business School
Information Service
Sussex Pl., Regent's Park
London NW1 4SA, England
TEL: 011-44-71-723-3404
FAX: 011-44-71-706-1897

London Chamber of
Commerce & Industry
33 Quinn St.
London EC4 R1AP, England
TEL: 011-44-71-248-4444

Lumbermen's Credit
   Association, Inc.
111 W. Jackson Blvd.
Chicago, IL 60604
TEL: 312-427-0733

M C B University Press Ltd.
62 Toller Ln.
Bradford, W. Yorkshire BD8
   9BY, England
TEL: 011-44-274-499821

M. Shanken Communications
   Inc.
387 Pane Ave., S.
New York, NY 10016
TEL: 212-684-4224

MH West Inc.
6633 Odessa Ave.
Van Nuys, CA 91406
TEL: 818-997-0644

MLR Publishing Company
229 S. 18th St.
Philadelphia, PA 19103
TEL: 800-223-2030;
   215-790-7000

Machinery Dealers National
   Association
1110 Spring St.
Silver Spring, MD 20910
TEL: 301-585-9494

Maclean Hunter Media
4 Stamford Forum
Stamford, CT 06901-3218
TEL: 203-325-3500
FAX: 203-324-8423

Maclean Hunter Publishing
   Company
300 W. Adams St.
Chicago, IL 60606-3298
TEL: 312-726-2802
FAX: 312-726-2574

Magellan On-Line Services
P.O. Box 2612
Denver, CO 80201
TEL: 800-525-5569

Management Publications Ltd.
30 Lancaster Gate
London W2 3LP, England
TEL: 011-44-71-402-4200
FAX: 011-44-71-402-5415

Manufactured Imports
   Promotion Organization
   (MIPRO) - U.S.
2000 L St., NW, Ste. 616
Washington, DC 20036
TEL: 202-659-3729
FAX: 202-887-5159

Manufactured Imports
   Promotion Organization
   (MIPRO) - Japan
6th Fl., World Import Mart
   Bldg.
1-3 Higashi Ikebukuro
3-chome, Toshima-ku,
   Tokyo 170, Japan
TEL: 011-81-33-988-2791
FAX: 011-81-988-1629

Manufacturers' Alliance for
   Productivity
1200 Eighteenth St., NW
Washington, DC 20036
TEL: 202-331-8430
FAX: 202-331-7160

Marc Publishing Company
600 Germantown Pike
Lafayette Hill, PA 19444
TEL: 215-834-8585

Market Research Society
15 Northburgh St.
London EC1 ZOAH, England
TEL: 011-44-71-490-4911

Marketing House Publishers
   Ltd.
Moor Hall, Cookham
Maidenhead, Berkshire SL6
   9QH, England
TEL: 011-44-6285-24922

Marketing Publications Ltd.
22 Lancaster Gate
London W2 3LY, England
TEL: 011-44-81-943-5000

Marquis Who's Who
121 Chanlon Rd.
New Providence, NJ 07974
TEL: 800-521-8110
FAX: 908-665-6688

Maruzen Company, Ltd.
3-10 Nihonbashi
2-chome, Chuo-ku,
   Tokyo 103, Japan
TEL: 011-81-33-409-0288

Massachusetts Institute of
   Technology
E38-754, 292 Main St.
Cambridge, MA 02139
TEL: 617-253-2839
FAX: 617-258-7432

Maxwell MacMillan
   Professional & Business
   Reference Publishing
910 Sylvan Way
Englewood Cliffs, NJ
   07632-3310
TEL: 800-562-0245
FAX: 201-816-3484

McFadden Holdings
233 Park Ave., S.
New York, NY 10003-1663
TEL: 212-979-4800

McGraw-Hill, Inc.
1221 Ave. of the Americas
New York, NY 10020
TEL: 212-512-2000

Mead Data Central Inc.
   (LEXIS, NEXIS)
9393 Springboro Pike,
   P.O. Box 933
Dayton, OH 45401
TEL: 513-865-6800
FAX: 513-865-6909

Medical Device Register
Five Paragon Dr.
Montvale, NJ 07645
TEL: 201-358-7641

Medical Economics Publishing
Five Paragon Dr.
Montvale, NJ 07645-1742

Mediobanca SpA, Banca de
  Credito Finanziario
Via Filodrammatici 10
20121 Milan, Italy
TEL: 011-39-2-88291

Merton Allen Associates
P.O. Box 15640
Plantation, FL 33318-5640
TEL: 305-473-9560
FAX: 305-473-0544

Metropolitan Cross-Reference
  Directory
2 Ripley Ave.
Toronto, M6S 3N9, Ontario,
  Canada
TEL: 416-763-5515

Micromedia Ltd.
20 Victoria St.
Toronto, Ontario, Canada,
  M5C 2N8
TEL: 416-362-5211
FAX: 416-362-6161

Midland Bank (England)
Poultry
London EC2P 2BX, England
TEL: 011-44-71-260-8000
FAX: 011-44-71-260-7436

Midland Bank (U.S.)
156 W. 56th St.
New York, NY 10019
TEL: 212-969-7060

Midland Bank Group
11th Fl., CITIC Bldg.,
  Jianguomenwali
Beijing, China
TEL: 011-86-1-504410

Miller Freeman Inc.
600 Harrison St.
San Francisco, CA 94107
TEL: 415-905-2200
FAX: 415-905-2232

Minda de Gunzberg Center
  for European Studies
Harvard University
27 Kirkland St.
Cambridge, MA 02138
TEL: 617-495-4303
FAX: 617-495-8509

Mining Journal Ltd.
151 Railroad Ave.
Greenwich, CT 06830-6381
TEL: 203-629-3400

Ministere de l'Economie des
  Finances et du Budget
192, rue Saint-Honore
75056 Paris, France
TEL: 011-44-1-42-61-33-04

Ministerium fuer Wirtschaft
(Federal Ministry of
  Economics)
Unter den Linden 44-60
O-1080 Berlin, Germany
TEL: 011-49-228-6151
FAX: 011-49-228-6154436

Ministero del Commercio con
  l'Estero
Viale America 341
00100 Rome, EUR
TEL: 011-39-6-5993

Ministero del Industria,
  Commercio e Artigianato
(Ministry of Industry,
  Commerce & Artisan Trade)
Via Molise 2
Rome, Italy
TEL: 011-39-6-4705

Ministry of Chemical Industry
Liupukang, Deshsengmenwai
Beijing, China
TEL: 011-86-1-446561

Ministry of Coal Industry
Xingua Rd., Andingmenwai
Beijing, China
TEL: 011-86-1-555891

Ministry of Commerce (China)
45 Fuxingmenwai
Beijing, China
TEL: 011-86-668581

Ministry of Electronics
  Industry
S. Sanlihe St., Fuxingmenwai
Beijing, China
TEL: 011-86-1-868451

Ministry of Finance (Japan)
Organization Div., Security
  Bureau
3-1-1 Kasumigaseki
Chiyoda-ku, Tokyo 100, Japan

Ministry of Foreign Affairs
  (Japan)
2-2-1 Kasumigaseki
Chiyoda-ku, Tokyo 100, Japan
TEL: 011-81-33-580-3311

Ministry of Foreign Affairs
  (Taiwan)
2 Chien Shou Rd.
Taipei, Taiwan
TEL: 011-886-2-311-9292

Ministry of Foreign Economic
  Relations and Trade
  (MOFERT)
2 Dongchangan Jie
Beijing, China
TEL: 011-86-1-512-6644

Ministry of Light Industry
12 Dongchangan Jie
Beijing, China
TEL: 011-86-1-556687

Ministry of Metallurgical
  Industry
46 Dongsi Xi Dajie
Beijing, China
TEL: 011-86-1-557031

Ministry of Petroleum Industry
Yuetan Nan Jie
Beijing, China
TEL: 011-86-1-444631

Ministry of Post and
  Telecommunications (Japan)
1-3-2 Kasumigaseki
Chiyoda-ku, Tokyo 10090,
  Japan
TEL: 011-81-33-504-4411

Ministry of Textile Industry
12 Dongchangan Jie
Beijing, China
TEL: 011-86-1-556831

Minitel Services Company
888 7th Ave., 28th Fl.
New York, NY 10106
TEL: 212-399-0080

Mitsubishi Bank
7-1 Marunouchi
2-chome, Chiyoda-ku,
   Tokyo 100, Japan
TEL: 011-81-33-240-1111

Mitsubishi Corp.
2-6-3 Marunouchi
Chiyoda-ku, Tokyo 100,
   Japan
TEL: 011-86-33-210-2121
FAX: 011-81-33-210-7359

Mitsubishi Research Institute
   in Tokyo
Time & Life Bldg.,
   2-3-6 Otemachi
Chiyoda-ku, Tokyo 100, Japan
TEL: 011-81-33-270-9211
FAX: 011-81-33-279-1309

Money Market Directories
320 E. Main St., P.O. Box 1608
Charlottesville, VA 22902
TEL: 800-446-2810

Monitor Publishing Company
104 Fifth Ave., 2nd Fl.
New York, NY 10011
TEL: 212-627-4140
FAX: 212-645-0931

Monopolies & Mergers
   Commission
New Ct., 48 Carey St.
London WC2A 2JT, England
TEL: 011-44-71-324-1407

Moody's Investors Service
99 Church St.
New York, NY
TEL: 212-553-0442
FAX: 212-553-4700

Mortgage Bankers Association
   of America
1125 15th St., NW
Washington, DC 20005
TEL: 202-861-6500

Motor Vehicle Manufacturers
   Association of the U.S.
7430 Second Ave., Ste. 300
Detroit, MI 48202
TEL: 313-872-4311

Murphy-Richter Publishing
   Company
230 W. Monroe St., #2210
Chicago, IL 60606
TEL: 312-454-9155

NCBFAA
One World Trade Center #1153
New York, NY 10048
TEL: 212-432-0050

National Customs Brokers
   Forwarders Association
NDT Update
P.O. Box 6273, FRD Station
New York, NY 10150

NIFTY Corporation
26-1, Minami-01 6-chome
Shinagawa-ku, Tokyo 140,
   Japan
TEL: 03 5471 5800
FAX: 03 5471 5890

NRF Enterprises
100 W. 31st St.
New York, NY 10001-3405
TEL: 212-244-8780

Nagoya Chamber of
   Commerce and Industry
10-19, Sakae 2-chome
Naka-ku, Nagoya, Aichi 46,
   Japan
TEL: 011-81-52-221-7211

Naha Chamber of Commerce
   and Industry
2-2-4, Kume Naha
Okinawa, Japan
TEL: 011-81-68-3758

Nan Tou Hsihn Chambers of
   Trade
24 Min-Chuan St.
Nan Tou City, Nan Tou
   Hsien, Taiwan
TEL: 011-886-49-222074

National Association of Chain
   Drug Stores
P.O. Box 1417-D49
Alexandria, VA 22313
TEL: 703-549-3001

National Association of Chain
   Drug Stores (NACDS)
c/o Ronald L. Ziegler,
   413 N. Lee St.
P.O. Box 1417 D49
Alexandria, VA 22313-1417
TEL: 703-549-3001

National Association of
   Chemical Distributors
1101 Seventeenth St., NW,
   Ste. 1200
Washington, DC 20036
TEL: 202-296-9200

National Association of
   Environmental Professionals
P.O. Box 15210
Alexandria, VA 22309-0210
TEL: 703-660-2364

National Association of Fleet
   Administrators
120 Wood Ave., S., Ste. 615
Iselin, NJ 08830
TEL: 908-494-8100

National Association of
   Photographic Manufacturers
550 Mamaroneck Ave.
Harrison, NY 10528
TEL: 914-698-7603
FAX: 914-698-7609

National Association of
   Plastics Distributors
6333 Long St., Ste. 340
Shawnee, KS 66216
TEL: 913-268-6273

National Association of
   Printers & Lithographers
780 Palisade Ave.
Teaneck, NJ 07666
TEL: 201-342-0700
FAX: 201-692-0286

National Association of
   Printing Ink Manufacturers
Heights Plaza, 777 Terrace Ave.
Hasbrouck Heights, NJ 07604
TEL: 201-288-9454

National Association of Quick
   Printers
404 N. Michigan Ave.
Chicago, IL 60611
TEL: 312-644-6610

National Computer Graphics
   Association
2722 Merrilee Dr., Ste. 200
Fairfax, VA 22031
TEL: 800-225-6242;
   703-698-9600

National Electrical
   Contractors Association
7315 Wisconsin Ave.,
   Ste. 1300W
Bethesda, MD 20814-3299
TEL: 301-657-3110

National Food Brokers
   Association
1010 Massachusetts Ave., NW
Washington, DC 20001
TEL: 202-789-2844
FAX: 202-842-0839

National Grocers Association
1825 Samuel Morse Dr.
Reston, VA 22090
TEL: 703-437-5300

National Live Stock and Meat
   Board
444 N. Michigan Ave.
Chicago, IL 60611
TEL: 312-467-5520

National Lumber & Bldg.
   Material Dealer's Assoc.
40 Ivy St.
Washington, DC 20003
TEL: 202-547-2230

National Paperbox &
   Packaging Association
1201 E. Abingdon Dr., Ste. 203
Alexandria, VA 22314
TEL: 703-684-2212

National Printing Equipment
   & Supply Association
1899 Preston White Dr.
Reston, VA 22091
TEL: 703-264-7200

National Private Truck Council
1320 Braddock Pl. #720
Alexandria, VA 22314-1649
TEL: 703-683-1300

National Productivity Board
   (Singapore)
2 Bukit Merah Central,
   NPB Bldg.
Singapore 0315
TEL: 011-65-278-6666
FAX: 011-65-278-6667

National Register Publishing
   Company
121 Chanlon Rd.
New Providence, NJ 07974
TEL: 800-521-8110
FAX: 908-665-6688

National Restaurant
   Association
1200 17th St., NW
Washington, DC 20036
TEL: 800-424-5156

National Retail Federation
100 31st St.
New York, NY 10001
TEL: 212-244-8780

National Science Council in
   Taiwan - Science &
   Technology
Information Center (STIC)
17-22 Fl., 106 Hoping E. Rd.,
   Section 2
Taipei 10636, Taiwan
TEL: 011-886-2-737-7500

National Science Foundation
   U.S.-Japan Program
4201 Wilson Blvd., Rm. 935
Arlington, VA 22230
TEL: 703-306-1710

National Society of
   Professional Engineers
1420 King St.
Alexandria, VA 22314-2794
TEL: 703-684-2875

National Soft Drink Association
1101 16th St., NW
Washington, DC 20036
TEL: 202-463-6732

National Standards
   Association Inc. (NSA)
1200 Euince Orchard Blvd.
Gaithersburg, MD 20878
TEL: 301-590-2300;
   800-638-8094
FAX: 301-990-8378

National Technical
   Information Service (NTIS)
5285 Port Royal Rd.
Springfield, VA 22161
TEL: 703-487-4650
FAX: 703-321-8547

National Telephone Co-op
   Association
2626 Pennsylvania Ave., NW
Washington, DC 20037
TEL: 202-298-2300

National Underwriter Company
420 E. 4th St.
Cincinnati, OH 45202
TEL: 513-721-2140

National Wholesale Druggists
   Association (NWDA)
1821 Michael Faraday Dr.,
   Ste. 400
Reston, VA 22090-5348
TEL: 202-787-0000
FAX: 703-787-6930

Neal-Schuman Publishers, Inc.
100 Varick St.
New York, NY 10013
TEL: 212-925-8650

Nelson Publications
One Gateway Plaza,
   P.O. Box 591
Port Chester, NY 10573
TEL: 914-937-8400

New Jersey Business and
   Industry Assn.
310 Passaic Ave.
Fairfield, NJ 07004
TEL: 201-882-5004

Newmedia International Japan
Avenida Infanta Carlota,
74, 5, 1
Barcelona 08029, Spain
TEL: 93 410 70 34

Newport Associates Ltd.
7400 E. Orchard Rd., Ste. 320
Englewood, CO 80111
TEL: 303-779-5515;
  800-733-5515
FAX: 303-779-0908

NewsNet Inc.
945 Haverford Rd.
Bryn Mawr, PA 19010
TEL: 215-527-8030;
  800-345-1301
FAX: 215-527-0338

Newsletters International Inc.
2600 S. Gessner
Houston, TX 77063-3297
TEL: 713-783-0100

Newspaper Association of
  America
11600 Sunrise Valley Dr.
Reston, VA 22091
TEL: 703-648-1000

Nihon Faxon Co. Ltd.
7-8-13 Nishi shinjuku
Xhinjukuku, Tokyo 160, Japan
TEL: 011-81-33-367-3081
FAX: 011-81-33-366-0295

Nihon Keieisha Dantai
  Renmei (NIKKEIREN)
4-6, Marunouchi 1-chome
Chiyoda-ku, Tokyo 100, Japan
TEL: 011-81-33-213-4463
FAX: 011-81-33-213-4466

Nihon Keizai Shimbun
  America, Inc.
1325 Ave. of the Americas,
  Ste. 2500
New York, NY 10019
TEL: 212-261-6240
FAX: 212-261-6249

Nihon Keizai Shimbun, Inc.
  (NIKKEI)
Databank Bureau - Nikkei
  Telecom, 9-5 Otemachi
1-Chome, Chiyoda-ku,
  Tokyo 100, Japan
TEL: 011-81-03-529-42407

Nippon Telegraph and
  Telephone Corp.
1-6-6 Uchisaiwai-cho
Chiyoda-ku, Tokyo, Japan
TEL: 011-81-33-509-5111

Nomura Research Institute
Data Bank Section, Dai-Ni
  Yamaman Bldg.
6-7 Nihonbashi, Chuo-ku,
  Tokyo 103
TEL: 011-81-03-324-99415

Nomura Research Institute
1-9-1 Nihonbashi
Chuo-ku, Tokyo 103, Japan
TEL: 011-81-03-211-1811
FAX: 011-81-03-278-0420

Nord Pas-de-Calais
  Development
16, Residence Breteuil
Parc Saint-Maur, 59800 Lille
TEL: 011-33-20-63-04-05
FAX: 011-33-20-55-39-15

North American Publishing
  Company
401 N. Broad St.
Philadelphia, PA 19108-1074
TEL: 215-238-5300
FAX: 215-238-5457

North American
  Telecommunications
  Association
2000 M St., NW, Ste. 550
Washington, DC 20036
TEL: 202-296-9800

Northern Development
  Company (NDC)
Great North House,
  Sandyford Rd.
Newcastle NE1 8ND
TEL: 011-44-91-261-0026
FAX: 011-44-91-232-9069

Northwestern Financial
  Review Communications Inc.
5270 84th St., Ste. 480
Minneapolis, MN 55437-1373
TEL: 612-835-5225

O.R. Telematique
7, rue de Sens, Rochecorbon
F-37210 Vouvray, France
TEL: 011-33-47-626262
FAX: 011-33-47-48973425

ORBIT Search Service
8000 Westpark Dr.
McLean, VA 22102
TEL: 703-442-0900;
  800-456-7248
FAX: 703-893-4632

Office of the Commercial
  Counselor
Ste. 380, 1990 M St., NW
Washington, DC 20036
TEL: 202-467-6790

Oildom Publishing Company
  of Texas Inc.
3314 Mercer St.
Houston, TX 77027-6082
TEL: 713-622-0676

Oryx Press
4040 N. Central Ave., Ste. 700
Phoenix, AZ 85012-3397
TEL: 602-265-2651

Osaka Chamber of Commerce
  and Industry
58-7, Uchihonmachi
Hashizume-cho, Higashi-ku,
  Osaka, Japan
TEL: 011-81-6-944-6215

Osaka Securities Exchange
2-1 Kitahama
Higashi-ku, Osaka 541, Japan
TEL: 011-81-6-229-8643

Overseas Private Investment
  Corp. (OPIC)
1100 New York Ave., NW
Washington, DC 20527
TEL: 202-336-8400
FAX: 202-408-9859

Oxbridge Communications
150 5th Ave., Ste. 302
New York, NY 10011
TEL: 212-741-0231
FAX: 212-633-2938

PSSI
840 N. Lake Shore Dr.
Chicago, IL 60611-2431
TEL: 312-943-0544

PTN Publishing Corp.
445 Broad Hollow Rd.
Melville, NY 11747
TEL: 516-845-2700

Pacific Coast Paper Box
    Manufacturer's Association
2301 Vernon Ave.,
    P.O. Box 60957
Los Angeles, CA 90060

Paint Research Association
Information Dept.,
    Waldegrave Rd.
Teddington, Middlesex TW11
    8LD, England
TEL: 081-977-4427
FAX: 081-943-4705

Paper Industry Management
    Association
2400 E. Oakton St.
Arlington Heights, IL 60005
TEL: 708-956-0250

Paris Stock Exchange
4 Pl. de la Bourse
75080 Paris, France
TEL: 011-33-1-49-27-1000
FAX: 011-33-1-49-27-1433

Patent Office of the People's
    Republic of China
Xuyuan Xi Lu, PO Box 8020
Beijing, China
TEL: 011-86-201-9221;
    201-4447 ext 2223

Paul Kagan Associates Inc.
126 Clock Tower Pl.
Carmel, CA 93923-8734
TEL: 408-624-1536
FAX: 408-625-3225

PennWell Books
P.O. Box 1260
Tulsa, OK 74101
TEL: 918-835-3161

PennWell Publishing Co.
1250 S. Grove Ave. #302
Barrington, IL 60010-5066
TEL: 708-382-2450

Penton Publishing Company
Cleveland, OH 44114-2518
TEL: 216-696-7658

People's Bank of China
San Li He, West City
Beijing, China
TEL: 011-86-863907

Pergamon ORBIT InfoLine,
    Inc. - ORBIT Search Service
8000 Westpark Dr.
McLean, VA 22101
TEL: 703-442-0900

Pergamon Press Ltd.
Headington Hill Hall
Oxford OX3 OBW, England
TEL: 011-44-865 794141

Permanent Hall for
    Negotiation and Exhibition
    of Xinjiang Export
Guangzhou Foreign Trade Ctr.,
    Hall #6, 2nd Fl.
Renmin Bei Lu, Guangzhou,
    China
TEL: 011-86-20-62290

Perry Publications (Holdings)
    Plc.
Compass House, 22 Redan Pl.
London W24SZ, England
TEL: 011-44-71-229-7799

Petroleum Abstracts
600 S. College
Tulsa, OK 74104
TEL: 918-631-2296

Petroleum Equipment Institute
P.O. Box 2380
Tulsa, OK 74101
TEL: 918-494-9696

Petroleum Information Corp.
P.O. Box 2612
Denver, CO 80201
TEL: 303-740-7100;
    800-525-5569

Pharmaceutical Manufacturers
    Association (PMA)
1100 15th St., NW
Washington, DC 20005
TEL: 202-835-3400

Phelon, Sheldon and Marsar,
    Inc.
15 Industrial Ave., Box 517
Fairview, NJ 07022
TEL: 800-234-8804
FAX: 201-941-8804

Phillips Business Information,
    Inc.
7811 Montrose Rd.
Potomac, MD 20854-3363
TEL: 301-340-2100

Photo Marketing Association
    International
3000 Picture Pl.
Jackson, MI 49201-8898
TEL: 517-788-8100

Photographic Manufacturers
    and Distributors Association
866 United Nations Plaza
New York, NY 10017
TEL: 212-688-3520

Practicing Law Institute New
    York
810 7th Ave., 29th Fl.
New York, NY 10019
TEL: 212-765-5700
FAX: 800-321-0093

Predicasts, Inc.
11001 Cedar Ave.
Cleveland, OH 44106
TEL: 800-321-6388

Prentice-Hall Legal and
    Financial Services
1090 Vermont Ave., NW,
    Ste. 430
Washington, DC 20005
TEL: 202-408-3120

Printing Industries of America
100 Daingerfield Rd.
Alexandria, VA 22314
TEL: 703-519-8100

Private Carrier Conference,
Inc.
1320 Braddock Pl., Ste. 720
Alexandria, VA 22314
TEL: 703-683-1300
FAX: 703-683-1217

Prodigy Services Company
445 Hamilton Ave.
White Plains, NY 10601
TEL: 914-993-8000

Produce Reporter Company
845 E. Geneva Rd.
Carol Stream, IL 60188-3520
TEL: 708-668-3500
FAX: 708-668-0303

Public Utilities Reports Inc.
2111 Wilson Blvd., #200
Arlington, VA 22201-3060
TEL: 703-243-7000

Putnam Publishing Company
301 E. Erie St.
Chicago, IL 60611-3059
TEL: 312-644-2020

QL Systems Limited
901 Ste., Andrew's Tower,
275 Sparks St.
Ottawa, Ontario, Canada,
K1R 7X9
TEL: 613-238-3499
FAX: 613-548-4260

Questel Inc. (France)
Le Capitole, 55, ave. des
Champs Pierreux
F-92029 Nanterre Cedex,
France
TEL: 011-33-1-46145660
FAX: 011-33-1-46145511

Questel Inc. (U.S.)
2300 Clarendon Blvd., Ste. 111
Arlington, VA 22201-3367
TEL: 800-424-9600

Quotron Systems, Inc.
77 Water St., 9th Fl.
New York, NY 10005
TEL: 212-898-7000
main headquarters

R.L. Polk & Company
2001 Elm Hill Pike,
P.O. Box 1340
Nashville, TN 37202
TEL: 615-889-3350

R.R. Bowker
121 Chanlon Rd.
New Providence, NJ 07974
TEL: 800-521-8110
FAX: 908-665-6688

RCC-IVEV Information
Services
Overschiestr. 65, Postbus 2624
NL-1000 CP Amsterdam,
Netherlands
TEL: 020 6157771
FAX: 020 6157109

Ranko International
390 Fifth Ave., Ste. 900
New York, NY 10018
TEL: 212-236-2790
FAX: 212-736-2796

Reed Business Publishing
205 E. 42nd St.
New York, NY 10017-5706
TEL: 212-867-2080
FAX: 212-687-6604

Reed Information Services
Ltd.
Windsor Court, E. Grinstead
House
E. Grinstead, W. Sussex
RH19 1XA, England
TEL: 011-44-342 326972
FAX: 011-44-342 335612

Reed Publishing
275 Washington St.
Newton, MA 02158
TEL: 617-964-3030
FAX: 617-558-4667

Reed Reference Publishing
New Providence, NJ 07974
TEL: 800-521-8110;
908-464-6800

Reed Travel Group
500 Plaza Dr.
Secaucus, NJ 07094-3602
TEL: 201-902-1792

Registre National du
Commerce
32 rue des Trois Fontanots
9200 Nanterre, France
TEL: 011-33-1-46-92-58-00

Reuters Information Services
Inc.
1333 H St., NW, Ste. 410
Washington, DC 20005
TEL: 202-898-8300;
800-426-4316

Reuters Ltd.
85 Fleet St.
London EC4P 4AJ, England
TEL: 011-44-71-250 1122

Robert Morris Associates
1 Liberty Pl., 1650 Market St.,
Ste. 2300
Philadelphia, PA 19103-7398
TEL: 215-851-9155
FAX: 215-851-9206

Rodman Publishing Corp.
26 Lake St.
Ramsey, NJ 07446
TEL: 201-825-2552

Royal Bank of Scotland
P.O. Box 31, 42 St.
Andrew Sq.,
Edinburgh EH2 2YE
TEL: 011-44-31-556-8555
FAX: 011-44-31-557-6565

Royal Bank of Scotland (U.S.)
63 Wall St.
New York, NY 10005
TEL: 212-269-1700
FAX: 212-269-8929

Royal Society of Chemistry
Info. Services, Thomas
Graham House
Science Pk., Milton Rd.
Cambridge CB4 4WF,
England
TEL: 011-44-223 420066
FAX: 011-44-223 423623

Royal Thai Embassy/Office of
  the Economic Counselor
Five World Trade Center,
  Ste. 3443
New York, NY 10048
TEL: 212-466-1745/6
FAX: 212-466-9548

Rubber Association of
  Singapore
14 Collyer Quay, #03-00
  Singapore Rubber House
Singapore 0104
TEL: 011-65-220-1205

S-N Publications Inc.
103 N. Second St.
West Dundee, IL 60118
TEL: 708-426-6100

SAE International
400 Commonwealth Dr.
Warrendale, PA 15096-0001
TEL: 412-776-4841

SARITEL S.p.A.
Via Aurelio Saffi 18, C.P. 512
I-10138 Torino, Italy

SEAT Divisione STET S.p.A.
Viale del Policlinico 147
1-00161 Rome, Italy
TEL: 011-39-6 84941
FAX: 011-39-6 8494421

SIETAR International
808 17th St., NW, Ste. 200
Washington, DC 20006-3953
TEL: 202-466-7883

SIRIO
Via Orazio 2
Milan, Italy
TEL: 011-39-2-88231

SMG Marketing Group, The
1342 N. LaSalle Dr.
Chicago, IL 60610
TEL: 312-642-3026
FAX: 312-642-9729

SRI International
333 Ravenswood Ave.
Menlo Park, CA 94025-3493
TEL: 415-326-6200

STN International
Karlsruhe Service Center,
  P.O. Box 2465
D-7500 Karlsruhe 1, Germany
TEL: 07-247-808555
FAX: 07-247-80866

SandPoint Corporation
One Canal Park
Cambridge, MA 02141
TEL: 617-868-4442
FAX: 617-868-5562

Savings & Community
  Bankers of America
900 19th St., NW, Ste. 400
Washington, DC 20006
TEL: 202-857-3100
merger occurred 6/1/92
between US League of
Savings Insts. & Nat. Council
of Community Bankers

Scan C2C, Inc.
13701 Georgia Ave.
Silver Spring, MD 20906
TEL: 301-949-8101
FAX: 301-942-0434

Schnell Publishing Company
80 Broad St., 23rd Fl.
New York, NY 10004
TEL: 212-248-4177

Scottish Enterprise
120 Bothwell St.
Glasgow G2 7JP
TEL: 011-44-41-248-2700
FAX: 011-44-41-221-5129

Securities Data Company Inc.
  (SDC)
1180 Raymond Blvd., 5th Fl.
Newark, NJ 07102
TEL: 201-622-3100

Securities Exchange of
  Thailand
Sinthon Bldg., 2nd Fl.,
  132 Wireless Rd.
Bangkok 10500, Thailand
TEL: 011-66-2-350-0001

Securities and Investments
  Board
2-14 Bunhill Row
London EC1Y 8RA, England
TEL: 011-44-71-638-1240

Shanghai Federation of
  Industry and Commerce
893 Huashan Lu
Shanghai, China
TEL: 011-86-21-433-5795

Shanghai International Trust
  and Service Corporation
521 Henan Rd., POB 3066
Shanghai, China
TEL: 011-86-21-332-1025;
  332-6650; 320-7412

Shanghai Overseas Enterprise
  Corporation
27 Shongshan Dong Yi Lu
Shanghai, China
TEL: 011-86-21-321-6965
FAX: 011-86-21-323-4701

Shanghai Patent Agency
601 Yanan Xi Lu
Shanghai, China
TEL: 011-86-385-668

Shanghai Trade and
  Transportation Company
74 Dianchi Lu, Rm. 316
Shanghai, China
TEL: 011-86-21-321-0718

Shore Communications Inc.
180 Allen Rd., Ste. 300-N
Atlanta, GA 30328
TEL: 800-241-9034

Silver Platter Information Inc.
100 River Ridge Rd.
Norwood, MA 02062-5026
TEL: 800-343-0064
FAX: 617-769-8763

Simmons Market Research
  Bureau
420 Lexington Ave.
New York, NY 10014-4590
TEL: 212-620-7200
FAX: 212-633-1165

Simmons-Boardman
 Publishing Corp.
345 Hudson St.
New York, NY 10014-4590
TEL: 212-620-7200
FAX: 212-633-1165

Los Angeles World Trade Ctr.
350 S. Figuero St., Ste. 909
Los Angeles, CA 90071
TEL: 213-617-7358/9
FAX: 213-617-7367

United Overseas Bank
Ste. 310, Vancouver Centre,
 PO Box 11616
650 W. Georgia St.
Vancouver BC V6B 4N9,
 Canada
TEL: 604-662-7055
FAX: 604-662-3356

Skilling's Mining Review
1st Bank Plz., Ste. 728,
 130 W. Superior
Duluth, MN 55802
TEL: 218-722-2310

Small Business Foundation of
 America Inc.
1155 15th St.
Washington, DC 20005
TEL: 202-223-1103

Societe Nouvelle d'Editions
 Industrielle
66 quai de Marechal Joffre
F-92600 Courbevoie, France
TEL: 01 43593759
FAX: 0145638348

Society for the Advancement
 of Material & Process
 Engineering
P.O. Box 2459
Covina, CA 91722
TEL: 818-331-0616

Society of Automotive
 Engineers (SAE)
400 Commonwealth Dr.
Warrendale, PA 15096-0001
TEL: 415-776-4841

Society of Manufacturing
 Engineers (SME)
One SME Dr., P.O. Box 930
Dearborn, MI 48121
TEL: 313-271-1500

Society of Soft Drink
 Technologists
4419 41st St., P.O. Box 259
Brentwood, MO 20722
TEL: 301-277-0018

Society of the Plastics Industry
1275 K St., NW, Ste. 400
Washington, DC 20005
TEL: 202-371-5200

Special Libraries Association
1700 18th St., NW
Washington, DC 20009
TEL: 202-234-4700

Specialized Agricultural
 Publishing
3000 Highwoods Blvd., Ste.
 300, Box 95075
Raleigh, NC 27604-1029
TEL: 919-872-5040

Sporting Goods Industries
 Clearing House
28 E. Jackson Blvd., Ste. 720
Chicago, IL 60604
TEL: 312-427-8699

Ssangyong Investment &
 Securities Co. Ltd. (U.S.)
1 World Trade Center,
 Ste. 8043
New York, NY 10048
TEL: 212-397-4000

Ssangyong Economic
 Research Institute
185, Euljiro 2-ka, Chung-ku
Seoul 100-192, Korea
TEL: 011-82-2-753-7800

Standard & Poor's Corp.
25 Broadway
New York, NY 10004
TEL: 202-208-8702

Standard Chartered Bank
 (China)
Box 2135, 4th Fl.,
 185 Yuan Ming Yuan Lu
Shanghai, China
TEL: 011-86-21-214245

Standard Rate & Data Service
3004 Glenview Rd.
Wilmette, IL 60091
TEL: 708-256-8333

State Administration for
 Industry and Commerce
8 Sanlihe Donglu, Xichengqu
Beijing, China
TEL: 011-86-801-3300 x211
FAX: 011-86-801-3300-2322

State Administration of
 Commodity Inspection
Bldg. 1212, Jianguomenwai
Beijing, China
TEL: 011-86-1-500-2387

State Statistical Bureau
38 Yuetan nan Jie, Xichengqu
Beijing, China
TEL: 011-86-1-868521

Statistical Office of the
 United Nations, Public
 Service
2 United Nations Plaza,
 N01420
New York, NY 10017
TEL: 212-963-8302

Statistiches Bundesamt
 (StaBuA)
(Federal Statistical Office)
Gustav-Stresesmann-Ring 11,
 Postfach 55 28
D-6200 Wiesbaden 1, Germany
TEL: 011-49-6121-4186511

Steel Foundries Society of
 America
455 State St.
Des Plaines, IL 60016
TEL: 708-299-9160

Stewart Directories
10540 J. York Rd.
Cockeysville, MD 21030
TEL: 410-628-5988

Stock Exchange of Singapore
 Ltd.
Publication/Research Dept.
PO Box 2306, One Raffles Pl.
#24/00 OUB Centre
Singapore 0104
TEL: 011-65-535-3788
FAX: 011-65-535-0985

Sumitomo Bank
22 Kitahama
5-chome, Higashi-ku,
    Osaka 541, Japan
TEL: 011-81-6-227-2111

T.K. Sanderson Organization
1115 E. 30th St.
Baltimore, MD 21218
TEL: 301-235-3383

TRW Business Credit Services
3110 Central Ave.
Riverside, CA 92506
FAX: 909-276-9442

Technical Insights, Inc.
P.O. Box 1304
Fort Lee, NJ 07024
TEL: 201-568-4744
FAX: 201-568-8247

Technology Transfer Service
    of Industrial Development
    and Investment
1st Fl., 7 Roosevelt Rd.,
    Section 1
Taipei, Taiwan
TEL: 011-886-2-322-2506
FAX: 011-886-2-396-3838

Technology Transfer Society
611 N. Capitol Ave.
Indianapolis, IN 46204
TEL: 317-262-5022
FAX: 317-262-5044

Teikoku DataBank Ltd.
5-20, Minami Aoyama,
    2-Chome
Minato-ku, Tokyo 107, Japan
TEL: 011-81-33-404-4311
FAX: 011-81-33-408-5519

TelTech
7890 12th Ave., S
Minneapolis, MN 55425
TEL: 800-233-2001
FAX: 612-854-8601

Telecom Publishing Group
1101 King St., Ste. 444
Alexandria, VA 22314
TEL: 703-683-4100
FAX: 703-739-6490
div. of Capitol Publications
    Inc.

Telecommunications
    Programming
432 N. Lake St.
Madison, WI 53706
FAX: 608-263-3160

Tennessee Bankers Association
201 Venture Cir.
Nashville, TN 37228-1603
TEL: 615-244-4871
FAX: 615-244-0995

Texas Bankers Association
P.O. Box 2007
Austin, TX 78768
TEL: 512-472-7980
FAX: 512-473-2560

Textile Information Users
    Council
School House Ln. &
    Henry Ave.
Philadelphia, PA 19144
TEL: 609-924-3150
FAX: 609-683-7836

Textile Research Institute
P.O. Box 625
Princeton, NJ 08542
TEL: 609-924-3150
FAX: 609-683-7836

Thomas Publishing Company
Five Penn Plaza
New York, NY 10001
TEL: 212-290-7262
FAX: 212-290-7373

Thomson & Thomson
500 Victory Rd.
North Quincy, MA 02171-1545
TEL: 800-692-8833

Thomson Financial Networks
11 Farnsworth St.
Boston, MA 02210
TEL: 800-662-7878
FAX: 617-330-1986

Thomson Financial Publishing
4709 W. Golf Rd., 6th Fl.
Skokie, IL 60076-1253
TEL: 708-676-9600

Time, Inc.
Time & Life Bldg.,
    Rockefeller Center
New York, NY 10020-1393
TEL: 212-522-1212

Tokyo Chamber of Commerce
    and Industry
2-2, Marunouchi 3-chome
Chiyoda-ku, Tokyo, Japan
TEL: 011-81-33-283-7500

Tokyo Keizai Inc.
1-2-1 Hongoku-cho
Nihonbashi, Chuo-ku,
Tokyo 103, Japan
TEL: 011-81-33-246-5655
FAX: 011-81-33-241-5543

Tokyo Shoko Research Ltd.
    (TSR)
Shinichi Bldg., 9-6
1-Chome, Shimbashi,
    Minato-ku, Tokyo 105
TEL: 81-33-574-2211

Tourism Authority
Five World Trade Center,
    Ste. 2449
New York, NY 10048
TEL: 212-432-0433

Tourist Promotion Office
3457 Wilshire Blvd.
Los Angeles, CA 90010
TEL: 213-387-2078

Toyo Information Systems Co.
    Ltd.
Shinbashi-Sanwa-Toyo Bldg.
1-11-7 Shinbashi, Minato-ku,
    Tokyo 105, Japan

Trade Promotion Center
1328 Broadway, Rm. #510
New York, NY 10001
TEL: 212-947-8889
FAX: 212-947-8866

Trademark Registration
    Bureau/State
Administration for Industry
    and Commerce
10 Sanlihe Dong Lu
Beijing, China
TEL: 011-86-801-3300 x324

U.S. Agricultural Trade
    Office (Korea)
63, 1-Ka, Eulchi-ro
Choong-ku, Seoul, Korea
TEL: 011-82-2-839-0218

U.S. Agricultural Trade
Office (Singapore)
1500 Liat Towers,
541 Orchard Rd.
Singapore 0923
TEL: 011-65-737-1233

U.S. Consulate Generals,
China
Don Fang Hotel, 11th Fl.,
Liu Hua Rd.
Guangzhou, China
TEL: 011-86-20-66-9900
FAX: 011-86-20-66-6409

U.S. Customs Service,
Intellectual Property
Rights Branch
1301 Constitution Ave., NW
Washington, DC 20229
TEL: 202-566-6956

U.S. Department of Commerce
14th & Constitution Ave., NW
Washington, DC 20230
TEL: 202-482-2000

U.S. Department of
Commerce/Bureau of
Export Administration
Office of Export Licensing,
Rm. H1099
Washington, DC 20230
TEL: 202-482-4811

U.S. Department of
Commerce/Bureau of the
Census
Customer Services,
Washington Plaza-Rm. 326
Washington, DC 20233
TEL: 301-763-4100

U.S. Department of
Commerce/Economic
Development Administration
14th & Constitution Ave., NW
Washington, DC 20230
TEL: 202-482-2000

U.S. Department of
Commerce/International
Trade Administration
14th & Constitution Ave., NW
Washington, DC 20230
TEL: 202-377-4767
Public Affairs Office:
202-482-3808

U.S. Department of
Commerce/U.S. Patent &
Trademark Office
Washington, DC 20321
TEL: 703-557-4636
FAX: 703-557-6369
USDOC, Patent & Trademark
Office, Washington, DC
20231

U.S. Department of Energy
OSTI, P.O. Box 62
Oak Ridge, TN 37831

U.S. Department of State/
Foreign Service Institute
4000 Arlington Blvd.
Arlington, VA 22204
TEL: 703-302-7143

U.S. Embassy, China
3 Xiushui Bei Jie 3
Beijing 100600, China
TEL: 011-86-532-3831
FAX: 011-86-1-532-3178

U.S. Environmental
Protection Agency
401 M St., SW
Washington, DC 20460
TEL: 202-260-2080
FAX: 202-260-6257

U.S. Export Development
Office (EDO)
7th Fl., World Import Mart
1-3 Higashi Ikebukuro
3-chome
Toshimi-ku, Tokyo 170, Japan
TEL: 011-81-33-987-2441
also known as the U.S. Trade
Center

U.S. Export-Import Bank
811 Vermont Ave., NW
Washington, DC 20571
TEL: 202-622-9823

U.S. Federal Communications
Commission (FCC)
1919 M St., NW
Washington, DC 20554
TEL: 202-632-6600
FAX: 202-632-6600

U.S. Food and Drug
Administration (FDA)
5600 Fishers Ln.
Rockville, MD 20857
TEL: 301-443-3285

U.S. Geological Survey
507 National Center
Reston, VA 22092
TEL: 703-648-6045

U.S. Government Printing
Office
Washington, DC 20402
TEL: 202-783-3238

U.S. Library of Congress
101 Independence Ave., SE
Washington, DC 20540
TEL: 202-707-5000

U.S. NASA Science &
Technology Info. Facility
P.O. Box 8757
BWI Airport, MD 21240
TEL: 703-271-5640

U.S. National Library of
Medicine
8600 Rockville Pike
Bethesda, MD 20894
TEL: 301-496-6193

U.S. Patent and Trademark
Office
Washington, DC 20321
TEL: 703-305-8600

U.S. Securities and Exchange
Commission
450 5th St., NW
Washington, DC 20549
TEL: 202-272-3100
FAX: 202-272-7050

U.S. Securities and Exchange
Commission/Public
Reference Rm.
500 N. Capital St., NW,
Mail Stop 1-2
Washington, DC 20549-1002
TEL: 202-272-7450

U.S. Technology Transfer
Institute
1500 Broadway, Ste. 501
New York, NY 10036
TEL: 212-719-5771
FAX: 212-719-5874

U.S. Telephone Association
900 19th St., NW, Ste. 800
Washington, DC 20006
TEL: 202-835-3100

U.S. Travel Data Center
1133 21st St., NW
Washington, DC 20036
TEL: 202-293-1040

U.S.-China Business Council
1818 N St., NW, Ste. 500
Washington, DC 20036
TEL: 202-429-0340
FAX: 202-775-4276

U.S.-Japan Business Council
1020 19th St., NW, Ste. 130
Washington, DC 20036
TEL: 202-728-0068

UMI/Data Courier
620 S. Third St.
Louisville, KY 40202-2475
TEL: 502-583-4111

Union Italiana delle Camere
de Commercio, Industria,
Artigianato e Agricoltura
Piazza Sallustio 21
00187 Rome, Italy
TEL: 011-39-6-47041
FAX: 011-39-6-4744741
Union of Italian Chamber of
Commerce, Industry,
Artisanship and Agriculture

United Asian Bank Berhad
PO Box 10753, Menara UAB,
6 Jalan Tun Perak
50724 Kuala Lumpur, Malaysia
TEL: 011-60-3-293-1722

United Engineering Center
345 E. 45th St.
New York, NY 10017
TEL: 212-705-7000;
800-221-1044

United Malayan Banking
Corporation Berhad
Bangunan UMBC, Jalan
Sultan Sulaiman
PO Box 12006
50935 Kuala Lumpur, Malaysia
TEL: 011-60-3-230-9866

United Nations Food and
Agriculture Organization
(UNIPUB)
P.O. Box 1222
Ann Arbor, MI 48106

United Nations Publications
2 United Nations Plaza,
Rm. DC 2-853
New York, NY 10017
TEL: 800-553-3210;
212-963-7680

University Microfilms
International
300 N. Zeeb Rd.
Ann Arbor, MI 48106
TEL: 313-761-4700

University R&D
Opportunities, Inc.
7 Mt. Lassen Dr., Ste. D251
San Rafael, CA 94903-1156
TEL: 415-507-0190
FAX: 415-507-0661;
800-733-1516

University of Illinois at
Urbana - Asean Library
1408 W. Gregory Dr., Rm. 325
Urbana, IL 61801
TEL: 217-333-1501
FAX: 217-244-2047

University of Rhode Island
PACAP Research Center
204 Ballentine Hall
Kingston, RI 02881
401-792-5807

University of Tsukuba
Science Information
Processing Center
1-1-1 Tenno-dai, Tsukuba-shi
Ibaraki-ken, 305 Japan
TEL: 011-02-98-532-2450

University of Wisconsin
Press, The
114 N. Murray St.
Madison, WI 53715-1199
TEL: 608-262-8782
FAX: 608-262-7560

Valeurs Actuelles
14 rue d'Uzes
75081 Paris, France

Value Line Publishing Inc.
711 Third Ave.
New York, NY 10017-4064
TEL: 212-687-3965
FAX: 212-986-3293

Vance Publishing Corp.
133 E. 58th St.
New York, NY 10022
TEL: 212-682-7777

Verband Deutscher
Adressbushverleger e.V.
Ritterstrasse 17-19
D-4000 Dusseldorf 1, Germany
TEL: 011-49-211-32-09-09
Federation of German
Address Book Publishers

Verlag Hoppenstedt
Havelstrasse 9, Postfach 4006
D-6100 Darmstadt 1, Germany
TEL: 01-49-61-513801

Verlagsbetriebe Walter Dorn
GmbH
AM Tuev #63000
Hannover 89, Germany
TEL: 011-49-511-830351

WEFA Group Inc.
150 Monument Rd.
Bala Cynwyd, PA 19004
TEL: 215-660-6000

Wales Investment Location
(WINVEST)
Greyfriars Rd.
Cardiff CF1 3XX
TEL: 011-44-222-223666
FAX: 011-44-222-223243

Walker's Western Research
1650 Borel Pl., Ste. 130
San Mateo, CA 94402
TEL: 415-341-1110

Wall Street Transcript Corp.
99 Wall St.
New York, NY 10005
TEL: 212-747-9500

Ward's Communications, Inc.
28 W. Adams
Detroit, MI 48226-1610
TEL: 313-962-4433
FAX: 313-962-4532

Warren Publishing, Inc.
2115 Ward Ct., NW
Washington, DC 20037-3435
TEL: 202-872-9200
FAX: 202-293-3435

Washington Researcher's Ltd.
2612 P St., NW
Washington, DC 20007-3062
TEL: 202-333-3499

Washington Service Bureau
655 15th St., NW, Ste. 275
Washington, DC 20005
TEL: 202-508-0600
FAX: 202-508-0694

Watt Publishing
122 S. Wesley Ave.
Mount Morris, IL 61081-1497

Weeks Publishing Company
601 Skokie Blvd., #202
Northbrook, IL 60062-2818
TEL: 708-559-0385

Welding Institute, The
Abington Hall
Cambridge CB1 5AI, England
TEL: 011-44-223-891-162
FAX: 011-44-223-892-588

Welsh Development
  International
Pearl House, Greyfriars Rd.
Cardiff, S. Glamorgan CF1
  3XX
TEL: 011-44-222-223666
FAX: 011-44-222-223243

West Publishing Company
610 Opperman Dr.
Eagan, MN 55123
TEL: 612-687-7000;
  800-328-0109
FAX: 612-687-7849

Wiesener Publishing Co.
7009 S. Potomac
Englewood, CO 80112
TEL: 303-397-7600
FAX: 303-397-7619

Woodward Directory Company
8609 Cheltenham Ct.
Louisville, KY 40222
TEL: 502-425-1054

World Bank - New York
115 W. 66th St.
New York, NY 10023

World Bank - Washington
2000 S. St.
Washington, DC 20008

World Chamber of Commerce
  Directory Inc.
P.O. Box 1029
Loveland, CO 80539
TEL: 303-663-3231
FAX: 303-663-6187

World Trade Academy Press
50 E. 42nd St., Ste. 509
New York, NY 10017-5480
TEL: 212-697-4999

World Trade Centers
  Association (WTCA)
1 World Trade Center,
  Ste. 7701
New York, NY 10048
TEL: 212-432-2626
FAX: 212-488-0064

Worldwide
  Telecommunications
  Directories Sdn Bhd
121A Jalan SS 17/1A,
  Subang Jaya
47500 Petaling Jaya, Selangor,
  Malaysia
TEL: 011-60-3-733-1592
FAX: 011-60-3-733-2524

Worldwide Videotex
P.O. Box 138, Babson Park
Boston, MA 02157
TEL: 617-449-1603

Xinhua Publishing House/
  Professional Book Company
5600 NE Asalo St.
Portland, OR
TEL: 503-288-1255

Yokohama Chamber of
  Commerce and Industry
2, Yamashita-cho
Naka-ku, Yokohama, Japan
TEL: 011-81-45-671-7400

Yomiuui Shimbun
1-7-1 Otemachi
Chiyoda-ku, Tokyo 100,
  Japan
TEL: 011-81-33-242-111
FAX: 011-81-33-279-6328

Yorkshire and Humberside
  Development Association
100 Wellington St.
Leeds LS1 4LT
TEL: 011-44-532-439222
FAX: 011-44-532-431088

Zhongguo Chaizheng Jingji
  Chubanshe
8 Dafosi Dongjie
Dongcheng District, Beijing,
  China
TEL: 011-86-1-441982
China Financial and
  Economic Publishing House

Ziff Davis Publishing Company
1 Park Ave., 3rd Fl.
New York, NY 10016-2100
TEL: 609-429-2100

INDEX